Rupert B...

University of North Carolina

Chapel Hill

June 23, 1949.

The NEGRO in the
UNITED STATES

THE MACMILLAN COMPANY
NEW YORK • BOSTON • CHICAGO
DALLAS • ATLANTA • SAN FRANCISCO

MACMILLAN AND CO., LIMITED
LONDON • BOMBAY • CALCUTTA
MADRAS • MELBOURNE

THE MACMILLAN COMPANY
OF CANADA, LIMITED
TORONTO

E. Franklin Frazier, Ph.D. PROFESSOR OF SOCIOLOGY
HOWARD UNIVERSITY

THE *Negro* IN THE UNITED STATES

THE MACMILLAN COMPANY · NEW YORK · 1949

To W. E. BURGHARDT DuBOIS *and*
to the Memory of ROBERT E. PARK
Two Pioneers in the Scientific Study
of the Negro

THE NEGRO in America has been the theme of many books. Since the publication of Myrdal's *An American Dilemma,* some explanation is needed for adding another to the long list which includes many distinguished volumes. The justification of the present book by Professor Frazier is to be found in the novelty of his approach as well as in the altered position of the Negro in the United States and of the United States in the world scene.

The epic of America offers the greatest example in the modern world of the building of a nation and a civilization out of the diverse peoples and cultures of the earth. The career of the Negro in America furnishes the most dramatic instance of the integration of one such element into our national life. The present book has traced this process with meticulous care. Professor Frazier has succeeded in depicting with clarity and understanding the adjustment of the Negro as a racial and cultural group to the life of the larger society and the responses that society has made to his presence.

We see in these pages something more, however, than the analysis of a unique minority. This work, while drawing its concrete materials from the experiences of the Negro in the United States, reflects the processes and problems generally associated with the emergence, the life cycle, and the integration of minorities wherever they may be found. Although the Negro minority, because of the racial factor and because of the complicating historical factor of the institution of slavery, represents certain unique features, there are many phases of the Negro's life in America that throw light on the position of all other minorities in this country.

This study is distinctive in another important respect. Whereas most of the studies of the Negro treat "the Negro problem" either in terms of a series of discrete conventional topics such as employment, education, housing, crime, health, religion, and cultural adjustment, the present study treats the Negro in his interaction with the larger American society of which he is a part. Professor Frazier has adopted a broad sociological perspective and has found that by portraying the experiences of the Negro in the context of his own community and institutions and the more inclusive American community and its institutions, it is possible to reveal with greater realism and balance the actual life of the Negro and of America.

As the reader and the student of this volume will note, the author has brought to his task a long and rich experience of research and study in this field. His pioneer work, *The Negro Family in Chicago*, his more comprehensive work, *The Negro Family in the United States*, and his penetrating study, *The Free Negro Family*, to cite only three outstanding examples of his previous contributions, have prepared him well for this major synthesis. What is offered here, therefore, is not an initial attempt to see the picture of the Negro in the United States as a whole, but a mature ordering and integration of the most important work that has been done so far to provide understanding of the life of the Negro people in America and of minorities on the road to integration.

The emphasis in this study is not upon the formulation of broad social policies, but upon the meticulous analysis of social processes. The choice of approach is not due to the author's disinterestedness in policies, but rather rests upon the belief that only through the understanding of the complicated processes of interaction of the various elements of society with one another can we arrive at a critical evaluation of policies and a realistic view of what is possible and what is desirable.

This work appears at a most propitious time in American and world history. There are many signs that the American people are more clearly conscious of the disparity between what Myrdal has referred to as "the American creed" and American practice in respect to the treatment accorded the racial and ethnic minorities comprising America. There is also ample evidence that the people who have hitherto occupied minority status in our national life, notably the Negro, are more than ever taking the promises of American democracy seriously. The new position of the United States in the world calls upon this nation to exercise an unprecedented role of leadership. This fact gives to our own minority problems and to our method of dealing with them a world-wide symbolic significance. What we do here to build a democratic society will influence the faith in the democratic ideal throughout the world. It will affect our capacity to play our part in shaping the world of the future.

Professor Frazier in this volume carefully refrains from telling us what we should do to realize more fully our ideal of a democratic society and thus to prepare ourselves for our role as responsible bearers of the democratic ideal throughout the world. He does, however, furnish us with an authentic and richly documented account of our record so far.

The thoughtful student of this record will be better equipped than those who think they already have all the answers to aid in formulating sound social policies to meet one of the most crucial problems of our troubled world.

Louis Wirth

The University of Chicago

THIS BOOK has grown out of the author's researches in the field of race relations and the problems of peasant people over a period of a quarter of a century. While carrying on research on the Negro in the United States, he was fortunate in having the opportunity to study similar problems of peoples in other countries. Soon after beginning the study of the Negro in the United States, the author received a fellowship from the American-Scandinavian Foundation which enabled him to spend a year in Denmark studying the rôle of the folk high schools in the life of the Danish peasants. Later, through a fellowship provided by the John Simon Guggenheim Foundation, he had the opportunity to carry on researches in Brazil and the West Indies on race relations and the Negro family. As the result of these studies, the author has approached his research on race relations and the social and economic problems of the Negro in the United States with a greater degree of objectivity and with a broader perspective than would otherwise have been possible.

The present study of the Negro is concerned with a phase of race and culture contact in the modern world or, more specifically, with the emergence of the Negro as a minority group and his gradual integration into American life. Consequently, the point of view of the present study represents a departure from the usual approach to the study of the Negro as a social problem. Studies of the Negro as a social problem usually treat Negroes as atomized individuals "floating about" in the American society. This atomistic approach to the Negro problem has not only tended to perpetuate outmoded and provincial notions of the Negro, but it has also given a false conception of his relation to American life. In the present study the aim was to study the Negro as a part of an organized (or disorganized) social life which forms a more or less segregated segment of American society.

This study was inaugurated at the time Dr. Gunnar Myrdal under-

took, with the support of the Carnegie Corporation and the cooperation of a large number of scholars, his monumental study of the
Negro which appeared under the title, *An American Dilemma*. The
author of the present work, who was closely associated with that work
and in fact prepared one of the memoranda upon which it is based,
was inclined not to continue this undertaking. Then came World
War II which forced the author to abandon altogether the writing
of this book. When he resumed the book after the War it became
apparent that the difference in the conception and standpoint of the
two studies provided sufficient justification for the completion of the
present work. The Myrdal study was concerned with broad social
policy in dealing with the Negro problem. The present study is not
concerned with social policy but rather with the processes by which
the Negro has acquired American culture and has emerged as a racial
minority or ethnic group, and the extent to which he is being integrated into American society. Moreover, unlike the Myrdal study,
the main emphasis of the present study is focused upon the Negro
community and its institutions and their interaction with other elements of American society. Thus the aim of the present work was to
study the Negro in a sociological frame of reference which would
throw light upon the problem of race and culture contact in other
parts of the world as well as in the United States.

It would be impossible for the author to make separate acknowl-
edgments of his indebtedness to all the individuals who have contributed in various ways to this work. There are, however, a number
of persons whose assistance has been so outstanding and indispensable that they merit special mention. First among these is Professor
Louis Wirth of the University of Chicago, who not only suggested
the writing of the book but read the manuscript through twice and
made many valuable suggestions and criticisms. The author takes
this opportunity to express to him appreciation for many improvements in both the organization and contents of the book. Next, he
acknowledges indebtedness with thanks to Professor Philip M.
Hauser, of the University of Chicago, for granting him permission
to use data from "Population Problems in the United States," an unpublished paper; and to Dr. Harold F. Dorn, United States Public

Health Service, who placed at his disposal the memorandum which he prepared for Gunnar Myrdal's *An American Dilemma.* To Dr. L. C. Gray the author is indebted, and he hereby expresses appreciation, for permission to reproduce the maps from his study, *History of Agriculture in the Southern United States to 1860.* Appreciation is expressed to Mrs. Dorothy Porter of the Moorland Collection of the Howard University Library who placed at the disposal of the author many valuable references, and to Dr. John Paul Stone, Librarian, San Diego State College, who helped the author at a crucial moment. The author takes this occasion to thank Mr. Richard Dempsey, who contributed to the book by preparing most of the diagrams and maps, and to Mr. Bunji Tagawa of Graphic Associates for the preparation of maps of the cities. Grateful acknowledgment is made to Mrs. Kathryn L. White, research assistant in the Department of Sociology at Howard University, who not only typed the entire manuscript several times but checked many of the references. The author is also indebted to Mr. G. Franklin Edwards and Dr. Harry J. Walker of the Department of Sociology at Howard University for their assistance in securing sources of information and for reading proofs of the book. Finally, grateful acknowledgment is made to Howard University for various forms of assistance provided the author while engaged in this undertaking.

E. Franklin Frazier

Howard University

CONTENTS

PART 4
Intellectual Life and Leadership

LIST OF TABLES

MAPS

xxix

DIAGRAMS

The Negro Under the Slave Regime

PART 1 is concerned with the process by which the Negro secured, first, a place in the economic organization of the South and, secondly, a peculiar status in the social organization dominated by the plantation system. A presentation of the influence of the Negro's African cultural heritage upon his development in the New World is followed by a study of the evolution of the slave status in relation to economic and social forces. Then there is a discussion of the Negro's rôle in the industrial and social organization of the plantation. The chief emphasis is upon his rôle in the social organization of the plantation because it was in this rôle that the Negro was able to take over the culture of the whites and there developed between the races a modus vivendi that provided patterns of race relations that have persisted to the present day. There follows a chapter on the emergence and rôle of the free Negro in a changing society with a commercial agriculture. The last chapter in this section, dealing with slave revolts and the Underground Railroad, not only indicates the extent to which the Negro made an external adjustment to slavery but also reveals how even his external adjustment to the slave status was affected by economic and social forces in American life.

CHAPTER I

Significance of the African Background

AMONG the "twenty Negers" who were brought in "a dutch man of warre" to Virginia in 1619, there were some whose names indicated that they had been baptized by the Spaniards.[1] But to what extent baptism and a new name were an indication that these slaves had lost their African cultural heritage or had acquired Spanish culture, the records do not inform us. Baptism and the acquisition of a Spanish name might have been artificial ceremonies, as they often were, when at the port of embarkation in Africa three or four hundred slaves were baptized and given a slip of paper in order that they might not forget their Spanish names.[2]

The manner in which young slaves were captured and sold on slave markets and confined in the slave pens in African ports had a more important effect upon the integrity of their cultural heritage. Such experiences, however, as well as the ordeal of the journey to the West Indies—the "middle passage"—did not destroy completely their African heritage. Individual slaves brought to America memories of their homeland and certain patterns of behavior and attitudes toward their fellow men and the physical world. It was in the New World, particularly in what became the United States, that new conditions of life destroyed the significance of their African heritage and caused new habits and attitudes to develop to meet new situations. Despite fresh importations from Africa, the process of sloughing off African culture continued. Since Emancipation this process has been

[1] Helen T. Catterall (ed.), *Judicial Cases Concerning American Slavery and the Negro* (Washington, D. C., 1926), Vol. I, pp. 55-56.

[2] Enrique de Gandia, *Francisco de Alfaro y la Condicion Social de los Indios* (Buenos Aires, 1939), p. 38.

so thoroughgoing that at the present time only in certain isolated areas can one discover what might be justly called African cultural survivals.[3]

OUR KNOWLEDGE CONCERNING AFRICAN BACKGROUNDS

Only recently have we begun to secure sufficiently exact knowl edge of the origin of the slaves brought to America to be in a position to identify African survivals. In the West Indies, the planters had some knowledge of the tribal backgrounds of the slaves; while in Brazil terms were used by the planters to indicate vaguely the area in Africa from which the slaves came. Recent investigations by Brazilian scholars have shown that "three great Negro peoples entered Brazil." "At the beginning of the slave trade," as pointed out by Ramos, "the largest number of those imported into Brazil were from Angola, the Congo and Guinea. When more active communication began with Bahia, the leading source of supply was Guinea and the western Sudan. There began a remarkable influx of Yorubas, Minas from the Gold Coast, Dahomans and various Islamized tribes such as the Hausas, Tapas, Mandingos, and Fulahs." [4] In the United States it has generally been assumed by scholars that throughout the slave trade slaves were drawn from far in the interior of Africa.[5] This assumption has been challenged recently by Herskovits who has studied the documents bearing on the slave trade, especially those collected and analyzed by Miss Donnan.[6] By analyzing the data

[3] The most comprehensive and systematic study of the problem of African cul tural survivals is to be found in Melville J. Herskovits, *The Myth of the Negro Past* (New York, 1942). Throughout this chapter there will be occasion to refer to this work, though our discussion will often be in disagreement with the conclusions of Herskovits, who attempts to show that African survivals can be discovered in practically every phase of Negro life in the United States.

[4] *The Negro in Brazil*, by Arthur Ramos, p. 11. Copyright 1939 by The Asso ciated Publishers, Inc.

[5] See for example U. B. Phillips, *American Negro Slavery* (New York, 1936), p. 31; Robert E. Park, "The Conflict and Fusion of Cultures," *Journal of Negro History*, Vol. IV, p. 117; and Edward Byron Reuter, *The American Race Problem* (New York, 1938), p. 123.

[6] Herskovits, *The Myth of the Negro Past*, pp. 35-53. See also Elizabeth Donnan, *Documents Illustrative of the Slave Trade to America*, Vols. I-IV (Washington, D. C., 1930-1935).

found "in manifests recorded from Virginia between the years 1710 and 1769" he was able to determine the specific areas from which came approximately 25,000 of the 45,000 slaves imported directly from Africa. The areas that figured most prominently were Guinea, "which means the west coast of Africa from the Ivory Coast to western Nigeria, Calabar, which represents the Niger Delta region, An-

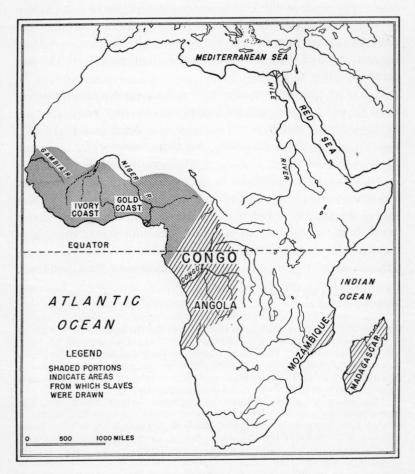

MAP I

Africa

gola, or the area about the lower Congo, and the Gambia." [7] As in the case of slaves imported into other states, only a few of these slaves— 1,011 out of a total of 52,504—were from Madagascar. During the last half of the eighteenth century, the vast majority of the slaves imported into the American colonies came from the areas described above; but toward the close of the century the number of slave ships coming from the Congo increased.[8] In the nineteenth century when efforts were made by the United States, England, and France to outlaw the slave trade in those parts of Africa under the control of the latter two powers, the Congo, which was under Portuguese control, became the chief source of slaves for the illegal trade to the United States as well as to Brazil.

This more precise knowledge of the areas from which the slaves came has not, however, enabled investigators to refer African survivals in the United States to a specific tribe or a definite area.[9] In fact, students of the Negro are agreed that there were fewer African survivals in the United States than in other areas of the New World.[10] This was due, first, to differences in the character of slavery and the plantation system in the United States and in other parts of the New World. In the West Indies and Brazil, large numbers of African slaves were concentrated on vast plantations for the production of sugar. Under such conditions it was possible for the slaves to reestablish their African ways of life and keep alive their traditions.

[7] *The Myth of the Negro Past*, by Melville J. Herskovits, p. 41. Copyright 1941 by Harper & Brothers.

[8] *Ibid.*, pp. 52-53. According to Herskovits' analysis of Miss Donnan's sources, approximately 22,000 of the 65,466 slaves imported into South Carolina between 1733 and 1738 came from Angola and the Congo. *Ibid.*, p. 48.

[9] ". . . one can set off the United States from the rest of the New World as a region where departure from African modes of life was greatest, and where such Africanisms as persisted were carried through in generalized form, almost never directly referable to a specific tribe or a definite area." *Ibid.*, p. 122.

[10] See *ibid.*, p. 16, where Herskovits arranges areas of Negro concentration in the New World on a scale according to the intensity of African survivals. The area of most intensive survivals is in Suriname (the Bush Negroes) while next to the last group at the other end of the scale appear isolated groups of Negroes on the coast of Georgia and South Carolina. "Finally," writes Herskovits, "we should come to a group where, to all intents and purposes, there is nothing of the African tradition left, and which consists of people of varying degrees of Negroid physical type, who only differ from their white neighbors in the fact that they have more pigmentation in their skins." *Ibid.*, p. 16.

But in the United States the slaves were scattered in relatively small numbers on plantations and farms over a large area. In 1860 in the South as a whole, three-fourths of the farms and plantations had less than fifty slaves.[11] Even in the lower South, where the slaveholdings were larger on the average, two-thirds of the holdings were less than fifty slaves. Only in Arkansas, Georgia, Louisiana, Mississippi, and South Carolina were there holdings with more than 500 slaves and such holdings constituted less than one per cent of the holdings in all these states except South Carolina.

SIZE OF PLANTATION AND AFRICAN SURVIVALS

The size of the slaveholdings on the farms and plantations significantly influenced both the extent and nature of the contacts between the slaves and the whites. There was little contact between the great body of field slaves and the whites on the large sugar and cotton plantations in the southern states, as was true also on the large sugar plantations in Brazil and in the West Indies. Concerning the situation in South Carolina, Mrs. Johnson writes: "On St. Helena Island, where there were some two thousand slaves to little more than two hundred whites, the Negroes learned very slowly the ways of the whites. Their mastery of English was far less advanced than that of the Piedmont slaves." [12] However, as we have seen, the majority of the slaves in the United States were on small farms and plantations. In some of the upland cotton regions of Alabama, Mississippi, Louisiana, and Arkansas the median number of slaves per holding did not reach twenty; while in regions of general farming based mainly upon slave labor in Kentucky, Maryland, Missouri, North Carolina, South Carolina, and Tennessee the median holdings were even less.[13] In some of these latter regions the close contacts between the slaves and whites extended to working together on the smaller farms.

Slaves freshly imported from Africa usually had to be "broken in"

[11] Lewis C. Gray, *History of Agriculture in the Southern United States to 1860* (New York, 1941), Vol. I, p. 529.

[12] Reprinted from *A Social History of the Sea Islands,* by Guion Griffis Johnson, p. 127, by permission of The University of North Carolina Press. Copyright 1930 by The University of North Carolina Press.

[13] Gray, *op. cit.,* Vol. I, pp. 534-35.

to the plantation regime. A traveler in Louisiana described the process as follows:

Negroes bought from the importers and carried home by the purchasers are ordinarily treated differently from the old ones. They are only gradually accustomed to work. They are made to bathe often, to take walks from time to time, and especially to dance; they are distributed in small numbers among old slaves in order to dispose them better to acquire their habits. These attentions are not usually due to sentiments of humanity. Interest requires them. It happens too often that poor masters, who have not other slaves, or are too greedy, require hard labor of these fresh negroes, exhaust them quickly, lose them by sickness and more often by grief. Often they hasten their own death; some wound themselves, others stifle themselves by drawing in the tongue so as to close the breathing passage, others take poison, or flee and perish of misery and hunger.[14]

It is likely that these new slaves with their African ways and memories of Africa had to face the disdain, if not the hostility, of Negroes who had become accommodated to the slave regime and had acquired a new conception of themselves.[15] They were most likely to meet such an attitude on the part of the household slaves, who because of their intimate association with the whites had taken over the culture of the latter.[16]

ADJUSTMENT OF SLAVES TO NEW ENVIRONMENT

Because of the fact that the manner of the Negro's enslavement tended to destroy so completely his African culture, some scholars have been inclined to dismiss the influence of the African culture on

---

[14] "Voyages . . . de la Louisiane," vol. iii, 169-70, by C. C. Robin, from *Plantation and Frontier: Documents: 1649-1863*, Vol. II, p. 31, by Ulrich B. Phillips. Copyright 1909 by A. H. Clark Company.

[15] The following newspaper account of the reception of four native Africans on a Georgia plantation, except for the inferred detail concerning the delight of the newcomers, is probably indicative of the general attitude of the slaves toward their African background: "Our common darkies treat them with sovereign contempt walking around them with a decided aristocratic air. But the Africans are docile and very industrious and are represented as being perfectly delighted with new homes and improved conditions. The stories that they are brutes and savages is all stuff and nonsense. It was put in the papers by men who do not know what they are talking about. As to their corrupting our common negroes, we venture the assertion would come nearer the truth if stated the other way." *Atlanta* (Ga.) *Daily Intelligencer*, March 9, 1859, from Phillips, *op. cit.*, 54-55.

[16] See Chapter III below.

the Negro's behavior. They have recognized, to be sure, that the speech of the Negro folk as well as their religious practices and family life differ from the behavior and customs of the whites; but these differences have been attributed to their isolation and incomplete assimilation.[17] On the other hand, there has been much speculation on the influence of African culture as a cause of these differences. In some instances this speculation has betrayed an ignorance of African cultures or has simply reflected popular prejudices in regard to "primitive" people or so-called "savages." But there has also been speculation of a nature that has led to fantastic conclusions concerning the influence of African survivals on the behavior of Negroes in the United States.[18] Only recently have competent scholars with a knowledge of the culture of the African areas from which the Negroes came attempted to identify definite African survivals.[19]

The first adjustment which the transported Negroes had to make in their new environment was to acquire some knowledge of the language of the whites for communication. Where the slaves, sometimes from childhood, were in close contacts with the whites, they took over completely the speech and language of their masters. On the other hand, the great masses of isolated slaves, as in the case of the slaves on St. Helena Island, acquired the speech and language of the whites more slowly. The peculiar speech of Negroes in such isolated places has generally been attributed to their isolation, their lack of appreciation of grammatical rules, or to the fact that they had preserved the characteristics of English as spoken at an earlier period. But

[17] See Reuter, *op. cit.*, pp. 129-31; and Park, *op. cit.*, pp. 115-17.

[18] For example, see Woodson, *The African Background Outlined or Handbook for the Study of the Negro*, pp. 168-75, where the author, among other equally untenable conjectures, states: "The industry of the Negro in the United States may be partly explained as an African survival. The Negro is born a worker. In the African social order work is well organized. Everybody is supposed to make some contribution to the production of food and clothing necessary for the whole community" (*The African Background Outlined or Handbook for the Study of the Negro* by Carter G. Woodson, p. 171. Copyright 1936 by Association for the Study of Negro Life and History. Reprinted by permission of The Associated Publishers, Inc.). The claim of a social worker (Corinne Sherman, "Racial Factors in Desertion," *Family*, III, 224) that she was not able to understand "the conjugal habits of colored clients" until she had gained a knowledge of African customs shows to what fantastic conclusions speculations about African survivals in America may lead one.   [19] See pp. 4ff. above.

Lorenzo D. Turner has discovered approximately four thousand words of West African origin in the Gullah vocabulary of Negroes on the coast of South Carolina and Georgia.[20] Moreover, he found numerous African given names and African phrases that had been translated into English. In view of Turner's researches, the current notion that African words have completely disappeared from the vocabulary of Negroes in all sections of the United States must be modified.[21]

DESTRUCTION OF AFRICAN FAMILY

In contrast to such concrete data on linguistic survivals, there is scarcely any evidence that recognizable elements of the African social organization have survived in the United States. This has been especially true in regard to those phases of the African social organization which had a political character.[22] A rare instance of such a survival may be found in the early history of New England, where it was customary for the Negroes to elect a "governor," who exercised an almost despotic discipline over local groups of slaves.[23] In regard to the African family organization there have been from time to time reports of survivals.[24] For example, in the autobiography of an ex-slave the following incident is related:

[20] See Herskovits, *op. cit.*, pp. 276-79.

[21] In the West Indies and Suriname, it has been easier to trace many words in the language of the Negroes to their African sources. See Melville J. Herskovits, "On the Provenience of New World Negroes," *Social Forces*, XII, 252-59. In Brazil, the Islamized Negroes who maintained connections with Africa not only continued to speak Arabic but also conducted schools. Among the non-Islamized Negroes, Yoruba was the chief means of communication, this language being preserved today in the religious practices of Brazilian Negroes about Bahia. See Arthur Ramos, *O Negro Brasileiro* (Rio de Janeiro, 1940) and Nina Rodrigues, *Os Africanos*, (2a Edição, São Paulo, 1935).

[22] In the West Indies and in Brazil, there were numerous instances where free Negroes and especially slaves that had revolted or escaped revived features of the traditional African political organization. See Chapter V below.

[23] H. S. Aimes, "African Institutions in America," *Journal of American Folklore*, Vol. XVIII, pp. 15-17.

[24] W. E. B. DuBois, who believed that careful research would reveal traces, but traces only, "of the African family in America" since "the effectiveness of the slave system meant the practically complete crushing out of the African clan and family life," nevertheless gives as an example of survival the case of a Negro country wedding in Lowndes County, Alabama, in 1892, in which the bride was chased "after the ceremony in a manner very similar to the Zulu ceremony." *The Negro Family* (Atlanta, 1908), p. 21.

I assisted her and her husband to inter the infant—which was a little boy—and its father buried with it, a small bow and several arrows; a little bag of parched meal; a miniature canoe, about a foot long, and a little paddle (with which he said it would cross the ocean to his own country), a small stick, with an iron nail, sharpened, and fastened into one end of it; and a piece of white muslin, with several curious and strange figures painted on it in blue and red, by which, he said, his relations and countrymen would know the infant to be his son, and would receive it accordingly, on its arrival amongst them. . . . He cut a lock of hair from his head, threw it upon the dead infant, and closed the grave with his own hands. He then told us the God of his country was looking at him, and was pleased with what he had done.[25]

If we can rely on the account of an old Negro woman that "a slave who married a girl from a group of native Africans just received on the plantation" was required "to obtain the consent of every member of the girl's group before he was allowed to marry her," [26] we have what might be an instance of the continued control of the extended family or clan organization. In his researches concerning linguistic survivals, Turner found that in isolated areas on the coast of Georgia and South Carolina, the Gullahs who often confine the use of African words to the intimate circle of the family reveal the influence of African traditions in the naming of their children. He writes:

Even though the Gullahs may not know the meaning of many African words they use for proper names, in their use of English words they follow a custom common in West Africa of giving their children names which suggest the time of birth, or the conditions surrounding it, or the temperament or appearance of the child. All twelve months of the year and the seven days of the week are used freely. In some cases the name indicates the time of day at which the birth occurs.[27]

These rare and isolated instances of survivals associated with the Negro family only indicate how completely the African social organization was wiped out by slavery.

[25] Charles Ball, *Slavery in the United States: A Narrative of the Life and Adventures of Charles Ball, A Black Man* (Lewistown, Pa., 1836), pp. 203-5.

[26] Reprinted from *Folk Beliefs of the Southern Negro* by Newbell Niles Puckett, p. 24, by permission of The University of North Carolina Press. Copyright 1926 by The University of North Carolina Press.

[27] *The Myth of the Negro Past* by Melville J. Herskovits, p. 192. Copyright 1941 by Harper & Brothers.

Although Herskovits agrees with other students of the Negro that the plantation system destroyed African family types as well as their underlying moral and supernatural sanctions, he nevertheless thinks that a diluted form of the African family continued to exist.[28] A diluted form of the African family may be recognized, he thinks, in the so-called common-law marriages among Negroes. "We . . . must recognize," he writes, "that the elasticity of the marriage concept among Negroes derives in a measure, largely unrecognized, from the need to adjust a polygynous family form to patterns based on a convention of monogamy, in a situation where this has been made the more difficult by economic and psychological complications resulting from the nature of the historical situation."[29] Likewise, he sees in the so-called "matriarchal" or "maternal" family among Negroes, in which the mother and grandmother play important rôles, evidence of the continuation in a diluted form of African traditions. "It cannot be regarded only as coincidence," he maintains, "that such specialized features of Negro family life in the United States as the rôle of women in focusing the sentiment that gives the family unit its psychological coherence, or their place in maintaining the economic stability essential to survival, correspond closely to similar facets of West African social structure."[30]

These statements concerning the continuation in a diluted form of the African family in the United States are not based upon any data showing continuity between African traditions and the familial behavior of American Negroes. They are only an ingenious attempt to show similarity between certain customs and practices of Negroes in the United States and in Africa in regard to sex and family behavior. However, the supposed similarities in attitudes and behavior are not real similarities in a cultural sense. When loose and unregulated sex behavior is encountered among American Negroes, it is not the same as the polygynous customs and practices of African Negroes. The latter are regulated by custom and tradition while the former

[28] "It goes without saying," writes Herskovits, "that the plantation system rendered the survival of African family types impossible, as it did their underlying moral and supernatural sanctions, except in dilute form." *Ibid.*, p. 139.

[29] *The Myth of the Negro Past* by Melville J. Herskovits, p. 170. Copyright 1941 by Harper & Brothers.   [30] *Ibid.*, p. 180.

lack the sanction of traditions and customs. Although in some areas "common-law" matings occur on a large scale among certain classes of Negroes, such behavior can be explained in terms of practices which sometimes have become customary as the result of social and economic forces in the American environment.[31] Moreover, such behavior is often recognized as being in conflict with the mores of the larger society.

The same fallacies appear in the attempt to explain illegitimacy among Negroes and the important position of the woman in the Negro family as a diluted form of African cultural survival. The argument that the impulsive and uncontrolled sex behavior of foot-loose Negro women which often results in illegitimacy has a basis in African traditions may be dismissed simply as unwarranted speculation. On the other hand, the statement concerning the survival of African customs in regard to the woman's place in the family deserves some consideration. It is probably true that the situation under the slave regime might have given support to those African traditions supporting the woman's important position in the family. But African traditions supporting male dominance were just as likely to survive in the New World. For example, even today it appears that the African pattern of family life is perpetuated in the patriarchal family organization of the West Indian Negroes.[32]

In the United States it is neither possible nor is it necessary to seek an explanation of the dominance of the male or the female in the family organization of Negroes in supposed survivals of the African

[31] See E. Franklin Frazier, *The Negro Family in the United States* (Chicago, 1939), Part II, "The House of the Mother."

[32] Martha W. Beckwith, *Black Roadways: A Study of Jamaican Folk Life* (Chapel Hill, 1929), p. 54. In the following observations of a visitor to the French West Indies about the year 1700 we have, doubtless, an example of this patriarchal authority which had its roots in Africa. Labat says: "I have often taken pleasure in watching a negro carpenter at Guadaloupe when he ate his meals. His wife and children gathered around him, and served him with as much respect as the best drilled domestics serve their masters; and if it was a fete day or Sunday, his sons-in-law and daughters did not fail to be present, and bring him some small gifts. They formed a circle about him, and conversed with him while he was eating. When he had finished, his pipe was brought to him, and then he bade them eat. They paid him their reverences, and passed into another room, where they all eat together with their mother." Pere Labat, *Voyage aux isles francoises*, II, 54, cited in Aimes, *loc. cit.*, pp. 24-25.

social organization. The important position of the mother in the Negro family in the United States has developed out of the exigencies of life in the new environment. In the absence of institutional controls, the relationship between mother and child has become the essential social bond in the family and the woman's economic position has developed in her those qualities which are associated with a "matriarchal" organization. On the other hand, the Negro family has developed as a patriarchal organization or similar to the American family as the male has acquired property and an interest in his family and as the assimilation of American attitudes and patterns of behavior has been accelerated by the breaking down of social isolation, sometimes through physical amalgamation.[33] Herskovits sees even in such well integrated patriarchal families, with a secure economic basis and traditions extending over several generations, evidence of the survival of the African ancestral cult in their family reunions when they praise the accomplishments of their ancestors or visit the family burying ground. Yet he admits that the overt manifestations of the ancestral cult have been obliterated and European religious beliefs have been taken over, and that only the "spirit" of ancestral culture has remained.[34] This simply means that the existence of such survivals cannot be validated on scientific grounds.

AFRICAN RELIGIOUS SURVIVALS

There can be no question about the survival of African religious ceremonies and rituals in some parts of the New World. In Brazil at the present time African religious survivals are easily recognized in the religious cults of the Negroes and people of Negro descent. The *macumbas* of the Negroes in the region about Rio de Janeiro are true African religious survivals that have become greatly "adulterated in contact with an elaborate and complicated urban civilization." [35] On the other hand, such religious cults as the *candomblés* of Bahia and some of the *shangôs* of the northeast have preserved many African elements. In these religious cults, formerly concealed from the

[33] See Frazier, *op. cit.*, Part III, "In the House of the Father."
[34] See Herskovits, *op. cit.*, p. 199.
[35] *The Negro in Brazil* by Arthur Ramos, p. 81. Copyright 1939 by The Associated Publishers, Inc.

whites, the worship of Yoruban deities was carried on for centuries; but at the present time African deities are becoming identified with Catholic saints and beliefs are becoming fused with spiritualism.[36] Likewise, in Haiti one may find African survivals in the religious beliefs and rituals of the peasantry.[37]

In the United States it has been more difficult to discover African survivals in the religious behavior of the Negroes. During slavery there were reports of the dancing and singing of the slaves which indicated that African religious ceremonies had been carried over. Moreover, there were reports of slaves praying in a manner that indicated that they had been converted to Mohammedanism.[38] Since the emancipation of the slaves, we have had accounts of authentic religious practices which were undoubtedly of African origin.[39] Then, too, on the Sea Islands, where the isolated unmixed Negroes speak a distinct dialect, the "praise house" probably represents a fusion of African culture traits and Christian practices.[40] However, except for such instances, generally occurring among isolated groups of Negroes, it has been difficult to identify religious traits that could correctly be called African survivals.

Despite the general absence of African beliefs and rituals in the religious behavior of the Negroes in the United States, there has been some speculation on the existence of less obvious African survivals. For example, the fact that the majority of the Negroes in the United States are affiliated with the Baptist churches seems to Herskovits to be due primarily to certain features in the Negro's African heritage. His first statement of this viewpoint was that

The importance of baptism in the ritual practices of Negro Christians has often been commented upon. It is not unreasonable to relate the

[36] *Ibid.*, pp. 82-93. See also Arthur Ramos, *O Negro Brasileiro*; Nina Rodrigues, *Os Africanos*; and Edison Carneiro, *Religioes Negras* (Rio de Janeiro, 1936).

[37] See Melville J. Herskovits, *Life in a Haitian Valley* (New York, 1937), pp. 139-248.

[38] See, for example, Ball, *op. cit.*, p. 127, where he tells of a slave "who prayed five times every day, always turning his face to the east."

[39] See George W. Cable, "Creole Slave Songs," *Century Magazine*, Vol. XXI, pp. 807-27.

[40] Guion G. Johnson, *A Social History of the Sea Islands* (Chapel Hill, 1930) pp. 147-53.

strength of adherence to this practice to the great importance of the river-cults in West Africa, particularly in view of the fact that, as has been observed, river-cult priests were sold into slavery in great numbers.[41]

Evidently after Herskovits became acquainted with the "aggressive proselyting activities of Protestantism" and the fact that white Baptists emphasized total immersion, he revised the statement of his position so as to include these facts.[42] He, nevertheless, maintains his position with reference to the rôle of priests of river-cults who were sold to rich Dahomean "conquerors of troublesome leaders." His most recent statement is as follows:

In the New World, where the aggressive proselytizing activities of Protestantism made the retention of the inner forms of African religion as difficult as its outer manifestations, the most logical adaptation for the slaves to make to the new situation, and the simplest, was to give their adherence to that Christian sect which in its ritualism most resembled the types of worship known to them. As we have seen, the Baptist churches had an autonomous organization that was in line with the tradition of local self-direction congenial to African practice. In these churches the slaves were also permitted less restrained behavior than in the more sedate denominations. And such factors only tended to reinforce an initial predisposition of these Africans toward a cult which, in emphasizing baptism by total immersion, made possible the worship of the new supernatural powers in ways that at least contained elements not entirely unfamiliar.[43]

The proselyting activities of the Baptists and Methodists provide an adequate explanation of the fact that the majority of the Negroes are members of the Baptist church. Moreover, they provide an adequate explanation of the fact that about a third of the Negroes are members of Methodist churches, which do not practice baptism by

[41] Melville J. Herskovits, "Social History of the Negro," in Carl Murchison, *A Handbook of Social Psychology* (Worcester, 1935), pp. 256-57.

[42] The backwoods preacher, Peter Cartwright, wrote as follows concerning the activities of the white Baptist preachers in Tennessee during the early years of the nineteenth century: ". . . indeed, they made so much ado about baptism by immersion, that the uninformed would suppose that heaven was an island, and that there was no way to get there but by diving or swimming." *Autobiography of Peter Cartwright*, edited by W. P. Strickland (New York, 1857), p. 134.

[43] Herskovits, *The Myth of the Negro Past*, p. 233.

immersion, a fact which the speculation about the influence of African river-cults fails to explain. The Negro slaves seemingly from the beginning of their residence in the United States took over the religious beliefs and rituals to which they were exposed. During the eighteenth century the Society for the Propagation of the Gospel in Foreign Parts operating through the ministers of the Established Church of England converted many slaves to Christianity. For example, in the Goose Creek Parish in South Carolina in 1705, a Reverend Samuel Thomas had given religious instruction to a thousand slaves, "many of whom could read the Bible distinctly and great numbers of them were engaged in learning the scriptures." [44]

Then came the revivals during the latter half of the eighteenth century which drew vast numbers of the slaves into the Methodist and Baptist churches. Around the opening of the nineteenth century appeared the camp meeting revivals that tended to revive and enforce the effects of the religious awakening of the preceding century.[45] The Methodist and Baptist preachers carried the "gospel of salvation" to the black slave as well as to the poor and ignorant white.[46] In King William County, Virginia, in 1789 the sheriff appealed to the Governor because the Baptists and Methodists were meeting with slaves several times a week and had ejected the patrollers from their meetings.[47] In fact, when the Methodists and Baptists began their proselyting among the slaves and poor whites they were outspoken against slavery. When they ceased to oppose slavery openly, they continued to present Christianity as an escape for the enslaved blacks from their earthly condition.

Although the Methodists made the same appeal as the Baptists, there were certain features in the Baptist church organization and in their policy with reference to the Negroes that caused the latter to enter the Baptist organization more freely than the Methodist church.

[44] *The History of the Negro Church* by Carter G. Woodson, p. 7. Copyright 1921 by The Associated Publishers, Inc.

[45] See Frederick M. Davenport, *Primitive Traits in Religious Revivals* (New York, 1917), pp. 60ff.

[46] The Presbyterian revivalists were also active at this time among the slaves.

[47] Luther P. Jackson, "Religious Development of the Negro in Virginia from 1760 to 1860." *The Journal of Negro History*, Vol. XVI, pp. 172-73.

The Baptists encouraged a form of local self-government that favored the growth of Negro congregations. Then, too, they permitted and encouraged Negroes to become preachers, at first to whites as well as Negroes, and later as leaders of Negro congregations. Because of these features of the Baptist church policy, the enslaved and free Negro was given an opportunity for self-expression not provided by the Methodist church.[48] Under the Methodist church organization he was not only subject to the control emanating from the bishops but he was generally under white leadership in churches.[49]

One may reasonably assume that among the Negroes who received the "call to preach," there were some who had been influenced by African traditions and that others cherishing memories of their African background found in the emotionalism and the ecstatic form of worship that characterized the Methodist and Baptist revivals an opportunity for self-expression. But such assumptions provide no proof for Herskovits' assertion that the emotionalism and ecstatic behavior that characterized the Great Awakening and the camp meetings were largely due to African influences and that contrary to usual accounts the whites took over the behavior of the Negroes.[50] In support of this view he cites Davenport's observation on the difference between the automatisms of the Kentucky and the Ulster revivalists, the former, he thinks, having been influenced by the Negroes.[51] This reasoning is in line with Herskovits' general belief in the "toughness of culture," which enables it to survive under

---

[48] See Chapter XIII below.   [49] See Jackson, *loc. cit.,* p. 147.
[50] Herskovits, *op. cit.,* pp. 227-32.
[51] Herskovits gives the following quotation from Davenport, *op. cit.,* p. 92: "I wish in closing to call attention to the difference in type of the automatisms of Kentucky and Ulster. In Kentucky the motor automatisms, the voluntary muscles in violent action, were the prevailing type, although there were many of the sensory. On the other hand, in Ulster the sensory automatisms, trance, vision, the physical disability and the sinking of muscular energy were the prevailing type, although there were many of the motor. I do not mean that I can explain it. It may be that as the Charcot and Nancy schools of hypnosis brought out by chance, each in its own field, different kinds of hypnotic phenomena which, when known, spread by imitation in the respective localities and under the respective influences, so in Kentucky and the north of Ireland by chance there appeared different types of physical manifestation which were then imitated in the respective countries." *The Myth of the Negro Past* by Melville J. Herskovits, pp. 230-31. Copyright 1941 by Harper & Brothers.

the most unfavorable conditions. However, such an argument fails to take into account the rôle of spontaneous impulses in human behavior, which probably account for the differences between the behavior of the Kentucky revivalists and those in Ulster. Likewise, much of the behavior of the Negroes was spontaneous and expressive and was not rigidly controlled by traditional patterns of behavior. It is significant that their religious behavior in the United States is similar to that of whites, while it differs markedly from that of Brazilian Negroes who have preserved African rituals and beliefs in their religious organizations.[52]

OTHER PHASES OF CULTURE

Herskovits' belief in the "toughness of culture" has led him to speculate upon the influence of African traditions upon various phases of Negro life. He thinks that economic cooperation among Negroes in the United States has been influenced by African traditions. Of the cooperation found in the lodges he writes:

Cooperation among the Negroes of this country is principally found in such institutions as lodges and other benevolent societies, which in themselves are directly in line with the tradition underlying similar African organizations.[53]

Even in the fraternal organization among Negroes in cities, he sees "deep-seated drives in Negro life; drives so strong, indeed, that it is difficult, if not impossible, to account for them satisfactorily except in terms of a tradition which reaches further than merely to the period of slavery." [54] In regard to such speculation, one can only say that historical data concerning the leadership, the needs of an isolated group laboring under economic disadvantages, and the manner in which these organizations developed provide an adequate explanation of such phenomena. The "deep-seated" drives, which are referred to, are strong because they represent general human needs and, as we shall see in a later chapter, they are provided for in a manner

---

[52] This statement is based upon the writer's uncontrolled observations as well as the accounts of others. See, for example, Arthur Ramos, *O Negro Brasileiro*, passim.
[53] *The Myth of the Negro Past* by Melville J. Herskovits, p. 161. Copyright 1941 by Harper & Brothers.   [54] *Ibid.*, p. 164.

consistent with the resources and the experiences of the people involved.

In some of the magic and folk beliefs of the rural Negroes in the United States, some African elements have probably been retained. But it is recognized by even Herskovits that "magic and other types of folk belief" originating in Africa and Europe have become amalgamated.[55] Therefore, the problem of the student seeking African survivals is to disentangle African from other elements in such beliefs and practices. On the basis of his knowledge of African cultures, Herskovits has attempted to show that unsuspected African elements have survived.[56] Puckett, who has devoted himself to the same task, concludes that the Negro has taken "over English practices in regard to the direct maintenance and perpetuation of life, while in things relating to pleasure, his customs seemingly have more of an African turn." [57] However, he adds that the African influence has been least where the Negro has had the most contact with the whites and that there are beliefs among Negroes "which seem to have no direct European or African parallels, and may represent independent Afro-American developments." [58]

The latter statement by Puckett concerning the appearance of new ways of thinking and acting applies to all aspects of Negro life in the United States. African patterns of thought and behavior could survive only where the Negroes were isolated and where there was sufficient common understanding among them to give significance to African survivals. But the isolation of the Negro from the whites was always limited by the fact that the majority of the slaves were scattered over a vast territory on small farms and plantations. Their isolation was further broken down by the organization of slave labor and the internal slave trade which created some mobility among the slave population. More important still was the fact that the African family system, the chief means of cultural transmission, was destroyed. Under such circumstances African languages were lost and the Afri-

---

[55] *Ibid.*, p. 235.   [56] *Ibid.*, pp. 235-51.
[57] Reprinted from *Folk Beliefs of the Southern Negro* by Newbell Niles Puckett, p. 78, by permission of The University of North Carolina Press. Copyright 1926 by The University of North Carolina Press.   [58] *Ibid.*

can social organization could not be reconstituted in the new environment. Consequently, Negroes acquired new habits and modes of thought, and whatever elements of African culture were retained lost their original meaning in becoming fused with their experiences in the New World. Beginning with emancipation Negroes have from time to time been uprooted from their customary ways of life and have gradually escaped from their isolation. As they have emerged from the world of the folk, they have been affected by the modes of thought and behavior characteristic of civilized or urbanized societies. This has constantly resulted in considerable social disorganization; but at the same time it has led to reorganization of life, at least among certain elements, on a pattern consistent with civilized modes of behavior. During this process of adjusting themselves to American civilization, the majority of the Negroes have sloughed off completely the African heritage.

CHAPTER II

Evolution of the Slave Status

IN 1619 twenty Negroes were purchased from a Dutch man-of-war by the Virginia settlers. Since there was no precedent in English law for slavery, these Negroes and those imported later were "absorbed in a growing system [servitude based upon English apprenticeship and vagrancy laws] which spread to all the colonies and for nearly a century furnished the chief supply of colonial labor." [1] The fact that the Negroes were an alien race bearing distinctive physical marks was, doubtless, the basis for differential treatment from the beginning and later facilitated their enslavement. But it was not due solely to difference in race that Negro slavery grew and finally supplanted white servitude. There were powerful economic factors, such as the demand for a cheap and permanent labor supply, that decided the fate of the Negro. Court decisions and statutes only gave legal sanction to customary practices or what was becoming an established fact. Later, because of the invention of the cotton gin and the rise of the textile industry in England, the slave system became the foundation of the economic life of the South. When, for economic as well as moral reasons, slavery was attacked by the North, the Bible and political philosophy were invoked to give an absolute sanction to the slave system.

[1] *A History of Slavery in Virginia* by James C. Ballagh, p. 32. Copyright 1902 by The Johns Hopkins Press. In fact, a large proportion of the white settlers had been impoverished agricultural laborers in England and had bound themselves to colonial capitalists for a period of servitude. In the same year in which Negroes were first introduced into Virginia, the existing system of servitude was given legal recognition in England. See Lewis C. Gray, *History of Agriculture in the Southern United States to 1860* (Washington, D. C., 1933), Vol. I, pp. 342-44.

STATUS OF NEGRO GRADUALLY DIFFERENTIATED
FROM THAT OF WHITE SERVANTS

Little is known of the fate of the first Negroes who were introduced
into Virginia. However, there is a record of the baptism of a child
of one couple among the original twenty Negroes. This is significant
because at the time, according to the law of England by which the
colony was governed, "a slave who had been christened or baptized
became 'infranchised.' " [2] That this law was recognized in the colony
is indicated in a case which came before the general court of Virginia in 1624. A Negro, John Phillip, was permitted to testify as a
free man and Christian in the trial of a white man because he had
been baptized twelve years previously in England.[3] During the following year another case came before the court which showed that
Negro servitude was clearly distinguished from Negro slavery. In
September 1625 the court ordered "the Negro that cam in with Capt.
Jones shall remaine with the La: Yardley till further order be taken
for him and that he shalbe allowed by the Lady Yardley monthly for
his labors forty pownd waight of good merchantable tobacco for his
labor and service so lone as he remayneth with her." [4]

Although the Negroes brought to Virginia during the early years
of the colony had the same legal status as white servants, there is evidence in the meager documents which have survived that they were
treated differently from the white servants. For example, note the
words of the court in the case of a white man who had sexual relations
with a Negro woman. The white man was ordered "to be soundly
whipt before an assembly of Negroes and others for abusing himself
to the dishonor of God and shame of Christianity by defiling his body
in lying with a Negro, which fault he is to actk. next sabbath day." [5]
If such language were provoked because the Negro woman was a
heathen or unbaptized, there is no doubt in a case brought before the
court in 1640 of the attitude of the white community. Three bound
servants, two white and one Negro, had been brought back from

---

[2] Helen T. Catterall (Ed.), *Judicial Cases Concerning American Slavery and
the Negro* (Washington, D. C., 1926), Vol. I, p. 55.
[3] *Ibid.*, p. 76.   [4] *Ibid.*   [5] *Ibid.*, p. 77.

Maryland after attempting to escape from servitude. The court ordered:

that the said three servants shall receive the punishment of whipping and to have thirty stripes apiece one called Victor, a dutchman, the other a Scotchman called James Gregory, shall first serve out their times with their master according to their Indentures, and one whole year apiece after the time of their service is Expired . . . and after that service . . . to serve the colony for three whole years apiece, and that the third being a negro named John Punch shall serve his master of his assigns for the time of his natural Life here or elsewhere.[6]

The sentence of the court that the Negro should serve for life reflected the change which was taking place at this time with reference to Negro servitude.

This change is indicated in other cases. There was a case in 1641 involving a Negro who had been permitted by his master to raise hogs on the condition that "half the increase" be given his master and "the other half reserved for his own benefit." [7] This Negro had a child by a Negro woman "belonging to Lieut. Robert Sheppard which he desired should be made a Christian" and brought up according to the religion of the Church of England. And for this reason he had bought his child from Sheppard. In order to establish his right to purchased property, it was necessary for his master to appear before the court, which ordered that the child should be free from his master and "remain at the disposing and education of [the Negro] and the child's godfather, who undertaketh to see it brought up in the Christian religion." It should be noted that the child's freedom was not established by Christian baptism but depended upon the property rights secured by the father. In fact, Virginia passed a law in 1667 to the effect that Christian baptism did not confer freedom upon slaves. This act read:

Whereas some doubts have risen whether children that are slaves by birth, and by the charity and piety of their owners made pertakers of the blessed sacrament of baptisme, should by vertue of their baptisme be made free; it is enacted . . . that the conferring of baptisme doth not alter the condition of the person as to his bondage or freedome;

[6] *Ibid.*, p. 77.   [7] *Ibid.*, p. 78.

that diverse masters, freed from this doubt, may more carefully endeavour the propagation of christianity by permitting children, though slaves, or those of greater growth if capable, to be admitted to that sacrament.[8]

Before this act was passed there were still other cases which indicated that the status of Negro servants was becoming differentiated from that of white servants. There was the case of a mulatto who had been "bought as a Slave for Ever but in September 1644 the said Servant was by the Assembly adjudged no Slave and but to serve as other Christian servants do and was freed in September 1665." [9] As Mrs. Catterall points out concerning this case, "other Christian servants" did not serve apprenticeships of twenty-one years. Another case of considerable importance during this transition period was that involving Anthony Johnson, who was probably among the original twenty Negroes imported in 1619. In 1653 John Casor, a Negro who had come to Virginia in 1640, and was the servant of Anthony Johnson, complained that he had been retained by Johnson beyond his seven years of indenture. At first Johnson refused to release Casor on the ground that he was a servant for life; but was later persuaded to release him because he was threatened with a suit by a white man. Johnson afterwards complained to the court that Casor was detained by the white man under the pretense that Casor was a free man. The court rendered the following decision:

The court . . . doe fynd that ye sd Mr. Robert Parker most unrightly keepeth ye sd Negro John Casor from his r[igh]t Mayster Anthony Johnson & . . . Be it therefore ye Judgment of ye court & ordered that ye sd Jno. Casor negro shall forthwith return into ye service of his sd Mayster Anthony Johnson and that the sd Mr. Robert Parker make payment of all charges in the suit and execution.[10]

Nine years after this case, Virginia incorporated into its laws the first reference to the Negro as a slave. This reference was in an act passed in 1662 dealing with the punishment of English servants who ran away "in company of any negroes who are incapable of making satis-

---

[8] Quoted in *ibid.*, p. 57.   [9] *Ibid.*, p. 58.
[10] *The Free Negro in Virginia: 1619-1865* by John H. Russell, p. 33. Copyright 1913 by The Johns Hopkins Press.

faction by addition of time." In the same year an act was passed concerning the status of the offspring of white men and Negro women. It was enacted that "wheras some doubts have arrisen whether children got by any Englishmen upon a Negro woman shall be slave or free . . . all children born in this colony shall be bond or free only according to the condition of the mother." [11] By this act the racial and hereditary principle in slavery became established.

SLAVE STATUS OF NEGROES BECOMES FIXED

The slave status of Negroes imported into Virginia was fixed in a law of 1670, regarding the status of "all servants not being Christians." According to this act such servants were divided into two classes: those coming by sea who "shall be slaves for their lives" and those coming by land who shall serve a period of apprenticeship. By this act the Indian could not be reduced to slavery; while all Negroes, except those having been converted to Christianity, were presumed to be slaves upon entering the colony. Twelve years later the law of 1670 was repealed and another substituted in its place, "making slaves of all persons of non-Christian nationalities thereafter coming into the colony, whether they came by sea or land and whether or not they had been converted to Christianity after capture." [12] For this reason the year 1682 is regarded by Russell as "the upper limit of the period in which it was possible for negroes to come to Virginia as servants and acquire freedome after a limited term." [13]

The legislators in the neighboring colony of Maryland apparently profited by the experience of Virginia in reducing the Negro to the slave status. In 1664 the Maryland legislature passed an act entitled, *An Act concerning Negroes and other Slaves*, in order that there might be no question about the slave status of Negroes entering the colony. The lower house requested the upper house "to draw up an Act obligeing negroes to serve *durante vita* they thinking itt very necessary for the provencion of the damage Masters of such Slaves

---

[11] *American Negro Slavery* by Ulrich B. Phillips, p. 77. Copyright 1918 by D. Appleton and Company. Reprinted by permission of D. Appleton-Century Company, Inc.

[12] *The Free Negro in Virginia: 1619-1865* by John H. Russell, p. 39. Copyright 1913 by The Johns Hopkins Press.   [13] *Ibid.*

may susteyne by such Slaves pretending to be christened And soe plead the lawe of England." [14] However, the act which was passed that year did not give as the reason for its adoption the "danger of enfranchisement of slaves through baptism." It was not until 1671 that an act was passed "for the Encourageing the Importacion of negroes and slaves into this Province," dealing with the problem of baptism. According to this act,

Severall of the good people of this Province have been discouraged to import into or purchase within this Province any Negroes or other Slaves and such as have Imported or purchased . . . have to the great displeasure of Almighty God and the prejudice of the Soules of those poore people Neglected to instruct them in the Christian faith or to Endure . . . they to Receive the holy Sacrament of Baptisme . . . upon a mistake and ungrounded apprehension that by becomeing Christians they . . . are actually manumited.[15]

Therefore, it was enacted,

That where any Negro or Negroes Slave or Slaves being in Servitude . . . is are or shall become Christian or Christians and hath or have Received or shall att any time Receive the Holy Sacrament of Baptizme before or after his or her or their Importacion in this Province the same is not . . . taken to . . . amount into a manumicion.[16]

The Maryland Act of 1664 was especially concerned with the problem of intermarriage between white women and Negro men and the status of their offspring. Virginia was confronted at the same time with this problem, which was dealt with in the law of 1691.[17] According to this law, if a white servant woman married a Negro or mulatto, she was condemned to five years of servitude; and for the same offense a free white woman was banished from the colony. Mulatto offspring of such unions were regarded as bastards and were bound as other bastards for a term of apprenticeship until they were thirty years of age. In Maryland the law of 1664 provided "That whosoever free borne woman shall inter marry with any slave . . . shall Serve the master of such slave dureing the life of her husband And that all the Issue of such free borne woemen soe marryed shall be Slaves as their

---

[14] Catterall, *op. cit.*, Vol. II, p. 1.   [15] *Ibid.*, Vol. IV, p. 1.   [16] *Ibid.*
[17] See Ballagh, *op. cit.*, pp. 44-45; and Russell, *op. cit.*, pp. 40-41; 124.

fathers were." [18] This act was repealed in 1681, largely because of the interest of Lord Baltimore in a case involving a white woman servant, brought by him into the colony, who had married a Negro. The repeal of the act of 1664, it was said, was also designed "to prevent persons from purchasing white women and marrying them to Negroes for the purpose of making slaves of them." [19] Although, according to the act of 1681, a white servant woman as well as her offspring became free, if her master knew of the marriage he was liable to a fine of 10,000 pounds of tobacco as well as the minister or magistrate who performed the service. In 1692 it was enacted that a white woman who married a slave or free Negro or had a child by a slave or free Negro became a servant for seven years and the Negro, if free, was given a similar sentence. After 1692 the mulatto offspring of white women and slave or free Negroes became servants for a long term.[20]

In Maryland and Virginia, the two colonies in which the slave system first took root, the institution developed slowly in the seventeenth century. Previous to 1650 only small lots of Negroes, not exceeding thirty, were imported from time to time into Virginia. This was probably due to the fact that during the first half of the century the slave trade was in the hands of the Dutch. But even after the Royal African Company was granted the exclusive right to import Negroes into the English colonies, the number of Negroes did not increase materially for there were only two thousand in the colony in 1671.[21] But during the closing decade of the seventeenth century, when England had achieved a dominant position in the struggle for colonial supremacy and thereby increased her slave trade, slaves began to pour into Maryland and Virginia. According to Gray, "Between mid-summer, 1698 and Christmas, 1707, a total of 2,290 slaves were brought into Maryland," and by 1712 there were 8,330 Negroes in the colony.[22] Likewise in Virginia during the ten-year period, 1699 to 1708, a total of 6,607 Negroes were brought to Virginia.[23]

[18] Catterall, *op. cit.*, Vol. IV, p. 2.   [19] *Ibid.*
[20] Jeffrey R. Brackett, *The Negro in Maryland* (Baltimore, 1889), p. 33.
[21] Phillip A. Bruce, *Economic History of Virginia in the Seventeenth Century* (New York, 1907), Vol. II, p. 77.
[22] Gray, *op. cit.*, Vol. I, p. 354.   [23] *Ibid.*, p. 355.

THE PLANTATION SYSTEM OF AGRICULTURE

The growth of the institution of slavery was inextricably tied up with the development of the plantation system of agriculture. As in other parts of the world, the plantation in America was a form of settlement requiring some form of forced labor.[24] Since it was generally difficult to force the native population to work, it was necessary to import laborers. In the beginning the great body of laborers on the plantations were white indentured servants, who were generally "bound" for seven years and under the "supervision" of the officers of the colony. The supervision which was exercised by the officers of the colony was another important element in the plantation. The plantation was not only an industrial institution; it was also a political organization.[25] Under the frontier conditions in which the plantations flourished the planter was the absolute ruler of a small principality. His supreme authority was exercised primarily in the maintenance of a disciplined and efficient labor force.

The plantation system began in the southern colonies as capitalistic undertakings of European associations which had the authority to establish colonies. When these undertakings failed, the initiative was assumed by private capitalists in establishing a commercial agriculture based upon tobacco, rice, indigo, and naval stores. Since profit was the main consideration in a system of commercial agriculture, the rela-

[24] According to Nieboer, the plantation type of exploitation requires some form of forced labor in regions of "open resources." In regions of "open resources," "the means of subsistence are open to all; everyone who is able-bodied and not defective in mind can provide for himself independently of any capitalist or landlord. Among some of these peoples capital is of some use, and some valuable lands are already held as property; but those who are destitute of such advantages can perfectly well do without them, for there are still abundant natural supplies open to them. Among the peoples of the other category (closed resources) subsistence depends on resources of which the supply is limited, and therefore people destitute of these resources are dependent on the owners . . . only among peoples with open resources can slavery and serfdom exist, whereas free labourers dependent on wages are only found among peoples with closed resources." *Slavery as an Industrial System* by H. J. Nieboer, 2nd ed., rev. 1910, p. 385. Reprinted by permission of Martinus Nijhoff, Modern and Antiquarian Bookseller N. V., The Netherlands.

[25] See Edgar T. Thompson, "The Plantation: the Physical Basis of Traditional Race Relations," in Edgar T. Thompson (Ed.), *Race Relations and the Race Problem* (Durham, N. C., 1939), pp. 180-218, for an exposition of the characteristics of the plantation system of agriculture.

tive costs of different types of labor were a primary consideration. Negro slavery displaced white servitude because of certain economic advantages to the planters. There was, first, the fact that it was more difficult for the Negro than for the white servant to escape and lose himself among the colonists. Then there was the economic advantage of employing the black women as field hands since white women were as a rule exempted from such work. But it appears that the cost of maintaining a white servant was only slightly greater than maintaining a black slave, the difference in cost of clothing being the chief item. The general economic superiority of the slave as compared with the white servant is summed up by Gray as follows:

About the beginning of the eighteenth century a servant for a four-year term could be obtained for £10 to £15, while adult slaves could be had on the average for £18 to £20. The services of the slave were for life, as compared with four years for the servant, and the descendants of the slave would also belong to the planter. In spite of the cost of raising them, slave children were of some value at birth. The slave would be more difficult to train to perform field labor, but when broken in, was probably as efficient for field cultivation as a servant, and generally more tractable.[26]

EXPANSION OF THE PLANTATION SYSTEM DURING THE COLONIAL PERIOD

Under a commercial system of agriculture, slavery and the plantation system tended to supplant other forms of economic exploitation. "Even in eastern North Carolina, in spite of its commercial handicaps, the plantation system made considerable progress during the first half of the eighteenth century, displacing in part the earlier regime of backwoods farmers." [27] But the plantation economy and slavery failed to develop on a large scale in North Carolina, despite the fact that slaves were prized as great riches by planters. "The insurmountable difficulty," as Miss Donnan points out, "was that North Carolina, in the first half of the eighteenth century, had no commodity with which to load English vessels, and it was at this time chiefly English vessels that were bringing slaves directly from Africa. This lack of a staple acceptable to England prevented her merchants from

---

[26] Gray, *op. cit.*, p. 371.   [27] *Ibid.*, pp. 444-45.

sending vessels to the colony and also made them unwilling to grant to North Carolina planters the liberal credit which was necessary if they were to become heavy purchasers of Negro cargoes." [28]

But in South Carolina the plantation economy based upon slave labor was foreshadowed from the beginning of its settlement. Many of the early settlers, who had come from the West Indies where they

MAP II

Geographic Expansion of the Slave Population
in the United States: 1790.*

* Maps II, III, IV, and V were prepared in the Bureau of Agricultural Economics, United States Department of Agriculture. They are reproduced with the permission of the Bureau of Agricultural Economics and of Dr. L. C. Gray in whose *History of Agriculture in the Southern United States to 1860*, 2 vols. (Washington, 1933), they appear on pp. 652-55.

had had experience with slavery, found in the colony a climate and soil congenial to the system. The Fundamental Constitution of the colony contained the provision that the owner of every Negro man or slave brought to the colony within the first year would receive "20

[28] Elizabeth Donnan, *Documents Illustrative of the History of the Slave Trade to America* (Washington, D. C., 1935), Vol. IV, p. 236.

acres, and for every woman Negro or slave 10 acres; and all men Negroes or slaves after that time and within the five years 10 acres; and for every woman Negro or slave 5 acres." [29] By the close of the seventeenth century, the number of Negroes had become so numerous that it was felt necessary to encourage the importation of white servants to secure the safety of the colony. Every owner of a plantation was required to have one white servant for every six Negroes over sixteen years of age.[30] But the profits that were to be derived from the expansion of the rice industry in the eighteenth century caused such regulations to lose their force.

The spread of slavery into Georgia provides a good example of the triumph of the plantation economy based upon slavery over the determination of the early settlers to develop an agricultural economy of small landowners. In establishing the colony in 1735, the Trustees prohibited the importation or holding of Negro slaves in order to render "the Colony of Georgia more Defencible." A section of the minutes of the Privy Council reads as follows: "Wheras Experience hath Shown that the manner of Settling Colonys and Plantations with Black Slaves or Negroes had obstructed the Increase of English and Christian Inhabitants therein who alone can in case of a War be relyed on for the Defence and Security of the same, and hath Exposed the Colonys so settled to Insurrections Tumults and Rebellions of such Slaves and Negroes and in Case of a Rupture with any Foreign State who should Encourage and Support such Rebellions might Occasion the utter Ruin and loss of such Colonys." [31] The action of the trustees was opposed by many of the planters, some of them complaining that South Carolina with slave labor was able to produce things more cheaply than Georgia. Prominent among the petitioners for the introduction of slavery was the Reverend George Whitefield who argued that it was necessary for the maintenance of his orphanage.[32] It was even proposed by some that since the Act only prohibited the importation of Negro slaves, free Negroes should be imported because they would work for less than white servants.[33] In 1750, because of the great pressure of the proslavery planters and the growing

[29] Quoted in *ibid.*, pp. 241-42.   [30] *Ibid.*, p. 250.   [31] *Ibid.*, pp. 587-88.
[32] *Ibid.*, p. 606.   [33] *Ibid.*, p. 598.

illicit importation of Negroes, who in fact had been in the colony from the beginning, the Trustees repealed the act excluding Negroes. After the repeal the number of Negroes increased rapidly. In 1750 it was reported that there were 349 Negroes in the colony; but only ten years later there were 3,578; and in 1773 the number had reached 15,000.[34]

The development of the plantation system in Louisiana followed a course similar to that in Virginia. Through a system of concessions

MAP III

Geographic Expansion of the Slave Population
in the United States: 1800.

resembling the joint-stock companies controlled by the English Virginia Company, quasi public plantations were first set up in a number of places in the colony. For a labor force, these plantations depended upon indentured white servants and slaves. However, because French laborers were disinclined to sell themselves into servitude in order to migrate, the concessionaries were forced to recruit criminals, vaga-

[34] See *ibid.*, p. 244; and Gray, *op. cit.*, Vol. II, p. 1025.

bonds, smugglers, and prostitutes. The development of the plantation during most of the colonial period was slow because of the restrictions upon the slave trade, due to the commercial policies of France and Spain. It was not until English settlers and merchants became influential and sugar and cotton became the staples that slavery began to assume importance.

Since the plantation system of agriculture did not exist in the North, Negro slavery did not develop there on a large scale. The majority of slaves in the North served as domestics and personal servants. When the first federal census was taken in 1790 there were 67,120 Negroes in the North, 40,086 of whom were slaves.[35] Over a half—21,324—of the slaves were in New York. By 1790 all of the 5,462 Negroes in Massachusetts were free, though a half of the 5,572 Negroes in Connecticut were still in slavery. Over a third of the 4,355 Negroes in Rhode Island were slaves, while about a third of the more than 10,000 Negroes in Pennsylvania were still in slavery. In the border state of Delaware there were nearly 9,000 slaves.

AN INTERLUDE OF IDEALISM AND DECLINING PRODUCTIVITY

During and for a brief period following the Revolutionary War, the system of Negro slavery was subject to attacks which seemed to portend the gradual disestablishment of the slave system.[36] Jefferson had attacked the system in his original draft of the Declaration of Independence, where he stated that the king of England had "waged cruel war against human nature itself" in maintaining the slave trade.[37] During the War the employment of black soldiers in the South was recommended by the Continental Congress to the southern states with the provision that the masters would be reimbursed and the slaves set free at the end of the War. In the North there were provisions in the various state constitutions that put an end to the slave system. In the majority of these states the abolition of slavery was achieved by making the children born of slave parents free

---

[35] See Evarts B. Greene, *American Population before the Federal Census of 1790.* (New York, 1932), *passim.*   [36] See Phillips, *op. cit.*, Chapter VII.
[37] See Carl Becker,*The Declaration of Independence* (New York, 1942), p. 212.

upon reaching a certain age. Although the measures providing for the emancipation of the Negro during this period reflected some of the current idealism respecting liberty, the attitude of the North as well as that of the South reflected economic interests. In the North Negro slavery was already dying a natural death because there was no demand for slave labor.[38] Likewise, opposition to Negro slavery or the importation of Negro slaves was expressed in Delaware, Mary-

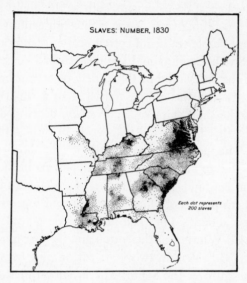

MAP IV

Geographic Expansion of the Slave Population
in the United States: 1830.

land, and Virginia where a diversified agriculture was supplanting the production of tobacco. In the lower South, where the production of tobacco, rice, and indigo was important, there was still strong opposition to the suspension of the slave trade as well as the emancipation of the Negro. When the states had achieved their independence, the provision that Congress could not prohibit the slave trade prior to

[38] See Cheesman A. Herrick, *White Servitude in Pennsylvania* (Philadelphia, 1926), where the author shows how the demand for laborers in diversified industry in Pennsylvania caused white servitude to displace black slavery in the state.

1808 was all that could be achieved in view of the fundamental conflict of interests in regard to slavery.

When the compromises on the status of slavery in the new Republic were embodied in the Constitution,[39] some of the Founding Fathers looked forward hopefully to the gradual disappearance of the institution. But soon after the birth of the Republic, the institution became even more deeply rooted in the economy of the South as the result of technological developments both in the South and in England. During the closing years of the eighteenth century the cultivation of the long staple sea-island cotton on the islands and adjacent mainland of South Carolina and Georgia reached considerable proportions. But the cultivation of this variety of cotton became a specialized industry and was always restricted to a small area of the South. It was the short staple upland variety, demanded by English manufacturers, that became the foundation of the Cotton Kingdom in the South. The increase in the demand for the short staple variety of cotton was due to inventions and developments in the cotton textile industry in England. In order to meet the demands it was necessary for southern planters to find some means of separating the seed from the close adhering lint. The problem was solved through the invention by Eli Whitney of the cotton gin, the first model of which appeared in 1793.[40] Within two years cotton gins began to appear on plantations all over the South. The invention of the cotton gin enabled American producers to meet the growing demands of the English market. Between 1780 and 1800 the annual importation of cotton into Great Britain increased eightfold.[41]

COTTON BECOMES KING

In response to the suddenly increased demands of English manufacturers for cotton, there was a rapid growth in cotton production in

[39] These compromises included the provisions that the slave trade could not be prohibited before 1808 and that a slave would be counted only as three-fifths of a person in determining the number of representatives which a state would have in Congress.

[40] A number of persons attempted to pirate the invention and as a result Whitney and his partner, Miller, were involved in numerous litigations. See Gray, *op. cit.*, Vol. II, pp. 680-81.   [41] *Ibid.*, p. 687.

the South. Up to 1815 the majority of the cotton was produced in the so-called "upper country" of South Carolina and Georgia. In 1811 three-fourths of the 80,000,000 pounds produced in the United States were produced in these two states, South Carolina producing twice as much as Georgia. In the same year Virginia and North Carolina produced 15,000,000 pounds of cotton, and in Tennessee the production of cotton had increased rapidly from 1,000,000 pounds in 1801

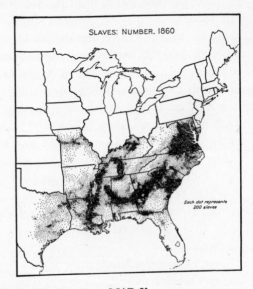

MAP V

Geographic Expansion of the Slave Population
in the United States: 1860.

to 3,000,000 pounds in 1811. Cotton production was spreading in the lower Mississippi region, 3,000,000 pounds or 10,000 bales having been produced in the Louisiana Territory as early as 1801.[42]

From 1815 onward the production of cotton increased at a phenomenal rate. This was in response to the rapid expansion of the foreign market for American cotton. Not only were the mills of England calling for cotton but also those of France. In 1821, when Eng-

[42] *Ibid.*, pp. 683-88.

land was importing nearly 100,000,000 pounds of cotton, France imported 27,000,000 pounds; but two decades later French cotton importations from the United States exceeded 100,000,000 pounds. After 1830 the expanding cotton textile industry on the European continent opened a new market for American cotton. By 1860 the exportation of cotton to the continent exceeded 1,000,000 bales as compared with two and a third million bales to England. The domestic consumption of cotton, which was small at first, reached nearly 1,000,000 bales by 1860.[43]

The phenomenal increase in cotton production to meet the demands of foreign and domestic markets was made possible by the abundance of suitable land in the southern states. In such marginal areas as Virginia, North Carolina, and Tennessee, cotton production thrived during the early decades of the nineteenth century and then declined. But south of these areas, from 1815 to 1840 cotton production and the plantation system spread almost to Texas. The expansion of cotton production in Georgia brought the white settlers into conflict with the Creek Indians, who were finally driven out. Before 1840 settlers from Virginia, Tennessee, Georgia, and the Carolinas had established their cotton plantations on the fertile lands of Alabama. Between 1840 and 1850 the plantation economy with cotton was established in northern and central Mississippi and the bottom lands of the Arkansas River. During the decade prior to the Civil War thousands of planters, ever seeking more fertile lands, established plantations in eastern Texas.

GROWTH OF THE SLAVE POPULATION

The growth of the slave population and expansion of the slave system coincided with the rapid growth of cotton production and the plantation economy. Although it is impossible to know the exact number, it appears that during the years 1790 to 1808, the year in which the external slave trade became illegal, over 100,000 slaves were brought into the United States. Even after 1808, because of the failure of the federal government to suppress the trade, between

[43] *Ibid.*, pp. 691-96. A bale of cotton weighed approximately 500 pounds. See *ibid.*, p. 1026n.

250,000 and 300,000 slaves were smuggled into the United States.[44] But, the chief source of growth in the slave population was through natural increase. Available statistics indicate that the rate of increase

TABLE I

Growth of the Slave Population in the United States: 1790–1860 *

CENSUS YEAR	1790	1800	1810	1820	1830	1840	1850	1860
Number	697,624	893,602	1,191,362	1,538,022	2,009,043	2,487,355	3,204,313	3,953,760
Decennial Increase		28.1	33.3	29.1	30.6	23.8	28.8	23.4

* *Negro Population in the United States, 1790–1915*, p. 53.

during the early decades of the nineteenth century was greater than toward the end of the slave period. This was probably due to the continued illegal entry of slaves during the earlier decades and the increasing number of old slaves in the slave population during the later years.

During the slave period there was a shift in the Negro population in response to the demands of the expanding plantation system. As the plantation system moved toward the Gulf States and the Mississippi Valley, it is estimated that three quarters of a million slaves were sold from the old slave states, Delaware, Maryland, Virginia, the District of Columbia, and North Carolina.[45] This shift is indicated by the fact that in each of the successive Federal censuses from 1800 to 1860 the percentage of slaves in the total population showed a decrease in the border states and a corresponding increase in the states of the lower South.[46] Thus the border states became in a sense the breeding ground for the slave system.

GROWING CONFLICT BETWEEN NORTH AND SOUTH

As the plantation economy spread over the South and became the basis of its culture, the interests of this section came into conflict with those of the North. The Missouri Compromise in 1820, which placed

[44] See W. E. B. DuBois, *The Suppression of the African Slave-Trade* (New York, 1869), pp. 123-24; 178-87.

[45] See estimate of Collins, "Domestic Slave Trade" in Gray, *op. cit.*, Vol. II, p. 651.   [46] See *ibid.*, Appendix A. Table I.

a limit upon the northward expansion of slavery, foreshadowed the growing conflict of interests between the two regions. Within another decade the southern planter interests began to resist the protective tariff program and in 1832 South Carolina came out for the nullification of the Federal tariff laws. The economic interests of the South and the East were becoming more sharply differentiated through the rapid industrialization of the East and the concentration of financial control in eastern cities.[47] The militant South, represented by the planter class, brought about the Mexican War in order to extend the Cotton Kingdom. Later there was agitation for the reopening of the slave trade. In the contest over western lands this class sought to maintain its political ascendency by increasing the number of slave states. The Compromise of 1850 was an attempt to reconcile the conflict between the two sections over the status of slavery in the western lands.[48] In the end the industrial and financial interests in the East were able to win the support of the western farmers and white laborers who did not want to compete with black slaves.

The conflict between the divergent economic interests of the two regions began to assume the character of a moral struggle over slavery after 1830. The moral attack upon slavery was led by northern abolitionists who were associated with the American Anti-Slavery Society organized in Philadelphia in 1833.[49] In reply to the moral attack upon slavery, the South passed more stringent laws respecting slavery, and its leading writers and thinkers developed an elaborate defense of the system. Slavery, it should be remembered, had become a part of the mores of this region as the cotton production and the plantation had become the basis of the economic life of the South. Therefore, the

[47] See William E. Dodd, *Expansion and Conflict* (New York, 1915), pp. 186-206.

[48] The so-called Compromise of 1850 included a number of acts passed by the Congress of the United States in 1850, embodying the right of Territories and newly created States to decide whether slavery should exist within their borders; an act suppressing the slave trade in the District of Columbia; and the Fugitive Slave Act.

[49] See Gilbert H. Barnes, *The Anti-Slavery Impulse: 1830-1844* (New York, 1933). See also Arthur Y. Lloyd, *The Slavery Controversy: 1830-1860* (Chapel Hill, 1939), which, despite its argumentative tone and passionate defense of the antebellum South, presents a good summary of the literature produced by the abolitionists and the southern defenders of slavery.

attack upon slavery by the North called forth moral and philosophical justification of a system that was considered indispensable to the welfare of the South.[50]

One of the most influential philosophical justifications of slavery was that of Thomas R. Dew, Professor of History, Metaphysics, and Political Law at William and Mary College, Virginia.[51] In a book published in 1832, which was the outgrowth of his testimony before a committee of the Virginia legislature, he presented a study of the origin and history of slavery from ancient times and an analysis of the economic and social aspects of the system in Virginia. He concluded that slavery was a positive good, that it was profitable in Virginia, and that it provided the only *modus vivendi* for the two races in Virginia. According to Professor Dew, the Negro possessed the form and strength of a man but had the intellect of a child and was therefore unfit for freedom. The justification of slavery was also set forth in 1854 in the first books on sociology published in America. In the preface of his *Treatise on Sociology, Theoretical and Practical,* Henry Hughes stated that those who understood the working of the slave system regarded it as "morally and civilly good" and that "its great and well-known essentials" should "be unchanged and perpetual." His treatise attempts "to expound the philosophy of the Perpetualists: or in other words, to express some of the views of the Southern people on Slavery." [52] During the same year there appeared a more important book, George Fitzhugh's *Sociology for the South; or the Failure of Free Society.*[53] As indicated in the title, this book was not only a justification of Negro slavery, but propounded a politi-

---

[50] See William Graham Sumner, *Folkways* (New York, 1906), "The mores are the folkways, including the philosophical and ethical generalizations as to societal welfare which are suggested by them, and inherent in them, as they grow" (p. 30).

[51] See "Professor Thomas R. Dew on Slavery" in *The Pro-Slavery Argument* (Philadelphia, 1853), pp. 287-490.

[52] Henry Hughes, *Treatise on Sociology, Theoretical and Practical* (Philadelphia, 1854), p. v. See also L. L. Bernard, "Henry Hughes, First American Sociologist," *Social Forces,* Vol. 15, pp. 154-74.

[53] George Fitzhugh, *Sociology for the South; or the Failure of Free Society* (Richmond, Va., 1854). See also Harvey Wish, *George Fitzhugh, Propagandist of the Old South* (Baton Rouge, La., 1943) and H. G. and W. L. Duncan, "The Development of Sociology in the Old South," *American Journal of Sociology,* Vol. 39, pp. 649-56.

cal philosophy directly opposed to the democratic theory of society. Fitzhugh declared that the Declaration of Independence was opposed to "all government, all subordination, all order." [54] Expressing a philosophy closely resembling recent Fascist doctrines, he declared that liberty, equality, and fraternity had brought crime and pauperism to Europe and that socialism and the struggle of women for equality with men were the results of the failure of a free society. Only in a society built upon slavery and Christianity, as the South was, could morality and discipline be maintained. The same author published three years later a book entitled *Cannibals All*, in which he elaborated the same doctrine, attacking the abolitionists, free labor, and socialism.[55]

Both Dew and Fitzhugh appealed to the Scriptures for a justification of Negro slavery. In fact, during the controversy over slavery the Bible became the chief source for its justification. Ministers all over the South searched the Scriptures to prove that the Negro had been cursed by God to serve other races or that Jesus had either approved slavery or at least had not condemned it. Two of the most sober and scholarly works justifying slavery on Scriptural grounds were by Presbyterian ministers. One was by the Reverend Armstrong of Norfolk, Virginia, who wrote a book entitled, *The Christian Doctrine of Slavery*, "With the hope of doing something towards bringing God's people North and South, to 'see eye to eye' on the much vexed question of Slavery." The author of this book felt that "It may be, that *Christian slavery* is God's solution of the problem (relation of labor and capital) about which the wisest statesmen of Europe confess themselves 'at fault.' " [56] The second book, entitled, *Slavery Ordained of God*, and dedicated to "The Men, North and South, Who Honor the Word of God and Love their Country," was by the Reverend Ross of Huntsville, Alabama. In this book the author presented the thesis "*that slavery is of God*, and to continue for the good of the

[54] Fitzhugh, *op. cit.*, p. 175.
[55] George Fitzhugh, *Cannibals All! or Slaves without Masters* (Richmond, Va., 1857).
[56] George D. Armstrong, *The Christian Doctrine of Slavery* (New York, 1857), p. 134.

slave, the good of the master, the good of the whole American family, until another and better destiny may be unfolded." [57]

In the year in which these books appeared, Chief Justice Taney of the Supreme Court, which was dominated by the South, handed down the famous decision, "A Negro has no rights which a white man need respect." In its examination of the meaning of the words, "people of the United States," in the newly formed Constitution, the court decided that Negroes did not come in this category. "On the contrary," according to the court, "they were at that time considered as a subordinate and inferior class of beings, who had been subjugated by the dominant race, and whether emancipated or not, yet remained subject to their authority, and had no right or privileges but such as those who held the power and the government might choose to grant them." [58] In this decision, the planter interest in the South finally succeeded in having the highest court of the land give legal sanction to a conception of the Negro's status that had already become a part of the southern mores. But Negro slavery was not a part of the mores of North and West; a fact that was to play an important rôle in the impending armed conflict.

[57] Rev. Fred. A. Ross, *Slavery Ordained of God* (Philadelphia, 1857), p. 5.
[58] See "Dred Scott Decision" in William MacDonald (Ed.), *Documentary Source Book of American History* (New York, 1914), p. 408.

CHAPTER III

The Plantation as a Social Institution

IN THE last chapter we have seen that the plantation was a type of settlement devoted to the production of the commercial staples: cotton, tobacco, sugar, indigo, and rice. Like similar types of economic organizations in other parts of the world, the plantation depended upon forced labor or slaves. Since the plantation was a capitalistic undertaking, the planter regarded the slaves as instruments of production to be utilized for the maximum profit. This required a large measure of coercion. Consequently, because of frontier conditions, the plantation became a political organization in which the planter exercised supreme authority in the disposal of the labor and lives of his slaves. But as frontier conditions tended to disappear in the South the state and public opinion began to restrict the absolute authority of the planter. Moreover, in certain parts of the South the plantation became a settled way of life with its peculiar traditions and culture. Where this occurred the plantation became a social as well as an industrial and political organization. The planter's authority often assumed a quasi-patriarchal character and the lives of slaves and masters became intertwined in a web of social relationships. Under such conditions the social organization of the plantation provided the channel by which the culture of the whites was mediated to the blacks. The pattern of race relations which developed on the plantation provided the traditional basis of future race relations in the South.[1]

[1] See Edgar T. Thompson, "The Plantation: the Physical Basis of Traditional Race Relations," in Edgar T. Thompson (Ed.), *Race Relations and the Race Problem* (Durham, N. C., 1939), *passim.*

TYPES OF PLANTATIONS AND SIZE
OF SLAVEHOLDINGS

The social organization of the plantation was influenced by the staples in which it specialized and the size of its slaveholdings. Although the economic, political, and cultural life of the South was dominated by the plantation economy, in 1850 only about 18 per cent of the farms in this region were classified as plantations. Slightly less than three-fourths of the so-called plantations specialized in cotton production. These plantations extended over a wide area of the South. Tobacco plantations, next in importance to cotton plantations from the standpoint of numbers, constituted 15 per cent of all plantations. However, tobacco production was carried on in connection with general farming in noncontiguous areas in Maryland, Virginia, North Carolina, and Kentucky. About 8 per cent of the plantations specialized in the production of hemp; these plantations were concentrated principally in Kentucky and Missouri. Only 2½ per cent of the plantations were devoted to sugar production and almost all of them were in Louisiana.[2]

Even many of the so-called plantations were farms with one or two slaves. This was especially true in the tobacco regions of Kentucky. In 1860 about 38 per cent of the 38,654 slaveholders in Kentucky had one or two slaves.[3] The size of slaveholdings on plantations devoted to cotton production varied according to soil conditions, climate, and accessibility to markets. Cotton plantations with the largest slaveholdings were in the alluvial lands of the Mississippi River and its tributaries, regions which were favorable for plantation economy. In 1860 "the four leading cotton producing counties in the South—Tensas, Carroll, and Concordia Parishes, Louisiana, and Yazoo County, Mississippi"—were located in this region.[4] The median size of slaveholdings was 87 for the Louisiana Parishes and 55 for the Mississippi county. But in Issaquena County, Mississippi and in Concordia Parish, Louisiana, the median size of slaveholdings on

[2] Lewis C. Gray, *History of Agriculture in Southern United States to 1860* (Washington, 1933), Vol. I, pp. 529-33.
[3] *Agriculture in the United States in 1860.* The Eighth Census (Washington, 1864), p. 247.　　[4] Gray, *op. cit.*, p. 533.

cotton plantations amounted almost to that of the rice and sugar plantations, where the median exceeded 100 slaves.[5] Generally, the size of slaveholdings was much larger in the lower South than in the border states. In 1850, the average number of slaves per slaveholding family was 15.0 in South Carolina, 13.4 in Mississippi, and about 11 in Louisiana, Alabama, and Florida. In Maryland, Missouri, and Kentucky the average number of slaves per slaveholding family did not reach six.[6] The size of slaveholdings was increasing particularly in the Southwest toward the end of the slave period. In the South as a whole, in 1860 about a fourth of the slaves were on plantations with less than ten slaves; and another fourth were on the larger plantations with 50 or more slaves. The remaining half of the slave population was on plantations with from 10 to 49 slaves.

THE DOMESTIC SLAVE TRADE

Since the Negroes were the chief capital investment in the plantation economy, the slave trade was an important feature in its operation. The domestic slave trade began to assume importance at the end of the eighteenth century when slaves were proving a liability on the tobacco estates in Maryland and Virginia. After the importation of African slaves became illegal, the demand for slaves in the expanding cotton regions caused the domestic trade in Negroes to become an important business undertaking. Despite the attempt of some southern writers to minimize the extent of the domestic slave trade and to say that it was generally condemned and held in disesteem, the domestic slave trade was necessary to a commercial system of agriculture, based upon slave labor, in which the chief motive was profit.[7] The slave trader, it is true, occupied a social position inferior to that of the planter and was hated because of his business methods. Nevertheless, the assertion of the Charleston *Mercury* that "Slaves . . . are as much and as frequently articles of commerce as the sugar

[5] *Ibid.*, p. 53.

[6] *Negro Population: 1790-1915.* Bureau of the Census (Washington, 1918), p. 56.

[7] See Ulrich B. Phillips, *American Negro Slavery* (New York, 1936), Chapter XI, where the author takes the position that slave-trading was an uneconomical practice and that it was generally condemned.

and molasses which they produce," indicates the importance of slave trading in the plantation economy.[8]

The slave trader was not only despised by the planters and execrated by antislavery advocates, but he was also feared and hated by the slaves. This was due to the fact that the most dehumanizing aspect of slavery was the trade in human beings. For the slave trader, who only had a temporary monetary interest in the slave, the slave was a commodity. As the slave trader drove his shackled cargo of human beings southward, his principal concern was to see that they did not die along the way. Charles Ball, an ex-slave, gives the following account of a slave coffle:

My new master, whose name I did not hear, took me that same day across the Patuxent, where I joined fifty-one other slaves, whom he had bought in Maryland. Thirty-two of these were men and nineteen were women. The women were merely tied together with a rope, about the size of a bed cord, which was tied like a halter round the neck of each; but the men, of whom I was the stoutest and strongest, were very differently caparisoned. A strong iron collar was closely fitted by means of a padlock round each of our necks. A chain of iron about a hundred feet in length was passed through the hasp of each padlock, except at the two ends, where the hasps of the padlocks passed through a link of the chain. In addition to this, we were handcuffed in pairs, with iron staples and bolts, with a short chain about a foot long uniting the handcuffs and their wearers in pairs.

In this manner, we were chained alternately by the right and left hand.[9]

At night the slave trader would lodge his slaves in jails, stockades, and warehouses and on the following day exhibit them for sale in the towns through which he passed. In the deep South, where the surplus value to be wrung from slave labor was high, he was sure to find a market.

[8] Frederic Bancroft, *Slave-Trading in the Old South* (Baltimore, 1939), p. 365.

[9] "Narrative of the Life and Adventures of Charles Ball, A Black Man," p. 30, from *Documentary History of American Industrial Society: Plantation and Frontier*, Vol. II, p. 59, by Ulrich B. Phillips. Copyright 1909 by A. H. Clark Company.

CHARACTER OF RACIAL CONTACTS
ON THE PLANTATION

Where the large plantation was essentially an industrial organization, as in some parts of the Southwest, the slaves had no contacts with whites except those with the overseer. On some of the larger plantations in South Carolina, Georgia, Mississippi, and Louisiana, a slave became, to use Aristotle's definition, a mere "animate tool" in the production of cotton, rice, and sugar. During the winter of 1853-54 Olmsted made the following observation regarding the larger plantations:

As a general rule, the larger the body of négroes on a plantation or estate, the more completely are they treated as mere property, and in accordance with a policy calculated to insure the largest pecuniary returns. Hence, in part, the greater proportionate profit of such plantations, and the tendency which everywhere prevails in the planting districts to the absorption of small, and the augmentation of large estates. It may be true, that among the wealthier slaveowners, there is oftener a humane disposition, a better judgment, and a greater ability to deal with their dependents indulgently and bountifully, but the effects of this disposition are chiefly felt, even on those plantations where the proprietor resides permanently, among the slaves employed about the house and stables, and perhaps a few old favorites in the quarters. It is more than balanced by the difficulty of acquiring a personal interest in the units of a large body of slaves, and an acquaintance with the individual characteristics of each. The treatment of the mass must be reduced to a system, the ruling idea of which will be, to enable one man to force into the same channel of labor the muscles of a large number of men, of various, and often conflicting wills.[10]

The slave gangs on these plantations were often under the sole direction of overseers, who were recruited from among the "poor whites," a class that regarded the slaves scarcely above animals. In the instructions which the overseers received from their employers, who were so often absentee owners of plantations, they were constantly reminded to treat their charges as human beings.

[10] Frederick L. Olmsted, *A Journey in the Back Country* (New York, 1907), Vol. I, p. 64.

In their isolation on industrialized plantations the slaves remained in a state of barbarism, which was worse than their native condition.[11] The same was true in other parts of the country where the great body of plantation Negroes were cut off from contacts with whites. For example, in the large isolated cotton plantations on the islands off the coast of South Carolina, the slaves were far behind the Negroes in the Piedmont region in the attainment of culture. In fact, those on large plantations on St. Helena Island were found by Sir Charles Lyell to be even less civilized than those on the smaller plantations on St. Simon's Island.[12] Thus, throughout the South the influence of the plantation as a civilizing agency depended upon the extent to which social relations developed between the master race and the slaves.

Where the plantation became a settled way of life and a type of patriarchal organization developed, as for example in Virginia, coercion tended to disappear. Social control was maintained by tradition, customs, and habits, and the sentiment of superordination and the feeling of responsibility on the part of the masters were matched by the sentiment of submission and a feeling of loyalty on the part of the slaves. Probably all masters, whether for economic or sentimental reasons, protected their slaves from molestation from outside the plantation. An ex-slave wrote that when fellow slaves killed patrollers who interfered with a dance, his master "was filled with sorrow for the loss of his slaves, but not alone, as is generally the case in such instances, because he had lost property. He truly regretted the death of his faithful servants, and boldly rebuked the occasion of their sudden decrease. When beset and harassed by his neighbors to give up his slaves to be tried for insurrection and murder, he boldly resisted, contending for the natural right of the slaves, to act in their own de-

[11] Olmsted was of the opinion that in the Southwest the slaves were compelled to work harder than in other sections of the slave states. *Ibid.*, p. 83. Charles Lyell observed that on the frontiers of the advancing Cotton Kingdom, "The condition of the Negroes is least enviable in such out-of-the-way and half-civilized districts, where there are many adventurers and uneducated settlers, who have little control over their passions, and who, when they oppress their slaves, are not checked by public opinion as in more advanced communities." "Second Visit to the United States," Vol. II, p. 181, by Charles Lyell, from *Plantation and Frontier*, Vol. II, p. 45, by Ulrich B. Phillips. Copyright 1909 by A. H. Clark Company.

[12] Guion G. Johnson, *op. cit.*, pp. 126-30.

fense, and especially when on his plantation and in their own quarters." [13] The actual situation regarding the relations of the masters and slaves are not to be found either in the stereotyped heart-rending scenes of abolitionist literature which was used for propaganda purposes or in the sentimental literature and the romantic tradition in which the ante-bellum South has been enshrined.[14] Despite legal definitions and the implications of the laws regulating the relations of masters and slaves, the human nature of the slave was bound to assert itself and the most cruel master had to take some account of it. Therefore, one must agree with Phillips, when he says that, "All in all, the slave regime was a curious blend of force and concession, of arbitrary disposal by the master and self-direction by the slave, of tyranny and benevolence, of antipathy and affection." [15]

THE SOCIAL RITUAL OF THE PLANTATION

As the plantation developed into a social institution the relations between the two races were regulated by a complex system of social ritual and etiquette.[16] The system of etiquette was especially important where the two races were brought into close association within the household. In fact, the social ritual and etiquette which developed within the household permitted the maximum degree of intimacy to exist in conjunction with the maximum difference in social status. For example, when members of the family left or returned home, the "mammy," because of the intimacy existing between her and the master's family, kissed not only the women in the household but very often the young men. The very term "mammy," which was the

---

[13] Austin Steward, *Twenty-two Years a Slave, and Forty Years a Freeman* (Rochester, 1857), p. 38. See also Ulrich B. Phillips, *American Negro Slavery* (New York, 1936), pp. 414-15. Another ex-slave reported, and there might have been other cases, that the regard of his master for his slaves was such as to prevent the employment of an overseer. See John Thompson, *The Life of John Thompson, a Fugitive Slave* (Worcester, 1856), pp. 64-65.

[14] See Francis P. Gaines, *The Southern Plantation* (New York, 1925) especially Chapters VII, VIII, and IX in which the author compares the actual facts with the romantic tradition which has grown up about the plantation.

[15] *Life and Labor in the Old South* by Ulrich B. Phillips, p. 195. Copyright 1929 by Little, Brown & Company.

[16] See Bertram W. Doyle, *The Etiquette of Race Relations in the South* (Chicago, 1937) Chapters II and III.

highest term of respect paid a slave, indicates her paradoxical position with relation to the family.[17] Though she was a slave, the young women and girls who were her special charges showed her deference and affection.[18] But in addressing members of the master's family, the "mammy" as well as the other slaves used the usual etiquette, though sometimes the "mammy" might address the mistress or her daughter as "Missy" without the Christian name.[19]

The social rituals regulating the relations of the two races carried with them an implication of their respective status in the plantation society.[20] From childhood, the slave children, who often played with the master's children, were expected to observe the etiquette which indicated their respective status. Besides the forms of address, there were certain forms of expected behavior which indicated the difference in status between the master and slave. The slave was never expected to sit or to wear his hat in the presence of his master's family. Then, there were certain voluntary or spontaneous forms of etiquette on the part of the slaves that assumed the nature, so to speak, of propitiatory offerings.[21] For example, when members of the master's family visited at the "quarters" on Sundays, as was customary on some plantations, the slaves generally offered small presents of eggs, vegetables, or a drink of milk.[22] Very often the two races associated in certain forms of recreation such as hunting and fishing. In such more or less informal relationships, the social rituals regulating the relations of the master and slave permitted the races a maximum freedom of action. The social ritual and etiquette did not divide master and slave but made them a part of the same social organization. This

[17] The term "Uncle" which, next to the term "Mammy," was the highest form of respect shown the slave, was used by the master's family in addressing old slaves, especially those who had served in a responsible capacity.

[18] Jessie W. Parkhurst, "The Role of the Black Mammy in the Plantation Household," *The Journal of Negro History*, Vol. 23 (Jan. 1938), pp. 349-69.

[19] Doyle, *op. cit.*, p. 15.

[20] Despite the position of the white overseer on the plantation, he was always considered an outsider and the slaves never accorded him the same respect as they accorded the master's family. In some cases they refused to work for the overseer who, in their opinion, was of "poor white" origin.

[21] See Herbert Spencer, *The Principles of Sociology* (New York, 1929), Vol. II, Chapter IV, concerning the rôle of presents in ceremonial institutions.

[22] Doyle, *op. cit.*, p. 20.

solidarity was often shown when death came to the plantation. A faithful slave was mourned by the household and the tombstone marking his burial place often commemorated his services. When the master of the household was on the verge of death, the slaves were often called to his bedside. One such occasion was described as follows:

The master's family and friends were gathered about his bedside when the time came for him to go. Having taken leave of his friends, he ordered his Negro laborers to be summoned from the field to take farewell of him. When they arrived he was speechless and motionless, but sensible of all that was occurring, as could be seen from his look of intelligence. One by one the Negroes entered the apartment, and filing by him in succession took each in turn the limp hand of the dying master, and affectionately pressing it for a moment, thanked him for his goodness, commended him to God, and bade him farewell.[23]

RELIGIOUS INSTRUCTION AND MORAL DISCIPLINE
OF SLAVES

On most plantations the religious instruction of Negro slaves was considered an indispensable part of plantation management. Among the instructions given to his overseers, the owner of a large plantation in Mississippi included the following:

I greatly desire that the Gospel be preached to the Negroes when the services of a suitable person can be procured. This should be done on the Sabbath; day time is preferable, if convenient to the Minister.[24]

On some of the plantations in the upland cotton region, where the contacts between the masters and slaves were close, the slaves attended the same churches as masters. The gallery or some section of the church was reserved for the slaves who enjoyed, as a Presbyterian minister reported to a meeting in Charleston on the Religious Instruction of Negroes, "the preached gospel in common with the

---

[23] Quoted in *ibid.*, p. 26.

[24] *Documentary History of American Industrial Society: Documents, 1649-1863, Plantation and Frontier*, Vol. I, p. 114, by Ulrich B. Phillips. Copyright 1909 by A. H. Clark Company.

whites." [25] Very often the master in the patriarchal household saw that the slaves gathered at family prayers and taught the catechism to the slaves one or two nights a week. Usually, however, the task of giving moral and religious instruction to the slaves fell upon the mistress in the household.

The historian of a Negro family, which developed considerable stability in a patriarchal household, wrote as follows concerning the mistress' care and discipline.

Among Miss Sallie's slaves were great grandmothers, grandmothers, mothers, children, grandchildren, and great grandchildren, for she seldom sold any of her people. Her women were taught and required to be as chaste, as were her nieces. All received great care, and much attention from "Miss Sallie" personally, requiring them to sleep in the great house until their marriage.[26]

According to the writer, the slave girls were allowed to be married with a ceremony in the dining room of the house.[27] It was under such conditions that the slaves assimilated the moral sentiments and ideals of the masters as well as the formal aspects of the white man's behavior.

DIVISION OF LABOR AND SOCIAL STATUS AMONG SLAVES

As the plantation was a more or less self-sufficient unit, there was a division of labor which provided some opportunity for the expression of individuality among the slaves. For example, the masters and overseers recognized certain personal qualities in the slaves when they

[25] Phillips, *American Negro Slavery*, p. 318. See also Guion Griffin Johnson, *A Social History of the Sea Islands* (Chapel Hill, 1930), p. 147. Writing of Mammy Mary, whom she regarded as "one of the most exalted Christians" whom she had ever met, Mrs. Smedes says: "She was a devout member of the Baptist Church, and attended it in Mrs. Moncure's carriage. For years her trim, neat figure, her snowy cap, and rapt face was a familiar picture to the congregation as she sat on the steps of the pulpit, a seat allowed her on account of her deafness. The church was built for the white people of the neighborhood, but a large number of benches were set apart for the negroes. They were well filled on 'meeting days.'" Susan Dabney Smedes, *A Southern Planter* (New York, 1890), p. 106.

[26] Nellie A. Plummer, *Out of the Depths* (Hyattsville, Md., 1927), p. 9.

[27] Sometimes the mistresses adorned their favorite slave girls with jewelry when the latter were married. See Doyle, *op. cit.*, p. 24.

raised them to the rank of drivers. Moreover, though the practice was not an established policy as in the West Indies and Brazil, mulatto slaves were often taken into the master's house as personal servants. Frances Kemble tells of a mulatto woman who came to her and begged to "be put to some other than field labor." [28] When the woman was asked why she wanted the change, "the principal reason she urged for her promotion to some less laborious kind of work was, that hoeing in the field was so hard to her on *'account of her color,'* and she therefore petitions to be allowed to learn a trade." Although Miss Kemble was shocked to learn that this woman felt that her white bastardy entitled her to special consideration, it was not unnatural that the mulatto was conscious of his relation to the master race.

Since the slaves tended to identify themselves with the master's family and the plantation, social distinctions among them were determined to some extent by the social standing and wealth of their masters. However, the most important distinctions in the slave population were due to advantages enjoyed by the domestic and personal slaves as compared with the field slaves. In a description of two large rice plantations with a patriarchal organization, in South Carolina, Olmsted gives the following account of the difference between the two classes:

The house-servants are more intelligent, understand and perform their duties better, and are more appropriately dressed, than any I have seen before. The labor required of them is light, and they are treated with much more consideration for their health and comfort than is usually given to that of free domestics. They live in brick cabins, adjoining the house and stables, and one of these, into which I have looked, is neatly and comfortably furnished. Several of the house-servants, as is usual, are mulattoes, and good looking. The mulattoes are generally preferred for in-door occupations. Slaves brought up to house-work dread to be employed at field-labor; and those accustomed to the comparatively unconstrained life of the negro-settlement, detest the close control and careful movements required of the house-servants. [29]

28 Frances A. Kemble, *Journal of a Residence on a Georgian Plantation in 1838-1839* (New York, 1863), pp. 193-94.
29 Frederick L. Olmsted, A *Journey in the Seaboard Slave States* (New York, 1856), p. 421.

During his second visit to the United States, Charles Lyell observed that "colored domestic servants were treated with great indulgence in Tuscaloosa," Alabama, and gave a description of a party which the slaves held in the house of a family which he visited.[30]

The house slaves were conscious of their superior status as well as the advantages which they enjoyed. A former slave emphasized the fact that "there was a social distinction among the slaves," and explained that the house slaves and personal servants were on a higher social plane than the field slaves.[31] Another ex-slave, Steward, recalled in his autobiography a party in which the distinction between the house and field slaves was shown in their dress and manners:

It was about ten o'clock when the aristocratic slaves began to assemble, dressed in the cast-off finery of their master and mistress, swelling out and putting on airs in imitation of those they were forced to obey from day to day.

House servants were of course, "the stars" of the party; all eyes were turned to them to see how they conducted, for they, among slaves, are what a military man would call "fugle-men." The field hands, and such of them as have generally been excluded from the dwelling of their owners, look to the house servant as a pattern of politeness and gentility. And indeed, it is often the only methods of obtaining any knowledge of the manners of what is called "genteel society"; hence, they are ever regarded as a privileged class; and are sometimes greatly envied, while others are bitterly hated.[32]

The superior status and prestige of the house servants were not due merely to artificial distinctions. Because of their close association with the master race, the house servants were able to assimilate their ideals and sentiments as well as their external forms of behavior. This was especially true when the association between the children of house

[30] "Second Visit to the United States," Vol. ii, p. 72, by Charles Lyell, from *Documentary History of American Industrial Society: Plantation and Frontier Documents: 1649-1863*, Vol. II, p. 46, by Ulrich B. Phillips. Copyright 1909 by A. H. Clark Company.

[31] Robert Anderson, *From Slavery to Affluence: Memoirs of Robert Anderson* (Hemingsford, Neb., 1927), pp. 29-30.

[32] Austin Steward, *Twenty-two Years a Slave, and Forty Years a Freeman; Embracing a Correspondence of Several Years, While President of Wilberforce Colony, London, Canada West* (Rochester, N. Y., 1857), pp. 30-32.

servants and the family of the master began at an early age.[33] When Olmsted inquired of the master, how "a respectable-looking, orderly, and gentlemanly-mannered mulatto," who was a trusted steward on the plantation, had developed such "trustworthiness and intelligence," he was given the following history of the slave:

Being the son of a favorite house-servant, he had been, as a child, associated with the white family, and received by chance something of the early education of the white children. When old enough, he had been employed, for some years, as a waiter; but, at his own request, was eventually allowed to learn the blacksmith's trade, in the plantation-shop. Showing ingenuity and talent, he was afterwards employed to make and repair the plantation cotton-gins. Finally, his owner took him to a steam-engine builder, and paid $500 to have him instructed as a machinist. After he had become a skillful workman, he obtained employment, as an engineer; and for some years continued in this occupation, and was allowed to spend his wages for himself.[34]

Frederick Douglass attributed his purity of speech to his close association with his master's son. "I have been often asked, during the earlier part of my free life at the North," he wrote, "how I happened to have so little of the slave accent in my speech. The mystery is in some measure explained by my association with Daniel Lloyd, the youngest son of Col. Edward Lloyd." [35] One of the most important advantages of becoming a house servant was summed up by another ex-slave in the remark that in "waiting at the table, and listening to the conversation going on, I learned many things of which the field hands were entirely ignorant." [36]

The division of labor on the plantation provided an opportunity for the expression and the development of individual talents among the slaves. As Bishop Coppin relates: "Those who had musical talent

[33] An ex-slave recalls: "The old colonel was a very easy going man, kind and generous, and loved by all the plantation people. We colored folks did what he asked us to because we liked him. He was kind to us and very seldom resorted to punishment. Almost as soon as I was able to toddle about, I would follow him over the plantation whenever he would let me. It was because of his fondness for me as a little fellow that I was given his name." Anderson, *op. cit.*, p. 19.

[34] Frederick L. Olmsted, *op. cit.*, p. 427.

[35] Frederick Douglass, *My Bondage and My Freedom* (New York, 1855), p. 33.

[36] Francis Frederick, *Autobiography of Rev. Francis Frederick of Virginia* (Baltimore, 1869), p. 15.

often became 'fiddlers,' and some of them became quite expert with the bow." [37] These musicians often appeared at the social functions given in the masters' homes. Because of their semiprofessional status, they enjoyed prestige among the slaves. Frederick Douglass has left us an excellent account of the division of labor on the plantation and the esteem in which the various occupations were held:

"Uncle" Tobey was the blacksmith, "Uncle" Harry the cartwright, and "Uncle" Abel was the shoemaker, and these had assistants in their several departments. These mechanics were called "Uncles" by all the younger slaves, not because they really sustained that relationship to any, but according to plantation etiquette as a mark of respect, due from the younger to the older slaves.

Among other slave notabilities, I found here one called by everybody, white and colored, "Uncle" Isaac Copper. Once in a while a negro had a surname fastened to him by common consent. This was the case with "Uncle" Isaac Copper. When the "Uncle" was dropped, he was called Doctor Copper. He was both our Doctor of Medicine and our Doctor of Divinity. Where he took his degree I am unable to say, but he was too well established in his profession to permit question as to his native skill, or attainments. One qualification he certainly had. He was a confirmed cripple, wholly unable to work, and was worth nothing for sale in the market. Though lame he was no sluggard. He made his crutches do him good service, and was always on the alert looking up the sick, and such as were supposed to need his aid and counsel. His remedial prescriptions embraced four articles. For diseases of the body, epsom salts, and castor oil; for those of the soul, the "Lord's prayer," and a few stout hickory switches.[38]

The mechanics on the plantations were chosen from among the slaves because of their intelligence and skill. They were highly valued by their masters and in turn developed a pride in their skill and standing in the plantation economy. Pennington, an ex-slave who had acquired his skill as a blacksmith from his father, wrote as follows concerning his pride in workmanship:

I had always aimed to be trustworthy; and feeling a high degree of mechanical pride; I had aimed to do my work with dispatch and skill; my blacksmith's pride and taste was one thing that had recon-

[37] Levi J. Coppin, *Unwritten History* (Philadelphia, 1920), p. 48.
[38] Douglass, *op. cit.*, pp. 30-31.

ciled me so long to remain a slave. I sought to distinguish myself in
the finer branches of the business by invention and finish; I frequently tried my hand at making guns and pistols, putting blades in
pen knives, making fancy hammers, hatchets, sword-canes, &c.,
&c., . . .[39]

Pennington, who ran away from slavery, states that pride in his
craftsmanship enabled him to endure slavery before the punishment
suffered by his father. But it was often slaves of his type who were
restless under the slave regime. Slaves, like Pennington, who had
assimilated the sentiments and ideals of the whites and were capable
of self-direction were inclined to resent the punishments to which
the ordinary slave was subject. In certain areas of Maryland and Virginia, where slaves were a liability, mechanics were often permitted
to hire their time and to work as free laborers. In bargaining with their
masters, they thus acquired a new status and were freed from the
discipline of the plantation regime. When they succeeded in earning sufficient money, they would often buy their freedom and become
a part of the growing number of free Negroes.

[39] J. W. C. Pennington, *The Fugitive Blacksmith; or Events in the History of
James W. C. Pennington* (London, 1850), pp. 7-8.

CHAPTER IV

The Free Negro

AS WE have seen in Chapter II, by the middle of the seventeenth century it was difficult for a Negro brought into the Virginia colony to escape becoming a slave. Nevertheless, the number of free Negroes in Virginia continued to increase up to Emancipation. The increase in the free Negro population came through five sources: (1) children born of free colored persons; (2) mulatto children born of free colored mothers; (3) mulatto children born of white servants or free women; (4) children of free Negro and Indian parentage; (5) slaves who were set free.[1] The increase in the free Negro population through the offspring of free colored parents, though difficult to estimate, contributed to the growth of this class until Emancipation. On the other hand, accessions to the free Negro population through unions of free and servant white women and Negro men, and free colored women and white men were kept at a minimum by the drastic laws against such unions.[2] It is difficult to determine to what extent the intermixture of free Negroes and Indians contributed to the growth of the free colored population, though there was always considerable association between the two races, both in areas given up to the Indian and outside these areas.[3]

[1] John H. Russell, *The Free Negro in Virginia: 1619-1865* (Baltimore, 1913), pp. 40-41.
[2] Virginia, in 1691, and Maryland, in 1692, enacted legislation restricting such unions. See Russell, *op. cit.*, p. 124, and Jeffrey R. Brackett, *The Negro in Maryland* (Baltimore, 1889), p. 33. Pennsylvania passed similar legislation in 1725-26. See Edward R. Turner, *The Negro in Pennsylvania* (Washington, 1911), p. 30. See also Carter G. Woodson, "The Beginnings of the Miscegenation of Whites and Blacks," *The Journal of Negro History*, Vol. III, pp. 335-53.
[3] See Carter G. Woodson, *Free Negro Heads of Families in the United States in 1830* (Washington, D. C., 1925), Introduction, p. vii, and Woodson, "The Relations of Negroes and Indians in Massachusetts," *The Journal of Negro History*, Vol. V., pp. 45-52.

MANUMISSION OF SLAVES

Manumission or the freeing of slaves was the chief means by which the free Negro class was increased. This was accomplished through both public and private action. The earliest known will emancipating Negroes is dated 1645. By its provisions a certain Vaughn in Virginia "freed his negroes at certain ages; some of them he taught to read and make their own clothes. He left them land." [4] Occasionally, public manumission came as a reward for meritorious public services. As early as 1710 the legislature of Virginia conferred freedom upon a Negro slave for discovering "a conspiracy of divers Negroes for levying war" in the colony.[5] Pierre Chastang of Mobile was bought and freed by popular subscription in recognition of public services in the war of 1812 and the yellow fever epidemic in 1819.[6] The philosophy of the Revolution was probably responsible for some of the early fervor in emancipating the slaves.[7] Individual manumission in Pennsylvania constantly increased the free class so that slavery became almost extinct through this means within two generations after 1750.[8] But private emancipation was not without legal restrictions. In Virginia private emancipation was forbidden by an act passed in 1723.[9] Owing chiefly to the persistent efforts of the Quakers and the Methodists, restrictions upon voluntary manumission were removed in 1782.[10] The subject of restoring the restriction was warmly debated in the 1804-1805 session of the legislature. In 1806 an act was passed requiring all slaves set free after May 1, 1806, to leave the state.[11] This law caused a large number of free Negroes to seek asylum in other states.[12] Following closely upon the Virginia act, Maryland, Kentucky, and Delaware passed laws prohibiting the entrance of free Negroes,

[4] Helen T. Catterall (Ed.), *Judicial Cases Concerning American Slavery and the Negro* (Washington, 1926), Vol. I, p. 59.   [5] Russell, *op. cit.*, p. 43.

[6] Ulrich B. Phillips, *American Negro Slavery* (New York, 1936), p. 428.

[7] Phillips, *op. cit.*, p. 425. Russell, *op. cit.*, pp. 54-55. John Daniels, *In Freedom's Birthplace* (Boston, 1914), pp. 7-9.

[8] Turner, *op. cit.*, p. 63. See also Cheesman A. Herrick, *White Servitude in Pennsylvania* (Philadelphia, 1926), pp. 12-13 and 25-26, for economic causes of the decline of slavery in Pennsylvania.

[9] Russell, *op. cit.*, pp. 52-53.   [10] *Ibid.*, pp. 58-59.   [11] *Ibid.*, pp. 67-70.

[12] David Dodge, "The Free Negroes of North Carolina," *Atlantic Monthly*, Vol. LVII, p. 23.

and within twenty-five years Ohio, Indiana, Illinois, Missouri, North Carolina, and Tennessee passed similar laws or placed rigid requirements upon the admission of free Negroes.[13]

The first act in Maryland dealing with the manumission of slaves was passed in 1752. This first act was designed to exercise some control over masters whose practice of setting their slaves adrift when they were no longer profitable placed a burden upon the community.[14] In this same act certain provisions concerning the form of manumissions and the age and fitness of the slaves for freedom placed restrictions upon the action of masters. The desire of individual slave owners and the incessant activities of the Society of Friends and the Society for the Abolition of Slavery were constantly in opposition to restrictions upon manumission.[15] The slave rebellion in Virginia caused the Maryland legislature to adopt the plan of colonizing the freed Negroes in Africa as a state policy.[16] According to this plan, it was provided that Negroes already free, who were willing to leave, should be colonized, and those who were subsequently set free should be forced to leave the state. There was the important proviso that annual permits might be granted to deserving freedmen to remain in the state.[17] Public sentiment failed to enforce the stringent provisions of this law. Between 1831 and 1845 some 2,350 manumissions were reported to the board of managers, which was empowered to carry out the provisions of the act of 1831. Of this number, 1,100 were freed outright, 170 upon the condition, usually, that they emigrate to Africa; and the remainder after service for a stated time.[18] Although it is not ascertainable how many freed slaves received annual permits to remain in the state, the continued residence of a large number of manumitted slaves is an established fact. In anticipation of the law of 1860, absolutely prohibiting emancipation, numerous slaves were freed.[19] Whereas in Maryland in 1830 there were 52,938 free blacks and 102,994 slaves, in 1860 there were 83,942 free blacks and 87,189 slaves.[20]

[13] Russell, *op. cit.*, p. 72.   [14] Brackett, *op. cit.*, p. 149.
[15] *Ibid.*, Chapter IV.   [16] *Ibid.*, p. 165.   [17] *Ibid.*, pp. 165-66.
[18] *Ibid.*, p. 167.   [19] Brackett, *op. cit.*, p. 171.
[20] *Negro Population in the United States, 1790-1915*, Bureau of the Census (Washington, 1918), p. 57.

GROWTH AND DISTRIBUTION OF FREE NEGROES

During the early years of the Republic the growth of the free Negro population was rapid, amounting to about three times that of the slave population.[21] But after 1810 there was a distinct decline in the rate of increase of the free Negro population, and during the next two

TABLE II

Growth of the Free Negro Population in the United States: 1790–1860 *

YEAR	1790	1800	1810	1820	1830	1840	1850	1860
Number	59,557	108,435	186,446	233,634	319,599	386,293	434,495	488,070
Decennial Increase		48,908	78,011	47,188	85,965	66,694	48,202	53,575
Per Cent Increase		82.2	71.9	25.3	36.8	20.9	12.5	12.3

* *Negro Population in the United States, 1790–1915, p. 53.*

decades there was only a small difference in the rate of growth of these two elements in the Negro population. It seems that the increase of 36.8 per cent in the free Negro population in 1830 was probably due to the gradual emancipation which was taking place in northern states.[22] Beginning in 1840, the rate of increase of the free Negro population was less than that of the slaves, and during the two succeeding decades it was so far below the rate for the slaves that it is difficult to account for the difference.[23]

Although the free Negro population did not grow as rapidly after 1840 as during the preceding decades, there was a steady growth in particular areas. Phillips has described the changes which had taken place in Virginia and Maryland by 1860:

[21] See Table I, p. 39 above.

[22] Woodson, *Free Negro Heads of Families in the United States in 1830,* Introduction, p. xviii.

[23] *Negro Population, 1790-1915,* p. 54. Concerning the decline in the rate of increase of the free Negro population the census report makes the following statement: "Census data do not very clearly account for this decline in the rate of increase of the free element in the Negro population, so far below the rate for the slave population, but it may be noted that, as compared with the slave population, the free colored were somewhat older, and on that account naturally subject to a higher mortality rate, and somewhat less normally distributed by sex and therefore, probably characterized by a marital condition less favorable to rapid natural increase."

Tidewater Virginia and the greater part of Maryland had long been exhausted for plantation purposes and were being reclaimed by farmers working with much the same methods as were followed in the northern states. The large land- and slave-owners mostly followed an example which George Washington had set and divided up their estates into small units, in each of which a few Negroes worked in the raising of varied crops under the control of a white man, who was more a foreman leading the squad than an overseer driving it. Planters who adhered to the old methods were now of decayed estate, supported more by the sale of slaves than by the raising of tobacco. Incidentally, eastern Virginia and Maryland had come to have a very large number of free Negroes.[24]

The relation between these changes and the growth in the free Negro population was more than accidental. Free Negroes did not constitute a conspicuous element in the Negro population where the plantation system flourished. The Alabama black lands and the Mississippi and Red River bottoms were still calling for slaves.[25] Consequently, the free Negro population was concentrated in seven characteristic areas: the Tidewater region of Virginia and Maryland; the Piedmont region of North Carolina and Virginia; the Seaboard cities of Charleston, South Carolina, Mobile, Alabama, and New Orleans; the northern cities, including Boston, New York, Chicago, Cincinnati, Philadelphia, Baltimore, and Washington; the Northwest Territory, comprising such settlements as Cass County, Michigan, Hamilton County, Indiana, and Wilberforce, Ohio; isolated communities of Negroes mixed with Indians; and, finally, the Seminoles of Florida.[26] In the case of Virginia, we find that of the 12,866 free Negroes in 1790, only 75 were in the Trans-Allegheny region, which is now mostly West Virginia; 815 in the Valley district; 3,640 in the Piedmont region and 8,330 in the Tidewater. In 1860 the Tidewater contained 32,841 of the total free Negro population of 58,042.[27] "It appears that Tidewater always had from one-half to two-thirds of the entire free negro class, although after 1830 that section contained less than one-

---

[24] *Documentary History of American Industrial Society: Plantation and Frontier Documents: 1649-1863,* Vol. I, Introduction by Ulrich B. Phillips, pp. 88-89. Copyright 1909 by A. H. Clark Company.   [25] *Ibid.,* pp. 89-90.
[26] From lecture notes on "The Negro in America," by Dr. Robert E. Park.
[27] Russell, *op. cit.,* p. 13.

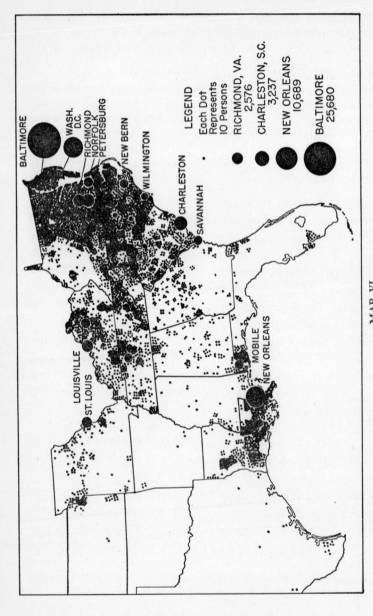

MAP VI

Distribution of Free Negroes in the United States According to Counties: 1860.*

* Based on *Population of the United States in 1860.*

fourth of the white people of the State." [28] In Nansemond County, in the Tidewater in 1860, there were 2,480 free Negroes and 5,481 slaves. Only in one county in the Piedmont did the free Negro population amount to as much as one-sixth of the total Negro population.[29]

In the New England states the free Negro population tended to

TABLE III

Distribution of the Free Negro Population According to States
in 1830 and 1860 *

STATE	1830	1860	STATE	1830	1860
Maine	1,190	1,327	Georgia	2,486	3,500
New Hampshire	604	494	Alabama	1,572	2,690
Massachusetts	7,048	9,602	Mississippi	519	773
Rhode Island	3,561	3,952	Louisiana	16,710	18,647
Connecticut	8,047	8,627	Tennessee	4,555	7,300
Vermont	881	709	Kentucky	4,917	10,684
New York	44,870	49,005	Ohio	9,568	36,673
New Jersey	18,303	25,318	Indiana	3,628	11,428
Pennsylvania	37,930	56,949	Illinois	1,637	7,628
Delaware	15,855	19,829	Missouri	569	3,572
Maryland	52,938	83,942	Michigan	261	6,799
Virginia	47,348	58,042	Arkansas	141	144
North Carolina	19,543	30,463	Florida	844	932
South Carolina	7,921	9,914	Dist. of Columbia	6,152	11,131
Minnesota	....	259	Oregon	....	128
Iowa	....	1,069	California	....	4,086
Kansas	....	189	Texas	....	355

* Bureau of the Census, *Negro Population 1790-1915* (Washington, 1918), p. 57.

remain stationary after 1840. In Vermont and New Hampshire there was an actual decline. After 1840, the number of free Negroes in New York remained about the same, whereas there were gradual increases in New Jersey and Pennsylvania. In the South Atlantic states there was a steady growth in the free Negro population, except Florida, where the number remained almost stationary. But the percentage of the total free Negro population living in the South Atlantic division declined from 53.8 in 1790 to 44.6 in 1860.[30] During the same period the percentage of free Negroes living in the North increased less than

[28] *Ibid.*, p. 14.   [29] *Ibid.*, p. 15.
[30] *Negro Population in the United States, 1790-1915*, p. 55.

one. In fact, between 1790 and 1830 there was a decline in the percentage of free Negroes living in the North, but after 1830 the proportion of free Negroes resident in the North increased. Those states in the North which showed the largest increase in the free Negro population were Ohio, Michigan, and Illinois, states bordering on Canada, whither many free Negroes fled after the passage of the Fugitive Slave Law in 1850.[31] In the states of Kentucky, Tennessee, and Alabama there was a significant increase, though the free Negro population in Louisiana showed a distinct decline after 1840. This decline was doubtless due to the stringent laws which were passed in 1830 to restrict the entrance of free Negroes as well as their activities. In Mississippi the number of free Negroes was always insignificant. The Supreme Court of that state held that "the laws of this state presume a negro *prima facie* to be a slave." Manumission was limited by a law passed in 1822 to cases in which the slave had performed some meritorious act for the owner or the state, and each proposed emancipation had to be validated by a special act of the legislature.[32]

When the first census was taken in 1790, free Negroes were found in considerable numbers in the four largest cities in the country. (See Table IV.) In fact, there was a general tendency for free Negroes to become concentrated in urban areas. In regard to Virginia, Russell writes: "In 1790, when the average ratio of free Negroes to slaves and to whites in the Tidewater section was 1 to 18, in Petersburg the free Negroes constituted one-fourth of the colored population of the town, and were to the whites as 1 to 4¼. In this town of 3,000 people there were 310 free Negroes." [33] In Virginia in 1850 nearly one-fifth of the total free Negro population lived in towns, while only about one-tenth of the whites lived in urban communities. "In 1860 between a fourth and a third of the whole free colored population lived in towns and cities." [34] A similar situation was to be found in other states. Of the 83,942 free Negroes in Maryland in 1860, 25,680 were in the city of

[31] Woodson, *Free Negro Heads of Families in the United States in 1830*, Introduction, p. xliii.

[32] Charles S. Sydnor, "The Free Negro in Mississippi Before the Civil War," *American Historical Review*, XXXII (July, 1927), p. 772.

[33] *The Free Negro in Virginia: 1619-1865* by John H. Russell, p. 14. Copyright 1913 by The Johns Hopkins Press.   [34] *Ibid.*, p. 15.

Baltimore.[35] In 1860, 10,689 of the 18,647 free Negroes in the State of Louisiana lived in New Orleans.[36] More than a third of the free Negro population of Pennsylvania was in Philadelphia in 1860.[37] Concerning Mississippi, Sydnor found that "Ten per cent of the slaves

TABLE IV

Number of Slaves and Free Negroes in the Total Population of Four Leading Cities in 1790 *

		Negro			
CITY	TOTAL	TOTAL	FREE	SLAVE	WHITE
New York	32,305	3,262	1,078	2,184	29,043
Boston	18,038	761	761	....	17,277
Philadelphia	28,522	1,630	1,420	210	26,892
Baltimore	13,503	1,578	323	1,255	11,925

* *Negro Population in the United States, 1790-1915*, p. 55.

in Adams County lived in the city of Natchez, 57 per cent of the whites and 73 per cent of the free colored. . . . Vicksburg contained 71 of the 102 free persons of color residing within the county." [38]

MIXED-BLOODS CONSPICUOUS AMONG
FREE NEGROES

The mulattoes and mixed-bloods were a conspicuous element in the free Negro population. Whereas about a twelfth of the slave population was regarded as of mixed blood, more than a third—37 per cent —of the free Negroes in the United States in 1850 were classed as mulattoes.[39] The large percentage of mulattoes in the free Negro population was not due to any legal presumption in their favor. Nor

[35] Brackett, *op. cit.*, p. 265.

[36] *Negro Population in the United States, 1790-1915*, pp. 195-96.

[37] Turner, *op. cit.*, p. 253.

[38] "The Free Negro in Mississippi Before the Civil War" by Charles S. Sydnor. *American Historical Review*, XXXII (July, 1927), p. 782. Copyright 1927 by The Macmillan Company.

[39] "At the censuses of 1850 and 1860 the terms 'black' and 'Mulatto' appear not to have been defined. In 1850 enumerators were instructed simply in enumerating colored persons to write 'B' or 'M' in the space on the schedule to indicate black or mulatto, leaving the space blank in the case of whites." *Negro Population in the United States, 1790-1915*, p. 207. See Edward Byron Reuter, *The Mulatto in the United States* (Boston, 1918), p. 116.

can the enormous increase in the number of free mulattoes be accounted for by natural increase. The increase in the number of free mulattoes came chiefly from the offspring of slave women and white masters, who manumitted their mulatto children. Russell says concerning the free mulattoes of Virginia: "The free mulatto class, which numbered 23,500 by 1860, was of course the result of illegal relations of white persons with Negroes; but, excepting those born of mulatto parents, most persons of the free class were not born of free Negro or free white mothers, but of slave mothers, and were set free because of their kinship to their master and owner." [40] Sydnor, in showing how the sex relations existing between master and slaves were responsible for the free class in Mississippi, cites the fact that "Of the 773 free persons of color in Mississippi in the year 1860, 601 were of mixed blood, and only 172 were black. Among the slaves this condition was entirely reversed. In this same year there were 400,013 slaves who were classed as blacks and only 36,618 who were mulattoes." [41] In regard to the mulatto character of the free Negro population, it should be noted that the association between the Indians and the Negro was responsible for mulatto communities of free Negroes in Virginia and elsewhere. In Florida, the Seminoles were mixed with the Negroes to such an extent that the Seminole War was due in part to the attempt of Indian fathers to prevent their Indian-Negro children from being enslaved.[42] There was also considerable interbreeding between the Indians and Negroes in Massachusetts. Many of the offspring of these relations passed into the colored community as mulattoes.[43] The predominance of the mulattoes among free Negroes was most marked in Louisiana, where 15,158 of the 18,647 free Negroes were mulattoes.[44]

[40] *The Free Negro in Virginia: 1619-1865* by John H. Russell, p. 127. Copyright 1913 by The Johns Hopkins Press.

[41] "The Free Negro in Mississippi Before the Civil War" by Charles S. Sydnor. *American Historical Review*, XXXII (July, 1927), p. 787. Copyright 1927 by The Macmillan Company.

[42] James Johnston, "Documentary Evidence of the Relations of Negroes and Indians," *The Journal of Negro History*, Vol. XIV, pp. 38-39.

[43] Woodson, "The Relations of Negroes and Indians in Massachusetts," *The Journal of Negro History*, Vol. V, pp. 45-57.

[44] *Population of the United States in 1860*, p. 194.

ECONOMIC STATUS OF FREE NEGROES

Most of the contemporary accounts of the free Negroes represent them as a dependent and despised class of pariahs.[45] But, in fact, the economic status of free Negroes was not the same in all sections of the country, and in all sections there were among the free Negroes wide variations in their economic condition. In the rural areas of the Piedmont they were not as well off generally as in the Tidewater. The following account is more descriptive of the free Negro in the Piedmont region of North Carolina than in the Tidewater:

A very few free Negroes prospered, bought larger and better farms, and even owned slaves—one as many as thirty,—which they held up to general emancipation. But generally when they bought land at all, the purchase was ludicrously small, and in the country phrase, "so po' it couldn't sprout er pea dout grunt'n." On these infinitesimal bits they built flimsy log huts, travesties in every respect of the rude dwellings of the earliest white settlers. The timber growth being often too scant to afford fence rails, their little patches of phantom corn mixed with pea-vines—or, rather, stubs, their little quota of hulls akimbo on top—were encircled by brush fences, which even by dint of annual renewals were scarcely to be regarded by a beast of average hunger and enterprise.[46]

In the rural counties of Maryland, especially in the Tidewater, the free Negroes were gradually acquiring land during the three decades prior to the Civil War.[47] Outside of the city of Baltimore about 5 per cent of the free Negroes had taxable property. Although their property included "small lots of land with inexpensive dwellings, horses, oxen, cows, hogs, sheep, petty furniture, farming implements, tools, and occasionally a carriage or gig, a watch, some plate and along

[45] See Ulrich B. Phillips, *American Negro Slavery* (New York, 1936), pp. 439-40; Olmsted, *A Journey in the Seaboard Slave States* (New York, 1856), pp. 125-26; and H. B. Schoolcraft, *By a Southern Lady: Letters on the Condition of the African Race in the United States* (Philadelphia, 1852).

[46] "The Free Negroes of North Carolina" by David Dodge. *Atlantic Monthly*, LVII, p. 24. Copyright 1886 by Houghton, Mifflin and Co. For a comprehensive study of the free Negro in North Carolina see John Hope Franklin, *The Free Negro in North Carolina* (Chapel Hill, 1943).

[47] James M. Wright, *The Free Negro in Maryland, 1634-1860* (New York, 1921), pp. 188-92.

the water courses watercraft," one-eighth of their holdings were valued at $500 or more.[48] The free Negroes in some counties in rural Virginia were indispensable as farm laborers. In other counties they were an important element in the rural tenantry. A small but an increasing number of free Negroes succeeded in buying land. Between 1830 and 1860 they increased the number of their holdings, the majority of which were small farm homes, a hundred per cent.[49]

On the whole, the free Negro had a more secure position in the economic life of southern cities than in the rural areas. For example, in Richmond County, Georgia, in 1819, where Augusta is located, there was a total of 194 free Negroes.[50] Of the 53 men listed only seven were classified as common laborers, the others being employed in boating, as carpenters, harnessmakers, and as wagoners; while the women were engaged in sewing and washing. In the cities of Virginia the free Negroes made considerable progress in the acquisition of property and in securing a place in the economic organization. In Petersburg, Richmond, and Fredericksburg, from a fourth to a third of the free Negroes owned some form of taxable property. Moreover, they enjoyed unusual opportunities for employment in the tobacco factories of Richmond and Petersburg.[51] However, it was in Charleston and New Orleans that the free Negroes acquired their most secure foothold in the economic organization. There were listed for 1860 among the taxpayers in Charleston 371 free persons of color, including 13 Indians, who were paying taxes on real estate valued at about a million dollars, and 389 slaves.[52] Because of their monopoly of the mechanical arts, the abortive attempt at insurrection by Denmark Vesey in 1822 was used as an argument for restricting the activities of free Negroes in the economic life of Charleston. In a memorial presented to the state legislature, it was argued that they constituted a

[48] *Ibid.*, p. 191.

[49] Luther P. Jackson, "The Virginia Free Negro Farmer and Property Owner," *The Journal of Negro History*, Vol. XXIV, pp. 390-408.

[50] Ulrich B. Phillips, *Documentary History of American Industrial Society: Plantation and Frontier Documents: 1649-1863*, Vol. II, pp. 143-44.

[51] Luther P. Jackson, "The Early Strivings of the Negro in Virginia," *The Journal of Negro History*, Vol. XXV, pp. 27-28. See also by the same author *Free Negro Labor and Property Holding in Virginia, 1830-1860* (New York, 1942).

[52] *List of the Tax Payers of the City of Charleston for 1860*, pp. 315-334.

menace to white society inasmuch as their monopoly of the mechanical arts caused German, Swiss, and Scotch immigrants to seek homes in the West.[53] In New Orleans, where there was a large free mulatto class, we find free Negroes in many skilled occupations. Of the occupations given for 1,463 mulattoes in 1850, 299 were carpenters, 213 masons, 143 cigar makers, 79 tailors, and 76 shoemakers. There were listed also 61 clerks, 12 teachers, 1 architect, and 4 capitalists.[54] The property owned by the free colored people in New Orleans in 1860 amounted to about fifteen million dollars.[55]

In northern cities, where free Negroes were faced with the competition of white labor, their economic condition was much less favorable than in southern cities. Moreover, they were frequently the object of violence on the part of white workers. This occurred especially during periods of economic depression in cities like Cincinnati and Philadelphia, to which runaway slaves and oppressed freedmen fled from the South.[56] Yet, even in northern cities some free Negroes managed to escape from the impoverished condition of the masses. A study of the Negro population in Philadelphia in 1847 showed the occupations of 3,358 Negro males to be as follows: mechanics 286; laborers 1,581; seafaring men 240; coachmen, carters, etc., 276; shopkeepers and traders 166; waiters, cooks, etc., 557; hairdressers 156; various 96. There were also among the employed men musicians, preachers, physicians, and schoolteachers. Although the majority of the 4,249 Negro women were classed as washerwomen and domestic servants, 486 were needlewomen and 213 were in the trades. The lowest class of colored people who were out of employment found a means of livelihood in "ragging and boning."[57] The Negro caterers, whose clientele included the wealthiest white families in Philadelphia, organized a guild around 1840 which continued in existence until about 1870. Through this organization many free Negroes were able

[53] Ulrich B. Phillips, *Documentary History of American Industrial Society: Plantation and Frontier Documents, 1649-1863*, Vol. II, p. 108.

[54] Charles H. Wesley, *Negro Labor in the United States, 1850-1925* (New York, 1927), pp. 37-38.   [55] *Ibid.*, p. 50.

[56] See Edward Turner, *The Negro in Pennsylvania* (Washington, 1911), pp. 150-56, and 196-205.

[57] *A Statistical Inquiry into the Condition of the People of Colour of the City and District of Philadelphia* (Philadelphia, 1849), pp. 17-18.

to overcome the disastrous competition of foreign labor and find a field in which they could achieve economic independence.[58] In Baltimore the free Negroes became formidable competitors of the white laboring population.[59] There is evidence also of a thrifty class in the free Negro population, since in 1860 the free Negroes had close to $21,000 in two of the leading banks in Baltimore.[60] In spite of the prejudice in New York against Negro labor, Negroes were engaged in skilled as well as unskilled occupations. In the census for 1850 they were listed chiefly as servants and laborers, but they were also found in the skilled occupations as carpenters, musicians, and tailors.[61] Between 1835 and 1840 the free Negroes of Cincinnati, despite the great hostility of white workers, succeeded in improving their economic position. According to Woodson, "2,255 Negroes accumulated, largely during this period, $209,000 worth of property, exclusive of personal effects and three churches valued at $19,000." [62]

EDUCATIONAL STATUS OF FREE NEGROES

The free Negroes in the cities were able to get some formal education. In New England, where educational opportunities were available to colored people almost from the beginning of their enslavement, the education of Negroes received an impetus after the Revolution.[63] A separate school for the colored children was established in Boston in 1798 with a white teacher.[64] According to Woodson, "An epoch in the history of Negro education in New England was marked in 1820, when the city of Boston opened its first primary school for the education of colored children." [65] By 1850 there were large numbers of Negroes attending schools in northern cities. (See Table V.) However, in New York and Philadelphia the free Negroes did not support their education to the extent that they did in Baltimore and Wash-

[58] W. E. Burghardt DuBois, *The Philadelphia Negro* (Philadelphia, 1899), pp. 32-39.   [59] Wesley, *op. cit.*, p. 32.

[60] Wright, *op. cit.*, p. 197.   [61] Wesley, *op. cit.*, pp. 37-38.

[62] "The Negroes of Cincinnati Prior to the Civil War" by Carter G. Woodson. *The Journal of Negro History*, Volume I, pp. 9-10. Reprinted by permission of The Associated Publishers, Inc.

[63] Carter G. Woodson, *The Education of the Negro Prior to 1861* (New York, 1915), p. 94.   [64] *Ibid.*, p. 95.

[65] *The Education of the Negro Prior to 1861* by Carter G. Woodson, p. 96. Copyright 1915 by G. P. Putnam's Sons.

ington.[66] In 1807 three former slaves built the first colored schoolhouse in the District of Columbia and employed a white teacher. Although this first venture was not successful, the school was reopened in 1818.[67] The first Negro to teach in the District of Columbia took charge of this school in 1824.[68] In Baltimore an adult Negro school had 180 pupils in 1860. "There were then in the Baltimore Sunday schools about 600 Negroes. They had formed themselves into a Bible association, which had been received into the connection of the Baltimore Bible Society. In 1825 the Negroes there had a day and night school, giving courses in Latin and French. Four years later there appeared an 'African Free School,' with an attendance of from 150 to 175 every Sunday." [69]

In the southern cities the free Negroes were under greater restrictions where education was concerned. The absence of census returns for school attendance in Virginia cities was due to the stringency of the laws against the instruction of Negroes. (See Table V.) The small number of persons reported as attending schools in Charleston, South Carolina, is attributable to the same cause. But it is significant that the number of adults who could not read or write was almost negligible. The restrictions upon the education of the free Negro population in Charleston were, probably, as one author holds, never enforced.[70] As early as 1790 the Brown Fellowship Society, an organization of free colored people, maintained schools for Negro children. Later, other societies were formed especially for the education of indigent and orphaned Negro children.[71] In New Orleans the free colored people openly enjoyed exceptional educational advantages.[72] Very often they attended special and parochial schools along with white children. However, generally the educational advantages which they enjoyed were the result of the enterprise of the progressive elements in the free colored population, some of whom sent their children to France to be educated.

[66] *Ibid.*, pp. 144-45.   [67] *Ibid.*, p. 131.
[68] *Ibid.*, p. 132.   [69] *Ibid.*, pp. 140-41.
[70] C. W. Birnie, "The Education of the Negro in Charleston, S. C. Before the Civil War," *The Journal of Negro History*, Vol. XII, pp. 17-18.
[71] *Ibid.*, p. 17. Woodson, *The Education of the Negro Prior to 1861*, p. 129.
[72] Woodson, *The Education of the Negro Prior to 1861*, pp. 128-29.

TABLE V

School Attendance and Adult Illiteracy Among the Free Negro Population
in 16 Cities: 1850 *

CITIES	FREE COLORED POPULATION TOTAL	NUMBER OF FREE COLORED ATTENDING SCHOOL FOR COUNTY IN WHICH CITY IS LOCATED	NUMBER OF ILLITERATE ADULT FREE COLORED IN COUNTY
Boston, Mass.[1] †	2,038	1,439	205
Providence, R. I.	1,499	292	55
New Haven, Conn.	989	360	167
Brooklyn, N. Y.	2,424	507	788
New York, N. Y.†	13,815	1,418	1,667
Philadelphia, Pa.	10,736	2,176	3,498
Cincinnati, Ohio	3,237	291	620
Louisville, Ky.	1,538	141	567
Baltimore, Md.†	25,442	1,453	9,318
Washington, D. C.[2]	8,158	420	2,674
Richmond, Va.	2,369	0	1,594
Petersburg, Va.	2,616	0	1,155
Charleston, S. C.†	3,441	68	45
Savannah, Ga.	686	0	185
Mobile, Ala.	715	53	12
New Orleans, La.	9,905	1,008	2,279

* Based on The Seventh Census of the United States, 1850.
† Indicates that city and county are coterminous.
[1] Includes Chelsea and North Chelsea.
[2] Statistics are for the city of Washington only.

CHURCH ORGANIZATION OF FREE NEGROES

Although free Negroes made tremendous sacrifices in order to
secure educational opportunities, it was not in the field of education
but in the field of religion that they built their major institutions. The
church organizations of the free Negroes were not simply religious
organizations. They were the centers of the social life of the free
Negro communities. Moreover, they provided a field of activities in
which free Negroes could acquire status and exercise leadership. This
was evident in the rise of independent church organizations toward
the close of the eighteenth and during the first two decades of the
nineteenth centuries.[73] The leaders in this movement had been asso-

[73] Carter G. Woodson, *The History of the Negro Church*, 2nd Edition (Washington, 1921), pp. 71-99.

ciated with white denominations in the North but had withdrawn from the white churches when colored members were segregated and their authority was restricted by the whites.[74] This had been the experience of Richard Allen and Absalom Jones, who founded the Free African Society in Philadelphia in 1787. Later Jones became the rector of the St. Thomas Episcopal Church and Allen, who was ordained by Bishop Asbury in 1799, founded the Bethel Methodist Church. By 1816 the Methodist Church organizations in various cities united into the African Methodist Episcopal Church organization with Allen as its first bishop. In New York in 1796 a group of Negroes seceded from the John Street Methodist Episcopal Church because of their "desire for the privilege of holding meetings of their own, where they might have an opportunity to exercise their spiritual gifts among themselves, and thereby be more useful to one another." [75] They were granted permission by Bishop Asbury to conduct their own services but rather than have separate meetings in the white church, they built their own church. From this sprang the African Methodist Episcopal Zion Church denomination. In 1809 the Negroes of Philadelphia organized the African Baptist Church. Similar movements were taking place in Baltimore, Boston, and Washington. The Negro Methodists in Baltimore merged in the African Methodist Episcopal Church organization.[76] The first Negro church in Boston, originally called the African Meeting House, was organized in 1809.[77] When the movement for separate church organizations began in Washington in 1820, the Methodist and Baptist Church organizations had acquired a dominant position in the institutional life of the Negroes.[78] The church became the repository of the Negro's oldest traditions.

[74] See Rt. Rev. Richard Allen, *The Life, Experience and Gospel Labors of Rt. Rev. Richard Allen* (Philadelphia, n.d.), and Charles H. Wesley, *Richard Allen, Apostle of Freedom* (Washington, D. C., 1935).

[75] Quoted in *The History of the Negro Church*, 2nd Edition, by Carter G. Woodson, p. 78. Copyright 1921, 1945 by The Associated Publishers.

[76] See Noah Davis,*The Narrative of the Life of Noah Davis, A Colored Man, Written by Himself at the Age of Fifty-four* (Baltimore, 1859), p. 85, for statistics on Negro churches in Baltimore in 1859.

[77] John Daniels, *In Freedom's Birthplace* (Boston, 1914), p. 21.

[78] John W. Cromwell, "The First Negro Churches in Washington," *The Journal of Negro History*, Vol. VII, p. 65.

FREE NEGROES AND THE ASSIMILATION PROCESS

The character of the institutions and organizations developed by the free Negroes as well as the general behavior of the free Negroes reflected the extent to which they had assimilated the white man's culture. There were, consequently, wide variations in the character of their institutions and in their standards of behavior. These variations in behavior were closely related to the extent of their social isolation and to their economic status. Where free Negroes, because of economic advantages and the attainment of a certain level of cultural development, enjoyed educational opportunities, their isolation was partially overcome. But the assimilation of the sentiments and ideals of the whites could not be acquired through formal education and imitation. Those among the free Negroes who had really assimilated the ideals and sentiments of the whites had either lived in close association with the whites, or their ancestors had enjoyed such advantages and white patterns of behavior had become incorporated into their family traditions.[79] Many of the most stable and most capable elements among the free Negroes in the North had migrated from the South where they had enjoyed these advantages.

In the South the two largest and most important communities of free Negroes were in Charleston, South Carolina, and New Orleans. Many of the free Negroes in Charleston, who numbered 586 in 1790, had no memory of slavery.[80] The origin of this class went back to the seventeenth century, when whites provided in their wills for the freedom and the economic welfare of their mulatto children. This class was constantly increased by mulattoes whose white fathers had provided for their freedom or they had gained their freedom through their own efforts. Generally through close and intimate association with the whites they had assimilated the ideals and patterns of behavior of the whites. Among them were some who acquired considerable property, including Negro slaves, toward whom they generally

[79] See E. Franklin Frazier, *The Negro Family in the United States* (Chicago, 1939), Chapters X and XIX. The family traditions of free Negroes will be considered in Chapter XIII below.

[80] E. Horace Fitchett, "The Traditions of the Free Negroes in Charleston, South Carolina," *The Journal of Negro History*, Vol. XXV, pp. 139-52.

had the same attitude as the whites. True to their conception of themselves, they organized the Brown Fellowship Society in 1790, which admitted only *brown* men of good character who paid an admission fee of fifty dollars. The society provided for the education of free Negroes, assisted widows and orphans, maintained a club house, and a cemetery for its members. They identified themselves with the slaveowning aristocracy and were loyal to the interests and ideals of this class. They did not permit any discussion of slavery and in turn the white slave-owning class accorded them special privileges.

The position of the free Negroes in New Orleans was such that they constituted, in fact, a separate or intermediate stratum in the community. Like the free Negroes of Charleston, they were largely of mulatto origin. The infusion of white blood was due originally to the association between Spanish and French settlers and Negro and Indian women because of the scarcity of white women.[81] By 1785 the free colored population of Louisiana numbered 1,303. At first the free Negroes were subject to sumptuary restrictions such as the prohibition against the wearing of diamonds and head-dress; but these restrictions could not be enforced as the free mulatto population was augmented by thousands of well-to-do and cultured mulatto refugees from Haiti.[82] By the time of the Louisiana Purchase the free Negroes had become important enough to protest against their not being included among the colonists who signed a memorial to Congress on the status of the colonists under the United States government.[83] Moreover, the free Negroes played an important rôle in the defense of New Orleans against the British in 1814. The condition of this class in 1830, which was known as *gens de couleur*, has been described as follows:

By 1830, some of these *gens de couleur* had arrived at such a degree of wealth as to own cotton and sugar plantations with numerous slaves. They educated their children, as they had been educated, in France. Those who chose to remain there, attained, many of them, distinction in scientific and literary circles. In New Orleans they became musicians, merchants, and money and real estate brokers. The

[81] See James A. Robertson (Tr.), *Louisiana Under the Rule of Spain, France, and the United States, 1785-1807* (Cleveland, 1911), Vol. I, pp. 71, 149, 150n4.

[82] Grace King, *New Orleans, The Place and the People* (New York, 1928), p. 342.　　[83] Robertson, *op. cit.*, Vol. I, p. 279.

humbler classes were mechanics; they monopolized the trade of shoemakers, a trade for which, even to this day, they have a special vocation; they were barbers, tailors, carpenters, upholsterers. They were
notably successful hunters and supplied the city with game. As tailors,
they were almost exclusively patronized by the *elite*, so much so that
the Legoasters', the Dumas', the Clovis', and Lacroix', acquired in-
dividually fortunes of several hundred thousands of dollars. This class
was most respectable; they generally married women of their own
status, and led lives quiet, dignified and worthy, in homes of ease
and comfort. A few who had reached a competency sufficient for it,
attempted to settle in France, where there was no prejudice against
their origin; but in more than one case the experiment was not satisfactory, and they returned to their former homes in Louisiana. . . .

In fact, the quadroons of Louisiana have always shown a strong
local attachment, although in the state they were subjected to griev-
ances, which seemed to them unjust, if not cruel. It is true, they possessed many of the civil and legal rights enjoyed by the whites, as to
the protection of person and property; but they were disqualified from
political rights and social equality. But . . . it is always to be remembered that in their contact with white men, they did not assume
that creeping posture of debasement—nor did the whites expect it—
which has more or less been forced upon them in fiction. In fact,
their handsome, good-natured faces seem almost incapable of despair.
It is true the whites were superior to them, but they, in their turn,
were superior, and infinitely superior, to the blacks, and had as much
objection to associating with the blacks on terms of equality as any
white man could have to associating with them. At the Orleans
theatre they attended their mothers, wives, and sisters in the second
tier, reserved exclusively for them, and where no white person of
either sex would have been permitted to intrude. But they were not
admitted to the quadroon balls, and when white gentlemen visited
their families it was the accepted etiquette for them never to be
present.[84]

Because of the extent to which the most favorably situated free
Negroes in Charleston as well as in New Orleans had become identified through blood and culture with the whites, it was natural that

[84] From an unpublished manuscript of Charles Gayarré in King, *op. cit.*, pp.
344-46. See also R. L. Desdunes, *Nos hommes et notre histoire* (Montreal, 1911).
Only the quadroon women, who were accompanied by their mothers or female
chaperons, were permitted at the quadroon balls, which were patronized by white
men.

they should have set themselves apart from the slaves and blacks. They were not only proud of their racial heritage but also of what they called their achievements in "culture." Because of their isolation, their "culture" became ingrown and their achievements in civilization were often only sorry imitations of white models. In their literary societies, which were similar to the literary aspirations of whites who thought that they had revived in a slave-owning community a modern Greek commonwealth, they sought to nurture their "cultural" heritage.

DEVELOPMENT OF RACE CONSCIOUSNESS AMONG FREE NEGROES

The free Negroes in the North did not form an intermediate stratum in a stable stratified society as did their brothers in the South. They were concentrated in cities where a great industrial civilization was coming into existence. They saw themselves disfranchised where universal suffrage was extended to the male population. They were generally excluded from public education which was becoming the right of all citizens. More important still, they were restricted in their efforts to make a living. Consequently, in their uncertain and precarious situation, they had to take thought and ally themselves with the developing ideals of the industrial society that was coming into existence. The efforts in this direction have become known as the convention movement among Negroes. The first important organized dissatisfaction of the free Negroes in the North had expressed itself in a local convention called in Philadelphia in 1817 to protest against the program of the American Colonization Society to remove free Negroes from the United States.[85] In 1830 a convention of free colored men in the North gathered to consider the condition of the Negro in the nation. The call was issued by Peter Williams, the rector of the St. Phillips Church in New York City, who was aware of the general feeling that such a convention should be called. Bishop Allen of the A.M.E. Church was elected president of the convention which was held in Bethel Church in which the A.M.E. denomination

[85] See John W. Cromwell, *The Early Negro Convention Movement, The American Negro Academy, Occasional Paper No. 9* (Washington, D. C., 1904).

was started. At this meeting strong resolutions were adopted against the action of the American Colonization Society. In addition to the parent organization, local auxiliary societies were provided for, primarily to raise funds for the establishment of a colony of free Negroes in upper Canada.

This convention reassembled each year for a number of years and then from time to time up to 1853. Among the resolutions adopted at the fifth annual convention, which met in Philadelphia, there was one endorsing the temperance movement and another appointing a committee to determine the names of colored slaveholders with a view "to remedy the evil." [86] Much of the attention of the members was directed to proposals for improving the educational and economic opportunities of free Negroes. One of the most important resolutions passed at this convention was that concerning the attitude of free Negroes toward runaway slaves. The resolution read as follows:

Resolved, that our duty to God, and to the principles of human rights, so far exceeds our allegiance to those laws that return the slave again to his master, (from the free states,) that we recommend our people to peaceably bear the punishment those inflict, rather than aid in returning their brethren again to slavery.[87]

By 1847 Frederick Douglass, the antislavery orator, had become interested in the convention movement and at the next meeting he was elected president of the organization. Largely under the leadership of Douglass, who was chairman of the business committee, the last and what has been regarded as the most important convention was held in Rochester in 1853. At this meeting, a three point program was adopted primarily to meet the economic problems of the Negro in the North. The program contained the following provisions: First, that an industrial college should be established and that Harriet Beecher Stowe should be requested to solicit funds for the school in England; second, that a registry be made of colored mechanics and of persons willing to employ colored men in business and to teach colored boys trades; and third, that statistics and other information

[86] *Minutes of the Fifth Annual Convention for the Improvement of the Free People of Colour in the United States, 1835* (Philadelphia, 1835).
[87] *Ibid.*, p. 18.

be collected and published on the condition of the Negro in order to counteract propaganda against free Negroes.

Many of the men who were responsible for this program had once been slaves. Though they had escaped from slavery, they found themselves isolated, disfranchised, and denied employment in the white communities of the North. Because of educational and other advantages, they became the leaders of free Negroes and began to make articulate the growing race consciousness among Negroes. With the assistance of white abolitionists, they agitated and fought not only for the improvement of their status in the North but also for the liberation of their enslaved brothers in the South.

CHAPTER V

Slave Revolts and the Underground Railroad

IN HIS study of the colonization of Africa, Sir Harry Johnston writes that "The Negro in a primitive state is a born slave." Then he goes on to describe the qualities of the Negro which fit him for this servile position:

He is possessed of great physical strength, docility, cheerfulness of disposition, a short memory for sorrows and cruelties, and an easily aroused gratitude for kindness and just dealing. He does not suffer from homesickness to the over-bearing extent that afflicts other peoples torn from their homes, and provided he is well fed, he is easily made happy. Above all, he can toil hard under the hot sun and in the unhealthy climates of the torrid zone. He has little or no race-fellowships—that is to say, he has no sympathy for other negroes; he recognizes, follows and imitates his master independently of any race affinities, and, as he is usually a strong man and a good fighter, he has come into request not only as a labourer but as a soldier.[1]

These same Negro characteristics, with the exception of the Negro's fighting qualities, have often been used to explain the fact that there were few serious insurrections among the slaves in the southern states, even during the Civil War, when their freedom was at stake. However, from what is known of the manner in which the Negro became accommodated to his slave status, it is not necessary to assume that the Negro possessed certain instinctive qualities which fitted him for slavery, in order to explain the absence of organized revolts on a large scale. Nor is it necessary to endow the Negro with such innate Chris-

[1] *A History of the Colonization of Africa by Alien Races* by Sir Harry H. Johnston, pp. 151-52. Published 1913. Reprinted by permission of the Cambridge University Press.

tian qualities as a natural forgetfulness of cruelties and a disposition to be grateful for kindness and just dealing to explain his faithfulness to his master during the Civil War.

RESISTANCE OF NEGROES TO ENSLAVEMENT

Those who traded in Negro slaves on the African coast did not have much faith in the docility of the Negro nor in his short memory of sorrows and cruelties. In Africa where the slave trader had to come to terms with the warlike tribes before buying captives, they could not even count upon the docility of conquered peoples. The *South Carolina Gazette* of July 7, 1759 carried the following news item concerning an incident which was not unique in the annals of slavers on the African coast:

A Sloop commanded by a Brother of . . . Capt. Ingledieu, slaving up the River Gambia, was attacked by a Number of the Natives, about the 27th of February last, and made a good Defence; but the Captain finding himself desperately wounded, and likely to be overcome, rather than fall into the Hands of such merciless Wretches, when about 80 Negroes had boarded his Vessel, discharged a Pistol into his Magazine, and blew her up; himself and every Soul on Board perished.[2]

The more seasoned slave traders generally took precautions against such incidents as that related by Joseph Hawkins who left Charleston, South Carolina, December 1, 1779, on the *Charleston* for the Guinea Coast.[3] Arriving off the coast of Africa, the ship's captain sought to buy a cargo of Gallas who had been defeated by the Eboes. Hawkins, who previously had rebuked himself for having embarked upon the African slave trade, said that he found consolation in the fact that he was doing an act of humanity in reducing the Galla captives to slavery. Moreover, he thought that he had convinced the captives that their lot would be better in America than in Africa. But in proceeding to the place of embarkation, he was impressed by the "sullen melancholy, and deep sighs of the Galla prisoners." He attempted to exhilarate their spirits and quiet their cares with liquor. When the

[2] Elizabeth Donnan, *Documents Illustrative of the History of the Slave Trade to America* (Washington, D. C., 1935), Vol. IV, p. 374.   [3] *Ibid.*, pp. 494-500.

slaves were placed aboard the shallop, a general revolt was started by six captives who were allowed to remain on deck. His story continues:

Two of them found means to jump overboard; a sailor who was in the small boat astern seized one of them by the arms, and the end of a rope being thrown to him, the slave was taken on board, though not without some difficulty. The others who had been at the oars, seeing their fellows, one of them seized, and the other struck on the head with a pole, set up a scream, which was echoed by the rest below; those that were loose made an effort to throw two of the sailors overboard; . . . they seized on the guns and bayonets that lay ready, and rushed upon the slaves, five of whom from below had got loose, and were endeavouring to set the rest free, while those we had to deal with above, were threatening to sacrifice us to their despair. . . . I had neither gun nor sword, and to retire in search of either, would have been to give the slaves a decisive superiority; I laid hold of the palloon stick, and had raised it to strike one of them who had nearly wrested a gun from one of the sailors, but before I could give the blow, I received a stroke of an oar, which severed my little finger from my hand; . . . the blow was broken that I had intended, but I renewed the effort, and with effect, for I levelled the fellow, and the sailor recovered his gun, whom I could not prevent from running the poor negro through the body; the hatch was open, and he fell among his fellows, who had, crouded tied, and ironed as they were, to assist as far as they were able, by holding our legs, encouraging their companions, and shouting whenever those above did any thing that appeared likely to overcome one or other of us. We at length overpowered them; one only having escaped and one being killed, the rest were immediately bound in double irons, . . . Five of the sailors were considerably, but not dangerously hurt, and of the slaves, those who had been riotous above and below, nine were severely wounded.[4]

Even after the slavers had placed their cargoes securely in the ships and had started on the Middle Passage, they were compelled to keep constantly on guard against uprisings and suicides on the part of the slaves. As a surgeon in the Royal British Navy wrote in 1721:

When we are slaved and out at Sea, it is commonly imagined, the Negroes Ignorance of Navigation, will always be a Safeguard; yet as many of them think themselves bought to eat, and more, that Death will send them into their own Country, there has not been wanting

4 *Ibid.*, pp. 498-99.

Examples of rising and killing a Ship's Company, distant from Land, tho' not so often as on the coast; but once or twice is enough to shew, a Master's Care and Dilligence should never be over till the Delivery of them.[5]

Despite the vigilance of the slavers, the slaves often succeeded in starting revolts.[6] In some cases the slave revolts during the Middle Passage ended in the capture of the vessel by the slaves. The *Boston Post Boy* of June 25, 1750 carried the following item:

By a Vessel lately arrived here from the West-Indies, we have Advice, that a Ship belonging to Liverpool coming from the Coast of Africa, with about 350 Slaves on board, and when in Sight of the Island Guardaloupe, the Slaves, as 'tis supposed, being admitted to come upon Deck to air themselves, took an Opportunity on the 28th of May, N. S. and kill'd the Master and Mate of the Ship and threw fifteen of the Men overboard, after which they sent the Boat with two white Lads and three or four others to discover what Land it was, meanwhile the Ship drove to the Leeward, which gave the Lads an Opportunity to discover the Affair to the Commandant of that Quarter of the Island, who immediately raised about 100 Men, and put them on board a Sloop, who went in Pursuit of the Ship, and in a few Hours took her and carried her into Port Louis.[7]

Because of their frequency, slave revolts during the Middle Passage were considered one of the principal hazards of the slave trade.

In the West Indies those who dealt in the slave traffic acquired some knowledge of the different cultural backgrounds of slaves, especially so far as this knowledge affected their adaptation to the requirements of the plantation economy. The Coromantyn or Gold Coast Negroes, who were distinguished for their firmness of mind and body and their ferociousness, were regarded as dangerous for West Indian plantations. It was said that the plantations on the island of Tobago

---

[5] *Ibid.*, pp. 281-82. Attempts on the part of the slaves to revolt were generally punished with the utmost barbarity. The author of the above account described the punishment of slaves in one revolt as follows: "Why, Captain Harding weighing the Stoutness and Worth of the two Slaves, did, as in other Countries they do by Rogues of Dignity, whip and scarify them only; while three other, Abettors, but not Actors, nor of Strength for it, he sentenced to cruel Deaths; making them first eat the Heart and Liver of one of them killed. The Woman he hoisted up by the Thumbs, whipp'd and slashed her with Knives, before the other Slaves till she died." *Ibid.*, p. 266.

[6] See *ibid.*, Vols. II and III under Insurrections.   [7] See *ibid.*, Vol. II, p. 485.

were destroyed during bloody insurrections because the planters were not acquainted with the different cultural backgrounds from which the slaves came.[8] The Negroes from the Congo, a very black, well-proportioned and handsome race of Africans, were considered good domestic servants and tradesmen. The Eboes were known to be "turbulent, stubborn and much addicted to suicide," whereas the Negroes from the Gaboon were regarded as totally unfit for slavery because of their physical weakness.[9]

Although American planters seemingly did not show such discrimination in regard to their African slaves, they were fearful from the beginning of insurrections.[10] As early as 1663, a favorite slave of a Virginia planter revealed a conspiracy of Negro and white indentured servants. During the remaining years of the seventeenth century several slave plots were reported in Virginia as the slave status of Negroes became fixed. A significant increase in the number of slave plots and revolts took place during the first half of the eighteenth century throughout the country. There were slave conspiracies in Virginia in 1709 and 1723. There was a recurrence of slave plots in Virginia in 1730. In the same year there was a plot formed among the rapidly growing slave population of South Carolina to exterminate the whites. In the North, the two most important slave plots were discovered in New York in 1712 and 1741. The suppression of the latter revolt was characterized by extraordinary cruelty. Thirteen of the conspirators were burned alive, eighteen were hanged and eighty deported. Toward the end of the eighteenth century there was unrest among the slaves because of the Revolutionary War, and in the first year of the following

[8] "Practical Rules for the Management and Medical Treatment of Negro Slaves in the Sugar Colonies" by a Professional Planter (London, 1803) in Ulrich B. Phillips *Documentary History of American Industrial Society: Plantation and Frontier Documents: 1649-1863* (Cleveland, 1909), Vol. II, pp. 127-28. See also Bryan Edwards, *The History, Civil and Commercial of the British Colonies in the West Indies* (London, 1801), Vol. II, pp. 74.

[9] "Practical Rules for the Management and Medical Treatment of Negro Slaves in the Sugar Colonies" by a Professional Planter from *Documentary History of American Industrial Society: Plantation and Frontier Documents, 1649-1863*, Vol. II, pp. 128-29, by Ulrich B. Phillips. Copyright 1909 by A. H. Clark Company.

[10] See Herbert Aptheker, *American Negro Slave Revolts* (New York, 1943), for a definitive study of slave revolts in America. See also Joshua Coffin, *An Account of Some of the Principal Slave Insurrections* (New York, 1860), and Ulrich B. Phillips, *American Negro Slavery*, pp. 467-73.

century there occurred the first of the three most important slave insurrections in the United States.

THREE IMPORTANT SLAVE INSURRECTIONS

In 1800 a well-planned insurrection, under the direction of a slave known as Gabriel, was discovered among the slaves near Richmond, Virginia.[11] Little is known of the leader of this attempted revolt. However, the thorough and elaborate manner in which it was planned indicated that Gabriel was an exceptional person. Although the conspiracy was betrayed by two slaves, the execution of part of the plot was frustrated by a torrential rain. It appears from the scanty information available that the Bible was used to impress the Negroes that they as the Israelites could throw off the yoke of slavery and that God would come to their aid. As this attempted insurrection occurred at the time when the Federalists were combating the rising democratic revolt led by Jefferson, the Federalists endeavored to place the blame upon their opponents and those influenced by the ideals of liberty growing out of the French Revolution. The latter charge found some support in the report that the Negroes intended to spare the French. When Gabriel was captured, he refused to implicate any of his fellow conspirators. Because of the large number of Negro slaves involved, the Governor of Virginia entered into secret correspondence with Jefferson with the view of securing a grant of land to which troublesome slaves could be banished. In 1805 a resolution containing the proposal to Jefferson was passed in a secret session of the Virginia legislature. But nothing was done about either the proposal to Jefferson or the resolution to the Virginia legislature.

The second most important and most elaborate slave uprising was that planned by Denmark Vesey in Charleston, South Carolina, in 1822.[12] Denmark Vesey was a free Negro who had purchased his free-

[11] T. W. Higginson, "Gabriel's Defeat," *Atlantic Monthly*, Vol. X (1862), pp. 337-45. See also Coffin, *op. cit.*, pp. 24-29.

[12] *An Official Report of the Trials of Sundry Negroes Charged with an Attempt to Raise an Insurrection in the State of South Carolina*, Prepared and Published at the Request of the Court by Lionel Kennedy and Thomas Parker (Charleston, 1822), hereafter referred to as *Attempt to Raise an Insurrection in the State of South Carolina*.

dom for $600 after drawing a prize of $1,500 in a lottery in Charleston, in 1800. As a boy he had been sold as a slave in San Domingo but was returned to his owner, the captain of the ship, because he was considered physically unsound and was subject to epileptic fits. He was brought back to Charleston by his master, whom he served as a faithful servant for twenty years. After obtaining his freedom, he worked as a carpenter and was respected by the slaves as well as the free colored people of Charleston. Vesey seems to have been acquainted with the successful uprising of slaves in Haiti since according to the testimony of some of the slaves he used the Haitian uprising to encourage them in their enterprise. He also had some knowledge of the principles of the French Revolution and was aware of the debates in Congress on the Missouri Compromise. Having such a knowledge, he used every occasion to instill in the Negroes confidence and a sense of their equality with whites. According to the report:

Even whilst walking through the streets in company with another, he was not idle; for if his companion bowed to a white person he would rebuke him, and observe that all men were born equal, and that he was surprised that any one would degrade himself by such conduct; that he would never cringe to the whites, nor ought any one who had the feelings of a man. When answered, We are slaves, he would sarcastically and indignantly reply, "You deserve to remain slaves"; and if he were further asked, What can we do, he would remark, "Go and buy a spelling book and read the fable of Hercules and the Waggoner"; which he would then repeat, and apply it to their situation.[13]

Vesey carefully selected four lieutenants, all of whom except one refused to reveal the names of the conspirators, which were kept in code. The conspiracy was betrayed by a faithful house slave who was asked to join the conspiracy. Although some members of the Negro Methodist Church were involved, the leaders in the church had kept clear of the conspiracy. The authorities gradually discovered the leaders in the plot, thirty-five of whom were hanged and thirty-seven were transported beyond the limits of the United States. Vesey accepted his fate courageously and was hanged without revealing the names of

[13] *Ibid.*, p. 19.

his confederates. His confederates with the exception of Gullah Jack who asked for a delay died likewise. The last words of Peter Poyas, a lieutenant of Vesey, to his confederates were: "Do not open your lips! Die silent as you shall see me do." [14]

The third important outbreak occurred in Southampton County, Virginia, in 1831.[15] This insurrection, which was led by Nat Turner, a slave and a Baptist exhorter, was not a well-planned enterprise like the Denmark Vesey plot. Turner was a mystic, who had found in reading the Bible what he regarded as a solution of the problem of Negro slavery. According to his testimony, for some years he had heard voices from heaven telling him to carry out the prophecy of Christ that the last should be first and first last. Instead of making careful preparations for his revolt, he spent his time during the months preceding the outbreak in prayer. Consequently, when he started on his enterprise he was accompanied by only a small group. He and his few followers began the assault on the whites by murdering his master's household. Then his band, which was increased from time to time by other slaves, roamed the country killing whites. In all, fifty-five whites were killed, including ten men, fourteen women, and thirty-one children. After the alarm was given, Turner and his followers, who probably never numbered more than sixty at any time, were easily suppressed by the whites with the assistance of the militia. After six weeks of hiding, Turner was caught and tried with forty-six other Negroes. He was hanged with sixteen of his followers.

During the nineteenth century many other slave plots and conspiracies were reported from various parts of the South. For example, in 1811 the people of New Orleans were thrown into consternation because of a revolt of slaves in two of the parishes near the city.[16] There was considerable slave unrest resulting in sporadic conspiracies and attempted uprisings during the decade prior to the Civil War. These conspiracies and outbreaks involved slaves in Kentucky, Arkansas, Tennessee, Mississippi, Louisiana, and Texas.[17] The unrest of the

[14] *Ibid.*, p. 45

[15] W. S. Drewry, *Slave Insurrections in Virginia, 1830-1865* (Washington, 1900). See also Ulrich B. Phillips, *American Negro Slavery* (New York, 1936), pp. 480-81 and Aptheker, *op. cit.*, Chapter XII.

[16] Aptheker, *op. cit.*, pp. 249ff.   [17] *Ibid.*, pp. 340-58.

slaves and their plotting were generally minimized and given little publicity by the whites. This was due partly to the effect which such knowledge would have had on public opinion, especially during the slave controversy. The suppression of news concerning the unrest was also regarded as a necessary precaution against spreading the unrest among the slaves. Throughout the period the unrest and disturbances were widespread and frequent enough to indicate that the Negro was not perfectly accommodated to the slave status.

WHY SLAVE INSURRECTIONS FAILED

However, even when one takes into account the numerous plots and conspiracies of slaves, which are usually ignored, one may still ask why the Negro slaves in the United States did not organize more widespread and more frequent revolts. The answer to this question may be sought, first, in the manner in which the Negroes were reduced to slavery. Although Phillips thinks that the Negro is naturally submissive, he admits that considerable coercion was necessary to make him submit to the requirement of the slave status.[18] Throughout slavery there were recalcitrant slaves who were beaten into submission or even killed. The idea once current that there was scarcely any crime among slaves has been shown to be false. Many of the crimes of the Negro slaves were aggressions or retaliations against whites if the record of Virginia is typical of the South. Of the 1,418 vouchers in the State Library of Virginia on the convictions of slaves, most of which were for the first five decades of the nineteenth century, 1,117 definitely stated the nature of the offense.[19] Of the 1,117 convictions stating the offense, 346 were for murder; 194 of the murdered persons being white, characterized as follows: master, 56; overseer, 7; white man, 98; mistress, 11; other white woman, 13; master's child, 2; other white child, 7. Among 60 more who were unidentified there might have been whites. For other assaults, such as attempts to murder, there were 111 convictions, only two of which were assaults against Negroes.

[18] See Phillips, *American Negro Slavery*, pp. 341-42, where he contrasts the heartlessness of the Roman latifundiarii with the paternalism of southern masters.
[19] Ulrich B. Phillips, "Slave Crime in Virginia," *The American Historical Review*, Vol. XX (1914), pp. 336-40.

The records of the slave regime are full of cases of unruly slaves who were subjected to whippings and when whippings proved futile they were sold into the lower South. The threat of selling slaves into the far South was always one of the effective means of controlling them. Runaways were not whipped but were branded as punishment and in order to make their escape more difficult. When the slaves revolted, those who were not hanged, were whipped and branded or expelled from the country. When slaves were hanged, or tortured, or merely whipped, this was generally done in the presence of other slaves in order to inspire terror. Then, too, all gatherings of slaves, even religious meetings, were under the surveillance of whites in order to prevent plots and uprisings. The system of patrollers, which was maintained in the South, was designed to keep a constant watch on the activities of slaves.

Although coercion and constant surveillance played an important rôle in maintaining the subordination of the slave population, there were important social factors which prevented concerted action against the masters. The first fact of importance regarding the Vesey plot was that it, like many other plots, was betrayed by a faithful personal slave.[20] Only a superficial understanding of human relations would attribute such behavior to what Sir Harry Johnston probably meant by lack of "race fellowship." The faithful house-servants were often bound, as we have seen, to their masters by close emotional ties and common interests. Peter Poyas, one of the heroic figures in the Vesey conspiracy, recognized this fact when he informed his lieutenant: "But take care and don't mention it [the plot] to those waiting men who receive presents of old coats, &c from their masters, or they'll betray us." [21] Likewise, in Jamaica and Brazil, where Negro revolts were generally more successful, it was always a faithful slave who revealed a conspiracy. The leaders of the Charleston conspiracy chose their followers from among carters, draymen, porters, laborers, and stevedores who were not attached to the whites by feelings of loyalty. But more important still, they chose them from among the neighboring country Negroes who had had little contact with the

[20] *Attempt to Raise an Insurrection in the State of South Carolina*, pp. 49-51.
[21] *Ibid.*, p. 26.

whites and had been influenced very little by the white man's culture.

The futile and desperate attempts of slaves in America to revolt have lacked generally the heroism of these well-organized and successful revolts in Jamaica and Brazil.[22] The Negro slaves in the United States, who were scattered over a wide territory, lacked a common medium of communication, and their cultural heritage was all but destroyed. In the process of "breaking" them into the plantation regime, some died of homesickness or were killed when they were recalcitrant. Newcomers were placed among seasoned Negroes, who had adapted themselves to the new environment and had forgotten

[22] In the revolts of Jamaican Negroes, known as the maroons (a word of Spanish derivation referring to the wild pigs on which the fugitive Negroes lived in the woods) the fact that their African traditions had remained intact was responsible for the solidarity and bravery of the Negro slaves in a revolt against the whites. Soon after the conquest of Jamaica by the British, the Negro slaves, who had fled to the mountain, began to harass the English settlers. Their mountain retreat became a refuge for other fugitive slaves. These Negroes under a chief, named Cudjoe, were able to wage war against the English until 1738 when a treaty was signed giving them rights to land, hunting grounds, and freedom of trade and movement. The maroons had scarcely been touched by the white man's culture, most of them not even being able to speak the English language. Their solidarity and loyalty to a despotic chief was secured mainly by religious practices and beliefs that were part of their African heritage. The same was true of the formidable insurrection which broke out in Jamaica in 1760. This insurrection was carried out by the fierce Coromantyn Gold Coast Negroes under an old man who used a fetish in administering a solemn oath to the conspirators. See R. C. Dallas, *The History of the Maroons*, 2 vols. (London, 1803), Vol. I, pp. 22-65. See also Edwards, *op. cit.*, Vol. I, pp. 522-45. The maroons were finally expelled from the island and settled first in Nova Scotia and later in Sierra Leone. In Brazil the isolation of the slaves from the white population and the moral solidarity which existed among them were often due to the influence of the Mohammedan religion rather than a sentiment of race. The leaders of the insurrectionary movements were often Mohammedan priests who could read and write Arabic and regularly gave instruction in Arabic. In an attempt to suppress these insurrections in northern Brazil, it was necessary to expel Mohammedan Negroes. The most famous of the insurrections in the northern part of Brazil was that which began in 1644 and developed into what was known as the Palmares Republic. The slaves built a fortified community of huts similar to those in the Congo and lived under a communistic regime with a fierce warrior as the absolute elected monarch. This Negro community was broken up from time to time. But from 1679 until 1695 these blacks defied the power of the Portuguese and when finally defeated, they preferred suicide and self-imposed starvation to surrender. See Arthur Ramos, *The Negro in Brazil*, translated from the Portuguese by Richard Pattee (Washington, D. C., 1939), pp. 24-41. See also João Dornas Filho, *A Escravidão No Brasil* (Rio de Janeiro, 1939), pp. 103-27, dealing with Negro insurrections in Brazil. See also Nina Rodrigues, *Os Africanos no Brasil* (São Paulo, 1935), p. 72.

most of their African heritage. The American Negro slave was a broken man and the only alternative left him was to acquire a motive for living under American culture or die. He found in Christianity a meaning for existence and a solace for his sorrows. But Christianity caused the Negro to accept his position as a slave and established the prestige of the white race.[23] The master was careful that the slaves should know only those sections of the Bible which would confirm his authority over them. It was only the literate Negro who could break through such mental isolation and use the Bible as an authority for slave revolts.

In the report on the Vesey insurrection, it is said that Denmark Vesey inspired his followers to revolt with citations from the Bible. In pronouncing the death sentence on Gullah Jack, the sorcerer, the Court first expressed its indignation against the fact that he had used superstition to give confidence to the slaves; and afterward the Court chided him with the statement that his sorcery would be of no avail in saving his life. "Let me then," stated the Court, "conjure you to devote the remnant of your miserable existence, in fleeing from the 'wrath to come'." [24] Despite the Court's judgment, Vesey had been wise not only in the use of the white man's Bible but in the selection of Gullah Jack, his lieutenant, who with his sorcery could use the fetishistic beliefs and practices of the country Negro as a basis for moral solidarity and control.

FUGITIVE SLAVES

Although there were few organized revolts on a large scale among the slaves in the United States, individual slaves constantly revolted against the system simply by running away. Runaway slaves were a problem throughout the entire period of slavery. In 1672, Virginia found it necessary to pass legislation to deal with runaway slaves who formed bands of armed outlaws and committed depredations upon the colony.[25] Early in the eighteenth century similar bands of outlaws

[23] In the insurrection in New York City in 1741, it was the Negroes who resisted Christian instruction who joined the revolt. See Coffin, *op. cit.*, p. 11.

[24] *Attempt to Raise an Insurrection in the State of South Carolina*, p. 179.

[25] Herbert Aptheker, "Maroons Within the Present Limits of the United States," *The Journal of Negro History*, Vol. XXIV, p. 168.

terrorized the colonists in South Carolina. In fact, many bands of runaway slaves established maroon communities in "the mountainous, forested, or swampy regions" of the southern states.[26] One of the largest maroon communities was located in the Dismal Swamp on the borders of Virginia and North Carolina. It was necessary at times for the authorities in the various states to send armed forces against these maroon communities. One instance in the lower South of such an expedition was the attack in 1827 of armed slaveholders against a maroon community in Mobile County, Alabama. This community comprised of men, women, and children was broken up at a time when the runaway slaves were constructing a fort.[27] During the Civil War, an increasing number of runaway slaves sought a refuge in such maroon communities.

For the vast majority of runaway slaves, flight from the plantation was an individual protest against enslavement. According to Phillips, who describes running away from slavery as a form of truancy,

Virtually all the plantations whose records are available suffered more or less from truancy, and the abundance of newspaper advertisements for fugitives reinforces the impression that the need of deterrence was vital. Whippings, instead of proving a cure, might bring revenge in the form of sabotage, arson or murder. Adequacy in food, clothing and shelter might prove of no avail, for contentment must be mental as well as physical.[28]

Psychological dissatisfaction with slavery appears to have been more important with runaways than physical mistreatment. Cartwright, a professor at the University of Louisiana, thought that running away from slavery was a peculiar mental disease, called by him *Drapetomania*, to which Negro slaves were subject.[29] He described the symptoms as follows: "Before negroes run away, unless they are frightened or panic-struck, they become sulky and dissatisfied. The cause of this sulkiness and dissatisfaction should be inquired into and removed, or they are apt to run away or fall into negro consumption." If the

26 *Ibid.*, p. 167.   27 *Ibid.*, p. 177.

28 *American Negro Slavery*, by Ulrich B. Phillips. Copyright 1918 by D. Appleton and Company. Reprinted by permission of D. Appleton-Century Company, Inc.

29 See Frederick L. Olmsted, *A Journey in the Seaboard Slave States* (New York, 1856), p. 191.

sulkiness or dissatisfaction were found to be without cause, then Dr. Cartwright advised "whipping the devil *out of them.*"

When the Negro slave exhibited sulkiness and dissatisfaction before running away, it was generally due to some cause less obscure than the fantastic disease invented by Dr. Cartwright. Slaves constantly ran away in order to escape harsh treatment and inhuman punishment. Then there was the fear of being sold into the far South which operated as a strong motive for attempting to escape. But even where slave life was not harsh, some crisis in the life of the slave might cause him to run away. The most important crisis in the life of a slave who was a part of a family group was the breaking up of his family. As one writer states:

So long as a black family remained together upon one plantation, the love of its members for one another operated as the strongest bond to prevent their unceremoniously leaving. But, upon the breaking up or separation of families, with no prospect of reunion, the firmest and often the sole tie which held them together was severed.[30]

Very often when the slaves were sold from the border states into the lower South, they ran away from their new masters in order to rejoin their families.

Although it is reasonable to assume that the majority of the slaves were accommodated to their status, there was a vast number of slaves who dreamed and yearned for freedom. News seeped through to many that if they could reach the North they would be free. This was especially true of the border states. In Kentucky, where the Ohio River separated them from the free states of Illinois, Indiana, and Ohio, the prospect of freedom was always close.[31] The knowledge that there was freedom beyond the Ohio gradually seeped into the lower South. By 1850 the number of runaway slaves had become large enough for the slaveholding power to have Congress pass the Fugitive Slave Law requiring citizens of the North to return fugitives to their owners. By this time a system for aiding slaves in reaching the North had developed to the extent that it had become known as the Underground

[30] Reprinted from *Slavery Times in Kentucky* by J. Winston Coleman, p. 61, by permission of The University of North Carolina Press. Copyright, 1940, by The University of North Carolina Press.　[31] See *ibid.*, pp. 218ff.

Railroad. The fugitive slave, following the North Star, ceased to be a "truant from the plantation" and became a seeker after freedom.

THE UNDERGROUND RAILROAD

The well-organized movement for assisting slaves to freedom, which became known as the Underground Railroad, had a long history.[32] From the beginning of the Negro's enslavement there were individual whites who assisted him when he fled from slavery. However, the Quakers were the first distinguishable group to become active as the friend of the fugitive slaves. In the South the Quakers often freed their slaves and provided them with means to begin life as freedmen. Because of the anti-slavery activities of the Quakers, Philadelphia became in the late eighteenth century an important center of the Underground Railroad movement. During the early nineteenth century the movement spread into western Pennsylvania, Ohio, Illinois and Indiana. Levi Coffin, one of the leaders in the Underground Railroad, became active in Indiana in 1826 after leaving North Carolina where he had been an apostle of anti-slavery and had aided many slaves to escape to the West.

The Abolitionist Movement found in the Underground Railroad one of its chief means of attack on the slave power. Each year after 1830, abolitionists as well as Quakers assisted hundreds of slaves to escape from slavery by means of the Underground Railroad. In the West there were hundreds of stations of the Underground Railroad in Illinois, Indiana, and Ohio. The routes connecting the stations in Illinois converged on Chicago, whence the slaves went by water to Canada. Because of its geographical position as well as the background of its settlers, Ohio was the chief center of Underground Railroad activities. After crossing the Ohio River, thousands of slaves found friends at numerous stations ready to assist them on their journey to Canada. In the East, the numerous stations around Philadelphia connected with routes leading westward to Buffalo and eastward to New England. However, the majority of slaves who used the Un-

---

[32] See Wilber H. Siebert, *The Underground Railroad from Slavery to Freedom* (New York, 1898), pp. 17-46; and Henrietta Buckmaster, *Let My People Go* (New York, 1941), pp. 11-47.

derground Railroad in Massachusetts in order to escape into Canada, were concealed on ships coming from southern ports.[33] It is difficult to determine how many slaves escaped from the South by means of the Underground Railroad. Siebert's work was based upon the activities of over 3,000 operators, 1,540 of whom were in Ohio alone.[34] Along the Ohio routes, according to Hesseltine, passed as many as 2,000 slaves a year during the period, 1830 to 1860.[35]

The rôle of the Negro in the Abolitionist Movement has generally been discounted or ignored, though the free Negroes of the North played an important part in assisting the enslaved members of the race to freedom.[36] There were many undistinguished Negroes who acted as guides along the routes of the Underground Railroad. But there were also Negroes of distinction, some of whom had escaped from slavery, who played important parts in the movement. Among them should be mentioned William Still, David Ruggles, Frederick Douglass, J. W. Loguen, Martin Delany, Lewis Hayden, and George DeBaptist. William Still was the chairman of the Acting Vigilant Committee of the Philadelphia Branch of the Underground Railroad.[37] There were also a number of fairly well-to-do free Negroes in the North who gave their time and money to the work. Outstanding among such people was the wealthy, cultured mulatto, Robert Purvis, who had helped to organize the first National Negro Convention and was among the signers of the declaration of the American Antislavery Society.[38] Frederick Douglass who had escaped from slavery became one of the great orators of the Abolitionist Movement. David Walker, who in 1829 issued his famous *Appeal* to the slaves to rise against their masters, aroused the slaveholders more than any other free Negro engaged in the movement.[39] When the state of Georgia was offering

[33] Wilber H. Siebert, "The Underground Railroad in Massachusetts," *Proceedings of the American Antiquarian Society*, Vol. 45 (April, 1935), pp. 25-100.
[34] *The Underground Railroad from Slavery to Freedom*, p. 351.
[35] William B. Hesseltine, *A History of the South 1607-1936* (New York, 1936), p. 258.
[36] See Herbert Aptheker, "The Negro in the Abolitionist Movement," *Science and Society*, Vol. V (1941), pp. 2-23.
[37] See William Still, *The Underground Railroad* (Philadelphia, 1872).
[38] Buckmaster, *op. cit.*, p. 107.
[39] *Walker's Appeal, in four Articles together with a Preamble* (Boston, 1856).

$4,000 for the arrest of Garrison, it offered $10,000 for Walker if taken alive and $1,000 if dead.[40]

There were many women among the free Negroes of the North who aided in the Abolitionist Movement and the Underground Railroad. One of the outstanding women was Sojourner Truth, who was born a slave in New York.[41] She became a quaint figure, known for her wit, as she went about speaking for the abolitionist cause. However, the most heroic figure in the Underground Railroad Movement was Harriet Tubman, who acquired the title of "The Moses of Her People." [42] She was introduced to Wendell Phillips by John Brown as "one of the best and bravest persons on this continent."[43] Harriet Tubman had earned this tribute because of her unexcelled bravery in the movement. After escaping from slavery in Maryland, in 1849, she made nineteen trips to the South and helped three hundred slaves to escape to freedom. She did this in defiance of the slaveholders when rewards amounting to $40,000 were offered for her capture. A deeply religious woman of indomitable courage, Harriet Tubman found it necessary at times to use a pistol in urging faltering slaves along the road to freedom.

JOHN BROWN AT HARPERS FERRY

While the free Negroes, from their secure position in the North, played an important rôle in the Underground Railroad, very few were willing to risk their lives in slave insurrections. With the exception of the Vesey plot in Charleston, the free Negroes in the South had played an inconspicuous part in the slave uprisings. These insurrections were instigated and led by slaves, who found in the Bible or within their African culture sufficiently strong imperatives to make them risk their lives in order to escape subordination to the white man. When John Brown started on his enterprise to liberate the slaves, the free Negroes gave the means and time to aid in its organization. But they refused to follow him and become martyrs in an

---

[40] See Buckmaster, *op. cit.*, pp. 43-58.

[41] *Narrative of Sojourner Truth* (Boston, 1875).

[42] See Sarah H. Bradford, *Harriet, The Moses of Her People* (New York, 1886). See also Siebert, *The Underground Railroad from Slavery to Freedom*, pp. 185-89.   [43] *Ibid.*, p. 185.

undertaking which was foredoomed to failure. Brown was especially disappointed in the withdrawal of Frederick Douglass, who had been his first confidant in his plan in Virginia and had helped to collect money and recruits for the undertaking.[44] When Douglass made his final decision to withdraw from the undertaking, Shields Green, a poor, illiterate slave at the conference, remarked: "I b'lieve I'll go wid de ole man." He with four or five other free Negroes followed Brown from the North to Virginia.

When Brown and his lieutenants attempted to arouse the slaves only thirty or forty responded and most of them deserted and returned to their masters with the excuse that they had been forced into the insurrection. To the slaves in Virginia, many of whom were accommodated to a patriarchal form of slavery, John Brown was a white man and an outsider. The slaves were probably even less affected by abstract ideas of human freedom than the free Negroes in the North. Nevertheless, John Brown was the extreme expression of social forces growing out of deeper economic developments in American life which were soon to decide the issue of freedom or slavery for the Negro.

[44] Oswald Garrison Villard, *John Brown* (New York, 1910), pp. 317, 412-13. See also W. E. Burghardt DuBois, *John Brown* (Philadelphia, 1901), pp. 343-46, for a defense of Douglass' withdrawal.

Racial Conflict and New Forms of Accommodation

PART 2 is concerned with the crisis in Negro life in America which resulted from the Civil War and Emancipation; the racial conflict which developed during and following Reconstruction; and the new types of accommodation between the races which grew out of this conflict. First, the economic and more especially the social consequences of Emancipation will be analyzed in relation to their effect upon race relations. This is followed by an analysis of the influence of Reconstruction upon the status of the Negro and his relations with whites. The last chapter in this section is concerned with the new forms of accommodation or external adjustment between the two races which emerged after "white supremacy" had been restored and a quasi-caste system had been established.

CHAPTER VI

The Civil War and Emancipation

SCARCELY a year before the opening of the Civil War it appeared from a set of resolutions adopted by the United States Senate that the slave status of the Negro had become established for a long period. According to these resolutions, sponsored by southern leaders and adopted on May 24-25, 1860,

. . . slavery is lawful in all the territories under the Constitution; neither Congress nor a local legislature can abolish it there; the federal government is in duty bound to protect slave owners as well as the holders of other forms of property in the territories; it is a violation of the Constitution for any state or any combination of citizens to intermeddle with the domestic institutions of any other state "on any pretext whatever, political, moral, or religious, with a view to their disturbance or subversion"; open or covert attacks on slavery are contrary to the solemn pledges given by the states on entering the Union to protect and defend one another; the inhabitants of a territory on their admission to the Union may decide whether or not they will sanction slavery thereafter; the strict enforcement of the fugitive slave law is required by good faith and the principles of the Constitution.[1]

The triumph of the Republicans at the polls in November of the same year, changed the political situation. It was a signal for the secession of the planter aristocracy. When the southern legislators withdrew, the Republicans, who were a minority in the Senate and House, were left in control of the federal government. Although the Republican party was opposed to the planter class, there was no unanimity among them on the question of the future status of the Negro.

[1] Charles A. Beard and Mary R. Beard, *The Rise of American Civilization* (New York, 1927), Vol. II, p. 29.

CONSERVATIVE AND RADICAL REPUBLICANS

The Conservative Republicans were not interested, on the whole, in the status of the Negro. Although Lincoln was the spokesman for the Conservative wing of the Republican party, William H. Seward of New York was its leader. As a United States senator, Seward had opposed slavery and the various compromises between the North and the South. But after he became Secretary of State, he opposed Emancipation until after a northern victory. The wing of the Republican party represented by Seward was interested primarily in shaping legislation to fit the economic progress of industrialization.[2] On the other hand, the Radical Republicans were divided into two factions: the Old Radicals who were not simply interested in making the industrial-capitalist class dominant but who were also concerned with the rights of the Negro; and the New Radicals who were interested in the triumph of the rising industrial class.

The two factions among the Radical Republicans agreed that the War could be won only by emancipating the Negro slave in order to destroy the political and economic power of the planter aristocracy. The Old Radicals in the Republican Party, represented by such men as Thaddeus Stevens and Charles Sumner, had carried on a long but losing struggle for the abolition of slavery. In the election of 1852 the Free Soil Party had not polled five per cent of the votes; and in 1859, "after Garrison had been at work for a quarter of a century, by a decision of more than three to one, even the mildest plank in the anti-slavery platform was overwhelmingly repudiated by the country at large." [3] In the campaign of 1860, the Abolitionist element in the Republican Party could secure only a declaration in the party's platform excluding slavery from the territories. However, with the outbreak of the Civil War, the Old Radicals with the support of the New Radicals were able to force upon Lincoln their ideas regarding abolition and equalitarian ideals in regard to the Negro. First, they were able to get Congress to pass two acts of Confiscation in 1861 and

[2] See Louis M. Hacker, *The Triumph of American Capitalism* (New York, 1940), p. 340.
[3] Beard and Beard, *op. cit.*, Vol. II, p. 24.

1862 confiscating the slaves and other property of the rebels.[4] In the latter year, two other acts, one abolishing slavery in the District of Columbia and the other abolishing slavery in the territories were passed.[5]

THE ENLISTMENT OF NEGRO SOLDIERS

The first and most important test of the status of the Negro during the Civil War was concerned with his employment as a soldier. At the opening of the War the services of free Negroes were refused by the Secretary of War.[6] In 1861 when General W. T. Sherman began operations on the coast of South Carolina he was instructed, as General Butler had been instructed in Virginia, not to return refugees to their masters and to use the "contrabands" as laborers. At the same time Sherman was also instructed to use the "contrabands" as he "may deem most beneficial to the service: this, however, not being a general arming of them for the service." [7] Although he was given this authority to use his discretion, Sherman did not receive Negroes into the armed forces and some northern officers even permitted the masters to retrieve escaped slaves who had sought refuge within the northern lines.[8] The action of these northern officers reflected a large section of northern opinion which was opposed to granting the Negro equality. Despite the growth in demoeracy during the three decades prior to the Civil War, the Negro outside of New England did not live under the same laws as the whites.[9] "To the Northern masses," writes DuBois, "the Negro was a curiosity, a sub-human minstrel, willing and naturally a slave, and treated as well as he deserved to be. He had not sense enough to revolt and help Northern armies, even if Northern armies were trying to emancipate him, which they were

[4] See William MacDonald, *Documentary Source Book of American History* (New York, 1914), pp. 442-44, and 454-57.

[5] *Ibid.*, pp. 450-52.

[6] Bell Irwin Wiley, *Southern Negroes, 1861-1865* (New Haven, 1938) pp. 295-96.

[7] *Southern Negroes, 1861-1865* by Bell Irwin Wiley, p. 296. Copyright 1938 by Yale University Press.

[8] W. E. Burghardt DuBois, *Black Reconstruction in America* (New York, 1935), p. 60.

[9] Carl R. Fish, *The Rise of the Common Man* (New York, 1927), pp. 280ff.

not. The North shrank at the very thought of encouraging servile insurrection against the whites." [10]

It was General David Hunter, an abolitionist and the successor to Sherman in South Carolina, who after applying to Washington for reinforcements recruited Negroes for the First South Carolina Volunteers. His action aroused both favorable and unfavorable comment in the Northern press and provoked a heated discussion in Congress.[11] Because of the attitude of the administration, Hunter's Negro regiment with the exception of one company was disbanded. However, as a result of the discussion Congress was compelled to take some action which was embodied in a bill providing for labor service on the part of Negroes in the War and "any war service." The vague language of the bill indicates the hesitancy on the part of Congress to enlist Negro soldiers. This hesitancy was due to the fear of a Negro insurrection and the unwillingness to accord the Negro equality of status with the white soldiers. Some members of Congress favored the enlistment of Negro soldiers because they thought it would enable the Negro to prove his right to equality; but the majority supported the measure as a means of weakening the South. It was only after the Emancipation Proclamation and the pressing need for Union troops in Louisiana that the enlistment of Negro soldiers became a definite policy of the North.[12] Before the War Department set up the Bureau of Colored Troops in May 1863, General Butler, commander of the Union forces in Louisiana, had accepted a free Negro regiment, which had been organized by the Confederate governor, for the defense of New Orleans.

THE EMANCIPATION PROCLAMATION

In a letter to Horace Greeley in August, 1862, Lincoln had made his position clear concerning the emancipation of the Negro. "My paramount object," he wrote, "in this struggle is to save the Union, and not either to save or destroy slavery." [13] Moreover, he stated that

[10] DuBois, *op. cit.*, p. 56.   [11] See Wiley, *op. cit.*, pp. 297-98.
[12] See Wiley, *op. cit.*, pp. 303-10, and DuBois, *op. cit.*, pp. 94-96.
[13] Merwin Roe (Ed.), *Speeches and Letters of Abraham Lincoln, 1832-1865* (New York, 1907), p. 194.

whatever he did "about slavery and the coloured race," he did because he believed it would help to save the Union. These statements contained, as he said, his views of his official duty and were not intended as a modification of his "personal wish that all men everywhere could be free." [14] Less than a month later, Lincoln admitted to an audience in Chicago that slavery was "at the root of the rebellion, or at least its *sine qua non.*" He also conceded that the emancipation of the Negro would help the Union cause in Europe.[15] Lincoln had little faith in the ability of the Negro to become a soldier. He expressed the opinion that if the Negroes were armed, within a few weeks their arms would be in the hands of the rebels. His opposition to the wholesale emancipation of the Negro was based upon his conviction that Negroes and whites could not live together in the same community.

Only nine days after his Chicago speech Lincoln issued his preliminary Emancipation Proclamation and on January 1, 1863 his final proclamation. The final proclamation declared that all persons held as slaves within the states that were in rebellion against the United States were free.[16] The emancipated Negroes were admonished to abstain from violence and to accept employment at reasonable wages. The proclamation also contained the important provision that the freedmen should be received into the armed forces of the United States.

Shortly after the Emancipation Proclamation the War Department authorized the Governor of Massachusetts to organize two Negro regiments—the famous Fifty-fourth and Fifty-fifth Negro regiments—

[14] *Ibid.,* p. 195.

[15] Because of the effect of the Union blockade on the textile industry, England and France—at least the upper classes—were favorable to the South. However, there were such men as John Bright in England who believed that the Civil War was a struggle for emancipation and democracy. They were supported by the English working class despite the hardships which this class suffered. The Emancipation Proclamation turned popular opinion in England decidedly in favor of the North. See Beard and Beard, *op. cit.,* Vol. II, pp. 81-84, and Karl Marx and Frederick Engels, *The Civil War in the United States* (New York, 1937), pp. 3-15, 41-42.

[16] The Thirteenth Amendment to the Constitution, which abolished slavery in the United States, was not declared in force until December 18, 1865. A resolution for an amendment abolishing slavery was first introduced in the Senate in January 1864; but it was not until January, 1865 that a joint resolution by the Senate and the House received the necessary two-thirds vote.

which were the first regularly authorized by the government.[17] Later Negro regiments were organized in New York and Pennsylvania. After the draft law was passed in 1863 the Negro became subject to its operation and as the Union army advanced into enemy territory the former slaves were recruited for military service. Half of the 186,017 Negro troops reported by the Adjutant General's Office were from the seceded states, and 40,765 from Kentucky, Maryland, and Missouri.[18] Because of the general attitude of the North in regard to the status of the Negro, the enlistment of them as soldiers was beset with many difficulties. When Negro soldiers were first authorized there was opposition in Congress to giving them the pay received by white soldiers. It was not until 1864 that the government finally agreed to give them the same pay as the whites. There was also the difficulty of securing white officers to command Negro troops because of the stigma attached to such service. In addition to the social stigma there was also the policy of assigning Negro soldiers to services which were thought unbecoming white soldiers. Then, too, the Confederate government, which toward the close of the Civil War began enlisting Negro soldiers,[19] threatened to shoot white officers commanding Negro units as felons until Lincoln threatened retaliation.[20]

There were grave doubts about the serviceability of Negro soldiers, but as the struggle progressed their fighting qualities warranted their continued enlistment. Although the Confederacy was inclined to disparage the fighting qualities of "an inferior race," the conduct of Negro soldiers was one of the arguments for enlisting Negroes in defense of the South.[21] Colonel Higginson, who commanded the *First South Carolina Volunteers*, which "contained scarcely a freeman, had

[17] The attitude of many northerners toward the enlistment of Negro soldiers is indicated by the fact that when it was planned for these regiments to pass through New York City, the chief of police warned that they would be insulted; therefore, it was necessary for them to go by sea to South Carolina. See DuBois, *op. cit.*, p. 97.   [18] Wiley, *op. cit.*, pp. 310-11.   [19] *Ibid.*, pp 146-62.

[20] *Ibid.*, pp. 311-12. The attitude of the Confederacy is indicated by the *Savannah Republican's* denunciation of General Hunter as "the cold-blooded abolition miscreant who, from his headquarters at Hilton Head is engaged in executing the bloody and savage behest of the imperial gorilla who, from his throne of human bones at Washington, rules, reigns and riots over the brutish and degraded north." *Ibid.*, p. 312, note. 55.   [21] *Ibid.*, pp. 152-53.

not one mulatto in ten, and a far smaller proportion who could read or write when enlisted," gives the following sober estimate of Negro soldiers:

The point of inferiority that I always feared, though I never had occasion to prove it, was that they might show less fibre, less tough and dogged resistance, than whites, during a prolonged trial,—a long, disastrous march, for instance, or the hopeless defence of a besieged town. I should not be afraid of their mutinying or running away, but of their drooping and dying. It might not turn out so; but I mention it for the sake of fairness, and to avoid overstating the merits of these troops. As to the simple general fact of courage and reliability I think no officer in our camp ever thought of there being any difference between black and white. And certainly the opinions of these officers, who for years risked their lives every moment on the fidelity of their men, were worth more than those of all the world beside.[22]

THE DISRUPTION OF THE PLANTATION REGIME

To the race-conscious free Negroes, especially those in the North, the Emancipation Proclamation meant the achievement of a new status in American life. On the other hand, the announcement of freedom created a state of bewilderment among the vast majority of illiterate slaves on southern plantations. One ex-slave recalled that the announcement sounded "like Greek" to him when his mother whispered, "Son, we have been slaves all our lives, and now Mr. Abe Lincoln done set us free, and say we can go anywhere we please in this country, without getting a pass from Marse Cage like we used to have

---

[22] Thomas W. Higginson, *Army Life in a Black Regiment* (Boston, 1870), p. 250. Many evaluations of the fighting qualities of Negro soldiers have been influenced, of course, by attitudes toward the Negro. Wiley, *op. cit.*, pp. 340-41, who constantly refers to Negroes as "darkies," concludes: "Generally speaking, the conduct of the Negroes in the war did not prove them good or bad fighters. It did show them capable of performing acts of reckless courage; it manifested their ability to go forward in impetuous charges under galling fire. The dependability in standing up against stubborn and sustained resistance was left for future determination." The Negro in Africa was an excellent warrior and the European colonizing powers have placed a high valuation upon his performance as a soldier in modern warfare. Therefore, his performance in the Civil War was due to such factors as morale, the influence of traditions, and other motivating forces. Unfortunately, no really scientific study has been made of the fighting qualities of Negroes in the Civil War.

to do." [23] A Negro minister tells the following story of the effects of the announcement of freedom on the plantation where his grand-father held a responsible position:

The slaves were in the fields chopping the cotton and chanting the rhythm of the day as a testimony to the drowsy overseer that they were doing his bidding. "Massah" Ridley was on the porch of the "big house" fast asleep. The Yankees had ridden up to the mansion, and the horses put their hoofs on the low and unrailed porch as if at home. Doctor Ridley awakened quickly, surprised, startled, bewildered, perplexed, a riot of color. Some words passed between the parties, and then one of the soldiers took something from his pocket and read it. By this time "Missus" Ridley had come from the house. She too heard the story and saw her husband's eyes suffused with tears, but said not a word. Doctor Ridley was trying hard to keep the tears back. He summoned Miles and spoke slowly with a tear in his voice: "Miles, call all the niggers together."

The slaves did not know the meaning of Miles' news to them, although they had heard rumors that they should sometime be free. Few could read, and none had access to newspapers. As they left the field they wondered who was to be whipped or who was to be sold or what orders were to be given. Half-startled, half-afraid, they wended their way through the fields in one silent mass of praying creatures. On seeing the Yankees they started back, but "Massah" Ridley beckoned.

The master was weeping bitterly. Finally he sobbed, "I called you together, Miles—" then he stopped. His words were stifled with sobs. The slaves were awe-stricken; they had never seen a white man cry. Only slaves had tears, they thought. All eyes were fastened on Doctor Ridley. He was saying something. "All you niggers—all you niggers are free as I am." The surprise was shocking, but in an instant in his usual harsh voice he added: "But there ain't going to be any rejoicing here. Stay here until the crop is made, and I'll give you provisions. Go back to work."

But the slaves did rejoice and loudly, too. Some cried; some jumped up and cracked their heels. Charlotte took her younger children in her arms and shouted all over the plantation: "Chillun, didn't I tell you God 'ould answer prayer?" [24]

[23] J. Vance Lewis, *Out of the Ditch: A True Story of an Ex-slave* (Houston, Texas, 1910), p. 9.

[24] Miles Mark Fisher, *The Master's Slave—Elijah John Fisher* (Philadelphia, 1922), pp. 6-8.

As indicated in the above document, the advance of the northern armies and the announcement of freedom tended to disrupt the plantation regime. But even before the northern armies had advanced far, it had become necessary in many parts of the South to tighten the state patrols and to institute supplementary military patrols.[25] When the patrols were withdrawn because of the diminishing man-power of the Confederacy, Negroes were likely to show insubordination. Many slaves exhibited loyalty toward their masters until the approach of the Union army, but then seized the first opportunity to escape. In fact, as the Union army advanced, it could generally rely upon the Negroes, especially the field slaves, to engage in espionage and furnish them with information.[26]

The behavior of the Negro toward his masters during the crisis created by the War was determined largely by the character of the relations that had developed between them. Where the slaves had been treated well and there had been close association between the races in the same household, the slaves generally remained loyal. On the other hand, the field slaves and those in the towns were more likely to utilize the opportunity to escape from a form of control that was external and formal.

Many of the slaves immediately left the plantations when they learned that they were free. This was natural since the right to move about freely was a crucial test of freedom.[27] On the other hand, the attitude of subordination was still strong in some slaves and they were afraid to assert their newly acquired rights. This attitude is shown in an incident related by Bishop Coppin:

Father Jones was promptly on hand with Lincoln's proclamation, but here was no one present with authority to say to the slave, you are free; so all were in suspense.

Uncle Jim Jones drove his mistress to Cecilton, and some one, a white person, told him that he was free now, and it was discretionary

---

[25] Wiley, *op. cit.*, pp. 33-40.   [26] *Ibid.*, p. 76.

[27] "After the coming of freedom," wrote Booker T. Washington, "there were two points upon which practically all the people on our place were agreed, and I find that this was generally true throughout the South: that they must change their names, and that they must leave the plantation for at least a few days or weeks in order that they might really feel sure that they were free." *Up from Slavery* (New York, 1902), p. 23.

with him whether or not he drove the carriage back. When Uncle Jim reached home he informed every one of what he had heard. When a few evenings after that, his old master himself drove the carriage to town and was late returning, Uncle Jim, in order to make a test case, would not remain to unharness the horses, but said, in a way that his master would be sure to hear it: "There has got to be a new understanding," which "new understanding," came promptly the next morning when "Mars Frankie" approached him to know about the strange doctrine which he was preaching around the place. Poor Uncle Jim begged pardon, saved his back, and said no more about a "new understanding."

He was too old to be very independent. He continued to live in the little house on the place, and work for Mars Frankie, who paid him about what he thought his services were worth. He never was able to throw off the terrible fear he always had of his master, who, by the way, was never cruel to him; but, he finally mustered enough courage to go and come at will.[28]

When the plantation system finally collapsed under the impact of war and the defeat of the southern armies, the spirit of submission tended to disappear and the traditional ties between the masters and slaves were disrupted.

SOCIAL DISORGANIZATION AMONG THE FREEDMEN

The collapse of the traditional forms of controls which had developed under the slave regime tended to demoralize the Negro. When Sherman's army swept through Georgia, it carried along with it thousands of Negroes from the plantations. The demoralization that resulted from the shock of war often caused mothers to leave their exhausted and dying children by the roadside. In some cases mothers put their children to death when they became too great a burden.[29] According to General H. W. Slocum commanding the left wing of the Army of Georgia:

Negro men, women, and children joined the columns at every mile of our march, many of them bringing horses and mules, which they cheerfully turned over to the quartermaster's department. I think at

---

[28] L. J. Coppin, *Unwritten History* (Philadelphia, 1920), pp. 91-92.
[29] Elizabeth Pearson, *War Letters from Port Royal, Written at the Time of the Civil War* (Boston, 1906), pp. 293-94.

least fourteen thousand of these people joined the two columns at different points on the march; but many of them were too old and infirm, and others too young, to endure the fatigue of the march, and were left in the rear. More than one-half of this number, however, reached the coast with us.[30]

Thousands of refugees flocked to the army camps and cities in search of work and new experience.[31] When Sherman's forces captured Savannah, Negroes from the surrounding plantations swarmed into the city. The flight of the refugees to the army camps and the cities created problems of discipline as well as of health and maintenance. An educated Negro minister from the North who began to work among the freedmen in South Carolina described the demoralization which he found as follows:

This whole section with its hundreds of thousands of men, women and children just broken forth from slavery, was so far as these were concerned, lying under an almost absolute physical and moral interdict. There was no one to baptize their children, to perform marriage, or to bury the dead. A ministry had to be created at once—and created out of the material at hand.[32]

Confronted with these conditions, General Sherman sent out an appeal to philanthropic people of the North for aid for the poverty-stricken and ignorant refugees. In response to this appeal Freedmen's Aid Societies were formed in Boston, New York, and Philadelphia. In March 1863, Edward L. Pierce, a representative of the Societies, sailed from New York with about forty-five men and fifteen women who were said to constitute "The first missionary expedition to propagate industry, religion, and education among the contrabands at Hilton Head (South Carolina), as well as encourage agriculture and like useful measures." [33] Although some of these missionaries became teachers among the freedmen, most of them acted as superintendents

[30] Quoted in Elizabeth Botume, *First Days Among the Contrabands* (Boston, 1893), p. 79.
[31] Carter G. Woodson, *A Century of Negro Migration* (Washington, D. C., 1918), pp. 101-07. It is estimated that in 1864, 30,000 to 40,000 Negroes came from southern plantations to the District of Columbia. *Ibid.*, p. 105.
[32] T. G. Steward, *Fifty Years in the Gospel Ministry* (Philadelphia, 1922), p. 33. [33] Botume, *op. cit.*, p. 19.

of the labor of the freedmen and distributed clothes and food among them. The number of teachers and superintendents increased to nearly one hundred within a few months and there were nearly four thousand freedmen working on 15,000 acres of corn, potatoes, and cotton by summer.[34] These missionaries and teachers formed the vanguard of the thousands of men and women who were to devote their lives to the task of fitting the Negro to assume the responsibilities of citizenship.

THE FREEDMEN'S BUREAU

The flight of Negro refugees to army camps and cities naturally required the federal government to assume some guardianship over the lives of the former slaves. This problem appeared first when the Union forces under General Butler occupied Fortress Monroe, Virginia.[35] Three Negroes who had escaped from their masters and entered the federal lines were held as "contrabands" of War, because they had been used in military operations by the Confederates.[36] When other slaves in the surrounding area learned of this action, they flocked in large numbers including women and children to the army camp. The men were put to work and all were provided with food and shelter. The same problem faced the Union army when it took possession of the Sea Islands on the coast of South Carolina. The southern planters fled, leaving thousands of slaves and large cotton crops. The Secretary of the Treasury sent "a special agent to visit this district for the purpose of reporting upon the condition of the Negroes who had been abandoned by the white population, and of suggesting some plan for the organization of their labor and the promotion of their general well-being." [37] Following the report of this agent, Edward L. Pierce, who had already shown much skill in handling the

[34] Pearson, *op. cit.*, Introduction, p. vii.

[35] See Edward L. Pierce, "The Contrabands at Fortress Monroe," *Atlantic Monthly*, Vol. VIII (Nov. 1861), pp. 626-40.

[36] After General Butler applied the term "contraband" to these escaped slaves, "contraband" was applied generally first to Negroes who had been used by Confederates for military purposes and later to all slaves of disloyal owners. See Wiley, *op. cit.*, pp. 176-77.

[37] Edward L. Pierce, "The Freedmen at Port Royal," *Atlantic Monthly*, Vol. XII (Nov. 1861), pp. 626-40.

"contrabands" in Virginia, was sent by the Treasury to take charge of the freedmen.[38]

As the Union army advanced in other sections of the country they had to face the problem of the "contrabands" who flocked to the army camps. In the West the problem was even more complicated because of the presence of loyal slaveholders.[39] In fact, the commander of the Military Department of the West issued an order that fugitive slaves were not to be permitted to enter the army camps and that those who were unemployed were to be turned out.[40] This order created a storm of protest in Congress and in the East and many subordinate officers refused to obey the order. General Butler attempted to exclude fugitive slaves from the Union camps in Louisiana but was forced to modify his orders. After the Congressional Act of 1862, confiscating the slaves of disloyal owners, the fugitives could not be turned away from the Union lines and some method had to be devised for their maintenance and discipline. They were employed first as laborers and servants and later as soldiers. "Through the wages and bounty money thus received [during the war]," writes DuBois, "a fund of something between five and ten millions of dollars was distributed among the freedmen—a mere pittance per capita, but enough in some cases to enable recipients to buy a little land and start as small farmers." [41]

The wages paid the servants and laborers in the army camps and the bounties given the soldiers did not provide the great mass of former slaves with the assistance which they needed to become established as free workers. In order to accomplish this purpose a bill had been introduced into Congress in 1863 providing for the establishment of a bureau to assist the freedmen. It was not, however, until 1864 that Congress, after receiving petitions from Freedmen's Aid Societies, gave serious attention to such a measure.[42] Charles Sumner was in favor of a bill establishing on a more or less permanent basis a department for dealing in a broad and fundamental manner with

38 See Edward L. Pierce, *The Negroes at Port Royal* (Boston, 1862).
39 Wiley, *op. cit.*, p. 181.   40 *Ibid.*, p. 181.
41 W. E. B. DuBois, *The Negro Landholders of Georgia*, "Bulletin of the Department of Labor," No. 35 (Washington, 1901), p. 647.
42 DuBois, *Black Reconstruction*, pp. 220ff.

the problem of inducting the freedman into citizenship. However, he was overruled by the opposition and a bill was passed in 1865 creating a Bureau of Refugees, Freedmen, and Abandoned Lands in the War Department, which became known as the Freedmen's Bureau. The Bureau was to last during the War and for one year thereafter. According to the provisions of the bill, the Secretary of War "may direct such issues of provisions, clothing, and fuel, as he may deem needful for the immediate and temporary shelter and supply of destitute and suffering refugees and freedmen and their wives and children." [43] Moreover, the commissioner, appointed by the President, was to have authority

to set apart, for the use of loyal refugees and freedmen, such tracts of land within the insurrectionary states as shall have been abandoned, or to which the United States shall have acquired title by confiscation or sale, or otherwise, and to every male citizen, whether refugee or freedman, as aforesaid, there shall be assigned not more than forty acres of such land, and the person to whom it was so assigned shall be protected in the use and enjoyment of the land for the term of three years at an annual rent not exceeding six per centum upon the value of such land, as it was appraised by the state authorities in the year eighteen hundred and sixty, for the purpose of taxation, and in case no such appraisal can be found, then the rental shall be based upon the estimated value of the land in said year, to be ascertained in such manner as the commissioner may by regulation prescribe. At the end of said term, or at any time during the said term, the occupants of any parcels so assigned may purchase the land and receive such title thereto as the United States can convey, upon paying therefor the value of the land, as ascertained and fixed for the purpose of determining the annual rent aforesaid. [44]

The stupendous labors which faced the Freedmen's Bureau are aptly summarized by DuBois as follows:

. . . : to make as rapidly as possible a general survey of conditions and needs in every state and locality; to relieve immediate hunger and distress; to appoint state commissioners and upwards of 900 bureau officials; to put the laborers to work at regular wage; to transport laborers, teachers and officials; to furnish land for the peasant; to open schools; to pay bounties to black soldiers and their families; to estab-

[43] MacDonald, *op. cit.*, p. 489.   [44] *Ibid.*, pp. 489-90.

lish hospitals and guard health; to administer justice between man and former master; to answer continuous and persistent criticism, North and South, black and white; to find funds to pay for all this.[45]

Despite the handicaps which the Bureau faced from its inception, it was fortunate in having as its head General Oliver O. Howard, a sympathetic and humane man who "tried with endless application and desperate sacrifice to do a hard, thankless duty." Concerning the conditions facing the Bureau, General Howard made the following statement:

In every state many thousands were found without employment, without homes, without means of subsistence, crowding into towns and about military posts, where they hoped to find protection and supplies. The sudden collapse of the rebellion, making emancipation an actual, universal fact, was like an earthquake. It shook and shattered the whole previously existing social system. It broke up the old industries and threatened a reign of anarchy. Even well-disposed and humane landowners were at a loss what to do, or how to begin the work of reorganizing society and of rebuilding their ruined fortunes. Very few had any knowledge of free labor, or any hope that their former slaves would serve them faithfully for wages. On the other hand, the freed people were in a state of great excitement and uncertainty. They could hardly believe that the liberty proclaimed was real and permanent. Many were afraid to remain on the same soil that they had tilled as slaves lest by some trick they might find themselves again in bondage. Others supposed that the Government would either take the entire supervision of their labor and support, or divide among them the lands of the conquered owners, and furnish them with all that might be necessary to begin life as an independent farmer.[46]

THE ESTABLISHMENT OF THE NEGRO AS A FREE MAN

The success or failure of individual Negroes in becoming established as free men capable of self-direction depended to a large extent upon their character, intelligence, and efficiency. These qualities reflected in turn the type of schooling they had received during slavery. The following is a description of the type of freedman who through

[45] DuBois, *Black Reconstruction*, p. 225.
[46] Quoted in *Black Reconstruction in America* by W. E. B. DuBois, p. 224. Copyright 1935 by Harcourt, Brace and Company, Inc.

his enterprise and intelligence showed himself capable of assuming the responsibilities of the newly acquired status:

He is a black Yankee. Without a drop of white blood in him, he has the energy and 'cuteness and big eye' for his own advantage of a born New Englander. He is not very moral or scrupulous, and the church-members will tell you 'not yet,' with a smile, if you ask whether he belongs to them. But he leads them all in enterprise, and his ambition and consequent prosperity make his example a very useful one on the plantation. Half the men on the island fenced in gardens last autumn, behind their houses, in which they now raise vegetables for themselves, and the Hilton Head markets. Limus in his half-acre has quite a little farmyard besides. With poultry-houses, pig-pens, and corn-houses, the array is very imposing. He has even a stable, for he made out some title to a horse, which was allowed; and then he begged a pair of wheels and makes a cart for his work; and not to leave the luxuries behind, he next rigs up a kind of sulky and bows to the white men from his carriage. As he keeps his table in corresponding style,— for he buys more sugar . . . than any other two families,—of course the establishment is rather expensive. So, to provide the means, he has three permanent irons in the fire—his cotton, his Hilton Head express, and his seine. Before the fishing season commenced, a pack of dogs for deer-hunting took the place of the net. While other families 'carry' from three to six or seven acres of cotton, Limus says he must have fourteen. To help his wife and daughters keep this in good order, he went over to the rendezvous for refugees and imported a family to the plantation, the men of which he hired at $8 a month. . . . With a large boat which he owns, he usually makes weekly trips to Hilton Head, twenty miles distant, carrying passengers, produce and fish. These last he takes in an immense seine,—an abandoned chattel—for the use of which he pays Government by furnishing General Hunter and staff with the finer specimens, and then has ten to twenty bushels for sale. Apparently he is either dissatisfied with this arrangement or means to extend his operations, for he asks me to bring him another seine for which I am to pay $70. I presume his savings since 'the guns fired at Bay Point'—which is the native record of the capture of the island—amount to four or five hundred dollars. He is all ready to buy land, and I expect to see him in ten years a tolerably rich man. Limus has, it is true, but few equals on the islands, and yet there are many who follow not far behind him.[47]

[47] Pearson, *op. cit.*, p. 37n.

Very often the slave who exhibited enough character to revolt against those in authority during slavery was the very one who was most capable of self-direction as a freedman. Concerning a freedman of this type, his employer wrote:

The one man on this plantation who, as a slave, gave most trouble, so much, in fact, that he was almost beyond control of the overseer, was Lem Bryant. Since he has been freed, he has grown honest, quiet, and industrious; he educated his children and pays his debts. Mr. Barrow asked him, one day, what had changed him so. "Ah, master!" he replied, "I'm free now; I have to do right." [48]

Despite the general confusion and disorder, the transition from servitude to freedom in many places was accomplished with scarcely any disturbance to the routine established under slavery. An ex-slave, who witnessed the peaceful transition on a plantation, gives the following account of the announcement concerning emancipation which his master made in "a calm, fatherly voice":

I have called you together to impart to you, officially, a piece of news that I myself do not regret that you receive. Three days ago Abraham Lincoln, the President of the United States, issued a proclamation whereby you are made free men and women. Some of you have been with me all your lives, and some of you I have bought from other owners, but you have all been well fed and clothed and have received good treatment. But now you are free to go anywhere you please. I shall not drive any one away. I shall need somebody to do my work still and every one of you who wants a job shall have employment. You may remain right here on the farm. You will be treated as hired servants. You will be paid for what you do and you will have to pay for what you get. The war has embarrassed me considerably and freeing you makes me a poorer man than I have ever been before, but it does not make me a pauper, and so I have decided to divide what I have with you. I shall not turn you a-loose in the world with nothing. I am going to give you a little start in life. I have made arrangements for every man and woman to receive ten dollars a piece and every child two dollars. I have also ordered that each family be issued enough food to last them a month. I hope you will be honest and industrious and not bring disgrace upon those who have brought you up. Behave yourselves, work hard and trust in God, and you will get

[48] David C. Barrow, "A Georgia Plantation," *Scribner's Monthly*, XXI (April, 1881), p. 836.

along all right. I will not hire anybody today, but tomorrow all who want to go to work will be ready when the bell rings.

It was a pathetic scene and there was hardly a dry eye amongst us. We had watched the master so closely that I had not seen young Mars Dunc in the crowd and was surprised when he cried out, "Say, Joe, dog-gone it, I told you you would not have to go away. Come on, and let us get our dogs and make Mollie Cottontail cut a jig from the cane patch to the woods." And so off to the woods we went in a jiffy.

All told, perhaps there were two hundred Negroes upon the plantation and when the big bell rang they all reported for duty. Mr. Cage, Sr., assigned Isham Stewart over the plow gang; Jeff Thomas over the hoe gang; Doc Lewis, my father, superintendent of the ditch gang—these being considered his most trustworthy men. Mansfield Williams was retained as family coachman, and the author of this book was given to understand that all time not spent in the ditch was to be at the disposal of D. S. Cage, Jr., and of his two brothers, Hugh and Albert. I ran errands and attended them when they were at school to look after the horses.

The devotion of these slaves would make a chapter of itself, but it is sufficient to say that at the writing of this book, Isham Stewart and Jeff Thomas remain upon the plantation, and but for the sarcasm of a schoolmate the author might be there, too. But that is another story and will be related in another place.[49]

Often the more ambitious among the emancipated Negroes were unwilling to remain as laborers or tenants on the plantation. As soon as they had accumulated sufficient money, they would begin payment on a farm.[50] When the freedman undertook to become a landowner, it not only changed his economic relationship with the whites; it affected the psychological relationship with the whites. For as the Negro escaped from economic dependence upon the whites, the old intimacy between master and slave, upon which the moral order of the slave regime rested, tended to disappear.

The extent to which the freedmen were able to secure an economic base for their freedom depended upon more than the character and ambitions of individual Negroes. The problem created by emancipation was of such magnitude that it required governmental action. The Freedmen's Bureau received nearly 800,000 acres of land and 5,000

---

[49] Lewis, *op. cit.*, pp. 12-14.   [50] See Fisher, *op. cit.*, p. 8.

pieces of town property which were leased to the freedmen.[51] But as the result of President Johnson's proclamation of amnesty, practically all of this land was restored to its former owners and the Negro tenants were dispossessed or became laborers. Another attempt in 1866 to make land available not only to the freedmen but also the landless whites was defeated.

Although the Freedmen's Bureau was set up with the avowed purpose of enabling the emancipated Negro to become established as a free man, there was opposition to the Bureau in the North as well as in the South and the work of the Bureau was subject to much criticism. There were northerners who while favoring the citizenship rights of the Negro were unwilling to make him a ward of the nation. They wanted the Negro to have the status of other free laborers and to be given the ballot in order to protect his rights. However, behind such objections to the Bureau was the opposition to the costs which a general program of social uplift would impose upon industry. Industrial capitalism was using the Civil War to consolidate its political power; therefore, it was more disposed to give votes to freedmen than to give them economic security. The South bitterly opposed the Bureau because it represented federal interference with its labor and the elevation of the freedmen to a position of equality.

A fair appraisal of the work of the Bureau shows that it accomplished much good in aiding the Negro to become a free worker and assume the obligations of citizenship. The educational work of the Bureau was of value to poor whites as well as Negroes. However, it was out of the work of the Bureau that a widespread system of public education for Negroes developed. "Between June 1, 1865 and September 1, 1871, $5,262,511.26 was spent on schools from Bureau funds, and in 1870 there were in day and night schools 3,300 teachers and 149,581 pupils. Nearly all of the present Negro universities and colleges like Howard, Fisk, and Atlanta, were founded or substantially aided in their earliest days by the Freedmen's Bureau." [52]

When the second Freedmen's Bureau Bill was passed in 1866, it

[51] DuBois, *The Negro Landholder of Georgia*, pp. 47-48.
[52] *Black Recontruction in America* by W. E. B. DuBois, p. 226. Copyright 1935 by Harcourt, Brace and Company, Inc.

was vetoed by President Johnson, who had begun his struggle against Congressional Reconstruction. Congress responded by passing first the Civil Rights Act and later the second Freedmen's Bureau Bill over the President's veto. By these acts Congress inaugurated the Reconstruction Period, which had tremendous consequences for the Negro. To a consideration of this period in the career of the Negro in the United States we shall turn in the next chapter.

CHAPTER VII

Reconstruction: Period of Acute
Race Conflict

LINCOLN'S attitude and views concerning Negroes gradually changed during the Civil War; but he did not live to formulate a consistent policy concerning the future status of the freedmen. At the beginning of the War he could not envisage the emancipation of the Negro unless it was associated with a plan for colonizing them outside the United States. He resisted the employment of Negroes as soldiers because he had little faith in their ability and courage to face white men in battle. The course of the War convinced him that the emancipation of the Negro was necessary. The behavior of Negro soldiers convinced him that they possessed courage and were effective soldiers. With his characteristic honesty, he acknowledged the contribution of Negro soldiers to the successful outcome of the War. Moreover, after he had issued the Emancipation Proclamation, he stood firmly for the freedom of the Negro. But still he had no definite plan for their future status in American society.

The issue of the future status of the freedman was forced upon Lincoln by the turn of the events in Louisiana. There the question of including the colored population among the citizens eligible to form a state government was raised by the colored people who had been free before the Civil War. As we have seen, the free colored population, chiefly of mulatto origin, was educated and had acquired considerable property. Moreover, during the War these colored people had fought to save the Union. Recognizing the justice of their demand that they be accepted as eligible voters, Lincoln suggested to the Governor of Louisiana in a letter of March 13, 1864, for his private consideration,

whether some of the colored people may not be let in, as, for instance, the very intelligent, and especially those who have fought gallantly in our ranks. They would probably help in some trying time in the future to keep the jewel of Liberty in the family of freedom.[1]

This suggestion was a modification of Lincoln's original proposal that the reconstitution of the governments of the states that had seceded should include only white voters. But Lincoln was not disposed to force any state to extend the franchise to colored citizens. In his last public address, he defended the government that had been set up in Louisiana, which provided "the benefits of public schools equally to black and white," and "empowered the legislature to confer the elective franchise upon the coloured man." [2]

STATUS OF NEGRO AND NATIONAL POLITICS

Lincoln's cautious policy in regard to the future status of the Negro reflected to a large extent the general attitude of the American people. During the crisis of the Civil War there had been an upsurge of idealism regarding human freedom. The abolitionists, who were influential among the Old Radicals in the Republican Party, attempted to utilize this idealism to secure complete equality for the Negro. They constantly prodded Lincoln to take a firm position on the side of the democratic implications of the Civil War and Emancipation. Lincoln was more sensitive to the traditional attitudes of the American people in respect to the complete admission of Negroes and colored people to equality. He was aware that even in the North the free Negro did not enjoy political rights and suffered discrimination in employment as well as in regard to civil rights. He was also aware of the attitudes of the nonslaveholding farmers and the middle class whites in the border and southern States.

Lincoln's successor, Andrew Johnson, came from the lower middle class, whose attitudes toward the Negro and slavery were embodied in Henry Helper's *The Impending Crisis*. Johnson was opposed to slav-

[1] Merwin Roe (Ed.), *Speeches and Letters of Abraham Lincoln* (New York, 1907), p. 216.   [2] *Ibid.*, p. 229.

ery and the planter aristocracy because the latter were opposed to the interests of his class. As provisional governor of Tennessee and during his first months in office as President, he was very outspoken in favor of democracy and in the denunciation of the Rebel leaders. He had sponsored the Homestead Bill because it would open up land for white farmers. Johnson envisioned the readmission of the seceded states upon terms which would place *white* small farmers in control of the federal and state governments. Thus, his conception of democracy did not include black men. After the War he was glad that slavery was destroyed but he was thankful because the War had "freed more whites than blacks." [3] Since, in his conception of a society of small farmers and mechanics, there was no place for black freedmen, his plan for the restoration of the seceded states did not include the ex-slave.[4] He recognized immediately the loyal governments in Arkansas, Louisiana, Tennessee, and Virginia and appointed to the remaining seven states provisional governors who were directed to call constitutional conventions in which all white men who had taken the oath of allegiance or had been pardoned could participate. These constitutional conventions were required to repeal the secession acts, repudiate the Confederate debt and abolish slavery. By December 1865 all the seceded states with the exception of Texas had fulfilled these requirements and were regarded as restored to the Union. Eight of these states together with a sufficient number of the northern states had also ratified the Thirteenth Amendment, abolishing slavery, which had been passed in Congress in 1865.[5]

In planning for the political ascendency of the small white farmers, Johnson was outspoken against the growing capitalism of the North.[6] Consequently, his program was opposed by the Republicans who saw their political ascendency threatened by the return to power of the planter class and farmers. By excluding the Negro from citizenship

---

[3] Robert W. Winston, *Andrew Johnson* (New York, 1928), pp. 228-29.

[4] W. E. B. DuBois, *Black Reconstruction in America* (New York, 1935), pp. 241-51.

[5] J. G. Randall, *The Civil War and Reconstruction* (New York, 1937), pp. 507-10.

[6] Louis M. Hacker, *The Triumph of American Capitalism* (New York, 1940), p. 375.

rights and at the same time counting him as a full person instead of three-fifths of a person for the purpose of determining congressional representation, the political power of the South would have been increased as the result of the War. As it happened the South itself provided a moral basis for the Republican opposition to the program by passing legislation that practically re-enslaved the Negro.

THE BLACK CODES

This legislation, which became known as the Black codes, dealt with apprenticeship, labor contracts, migration, vagrancy, and civil and legal rights. Mississippi practically re-enacted its slave code when it declared .

That all the penal and criminal laws now in force in this State, defining offenses, and prescribing the mode of punishment for crimes and misdemeanors committed by slaves, free Negroes or mulattoes, be and the same are hereby reenacted, and declared to be in full force and effect, against freedmen, free Negroes, and mulattoes, except so far as the mode and manner of trial and punishment have been changed or altered by law.[7]

The Mississippi code also provided that sheriffs and justices of the peace should report to the courts semiannually all freedmen, free Negroes, and mulattoes under eighteen years of age who were orphans or whose parents were unable or unwilling to support them and that such minors should be apprenticed to some person preferably the former owners of such minors. Moreover, freedmen without lawful employment and white people associating with freedmen on terms of equality were declared vagrants. Though the right to buy and sell property was granted freedmen, they were not allowed to rent or lease land except in incorporated towns and cities provided, of course, they were not denied this right by local authorities.

Other southern states followed the example of Mississippi in limiting the movement and the rights of the freedmen.[8] South Carolina forbade the entrance of persons of color unless two freeholders gave

[7] Quoted in *Black Reconstruction in America* by W. E. B. DuBois, p. 177. Copyright 1935 by Harcourt, Brace and Company, Inc.

[8] See Walter L. Fleming, *Documentary History of Reconstruction* (Cleveland, 1906), Vol. I, pp. 243-312.

a bond of a thousand dollars for their good behavior. Freedmen were not permitted to enter any occupation, except that of a farmer or servant, unless they secured a special license and paid an annual tax. In the same state there were laws concerning labor contracts between Negro servants and white masters. Louisiana passed a law regulating agricultural labor in which it was stated that laborers should make contracts with their employers at the beginning of the year and that if they failed to fulfill their contract or left the premises, they forfeited all their wages. The Florida code stated that if any person of color failed to fulfill the stipulations of a contract into which he entered with a plantation owner or was impudent to the owner, he should be declared a vagrant and be subject to punishment for vagrancy. Despite the argument that the chaotic conditions created by the War and emancipation required special legislation for controlling the freedmen, the Black Codes attempted on the whole to re-establish the old master and slave relationship.

From the most trustworthy reports on the situation in the South at the end of the Civil War, it appears that the great body of white people were not willing to accord the Negro the status of a free man.[9]

[9] The Black Codes and other phases of Reconstruction have been warmly defended but more often vigorously condemned by historians of the period. For example, Randall, who admits that "Torture and mutilation were in some cases the penalty for perjury," nevertheless, states that "Under the circumstances the passing of new Negro codes was a social and economic necessity with which the Southern states had to deal in setting their houses in order." *The Civil War and Reconstruction* by J. G. Randall, pp. 726-27. Copyright 1937 by J. G. Randall. Reprinted by permission of D. C. Heath and Company. On the other hand, DuBois states: "Making every allowance for the excitement and turmoil of war, and the mentality of a defeated people, the Black Codes were infamous pieces of legislation." *Black Reconstruction in America* by W. E. B. DuBois, p. 176. Copyright 1935 by Harcourt, Brace and Company, Inc. In the preface of his book, DuBois says that "If he [the reader] believes that the Negro in America and in general is an average and ordinary human being, who under given environment develops like other human beings, then he will read this story and judge it by the facts adduced." In the body of his work, he states (pp. 165-66) what "a small but determined and clear-thinking group of men" might have said in regard to adjusting the freedmen to his new status. In fact, during the Reconstruction period, not many people in the North and very few in the South regarded the Negro as an "ordinary human being." Even today, it is doubtful that the majority of the people even in the North believe that the Negro "under given environment develops like other human beings." In regard to DuBois' hypothetical "clear-thinking" and "far-sighted" men in the South, it might be said that the circum-

Some of the whites accepted the verdict of the Civil War and were disposed to accommodate themselves to the new situation. There were others who were willing to make such concessions as the adoption of the Thirteenth Amendment. By acknowledging the new status of the Negro resulting from the war they thought they would be allowed to regulate their own affairs, including race relations, as they chose. Then there were those who were irreconcilable and who utilized the prejudices of the white masses for their own ends. The attitude of the majority of the whites, who had suffered the loss of property and friends and relatives and were embittered by defeat on the battlefield, is probably correctly presented by Carl Schurz in the following statement:

Wherever I go—the street, the shop, the house, the hotel, or the steamboat—I hear the people talk in such a way as to indicate that they are yet unable to conceive of the Negro as possessing any rights at all. Men who are honorable in their dealings with their white neighbors, will cheat a Negro without feeling a single twinge of their honor. To kill a Negro, they do not deem murder; to debauch a Negro woman, they do not think fornication; to take the property away from a Negro, they do not consider robbery. The people boast that when they get freedmen's affairs in their own hands, to use their own expression, 'the niggers will catch hell.'

The reason of all this is simple and manifest. The whites esteem the blacks their property by natural right, and however much they admit that the individual relations of masters and slaves have been destroyed by the war and by the President's emancipation proclamation, they still have an ingrained feeling that the blacks at large belong to the whites at large.[10]

---

stances did not produce such men or that they were an ineffectual minority. In view of the "mentality of a defeated people," the existing racial feeling, and the traditional views concerning the Negro, it was to be expected that southern whites would enact harsh and even brutal legislation with a view to keeping the Negro in an inferior economic and social position. Therefore, while DuBois assumes that the South should or could have acted "rationally" in the situation, Randall and other defenders of the Black Codes have simply attempted to "rationalize" the acts of the southern states.

[10] Report of Carl Schurz. Senate Executive Document. Number 2. 39th Congress. 1st Session in *Black Reconstruction in America* by W. E. B. DuBois, p. 136. Copyright 1935 by Harcourt, Brace and Company, Inc.

STATUS OF NEGRO BECOMES A NATIONAL ISSUE

When Congress met in December, 1865, the Radicals had determined that Congress should control the restoration of the southern states. One of its first acts was the creation of the Joint Committee of Fifteen which was to inquire into the condition of the "so-called Confederate States." This committee recommended the submission to the states of an amendment to the Constitution guaranteeing the civil rights of the Negro. In fact, the Fourteenth Amendment embodied two major provisions; one declaring the Negro to be a citizen of the United States, and the other that when a state denied the right to vote to any of its male inhabitants, the basis of representation of such a state in Congress should be reduced proportionately.[11] With the support of President Johnson, the southern states with the exception of Tennessee rejected the Fourteenth Amendment. But in the meantime the Radicals, led by Charles Sumner in the Senate and Thaddeus Stevens in the House, secured the enactment of a Civil Rights bill over the veto of President Johnson. The Civil Rights bill nullified the Black Codes and granted the Negro equal protection of the laws under the jurisdiction of the federal courts. During the congressional elections of 1866 the President attempted to convince the country that his plans for the restoration of the states were expedient and just. But the country responded by electing to Congress a larger Republican majority than the party had had in the previous Congress.

In attacking southern legislation, Sumner and Stevens were not calculating politicians bent upon the security of industrial capitalism. Both men had a sincere faith in democracy and in the equality of men. In 1866, Sumner expressed this faith in a speech before the Senate:

The freedmen must be protected. To this you are specially pledged by the Proclamation of President Lincoln, which, after declaring him 'free,' promises to *maintain* this freedom, not for any limited period, but for all time. But this cannot be done so long as you deny him the shield of impartial laws. Let him be heard in court and let him vote.

[11] William MacDonald, *Documentary Source Book of American History, 1606-1898* (New York, 1914), pp. 536-38.

Let these rights be guarded sacredly. Beyond even the shield of impartial laws, he will then have that protection which comes from the consciousness of manhood. Clad in the full panoply of citizenship he will feel at last that he is a man. At present he is only a recent chattel, awaiting your justice to be transmuted into manhood. If you would have him respected in his rights, you must begin by respecting him in your laws. If you would maintain him in his freedom, you must begin by maintaining him in the equal rights of citizenship. . . .

Foremost is the equality of all men. Of course, in a declaration of rights, no such supreme folly was intended as that all men are created equal in form or capacity, bodily or mental; but simply that they are created equal in rights. This is the first of the self-evident truths that are announced, leading and governing all the rest. Life, liberty, and the pursuit of happiness are among inalienable rights; but they are all held in subordination to that primal truth. Here is the starting-point of the whole, and the end is like the starting-point. In announcing that governments derive their just powers from the consent of the governed, the Declaration repeats again the same proclamation of Equal Rights. Thus is Equality the Alpha and the Omega, in which all other rights are embraced. Men may not have a natural right to certain things, but most clearly they have a natural right to impartial laws, by which they shall be secured in Equal Rights.[12]

Stevens' position in regard to the ignorant Negro who was helpless before his former master had been expressed in his argument in favor of the Thirteenth Amendment:

The Congress owes it to its own character to set the seal of reprobation upon the doctrine that 'this is the white man's government.' . . . Wherein does this differ from slavery except in degree? Our fathers repudiated the whole doctrine of the legal superiority of families or races, and proclaimed the equality of men before the law. . . . They were prevented by slavery from perfecting the superstructure whose foundation they had thus broadly laid. . . . They consented to wait, but never relinquished the idea of its final completion. . . . It is our duty to complete their work.

This is not a 'white man's government' in the exclusive sense in which it is used. . . . This is man's Government, the Government of all men alike; not that all men will have equal power and sway within it. . . . But equal rights to all the privileges of Government are in-

[12] Speech of Hon. Charles Sumner, of Massachusetts in the United States Senate, February 6 and 7, 1866, *The Congressional Globe* (Washington, 1866), pp. 7, 18.

nate in every immortal human being, no matter what the shape or color of the tabernacle it inhabits. . . .

If equal privileges were granted to all, I should not expect any but white men to be elected to office for long ages to come. . . . But it would still be beneficial to the weaker races. Without the right of suffrage in the late slave States (I do not speak of the free States), I believe the slaves had far better have been left in bondage.[13]

In view of the reaction of the white South to the Civil War and Emancipation, the democratic doctrine expounded by Sumner and Stevens implied a social revolution in the South. In order to carry out such a revolution it was necessary to use the military power of the federal government.

RIGHTS OF THE NEGRO ESTABLISHED BY MILITARY RULE

As a part of the plan to guarantee the rights of the Negro as a citizen, the Fourteenth Amendment to the Constitution was passed by the Congress of the United States in 1866. The rejection of this Amendment by the southern states together with race riots in the South during which hundreds of Negroes were killed was evidence in the eyes of the northern Radicals that the southern states were determined that the emancipated Negro should not enjoy the rights of a free man. These representatives of industrial capitalism were depending, of course, upon the votes of the Negroes to help maintain the Republican Party in power. Therefore, in March, 1867 they secured the passage of the First Reconstruction Act, which displaced the ten southern state governments created by President Johnson. According to the provisions of the Act, the ten southern states were divided into five military districts; the Negro was granted the right to vote; and high civil and military officials in the Confederacy were excluded from participation in the election of the new state conventions which were authorized.[14] The state legislatures set up by the new state conventions were to enfranchise the Negro and to ratify the Fourteenth Amendment before the military governments were

[13] Quoted in *Thaddeus Stevens* by Alphonse B. Miller, pp. 237-38. Copyright 1939 by Harper & Brothers.   [14] MacDonald, *op. cit.*, pp. 502-04.

removed and congressmen and senators from the seceded states were admitted to Congress. Two other Reconstruction Acts were passed in 1867, providing for the registration of male citizens twenty-one years of age and over and the calling of state conventions; and a fourth Reconstruction Act was passed in 1868 dealing with elections.[15]

In accordance with the Reconstruction Acts, the qualified white and black voters of ten southern states registered in 1867.[16] In five of the southern states—South Carolina, Alabama, Mississippi, Florida, and Louisiana—the number of Negroes registering outnumbered that of whites. However, it is likely that a larger number of poor whites registered and participated in the election than at any previous election. When the delegates were elected to the state conventions in 1868, Negroes were in a majority in only one state—South Carolina—and constituted a half of the delegates in Louisiana. In North Carolina, Arkansas, Alabama, Mississippi, Georgia, the proportion of Negroes among the delegates ranged from 10 to 19 per cent. During 1868 North Carolina, South Carolina, Louisiana, Georgia, Alabama, and Florida fulfilled the requirements of the Acts and their representatives were admitted to Congress.[17] The readmission of Georgia was delayed until 1870 because when the military authority was withdrawn, Negro members of the legislature were denied their seats and ex-Confederates were admitted. The fight against proscription of ex-Confederates and the refusal to ratify the Fifteenth Amendment delayed the restoration of Mississippi until 1870. Texas was also admitted in 1870 after much dispute over the status of the ex-Confederates, and Virginia in the same year when a compromise was effected on the question of Negro suffrage and the participation of ex-Confederates in the government of the state.

NEGRO EQUALITY VIS-À-VIS SOCIAL
AND ECONOMIC REALITIES

Historians have primarily been concerned with the political aspects of Reconstruction in the South. In the drama of the "bad government of the period," they have presented three chief actors, the carpet-

---

[15] *Ibid., op. cit.*, pp. 508-11, 514-18, 529-30.
[16] DuBois, *op. cit.*, pp. 371-72.　　　[17] See Randall, *op. cit.*, pp. 784-94.

bagger,[18] the scalawag,[19] and the Negro, engaged against the prostrate white South struggling to heal her wounds and restore her wasted lands. The carpetbagger has been pictured as the unscrupulous northern adventurer who, backed by the Freedmen's Bureau and the Union League clubs, used the ignorant Negro to loot the South. The scalawag has been portrayed as the degenerate poor white man and a traitor to the white race who aided the carpetbagger in looting the South. The Negro has been presented as a clown and a barbarian who spent his time in robbing State treasuries and was instigated by the carpetbagger to seek equality with the whites. Since the historian of Reconstruction has been interested in the drama of history, he has focused attention upon episodes and personalities in order to fix blame and innocence. However, behind the drama of Reconstruction, there were fundamental social and economic forces in the southern situation which determined the course of events more than the behavior of individuals or, in fact, the ethical codes upon which their behavior was based.

The imposition of military rule upon the South—whatever other motives may have entered into it—was a genuine attempt to establish democracy there.[20] In order to establish democracy in the South, it was necessary to destroy the political power of the landowning class by the enfranchisement of the poor whites and the Negro masses. In the legislation known as the Black Codes the landowning or planter class had shown its determination to control the labor of the Negro and keep him in a subordinate status. Consequently, their opposition to the enfranchisement of the Negro and even the general enfranchisement of the whites was based upon their desire to retain political power. Their opposition to the enfranchisement of the Negro was re-enforced by traditional ideas and prejudices con-

[18] This term was applied indiscriminately to northern whites who went to the South to work among Negroes as teachers and missionaries, the agents of the Freedmen's Bureau, and those who honestly worked for the reconstruction of the South as well as whites who went there to plunder the South and seek their fortunes as politicians.

[19] This term was applied to southern whites who accepted and cooperated with the Reconstruction governments.

[20] See James S. Allen, *Reconstruction: The Battle for Democracy* (New York, 1937).

cerning the Negro as a race and his proper place in society. The general attitude of this class was expressed in a convention in South Carolina in 1867. A section of the resolutions of that convention read as follows:

We, therefore, feeling the responsibility of the subject and the occasion, enter our most solemn protest against the policy of investing the negro with political rights. The black man is what God and nature and circumstances have made him. That he is not fit to be invested with these important rights may be no fault of his. But the fact is patent to all that the negro is utterly unfitted to exercise the highest functions of the citizen. The government of the country should not be permitted to pass from the hands of the white man into the hands of the negro. The enforcement of the Reconstruction acts by military power under the guise of negro voters and the negro conventions cannot lawfully reestablish civil government in South Carolina. It may for a time hold us in subjection to a quasi-civil government backed by military force, but it can do no more. As citizens of the United States we should not consent to live under negro supremacy, nor should we acquiesce in negro equality. Not for ourselves only, but on behalf of the Anglo-Saxon race and blood in this country, do we protest against this subversion of the great social law, whereby an ignorant and depraved race is placed in power and influence above the virtuous, the educated and the refined. By these acts of Congress intelligence and virtue are put under foot, while ignorance and vice are lifted into power.[21]

As President Johnson and others had seen, the destruction of slavery liberated the poor whites as well as the black slaves. The Reconstruction Acts, granting manhood suffrage without property qualifications in the southern states, provided the poor whites with the means for achieving democracy. However, this involved cooperation with the newly emancipated blacks. An obstacle to this cooperation was the traditional antagonism that had existed between the poor whites and Negroes during slavery. The crisis created by the Civil War and especially Reconstruction with its democratic tendencies might have modified these traditional attitudes. Since both the poor whites and the Negroes were dependent upon the planter class in their struggle for existence, the two groups had much in common. But during these

[21] Fleming, *op. cit.*, Vol. I, pp. 425-26.

critical times the poor whites and Negroes were thrown into competition for the first time on a large scale. Since this competition assumed a racial character, it tended to intensify racial prejudices and re-enforce traditional prejudices. The planter and propertied classes did not fail to take advantage of the traditional prejudices of the poor whites and the competition between the latter and the Negro to destroy any cooperation between the two groups. The poor whites were constantly subjected to propaganda concerning their obligation to maintain the supremacy and purity of the white race. Typical of this propaganda are the contents of a book entitled *Nojoque*, by the author of the *Impending Crisis*.[22] Yet, despite the appeals to race prejudice and the propaganda against the Negro, many of the so-called scalawags were poor whites, who regarded their interests as identical with those of the Negroes and voted with the latter against the planter class.[23]

Since the governments set up under military rule did not expropriate the white landlords, the great body of illiterate and impoverished Negroes were dependent upon them for subsistence. Some of the Negroes were disposed to accept their traditional dependence upon the whites. But many more were eager to take advantage of the opportunity to assert their rights as free men. Nothing symbolized their rights as free men so much as the right to vote along with white men.

THE NEGRO IN POLITICS

The great mass of ex-slaves, who had been kept in ignorance during slavery and many of whom had become demoralized during the up-heaval of the Civil War and Emancipation, were naturally not as prepared to use the ballot as voters with political experience or traditions of self-government. It was not strange, therefore, that they were often misled by scheming politicians, and their ignorance and super-

[22] See Hinton R. Helper, *Nojoque* (New York, 1867). In this book, the author stated that the Negro was a subhuman species and advocated that he should be removed from the confines of the United States.

[23] The cooperation of the poor whites and freedmen has been presented in fictionalized form in Howard Fast's novel, *Freedom Road*.

stition were utilized for selfish purposes by unscrupulous leaders.[24] The support of the demoralized elements among the freedmen was often secured through money and other considerations. Then there was disorder during the campaigns and elections which shocked some of the most staunch believers in the democratic process. Yet when one takes into account the fact that the established social order in the South had collapsed and that a social revolution was being undertaken, the ignorance and ineptitude and even the venality of the newly enfranchised Negro were to be expected. In fact, if the situation in the South is compared with revolutionary situations in other parts of the world, the Negroes exhibited considerable restraint and intelligence during the transition to their new status.

This was because there arose from among the ex-slaves leaders who were intelligent and showed sound judgment with reference to the Negro's new status. They were keenly aware of the inadequacies of the Negro in the face of the responsibilities that had been placed upon him as a citizen. Moreover, they showed an understanding and appreciation of the feelings and attitudes of their former white masters who had lost political power and prestige. Yet these men wanted to be free and enjoy the rights of citizenship. We may take as an example of such leadership, Beverly Nash, an ex-slave who, while a member of the constitutional convention of South Carolina, expressed himself as follows on the problems of Reconstruction:

I believe, my friends and fellow-citizens, we are not prepared for this suffrage. But we can learn. Give a man tools and let him commence to use them, and in time he will learn a trade. So it is with voting. We may not understand it at the start, but in time we shall learn to do our duty. . . . We recognize the Southern white man as the true friend of the black man. You see upon that banner the words, 'United we stand, divided we fall,' and if you could see the scroll of the society that banner represents, you would see the white man and the black man standing with their arms locked together, as the type of friendship and the union which we desire.

It is not our desire to be a discordant element in the community, or to unite the poor against the rich. . . . The white man has the land,

[24] In this respect the behavior of the freedmen was the same as that of many white voters in the South today. See, for example, Allan A. Michie and Frank Ryhlick, *Dixie Demogogues* (New York, 1939).

the black man has the labor, and labor is worth nothing without capital. We must help to create that capital by restoring confidence, and we can only secure confidence by electing proper men to fill our public offices.

In these public affairs we must unite with our white fellow-citizens. They tell us that they have been disfranchised, yet we tell the North that we shall never let the halls of Congress be silent until we remove that disability. Can we afford to lose from the councils of state, our first men? Can we spare judges from the bench? Can we put fools or strangers in their positions? No, fellow-citizens, no! gloomy, indeed, would be that day. We want in charge of our interest only our best and ablest men. And then with a strong pull, and a long pull and a pull together, up goes South Carolina.[25]

Many of the political leaders among the freedmen came from the class of Negroes who were free before Emancipation. The Negro leaders of free ancestry were educated men who were more capable than the majority of the enfranchised whites to exercise the right of the franchise and to hold office. A typical representative of this class was Francis L. Cardozo, who became Treasurer of the state of South Carolina. These Negro leaders were as interested in maintaining law and order and preserving civilization as the whites who complained of Negro rule. They had the same ideas as the conservative whites about economic and political rights, except that they were opposed to a caste system based on racial descent. In fact, in Louisiana many of the educated and wealthy mulattoes of free ancestry were opposed to the general enfranchisement of the illiterate masses of emancipated blacks.[26]

The acts of the Reconstruction governments have been popularly regarded as the work of incompetent, criminal, and savage Negroes who under the protection of federal bayonets imposed black domination upon the white South. This popular belief has been the result largely of a myth which had its origin in the editorials and reports in Southern newspapers. As it has been stated in a work on Reconstruction in South Carolina: "One unfamiliar with the situation would think the editors and their correspondents had gone crazy with anger or obsessed with

[25] Quoted in *Black Reconstruction in America* by W. E. B. DuBois, p. 391. Copyright 1935 by Harcourt, Brace and Company, Inc.
[26] See Fleming, *op. cit.*, Vol. II, pp. 279-80.

some fearful mania, so great was the ridicule, contempt, and obloquy showered upon the representatives of the state." In support of this observation, the authors present the following comment from the *Fairfield Herald*, which battled

against the hell-born policy which has trampled the fairest and noblest States of our great sisterhood beneath the unholy hoofs of African savages and shoulder-strapped brigands—the policy which has given up millions of our free-born, high-souled brethren and sisters, countrymen and countrywomen of Washington, Rutledge, Marion, and Lee, to the rule of gibbering, louse eaten, devil worshipping barbarians, from the jungles of Dahomey, and peripatetic buccaneers from Cape Cod, Memphremagog, Hell, and Boston.[27]

When the rôle of Negroes in the Reconstruction governments is studied, it is found that they were not dominated by Negroes. Even in South Carolina, where Negroes formed about 60 per cent of the population, the whites were always in a position to block the acts of Negro legislators. In the state Senate the whites were in the majority from 1868 to 1878; while in the House Negroes were in the majority only during the first five years of this period.[28] Likewise in Mississippi, where Negroes also formed a majority of the population, the whites were always in control. Only 17 of the 97 members of the constitutional convention of 1868 were colored. Of the 115 members elected to the lower house of the state legislature in 1871, only 38 were colored; and in the state Senate the proportion of colored members was still smaller.[29] A relatively small number of Negroes were sent from the southern states to the national Congress. The reconstructed states elected only 20 Negro congressmen and two senators, both from Mississippi, during the period from 1870 to 1901.[30] These Negro members of Congress were elected from only eight of the southern states and from districts in these states where there were large concentrations of Negroes. It is probably true that the Negroes elected to Congress were superior on

[27] Francis B. Simkins and Robert H. Woody, *South Carolina During Reconstruction* (Chapel Hill, 1932), p. 122.   [28] DuBois, *op. cit.*, p. 404.

[29] John R. Lynch, *The Facts of Reconstruction* (New York, 1915), p. 93.

[30] Reprinted from *The Negro in Congress, 1870-1901* by Samuel Denny Smith, pp. 3-6, by permission of The University of North Carolina Press. Copyright 1940, by Samuel Denny Smith.

the whole to those active in state governments. According to a recent study, they "were rather well equipped by education, previous political experience, and wealth." [31] However, the work of the Negroes in Congress was of less significance than that of those in the state legislatures.

In assessing the work of these state legislatures one must understand the economic interests that were involved at the time in the political situation in the South. With the passing of Thaddeus Stevens in 1868 and the supremacy of the New Radicals after 1870, the equalitarian and democratic ideals of the Old Radicals ceased to influence Reconstruction. After the election of Grant the Fifteenth Amendment, safe-guarding the right of the Negro to vote, was passed by Congress in 1869 and declared in effect in 1870. During the same year Congress passed an act to enforce the Fifteenth Amendment and during the following year it was necessary to pass a drastic law to deal with the Ku Klux Klan. It was also necessary to use federal troops in order to suppress this organization, which had introduced a reign of terror in some places in the South. Despite these measures which were designed to protect the right of the Negroes to vote, the Radical Republicans were not sympathetic toward the Negro's struggle for land, but were concerned with their own plans for the investment of capital in the South. Therefore, a judicious appraisal of the constitutions of the Reconstruction legislatures may be summed up in the words of Hacker, who writes:

. . . as a result of the combination of Negroes and white scalawags and carpetbaggers, they established the supremacy of petty-bourgeois enterprise in the South. They were, in short, leveling documents which sought to defend the civil and economic rights of men of small property, both white and black. And, interestingly enough, because they were so satisfactory to the majority of *whites* in the South, they were maintained long after the southern Reconstruction governments were overthrown. Thus, the Florida constitution, written in 1868, was kept on until 1885; the Virginia constitution survived from 1870 to 1902; the South Carolina constitution from 1868 to 1895; and the Mississippi constitution from 1868 to 1890.[32]

[31] *Ibid.*, p. 144.
[32] Reprinted from *The Triumph of American Capitalism* by Louis M. Hacker, pp. 378-79. Copyright 1940 by Simon and Schuster, Inc.

THE NEGRO'S STRUGGLE FOR LAND

Political participation was only one of the means by which the Negroes attempted to utilize the revolutionary change in their status. For the vast majority who were concerned with the everyday problem of making a living, land ownership was of paramount importance. Their desire to acquire land and their expectation that the government would provide them with "forty acres and a mule" has generally been derided as a naïve and childish hope. On the contrary, their hopes concerning land ownership indicated that they had sound ideas concerning the real meaning of freedom. In fact, the newly emancipated Negroes had been led to believe that the federal government intended to give substance to their free status by making it possible for them to secure land. Thaddeus Stevens had advocated the confiscation of the lands of the planter aristocracy and their distribution among the freedmen. On one occasion he had said: "In my judgment, we shall not approach the full measure of justice until we have given every adult freedman a homestead on the land where he was born. . . . Forty acres of land and a hut would be more valuable to him than the immediate right to vote." [33] Moreover, Sherman as well as other army commanders had confiscated the abandoned plantations on the sea islands along the coast of South Carolina and Georgia and distributed them among the freedmen.[34] Then, too, as we have seen in the last chapter, the Freedmen's Bureau bill provided that lands be set aside for refugees and freedmen, but because of President Johnson's policy of restoring the land to the planters, only an insignificant number of Negroes had secured homesteads.[35] The emancipated Negro continued to struggle for landownership until the industrial leaders of the North as well as southern landowners forced him into the status of day laborer and sharecropper.[36] The struggle of the freedman to secure land was carried to the newly created legislatures. In South Carolina it was proposed that Congress be asked to lend the

[33] Quoted in *Thaddeus Stevens* by Alphonse B. Miller, p. 265. Copyright 1939 by Harper & Brothers.

[34] Fleming, *op. cit.*, Vol. I, pp. 350-52.　　　[35] See *supra*, p. 120.

[36] See James S. Allen, "The Struggle for Land During Reconstruction," *Science and Society*, Vol. I, pp. 378-401.

state a million dollars to purchase land for the Negroes.[37] This move was dropped when it was found to be impractical. The masses of Negroes were doomed to continue in their dependence upon the white landlords; while a minority through their thrift and self-denial gradually acquired title to relatively small holdings in a region dominated by the plantation system and cotton culture.

THE NEGRO'S STRUGGLE FOR EDUCATION

The freedmen were more successful in establishing their right to education than in their efforts to acquire land. In South Carolina the constitution of 1868 provided for a system of universal education. This was a revolutionary proposal, even more so since it provided that ultimately the two races should attend the same schools. However, the colored leaders did not show any desire to enforce such a system immediately, though they believed that the association of the children of the two races would wipe out race prejudice.[38] The attempt of the freedmen in South Carolina to secure education for their children was not unique. In those southern states where Negroes formed an important part of the electorate, the education of Negro children was placed on a basis of equality in the law with that of white children.[39] In Tennessee, where the Reconstruction government was supported by the nonslaveholding mountain whites in the eastern part of the state, this class as well as the Democrats from the black counties in western Tennessee opposed the education of the Negro. However, it was the Democrats or conservatives in the states where Negroes formed the majority of the electorate who were the chief opponents of Negro education. This opposition was based not only on racial reasons but more especially on the ground that it meant the levying of taxes on the propertied classes.

The desire on the part of the ex-slaves for education was closely

[37] Simkins and Woody, *op. cit.*, pp. 98-99.

[38] *Ibid.*, pp. 436-37. In Louisiana where the mulatto leaders insisted upon mixed schools, the public school system collapsed because of racial prejudice as well as fraud and inefficiency. See Roger W. Shugg, *Origins of Class Struggle in Louisiana*. University, La.: Louisiana State University Press, 1939, p. 226.

[39] Horace M. Bond, *The Education of the Negro in the American Social Order* (New York, 1934), p. 49.

tied up with their struggle for status as free men and citizens. Old as well as young flocked to the schools provided by the white teachers from the North. These teachers were sympathetic toward the Negro's striving for an education because they believed in the essential humanity of the Negro and believed that through education he would acquire a sense of personal worth and dignity. But the sincere efforts of these teachers only aroused the indignation of the southern whites, who constantly complained that the northern teachers were communicating to Negroes ideas of social equality with the whites.[40] In order to offset this influence, it was even urged in an Alabama paper that southern whites teach their former slaves.[41] However, there was no general disposition on the part of the whites to follow any such policy and the schools established by northern white missionaries were often burned and the teachers were driven out.

It was probably because of the Negro's interest in acquiring an education that he sought the superintendency of education in the reconstructed governments. Concerning the Negro superintendents, Bond writes:

In five states—Arkansas, Louisiana, Mississippi, Florida, and South Carolina—Negroes were elected to the state superintendency of education. Two of these men were alleged to be notoriously corrupt. The other men were never accused of either inefficiency or dishonesty, even by their bitterest political opponents. In Louisiana, the Negro superintendent James Brown "was a quiet, inoffensive man," who did not "obtrude himself" into white schools where he was unwelcome, according to the testimony of one of the Democratic legislators of the day. In Florida, Jonathan C. Gibbs became Superintendent of Education in 1872. He was a graduate of Dartmouth College and of the Theological Seminary at Princeton, New Jersey. His administration was marked by ability and character.

In Arkansas, J. C. Corbin was Superintendent of Schools for two years during the Reconstruction regime. Corbin was a graduate of Ohio University in the class of 1853 and had conducted a private school for free Negroes in the city of Louisville before the Civil War. He was a man of distinguished honesty, and after the overthrow of the Republican Party in Arkansas was appointed to the principalship

40 See Fleming, *op. cit.*, Vol. II, pp. 183-84.   41 *Ibid.*, p. 181.

of the state school for Negroes at Pine Bluff. This appointment was made by a Democratic administration.[42]

THE RACIAL CONFLICT

Throughout the Reconstruction period there was racial conflict. Under slavery whatever racial antagonism there might have existed between masters and slaves was reduced to a minimum by the social controls regulating their relations. Emancipation and the endowment of the slaves with citizenship removed the normal expectations that had characterized race relations. This aroused a sense of insecurity and fear in the former slaveholding class in regard to the Negro. These fears and anxieties became fixed upon the alleged racial character of the Negro. Among the nonslaveholding whites there had been a tradition of racial antagonism. This racial antagonism was intensified when the races were thrown into competition. It was constantly stimulated by politicians and other leaders of the poor whites, who constantly represented the Negro race as a menace to their economic and social welfare.

All of the various factors contributing to the development of racial conflict were focused upon the question of the status of the Negro. When the Negro failed to observe the traditional forms of etiquette toward the whites, when he exercised his right to vote, even when he acquired land and attended school, such actions were an indication that the Negro was "getting out of his place." Thus it was inevitable that the Negro should "get out of his place" if he were to act according to his new rôle in southern society. There were numerous reports of violence between individual whites and blacks due to the fact that the Negro was considered arrogant or had failed to show the proper respect toward whites.[43] The Ku Klux Klan developed as the result of an organized attempt on the part of southern whites to force the Negro to accept a subordinate status in the social organization. In order to become a member of this organization, a candidate had to

[42] *The Education of the Negro in the American Social Order* by Horace M. Bond, p. 49. Copyright 1934 by Prentice-Hall, Inc.

[43] See Bertram Doyle, *The Etiquette of Race Relations in the South* (Chicago, 1937), Chapter IX, for a discussion of race conflict arising from the breakdown of the etiquette which had governed race relations during the slavery period.

declare himself opposed to the social and political equality of the Negro. In Tennessee where the Klan was founded, northern missionary societies reported that this organization was responsible for the burning of numerous schoolhouses.[44] The outrages committed by the Klan against the Negro and his white supporters were seldom due to individual acts of Negroes. The organization assumed a political character in that it became a powerful instrument of the conservatives and Democrats in their efforts to control Negro labor and to regain their political power.

When the traditional forms of race relations were uprooted, it appears that most whites felt that the only basis upon which they could carry on a common life with Negroes had been destroyed. Even when Negroes exhibited intelligence, efficiency, and honesty in their new rôle, this fact did not affect their feelings and attitudes toward the changed status of the Negro. Cardozo probably had this in mind when he said on one occasion in the constitutional convention of South Carolina, "There is an element [white] that is opposed to us no matter what we do, which will never be conciliated." [45] There were Negroes who would have been inclined to accept the political leadership of southern whites, but southern whites were not interested in helping the Negro to secure the status of a citizen. They were even opposed to the most reasonable efforts of the agents of Freedmen's Bureau to protect the Negro in his labor contracts.[46] It was natural that the ex-slaves should have turned to those who were disposed to protect them and to give them some of the rights of free men. Sometimes the acts of the Ku Klux Klan have been justified on the ground that they counteracted the lawlessness of the Union League clubs, organizations through which the Republican Party mobilized the support of the freedmen and sympathetic whites. But such an argument is untenable in that the Union League clubs were organiza-

[44] Bond, *op. cit.*, p. 48.

[45] Quoted in *Black Reconstruction in America* by W. E. B. DuBois, p. 397. Copyright 1935 by Harcourt, Brace and Company, Inc.

[46] Even southern critics of the Freedmen's Bureau are forced to admit that the Freedmen's Savings Bank trained Negroes in business methods and developed habits of thrift among the ex-slaves. See Walter L. Fleming, *The Freedmen's Savings Bank* (Chapel Hill, 1927), Chapter IV.

tions for the political education of the Negroes and were not designed to commit acts of violence upon whites. The Union Leagues were opposed by southern whites, not because of lawless acts, but because they educated the Negro for his new status as a voter. The same might even be said concerning the Negro militias. Of course, it is true that Negro soldiers committed depredations, but similar charges were brought against the white militias. But the very fact that the Negro wore a uniform and thereby enjoyed certain rights was an affront to most southern whites. Hence, when the social forces in the situation are properly understood, it is clear that the situation was such as to produce an inevitable and real conflict of interests that could not have been avoided simply by "reasonableness" on either side.

If the Reconstruction period may be called a "tragic era," it was the Negro who played the truly tragic rôle. He was the element in those fateful times who became the victim of social and economic forces which he did not understand and which, if he had understood, he would not have had the power to influence. He was the victim of racial prejudice, which only became the more violent when he attempted to realize the hopes that Emancipation had inspired. He was the victim of the clash of large economic and class interests. If he sided with the remnants of the old planter class, the only class that had a tradition, at least, of sentimental or paternalistic regard for him, he became the opponent of the interests of the rising merchant class and the democratic aspirations of the poor whites. When he sided with the democratic aspirations of the poor whites, he was spurned because of his race. History has charged him with piling up heavy public debts through graft and the looting of the state treasuries for personal consumption. But as a matter of fact, the Negro secured only an inconsequential part of the graft and loot.[47] The Negro had no share in the really consequential wealth of the states such as the control of the financial manipulations and mining and railroad rights. For example, the Union League clubs, which were controlled from the North, were the agents of capitalistic enterprise in Ala-

[47] See Roger W. Shugg, *Origins of Class Struggle in Louisiana* (Baton Rouge, 1929), pp. 226-27.

bama.[48] Slogans concerning white supremacy and equal rights which were used in political contests concealed the struggle for control over railroads, mining rights, and state subsidies. In these struggles the welfare of poor whites as well as that of Negroes was subordinated and the way was prepared for the triumph of the Bourbons, who represented the interests of landlords and the new capitalism of the South allied with northern financial, mining, and railway interests.

[48] See Horace M. Bond, "Social and Economic Forces in Alabama Reconstruction," *Journal of Negro History*, Vol. XXIII, pp. 290-348; and by the same author, *Negro Education in Alabama. A Study in Cotton and Steel* (Washington, D. C., 1939), Chapter IV.

CHAPTER VIII

New Forms of Accommodation

WHEN Congress undertook through military force to establish a democratic organization of society in the South, in which the Negro would enjoy the same rights as the whites, it was attempting to carry out what was in fact a social revolution. The way was prepared for a counter-revolution, when Congress in 1872 removed the Civil Disabilities imposed upon the Confederate leaders by the Fourteenth Amendment.[1] The leaders of the old planter class were thus able to take over the direction of the campaign for the "redemption" of the South through the triumph of the Democratic Party. Through the work of the Klan, which continued its depredations upon Negroes and their white allies after being outlawed by Congress in 1871, the white propertied classes were able to enlist the support of the poor whites in a struggle that identified the triumph of the Democratic Party with the movement for "white supremacy." At the same time, the experienced leaders of the old planter class found it possible to make common cause with the rising commercial and industrial classes.[2] The power of the planters was strengthened when the Freedmen's Bureau was discontinued in 1872. Since their Negro laborers and tenants could no longer receive assistance from the Bureau, the planters were able to force them to refrain from political activities. Therefore, as the federal government ceased to provide military protection for the

[1] See James S. Allen, *Reconstruction; The Battle for Democracy* (New York, 1937), pp. 181-206; and W. E. B. DuBois, *Black Reconstruction in America* (New York, 1935), pp. 580-635.

[2] The members of this new class alliance, dominated by businessmen, became known as the Bourbons.

Negroes and their white allies, the Bourbons succeeded within a few years in restoring the state governments to "native white" control.

Virginia, Georgia, and North Carolina were the first states to restore their State governments to "native white" control; and later Mississippi, Alabama, Arkansas, and Texas were "redeemed." By the time of the presidential election of 1876, only three states— Florida, Louisiana, and South Carolina—were still in control of the Radical Republicans, who were to lose their control after the election.

THE RESTORATION OF "WHITE SUPREMACY"

Despite the conflicting economic and class interests among the whites, they were eventually mobilized for the "redemption of the South," which they defined as the restoration of "white supremacy." In order to achieve this purpose the leaders of this movement did not hesitate to use fraud and organized violence which were justified on grounds that their use was necessary in the defense of civilization. In the election of the governor of Louisiana in 1872, the contest between the Radical Republicans on one hand and anti-Grant faction which had combined with the Democrats on the other hand resulted in civil war in some localities. The White League in Louisiana was organized and armed for the purpose of restoring "white supremacy," which meant in fact the supremacy of the planters and the capitalists. In South Carolina, where the Democrats cooperated from 1872 to 1874 with the Radical Republican governor, the whites decided in 1876 to elect a "straightout" Democratic candidate even if they had to resort to violence.[3]

To Mississippi, which had provided the pattern for the Black Codes, the whites in South Carolina were indebted for the technique which they used in restoring white supremacy. This technique involved the organization of "rifle clubs" among the whites. These "rifle clubs," according to Randall, used methods analogous to those used in the American Revolution by the colonists in order to "supplement or circumvent the regular government." He described these methods as follows:

[3] Francis B. Simkins and Robert H. Woody, *South Carolina During Reconstruction* (Chapel Hill, 1932), p. 500.

Armed usually with pistols they would invade Republican political meetings, heckle the speakers, and insist on their own speakers being heard. In the course of the meeting they would move about in the crowd, persuading Negroes and white Radicals that the healthy course would be to vote Democratic. If forced to disband they would reorganize as missionary societies or dancing clubs and carry on as before. . . . By such means Negroes in large numbers, and a great many white Republicans as well, were induced, usually without actual violence, to "cross Jordan" (i.e. shift to the Democratic party).[4]

Wade Hampton, an ex-Confederate general and large plantation owner, became the Democratic candidate for governor in South Carolina. During the campaign Hampton solicited the votes of Negroes with the promise that he would protect their political rights. Although many Negroes accepted this promise in good faith and supported Hampton, the promise was never fulfilled. As the result of the election in which both Democrats and Republicans claimed the election of state officials and a majority in the General Assembly, a dual government was set up.[5] That the Democratic Party was admittedly responsible for most of the fraud did not affect the outcome since this was to be decided by the turn of events in the Presidential election of the same year. As the result of the Presidential election in 1876, federal troops were withdrawn from South Carolina, thus leaving the white Democratic Party of the state in control.[6]

4 *The Civil War and Reconstruction* by J. G. Randall, p. 886. Copyright 1937 by J. G. Randall. Reprinted by permission of D. C. Heath and Company. See Simkins and Woody, *op. cit.*, pp. 499-509.

5 Simkins and Woody, *op. cit.*, pp. 514-41.

6 In the Presidential election of 1876, it appeared at first that Tilden, the Democratic candidate, had won; but since fraud and violence had been used extensively in Florida, Louisiana, and South Carolina, the Republicans had grounds for contesting the election. Since the electoral boards, which were under Republican control in the three States, certified Republican electors, Congress was confronted with two sets of electors. Thereupon, Congress appointed an electoral commission of fifteen members, on which the Supreme Court, the Senate, and the House were each represented by five members. After much suspense on the part of the country, the commission recognized the electors certified by the Republicans in the three southern States (and the contested Republican elector from Oregon) and declared the election of Hayes. The decision on the part of the commission was undoubtedly a part of a bargain involving the withdrawal of federal troops from Louisiana and South Carolina. Soon after his inauguration, Hayes withdrew the federal troops from South Carolina and Louisiana and thus left the South under the control of the white Democratic Party. In thus abandoning the southern

When the federal government withdrew its military forces from the South the Negro was left to the mercy of the whites. Some of the Negro and white Republican leaders were indicted for frauds, but the indictments were usually dropped since they were essentially political reprisals. Many of the Negro and white leaders during Reconstruction migrated to Washington, D. C., and to the North in order to escape the vengeance of the southern whites. But the masses of ignorant and propertyless Negroes had to come to terms with their former masters and the "poor whites."

During the upheaval of the Civil War and Reconstruction, the majority of the Negroes had solved the problem of everyday living by becoming tenants and laborers on the plantations which were in the hands of the white planters. In numerous cases the old paternalistic attitude of the planter toward the former slaves was scarcely disturbed. Even during the turmoil of the Reconstruction period, the ties of affection and loyalty that had held master and slave together under slavery were not always broken.[7] Many of the ex-slaves, after wandering about the country, returned to their former homes and settled down. But, on the whole, the new status of the Negro had to be recognized if only in his right to move about at will. Moreover, not even the strongest attachments between individual white planters and their black laborers and tenants could overcome the estrangement between the two races which had resulted from the political activities of Negroes during Reconstruction. Describing this estrangement, an observer wrote:

Even when he [the white planter] feels any interest in their moral education, irrespective of their connection with the government of his own estate, he finds it impossible to come near enough to them to win and hold their attention, for child and parent alike shrink from asso-

---

Negro and white Republicans, the leaders of the party in Washington were not unconscious of the fact that the domination of industrial capitalism had been assured. During the congressional elections from 1870 to 1876, the Republicans had steadily increased their representation from the agrarian states of the Old Northwest. Republican votes from these States were sufficient to offset the loss of representation from the South. By 1880 the triumph of the Republican Party in Illinois, Indiana, Michigan, Ohio, and Wisconsin was complete. See Louis M. Hacker, *The Triumph of American Capitalism* (New York, 1940), pp. 384-85.

[7] See C. W. Tebeau, "Some Aspects of Planter–Freedman Relations, 1865-1880," *The Journal of Negro History*, Vol. XXI, pp. 130-50.

ciation with him. His advances are not cordially met. However keen his sense of moral responsibility, therefore, and however earnestly he may wish to prosecute a plan of moral education among the children of his laborers, he runs upon an almost insurmountable obstacle in his path at the very beginning, and he is generally discouraged from going any further.[8]

As the result of the breaking down of the moral order upon which slavery and the plantation had rested and the racial conflict during the Reconstruction period, the Negro emerged as a race problem in the South.

CLASS CONFLICT AND THE NEGRO

The crisis produced by the Civil War and Reconstruction brought into the open the latent conflict of class interests that had always existed in the South.[9] During the racial conflict growing out of Reconstruction, the conflict of various class interests was intertwined in the struggle of whites and blacks.[10] The leaders of the rising industrial and commercial classes and the large plantation owners were able to soften the class conflict by leading the crusade for white supremacy. But the conflict of economic interest could not be removed especially when the landless whites and poorer farmers began to suffer as the result of declining farm prices and foreclosures which were affecting the West and South. The agrarian discontent which began in the seventies became an organized revolt in the eighties and nineties.[11] The Bourbons became "the target of the agricultural radical, the perennial debtor, and in a period which was full of disaster for him, his protest brought on a political revolution." [12] The poor whites had begun to realize that the various devices which were used to disfranchise the Negro and keep

[8] Phillip A. Bruce, *The Plantation Negro as a Freeman* (New York, 1889), p. 4.

[9] See Roger W. Shugg, *Origins of Class Struggle in Louisiana* (Baton Rouge, 1929), Chapter VI.

[10] See *ibid.*, Chapter VII. Paul Lewinson, *Race, Class and Party* (New York, 1932), pp. 69-70.

[11] See Louis M. Hacker and Benjamin B. Kendrick, *The United States Since 1865* (New York, 1937), pp. 295-320; and John D. Hicks, *The Populist Revolt* (Minneapolis, 1931), Chapters IV and V.

[12] *Race, Class and Party* by Paul Lewinson, p. 71. Copyright 1932 by Oxford University Press.

down Republicanism could be used to stifle their discontent. But, the southern representatives who dominated the Farmers' Alliance which met in Ocala, Florida, in December, 1890, and included representatives of the Colored Farmers' Alliance, were opposed to the creation of a third party. The southern Populists who had succeeded in capturing the Democratic party in two states were not prepared to deal frankly with the problem of Negro voters. They were opposed to a third party because it would destroy the solidarity of the white voters and open the way for Negroes to re-enter politics.

In South Carolina, where the agrarian movement was dominated by Benjamin Tillman, who was really a conservative landowner, the Negro did not play an important rôle. In the gubernatorial election of 1890, Tillman's oponent, Haskell, threatened to seek the support of Negro voters. But the Negroes had little faith in Haskell and being mindful of the terroristic methods used against them in previous elections they refrained on the whole from voting.[13] In fact, during the election campaign Tillman intimated that participation by Negroes on a large scale would result in violence. After he became governor, he declared that his victory was a complete "triumph of Democracy and white supremacy over mongrelism and anarchy." [14] He stated frankly that the white people of South Carolina had absolute control of the government and intended to keep it at any hazard. The Negro, in his opinion, lacked the capacity to exercise intelligently the right of suffrage. However, in other southern States Negro voters were used more extensively by both Bourbons and agrarians. In Alabama the large landowners in the Black counties secured the black vote by promises and bribes in order to defeat the Populists in the white counties.[15] The success of the Bourbons in Georgia in the elections for state officers in 1892 was attributed to the fact that the planters and owners of turpentine farms marched their black workers to the polls.[16] During the elections of 1896

[13] See Francis B. Simkins, *The Tillman Movement in South Carolina* (Durham, 1926), pp. 103-34.

[14] *The Tillman Movement in South Carolina* by Francis B. Simkins, p. 137. Copyright 1926 by Duke University Press.

[15] See John B. Clark, *Populism in Alabama* (Auburn, Ala., 1927), pp. 178-80.

[16] There is also evidence that white as well as black mill workers in Augusta were used in the same manner. Lewinson, *op. cit.*, p. 77.

in Louisiana, the registration of Negroes by Republicans and Populists in one parish resulted in the slaying of many Negroes.[17]

The agrarians attempted in some cases to enlist the support of the exploited Negro farmers. In Georgia, Tom Watson in 1892 appealed to white and Negro farmers to form a united front.

> Now the People's Party says to these two men, "You are kept apart that you may be separately fleeced of your earnings. You are made to hate each other because upon that hatred is rested the keystone of the arch of financial despotism which enslaves you both. You are deceived and blinded that you may not see how this race antagonism perpetuates a monetary system which beggars both." [18]

Watson declared that the object of the Populist party was to "make lynch law odious to the people" and nominated a Negro for membership on the state executive committee of the party.[19] He defended the right of the Negro to citizenship rights and declared that social equality was something for each individual to decide for himself. When South Carolina, under Tillman's leadership changed its constitution in 1895 in order to disfranchise the Negro, Watson called such action reactionary and stated that it was done in order to perpetuate the rule of the Democratic party.[20] It is impossible to know what influences caused Watson later to become like Tillman a defender of white supremacy and one of the worst enemies of the Negro.[21]

There were class contradictions in the Populist movement as well as the racial issue which help to account for its failure. In South Carolina, where Tillman dominated the movement, the struggle for land was turned into a struggle for a share in political offices. Likewise, in Alabama the economic interests were submerged in a purely political struggle.[22] The various propertied interests represented by the Demo-

17 *Ibid.*, pp. 77-78.
18 Quoted in C. Vann Woodward, *Tom Watson Agrarian Rebel* (New York, 1938), p. 220.   19 *Ibid.*, p. 221.   20 *Ibid.*, p. 371.
21 After Watson became a defender of white supremacy, he declared that "In the South, we have to lynch him (the Negro) occasionally, and flog him, now and then, to keep him from blaspheming the Almighty, by his conduct, on account of his smell and his color." Quoted in *ibid.*, p. 432. Watson was aware, it might be pointed out, that if the Negro was eliminated from politics, the Populists under his leadership would hold the balance of power in the Democratic Party.
22 Clark, *op. cit.*, p. 178.

cratic party in Georgia took advantage of the weaknesses in the Populist movement and utilized the racial issue to their own advantage. In fact, throughout the South the propertied classes were able, after the collapse of the agrarian revolt as a national movement, to make deals with the leaders of the agrarians that would bring the white voters back into the Democratic party. During the nineties the southern whites became united once more and the disfranchisement of the Negro became the chief issue.

THE NEGRO SEEKS A PROMISED LAND

After the fall of the Reconstruction governments in the South, many of the Negro's leaders still hoped that the federal government, through the Republican Party, would coerce the South into according the Negro equality.[23] On the other hand, the illiterate and impoverished Negro masses had gradually given up the hope that the government would provide them with land and protect them in their rights. But the new hope of acquiring land and freedom had not died out altogether and though they were completely under the power of whites, they could still move about.

A movement embodying these hopes developed in the lower South. This movement, which was stimulated by the debt-servitude which

[23] The withdrawal of federal troops from the South after the Presidential election of 1876 was an indication of the changing attitude of the North toward the question of the rights of the Negro in the South. (See Paul H. Buck, *The Road to Reunion.* Boston, 1938.) In 1875, Congress had passed a second Civil Rights Act guaranteeing the Negro civil rights, such as equal accommodation on public conveyances and in public places, and the right to serve on juries. Eight years later this law was declared unconstitutional on the grounds that it interfered with state rights. In 1890, the Republicans made a last unsuccessful attempt to secure the political rights of the Negro through the enactment of law for the federal supervision of elections. This law failed to accomplish its purpose because of the lack of an appropriation and an unwillingness on the part of the federal government to use military force in the South. Moreover, the federal courts had handed down decisions which had really destroyed the effect of the Fifteenth Amendment. The Supreme Court had taken the position that, "A denial of the right to vote by the states must, to make a case for the Federal courts, be on grounds of race, color, or previous condition of servitude, and such discrimination must be alleged in any indictment under the Amendment or what remains of the Enforcing Act." (*Race, Class and Party* by Paul Lewinson, p. 59. Copyright 1932 by Oxford University Press.) Such was the general attitude of the North when the southern states began in the eighteen nineties to give legal sanction to the disfranchisement and segregation of the Negro and other forms of social and civil discriminations.

had grown out of the crop lien system, developed into an exodus in 1879 from the States along the Mississippi River to Kansas.[24] Following the downfall of the Reconstruction governments, the Negroes in Louisiana had become the object of the vengeance of the whites. Thousands of Negroes were injured and killed for political reasons. In Alabama, Mississippi, and Texas as well as in Louisiana the Negroes had no redress in the courts and were denied educational opportunities. Moreover, in these states there were laws in accordance with which convicts were leased to plantation owners, thus inaugurating a system of peonage. Consequently, when there was a failure of the cotton crop in Mississippi and Louisiana in 1879, the impoverished blacks eagerly listened to the appeal of agents who painted a picture of a Canaan in Kansas. The leader of the movement was a shrewd Negro named Benjamin Singleton, nearly seventy years of age, known as "Pap" Singleton, but who called himself "The Moses of the Colored Exodus." [25] After the Negroes had failed to acquire land in the South, Singleton hoped to lead them to a country where they might realize their freedom as landowners. Thousands of Negroes, unprepared for the rigor of the Kansas climate, left Alabama, Georgia, Mississippi, and Texas to start life anew in Kansas. Although about a third of the "Exodusters" remained in Kansas and prospered on the whole, many of the migrants returned home with reports of the bleak climate and barren country. The movement attracted nation-wide attention and Negro leaders were divided on the question whether the Negro should seek escape from his condition in the South through migration.

"RISE OF THE POOR WHITES" AND LEGISLATION OF NEGRO'S INFERIOR STATUS

The agrarian discontent which found political expression in the Populist movement in the South created the popular but false belief that the "poor whites" had captured political power. This belief became current because of the large number of state and national

[24] See John G. Van Deusen, "The Exodus of 1879," *The Journal of Negro History,* Vol. XXI, pp. 111-29.
[25] See Walter L. Fleming, "Pap" Singleton, The Moses of the Colored Exodus," *American Journal of Sociology,* Vol. XV, pp. 61-82.

officials who were elected from among the common people.[26] Although the type of political leaders represented by Vardaman, Blease, and others secured office because of the deplorable economic and social condition of the white masses, their means of attaining political power was through arousing race prejudice. The emergence of this type of leadership has brought no improvement to the social and economic condition of the white masses.[27] They have been the spokesmen of the oligarchy which has controlled the South since the overthrow of the Reconstruction governments.[28]

The leaders who used the general unrest among the whites to attain political power succeeded in persuading the poor whites that the Negro was the cause of all their troubles. Mississippi, which had taken the lead in the enactment of the Black Codes and in the formation of the "rifle clubs" for the restoration of white supremacy, once again took the lead in 1890 in enacting constitutional provisions for disfranchising the Negro. Following the example of Mississippi, South Carolina and Louisiana adopted new constitutions in 1895; North Carolina amended its constitution in 1900 and 1905; Alabama and Virginia adopted new constitutions in 1901; Georgia in 1908 and Oklahoma in 1910.[29] By statutory provisions other southern States were able to accomplish the same purpose. In order to disfranchise the Negro it was necessary, of course, to circumvent the Fifteenth Amendment. This was achieved, first, by requiring the payment of poll taxes and other taxes, and providing for registration of voters months in advance of voting. The ownership of small amounts of property was also generally included among the qualifications for the right to vote, but since the purpose of these constitutions was to disfranchise Negroes alternative qualifications were provided for. A voter might qualify on the basis of literacy or under an "understanding clause," according to which he must demonstrate to the election official that he could read and interpret the federal or state constitution. The white election officials were, of course, to determine whether a voter could meet these qualifications. In order that these requirements

[26] Cf. Shugg, *op. cit.*, pp. 274-76.   [27] *Ibid.*, pp. 276ff.
[28] See William H. Skaggs, *The Southern Oligarchy* (New York, 1924).
[29] See Lewinson, *op. cit.*, p. 260, note 5.

would not disqualify any white voters, the "grandfather clause" was included in most constitutions According to the "grandfather clause," a person might become a registered voter if he had served in the armies of the United States or the Confederacy or was a descendant of such person, or had the right of franchise before 1867. By these constitutional provisions, the southern states were able to disfranchise practically all Negroes.

In making constitutional changes, in order to disfranchise the Negro, the aim was not simply to exclude from the electorate the ignorant, shiftless, and irresponsible Negroes. The purpose was primarily to exclude all Negroes from participation in the political life of the South and to reduce them to a subordinate status. Once in stating his opposition to the Negro's voting, Senator Vardaman of Mississippi declared:

. . . it matters not what his [the Negro's] advertised mental and moral qualifications may be. I am just as much opposed to Booker Washington as a voter, with all his Anglo-Saxon re-enforcements, as I am to the cocoanut-headed, chocolate-colored, typical little coon, Andy Dotson, who blacks my shoes every morning. Neither is fit to perform the supreme function of citizenship.[30]

Some of the leaders of the movement to disfranchise the Negro were afraid that the Negro would be encouraged to get an education in order to qualify as a voter. In fact, in the conventions in which the disfranchising constitutions were formed, the leaders made it clear that the purpose was to reduce the Negro to a subordinate caste. These constitutions provided for the separation of the races in all public conveyances, following the example of Mississippi where separate coaches for Negroes or the "Jim Crow" car was inaugurated in 1865.[31] The same principle was embodied in these constitutions in

[30] Quoted in *Race, Class and Party* by Paul Lewinson, pp. 84-85. Copyright 1932 by Oxford University Press.

[31] It appears that the earliest use of the term "Jim Crow" was in 1835 when Thomas D. Rice, the first Negro minstrel presented in Washington, D. C., a song and Negro dance entitled "Jim Crow." In 1841 the term was applied to a railroad car set apart for Negroes in Massachusetts. After the emancipation of the Negro, the term was applied to all the laws providing for the separation of the races in the South. See Gilbert T. Stephenson, *Race Distinctions in American Law* (New York, 1911), pp. 208ff.

regard to charitable and penal institutions and schools. However, the provisions concerning separate educational systems were designed to accomplish more than the mere separation of the two races. The conservative Democrats who had gained political control after the overthrow of the Reconstruction governments were lukewarm toward the support of the education of both white and Negro children at the expense of the taxpayer. But when the representatives of the "poor whites" assumed political control, they had to meet the demand of the "poor whites" for education at public expense. In order to meet this demand they resorted to the expedient of granting considerable discretionary power to local school boards. These boards diverted state funds, appropriated on a per capita basis, from Negro to white children.[32] In order to justify such action, the demagogic leaders of the "poor whites" attacked the principle of Negro education. Typical of such attacks is the following excerpt from a speech which Vardaman made in 1906 while governor of Mississippi.

The State, for many years, at great expense to the tax-payers, has maintained a system of negro education, which has produced disappointing results, and I am opposed to the perpetuation of that system. My own idea is that the character of negro education ought to be changed. If, after forty years of earnest effort and the expenditure of fabulous sums of money to educate his head, we have succeeded only in making a criminal of him and impairing his usefulness and efficiency as a laborer, wisdom would suggest that we make another experiment, and see if we cannot improve him by educating his hand and heart. There must be a moral substratum upon which to build, or you cannot make a desirable citizen. The negro, as a race, is devoid of that element. He has never felt the guilt of sin, and the restraining influences of moral scruples or the goading of an outraged conscience are unknown to the negro. Slavery is the only process by which he has ever been partially civilized. God Almighty created the negro for a menial—he is essentially a servant. . . . When left to himself he has universally gone back to the barbarism of his native jungles. While a few mixed breeds and freaks of the race may possess qualities which justify them to aspire above that station, the fact still remains that the race is fit for that and nothing more. At any rate, that is all that he will ever

32 Horace M. Bond, *The Education of the Negro in the American Social Order* (New York, 1934), pp. 86-115.

accomplish in Mississippi, and as it is in Mississippi, so will it be in all the states ultimately.[33]

As a consequence of the attack upon Negro education and the diversion of state funds to white schools, a general improvement occurred in the education of white children, while the condition of Negro schools was scarcely better in 1900 than in 1875.

RACIAL CONFLICT AND NEW FORMS OF ACCOMMODATION

During the period when "white supremacy" was being established in the South there was continual racial conflict. Sometimes there was conflict between individual whites and Negroes; at other times racial conflict took the form of organized violence. During Reconstruction the Negroes met the organized violence of the whites with some type of collective action on their part and the racial conflict developed into race riots. But gradually the organized resistance of the Negroes decreased and individual Negroes became the victims of the organized violence of the whites. A rough indication of this type of violence is provided in the statistics on Negroes lynched in the South. Lynchings in the South increased rapidly from 1882, the first year for which statistics are available, up to 1890 and then showed a sharp rise in the early nineties when the white South began to legalize the subordinate status of the Negro. (See Diagram I) Although the majority of the Negro victims were lynched for homicide,[34] the avowed justification for lynching was the raping of white women. In over 10 per cent of the cases the alleged cause for lynching Negroes included insulting white persons, robbery and theft, and a host of minor offenses. It appears that the lynching of Negroes was essentially an informal type of "justice" designed to "keep the Negro in his place." Community sanction for this type of "justice" was based upon the general belief that the Negro was a subhuman species and the fear that the Negro would get "out of hand." Lynching has been one of the fruits of the crusade to establish "white supremacy."

[33] Quoted in *The Education of the Negro in the American Social Order* by Horace M. Bond, p. 102. Copyright 1934 by Prentice-Hall, Inc.

[34] See Monroe N. Work (Ed.), *Negro Year Book, 1937-1938* (Tuskegee Institute, Ala., 1937), p. 157.

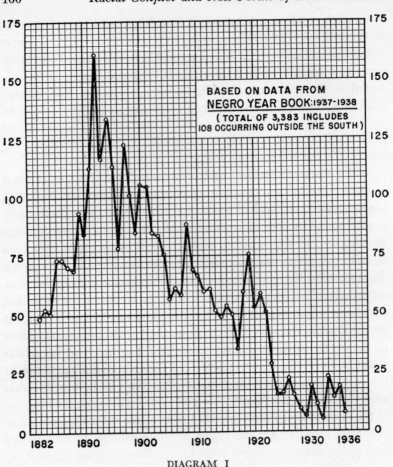

BASED ON DATA FROM
NEGRO YEAR BOOK:1937-1938
(TOTAL OF 3,383 INCLUDES
108 OCCURRING OUTSIDE THE SOUTH)

DIAGRAM I

Negroes Lynched In the United States: 1882–1936.

During the period when the Negro was being reduced by legal en-
actments and violence to a subordinate status in the South, a race
riot occurred in Wilmington, North Carolina, which signalized the
triumph of the counterrevolution in the South.[35] This riot was the
result of the Populist victory of 1896, when a fusion with the Republicans had been effected. In some of the eastern counties with large

[35] See Henry L. West, "The Race War in North Carolina," *The Forum*, Vol.
XXVI, pp. 578-79.

concentrations of black voters, Negroes had been elected to office. The large number of Negro officeholders in Wilmington was the occasion for the defeated Democrats to raise the cry of Negro domination. When the election of 1898 approached, the whites led by the Chamber of Commerce, the president of which was a New England Republican, determined to overthrow Negro rule. The whites formed armed units on a block basis in which "lawyers, doctors, merchants, railroad officials, cotton exporters, and . . . the reputable, taxpaying, substantial men of the city," participated.[36] In order to remove the incentive for the Negro to vote, a compromise among the whites was reached whereby the Democratic candidates withdrew and were replaced by "two gentlemen named by the businessmen." [37] Despite the fact that the Negroes did not vote and the whites triumphed throughout the State, on the day following the election the armed whites descended upon the Negro community.[38] Their first act was the destruction of the offices of a Negro newspaper, whose editor in an editorial had shown contempt, it was said, for "the white woman's purity." [39] After a number of Negroes had been killed and driven out of the city, the Negro officeholders and policemen were replaced by whites. Thus "white supremacy" was restored in North Carolina. But even before the Wilmington Riot, newspapers in control of the Democrats had used the Wilmington situation to drive white Populists back into the Democratic Party.[40]

The Wilmington Riot marked the end of the Negro's resistance to the determination on the part of the white South to reduce him to a

[36] "The Race War in North Carolina" by Henry L. West. *The Forum*, Vol. XXVI, p. 579. Copyright 1898 by The Forum Publishing Co.

[37] *Ibid.*, p. 583. West naively assumes that this compromise showed how "far removed politics was from the situation." As a matter of fact, there can be no clearer instance of the relation between class interests and politics. Since the respectable men of property were white and the propertyless workers were black, it was natural that the cause of "white supremacy" included Republicans as well as Democrats.

[38] The Negro leaders had been called before a committee of whites and ordered, without being permitted to discuss the issue, to send a statement by the next morning indicating their agreement or refusal to accede to the demands of the whites that they withdraw from politics and accept a subordinate status in the community. The Negro leaders sent a letter in which they acceded to the demands of the whites but the letter arrived late. See West, *loc. cit.*

[39] *Ibid.*, p. 582.   [40] Hicks, *op. cit.*, pp. 391-93.

subordinate status. When Booker T. Washington made his famous speech in Atlanta in 1895, in which he announced his widely quoted formula for the accommodation of the two races, the Negro had already been gradually forced to accept an inferior status in the South and the period of acute race conflict was drawing to a close. At the very time when Washington was announcing his formula, the South was giving content to the first part of his formula: "In all things that are purely social we can be as separate as the fingers, yet one as the hand in all things essential to mutual progress." This was accomplished, as we have seen, in the attempt to maintain the Negro in a subordinate status, through the disfranchisement of the Negro and the enactment of laws enforcing the separation of the races in all phases of life.[41] The downward trend in the number of Negroes lynched after 1893 coincided with the growing tendency on the part of Negroes to accept outwardly at least the status accorded them by the whites.

As in all cases of accommodation or external adjustments between groups with conflicting interests, there was still a latent conflict between the two races which flared up occasionally. The most important

[41] Charles Sumner had foreseen that the only alternative to the equality of the Negro under the law would be the creation of a quasi-caste system based upon color. He stated his position in a speech, before the Senate in 1869, in support of the Fifteenth Amendment. See *Speech of Hon. Charles Sumner, of Massachusetts, delivered in the Senate of the United States, February 5, 1869* (Washington, 1869). Buck thinks, on the other hand, that the discipline of the Negro under white supremacy "possessed advantages which far outweighed its evils" since "the discipline prevented the Negro from slipping into semibarbarism, gave him a job and a permanent place in Southern life, and permitted a slow but definite progress for the race as a whole." See Buck, *op. cit.*, pp. 269-70. This statement indicates a lack of knowledge of the manner in which "white supremacy" has operated in the South. The so-called "discipline" has turned out to be a system of widespread exploitation and the denial of human rights. It is difficult to discover advantages in a type of social organization in which a group is reduced to the position in which no premium is placed upon intelligence, efficiency, and civilized behavior and even such usually recognized human virtues as honesty and courage. The theory of "white supremacy" and the practices based upon it tended to weed out and destroy the intelligent Negroes and debase all of them as human beings. Moreover, instead of being a discipline fitting the Negro for citizenship it really unfitted him for responsibility in a civilized community. The progress made by the Negro has been owing to his ability to escape from such conditions. Even liberal whites in the South today deny the advantages of the so-called "discipline" to which the Negro was subjected.

of these conflicts occurred in Atlanta in 1906 as a sequel to an election in Georgia where the disfranchisement of the Negro had been delayed because of the conflict between various industrial and landowning interests. During the gubernatorial campaign of 1906, the Democratic Party was split between two factions, one favorable to the railroads and the industrialists and the other favorable to the agricultural interests.[42] Hoke Smith, the candidate favorable to the agricultural interests, had come out for the elimination of the Negro from politics by legal and constitutional methods. He was supported by Tom Watson, who used his influence to swing the Populists to Smith. During the campaign Watson had to overcome the suspicions of the white farmers who were afraid that the disfranchisement of the Negro would lead to the disfranchisement of illiterate whites. Since the main issue of the campaign was the disfranchisement of the Negro, much racial antagonism was stirred up against the Negro. Clark Howell, the representative of the railroads and industrialists, was also in favor of Negro disfranchisement but opposed the proposal because he thought it would not be effective and would disfranchise some whites. Thus the stage was set for the riot which followed Hoke Smith's triumph on the issue of White Supremacy.

Some months prior to and during the campaign there had been a number of crimes committed by Negroes against white women. The number of such crimes had been exaggerated and played up by the newspaper.[43] The riot which broke out on September 22, 1906, was fomented by flaming headlines in the newspapers reporting four assaults on white women by Negroes. The *Atlanta News* printed four extras, which were carried through the streets by newsboys crying out

[42] Woodward, *op. cit.,* pp. 370-79.

[43] See Baker, *Following the Color Line,* pp. 3-25. The author "had a personal investigation made of every crime against a white woman committed in the few months before and after the riot. Three, charged to white men, attracted comparatively little attention in the newspapers, although one, the offence of a white man named Turnadge, was shocking in its details. Of twelve such charges against Negroes in the six months preceding the riot two were cases of rape, horrible in their details, three were aggravated attempts at rape, three may have been attempts, three were pure cases of fright on the part of the white woman, and in one the white woman, first asserting that a Negro had assaulted her, finally confessed attempted suicide." *Following the Color Line* by Ray Stannard Baker, p. 5. Copyright 1908 by Doubleday & Company, Inc.

each successive assault. A later investigation showed that two of the cases reported might have been attempts at assaults, but that two were undoubtedly cases of fright on the part of the Negroes as well as the white women because of the tense situation.[44] However, the white mobs that had been incited by the newspapers began to assault or murder every Negro within reach. The pent-up vengeance of the "poor whites" was shown by their attack upon a large settlement of respectable Negro homeowners. In a meeting later called by the respectable propertied whites, a prominent Negro physician, a graduate of Yale University, who had been sought by the mob made the following statement:

We have been disarmed: how shall we protect our lives and property? If living a sober, industrious, upright life, accumulating property and educating his children as best he knows how, is not the standard by which a coloured man can live and be protected in the South, what is to become of him? If the kind of life I have lived isn't the kind you want, shall I leave and go North?

When we aspire to be decent and industrious we are told that we are bad examples to other coloured men. Tell us what your standards are for coloured men. What are the requirements under which we may live and be protected? What shall we do? [45]

In response to this frank statement of the dilemma of the Negro who aspired to meet the demands of a civilized community, the respectable and propertied whites, who had helped to make the Negro defenseless by disfranchising him, expressed their paternalistic regard for the Negro victims by starting a fund for their relief. The helplessness of the Negro, on the one hand, and the paternalistic attitude of the whites, on the other, indicate the terms upon which the accommodation of the races had been established during the first decade of the present century.

AFTER FIFTY YEARS OF FREEDOM

Despite racial violence and the denial of civil rights, a half-century after Emancipation nine-tenths of the Negroes were still in the South.

44 *Ibid.*, p. 9.
45 *Following the Color Line by Ray Stannard Baker*, pp. 19-20. Copyright 1908 by Doubleday & Company, Inc.

At one time there had been some discussion among Negro leaders concerning a wholesale migration from the South. But the question of the Negro's leaving the South could not be settled in debates or on the basis of theoretical arguments. The masses of Negroes remained in the South primarily because it was the place where they were able to secure a living. The majority of the Negroes in the North carried on a precarious existence because they had never been able to secure a foothold in industry.[46] The great body of Negro workers were concentrated in unskilled occupations and domestic service. Even in the South he had lost his privileged position as a skillful artisan. At the close of the Civil War there were 100,000 Negro mechanics as compared with 20,000 white mechanics in the South,[47] but between 1865 and 1890 the proportion of Negro artisans decreased as the result of the competition of white labor.[48] However, from 1890 on the Negro artisan was able to hold his own and in fact the Negro industrial worker gained a foothold in the developing steel industry in the South.[49]

The great majority of the Negro population continued to find its chief means of livelihood in agriculture. In 1910 three-fourths of the Negro farms as compared with two-fifths of the white farms in the South were operated by tenants. (See Table VI) About 40 per cent of the Negro tenants paid a stated sum for the rental of their farms while most of the remaining Negro tenants gave a share, usually a half of the crop, in return for the use of the land. About a fourth of the Negro farmers had managed to become landowners. The average size of their holdings was about one-half that of the farms of white owners.[50] Between 1900 and 1910 the value of their holdings increased from $123,754,396 to $375,323,227, which was slightly higher than the relative increase in the value of white holdings.[51]

[46] See Alfred H. Stone, *Studies in the American Race Problem* (New York, 1908), pp. 149-208; and Baker, *op. cit.*, pp. 109-47.

[47] Charles H. Wesley, *Negro Labor in the United States* (New York, 1927), p. 142.

[48] Carl Kelsey, "The Evolution of Negro Labor," *Annals of the American Academy of Political and Social Science*, Vol. 21, pp. 55-76.

[49] Sterling D. Spero and Abram L. Harris, *The Black Worker* (New York, 1931), p. 247.

[50] United States Bureau of the Census, *Negro Population, 1790-1915* (Washington, 1918), p. 577. [51] *Ibid.*, p. 578.

There was also a marked decrease in the illiteracy of the Negro in the South. From 1880 to 1910, there was a decline from 70 to 33.3 per cent in the proportion of illiterates ten years of age and over among southern Negroes. Impressed by the progress which the Negro had made in acquiring land and in conducting small business enterprises, some of his leaders started a movement for the development of

TABLE VI

Number and Percentage Distribution of Colored and White Farms
According to Tenure in the South: 1910 *

Tenure	Number		Percentage Distribution	
	COLORED	WHITE	COLORED	WHITE
Total	890,141	2,207,406	100.0	100.0
OWNERS	218,467	1,326,044	24.5	60.1
Free	128,557	908,211	14.4	41.1
Mortgaged	46,733	245,889	5.3	11.1
Part	43,177	171,944	4.9	7.8
TENANTS	670,474	866,278	75.3	39.2
Cash	260,966	192,094	29.3	8.7
Share	370,306	611,370	41.6	27.7
Share-cash	14,218	25,447	1.6	1.2
Not specified	24,984	37,367	2.8	1.7
MANAGERS	1,200	15,084	0.1	0.7

* *Negro Population, 1790-1915*, p. 572.

economic self-sufficiency as a solution of his problem in the South. In 1900 the National Negro Business League was organized under the leadership of Booker T. Washington. In fact, because of the uncertain economic status of the Negro in the North, the belief that the Negro could best work out his destiny in the South despite segregation and disfranchisement gained acceptance among some Negroes as well as among whites.

In 1913 a group of white and colored leaders and scholars made an assessment of the Negro's progress during fifty years of freedom.[52] In the various articles dealing with different phases of Negro life, there was a general agreement that the Negro had made considerable

[52] See *The Negro's Progress in Fifty Years*. The American Academy of Political and Social Sciences, Philadelphia, 1913.

progress since Emancipation. In a paper dealing with the work of the southern universities on the race question, a liberal southern university professor concluded his discussion with a passionate defense of racial integrity in which he stated that "ours is a noble mission, that of discussing the ways and means of bettering the religious, educational, hygienic, economic, and civic conditions of an inferior race." [53] Another southern professor gave an account of the improvements in race relations which, according to him, had been brought about as the result of the separation of the races. In the conclusion of his paper appears the following:

When the Negro has become economically efficient, intellectually more advanced, racially self-conscious, there will be far 'less friction, for he will then feel as the white man feels that racial integrity and social separation are best for both races. Indeed most of the best trained Southern Negroes I know at present feel as the white man does about this matter—that each race can make its largest contribution to humanity if it develops its own race life and race consciousness. It has been the fear on the part of the Southern white man that development of the Negro intellectually and economically would mean race amalgamation. But as this race consciousness grows stronger and stronger in the Negro race this feeling will be allayed and the two races will dwell side by side in a spirit of increasing brotherhood.[54]

Some of the papers dealt with the problems of the Negro: crime, unemployment, health, and the problems raised by the migration of Negroes to cities. The problems of Negroes in cities, especially southern cities, were analyzed by a Negro sociologist. The first of his recommendations for dealing with these problems contained the statement that there "should be an organized effort to acquaint the Negro in the country with the desirability of remaining where he is unless by education and training he is prepared to meet the exactions of adjustments to city life." [55] None of the contributors to this symposium could foresee at the time that the drift of Negroes to cities would de-

[53] See Charles H. Brough, "Work of the Commission of Southern Universities on the Race Question," *Loc. cit.*, p. 57.
[54] W. D. Weatherford, "Race Relationship in the South," *Loc. cit.*, p. 172.
[55] See George E. Haynes, "Conditions Among Negroes in Cities," *Loc. cit.*, p. 105-19.

velop, as the result of a world war, into a mass migration to northern cities which would change the relation of the Negro to American society. Nevertheless, the change in the relation of the Negro to American life had its roots in the social and economic background which has been presented in the foregoing pages.

PART 3

The Negro Community and Its Institutions

HAVING traced the emergence of Negro-white relations through slavery, Reconstruction, and restoration of "white supremacy," we now turn to an analysis of the character of the Negro communities which have emerged as the result of interaction of Negroes and whites in American life. Basic to an understanding of this is an account of the growth and distribution of the Negro population and the organization of both rural and urban communities. Because of the importance of the increasing stratification of Negro communities, a special chapter is devoted to this subject. In the succeeding chapters, there is an analysis of the institutions that have evolved in Negro communities. There is first a discussion of Negro family life, with emphasis on an analysis of the Negro family as a social institution. Then follow chapters on the development and function of such important institutions as the church, mutual aid societies, and fraternal organizations. In the last chapter, business institutions are analyzed both in relation to their rôle in the Negro community and in relation to the economic organization of American life.

CHAPTER IX

The Growth and Distribution of the Negro Population

W HEN the first federal census was taken in 1790, one person out of five (19.3 per cent) in the United States was a Negro. However, the 757,208 Negroes in the country at that time were not evenly distributed.[1] More than nine-tenths of them were concentrated in the South where the plantation system of agriculture had grown up. Though in Virginia the cultivation of tobacco was being rapidly replaced by wheat and corn, 305,493 Negroes or 40 per cent of the entire Negro population were still in that State. There were three other southern states—Maryland, North Carolina, and South Carolina—in which the Negro population numbered more than 100,000 persons. The 111,079 Negroes in Maryland, where tobacco cultivation was also declining, constituted over a third (34.7 per cent) of the total population. Because of the movement of farmers from the North and from Europe into the back country of the South, the white population of the southern states had increased considerably during the latter part of the eighteenth century. The 105,547 Negroes in North Carolina did not number quite three persons in ten (29.4 per cent) in the population of the state. In South Carolina, where the cultivation of rice and indigo required large numbers of slaves, there were 40,000 whites and 90,000 blacks in 1765,[2] but by 1790 the white population exceeded the black population. Yet in South Carolina as in Virginia in 1790

[1] United States Bureau of the Census, *Negroes in the United States, 1920-32* (Washington, 1935), pp. 10-11, 14-15.

[2] Lewis C. Gray, *History of Agriculture in the Southern United States to 1860* (Washington, 1933), Vol. II, p. 614.

the Negroes accounted for more than two persons in five in the population. In the part of Georgia included in the federal enumeration there were slightly less than 30,000 Negroes, but they accounted for over a third (35.9 per cent) of the inhabitants. There were still fewer Negroes in Kentucky and Tennessee, and because of the large number of white farmers engaged in general farming, the blacks constituted a much smaller proportion of the population. In Kentucky one person in six, and in Tennessee only one in ten was a Negro.

Turning to the North, one finds that the proportion of blacks in the population was extremely small, one person in thirty being of Negro extraction. The proportion was relatively large in three states; Rhode Island had one person in sixteen of Negro descent, and in New York and New Jersey one in thirteen was of Negro origin.

During the 150 years since the first census was taken, the proportion of Negroes in the population of the South has declined from slightly more than one person in three to less than one in four. This decline has been due partly to the decline in the Negro birth rate and partly to the migration of large numbers of Negroes to the North. The proportion of persons of Negro descent in the population of the North at present, however, is about what it was at the first census.

GROWTH OF NEGRO POPULATION IN DIFFERENT REGIONS

From 1790 to 1830 the rate of increase in the Negro population of the country was slightly less than that of the whites, though there was a large increase in the slave population during the decade 1800 to 1810, especially during the years before the prohibition of the slave trade (in 1808).[3] During the entire period from 1790 to 1830, there was an increase in the proportion of Negroes in the population of all southern states, with the exception of Delaware, Maryland, and the District of Columbia, in which states the proportion of Negroes in the population remained stationary on the whole. In the northern states, there was not much change in the number of Negroes and as a result of the increase in the white population their proportion of the total

[3] United States Bureau of the Census, *Negro Population, 1790-1915* (Washington, 1918), pp. 28-?0

showed a decrease. During this same period the free Negroes increased much more rapidly than the slaves, but beginning in 1840 the slaves increased more rapidly than those of free status.[4] From 1840 on there was a decline in the relative number of Negroes in the border states—Missouri, Kentucky, Delaware, Maryland, the District of Columbia, and even in Virginia. On the other hand, though there was a decline in the South as a whole, the proportion of Negroes in the population of the lower South with the exception of Florida continued to increase until 1860. In the North the decline in the relative numbers of blacks in the population continued until 1860, at which time Negroes numbered less than one person in fifty. Beginning in 1840, the country as a whole showed a much higher rate of increase for the whites than for the Negroes, and from that time onward the proportion of Negroes in the total population began to decline significantly. From one person in six in 1840, the proportion of Negroes in the total population declined to one person in seven just before the outbreak of the Civil War.

The Negro population doubled during each of the thirty-year periods from 1790 to 1850; but during the next thirty-year period the rate of increase was only 80.9 per cent as compared with 122.0 per cent for the whites.[5] Although in the South as a whole the proportion of Negroes in the population did not increase during the thirty-year period from 1850 to 1880, a number of southern states showed an increase in the proportion of Negroes in their population. In the lower South the largest increases were in Mississippi, Georgia, and Alabama; and there were smaller increases in North Carolina, South Carolina, and Louisiana. Moreover, while the proportion of blacks in the population of Delaware, Maryland, and Kentucky decreased significantly from 1850 to 1880, there were marked increases in the District of Columbia and Virginia. At the same time the proportion of Negroes in the population of the North began to increase slightly.

---

[4] See Table II, p. 62 above.

[5] United States Bureau of the Census, A *Century of Population Growth, From the First Census to the Twelfth, 1790-1900* (Washington, 1909), p. 81. See Bureau of the Census, *Negro Population, 1790-1915*, pp. 25-27, concerning undercount of Negro population at the census of 1870 and the estimates of its real increase during the decade from 1860 to 1870.

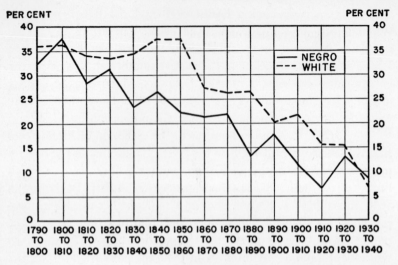

DIAGRAM II

Percentage Increase in the White and Negro Population in the
United States for Each Decade: 1790–1940.*

* Based on Table VII.

After 1880 the proportion of Negroes in the population of the
South began to decline rapidly. Even in the border states where
Negroes in the population had increased following the Civil War, the
proportion of blacks in the population began to decline. In all of the
states of the lower South, with the exception of South Carolina, Mississippi, and Louisiana, there was a decrease after 1880 in the percentage of Negroes in the population. Beginning in 1900 the proportion of the Negroes in the population of South Carolina and
Louisiana has followed the trend in the South as a whole.[6] Since 1900
the proportion of Negroes in the population of all southern states has
continued to decrease.[7] From one person in three in 1900 the pro-

[6] See Bureau of the Census, *Negro Population, 1790-1915*, pp. 27-28, concerning the undercount of the Negro population in 1890.

[7] The increase of only 6.5 per cent in the Negro population between 1910 and
1920 as compared with an increase of 13.6 per cent between 1920 and 1930 has
caused students of the Negro to believe that because of the northward migrations
between 1910 and 1920, there was an underenumeration of Negroes in 1920.
According to the *Fifteenth Census of the United States: 1930*, Vol. III, Part I,

TABLE VII

White and Negro Population of the United States, with Decennial Increase: 1790–1940 *

YEAR	ALL CLASSES	WHITE	Negro		Preceding Increase During Percentage 10 Years	
			NUMBER	PER CENT	NEGRO	WHITE
1940	131,669,275	118,214,870	12,865,518	9.8	8.2	7.2
1930	122,775,046	108,864,207	11,891,143	9.7	13.6	15.7
1920	105,710,620	94,120,374	10,463,131	9.9	6.5	15.7
1910	91,972,266	81,364,447	9,827,763	10.7	11.2	21.8
1900	75,994,575	66,809,196	8,833,994	11.6	18.0	21.2
1890	62,947,714	55,101,258	7,488,676	11.9	13.8	27.0
1880	50,155,783	43,402,970	6,580,793	13.1	22.0	29.2
1870	38,558,371	33,589,377	4,880,009	12.7	21.4	24.8
1860	31,443,321	26,922,537	4,441,830	14.1	22.1	37.7
1850	23,191,876	19,553,068	3,638,808	15.7	26.6	37.7
1840	17,069,453	14,195,805	2,873,648	16.8	23.4	34.7
1830	12,866,020	10,537,378	2,328,642	18.1	31.4	33.9
1820	9,638,453	7,866,797	1,771,656	18.4	28.6	34.2
1810	7,239,881	5,862,073	1,377,808	19.0	37.5	36.1
1800	5,308,483	4,306,446	1,002,037	18.9	32.3	35.8
1790	3,929,214	3,172,006	757,208	19.3	....	....

* *Negroes in the United States, 1920-32*, p. 1, for years 1790 to 1940; and *Sixteenth Census of the United States: 1940*, Series P-10, No. 1.

portion of Negroes in the population of the South declined to 23.4 per cent in 1940. The number of Negroes in the North more than tripled (from 880,771 to 2,790,193) between 1900 and 1940 because of the migrations during and following the World War. Thus whereas in 1900, only one Negro out of ten in the United States was in the North, in 1940 more than one Negro out of five (21.7 per cent) lived in the North. Despite this large increase in the number of Negroes in the North, their relative numbers in the population of the North in 1940 were practically the same (3.6 per cent) as in 1790. Likewise in the West, where Negroes did not exceed 10,000 until 1880, the rel-

p. 7, the undercount may have been as high as 150,000. See also T. J. Woofter, "What Is The Negro Rate of Increase?" *Journal of the American Statistical Association*, Vol. 26, n.s. (December, 1931), pp. 461-62; and Kelly Miller, "Enumeration Errors in Negro Population," *Scientific Monthly*, Vol. 14, (1922), pp. 167-77.

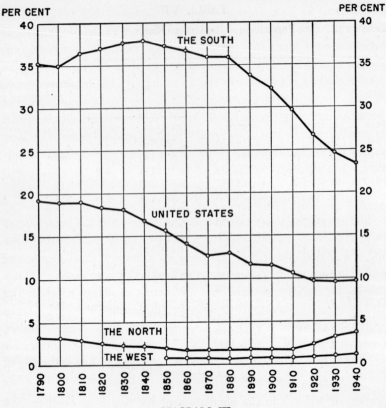

DIAGRAM III

Percentage of Negroes in the Total Population of the United States, of the South, of the North, and of the West: 1790–1940.*

* Based on *Negro Population 1790-1915*, p. 33; *Negroes in the United States, 1920-32*, p. 5; and *Sixteenth Census of the United States: 1940. Population.* Vol. II, "Characteristics of the Population," p. 55.

North: Maine, New Hampshire, Vermont, Massachusetts, Rhode Island, Connecticut, New York, New Jersey, Pennsylvania, Ohio, Indiana, Illinois, Michigan, Wisconsin, Minnesota, Iowa, Missouri, North Dakota, South Dakota, Nebraska, Kansas.

South: Delaware, Maryland, District of Columbia, Virginia, West Virginia, North Carolina, South Carolina, Georgia, Florida, Kentucky, Tennessee, Alabama, Mississippi, Arkansas, Louisiana, Oklahoma, Texas.

West: Montana, Idaho, Wyoming, Colorado, New Mexico, Arizona, Utah, Nevada, Washington, Oregon, California.

atively large increase since 1900 has not increased their relative numbers in the total population. Although Negroes in the West have increased almost fifteenfold since 1880, they constitute at present only slightly more than 1 per cent of the population of the West. Since 1900 the white population in the United States has increased almost 80 per cent while the Negro population has increased by only 45.6 per cent. Yet Negroes still constitute about one-tenth of the entire population and their relative numbers in the nation's population have declined less than two per cent since the opening of the present century.

BIRTHS AND DEATHS

The growth of the Negro population since 1810 has been due almost entirely to the excess of the number of births over deaths.[8] During the period of slavery, according to common observations and available sources of information, the Negro was very prolific.[9] Statistics on the number of children under five years of age to women of childbearing age enable us to compare the fertility of Negro women with that of white women. In 1820 there were 810 Negro children under five years of age for each 1,000 Negro women of childbearing age (15 to 44) as compared with 905 white children to 1,000 white of the same age group.[10] Though the ratio of white children to white women was greater than that of Negro children in 1830 and 1840, the difference was very small. By 1850 the ratio of Negro children to Negro women had begun to exceed the ratio of white children to white women. In 1860 there were 724 Negro children under five years of age to each 1,000 Negro women of childbearing age as compared with 675 white children to white women of childbearing age. After the Civil War the ratio of Negro children continued to exceed the ratio of white children until 1920, when the ratio for white children was 471 against 429 for the Negro population. However, in 1930 the

[8] The number of foreign-born Negroes in the United States increased from 40,339 or 0.4 per cent of the Negro population in 1910 to 83,941 or 0.7 per cent in 1940.

[9] See S. J. Holmes, *The Negro's Struggle for Survival* (Berkeley, Calif., 1937), pp. 142ff.

[10] Warren S. Thompson and P. K. Whelpton, *Population Trends in the United States* (New York, 1933), pp. 262-67.

ratio of children to Negro women of childbearing age slightly exceeded the ratio among whites.

Since the opening of the present century the decline in the ratio of children to women of childbearing age in the Negro population has been greater than in the white population. Among Negroes the ratio of children declined from 582 in 1900 to 420 in 1940; whereas among whites the ratio of children declined from 508 to 399. At the opening of the century, "there were 14 States, all in the South, in which the proportion of [Negro] children to 1,000 females ranged from 500 in Delaware to 712 in South Carolina," but by 1910 the number of such states had been reduced to 10.[11] In 1920 there were only two states, North Carolina and South Carolina, with 500 or more children to 1,000 Negro women and by 1930 North Carolina was the only state with this ratio. The low ratio of children to Negro women of childbearing age in 1920 was probably due to conditions growing out of the migrations during the World War.[12] This explanation is supported by the fact that between 1920 and 1930 there was an increase in the ratio of Negro children in 26 states and the District of Columbia, nine of these states being industrial areas to which Negroes migrated.[13] It appears, however, that urban life has a more adverse effect upon the fertility of the Negro women than upon that of the white women. In 1940 the ratio of children in the rural-farm white population was 180 per cent of the ratio among urban whites, whereas the ratio of children in the rural-farm Negro population was 238 per cent of the ratio among urban Negroes.[14]

The early reports from the Birth Registration Area,[15] which was established in 1915 and included principally northern states, indicated that the birth rate among Negroes was lower than among whites. But

[11] Bureau of the Census, *Negroes in the United States, 1920-1932*, p. 201.

[12] Warren S. Thompson, *Ratio of Children to Women: 1920*. Census Monograph (Washington, 1931), p. 149.

[13] Bureau of the Census, *Negroes in the United States, 1920-32*, p. 201.

[14] See T. Lynn Smith, "A Demographic Study of the American Negro," *Social Forces*, Vol. 23, p. 384.

[15] In 1880, the Bureau of the Census established a national "registration area" for deaths because some of the states "had efficient systems for the registration of vital statistics." The original "registration area" grew as the different states adopted adequate systems for the registration of births and deaths. See Bureau of the Census, *Vital Statistics of the United States, 1943* (Washington, 1943), p. 1.

beginning in 1919, the statistics for the Birth Registration Area have shown a higher birth rate for Negroes than for whites.[16] When crude birth rates are calculated on a basis allowing for an estimated undercount in the white as well as in the Negro population, the difference between the birth rates for the two races has been even greater.[17] In 1920 the crude birth rate for Negroes was 31.3 per 1,000 as compared with 26.1 for whites. Reports for the Registration Area show that though the birth rates of whites and Negroes have declined since 1920, the Negro birth rates have continued to be higher than white birth rates. By 1930 the crude white birth rate had declined to 18.7 and the Negro rate to 21.7.[18] For the 1919 Registration Area specific birth rates for native white, foreign-born white, and Negro women declined between 1920 and 1929, the decline for each group increasing with the rise in age.[19] Although the specific birth rates for native white and Negro women were about the same in 1929, when adjustments are made for nonregistration the standardized rate of Negroes is 15 per cent higher than whites in 1920 and 17 per cent higher in 1929.[20] During this same period and up to 1933, although Negro mothers lost a larger number of children than white mothers, they still had a larger number of surviving children than all white mothers and native white mothers, though in some years foreign-born white mothers had more surviving children.[21]

The growth of the Negro population has been affected, of course, by the trend of Negro mortality as well as by birth rates. The meager statistics on death rates among Negroes before the Civil War indicate that they were lower than among whites.[22] But reports on conditions following the Civil War and during Reconstruction show that the mortality of the Negro increased greatly. It was not until 1900 that reliable statistics were available on the Negro population. In the

[16] Holmes, *op. cit.*, pp. 146-47.   [17] Thompson and Whelpton, *op. cit.*, pp. 263-64.

[18] Bureau of the Census, *Summary of Vital Statistics: United States, 1940*, (Washington, November 7, 1941), p. 9.

[19] Thompson and Whelpton, *op. cit.*, pp. 270-71.   [20] *Ibid.*, p. 272.

[21] Holmes, *op. cit.*, p. 151-53. Calculations were made by Holmes for the years 1924 to 1933, since no data on average number of children born and living were published after 1923.

[22] Holmes, *op. cit.*, p. 39. The Census of 1850 reported a death rate of 16.4 per 1,000 in the slave population. Bureau of the Census, *Negro Population, 1790-1915*, p. 298.

Registration Area, which contained only 13.4 per cent of the Negro population, the death rate for Negroes in 1900 was 30.2 as compared with 17.3 for whites.[23] By 1910, when the Registration Area had been extended to include Maryland and a number of southern cities, there were indications that the death rate among Negroes had declined rapidly, largely because of the decline in infant mortality. From 18.7 in 1920 the death rate declined to 16.5 in 1930, and by 1940 it had reached 13.8 per 1,000.[24] During this period the rate has fluctuated considerably and has varied in urban and rural areas. These variations as well as the influence of different diseases upon the survival of the Negro will be considered in a later chapter. Here it is only necessary to note that the decline in the death rate of the Negro together with a relatively high birth rate, which stood at 23.2 in 1940, accounts for the increase of 8.2 per cent in the Negro population during the decade 1930 to 1940. According to the latest census reports the net reproduction rate [25] of the white population in 1940 was 95 as compared with 107 for the nonwhite population.[26] The higher net reproduction rate of the nonwhite population is due to the fact that it has a larger proportion in rural-farm areas than the white population. In the urban areas both groups have the same net reproduction rates.

SEX RATIO

At each census from 1840 to 1940, there has been an excess of females in the Negro population.[27] In 1870 there were only 96.2 males per 100 females and though the ratio of males increased at the follow-

23 United States Bureau of the Census, *Negroes in the United States* (Washington, 1904), p. 64.

24 Bureau of the Census, *Negro Population, 1790-1915*, p. 300; Holmes, *op. cit.*, p. 40; Bureau of the Census, *Vital Statistics Rates in the United States, 1900-1940*, p. 127.

25 "The net reproduction rate is the ratio of (1) the number of daughters which would be borne by a cohort of newborn girls if age and specific fertility rates for female births continued at the same level, *but with effects of mortality on the cohort taken into account*, to (2) the number of newborn girls in the original cohort." Margaret J. Hagood, *Statistics for Sociologists* (New York, 1941), p. 891.

26 Bureau of the Census, *Vital Statistics Special Reports. The Net Reproduction Rate* (May 9, 1941), p. 402. The nonwhite population in 1940 included 588,887 who were classified as other races, for whom 13,577 births were reported.

27 Bureau of the Census, *Negroes in the United States, 1920-32*, p. 78. The ratio of males to females in 1820 and 1830 were 103.4 and 100.3 respectively.

ing censuses, it declined to 95 in 1940. Thus in respect to sex distribution, the Negro population has shown a trend opposite to that in the white population. Since 1820 there has been an excess of males in the white population, the ratio of males to females being 101.2 in 1940. The excess of females has been more marked in the Negro population of the South, especially in the "Black Belt" or those counties with a population 50 per cent or more Negro, than in other areas. In the "Black Belt" in 1930 the excess of females was probably the result of the migration of Negroes from that area, more Negro males having migrated than females.[28] However, in three southwestern states—Arkansas, Oklahoma, and Texas—there was an excess of males from 1890 until 1930, when there appeared an excess of females in Arkansas and Texas. In West Virginia, where large numbers of Negroes have been employed in mining, there has always been a large excess of males, though the ratio of males declined between 1910 and 1940 from 132.8 to 106. In Maryland females predominated in the Negro population from 1880 on, but since 1920 there has been an excess of males, which has probably been the result of increased employment opportunities for Negro men in industry. On the other hand, in the District of Columbia, where Negro women have found ready employment as teachers and in government service as well as in domestic service, there has been a large excess of females. However, with the increasing opportunities for the employment of Negro men, the sex ratio has increased from 78.7 in 1880 to 89.9 in 1940.

In the North as a whole there has been an excess of males in the Negro population since 1890. The excess of males has not been large (the ratio being 102 or 103 males per 100 females) but in 1920, following the migrations during the War period, when Negro men migrated in large numbers to northern industries, the ratio of males to females increased to 106.1. The excess of males in the Negro population of the North has been generally greater in those states where there were few Negroes and there were few opportunities for the employment of Negro women in domestic service. For example, in Maine, New Hampshire, and Vermont, the ratio of males to females has ranged from 120 to over 200 since the opening of the present century. On

28 *Ibid.*, p. 78.

the other hand, in Massachusetts, Rhode Island, Connecticut, New York, and New Jersey, states in which Negro women have found employment, there has been an excess of Negro females. However, in the industrial cities of New York, Pennsylvania, Ohio, and Indiana where there has been a demand for the labor of Negro men, there has been an excess of males since 1900. The excess of females has been reduced or has disappeared altogether in some cities. For example, in Akron, Ohio, in 1910, there were 119 males per 100 females and following the migrations during World War I the ratio of males to females increased to 175.4 in 1920; but by 1940 the ratio of males to females had declined to 97.9. In Chicago, Illinois, there were 104.5 males per 100 females in 1920, as a result of the great demand for the labor of Negro men; but by 1940 there were only 88.7, as a consequence of the increased employment opportunities for Negro women.

In the South with the exception of Wilmington, Delaware, there was not a city with 10,000 or more Negroes in 1930 with an excess of males. The same was true of smaller cities in the South with Negro populations ranging from 2,500 to 10,000. This situation, which has existed with few exceptions in southern cities since 1910, is a result of the fact that Negro females have had a better opportunity for employment in southern cities than Negro males. A similar situation in regard to the sex ratio has existed among whites in southern cities.

Males have always predominated in the Negro population of the West, and since 1880 the excess of males has been greater in the West than in the North. However, in the urban Negro population of the West as a whole there has been an excess of females. In Los Angeles, where Negro women have found employment in large numbers, there were 88.2 males per 100 females in 1940. Only in San Francisco and Seattle, Washington, did males outnumber females in 1940. But in the rural-farm population and the rural nonfarm population the ratios of males to females were 127.8 and 155.9 respectively.

AGE DISTRIBUTION

The median age of the Negro population has steadily increased since 1850.[29] In 1850 the median age was 17.3 and by 1900 it had

[29] Bureau of the Census, *Negroes in the United States, 1920-32*, p. 87.

increased to 19.4 years. Since 1900 the median age has increased to 22.3 years in 1920 and 25.3 years in 1940. In 1940 the median age of Negro males and females was the same, while the median ages of both Negro males and Negro females were lower than those of native white males and white females.[30] The increase in the median age of the Negro population has been a result of the increase in the average length of life and the decline in the proportion of children. The proportion of the Negro population under five years of age declined from 16.5 per cent in 1850 to 9.7 per cent in 1940.[31] From 1850 to 1940 the proportion of Negroes between 45 and 64 years of age increased from 8.7 per cent to 15.1 per cent, as compared with an increase of from 10.1 to 20.3 in the white population. The proportion of Negroes 65 years of age and over has increased from 2.4 to 4.8 per cent since 1850, while the increase in the white population has been much greater.[32] The smaller proportion of Negroes in the older age groups has been due to the higher death rate among Negroes than among whites. The Negro population like the white population is becoming older but at a slower rate.

The age composition of the Negro population has varied with respect to regions, and the size and character of the community. In the South the proportion of children under 5 years of age has been higher than in the North. However, the proportion of children under five years of age in the South declined from 16.7 to 10.9 per cent between 1850 and 1930. In the Northeast and North Center, the decline during this period was from 12.7 to 8.9 per cent in the Northeast and from 17 to 8.1 per cent in the North Center.[33] The propor-

[30] *Sixteenth Census of the United States. Population.* Second Series. United States Summary. Washington, 1943, p. 16. The median age of native white males and females was 26.7 and 27.1 respectively.

[31] *Negroes in the United States, 1920-32,* and *Sixteenth Census of the United States: 1940. Population,* Vol. II, Part I, Washington, 1943.

[32] There are many irregularities in the reported ages of Negroes. These irregularities have been especially conspicuous in the ages of older Negroes. For example, "Of the 3,555 centenarians reported in the total population of all classes at the census of 1910, 2,675, or more than three-fourths were Negroes, the number of centenarians per 100,000 of all ages being for Negroes 27.2, and for whites 0.9." *Negro Population, 1790-1915,* p. 162. The proportion of centenarians reported for Negroes was inconsistent with the age distribution of the Negro population. *Ibid.*

[33] See Thompson and Whelpton, *op. cit.,* Table 20. Appendix, pp. 375-76.

tion of the Negro population in the age group 5 to 19 years declined nearly a third in the Northeast and nearly 50 per cent in the North Center from 1850 to 1930.[34] In fact, the small proportion (about 23 per cent) of Negroes in this age group in the North in 1930 as compared with the proportion (35.1 per cent) in the South can be explained only by the northward migrations during and following World War I. The northward migrations also explain a higher percentage of Negroes between the ages of 20 and 44 years in the Negro population of the North than of the South. In 1930 about a half of the Negro population of the North was within this age group as compared with 37 per cent in the South. Since 1850 there has been a larger percentage of Negroes 45 to 64 years of age in the Negro population of the North than the South.

The difference between the proportion of the Negro population under five years in larger cities and rural areas has been greater among Negroes than among whites.[35] In 1890 the proportion of the Negro population in this age group in rural communities was 14.5 per cent as compared with 7.3 per cent for cities with 500,000 population or over. At each census from 1890 to 1920 the proportion of Negroes under 5 years of age showed a decrease as the size of the community increased. But in 1930 the proportion under five was slightly higher in cities of 500,000 population and over than in communities with 100,000 to 500,000 population. In respect to the age group 45 to 64 years there has been little difference between the proportion in the cities and in rural areas. However, the relative size of the older age group, 65 years and over, decreased in urban communities and increased in rural areas during the decade, 1920 to 1930. The highest proportion of Negroes 65 years and over was not in the rural South but in the smallest cities and rural districts of the North Center. Area.[36]

[34] Northeast includes the New England and Middle Atlantic States; and the North Center the States in the East North Central and West North Central divisions. Thompson and Whelpton, *op. cit.*, note b, p. 340.

[35] *Ibid.*, pp. 155-59.　　[36] *Ibid.*, p. 159.

BLACK AND MULATTO ELEMENTS

During the 60-year period from 1850 to 1910, the proportion of mulattoes in the Negro population nearly doubled.[37] According to the census figures for 1850, about one Negro in nine was classified as a mulatto.[38] During the next 20 years there was very little increase in the proportion of mixed-bloods but by 1890, the proportion had increased to 15.2 per cent. There was an even greater increase in the proportion of mulattoes during the next 20 years. In 1910 one Negro out of five was classified as a mixed-blood, though in 1920 the proportion had declined to 15.9 per cent. The increase in the mulatto element up to 1910 was not owing solely or primarily to the continuous infusion of white blood, but largely to the intermarriage of blacks and mulattoes. In fact, it appears that in view of race relations in the South during the past fifty years, there has been less infusion of white blood than during the quarter of a century following emancipation.

Among mulattoes there has been a much smaller ratio of males to females than among blacks. In 1860 there were 90.9 males per 100 females among mulattoes as compared with 101 males per 100 females among blacks and in 1910 the sex ratio for mulattoes was 88.6 as against 101.8 for blacks.[39] One explanation for this difference has

[37] The census definition of a mulatto has not been the same at each census in which the classification has been used. "At the censuses of 1850 and 1860 the terms "black" and "mulatto" appear not to have been defined. In 1850 enumerators were instructed simply in enumerating colored persons to write "B" or "M" in the space on the schedule, to indicate black or mulatto, leaving the space blank in the case of whites. In 1860 no instructions are known to have been given to enumerators. No data are available in published reports for the census years 1880 and 1900." In 1870 the term "mulatto" was defined "to include quadroons, octoroons, and all persons having any perceptible trace of African blood." Instructions at the census of 1890, however, differed materially from those of 1910 and 1870. In 1890 the term "black" was defined to include all persons "having three-fourths or more 'black blood,'" other persons with any proportion of "black" blood being classified as "mulattoes," "quadroons," or "octoroons." According to the census of 1910, "the term "black" included all persons who are evidently full-blooded Negroes, while the term "mulatto" includes all other persons having some proportion or perceptible trace of Negro blood." Bureau of the Census, *Negro Population, 1790-1915*, p. 207. The enumerators were given practically the same instructions in 1920 as in 1910. *Fourteenth Census of the United States*, Vol. II, "Population," p. 16.

[38] The proportion of mulattoes was higher among the free Negroes than among the slaves. See pp. 67-68 above.

[39] Bureau of the Census, *Negro Population, 1790-1915*, p. 211.

TABLE VIII

Number and Percentage of Blacks and Mulattoes in the Negro Population
of the United States: 1850–1920 *

			Mulatto [1]	
YEAR	TOTAL	BLACK	NUMBER	PER CENT
1920	10,463,131	8,802,577	1,660,554	15.9
1910	9,827,763	7,777,077	2,050,686	20.9
1900	8,833,994	....	....	....
1890	7,488,676 [2]	6,337,980	1,132,060	15.2
1880	6,580,793	....	....	....
1870	4,880,009	4,295,960	584,049	12.0
1860	4,441,830	3,853,467	588,363	13.2
1850	3,638,808	3,233,057	405,057	11.2

* Source: *Negro Population, 1790-1915*, p. 208, for years 1850 to 1910; and
Fourteenth Census of the United States, Vol. II, Population, p. 35, for 1920.

[1] No data for 1880 or 1800.

[2] Includes 18,636 Negroes in Indian Territory, not distinguished as black or
mulatto.

been that the mulatto man has been more mobile than the woman
and has more frequently passed into the white race. At least the
mulatto man has tended to migrate from the South since the ratio
of males in the mulatto population of the North has been greater than
in the mulatto population of the South. In fact, the mulatto element
in the Negro population at the different censuses has been higher in
the North and the West than in the South. From 1850 to 1890,
the proportion of mulattoes in the Negro population of the North
was about twice as great as the proportion in the Negro population
of the South. However, since the opening of the present century the
proportion of mulattoes in the Negro population of the North has
declined and approximated what it is in the South. At the same time
the mulattoes have formed a larger proportion of the urban than of
the rural Negro population. In 1910 the mulattoes formed 27.2 per
cent of the urban and 18.5 per cent of the rural Negro population in
the country. Among the 96 cities in the country with a Negro population of 5,000 or more in 1910, there were 20 in the South, 7 in the
North, and 1 in the West in which mulattoes constituted a third or
more of the Negro population. After the mass migrations from the
South during World War I the proportion of mulattoes in north-

ern cities declined. For example, the percentage of mulattoes in the Negro population in Chicago declined from 41.6 in 1910 to 27.4 in 1920; and in New York City from 24.9 to 14.1 during the same period.[40] Although the decline in the proportion of mulattoes in the Negro population of these cities was primarily the result of the migration of the unmixed Negroes or Negroes of dark complexion from the South, the decline may have been affected by the "passing" of mulattoes for whites. It was during the decade, 1910 to 1920, that the proportion of mulattoes in the Negro population as a whole declined from 20.9 per cent to 15.9 per cent.

THE "BLACK BELT" OF THE SOUTH

Since 1860 a large proportion of the Negro population of the South has been concentrated in an area which includes "a group of counties in eastern Virginia and North Carolina; a belt of counties extending from the South Carolina coast through South Carolina, central Georgia, and Alabama; and a detached area embracing a portion of the lower Mississippi River Valley." [41] In the counties included in this area, which is known as the "Black Belt," the Negro population has constituted 50 per cent or more of the total population.[42] The number of counties included in the "Black Belt" declined during the present century from 286 in 1900 to 180 in 1940.[43] Up to 1900 the total Negro population of the "Black Belt" increased, but from 1900 to 1940 the Negro population declined from 4,057,619 to 2,642,808. Moreover, since 1880 the percentage of the Negro population of the South resident in the "Black Belt" has steadily declined. In 1880, the Negroes in the "Black Belt" constituted 57 per cent of the total Negro population of the South; 51.2 per cent in 1900; and 26.5 per cent in 1940.

The decline in the number of "Black Belt" counties and in the

[40] *Fourteenth Census of the United States.* Vol. II, "Population," p. 35.

[41] Bureau of the Census, *Negro Population, 1790-1915,* p. 125. See also Bureau of the Census, *Negroes in the United States: 1920-32,* p. 70.

[42] According to the Bureau of the Census, "This area of relatively high proportion Negro in the population corresponds generally with the area of relatively high density of Negro population, and it is the area popularly designated as the 'black belt.' " *Ibid.,* p. 125.

[43] Bureau of the Census, *Population—Special Reports,* Series P-45, No. 3, March 29, 1945.

Negro population of the "Black Belt" has been greater in some states than in others. There were three "Black Belt" counties in Maryland in 1880, but the number of counties declined to one by 1910 and such counties had disappeared by 1920. In Virginia the number of "Black Belt" counties decreased 50 per cent (36 to 18) between 1900 and 1940 while the Negro population decreased from 286,733 to 141,009. Among the South Atlantic states the greatest decline in the Negro population of "Black Belt" counties occurred in Georgia, where low farm incomes and boll weevil invasions have caused the rural population to leave the land. Though the number of such counties decreased only 34 per cent (67 to 46), the Negro population decreased from 708,765 to 350,991 or 51 per cent. However, it was in Florida where urbanization is proceeding at a more rapid rate than in any state in the South with the exception of Texas, that the relative decline in the Negro population of the "Black Belt" counties was greatest. From 1900 to 1940 the number of such counties declined from 12 to 3 and the Negro population from 134,784 to 41,616 or 69 per cent.

Of the three states in the East South Central division—Tennessee, Alabama, and Mississippi—only the first two states showed a decline in the total Negro population of the "Black Belt" counties between 1900 and 1930, the relative decline being greater in Tennessee than in Alabama. In 1900 there were only three "Black Belt" counties in Tennessee, with a total Negro population of only 39,543. During the same period the number of "Black Belt" counties in Alabama declined from 22 to 18 and the total Negro population from 505,576 to 389,068. In Mississippi the number of such counties decreased from 38 to 35 while the total Negro population of the 34 counties which were in the "Black Belt" in 1930 and 1940 increased from 690,416 to 729,713. Among the states in the West South Central division, which have had a much smaller total Negro population than the other southern divisions, Texas had the largest relative decline in the Negro population of its "Black Belt" counties. From 12 "Black Belt" counties in 1900, the number of such counties decreased to 3 in 1940, the total Negro population of these counties declining from 120,078 to 41,050. In Louisiana the number of "Black Belt" counties declined about 50 per cent (from 31 to 15) and the total population of such counties decreased about 52 per cent. Although the number of "Black Belt" counties in Arkansas decreased 40 per cent (from 15 to 9) during this period, the total Negro population showed a marked increase in 1910 and 1920, and in 1940 there were 193,308 Negroes in the 9 counties.

TABLE IX

Decrease in the Number of Counties and in the Total Negro Population of Counties With Populations 50 Per Cent or More Negro in the South and By Divisions: 1910–1940 *

State	1940	1930	1920	1910	1900
THE SOUTH					
POPULATION	2,642,808	2,738,432	3,251,440	3,932,484	4,057,619
NO. COUNTIES	180	191	221	264	286
Alabama	18	18	18	21	22
Arkansas	9	9	11	14	15
Florida	3	4	5	10	12
Georgia	46	48	58	66	67
Louisiana	15	16	22	25	31
Maryland	. .	. .	. .	1	2
Mississippi	35	35	34	38	38
North Carolina	9	9	12	14	18
South Carolina	22	25	32	33	30
Tennessee	2	2	2	2	3
Texas	3	4	4	8	12
Virginia	18	21	23	32	36

* Bureau of the Census, *Population—Special Reports*. Series P-45, No. 3.

The decrease in the number and in the total Negro population of the "Black Belt" counties was the result partly of migration from the "Black Belt" to counties with smaller proportions of Negroes in their population.[44] This movement has brought about greater diffusion of the Negro population of some states than of others. For example, between 1910 and 1930 the proportion of the Negro population of Virginia increased in all classes of counties in which the Negro population amounted to less than 50 per cent. In North Carolina during this period the increase in the proportion of Negroes of the state resident in counties 12.5 to 24.9 per cent Negro was much more marked than in counties with larger or smaller percentages of Negroes. The

[44] The census classifies such counties as follows: less than 12.5 per cent; 12.5 to 24.9 per cent; and 25 to 49.9 per cent Negro.

movement of Negroes in Florida was similar to that in North Carolina. But in Georgia and in Louisiana the proportion of the Negro population resident in counties with from 25 to 49.9 per cent Negro increased more than in counties with smaller percentages of Negroes. On the other hand, in Tennessee and in Texas the proportion of the Negro population resident in counties 25 to 49.9 per cent Negro declined along with the proportion in their "Black Belt" counties. The total result of these changes has been the diffusion of the Negro population in the rural South.

URBANIZATION OF THE NEGRO POPULATION

When the first census was taken in 1790, Negroes were found in considerable numbers in the four large cities of the country. In New York City and Baltimore they constituted more than 10 per cent of the population, and in Philadelphia and Boston their relative numbers were about half as great.[45] During the period of slavery, as we have seen, the free Negroes were concentrated in urban areas.[46] After Emancipation Negroes migrated in large numbers to the cities of the North as well as the South. Between 1860 and 1870 the Negro population increased 90.7 per cent in fourteen southern cities as compared with an increase of 16.7 per cent of the white population in these same cities.[47] During this period the Negro population of eight Northern cities increased 51 per cent. The cityward movement of Negroes during the next two decades continued but slowed down. In 1890 four out of five Negroes still lived in rural areas. Those who had moved from rural areas had gone principally to southern cities. As late as 1910, nearly seven-tenths (69.0 per cent) of the urban Negro population was in the South.[48] The movement to southern cities was in response to the demand for labor created by railroad building and growing industrial and commercial enterprise in the South.

[45] Bureau of the Census, *A Century of Population Growth*, p. 84. The percentages for the four largest cities were as follows: New York, 10.1; Philadelphia, 5.7; Boston, 4.2; and Baltimore, 11.7. [46] See pp. 66-67 above.

[47] George E. Haynes, "Conditions Among Negroes in the Cities," in *The Negro's Progress in Fifty Years*, p. 106.

[48] The majority of the Negroes in the North have always been concentrated in urban areas. The proportion of the Negroes of the North in urban areas increased from 76.9 in 1910 to 89.4 in 1940.

The urbanization of the Negro population during the present century has followed a similar trend in the white population and has been influenced largely by the same social and economic factors. From 1900 to 1940 the proportion of whites living in urban areas increased from 43 per cent to 57.8 per cent. During this same period the proportion of the Negro population resident in urban areas increased from 22.7 per cent to 48.2 per cent. Between 1900 and 1930, about two and a quarter million Negroes left the farms and small villages of the South for the cities.[49] According to Ross, "During the first decade of the present century the volume was somewhat over a third of a million, during the second decade nearly three-quarters of a million, and between 1920 and 1930 nearly one and one-quarter million." [50] During these thirty years, the rural Negro population in the South decreased 262,921 while the urban Negro population in the country increased by 3,191,905. A million rural Negroes moved from rural areas into 78 southern cities with a population of 25,000 and over and into 773 towns and cities with populations ranging from 2,500 to 25,000.[51] The movement of Negroes to southern cities was inconspicuous, while the mass migrations to northern cities during the War period were replete with dramatic incidents and were directed to a few cities— New York, Chicago, Philadelphia, and Detroit. During the decade from 1910 to 1920 the total Negro population of these four cities increased by nearly three-quarters of a million.

Of the 14 southern cities having 25,000 or more Negroes in 1920, Norfolk had the largest increase in its Negro population between 1910 and 1920. Because of the great demand for labor in its shipyards, the Negro population of Norfolk increased from 25,039 in 1910 to 43,392 in 1920 or 73.7 per cent. The Negro population of Houston, Texas, and Jacksonville, Florida, increased over 40 per cent and that of Birmingham, Alabama, about a third during this decade. On the other hand, of the 10 northern cities with 25,000 or more Negroes in 1920, all except Pittsburgh and Kansas City, Missouri, showed an increase of over 50 per cent in their Negro population between 1910 and

[49] Frank A. Ross, "Urbanization and the Negro," *Publication of the American Sociological Society*, Vol. XXVI, p. 118.
[50] *Ibid.*, p. 118.   [51] Ross, *Urbanization and the Negro*, p. 12.

1920.[52] The greatest relative increase in the Negro population occurred in Detroit where the number of Negroes increased from 5,741 in 1910 to 40,838 in 1920, or 611.3 per cent. Cleveland came next with an increase from 8,448 to 34,451 Negroes, or 307.8 per cent. The Negro population of Chicago increased from 44,103 in 1910 to 109,-458 in 1920, or 148.2 per cent; while the number of Negroes in Indianapolis, who were half as numerous as those in Chicago in 1910 increased 59 per cent. Philadelphia, one of the three northern cities with 100,000 and more Negroes in 1920, showed an increase of 58.9 per cent in its Negro population. There were other northern cities with very small Negro populations that showed a much higher relative increase in the number of Negroes. For example, Gary with only 383 Negroes in 1910, had 5,299 Negroes in 1920, an increase of 1,283.6 per cent. Likewise, in Akron, Ohio, the Negro population of only 657 in 1910 increased to 5,580 in 1920 or 749.3 per cent.

The movement of southern Negroes to northern urban centers between 1910 and 1920 differed fundamentally from earlier northward migrations. During previous migrations Negroes had moved from the border states into the North. The difference between the two movements is summarized by J. A. Hill, of the United States Census Bureau, as follows:

Even as recently as 1910, 48 per cent, or nearly one-half, of the southern-born Negroes living in northern States came from two States—Virginia and Kentucky. The migration between 1910 and 1920 reduced the proportion born in these two States to 31.6 per cent. On the other hand, the proportion of northern Negroes coming from the States farther south, or from what we may term the cotton-belt States, including in this class South Carolina, Georgia, Florida, Alabama, Mississippi, Arkansas, Louisiana, and Texas, increased from 18.2 per cent of the total number of southern-born Negroes living in the North in 1910 to 40.5 per cent of the total in 1920. The absolute number of Negroes in the North who were natives of these States increased from 75,517 in 1910 to 298,739 in 1920, so that there were nearly four times as many in 1920 as there were in 1910.[53]

[52] In Pittsburgh and Kansas City, Mo., the increases were 47.2 per cent and 30.4 per cent respectively.
[53] Quoted in Louise V. Kennedy, *The Negro Peasant Turns Cityward* (New York, 1930), p. 30.

On the basis of special census tabulations for cities, Ross was able to discover five distinct types of Negro population origins:

(1) widespread drawings to many of the larger and more northerly of the northern cities, as exemplified by Chicago; (2) accretions to certain northern Atlantic coast cities almost exclusively from southern states on the Atlantic Seaboard as in Baltimore; (3) strictly local increases in most of the cities of the deep South, as demonstrated by Atlanta; (4) acquisitions from the Mississippi Basin by cities of the middle western, border and lower tier states, for example St. Louis; (5) increments to far western cities from East South Central and more strikingly West South Central states, as found in Los Angeles.[54]

Although the northward migration of Negroes was influenced by social factors, the basic cause was undoubtedly economic.[55] During and following the War there was a great demand for unskilled labor to fill the gap created when immigrants returned to Europe and immigration from Europe ceased. At the same time economic conditions in the South growing out of the tenancy system tended to "push" the Negro out of the South. During 1915 and 1916, crop failures, floods, and the ravages of the boll weevil resulted in the widespread disorganization of the plantation economy. In a study which was designed to measure the relative strength of the "pull" of northern industries and the "push" of southern agriculture, Lewis concluded that the "pull" of the North was primarily responsible for the migrations.[56]

During the industrial depression of 1920, the northward migrations slowed up, but when industrial activities in the North increased in 1922 the northward migrations were resumed. According to a press release of the United States Department of Labor on October 24, 1923, nearly half a million Negro migrants left the 13 southern states during the twelvemonth period ending August 31, 1923.[57] The effect of these movements was seen in the growth of the Negro population in northern cities. Between 1920 and 1930 the Negro population in New York City and in Chicago increased 114 per cent while in Detroit

[54] Ross, *op. cit.*, p. 124.
[55] Kennedy, *op. cit.*, pp. 41-57 for a systematic analysis of the causes of the mass migration of Negroes to northern cities.
[56] See Edward E. Lewis, *The Mobility of the Negro* (New York, 1931), pp. 129-33.   [57] Quoted in Kennedy, *op. cit.*, p. 35.

the increase amounted to 194 per cent.[58] During the same period the Negro population of Cleveland increased 108.7 per cent; that of Gary 238.2 per cent; and that of Buffalo, New York, 200.7 per cent. The Negro population of Los Angeles, the only city in the West with 10,000 or more Negroes in 1920, increased 105 per cent between 1910 and 1920 and 149.7 per cent between 1920 and 1930. Even during the depression years, 1930 to 1940, the cityward movement of Negroes continued, though at a slower rate. The Negro population of New York City increased 40 per cent; that of Detroit 24 per cent; and that of Chicago only 19 per cent. On the other hand, the Negro population of the District of Columbia increased 42 per cent; that of Miami, Florida, 47 per cent; and that of Houston, Texas, 36 per cent.

From federal census data we are able to secure information on the volume and the direction of Negro migration during the years 1935 to 1940.[59] In 1940, 1,141,920 nonwhite persons in the United States had migrated from the county in which they were living in 1935. The vast majority, 808,833, or about 70 per cent, of the nonwhite migrants were resident in the South in 1940. In fact, most of the nonwhite or Negro migrants in the South had moved about in the state of their residence in 1935 or had moved to other southern states.[60] There were more men than women among the Negro migrants who had remained in southern states. On the other hand, women predominated among the 253,083 nonwhite migrants who were living in the North in 1940. About nine-tenths of these nonwhite migrants living in the North had come from southern states. As the result of interregional migration the South lost 106,610 Negroes and 165,701 whites. All of the southern states with the exception of West Virginia showed a net loss in Negro population, the greatest loss—30,801—being in the state of Georgia. In the South as a whole the greatest net loss of Negro population was in the rural-farm regions, though the migration of

[58] See Bureau of the Census, *Negroes in the United States, 1920-32*, p. 55.

[59] *Sixteenth Census of the United States: 1940. Population.* "Internal Migration, 1935 to 1940." Color and Sex of Migrants. Washington, 1943.

[60] See Preston Valien, "Southern Negro Internal Migration, 1935 to 1940." Unpublished paper presented to the Fourth Annual Conference of the Negro Land Grant Colleges Cooperative Social Studies Project. Howard University. Washington, D. C., May 7, 1948. The discussion here is based partly upon this paper.

Negroes from the South had been principally from southern cities to the large urban areas of the North.[61]

As the result of the growth of the centers of defense industries prior to and during World War II, there was an increase in the migration of Negroes from the state of their residence in 1940. Between 1940 and 1947, 1,187,000 Negroes moved from the state of their residence in 1940 to a nonadjacent state. A large proportion of the migrants from the South took a westward direction for the first time. It is estimated that 250,000 Negroes migrated to the cities on the Pacific Coast where defense industries were located.

The urbanization of the Negro population during the past four decades is another instance of the fact that its growth and distribution in the country has been determined by economic and social forces in the growth of the nation. By 1930 there were some Negroes in 2,855 of the 3,100 counties in the country. There were no Negroes in only 20 of the 1,415 counties of the South; whereas no Negroes were found in 156 of the 1,274 counties of the North; and none in 69 of the 411 counties of the West. But over one-half of the counties of the North with Negroes and three-fourths of such counties in the West had less than 100 Negroes; whereas about 70 per cent of the counties in the South had 1,000 or more Negroes. Thus during its growth the Negro population has become concentrated on the whole in those areas where there has been a demand for the type of labor which Negroes have been able to supply. Originally, they were concentrated in the South because a commercial system of agriculture without machinery required a large supply of cheap unskilled labor. When Emancipation came, Negroes were still held to the plantation South because it provided them the chief means of subsistence in a competitive society. Toward the end of the last century Negroes began to move in small numbers into numerous towns and cities in the South. But when, during and following World War I, a demand for unskilled workers was created in the heavy industries of the North, large numbers were drawn into the urban areas of that section. As the result of

[61] Since about 70 per cent of the 80,000 nonwhite migrants, the majority of whom were males, resident in the West in 1940 were from the South, Negroes comprised the majority of these migrants.

mass migrations to the North, large urban Negro communities have grown up in the North, with an aggregate population equal to about half of the rural Negro farm population. These urban communities and those in the South and in the West continued to grow during World War II. In the following two chapters, we shall consider the economic and social organization of both the rural and urban Negro communities and their relation to the larger white communities of which they are a part.

CHAPTER X

Rural Negro Communities

RURAL NEGRO SETTLEMENTS IN THE NORTH

ONLY a small proportion of the Negro population in the United States has ever been located in the rural areas of the North. In 1940 there were less than 300,000 Negroes in the rural areas of this section and they constituted only 10 per cent of the entire Negro population there.[1] The rural Negro population has always consisted of widely scattered individuals and small groups in the various northern states.[2] The larger concentrations of rural Negroes have generally represented communities formed by related family groups. Some of the communities concerning which we have information grew out of free mulatto families or groups of ex-slaves who attempted to establish themselves in an environment of free men. There were also rural communities that were indigenous to the North, having developed out of mulatto families that were bound together in a clan organization through kinship ties and intermarriage. The oldest and best known community of this type was the Gouldtown settlement near Bridgeton, New Jersey, concerning which there is a well-documented record.[3] This community originated in what remains of the original settlement during the latter half of the seventeenth century. The

[1] From 1890 to 1920 the rural Negro population of the North decreased from 267,685 to 221,997, but increased to 294,556 in 1940. In the West the rural Negro population was only 28,873 in 1940.

[2] For example, in New York State in 1940 there were 3,835 Negroes in rural-farm areas and 27,699 in rural-nonfarm areas. In 46 of the 62 counties the rural-farm Negro population numbered less than 50 and in only 7 counties did it exceed 100.

[3] William and Theophilus G. Steward, *Gouldtown: A Very Remarkable Settlement of Ancient Date* (Philadelphia, 1913).

original settlers were three families growing out of the marriage of Negro men and white and Indian women. Another such community is located in the Ramapo Hills about thirty miles north of New York City.[4] This rural settlement grew out of mulatto families of Boer, English, Indian, and Negro ancestry. A similar but more prosperous community of southern origin is located in Darke County, Ohio, where free Negroes of white, Indian, and Negro ancestry settled around 1800.[5] In Cass County, Michigan, a Negro rural community grew out of a group of ex-slaves who were liberated and brought there by their Virginia master in 1847.[6] Later free Negroes from Ohio, Indiana, and Illinois swelled the population of the settlement to 1,368 in 1860, of whom 981 were mulattoes. These settlements are representative of the more prosperous Negro rural communities of the North which were able to survive and maintain a standard of living comparable to their white neighbors.[7] They have all been affected by the movement of Negroes to cities. The Gouldtown settlement, which has been especially prolific in the number of leaders which it has furnished the Negro group, has all but disappeared.

THE RURAL NEGRO POPULATION AND SOUTHERN REGIONS

Contrary to popular notions, the South of the present day, as the South of the ante-bellum period, is neither a geographic nor a cultural unit.[8] From a physiographic standpoint the South may be divided into seven regions, though each of these regions exhibits some diversity with reference to soil and topography. Although the mode of life of the inhabitants in each of these seven physiographic regions exhibits some characteristic features, physiographic differences have

[4] See E. Franklin Frazier, *The Negro Family in the United States* (Chicago, 1939), pp. 226-29.   [5] *Ibid.*, pp. 221-26.

[6] James D. Corruthers, *In Spite of Handicaps: An Autobiography* (New York, 1916), pp. 17-18.

[7] Huntington has attributed the higher efficiency and greater productivity of northern Negro farmers as compared with southern Negro farmers to the climate of the North. See Ellsworth Huntington, *Civilization and Climate* (New Haven, 1924), pp. 37ff. But it appears that in addition to the difference in the economic organization of farming in the North, the northern Negro farmer has a cultural heritage which would account for his higher efficiency.

[8] Rupert B. Vance, *Human Geography of the South* (Chapel Hill, 1935), p. 23.

less significance for the various economic and social cultures of the South than soil and crop belts. During the first decade of the present century, before the advent of the boll weevil, the distribution of Negroes, of the plantation system, and of cotton culture were closely associated with fertile soils.[9] The boundaries of the area of cotton culture have been determined by temperature and rainfall.

The Cotton Belt, one of the most highly specialized agricultural regions in the world, consists of many sub-regions, but is bound by temperature and rainfall. On the north it follows the summer average temperature of 77 degrees; on the south the belt has its bounds set along the Gulf and Atlantic Coast by an average rainfall limit of over 10 inches during the autumn. Beyond the northern temperature boundary the growing season is too short; below the southern limits the picking season is likely to be ruined by rains. Cotton production is found throughout the southern states extending from eastern North Carolina to Western Texas. The Belt is 1,600 miles long and varies from 125 to 500 miles in width, the average width being 300 miles. In an area of 295,000,000 acres, less than 3 per cent of the world's land area, is grown about 55 per cent of the world's cotton.[10]

In 1910 when 78.8 per cent of the Negroes in the South lived in the rural areas, the majority of them were in the Cotton Belt. However, as the Cotton Belt has moved westward into Texas and Oklahoma and the cotton production areas in the Southeast have been abandoned, the Negro has not followed the movement to any great extent.[11] The concentration of Negroes in the "Black Belt" counties, as we have seen, has decreased and the Negro population has become more evenly distributed over the South. This has not resulted in the distribution of Negroes in areas where there were no Negroes, but in an increase in the number of Negroes in counties with relatively few Negroes.[12]

Because of the widespread distribution of the Negro population in the South, rural Negro communities vary according to their location

[9] *Ibid.*, p. 99.

[10] Reprinted from *Human Geography of the South* by Rupert B. Vance, p. 185, by permission of The University of North Carolina Press. Copyright, 1929, by The University of North Carolina Press.

[11] See Robert B. Vance, *All the People* (Chapel Hill, 1945), p. 236.

[12] See Monroe N. Work, "Racial Factors and Economic Forces in Land Tenure in the South," *Social Forces*, Vol. XV, pp. 205-15.

in certain cultural regions which are closely identified with the soil and crop belts in the South.

RURAL-CULTURAL REGIONS OF THE COTTON BELT

On the basis of a recent division of the country into rural cultural regions, the Cotton Belt embraces three such regions: the Eastern Old South, the Mississippi Delta, and the Western Old South.[13] (See Map VII) The Eastern Old South Region (Region 7 on the map) consists of

The vast region stretching from southern Virginia through the Piedmont upland and coastal plains of the Carolinas, Georgia, Alabama, Mississippi, and southwestern Tennessee to the Mississippi Delta, together with five Florida counties and three Louisiana counties. . . . Cotton farms are the major agricultural type throughout most of the region, but the tobacco areas of Georgia, North Carolina, and Virginia, the peanut area of Virginia and North Carolina, fruit areas of Georgia, and a truck area in Copiah County, Miss., are also included.[14]

The population of the region is about 75 per cent rural, Atlanta and Birmingham being the only large urban centers of population. This region ranked near the bottom of all rural farm regions in respect to plane of living, capital, farm land value, and percentage of foreign born. It ranked near the top in respect to percentage of farms with low income, farm tenancy, and ratio of children to women. Of the

---

[13] A. R. Mangus, *Rural Regions of the United States* (Washington, 1940). The system of regionalism used in this work divides the country into 32 rural-farm regions and 34 rural cultural regions. The first system of classification was used for considering farm characteristics alone and the second for considering rural nonfarm characteristics, where "the nonfarm population is dependent on agriculture" and for regions in which the nonfarm population is "suburban or dependent on particular rural industries." (*Ibid.*, p. 3.) "The general boundaries of these 34 regions follow closely those of the 32 rural-farm regions with few exceptions." (*Ibid.*, p. 4.) The Mississippi Delta and the Western Old South were two of the six rural-farm cultural regions which remained practically the same as the rural cultural regions. (*Ibid.*, p. 88.) The West Old South as a rural cultural region is the same as the rural-farm region of the same name with the exception of minor changes in boundaries involving two counties. (*Ibid.*, p. 59.) The descriptions of the rural cultural regions in our discussion are concerned primarily with the rural-farm population; however, where the boundaries of the rural cultural regions are markedly different from those of the rural-farm cultural regions, the difference will be noted.   [14] *Ibid.*, p. 21.

eleven and one-half million inhabitants in this region in 1930, more than six million comprised the farm population or 21 per cent of the farm population in the United States. The 2,650,740 Negroes in the rural-farm population constituted 42.5 per cent of the total in the region and 57 per cent of the entire rural farm Negro population in the United States.

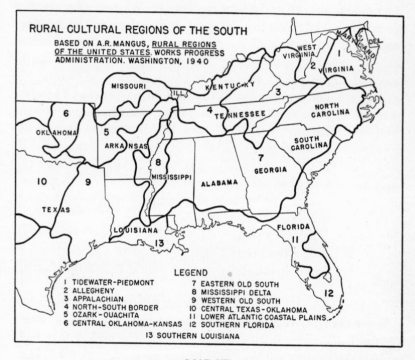

RURAL CULTURAL REGIONS OF THE SOUTH

BASED ON A.R. MANGUS, <u>RURAL REGIONS</u>
<u>OF THE UNITED STATES</u>. WORKS PROGRESS
ADMINISTRATION. WASHINGTON, 1940

LEGEND

1 TIDEWATER-PIEDMONT	7 EASTERN OLD SOUTH
2 ALLEGHENY	8 MISSISSIPPI DELTA
3 APPALACHIAN	9 WESTERN OLD SOUTH
4 NORTH-SOUTH BORDER	10 CENTRAL TEXAS-OKLAHOMA
5 OZARK-OUACHITA	11 LOWER ATLANTIC COASTAL PLAINS
6 CENTRAL OKLAHOMA-KANSAS	12 SOUTHERN FLORIDA
13 SOUTHERN LOUISIANA	

MAP VII

"The Mississippi Delta Region (Region 8 on the map) includes those counties in Mississippi, Arkansas, and Louisiana located in the bottom lands of the Mississippi River and Shelby County, Tenn." [15] In this region in 1930 there were over one and a third million people, nearly three-fourths of whom were Negroes. Although 30.9 per cent

[15] *Ibid.*, p. 22. The facts given here are concerning the rural-farm cultural region which coincides with the rural cultural region. For cultural indices in the 32 rural farm regions, see *ibid.*, pp. 37-38.

of the people of this region live in urban areas, more than a half of them being in Memphis, Tennessee, it is the most thickly settled rural-farm region in the United States. The rural population is engaged almost entirely in cotton production, from which it derives nearly all of its income. Though there are only 33 counties in this region, they produced 21 per cent of the country's cotton in 1939. But since 86 per cent of the farm operators in 1935 were croppers, the plane of living was lower than in any other major region. Unlike other regions with a low plane of living, this region has a low ratio of children to women of childbearing age because of high infant death rates and the emigration of persons in the productive age groups.

The third rural region in the Cotton Belt is the Western Old South (Region 9 on the map), which lies "within the Mississippi alluvial plain bordering on the Delta Region in Arkansas, Missouri, and Louisiana and within the Gulf Plain in eastern Texas, Arkansas, and Louisiana." [16] In 1930 over a million persons in this area lived in urban areas, a third of whom were in two cities, Little Rock, Arkansas, and Houston, Texas. The residents in urban areas together with those in the nonfarming rural areas constituted about a half of the nearly four million inhabitants in the region. Of the nearly two million persons on farms, a third were Negroes. The plane of living among the farm population in this region was the same as that in the Eastern Old South.

The rural-farm regions within the Cotton Belt are dominated today as before the Civil War by the plantation system of agriculture. During the half-century from 1860 to 1910 the plantations that had existed prior to the Civil War were broken up to some extent.[17] The

---

[16] *Ibid.*, p. 24. "The region extends from the southeastern Missouri boot heel just north of the Delta Region southward and eastward along a central axis through Little Rock and Houston to the Gulf of Mexico. Its eastern boundary is the Mississippi Delta Region; its western boundary is the Ozark-Ouachita Region and the Black Prairie in Texas; and its southern boundary is the southern Louisiana sugar and rice area and the Texas coast."

[17] Between 1860 and 1910 the average number of acres of land per farm in the South declined from 335.4 to 114.4 as compared with an increase of from 126.4 to 143 acres in the North. These statistical averages were obtained by counting each tenant farm in the South as a unit, whereas a plantation comprises a number of farms operated by tenants. See Bureau of the Census *Plantation Farming in the United States* (Washington, 1916), pp. 8-11.

division of the large plantations had resulted not only from the ravages of the Civil War but also from the fall in cotton prices after 1871.[18] However, the trend toward landownership by small farmers was checked by economic forces inherent in cotton production. The rising middle class—comprised of merchants, lawyers, and doctors— in the South, stepped into the place of landlord and "bought plantations as speculative investments." [19] Thus farming became, as Vance has pointed out, "a financial instead of an agricultural interest" and landlords living in towns required tenants to raise cotton, the money crop, instead of food stuffs.[20] Cotton became a "tenant crop," and "supervision," which was the outstanding feature of the plantation system under slavery, has continued to the present day.[21]

In 1910 the average size of a plantation was 724 acres and 68 per cent of the plantations had from five to nine tenants.[22] A study of southern plantations indicates that they are becoming larger units and that the increase in size has coincided with an increase in the area devoted to crops.[23] For the 246 plantations studied, the total average acreage increased from 955 to 1,014, while the average crop acreage increased from 417 to 477.[24] Although other crops, especially corn, are planted on practically all the plantations, cotton is planted on a half and in individual cases as much as four-fifths of the acreage of the plantations.[25] Because of the primary importance of cotton as a cash crop, landownership is concentrated, and the types of manage-

[18] Rupert B. Vance, *Human Factors in Cotton Culture* (Chapel Hill, 1929), pp. 60-63.

[19] *Ibid.*, p. 65. In order to compare the situation in the southern States in this respect with that in Russia after the emancipation of the serfs in 1861, one may consult Stepniak, *The Russian Peasantry* (London, 1905), pp. 54-78.

[20] Vance, *Human Factors in Cotton Culture*, p. 65.

[21] As defined by the Census Bureau, "A tenant plantation is a continuous tract of land of considerable area under the general supervision or control of a single individual or firm, all or a part of such tract being divided into at least five smaller tracts, which are leased to tenants." Bureau of the Census, *Plantation Farming in the United States*, p. 13.

[22] Bureau of the Census, *Plantation Farming in the United States*, pp. 19-20.

[23] See William C. Holley, Ellen Winston, T. J. Woofter, *The Plantation South: 1934-1937* (Washington, 1940), p. 3 for a study of changes in 246 plantations. Although the areas used in this study do not coincide with those used in *Rural Regions of the United States*, data from the study by Holley, *et al.*, may be utilized in our discussion.

[24] Holley, *et al.*, *The Plantation South: 1934-1937*, p. 2.   [25] *Ibid.*, p. 5.

ment reflect the various types of ownership. On the basis of management, the plantations in the Cotton Belt fall into three classes:

the small plantation, managed by the landlord who lives on it and directs to some extent the work; the large plantation, owned by a well-to-do capitalist or possibly a corporation and run by a managerial staff; and the plantation bought as a speculation by one engaged in another business who attempts to operate it as an absentee landlord. The management of a plantation owned by a corporation is likely to be most efficient; the smaller plantation on which the landlord lives usually possesses a well-developed social system as well as economic organization. The plantation bought as a speculative venture and owned by an absentee landlord is likely to be least efficiently managed and to offer its tenants a lower economic status.[26]

PHYSICAL CHARACTER OF NEGRO COMMUNITIES IN PLANTATION AREA

The general spatial pattern of the rural Negro communities in the Cotton Belt has been determined by the plantation organization. Following the Civil War and Emancipation, the attempt to keep the Negroes in the slave quarters and to organize black laborers into gangs proved unsuccessful.[27] Consequently, the land was divided among Negro families and the work animals were sold to the Negroes, upon whom responsibility was placed for their care. Part of the plantation was generally set apart for a school and a church. In rare instances today the cabins on a large plantation are clustered in a manner to provide easy access to the cotton fields. But generally, as the result of the division of the plantations into small units formed by family groups, the cabins are scattered in the open country so that the development of village communities has been impossible. Consequently, communication between rural families as well as the development of rural institutions has been limited by the wide dispersion of the population.

[26] Reprinted from *Human Factors in Cotton Culture* by Rupert B. Vance, p. 71, by permission of The University of North Carolina Press. Copyright, 1929, by The University of North Carolina Press.

[27] See David C. Barrow, "A Georgia Plantation," *Scribner's Monthly*, XXI (April, 1881), pp. 830-36; and Ulrich Bonnell Phillips and J. D. Glunt (Eds.), *Florida Plantation Records from the Papers of George Noble Jones* (St. Louis, 1927), p. 193.

From a physical standpoint the rural Negro communities in the Cotton Belt are characterized, as the region in general, by the poor housing facilities.

The observing traveler in the deep South is rudely shocked when he sees for the first time the widespread evidences of rural poverty revealed by farm homes. Houses, of poor construction to begin with, seldom are repaired either by the landlord or the occupant. Roofs and walls that need repairs, inadequate lighting, overcrowding, lack of other than primitive sanitary facilities, and bare yards edged by cotton fields are characteristic. A painted house is often indicative of considerable social as well as economic standing.[28]

According to a survey made in 1934, from 95 to 98 per cent of the farm houses in the seven states of the southeastern Cotton Belt were frame buildings, over two-thirds of which were from 25 to 49 years old.[29] In North Carolina and Arkansas 59.3 and 68.4 per cent, respectively, of the farm houses were unpainted, while in the remaining five states three-fourths to four-fifths of the houses were in this condition. The run-down condition of these houses is indicated by the fact that the foundations, exterior walls, and roofs of from a third to a half of them were in poor condition.[30]

In his survey of 612 families in Macon County, Alabama, Johnson has presented an excellent picture of a typical Negro house in the Cotton Belt:

The home of the Jenifers is set in the midst of a new stretch of cotton beyond the trees, and once there, no other dwelling is visible. Around the dwelling is a cleared space packed hard and yellow. On the left, and beginning a few feet from the house, is an inclosed area about the size of a bedroom. It is the family garden, and into it has been crowded a patch of cabbage, greens, and onions which the family has attempted to shield from marauding animals and the younger children by a fence randomly constructed of sticks, tin advertising signs, tar paper, and stray bits of canvas. The house itself is constructed of upright boards about a foot wide with thin strips down the seams to keep out the weather. It is set rather precariously about a foot from the ground upon four uprights of rocks placed one upon the other

[28] Holley, *et al.*, *op. cit.*, p. 58.
[29] Bureau of Home Economics, *The Farm Housing Survey* (Washington, 1939), pp. 4-5.   [30] *Ibid.*, pp. 22-44.

and held plumb by the weight of the house alone. On first sight it gives the appearance of two single-room cabins set close together and joined by a roof. The passageway, however, has a rough flooring like the two inclosed rooms, and this passageway is called the "dog-run." The soft wood of the floor has been worn into smooth and grimy ruts, testifying to the habits of the family.

The dog-run is an important part of the house. It is the sitting-out place, and in summer, especially, it is the meeting place for the family. They rest, eat, doze, and gossip there. Two benches fashioned after a simple pattern are planted against the wall. On the end of one of these is a battered wooden water pail covered over with a damp cloth. A pair of overalls and a man's hat, both frayed and dusted white with earth, hang from a nail support. A tub and washing stick, a pair of men's heavy shoes, a rusty water-dipper, and pieces of firewood also find a place in this areaway. From the front of the house there is a sweep which permits a view of the family well at the rear with its box-shaped covering, its sagging and insecure sides, its top open and exposed to sundry deposits.

Doorways lead off the dog-run into the two rooms. In one of these rooms, where Father and Mother Jenifer sleep, there is a large bed with a double mattress, one of shucks, the other of feathers, and they are covered over with a quilt patched laboriously from an indeterminate variety of cloth scraps into an intricate pattern of squares. They call it, modestly, a "crazy quilt." The bed is the outstanding piece of furniture. Besides this article there is a wooden box spread over with a newspaper, a rocking chair, and a small table on which stands a kerosene lamp with a broken chimney. Some pride of home has gone into the effort to select newspapers with colored pictures for the wall covering and to keep it reasonably fresh. There are no glass windows. For light and air a board window is pushed open. But this can be done comfortably only in spring and summer, and at other times the family contents itself with light from the open fireplace, where, incidentally, the cooking is also done. On any day when the window and door are closed, sharp slices of light, from the sides of the house and from the roof, spatter the room with shadows. When it rains or the winds blow cold, these interstices bring a great deal of inescapable discomfort.[31]

[31] *Shadow of the Plantation* by Charles S. Johnson, pp. 91-92. Copyright 1934 by the University of Chicago Press. Concerning the housing of Negroes in two Black Belt counties in Georgia, Raper writes as follows: "In both counties the sturdy, stolid log cabins which once stood behind the big house have been replaced by small frame houses of the "shot gun" type, which rest on stones or blocks furnishing a sheltered place for perhaps a hound or two, couple of bony porkers, a half-

The "dreary monotony of weatherworn cabins" is broken, as Johnson points out, by the better homes of owners, who are not numerous in the Cotton Belt.[32]

LAND TENURE AMONG NEGRO FARMERS

The number of Negro farm owners in the South gradually increased until 1910 when they owned 24.5 per cent of the farms operated by Negroes. But during the following 20 years tenancy among Negroes as among whites steadily decreased until by 1930 only one out of five Negro farmers in the South was an owner.[33] In 1929 Negro owners

---

dozen chickens. As a rule, the difference in appearance of long-residence and short-residence tenant dwelling is due not to differences in the houses but in upkeep. Tenants who move every year or so, whether white or black, seldom take much interest in the appearance of their dwellings. . . . Taking the two counties as a whole, the rural dwellings have an average of between three and four rooms; the white owners have the largest houses and the croppers and wage hands, irrespective of race, live in the fewest rooms. There are exceptions, particularly in the abandoned plantation areas of Greene, where a Negro or white tenant now lives in the house formerly occupied by a plantation owner. As a general rule, the tenant family uses only two or three rooms on the first floor. In several instances the upstairs windows are gone and rough pine boards have been nailed over them to keep out the rain. Sometimes the unused parts of these houses are entirely neglected. . . . The vast majority of the houses occupied by tenants fall in one of three distinct classes: houses built by landlords for tenants, with two or three rooms; houses built by small owners for themselves, with three to five rooms; houses built by planters for themselves, with a half-dozen or more rooms. With an average of nearly six persons to the tenant family, the overcrowding in the typical tenant house is evident. It is not unusual to find a family of ten living in two or three rooms. In most tenant houses the kitchen is also the dining-room, while the living-room is the bedroom for the parents and the smaller children. The kitchen may serve not only as dining-room for the entire family, but as a bedroom for two or three of the older children." Reprinted from *Preface to Peasantry* by Arthur F. Raper, pp. 61-63, by permission of The University of North Carolina Press. Copyright, 1936, by The University of North Carolina Press.

[32] In an analysis of socioeconomic indices of 1104 southern counties, Johnson found that in 155 or 28.1 per cent of the 551 "cotton counties," Negroes comprised 50 per cent or more of the population and that there was a statistical correlation of +.50 between the percentage of the population of the counties that was Negro and the percentage of farm operators who were tenants. Charles S. Johnson *et al., Statistical Atlas of Southern Counties* (Chapel Hill, 1941), pp. 13-14.

[33] Likewise in the North and West, where the rate of farm ownership has been higher among Negroes, the proportion of owners declined from 62.2 per cent to 39.8 per cent in the North and from 80.3 per cent to 57 per cent in the West. See Bureau of the Census, *Negroes in the United States: 1920-32,* p. 577.

of farms produced only 3.8 per cent of the cotton in the South, whereas 28.6 per cent of the entire cotton crop was produced by Negro tenants.[34] During the decade, 1930 to 1940, there were important changes in the rural Negro population both in respect to numbers and land tenure.[35] The number of owners continued to decline; but

TABLE X

Number and Percentage Distribution of Farms of Nonwhite Operators According to Tenure, for the South, 1910–1940 *

TENURE	1940		1930		1920		1910	
	Number	Per Cent	Number	Per Cent	Number	Per Cent	Number	Per Cent
Owners	173,263	25.5	182,019	20.6	217,589	23.6	218,467	24.5
Full Owners	141,902	20.9	140,496	15.9	178,558	19.3	175,290	19.7
Part Owners	31,361	4.6	41,523	4.7	39,031	4.2	43,177	4.9
Managers	365	0.1	829	0.1	1,770	0.2	1,200	0.1
All Tenants	506,638	74.5	698,839	79.3	703,555	76.2	670,474	75.2
Cash	64,684	9.5	97,920	11.1	100,275	10.9	260,966 [3]	29.3 [3]
Share-cash	6,547	1.0	¹	¹	8,207	0.9	14,218	1.6
Share	89,483	13.2	¹	¹	176,711	19.1		
Croppers	299,118	44.0	392,897	44.6	333,713	36.2	370,306	41.6
Other	46,806	6.9	²	²	84,649	9.2	24,984 [3]	2.8 [3]
Total	680,266	100.0	881,687	100.0	922,914	100.0	890,141	100.0

* *Sixtenth Census of the United States. Agriculture,* Vol. III. Washington, 1943, p. 151. Nearly all the nonwhite operators in the South were Negroes.

1 Not available

2 Not comparable

3 For 1910, renters paying a fixed quantity of products were included with "cash tenants."

there was also a decline of almost 200,000 in the number of tenants. (See Table X.) As a result there was a small increase in the proportion of owners among Negro farm operators as compared with a much higher increase in this class among whites. In 1940 there was about the same number of Negro landowners as in 1900; and they represented the same proportion among farm operators in 1940 as in 1900. On the other hand, while the number of Negro tenants and croppers had decreased through migrations, the proportion of tenants among

34 *Ibid.,* p. 570.

35 *Sixteenth Census of the United States. Agriculture,* Vol. III (Washington, 1943), p. 151.

farm operators had remained the same.[36] However, it should be noted that the proportion of croppers among these tenants had increased during the four decades.

PLANE OF LIVING IN PLANTATION AREAS

As we have indicated, the plane of living in the three rural-farming regions of the Cotton Belt is the lowest for rural regions in the entire country. The Negro has long been the scapegoat upon whom blame has been placed for the economic condition of the South.[37] But, as Vance shows, certain practices involved in the production of cotton have affected white croppers, tenants, and small farmers in the same manner in which they have affected the behavior and attitudes of Negro farmers in these classes.[38] A study in 1934 of 646 plantations located in 11 areas in the eastern Cotton Belt revealed that the average annual net income of wage hands, croppers, other share tenants, and renters was $309 per family.[39] The wage laborers had a net income

[36] See T. J. Woofter, *Landlord and Tenant on the Cotton Plantation* (Washington, 1936), pp. 9-10. A cash or standing tenant is usually provided with the land, a house or a cabin, and fuel, by the landlord who receives in return a fixed amount in cash or lint cotton. The cash tenant supplies the labor, work stock and feed for the work stock, tools, seed and fertilizer, and receives the entire crop minus the fixed amount in cash or lint cotton. A share tenant is provided with some fertilizer in addition to the land, house, and fuel, by the landlord who receives one-fourth or one-third of the crop, while the share tenant receives the remainder of the crop. The cropper is generally supplied with everything, except one-half of the fertilizer, by the landlord who receives one half of the crop. The cropper, who furnishes his labor and one-half of the fertilizer, receives one-half of the crop. There are many modifications and combinations of these arrangements and some farm families have the status of "wage hands" or laborers.

[37] Vance, *Human Geography of the South*, p. 192.

[38] *Ibid.*, p. 193. These practices involve "(1) a large proportion of expensive credit, (2) in connection with a small percentage of other crops, (3) under a system of supervision and regimentation as in plantation and tenancy, (4) calling for a maximum amount of manual labor much of which is furnished by women and children. Moreover, (5) in prosperity cotton creates a vested interest in credit institutions to maintain it, (6) in times of depression, it enables failing farmers to continue in the cotton system by receding to the lower levels of tenure, and (7) at all times it encourages speculation, overexpansion, and overproduction. Finally, (8) the crop is sold in a marketing system which the growers do not understand and over which they exercise little or no control." Reprinted from *Human Geography of the South* by Rupert B. Vance, pp. 193-94, by permission of The University of North Carolina. Copyright, 1935, by The University of North Carolina Press.

[39] Woofter, *op. cit.*, p. 83, "Most of the croppers and other share tenants on the plantations of the South do not buy their supplies and equipment or sell their prod-

of $180 and sharecroppers, who comprised the majority of the families studied, $312. The families of share tenants received on an average $417 and the families of cash tenants $561. This study brought out the significant fact that as the acreage devoted to cotton increased the average income of croppers and share tenants decreased. Where tenants and croppers are required to devote more acreage to the growing of cotton, they devote a smaller proportion of their time and crop land to home-grown foodstuffs. Although these figures are for both white and Negro farmers in the various classes, one is able to compare areas with larger concentrations of Negroes with areas with smaller percentages of Negroes. In the Delta areas the average family income of wage laborers was above that of the same class in other areas. But in the Delta areas and in the "Black Belt" the average family incomes of croppers, share tenants, and cash tenants were generally lower than the averages for areas with smaller percentages of Negroes.[40]

More specific information concerning the incomes of Negro farmers in the Cotton Belt is found in the two studies referred to above. Of the 612 families in Macon County, Alabama, studied by Johnson, 56 per cent had a gross annual income of less than $100, which did not include food raised by the families in their gardens.[41] However, it should be noted that 26 per cent of these families went into debt to their landlord and that 61.7 per cent "broke even." Raper's study provides a more detailed study of the incomes of the various classes of white and Negro farmers in two counties in Georgia.[42] The first fact to be noted is that as the result of the depression, the average cash income of Negro families decreased and that the value of home grown foodstuffs increased between 1927 and 1934. Second, it is evident that

ucts in the manner ordinarily followed by small farmers in other areas. They are usually advanced their seed, feed, fertilizer, and items for family living by the landlord, and they commonly turn their crops over to him for sale. Consequently, they are not familiar with the details of the nature or amount of their individual receipts and expenses. They usually know only the total amount of their seasonal indebtedness to the landlord and the amount of cash which they received or the amount which they still owed at settlement time. In addition, they are familiar with the few minor expenses and sales arising from transactions with persons other than the landlord." *Ibid.*, p. 82. Since this study was made during the depression, these incomes include Agriculture Adjustment Administration benefits.

[40] See *Ibid.*, Table 38, p. 220.   [41] *Shadow of the Plantation*, p. 124.
[42] *Op. cit.*, pp. 45-56.

the incomes of whites and Negroes of all tenant classes are affected
by the type of soil upon which they work. In 1934 Negro owners in
Greene County had a total income of $500 as compared with $647 for
white owners; while for the same class in Macon County the average
income for Negroes was $1,132 as compared with $1,198 for whites.
In Greene County where white farmers were evenly distributed in the
three tenure classes (cash tenants, share tenants, and croppers), the
average family incomes of white renters and croppers were $550 and
$384 respectively, while the average incomes for Negroes in these two
classes were $417 and $281. In Macon County where three-fifths of
the white and four-fifths of the Negro farmers were croppers, the differential between the income of white and Negro renters and croppers
was much greater. The average family incomes of white renters and
croppers were $1,150 and $1,007 respectively, while the average family
incomes of Negroes in the same classes were $644 and $519 respectively. White wage hands in both counties received more than twice
the amount received by Negro wage hands in the two counties.

The differences in income between Negroes and whites in the various tenure classes are reflected in differences in planes of living. According to the 1930 census reports for the seven states in the southeastern
cotton area, the average value of the dwellings of white farmers was
more than twice as high as the average for Negro farmers.[43] Whereas
the average value of white owners' dwellings was more than twice that
of white tenants' dwellings, the average value of Negro owners' dwellings was about the same as the average for white tenants and only 52
per cent greater than the average value of Negro tenants' dwellings.
In the two Black Belt counties studied by Raper, Negro dwellings
were decidedly inferior to white dwellings and white croppers lived in
plastered houses almost as often as Negro owners.[44] One-fourth of the
houses occupied by whites had leaky roofs whereas slightly more than
two-thirds of the houses of Negroes were in this condition. On the
other hand, screened houses were extremely rare among both races, the
whites being little better off than Negroes. For water white and Negro
families alike depended upon springs and more generally upon wells,
neither of which as a rule was of a character to safeguard health. The

[43] Woofter, *op. cit.*, pp. 94-95.   [44] Raper, *op. cit.*, pp. 63-68.

same lack of sanitation was apparent in the inadequate facilities or lack of facilities for the disposal of human excrement.

In regard to household furnishings of the two races, Raper makes the following important observations:

The white tenants as a whole seem to have better furnishings than the Negro tenants, but some of the latter have considerably more than any of the landless whites. The Negro rural family often has the savings of a lifetime invested in household furnishings, including showy enlarged pictures of relatives and friends, sewing machines, phonographs, organs and pianos, gilt bedsteads, ornate bureaus, and expensive cook stoves. Whereas more land is an available and attractive repository for the cash surpluses of a considerable element of the owners and some few tenants of either race, the typical landless Negro usually puts his savings, when he has any, in a "big time"—which includes some "Sunday" clothes and an automobile—or in household furnishings. Some Negro families have valuable old pieces which came into their possession when landed white acquaintances secured new furniture or moved to a distant community. This collecting and hoarding of miscellaneous furnishings is more noticeable among old women who have made their living by doing the weekly wash and other housework for prominent white families.

Of the Negro families studied intensively, 82 per cent have dressers or bureaus; 55 per cent have sewing machines; 23 per cent have pianos or organs, most often the latter; 19 per cent have phonographs; and 15 per cent have ranges to cook on. All the families use oil lamps, and not one of them has a radio.[45]

More than a fifth of the Negro families had no printed matter in their homes. In homes where there was printed matter, the Bible and schoolbooks constituted the majority of the reading materials. Only an eighth of the Negro families as compared with three-fourths of the white families subscribed to newspapers and magazines. The proportion of Negro families with reading materials in their homes was, as in the case of the white families, highest among owners and was progressively smaller for renters and croppers. However, white families in each tenure class had more reading materials in their homes than Negro families in corresponding tenure classes. This difference is

[45] Reprinted from *Preface to Peasantry* by Arthur F. Raper, by permission of The University of North Carolina Press. Copyright, 1936, by The University of North Carolina Press.

partly accounted for by the greater illiteracy among the Negroes. One of these counties was typical of the rural-farming sections of the South, where 23.4 per cent of the Negroes and 5.6 per cent of the whites were illiterate in 1930.[46] Negro illiteracy in the other county amounted to 29.3 per cent.

The low plane of living of Negroes in the Cotton Belt was indicated by their dietary habits. The average tenant, who lived on an advance by his landlord of $13 a month for eight months, had to purchase kerosene, clothing, medicine, and tobacco, in addition to food.[47] Food items included flour, lard, and principally meat which "is almost universally fat salt pork." Very little foodstuffs are secured from a garden because gardening is "foreign to the habits of most tenants," and landlords are not disposed generally to advance credit for gardening which would reduce the profit which they derive from advances for foodstuffs. Scarcely more than half of the tenants have cows, which fact accounts for the lack of milk and butter in their diet. Since a relatively large number of the tenants have pigs, during the fall and winter pork forms an important addition to their diet. In general, the diet of both white and Negro tenants in the Cotton Belt consists, as Raper has said, of "the three M's—meat, meal, and molasses—and baked potatoes, called 'taters.'"[48] The tenants fare better than the croppers and the owners of both races enjoy on the whole a better diet than the renters.

FAMILY LIFE IN THE PLANTATION AREA

Attention has already been called to the fact that the distribution of family units in the open country has hindered the development of village communities or other forms of well-knit community life. But even more important still has been the influence of the mobiliity of the population upon the stability of the social organization in these rural areas. Because of the system of tenure, there is a high rate of mobility among both white and Negro farmers, especially the croppers, in the Cotton Belt. "Every year," as Woofter has pointed out, "thou-

[46] Bureau of the Census, *Negroes in the United States: 1920-32*, p. 238.
[47] See Woofter, *op. cit.*, pp. 101-104. See also Johnson, *Shadow of the Plantation*, pp. 100-102; and Raper, *op. cit.*, pp. 52-54. [48] *Ibid.*, p. 52.

sands of cotton tenant farmers place their household goods and other belongings in wagons and trucks and move on to other quarters. Sometimes the destination is another farm at no great distance; sometimes it is a nearby village or town where the tenant expects to engage in industrial activities. . . ." [49]

Studies indicate that Negro families are less mobile than white families.[50] However, the difference between the two races is not great and the mobility of Negroes has been sufficiently great to affect the social organization and culture of their rural communities. In the Cotton Belt one does not find rural communities similar to the old Russian mir or an Irish village community, where deeply rooted customs and traditions govern the relations of life.[51] Nor does one find rural Negro communities like those in Haiti, where a landowning peasantry has preserved over five or more generations a cultural heritage embodying many elements of African culture.[52] At its worst, the rural Negro community, with its dependence upon the exigencies of a capitalistic agriculture and the dominant white community, shows, as DuBois pointed out fifty years ago, the degradation of the impoverished country Negro.[53] However, in the majority of communities mobility and other secularizing influences have not completely wiped out plantation traditions and folk customs that often have their roots in

[49] Woofter, *op. cit.*, p. 106. Cf. Johnson, *Shadow of the Plantation*, p. 25. "Year after year these families continue to live and move about within the county, but rarely leaving it."

[50] Woofter, *op. cit.*, pp. 123-24. According to this study Negro families had lived 8.6 years and white families 5.9 years on the farm where they resided in 1934. Negro heads of families had lived on an average of 6.1 years on a farm since they were 16 years of age as compared with an average of 4.8 years for white heads of families. Negro families had lived on an average of 3.7 farms as compared with 4.3 farms for white families. Raper's study showed that Negro families of all four tenure classes (owners, renters, croppers, and wage hands) had lived longer in one house than white families in corresponding tenure classes. *Ibid.*, p. 61. In view of these facts, it is unnecessary to assume, as John Dollard, *Caste and Class in a Southern Town* (New Haven, 1937), p. 395, that the mobility of Negro tenants is the result of sexual entanglements and the quest for new fields for "erotic operations."

[51] See Stepniak, *op. cit.*, pp. 125-39; and Conrad M. Arensberg and Solon T. Kimball, *Family and Community in Ireland* (Cambridge, 1940).

[52] See Melville J. Herskovits, *Life in a Haitian Valley* (New York, 1937); and George E. Simpson, "Haitian Peasant Economy," *The Journal of Negro History*, Vol. XXV (October, 1940), pp. 498-519.

[53] W. E. B. DuBois, "The Negro in the Black Belt: Some Social Sketches," *Bulletin of the Department of Labor*, 22 (May, 1899), p. 401.

the ante-bellum society. This has been due to the social isolation of these rural folk, who in their physical characteristics show less admixture of white blood than Negroes in other sections of the country.[54]

The family among the rural Negroes in the Cotton Belt is, as in all peasant societies, the basic and most important social group. However, it lacks the definite organization which is found in peasant communities in some parts of the world.[55] The Negro family in these rural communities has grown out of customary practices which originated during slavery or developed after slavery in response to the conditions on the plantations. Since legal sanctions have had little control over sex relations, many of the families originated in illegitimacy, a condition which gave rise to a maternal family organization.[56] For example, in 1920 in Macon County, Alabama, nearly a third and in Issaquena County, Mississippi, a fifth of the Negro families had a woman head.[57] Very often the so-called marriages lack legal sanction. They develop out of individual wishes, where the couple decide to live together for sexual satisfaction and economic cooperation. Sometimes the basis of the association has been established through sexual intercourse over a considerable period during which children have been born. The children are cared for by the mother and are taken into the girl's family until she decides to "marry" or establish her own household. In a loose family organization of this type, there are many adopted children who may be blood relations or children whose parents have died.

[54] In 1910 the percentage of mulattoes in the rural Negro population of the seven states of the southeastern Cotton Belt ranged from 14.3 in South Carolina to 40.4 in North Carolina, which has a relatively few cotton-growing counties. Bureau of the Census, *Negro Population in the United States: 1790-1915*, p. 228. At the same census there were in Issaquena County, Mississippi, 166 mulatto couples as compared with 1,882 black couples. See Frazier, *op. cit.*, p. 588.

[55] See for example Conrad M. Arensberg and Solon T. Kimball, *Family and Community in Ireland*, p. 61 (Harvard University Press, copyright 1940), where appears the following description of the Irish peasant family: "The relations of the members of the farm family are best described in terms of the patterns which uniformity of habit and association build up. They are built up within the life of the farm household and its daily and yearly work. The regulations of the fathers to sons and mothers to sons fall repeatedly in regular and expectable patterns of this kind that differ very little from farm to farm."

[56] See Frazier, *op. cit.*, pp. 112-19.   [57] *Ibid.*, p. 128.

These families, which are held together by habit and sentiment and the common interests which develop between their members, may continue to maintain their identity over two or three generations. But usually families, especially among the cropper class, do not have such stability. They are constantly breaking up and changing their composition by the mobility of the population. The male members are drawn into lumber mills and work on the roads while the female members seek a living in domestic work in the towns. This often involves new "marital arrangements," which where there has been legal marriage are entered without legal divorce. Since institutional controls are generally weak or absent, such behavior is not only tolerated by the community but does not violate the mores of the community.

There are communities scattered throughout the Black Belt in which sex and familial relations are under greater institutional control and conventional standards have the support of a large element in the community. This stable element has a large proportion of mixed-bloods, with family traditions, who have managed to become landowners. Whatever social differentiation one finds in these Black Belt communities is based upon the status and influence of these families. Landownership is not, however, the basis of social distinctions nor is it a certain index to family stability and conformity to conventional standards of sex and family behavior. In a region where tenancy is the dominant form of tenure, traditional and other social and cultural factors often play a more important rôle. But usually croppers are as poor in social inheritance as in worldly goods and their family life reflects the poor social inheritance.

CHURCHES, LODGES, AND ORGANIZATIONS
FOR MUTUAL AID

Next to the family the church is the most important association in rural Negro communities. In fact, the church often defines the limits of the community which often derives its name from the church organization. The numerous Negro church organizations in the Black Belt are generally affiliated with the Baptist and Methodist denominations, the former denomination having the larger following. The Negro church not only provides the most important means of community expression but it enlists the deepest loyalties of the Negro.[58] The church owes its existence largely to the initiative of the Negro who is generally willing to make financial and material sacrifices in order to maintain it. Between the various church organizations affiliated with the Baptist and Methodist denominations, there are often keen rivalries and bitter dissensions over matters of faith and ritual. As a social institution the Negro church embodies many activities not of a religious nature. It is the center for recreational activities and the church building very often serves as the school house.[59] Although the church is undoubtedly an important agency of social control, its influence does not transcend the dominant mores and folkways of the community. While the church often attempts to discipline its members for immoral conduct, its discipline is generally ineffective unless it represents the dominant attitudes of the community. Moreover, these churches have a decidedly other-worldly outlook and consequently leave the retribution of the sinner to life after death.

Organizations for mutual aid, the chief purpose of which has been to provide proper burial for their members, form an important part of the traditions of these rural communities. Such organizations grew up in connection with the church organizations. They often developed into lodges or were absorbed by the lodges, which with their rituals and a more formal organization, performed a similar function. Some of the lodges were local organizations with names taken from the Bible, while others were national organizations such as the Masons and Odd Fellows. In either case the lodge was closely affiliated with the church and functioned as a sacred brotherhood. Consequently, close by the church in most rural communities one may see today one or more lodge halls.[60] The lodges usually have insurance features, including both sick- and death-benefits. The cost of the insurance has generally been high and not on a sound actuarial basis. As a consequence, membership in the lodges has fluctuated partly because of the costs and partly because of the failure of the lodges to meet their obliga-

[58] This as well as other aspects of the Negro church will be discussed in greater detail in Chapter XIV below.

[59] In the two counties studied by Raper, nearly a third of the Negro schools were housed in churches. *Op. cit.*, p. 325.   [60] Cf. *Ibid.*, pp. 373-81.

tions. Then, too, the purely secular business organization, the insurance company, with sounder business methods, has entered into competition with the lodges. The lodge has been able to meet this competition because of its secret rituals and uniforms, which provide an opportunity for display especially during the pageantry at funerals. However, because of the low economic status of these rural folk, the tradition of the simple burial society persists since it holds out to the poorest member of the community the prospect of a decent burial.

EDUCATION

Unlike the church and the lodge, the school is an institution that is alien to the plantation tradition and represents the impact of the larger world upon these rural folk. Many of the older generation have never had any schooling, and the educational provisions for their children are far below what is provided for white children. The per capita spent upon white children is from twelve to eighteen times as much as that spent upon Negro children. A large proportion of the school houses attended by Negro children are not owned by the county. For example, in the two counties studied by Raper, only 15 of the 58 schools for Negro children were owned by the county. Of the remaining buildings in which school was held for Negro children, 24 were lodge halls, 16 churches and 3 abandoned tenant houses.[61] The school term for Negro children is from one-third to two-thirds as long as the term for white children. Moreover, the attendance of the children of tenants is limited by labor requirements and the mobility of the population. As a consequence of inferior educational facilities and lower pay for Negro teachers, Negro children are taught by unprepared teachers who attempt to give them formal instruction in subjects which have little meaning for them. After sitting listlessly through three or four terms, many of the children drop out of school. If they are fortunate enough to have parents who are able to send them out of the community where they can get an adequate education, they seldom return. Because of its gross inadequacies, the Negro school does little to solve the simple problem of illiteracy, much less the

[61] *Ibid.*, pp. 324-25.

broader problem of educating a peasantry for participation in the modern world.

RECREATION

The recreational life of the Negro in the Cotton Belt revolves principally about the rural institutions and is conditioned by the routine of work on the plantation. Visiting friends and relatives is one of the most important leisure time activities for both men and women.[62] On Saturday evenings and Sunday afternoons whole families go by wagons or on foot to the home of a friend or relative. Many of the men find a source of recreation in hunting and for women as well as men fishing is one of the chief pastimes. As an escape from the dull routine of labor and the isolation in which they live, church services, more especially the "big meetings" and the revivals, serve as a form of recreation for many members of these communities. On such occasions as well as at the church suppers families gather with their neighbors for feasting and the enjoyment of social intercourse. The lodge with its barbecue suppers and the school on holidays and at the close of the term also provide an occasion for escape from the daily routine. It is through the schools that athletics is beginning to play a larger part in the recreational life of the young people. The younger members of the community generally seek a more exciting form of amusement in the frolics or parties where they can indulge in dancing. Usually such forms of amusement are condemned by the churches but as the young people gain access to the larger world, they are more inclined to ignore the opposition of the church. Escape from the isolation and routine of the countryside has long been possible through the regular trip to town on Saturday afternoons. With the advent of movie theaters and the radio, the trip to town is bringing the black peasant into contact with the world beyond the small town. Moreover, many of the dance halls against which the rural church rails are located in the towns, where socially tabooed patterns of behavior are acquired. It is through contacts in the town that sexual indulgence,

[62] See Raper, *op. cit.*, pp. 387ff., and Johnson, *Shadow of the Plantation*, pp. 180ff. See also Carter G. Woodson, *The Rural Negro* (Washington, 1930), pp. 132ff.

which has always formed a part of the recreation of these rural folk, is acquiring a new meaning and is affecting customary family relations.

RACE RELATIONS IN PLANTATION SOUTH

The relations between rural Negro communities and the larger white communities are determined by the economic and social factors which have characterized the plantation system in the South. Although following Emancipation the poor whites of the South became competitors of the freedmen, rarely has this competition in agricultural pursuits become the basis of social conflict.[63] This has been true despite the fact that since the Civil War there have appeared in the South over three quarters of a million white tenants and laborers who are competing with Negroes for a place on the land.[64] During the 1910's, when the Negro was showing rapid gains in landownership, the segregation of the rural Negro became a political issue.[65] However, in North Carolina where the agitation was centered, the legislatures voted down the measure and the agitation died down. The absence of social conflict has been due partly to the spatial separation of the races in rural areas but more especially to the fact that the Negroes have not crowded whites off the land. In those counties which comprise the "Black Belt" there has been a proportional and an absolute decline over the years in the Negro population. Since the 1860 census, the "Black Belt" has shrunk in area and in the proportion of the Negroes living in these areas.[66] Since the movement of the Negro population from "Black Belt" counties to counties in which whites predominate has been a movement from the richer to the poor lands

[63] See Rupert B. Vance, "Racial Competition for the Land," in Edgar T. Thompson (Ed.), *Race Relations and the Race Problem* (Durham, N. C., 1939), pp. 97-124.   [64] Woofter, *op. cit.*, pp. 11-13.

[65] The proposal for the rural segregation of Negroes in North Carolina read as follows: "That wherever the greater part of the land acreage in any given district that may be laid off, is owned by one race, a majority of the voters in such a district may say, if they wish, that in the future no land may be sold to a person of a different race, provided such action is approved or allowed (as being justified by considerations of the peace, protection, and social life of the community) by reviewing judge or board of county commissions." Vance, in Thompson, *Race Relations and the Race Problem*, p. 107. See also W. D. Weatherford, "Race Segregation in the South," *The Survey*, Vol. XXXIII, pp. 375-77.

[66] See pp. 187-90 above and Work, *op. cit.*, pp. 205-15.

in the Cotton Belt, this movement has also tended to allay conflict.[67]

Economic and social factors have played a more important rôle than such physical factors as the density and the distribution of the Negro population in preventing competition between the two races from developing into conflict. Undoubtedly, the traditional association of the Negro with the land has been an important social factor. But more important has been the fact that the proportion of Negro farmers who have risen to the status of owners, though a notable achievement in view of prevailing racial attitudes and economic factors inherent in the plantation system of agriculture, has not affected fundamentally the relations between the races.[68] Even the acquisition of land by a Negro in the Cotton Belt is not simply an economic transaction. As a rule it can only be accomplished when the transaction is in accordance with the traditional relations of the races. Since prospective Negro owners must acquire land from whites, they must be acceptable to white sellers in the sense that they are industrious, their credit is good, and they know their "place" as Negroes and stay in their "place." [69] It is the white owner, whether absentee landowner or the owner upon whom the Negroes have been dependent as tenants, who generally takes the initiative in the transaction.[70] Then too the land which is placed at the disposal of prospective Negro owners is land least desired by whites. The Negro owner in the Cotton Belt is generally found in areas where renters cultivate the poorer lands and in out-of-way places. As Vance has pointed out, the 1940 federal census of agriculture shows that the Negro owners operate smaller farms valued at less per acre on the average than white tenants. And while Negro owners operate larger farms than Negro tenants, the value

[67] Cf. Rupert B. Vance, *op. cit.*, p. 114.

[68] During the period from 1925 to 1930 farm ownership tended to increase among Negroes and whites in a large part of the Cotton Belt. The increase was appreciably more widespread among Negroes than among whites, because, it appears, the Negroes had greater interest in landownership and they bought land in areas where unfavorable economic conditions had thrown land on the market. Edward E. Lewis, "Recent Farm-Ownership changes in the Cotton Belt and their Significance for Migration," *Social Forces*, Vol. 13 (December, 1934), pp. 238-44.

[69] See Raper, *op. cit.*, pp. 121-37.

[70] In some cases the white owner is a relative of the Negro purchaser or has provided in his will for the Negro to have the opportunity to purchase his land.

of the land per acre is less than that of Negro tenants.[71] Consequently, because of the social subordination of the Negro, landownership does not bring to him the economic and cultural advantages which it brings to whites.

For the great mass of the Negro population in the Cotton Belt, their position as tenants and croppers has been sufficient to keep them in their traditional dependence upon the whites and in a subordinate social status. The fact, noted above, that Negroes are less mobile than whites is owing partly to their inability to move about as freely as white tenants.[72] Though whites and Negroes are found on the same plantations, the white tenants and croppers, who are imbued with the idea of their racial superiority, can assert themselves more freely than Negroes. It is probably for this reason that landlords generally prefer Negro tenants to white tenants. In his dealings with his black tenants, the white landlord has absolute control both because of his economic position and his identification with the white ruling group. Since agreements are worked out informally and there are no written contracts, settlements are dependent entirely upon the landlord's sense of justice. There is evidence that the Negro cash tenants are forced to pay more than whites of the same status in order to penalize Negroes who attempt to rise from the cropping and share-renting class.[73] Moreover, the Negro farmers in the tenant classes find it more difficult to move up into a higher tenure class than white tenants.[74]

Throughout the Cotton Belt race relations are characterized by the complete social subordination of the Negro. This is maintained partly by the force of tradition and partly by the Negro's economic dependence upon the whites. Where whites and Negroes are concerned, equality before the law is out of the question, since the courts only give legal sanction to current prejudices and practices in regard to the Negro's inferior status. But in addition to this, the total disfranchisement of the Negro, whether because of his apathy, the poll tax, or the threat of force, has helped to "keep him in his place." In areas where

71 Vance, *All These People*, p. 241.
72 Cf. Woofter, *Landlord and Tenant on the Cotton Plantation*, p. 123.
73 Rupert B. Vance, "Racial Competition for the Land," *loc. cit.*, pp. 108-10.
74 T. J. Woofter, *Landlord and Tenant on the Cotton Plantation*, p. 124.

Negroes outnumber whites nine or ten to one, as in some parts of the Mississippi Delta, social controls are likely to be more rigid and any violation of the "etiquette of race relations" is likely to provoke violent repression on the part of the ruling whites.[75]

From these three Rural-Cultural Regions of the Cotton Belt, in which about three-fourths of the rural southern Negroes live, we now turn to the other Rural-Cultural Regions of the South where the remainder of the rural Negroes are found.

SOUTHERN LOUISIANA AND THE LOWER ATLANTIC COASTAL PLAIN

In the lower South there are two rural regions with large concentrations of Negro population. One of these is Southern Louisiana (Region 13 on map) where the rural population contains "large numbers of Negroes and descendants of French immigrants who have maintained the original French culture." [76] The region is thickly settled, with over a half million residents in rural areas, though over 40 per cent of them are in nonfarming areas. Sugar cane, rice, fruits, and cotton are the chief agricultural products. The majority of the Negro farmers, who constitute 35 per cent of the rural population, are tenants and croppers on the sugar and cotton plantations. Nearly a half century ago a study of the Negro on the sugar plantations in this area, where Negroes still lived in "quarters" as in slavery times, concluded that their condition had "improved but little, if any, since freedom was given them." [77] The social disorganization which existed in this

[75] The lynching rate, according to Raper, is lower in the Black Belt than in other parts of the South because relations between whites and Negroes are well defined and there are fewer possibilities for contacts between the two races. Arthur F. Raper, *The Tragedy of Lynching* (Chapel Hill, 1933), p. 27. However, the lynching rate has been higher in cotton counties than in other types of farming areas. See Johnson, *Statistical Atlas of Southern Counties*, pp. 31-32. Commenting upon a lynching in Bolivar County, "Mississippi's banner county," where there were three Negroes to one white, Raper says: "The whole tradition of Bolivar County, accepted by officers, churches, and other agencies and institutions, is that each planter, much as in slave days, shall be allowed complete control of his tenants and wage hands. To all practical purposes a dead 'nigger' is just a worker gone, and of no concern to the public." *Tragedy of Lynching*, p. 105.

[76] Mangus, *Rural Regions in the United States*, p. 61.

[77] J. Bradford Laws, "The Negroes of Cinclare Central Factory and Calumet Plantation, Louisiana," *Bulletin of the Department of Labor*, No. 38 (Washington, 1902), p. 119.

area was due to the highly commercial type of farming. Recent studies of the sugar plantations in the area show the sugar plantations still depend largely upon resident laborers who live in "quarters" and that the demand for laborers is seasonal.[78] The majority of the resident laborers and croppers were Negroes. The resident laborers as a whole had a gross income between $250 and $500 including the work of their wives and children. The gross income of Negro laborers was less than that of whites though Negro family members contributed more labor than white family members. In this region as in the Cotton Belt the Negro laborer and cropper are dependent upon the landlord and merchant for advances and the same system of social controls is utilized to keep the Negro in a subordinate position. As in the Cotton Belt the social life of the Negro in these rural communities revolves about the churches and the lodges.

The other rural region in the lower South with a large percentage of Negroes is the Lower Atlantic Coastal Plains (Region 11 on the map), which extends from Wilmington, North Carolina, southward through northern Florida and westward to New Orleans. This is an area of a mixed type of farming in which truck, potatoes, dairy products, poultry, livestock, and cotton are of chief importance. Like the adjoining southeastern Cotton Belt this is an impoverished agricultural area, though a majority of the farmers are owners of their land. A large percentage of the Negroes, who constitute a third of the rural population, are like the white farmer landowners. In this region there are areas along the coasts of South Carolina and Georgia, including the sea islands, where a Negro yeomanry exists upon land once devoted to the production of rice and long staple cotton.[79] In these areas, as Woofter remarks, "Landownership—that most powerful factor differentiating these farmers from the farm tenants of the interior black belt—came in reconstruction days." [80] The isolation of

[78] See Harold Hoffsommer, *The Sugar Cane Farm*, Louisiana Bulletin No. 320 (Louisiana State University, 1940); and by the same author, *The Resident Laborer on the Sugar Cane Farm*, Louisiana Bulletin No. 334 (Louisiana State University, 1941).

[79] See Guion G. Johnson, *A Social History of the Sea Islands* (Chapel Hill, 1930).

[80] *Black Yeomanry* by T. J. Woofter, p. 10. Copyright 1930 by Henry Holt and Company, Inc. See also Niels Christensen, "Fifty Years of Freedom: Conditions in the Sea Coast Regions," in *The Negro's Progress in Fifty Years*, pp. 58-66.

the Negroes in these areas is indicated by the fact that they are of unmixed African ancestry and have preserved more of their African heritage than Negroes in other parts of the country.[81] They speak a dialect, known as Gullah, which contains words of African origin, and other phases of their folk culture have undoubtedly been mixed with African elements.[82] Even in this isolated community of black yeomanry, the Negroes are disfranchised and the few whites have the political power in their hands.[83]

THE TIDEWATER-PIEDMONT REGION

The Eastern Old South region merges in North Carolina and Virginia with the Tidewater-Piedmont Region (Region 1 on the map) where there is a varied type of farming.[84] In the Virginia Tidewater section self-sufficient, truck and part time farming is carried on, while in the Eastern Shore section general farming, poultry, truck, fruit, and potatoes are of primary importance. In southern Maryland there are tobacco farms, while mixed farming is carried on in the coastal section of North Carolina. Of the more than 600,000 residents on farms in this region in 1930, about 37 per cent were Negroes. The Negro farmers in this region are differentiated from those in the Cotton Belt by the high rate of ownership. With the exception of a few counties in North Carolina, from a third to two-thirds of the farmers in the counties comprising this region are farm owners. In some counties in Virginia the rate of ownership is much higher, amounting in one county to 84 per cent. The high rate of ownership among the Negro farmers in this region is related to other advantages which they have enjoyed in contrast to the Negroes in the Cotton Belt. Many of the Negroes are descendants of Negroes who obtained their freedom before the Civil War and therefore have had a longer history of freedom. More-

[81] See p. 11 above.

[82] See Guy B. Johnson, *Folk Culture on St. Helena Island, South Carolina* (Chapel Hill, 1930), and Melville J. Herskovits, *The Myth of the Negro Past* (New York, 1941), pp. 276-79.   [83] Woofter, *Black Yeomanry*, p. 9.

[84] The Tidewater-Piedmont rural region "includes southern Maryland, the Virginia and Maryland Eastern Shore, southern Delaware, eastern Virginia, and northeastern North Carolina" and a number of counties in the Pamlico and Albemarle Sound section of North Carolina. Mangus, *Rural Regions in the United States*, pp. 18, 51-52.

over, Negroes in this region, especially in Virginia, have not been as isolated, either biologically or sociologically, as the Negroes in the lower South. In 1910 one-third of the Negroes of Virginia as contrasted with one-sixth of the Negroes of Alabama and Mississippi were mulattoes. Moreover, since in this region the differential between the money spent for the education of Negro and white children is not as great as in the Cotton Belt, Negroes have a lower illiteracy rate. Because of these various economic and social factors, the social organization of rural Negro communities in these areas is different from that of rural communities in the Cotton Belt.

The following description of a rural Negro community in this region is typical of the better communities:

The Holy Neck Community of Nansemond County, about 15 miles southwest of Suffolk, is one of the best developed rural Negro communities in the state. The large number of well kept homes and the fine school and church indicate a well-being not found in many Negro communities. This community has approximately 100 Negro families, the majority of whom are home owners.

The economic base of the community is farming, although some depend on industrial employment for at least part of their living. Cotton and peanuts are the chief cash crops. Hogs are also a source of income for some. Corn is raised, but chiefly for feed. Under the leadership of the county agent and the agricultural teacher of the high school, good farming practices are being introduced.

The homes of the community vary from the primitive type to relatively new cottages of the more modern type with modern conveniences. Eight had electric lights, and 12 running water in the house. Pride in home beautification is growing.

Much of the life of the area centers around the high school (the Nansemond County Training School) and the Mt. Sinai Baptist Church. In 1919 four neighborhood schools were consolidated into what became the county training school, and an eight-room frame building was erected. The people of each of the four supporting neighborhoods raised $550 for this building or $2,200 in the community as a whole.

Practically none of the farm produce is now sold cooperatively, although Negro farmers of the area belonged to and patronized the peanut growers cooperative marketing association when that was functioning. Some fertilizer is bought cooperatively. Securing needed credit on the most advantageous terms is difficult, but not as serious here as in places where there is exclusive dependence on the time merchant system with all of its accompanying abuses.

Community recreational activities center around the school and the churches, especially the former. The 4-H club and the NFA [New Farmers of America] group of the school help to furnish recreation for the young people. Baseball games are popular in the summer. A community club, under the leadership of the farm demonstration agent, and church meetings help furnish recreation for the adults. Before the 1929 depression, car riding was a popular pastime and still is to a somewhat reduced extent.[85]

In some areas of this region, especially in the Piedmont and in the tobacco counties, the Negro communities present a different picture. The inhabitants may live on small plots of land but must depend for a livelihood upon outside work or they may work as laborers and tenants.

OTHER REGIONS

More than 96 per cent of the rural Negro population of the South is found in the rural regions which we have considered. However, in 1930 there were 15,000 Negroes among the 90,000 residents in the rural region known as Southern Florida (Region 12 on the map). The majority of Negro farmers in this region find employment as tenants and laborers on the fruit and truck farms. In still another rural region, North-South Border (Region 4 on the map), there were over 100,000 Negroes who constitute about a fourteenth of the entire population. The majority of these Negroes were in the part of this region which includes sections of Kentucky and Tennessee. The agricultural activities in this region are devoted to general farming and Negro farmers like white farmers in the area have a relatively high rate of land ownership.

At the opening of the present century 77 per cent of the Negro

[85] William E. Garnett and John M. Ellison, *Negro Life in Rural Virginia: 1856–1934*, Virginia Polytechnic Institute, Bulletin, 295 (June, 1934), pp. 33-35. See also C. Horace Hamilton and John M. Ellison, *The Negro Church in Rural Virginia*, Virginia Polytechnic Institute, Bulletin, 273 (June, 1930).

population was in the rural areas of the South and in 1940 about 47 per cent of the Negroes in the country were still in the rural South. It was in the rural areas of the South that organized social life first took shape among the majority of the Negroes. In these same areas today between four and five out of every ten Negroes in the country earn their livelihood, and are still controlled by, the folkways and institutions indigenous to the region. Since 1900 an increasing number of Negroes have been drawn out of these rural communities into the urban areas of the South and the North. These migrants from the rural South, like the European peasants coming to the cities of the United States, have carried to the urban areas the patterns of behavior and the conceptions of life that characterized their lives in the rural environment. In the following chapters we shall study the adjustments which they have made to the urban environment, the organization and culture of the more or less segregated Negro communities in cities, and their relations to the larger urban communities.

CHAPTER XI

Urban Negro Communities

T HE growth of urban Negro communities in the United States is a phase of the urbanization of the population of the country as a whole.[1] From 1900 to 1940, the number of cities with 50,000 or more inhabitants increased from 78 to 199.[2] In 17 of the 78 cities with 50,000 or more population, in 1900, there were Negro communities numbering 10,000 or more persons. In 1900 there were also 15 other cities of less than 50,000 population with Negro communities numbering at least 10,000 persons.

Ten years later the number of such Negro communities had increased from 32 to 43. In 1910, as in 1900, the majority of these communities were in the South and in the border states.[3] Washington, D. C. with 86,702 Negroes in 1900 and 94,446 Negroes in 1910, ranked first among these cities; while New York which ranked fourth in 1900 moved up to second place in 1910 with 91,709 Negroes. In 1910 as in 1900 there were three northern cities, New York, Philadelphia, and Chicago, among the ten cities having the largest Negro communities.

As the result of the northward migrations, during the next decade, from 1910 to 1920, the number of northern cities with 10,000 or more Negroes increased to fifteen. The Negro communities in New York City, in Chicago, and in Philadelphia became in the order named the three largest Negro communities in the country.

[1] In 1920 there were 300 times as many people in urban areas as in 1790. National Resources Committee, *Our Cities. Their Role in the National Economy* (Washington, 1937), p. 1.

[2] *Sixteenth Census of the United States, Population* (Washington, 1941), pp. 18-19.

[3] In 1900 there were seven northern cities and in 1910 there were nine northern cities with 10,000 or more Negroes.

Between 1920 and 1930, Negro communities in other northern cities continued to increase in population with the result that 24 of the 80 cities with 10,000 or more Negroes in 1930 were in the North. Although by 1940 the number of cities in the country with 10,000

TABLE XI

Cities With a Negro Population of 100,000 or more in 1940 with Comparative Figures for 1930, 1920, 1910, and 1900.*

CITY	1940	1930	1920	1910	1900
		NORTH			
New York	458,444	327,706	152,467	91,709	60,666
Chicago	277,731	233,903	109,458	44,103	30,150
Philadelphia	250,880	219,599	134,229	84,459	60,613
Detroit	149,119	120,066	40,838	5,741	4,111
		BORDER			
Washington	187,266	132,068	109,966	94,446	86,702
Baltimore	165,843	142,106	108,322	84,749	79,258
St. Louis, Mo.	108,765	93,580	69,854	43,960	35,516
		SOUTH			
New Orleans	149,034	129,632	100,930	89,262	77,714
Memphis	121,498	96,550	61,181	52,441	49,910
Birmingham	108,938	99,077	70,230	52,305	16,575
Atlanta	104,533	90,075	62,796	51,902	35,729
TOTAL	2,074,051	1,684,362	1,020,271	695,177	538,944

* United States Bureau of the Census, *Negroes in the United States 1920-1932* (Washington, 1935) p. 55, and *Sixteenth Census of the United States: 1940, Population*, Vol. II, "Characteristics of the Population" (Washington, 1943), p. 114.

or more Negroes had declined to 72; the number of such cities in the North had increased to twenty-six (See Map VIII). Among these 72 cities, there were 11 cities with Negro communities numbering over 100,000 which had a total Negro population of over two million persons (See Table XI). The 11 cities included four southern cities: New Orleans, Memphis, Birmingham and Atlanta; three border cities: Washington, Baltimore, and St. Louis; and four northern cities: New York, Chicago, Philadelphia, and Detroit. The classification of urban Negro communities according to their location is not a mere formal division on the basis of geography. It will be shown in the description and analysis of these communities that their social and economic or-

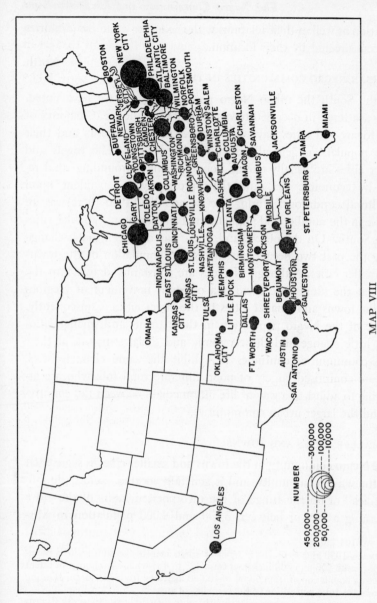

MAP VIII

Seventy-two Urban Negro Communities with 10,000 or More Population in 1940.*

* Based on Sixteenth Census of the United States: 1940. Population. "Characteristics of the Population."

ganization as well as their relations with the larger white communities has been affected by their location.

URBAN NEGRO COMMUNITIES IN THE SOUTH

In the South the urban Negro population is, as we have noted, widely scattered in over 850 towns and cities.[4] The great majority of these towns and cities have less than 25,000 inhabitants and their Negro populations generally do not exceed 5,000. The towns and smaller cities are usually closely bound to the surrounding rural regions by economic ties, and their prosperity is dependent upon agricultural conditions. During the decade 1930-1940 there was an increase in the number and population of the towns and smaller cities of the South.[5] On the other hand, there has not been much change during the past two decades in the Negro population of the towns and smaller cities. Although Negroes are constantly drawn into the towns, at the same time there is a constant movement of Negroes from the towns and smaller cities to the larger cities. Consequently, the size of the Negro population in these towns and smaller cities shows little change and the economic and social structure of their Negro communities continues to exhibit the same characteristics. They are comprised largely of poor, illiterate rural folk who are attempting to adjust to a way of life intermediate between the countryside and the larger urban communities.

SMALLER CITIES AND TOWNS

The Negro community in the towns and smaller cities is segregated from the white community, and is generally located "across the railroad track" or on the fringe of the incorporated limits of the city.[6] Concerning a city of between 3,000 and 4,000 population in Mis-

[4] See p. 191 above.

[5] Between 1930 and 1940, the number of urban areas in the South with a population of from 2,500 to 5,000 increased from 427 to 485 while the number of urban areas with a population of from 5,000 to 10,000 increased from 221 to 267. During this period the total population of the first class of areas increased less than 200,000 and of the second class of urban areas slightly more than 300,000. *Sixteenth Census of the United States, Population*, p. 21.

[6] The spatial pattern with reference to Negro residence differs, as we shall see, from that in the larger cities of the South and the large cities of the North.

sissippi, with a fairly well-off Negro community, Powdermaker writes:

> The railroad divides the town roughly according to color. "Across the tracks" is used as the name of the Negro district, a label with obvious implication. . . .
>
> In contrast to the homogeneous aspect of the white section, Across the Tracks runs the gamut of possibilities between comfort and poverty, although there is no house here as pretentious as the finest on the other side of the tracks. The main street of this district is paved, and flanked by modest cottages in fairly good condition, most of them owned by their occupants. It also boasts two churches, one Baptist and one Methodist, a decrepit barn-like building where the Church of God in Christ holds its services, and another building, smaller and better kept, used by those who call themselves simply "Christians." Further up are several small stores in private houses, selling groceries and soft drinks—occasionally also a hard one—as well as a shoemaker's shop and a barber shop. Further down is a playground, recently opened, for colored children. This street is the axis of the colored section, and most of the Negroes pass up and down its sidewalks every day.
>
> The other paved street Across the Tracks runs parallel to the main street. It too is wide and lined with small houses in respectable repair, a few of which serve also as shops; it contains in addition two of the leading churches, and a couple of houses of bad repute. Other, unpaved streets of varying widths run parallel to these two, and still others intersect them. Some of good proportions and reputations; others are narrow alleys with dilapidated red shanties straggling along the borders. The latter form a section known as "the Flats," which, with its drinking, gambling, and fighting, is the most disreputable part of town.[7]

The areas of Negro residence are generally characterized by unpaved streets and sidewalks and unpainted shacks. Among the shacks of the great body of poorer Negroes there generally appears a sprinkling of

[7] Hortense Powdermaker, *After Freedom* (New York, 1939), pp. 11-12. In Charlottesville, Va. "The areas of the city occupied by Negroes lie near the railroads and in low-lying regions. These areas represent in many instances places of settlement and transition. The Negro is gradually encroaching upon the white settlement. Frequently and unfortunately he is occupying insanitary and unsightly former homes of the white people. The areas occupied by Negroes in Charlottesville are clearly defined—their homes and businesses set apart from white occupation, . . ." *Charlottesville—A Study of Negro Life and Personality* by Helen DeCorse, p. 7. Published 1933 by The University of Virginia.

more comfortable homes of the educated and economically better-off families.

The dwellings reflect the different status of their inhabitants. Even on the respectable main street there is a tumbledown little shanty of one and a half rooms, unpainted outside and with newspapers covering the inner walls by way of decoration and protection. It is lighted by oil lamps and has no running water or plumbing. In it lives an illiterate old woman who firmly believes in the current superstitions, and has implicit faith in voodoo doctors. Directly opposite stands a new five-room house equipped with electricity, modern heating, and plumbing, and furnished according to the highest dictates of mail-order fashion. The couple who own it are both college graduates. . . .

The two contrasting houses stand face to face, both part of the same section. Their proximity and their incongruity are typical of Across the Tracks, where side by side live the respectable and the disreputable, the moderately well-to-do and the very poor, the pious and the unsaved, the college graduates and the illiterates, the dusky blacks, the medium browns, and light creams, all thrown together because all are Negroes.[8]

The majority of the Negro males in the small urban areas are employed as common laborers while most of the employed women are engaged in domestic service. In the smaller towns some of the Negroes continue to work as farm laborers and supplement their incomes with produce from gardens about their homes.[9] In the larger cities where there is more industry opportunities for more varied types of employment are afforded Negro men. However, in the larger cities as well as in the towns the great body of Negro workers find a living as unskilled workers and in domestic service. In the twelve largest Mississippi cities in 1940, from 60 to 75 per cent of the Negro women 14 years of age and over were employed in domestic service and about a third of the Negro men of the same age were employed as common laborers.[10] A sixth to a fifth of the men in these cities were engaged

[8] Powdermaker, *op. cit.*, p. 13.

[9] *Ibid.*, pp. 113-14. See William L. Leap, *Red Hill—Neighborhood Life and Race Relations in a Rural Section* (Charlottesville, Va., 1933), pp. 42-43, concerning economic activities of the Negro community on the outskirts of Charlottesville, Va.

[10] *Sixteenth Census of the United States. Population—Second Series* (Washington, D. C., 1943), p. 114. Jackson was the largest city with a total population of 62,107.

in domestic service. In the town studied by Miss Powdermaker Negro men also found employment as janitors, helpers at gasoline stations, truck drivers, chauffeurs and as delivery boys.[11]

The incomes of the great majority of Negro wage earners in the towns and smaller cities of the South are exceedingly low. A study of family incomes and expenditures in small cities and villages of the southeastern region in 1936 revealed that four-fifths of the Negro families in South Carolina and Georgia villages had incomes less than $500 and that median incomes of families in North Carolina and Mississippi villages were $373.[12] In two small cities, Sumter, South Carolina, and Griffin, Georgia, the median income of Negro families was $430 and $397, respectively. Studies of the incomes of Negro families in other small cities of the South reveal a similar situation. In Gastonia, North Carolina, the median income of Negro families was $414 and in Albany, Georgia, three-fourths of the Negro families had incomes of less than $500 during the year.[13] Though the father was the chief wage earner the incomes secured by nearly three-fourths of these families represented the efforts of several members of the family. Since nearly nine-tenths of the Negro families in the smaller cities were wage earners, these figures represent the incomes for the vast majority of the Negro population.

In the towns and smaller cities of the South there has always been some social differentiation in the Negro population which has been the basis of a class structure. The class structure in these towns and smaller cities of the South has been based primarily upon social distinctions that grew up among the slaves and the Negroes who were free before the Civil War. Usually mixed ancestry combined with cultural advantages and conventional family and sex behavior have been the basis of upper-class status. Historical circumstances as well as the size of the Negro population has determined the size and growth of a substantial middle class of self-respecting workers with a fairly stable family life. In all of these communities there has al-

[11] Powdermaker, *op. cit.*, p. 114.

[12] Bureau of Home Economics, *Family Income and Expenditures Southeastern Region*, Part I, Family Income (Washington, 1940), p. 177.

[13] Bureau of Labor Statistics, *Family Income and Expenditure in the Southeastern Region*, 1935-36, Vol. I, Family Income (Washington, 1939), pp. 12-13.

ways been a relatively large lower class, with unstable family relations, including the shiftless and criminal elements. The composition of these classes as well as the changes which have occurred in their character during the past two decades will be considered in the next chapter.

The organized social life among Negroes in the towns and smaller cities consists chiefly of churches, fraternal organizations, and mutual aid societies. The church today, as in the past, is the center of the social life of the community. At the same time the secular rôle of the church has increased as the masses have acquired education and have had contacts with the larger world. In its secular rôle the church is the center of recreation and organized efforts for social welfare.[14] The school plays a minor rôle in the plantation area, where education is still something of a novelty, and the whites make little provision for the education of the Negro. In the towns and smaller cities outside the plantation area, the school may be the center of the social life of the community.

Race relations in the smaller cities and towns, especially in the deep South, resemble a caste system in many important features.[15] The subordination of the Negro is sanctioned first by beliefs concerning his mental and moral inferiority. Then in all the relations between the two races there are symbols and rituals, designed to confirm the Negro's inferior status. The social subordination of the Negro is maintained partly by his economic subordination, which results in economic advantages for the white middle class. Moreover, the social subordination of the Negro provides, as Dollard has pointed out, a certain "sexual gain" for white men in that they have sexual access to both white and Negro women.[16] Then the system of social subordination of the Negro maintains the prestige of the whites. At all times the Negro is supposed to use deferential behavior toward whites. Except for those relationships in which the Negro man is a servant,

14 See Powdermaker, *op. cit.*, pp. 274ff.
15 John Dollard, *Caste and Class in a Southern Town* (New Haven, 1937) and Allison Davis, Burleigh B. Gardner, and Mary R. Gardner, *Deep South: A Social Anthropological Study of Caste and Class* (Chicago, 1941), give a comprehensive and thoroughgoing analysis of race relations in two towns in Mississippi.
16 See Dollard, *op. cit.*, pp. 134ff.

contacts between white women and Negro men are tabooed. Infractions of these regulations regarding Negro-white relations provoke a violent reaction on the part of the whites. The violation of the taboo on contacts between white women and Negro men usually ends in the killing of the latter. The rigidity of these quasi-caste relations and the severity of the punishment for the infringement of the corresponding controls are not the same throughout the South. In the towns and smaller cities of the upper South, there may be some relaxation of the castelike regulations and the punishment for their infringement by Negroes is less severe.

NEGRO COMMUNITIES IN LARGE CITIES

The location of Negro communities in the large cities of the South is different, on the whole, from that in the smaller cities and towns. In the large cities the location of Negro communities reveals two general patterns. In the older cities, like Charleston, with a large Negro population, the Negroes are widely scattered.[17] The location of the widely scattered Negro population in the older cities is due largely to historical factors. Small Negro settlements, comprised mostly of servants, have grown up close to the houses of the whites in which Negroes served. These settlements thus took root before the spatial pattern of the cities was affected by the economic forces which have shaped the pattern of our modern industrial and commercial cities. The second general pattern appears in the newer cities of the South, or in cities where industry and commerce have determined their spatial pattern. In these latter cities, there are several large concentrations of Negroes and the remainder of the Negro population is scattered lightly over a large area. The light scattering of Negroes over a large area is attributable, as was noted above, to historical factors, while the large concentrations of the Negro population reflect the increasing influence of economic and social forces inherent in the growth of the modern city.

There were four cities in the South in 1940 with Negro communities numbering 100,000 or more (See Table XI). The largest of these communities was in New Orleans, where since 1900 there has

[17] T. J. Woofter, Jr., *Negro Problems in Cities* (New York, 1928), p. 38.

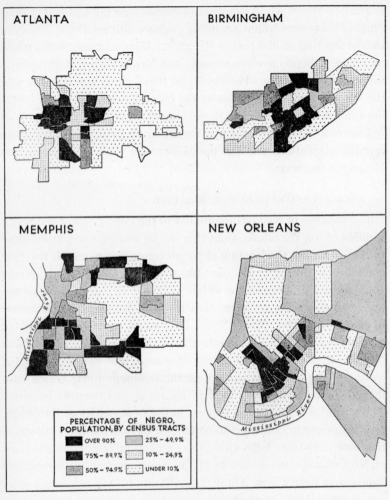

ATLANTA

BIRMINGHAM

MEMPHIS

NEW ORLEANS

PERCENTAGE OF NEGRO,
POPULATION, BY CENSUS TRACTS

OVER 90%   25% - 49.9%

75% - 89.9%   10% - 24.9%

50% - 74.9%   UNDER 10%

MAPS IX, X, XI, XII

Distribution of the Negro Population, According to Census
Tracts, in Four Southern Cities: 1940.*

* Based on the *Sixteenth Census of the United States*, 1940, "Population and
Housing."

developed one of the largest Negro communities in the country. This Negro community is unique in that a large proportion—a third—of the Negroes are of mixed ancestry, many of whom have a background of French culture. These so-called "creoles" have tended to remain apart from the great mass of the Negro population. In Memphis, with the second largest Negro community, the Negro population has more than doubled during the present century. The Negro population of Memphis has been drawn largely from the rural areas of the neighboring states. The third largest Negro community is in the relatively new city of Birmingham, where the Negro population has increased almost sevenfold since 1900. Into this rapidly developing industrial area, large numbers of Negroes have been drawn, mostly from the plantation areas in Alabama. In Atlanta, the location of the fourth community with over 100,000 Negroes, the Negro population has been drawn largely from the rural areas of Georgia, and has more than tripled since 1900.

In the larger cities of the South the majority of the Negro residents are concentrated in the slum and blighted areas. At the same time there are areas of Negro settlement which are sharply differentiated from these slum areas. They are the areas in which upper- and middle-class Negro families are able to buy homes. Quite often the better residential areas are found in close proximity to the Negro colleges.[18] The housing of Negroes in the larger southern cities was improved through public housing before and during World War II. Of the projects built under the United States Housing Act, 36.5 per cent of the units were for Negroes.[19] The majority—58.7 per cent—of the urban dwelling units in the United States Housing Authority projects were in the South.[20] In the program of war-housing, the Negro did not share as largely as in the low-rent housing program. Only a sixth of the war-housing units were for Negroes.[21] Less than a fourth—97 out of 408—of the war-housing projects for Negroes were located in

[18] Committee on Negro Housing, The President's Conference on Home Building and Home Ownership, *Negro Housing*. Prepared by Charles S. Johnson (Washington, D. C., 1932), pp. 17ff.
[19] National Housing Agency, Federal Public Housing Authority, Report S-602.
[20] Richard Sterner, *The Negro's Share* (New York, 1944), p. 319.
[21] National Housing Agency, Report S-602.

southern cities. Moreover, over three-fourths of these war-housing projects were temporary and convertible family dwellings or demountable family dwellings.[22] In Birmingham, there was one project —a permanent family dwelling development with 90 units; in Memphis, a permanent family dwelling project with 342 units; and in New Orleans, a permanent family dwelling project with 198 units.

OCCUPATIONAL STATUS OF NEGROES IN LARGE CITIES

Although the occupational differentiation of the Negro population of these large cities has progressed further than in the smaller cities and towns, the majority of the Negroes derive a living from common labor and unskilled occupations (See Table XII). In Birmingham, Memphis, and New Orleans, a third, and in Atlanta a fourth, of the

TABLE XII

Percentage of Employed Negro Males in Each Employment Status in Four Southern Cities with a Total Negro Population of 100,000 or More: 1940 *

EMPLOYMENT STATUS	ATLANTA	BIRMINGHAM	MEMPHIS	NEW ORLEANS
Professional and Semiprofessional	2.4	2.0	2.2	2.3
Proprietors, Managers, etc.	1.9	1.2	1.6	1.8
Clerical	3.9	2.7	3.4	4.9
Craftsmen	8.9	9.0	9.5	10.4
Operatives	22.7	34.4	24.6	22.6
Domestic Service	5.2	3.1	3.6	2.5
Service Workers	29.4	13.6	17.6	19.1
Laborers	24.5	32.6	35.5	34.9

* *Sixteenth Census of the United States: 1940 Population,* Vol. III. "The Labor Force."

Negro men are employed as common laborers. In Atlanta there is a relatively large number—30 per cent—of Negro men employed in the service occupations as porters, janitors, cooks, and barbers. More than a fifth of the Negro men in three of these cities derive a livelihood from unskilled work (operatives) in industry. In Birmingham more than a third of the employed Negro men are engaged in unskilled industrial occupations and consequently a smaller proportion of Negro

[22] *Ibid.*

men are in service occupations. In all of the four cities a relatively small proportion of the Negro men are employed as skilled craftsmen. The proportion of skilled craftsmen is highest in New Orleans, where the "creoles" or mulattoes with a background of French culture have a long tradition of skilled craftsmanship.[23]

The pattern of Negro employment in these four cities is characteristic of the employment of Negroes in the cities of the South. In 1940 a fifth of the employed Negro males in the South were employed as common laborers in industry. A tenth of the employed Negro men were in semiskilled jobs. The majority of Negro women—58.2 per cent—were in domestic service. In some cities as, for example, Richmond and Birmingham, Negro women have found employment as unskilled workers in industry. The employment of both Negro men and women in skilled occupations in southern cities has been kept at a minimum.

The occupational "ceiling" for the employment of Negro men and women has been due to the principle of "color-caste" in southern cities. Negro men and women are excluded from clerical and other white-collar occupations because these occupations are associated with a social status to which Negro workers cannot aspire. Consequently, Negro men and women can find employment in clerical and white-collar occupations only in the segregated Negro community. In Atlanta and New Orleans the presence of Negro colleges increases the opportunity for the employment of Negroes in clerical and white-collar occupations. In Birmingham and Memphis Negroes must depend almost entirely upon Negro business and fraternal organizations for employment in white-collar occupations. The principle of "color-caste" in employment extends to skilled occupations, which presuppose a larger amount of education and are generally cleaner and lighter types of work.

In response to the demand for workers in the areas where there were factories manufacturing munitions, there was a movement of Negroes from farms to these areas. But despite the emergency created by World War II, there was only a slight modification of the pattern of employment of Negroes in southern cities. Both employers and

[23] See p. 71 above.

workers in southern cities undertook to maintain the pattern of Negro employment. For example, in 1942 when plans were being made for bringing 9,000 white workers into Charleston, S. C., to work in defense plants, there were 4,000 Negro workers registered with the local United States Employment Service.[24] In order to maintain the traditional pattern of Negro employment, Negroes were kept from receiving the defense training courses or relegated to inadequate training centers.[25] In southern cities where there was a "tight" labor market, Negroes were more likely to be given employment in industry. But even in such cases Negroes were generally restricted to unskilled occupations. It was not until 1942 that Negroes succeeded in being upgraded in some southern cities. This was the result of governmental pressure exerted through the Fair Employment Practices Committee. This pressure was brought to bear on defense training programs for Negroes and on the United States Employment Service. For example, by 1944 Negroes were being trained in Atlanta for production jobs in the aircraft plants.[26] But, on the whole, the Negro was confined to the unskilled jobs in the industries of the South.

The relations of the Negro community to the larger urban communities in the South are very similar to the relations in the smaller cities and towns.[27] There is some relaxation of taboos because of the greater mobility and anonymity of the larger cities. In the larger cities there is a tendency for relations between the members of the two races to become more impersonal and formal. But the white and colored communities are separated in regard to their institutions. The outstanding exception has been the organization of the Negro and white workers in the United Mine Workers Union in the Birmingham area.

URBAN NEGRO COMMUNITIES IN BORDER STATES

The border states became differentiated from the lower South during the growth of the plantation system and cotton culture. As the Cotton Kingdom moved westward, slavery was introduced into Missouri but it did not thrive there as in the lower South. Likewise, great

[24] Robert C. Weaver, *Negro Labor* (New York, 1946), p. 23.
[25] *Ibid.*, Chapter 4.   [26] *Ibid.*, p. 86.
[27] Race relations in southern cities will be discussed in greater detail in Chapter XXVIII.

plantations with hordes of slaves did not find a congenial soil in Kentucky. For a time slavery was confined to the eastern tidewater region of Maryland, but the slave system was fast disappearing at the outbreak of the Civil War. In Delaware and in the District of Columbia there had never been more than a sprinkling of slaves. Since the plantation system of agriculture did not develop on a large scale in the border states the proportion of Negroes in their population was smaller than in the lower South. Only in the District of Columbia have the Negroes numbered more than one person in six. In Kentucky and Missouri Negroes have numbered only one person in sixteen. Moreover, since 1900 the Negro population of the border states as a whole has increased slowly. The increase has been greatest in West Virginia, while in Kentucky there has been a decrease of nearly 50,-000. The border states have been differentiated from the lower South by the large proportion of Negroes in urban areas.[28] In 1940 two-thirds of the 1,101,244 Negroes in the border states were in urban areas. Over a half-million of them were resident in four cities—Louisville, St. Louis, Mo., Baltimore, and Washington.

The location of the Negro communities in the border cities tends to conform to the pattern of southern cities though there are large concentrations of Negroes similar to those in northern cities. In all of the four large border cities, there are large concentrations of Negroes in a few areas but there are scattered areas of Negro residence outside the main areas of concentration. In the border cities, both historic and economic factors have determined the location of Negro communities. It seems probable that because of this fact, the major battles over the residential segregation of Negroes were first fought in the courts of these border cities.[29] Although in Louisville there are scat-

[28] In West Virginia, the rural Negro population exceeded the urban population in 1940, however, over 90 per cent of the rural Negro population was in rural nonfarming areas, which are industrialized areas.

[29] In St. Louis the first popular vote on the residential segregation of the Negro in the United States was held in 1916. It was in the Louisville segregation case that the United States Supreme Court handed down the unanimous decision that it was unconstitutional to prohibit Negroes by law from buying and occupying property. The United States Supreme Court decisions of May 3, 1948, outlawing the enforcement by state or federal courts of covenants restricting the sale or rental of property to Negroes, were based upon two covenant cases from the District of Columbia, one case from St. Louis, and a fourth case from Detroit.

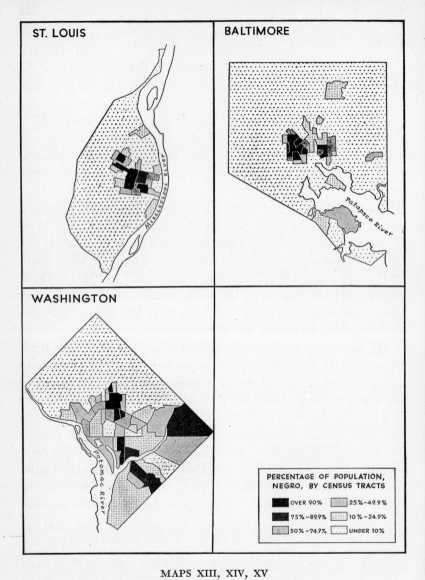

ST. LOUIS

BALTIMORE

WASHINGTON

PERCENTAGE OF POPULATION,
NEGRO, BY CENSUS TRACTS

OVER 90%   25%-49.9%

75%-89.9%   10%-24.9%

50%-74.9%   UNDER 10%

MAPS XIII, XIV, XV

Distribution of the Negro Population, According to Census
Tracts, in Three Border Cities: 1940.*

* Based on the *Sixteenth Census of the United States, 1940,* "Population and
Housing."

tered areas of Negro residence, the areas of greatest concentration are located just outside the central business zone.[30] In one of these areas in 1930 there were approximately 20,000 Negroes, who comprised nearly two-thirds of the total Negro population in Louisville. This area, which is seven blocks wide, extends westward for 25 blocks. These 25 blocks may be divided into three zones marking the westward expansion of the Negro population. The first zone, or the zone nearest the center of the city, is essentially a slum area where all forms of vice flourish. At the same time it is the location of Negro business and recreational institutions. The second zone is characterized by better dwellings and in this zone are located the most exclusive Negro church and the better public schools for Negroes. In the third zone, which marks the farthest expansion of the Negro community, is found the most desirable Negro residential area. There are other areas of Negro residence which reveal in their location in respect to the growth of the city and the character of Negro population and institutions the same processes of segregation and selection as this main area of concentration.

WASHINGTON, D. C.

Following the Civil War, Washington was considered a promised land by the freedmen. Here, under the protection of the government that had been responsible for their emancipation, the Negroes expected to enjoy the full benefits of freedom. During the decades from 1860 to 1940, the greatest increase in the Negro population occurred between 1860 and 1870, when thousands of ignorant and impoverished Negroes flooded the District and naturally created a tremendous social problem. According to a report made to the Senate at the time by General O. O. Howard of the Freedmen's Bureau, many of the refugees were crowded into filthy, floorless hovels unfit for human habitation, for which they were forced to pay exorbitant rents. In order to relieve this situation the Freedmen's Bureau provided tenements in public buildings and fitted up barracks in and near Washington. Yet the sordid realities of living in the nation's capital failed

[30] See E. Franklin Frazier, *Negro Youth at the Crossways* (Washington, D. C., 1940), pp. 14-18.

to dissipate the illusion that drew thousands of emancipated blacks to Washington. Some of those seeking a refuge in the capital following Reconstruction were the educated and more prosperous leaders, who fled from the wrath of southern whites when "white supremacy" was re-established.

Although the Negro inhabitants before the Civil War were badly enough housed, it was not until after the Civil War that the alleys of Washington became the special abode of Negroes. In 1872 it was estimated that 3,000 whites as against 22,000 Negroes or about half the Negro population lived in alleys. Forty-one years later, the Negro population in the alleys, according to a police census, had declined one-half and the white population to less than a thousand. In 1927, a firsthand investigation of 206 alleys in which 2,489 houses were located in 1912, revealed that only 150 of these alleys were inhabited and that they contained 1,495 houses.[31] During the depression, many of the uninhabited alleys once again became a refuge for dispossessed families. According to the estimates of the Alley Dwelling Authority made in 1937 there were 176 inhabited alleys containing 2,500 houses.

From time to time, welfare workers and humanitarians have protested against the condition of the Negro in the alley, but the power of landlords has been sufficient to halt periodic attempts to condemn alley dwellings. Consequently, many impoverished and ignorant Negroes continued to live in the alleys until the inauguration of a more enlightened social policy. This appeared in the creation of the Alley Dwelling Authority in 1934, which has cleared up many of the worst sore spots and has built several low-cost housing projects for Negroes.

Although the Negro population appears to be widely scattered over the District, the heavy concentrations of Negroes encircle the central business area of the city [32] (See Map XIV). Within the central business section, covering a half-mile area and including two census tracts,

[31] William H. Jones, *The Housing of Negroes in Washington, D. C.* (Washington, D. C., 1927), pp. 161ff.

[32] The city of Washington, which has been coterminous with the District of Columbia since 1895, was laid out in quadrants corresponding to the four points of the compass with the Capitol as the center; but in the natural organization which has grown up, the central business area is located roughly in the neighborhood of F and Thirteenth Streets, Northwest.

there were only 330 Negroes in 1930 and 255 in 1940 (See Table XIII). But within the next three-quarter mile zone (Zone II) encircling the business area nearly three-eighths of the entire Negro population was concentrated in both 1930 and 1940. This zone embraces a large part of the old Southwest community described in a Senate Report as follows:

The Southwest section has been the "problem child" of Washington housing students for three generations. Separated from the Northwest by the Mall and bounded by waterfront on two sides, the Southwest

TABLE XIII

Distribution of the Negro Population in the District of Columbia According to Zones, 1940 and 1930 *

ZONES	1940		1930	
	NUMBER	PER CENT	NUMBER	PER CENT
Zone I—½ Mile	255	0.1	330	0.2
Zone II—¾ Mile	68,207	36.4	48,447	36.7
Zone III— 1 Mile	70,120	37.5	51,669	39.1
Zone IV— 1 Mile	28,266	15.1	19,212	14.6
Zone V—To Boundary	20,418	10.9	12,410	9.4
Total	187,266	100.0	132,068	100.0

* Source: *Real Property Inventory for the District of Columbia, 1934.* Federal Housing Administration, and *Sixteenth Census of the United States: 1940, Population and Housing,* "Statistics for Census Tracts, Washington, D. C." (Washington, 1942).

is characterized by old and depreciated housing, the second largest number of inhabited alleys in any police precinct, and a fair percentage of old family residences whose owner-occupants, loyal to their neighborhood, see themselves more closely hemmed in each day by decaying housing. Census statistics show a steady diminution in the population of the Southwest. This reduction in population . . . has been halted, probably by the reduced economic status of families who moved to the Southwest in quest of lower rents.[33]

In the next zone (Zone III) there is another concentration of Negroes, comprising a slightly larger proportion of the Negroes in

[33] *Rent and Housing Conditions in the District of Columbia,* 73rd Congress, 2nd Session, 1934. Senate Document No. 125, Part 2, pp. 8-9.

the District. Between 1930 and 1940 the number of Negroes in each of these two zones had increased by about 20,000. The increase in the Negro population in Zone II had been caused chiefly by the poorer newcomers to the city, while the increase in Zone III had resulted partly from movements from Zone II. The number of Negroes and the proportion of the Negro population decline sharply in Zone IV. The decline in both numbers and proportion of Negroes continues in Zone V, where only about a tenth of the Negro population is located. The distribution of the Negro population for 1930 and 1940 indicates that whereas there has been a slight movement from the two main zones of Negro concentration, Negroes have been held within these two zones despite an increase of 55,000.

In Baltimore more than two-thirds of the Negro families are concentrated in four of the twenty statistical areas into which the city is divided.[34] A study of six "housing areas" in which Negroes predominated in 1933 revealed that all of them were blighted areas.[35] The housing situation among Negroes at that time was worse than that in Washington.[36] In both cities, however, the housing situation has become worse since these studies were made. It became worse in Washington as the result of the increasing activities of the governmental agencies under the New Deal and during the War emergency, which caused a large influx of residents without a corresponding increase in housing facilities. During the War emergency 22 public war-housing projects comprising 4,426 dwelling units were constructed for Negroes.[37] They consisted of four dormitory projects, 17 temporary and demountable dwelling projects, and four permanent family dwelling projects. These public war-housing projects together with the low-cost housing projects in the border cities have scarcely begun to solve the problems of housing facing Negro families. In the District of Columbia the problem is complicated by the opposition of whites to the locations chosen for housing projects for Negroes.

[34] Ira DeA. Reid, *The Negro Community in Baltimore. A Social Survey* (Baltimore, October 1, 1934), p. 26.
[35] *Ibid.*, p. 28.　　[36] Jones, *op. cit., passim.*
[37] National Housing Agency, Federal Public Housing Authority, Report S-602A.

OCCUPATIONAL STATUS OF NEGROES IN BORDER CITIES

Except in the District of Columbia Negro workers are not better off in the border cities than in the southern cities. In fact, in southern cities a larger proportion of Negro male workers have achieved the status of skilled craftsmen than in border cities. In most of the border cities there is a slightly larger professional and business class. But in the District of Columbia, where many Negroes are in government employment, the proportion of clerical workers is much larger than in southern cities. The chief difference between the Negro workers in the cities of the two sections is that a larger proportion of service workers are found in the border cities. In the case of Baltimore the generally low status of Negro workers is indicated by the fact that 43 per cent of them are common laborers.

TABLE XIV

Percentage of Employed Negro Males in Each Employment Status in Three Border Cities with a Total Negro Population of 100,000 or More and Louisville: 1940 *

EMPLOYMENT STATUS	BALTIMORE	DISTRICT OF COLUMBIA	ST. LOUIS, MO.	LOUISVILLE
Professional and Semiprofessional	2.4	2.9	3.3	3.2
Proprietors, Managers	2.8	1.4	2.8	2.8
Clerical	3.8	9.6	4.9	3.1
Craftsmen	5.3	6.3	6.6	5.9
Operatives	17.1	18.7	18.4	16.3
Domestic Service	3.2	2.4	2.5	5.5
Service Workers	20.9	28.9	31.7	29.6
Laborers	42.9	28.0	28.5	32.1

* *Sixteenth Census of the United States: 1940 Population*, Vol. III. "The Labor Force."

In Baltimore as in the other border cities, Negroes are regarded as the chief source of common labor by the industrialists.[38] They are employed as laborers in fertilizer plants, steel mills, and chemical factories, on roads and street railways, in stores, and in coal and lumber yards. The vast majority of Negro women workers are employed as

[38] Reid, *op. cit.*, pp. 38ff.

laundresses, servants and waitresses. The "ceiling" which keeps Negroes in the least desirable forms of employment is maintained by both employers and white workers. The workers limit this employment by excluding Negroes from their unions and from the training and apprenticeship necessary for entering certain occupations. Moreover, even in the border cities, with the exception of the District of Columbia, the Negro is excluded from public service. As the result of the exclusion of the Negro from skilled occupations, the income of the average Negro worker's family is far below that of the white working class family. A study of the income of a group of Negro male heads of families in Baltimore revealed their weekly incomes to range from $10 to $22.50 a week.[39]

During the War emergency the Negro worker was able to improve his status to a greater extent in border cities than in southern cities. At the beginning of the War emergency there was much opposition to the employment of Negroes in defense industries. In St. Louis Negroes were excluded from skilled craft unions and closed shop agreements continued to limit their employment.[40] Likewise, in Baltimore during the summer of 1941, Negroes were being excluded from defense plants although there was a manpower shortage. But because of economic needs and governmental pressure, by 1942 Negroes had begun to secure a foothold in the Baltimore industries. In 1943 Negroes constituted 63.1 per cent of pre-employment courses and about a sixth of the workers in the war plants.[41] Moreover, Negro workers had been upgraded and Negro and white workers were working together and using the same toilet facilities, which was opposed to the traditional pattern. In the District the improvement in the status of Negro workers was most marked in regard to government employment. Before Executive Order 8802 created the Fair Employment Practices Committee in 1941, about 8 per cent of the federal employees were colored and 90 per cent of the colored employees were in subclerical occupations. But by November, 1942, Negroes constituted about 17 per cent of the government employees and nearly half of the Negro employees were in clerical and professional occupations.[42]

[39] *Ibid.*, p. 53. [40] Weaver, *op. cit.*, pp. 31, 36. [41] *Ibid.*, pp. 84-85.
[42] *Ibid.*, p. 137.

RACE RELATIONS IN BORDER CITIES

The relations of the members of the Negro community to whites and the institutions of the larger community in border cities involve many contradictions. Unlike the pattern of race relations in southern cities, the separation of the races varies considerably. In the District of Columbia, Negroes enjoy fewer rights and privileges in some respects than they did thirty-five or forty years ago. When Negro residents undertake to fix the date for the change and attempt to place responsibility for the change, they usually say that it dates from the inauguration of President Woodrow Wilson, and that his wife became a leader in the movement to segregate the Negro after her visit to the Bureau of Printing, where she saw white and colored people working together and using the same toilet facilities. More important than the influence of the President's wife was that of the large number of southern whites who came to Washington during the Wilson administration. However, the Wilson administration and the influence of southern whites seemed to have brought to a climax the restrictions and discriminations that had always existed in the District. As in other border cities, there is a color line in employment.[43] Even in the government there has been a color line though the principle of "color-caste" has not been so rigid. During the extension of federal activities under the New Deal, a large number of Negroes were employed in clerical and some in administrative positions in separate Negro units. We have noted some of the changes in employment which occurred during the War emergency. Moreover, discrimination in regard to eating facilities and the use of lavatories has been removed in a number of government agencies.

But none of these changes have had much influence on the practices of the community. The CIO government unions have been most active in breaking down color barriers. Their canteen, to which men and women of all races in the armed forces were admitted, symbolized the most revolutionary advance in the social relations of the races since the Civil War. But the traditional institutions of the

[43] See Lorenzo J. Greene and Myra Colson Callis, *The Employment of Negroes in the District of Columbia* (Washington, D. C.).

community are still organized according to race. There are white and colored churches and the association of white and colored ministers is only a formal gesture. There is a separate school system in the District as in other border cities. Although the Negro children are supposed to receive the same education as the white children, there are discriminations.[44] In the District Negroes are excluded from places of amusement and restaurants with the exception of the restaurant in Union Station and in such places as the National Art Museum, the Supreme Court Building, and cafeterias in other government buildings. In some of the department stores Negroes may eat at the lunch counter where the patrons stand but are not permitted at the tables. As an indication of the attitude of the white community in regard to the status of the Negro, a large proportion of the whites of the District would rather remain without the suffrage than have the Negroes vote.[45]

URBAN NEGRO COMMUNITIES IN THE NORTH AND WEST

From three-fourths to nine-tenths of the Negroes in the North have always lived in cities. However, there has been a tendency for them to live in the larger cities. Consequently, little attention has been given to the Negro communities in the smaller cities.[46] Yet in these smaller cities of the north the Negro has faced more acute problems of

[44] See Howard H. Long, "The Support and Control of Public Education in the District of Columbia," *Journal of Negro Education*, VII (July, 1938), pp. 390-99. Harlan E. Glazier, *The Color Line in Our Public Schools* (Washington, D. C., 1937).

[45] Although Louisville is located in a state with segregation laws, Negroes are not "Jim-Crowed" on the streetcars; and at the railroad station they buy tickets at the window with whites and are not forced to remain in the separate waiting room. On the other hand, white people in Louisville are generally opposed to the use of Mr., Mrs., and Miss in addressing colored people and the newspapers avoid the term altogether. Likewise in Baltimore in a renowned institution like the Johns Hopkins Hospital the nurses are instructed in their class in Social Ethics not to use Mr., Mrs., and Miss in addressing colored people. Not many years ago when the father of a Howard University professor was taken to the Johns Hopkins Hospital and refused to reply when addressed by his first name, the medical authorities informed the professor that his father was apathetic to his environment and was giving negative responses. See Frazier, *Negro Youth at the Crossways*, pp. 29-38.

[46] Since the migrations during and following World War II, the National Urban League has made surveys of Negroes in the smaller industrial centers of the North.

employment and integration into communities than in the larger urban areas because the Negro population has been too small to develop a substantial separate community life. For example, in Muncie, Indiana, in 1940 there were 2,965 Negroes, who formed 6 per cent of the total population of 49,720. The Negroes in Muncie are concentrated in two sections: the largest and most important is comprised almost entirely of Negroes on the outskirts of the city and in the other, adjacent to it, Negroes are mingled with poor whites.[47] For a livelihood Negroes are employed in unskilled jobs in the building trades and at common labor. Between the Negro and white populations there is a deep cleavage though at some points the color line tends to give a little at times. But on the whole the Negro community tends to reproduce the institutions of the larger community. The more enterprising among the Negro population tend to migrate to the Negro communities in large northern cities.

Similar isolation of Negroes is found in other northern cities where their members have not increased to the point where they constitute a "problem." In the town of Milton, Pennsylvania, there were only 28 Negro families comprising a total of 100 people in a population of approximately 9,000 in 1940. The population of this town had continued inconsequential until Negro laborers were brought in during World War I. Before that time the few Negroes had found employment in personal and domestic service among the well-to-do white families.[48] Negroes had been accepted to the extent that white and colored children went to school together and they mingled socially to some extent. The importation of Negro laborers from the South created race consciousness among both Negroes and whites. Since the Negro laborers have left, race relations have tended to assume their former character. But for educated Negro youth there is no future in such towns in the North. They have no opportunities for employment and as they become adults, they are barred from full participation in the community because of barriers preventing intimate association between the races.

[47] Robert S. Lynd and Helen M. Lynd, *Middletown in Transition* (New York, 1937), p. 463.
[48] See J. Howell Atwood, Donald W. Wyatt, Vincent J. Davis, and Ira D. Walker, *Thus Be Their Destiny* (Washington, D. C., 1941), p. 6.

In the smaller cities of the North to which Negroes have been attracted because of the demand for unskilled workers, the barriers between the white and Negro population are greater. This is especially true of the cities in New Jersey. In the towns and cities of New Jersey the vast majority of the Negro population is located in blighted areas which are located "across the tracks," "over the creek," "by the dump," or "back of the hill." [49] The masses of Negro male workers are employed in unskilled and semiskilled occupations while Negro women are employed in domestic service. During World War II Negro workers were drawn into the industrial areas of New Jersey and their position in industry has been improved.[50] At the same time, the occupational differentiation of the Negro population has increased and Negroes have been able to acquire to a large extent property and homes in more desirable areas.

The situation is somewhat different in the cities of New England. In Boston, where the Negro population has increased only from 2 to 3 per cent of the total from 1910 to 1940, the Negro population is widely scattered over the city. But over a period of three hundred years the Negro population, as a whole, had remained distinct from the larger community.[51] There had been a slow occupational differentiation of the Negro population and as a result there was a tendency for Negroes of mixed ancestry to become integrated to some extent into the economic and cultural organization of Boston. Even this group met barriers against the more intimate association of the races, especially in marriage relations. The increase in the Negro population during and following World War I accentuated race consciousness among Negroes as well as whites.

In New Haven, Connecticut, the distribution of Negroes in the city was similar to that in Boston. At the same time, the color line in New Haven has been more rigid. The small Negro population of 6,235 in 1940, which was only 4 per cent of the total, formed a distinct

[49] *The Negro in New Jersey*. Report of a Survey by the Interracial Committee of the New Jersey Conference of Social Work in Cooperation with the State Department of Institutions and Agencies, December, 1932.

[50] Weaver, *op. cit.*, pp. 83, 87.

[51] See John Daniels, *In Freedom's Birthplace* (Boston, 1914), *passim*.

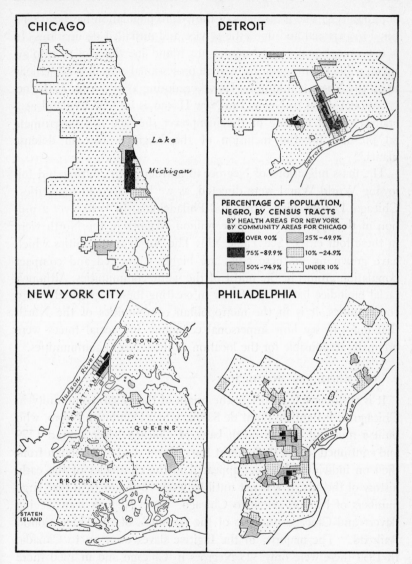

CHICAGO

Lake Michigan

DETROIT

Detroit River

PERCENTAGE OF POPULATION,
NEGRO, BY CENSUS TRACTS
BY HEALTH AREAS FOR NEW YORK
BY COMMUNITY AREAS FOR CHICAGO

OVER 90%   25% –49.9%
75% –89.9%   10% –24.9%
50% –74.9%   UNDER 10%

NEW YORK CITY

Hudson River
MANHATTAN
BRONX
QUEENS
BROOKLYN
STATEN ISLAND

PHILADELPHIA

Delaware River

MAPS XVI, XVII, XVIII, XIX

Distribution of the Negro Population, According to Census
Tracts, in Four Northern Cities: 1940.*

* Based on the *Sixteenth Census of the United States, 1940,* "Population and
Housing."

community.[52] The great mass of the Negro population has been confined to personal and domestic service and unskilled occupations. In a few exceptional cases Negroes are found in white-collar employment, while the insignificantly small professional class depends chiefly upon the Negro community. However, during World War II the occupational status of Negroes in New Haven as in New England generally changed because of the manpower shortage and governmental pressure for the inclusion of the Negro worker in defense plants.[53]

The mass migrations of Negroes to northern cities during and following World War I were directed, as we have seen to four cities: Chicago, Detroit, New York, and Philadelphia. In 1940, over a million of the approximately three million Negroes in the North were in these four cities (See Table XI). The Negro communities which have grown up in these cities are highly segregated and compact population groups in the midst of the white communities. Although racial prejudice has been a factor in creating these segregated Negro communities, it is in the metropolitan communities of the North that one can see how impersonal economic and social forces were originally responsible for the location of these Negro communities.

THE SOUTH SIDE IN CHICAGO

It is customary to associate the origin of the Negro community in Chicago with Baptiste Point de Saible, a San Domingan Negro, who built a rude hut on the north bank of Chicago River around 1779 and continued to live there for at least fifteen years.[54] Although from then on individual Negroes appeared in the chronicles of the early history of the city, it was not until between 1840 and 1850 that large numbers of Negroes came to Chicago. These Negroes were fleeing slavery and Chicago was one of the terminals of the Underground Railroad.[55] The majority of the fugitive slaves went on to Canada. In 1850 there were only 323 Negroes in Chicago and in 1860 there

[52] See Robert A. Warner, *New Haven Negroes* (New Haven, 1940), pp. 182-226.
[53] Weaver, *op. cit.*, pp. 34, 38.
[54] E. Franklin Frazier, *The Negro Family in Chicago* (Chicago, 1932), p. 86.
[55] St. Clair Drake and Horace R. Cayton, *Black Metropolis, A Study of Negro Life in a Northern City* (New York, 1945), p. 32.

were less than a thousand. Following the Civil War Negroes came to Chicago in such numbers that by 1870 there were 3,696 in the city. From then on the Negro population doubled each decade until 1900. Between 1900 and 1910 the rate of increase declined to 50 per cent. Then came the mass migration during and following World War I and the number of Negroes increased from 44,103 in 1910 to 109,594 in 1920, or 148.2 per cent. The migrations continued during the prosperous twenties and the population more than doubled between 1920 and 1930. Then came the depression years and the rate of increase diminished. Between 1930 and 1940 the Negro population increased from 233, 903 to 277, 331 or 18.7 per cent. World War II stimulated once more the migration of Negroes to Chicago and it was estimated that 60,000 came to the city.[56]

In the early history of the Negro community in Chicago, there was a settlement in the area near the center of the city but over a half of the Negro population was resident outside this small Black Belt.[57] But after the migrations during World War I the Negro population became more concentrated in the Black Belt (See Map XVI). Nevertheless, the expansion of the Negro community was similar, on the whole, to that of other racial and cultural groups.[58] The Negroes had gained a foothold in and near the center of the city and as the city expanded, the segregation of the Negro population was part of the general process of segregation of different racial, economic, and cultural groups. Moreover, as the Negro community moved southward there was a process of selection and segregation of various elements in the Negro community on the basis of occupation, intelligence and ambition.[59]

It was possible to measure the process of selection and segregation in the Negro community in 1920 by dividing the community into zones coinciding more or less with the expansion of the city as a

[56] *Ibid.*, p. 8.   [57] *Ibid.*, pp. 175-76.

[58] Ernest W. Burgess, "Residential Segregation in American Cities," *The Annals*, CXL (November, 1928), p. 110.

[59] Robert E. Park, "The Urban Community as a Spatial Pattern and a Moral Order," in *The Urban Community*, edited by Ernest W. Burgess (Chicago, 1926), p. 9.

whole [60] (See Map XX). In the process of selection and segregation it will be observed that the more recent migrants tend to be concentrated in the areas near the center of the city (See Table XV). In the first zone over three-fourths of the heads of families were southern-born. The proportion of southern-born heads of families decreased in

TABLE XV

Characteristics of the Negro Population in Seven Zones of the South Side Negro Community, Chicago, Illinois, 1920 *

ZONE	HEADS OF FAMILIES SOUTHERN-BORN	PERSONS TEN YEARS AND OVER ILLITERATE	Mulattoes Fifteen Years and Over	
			MALE	FEMALE
I	77.7	13.4	19.9	27.2
II	77.0	4.6	19.0	23.8
III	74.7	3.2	33.5	40.2
IV	73.8	2.3	19.2	24.0
V	72.6	3.3	22.8	24.7
VI	69.0	2.9	31.3	32.8
VII	65.2	2.7	49.7	48.5

* Reproduced with permission from *The Negro Family in the United States* by E. Franklin Frazier, p. 305. Copyright 1939 by The University of Chicago Press.

the successive zones marking the expansion of the Negro community from the center of the city. The same process of selection was evident in regard to the literacy of the Negro population. In the first zone, where the poorer newcomers to the city gained a foothold in the blighted areas of cheap rents outside the business area, 13.4 per cent of the Negroes were illiterate. The illiteracy rate declines in the successive zones as one goes from the center of the city. The process of selection and segregation is even evident in regard to the mulatto elements in the Negro population.[61] In Zones I and II, near the center

[60] Burgess has shown that the process of urban expansion can be measured by the rate of change in poverty, home ownership, and other variable conditions for unit areas along the main thoroughfares radiating from the center of the city. Ernest W. Burgess, "Determination of Gradients in the Growth of the City," *Publication of the American Sociological Society*, XXVI (1927), pp. 178-84.

[61] As we have seen, the mulattoes or mixed-bloods have enjoyed, on the whole, superior cultural and economic advantages which have caused them to comprise a large proportion of Negro leaders and professional men and women. See Edward B. Reuter, *The Mulatto in the United States* (Boston, 1918).

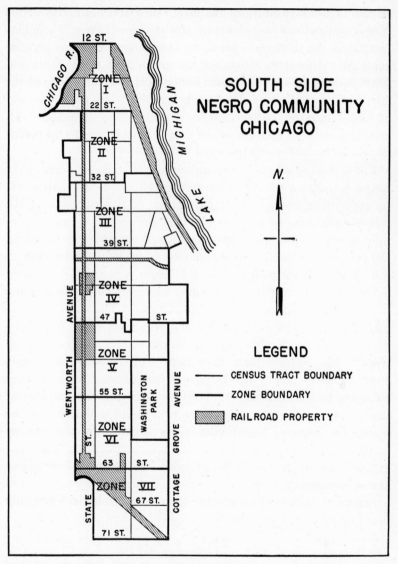

MAP XX

South Side Negro Community: Chicago.

Reproduced with permission from *The Negro Family in the United States* by
E. Franklin Frazier. Copyright 1939 by the University of Chicago Press.

of the city, only one-fifth of the Negro men and one-fourth of the Negro women show any admixture of white blood. There is a sudden increase in the third zone, where the disorganized elements are concentrated.[62] Except for the sudden rise in this zone, the proportion of Negroes of mixed-blood increased as one went from the center of the city. In the seventh zone about one-half of the Negro population was of mixed ancestry. The increase in the proportion of mixed-bloods coincided with an increase in the proportion of Negroes in professional and clerical occupations and in business.[63]

The process of selection and segregation of various elements in the Negro population which we have described occurs when there are no artificial or consciously created barriers to the expansion of the Negro community in northern cities. In the case of Chicago, as in most northern cities, there have been conscious attempts to restrict the expansion of the Negro community. Since 1920 the attempts to restrict the normal expansion of the Negro community have been mainly through restrictive covenants, or agreements among white property owners not to rent or sell to Negroes.[64] The restrictive covenant is, in fact, one of a number of instruments which have been devised to confine the Negro population to certain areas in northern cities.[65] In addition, there have been neighborhood associations and agreements among real estate operators seeking the same end. Even the Federal Housing Authority has accepted and perpetuated the practices of the real estate operators in regard to the financing of homes for Negroes. Nevertheless, the restrictive covenant has remained the most important instrument for maintaining the segregation of the Negro since it has provided legal sanction for the practice of segregation.

For short periods the restrictive covenants, which are generally made by property owners on the periphery of Negro neighborhoods,

---

[62] See Frazier, *The Negro Family in Chicago*, p. 103.   [63] *Ibid.*, p. 107.

[64] Drake and Cayton, *op. cit.*, pp. 179ff and pp. 382-83.

[65] See Robert C. Weaver, *The Negro Ghetto* (New York, 1948), pp. 21ff. This book is the most recent and at the same time the most comprehensive and thoroughgoing study of the social and economic aspects of the residential segregation of Negroes in northern cities. See also Herman H. Long and Charles S. Johnson, *People vs. Property* (Nashville, Tennessee, 1947), concerning restrictive covenants in housing in Chicago and St. Louis.

have succeeded in confining the Negro population to certain areas. But in the long run the restrictive covenants have not proved effective because they are opposed to the interests of some landlords and real estate operators. As the population of the northern city has expanded and changes have occurred in the character of the white areas adjacent to Negro neighborhoods, white owners and real estate operators have sought to profit from these changes. Consequently, the Negro population breaks through the ring of covenants about the areas of Negro residence. One of the immediate results of the attempts to confine the Negro to certain areas by these artificial agreements has been an increase in racial tensions. Another result has been the numerous legal battles, which have been fought over the restrictive covenants. In the course of these legal battles, covenants have been upheld and enforced by the local courts in at least 17 states, while in only one or two states have the courts in recent years refused to sanction them.[66] Until its decision in 1948, the Supreme Court evaded the issue or its decisions were not definitive. But on May 3, 1948, the Supreme Court ruled that covenants restricting the sale and occupancy of property on racial grounds could not be enforced by either state or federal courts.[67]

While it is impossible to forecast the consequences of these decisions, there can be no question about the moral consequences of these rulings.[68] As for the effects of the decisions on the housing of Negroes, it appears that more housing facilities will be made available for them. Real estate operators will probably take advantage of the new demand for houses in declining white areas adjacent to Negro neighborhoods. It is also likely that tensions will develop in these same areas where whites resist the expansion of the Negro population. Undoubtedly, white owners and real estate operators will undertake to devise new instruments in order to restrict the free movement of the Negro population. But it is not likely that such action will have much effect, especially if adequate housing is made available to the community as a whole.

[66] Weaver, *op. cit.*, p. 243.
[67] See *Supreme Court of the United States*, Nos. 72 and 87, and 290 and 291.
[68] See American Council on Race Relations, *Report*, May, 1928.

NEGRO HARLEM IN NEW YORK CITY

When one turns to New York City, one finds that not only has the location of the Negro community been determined by economic and social forces inherent in the growth of the city but that the expansion of the Negro community has assumed the pattern of a self-contained city.[69] Although there is disagreement as to the historical events leading to the settlement of Negroes in the Harlem area, there seems to be no question that Harlem had deteriorated as a residential area for the whites when Negroes first gained an entrance, around the beginning of the present century.[70] From a small settlement in a block on 135th Street, the Negro community spread out in all directions.

The radial expansion of the Negro population from the area about 135th Street and Seventh Avenue may be represented ideally by drawing concentric circles about the census tract in which the intersection of these two main thoroughfares is located (See Map XXI). The expansion of the community from the standpoint of numbers is shown in the increase in the number of Negroes in each of the five zones since 1910 (See Table XVI). In 1910 more than half of the Negro population was concentrated in the first two zones, where they constituted 18 per cent of the resident population. By 1920 the Negro population, which had more than trebled, had begun to fill up the first two zones and to overflow into the third zone. But it will be observed that the number of Negroes increased very little in the fourth and fifth zones. During the decade from 1920 to 1930 the Negro population of Harlem more than doubled. The population of the first zone was 99 per cent Negro while in the second zone seven out of every eight persons were Negroes. The absolute number of Negroes and their relative numbers in the population of the third zone had tripled and it is significant that the Negroes had become a large proportion of the population of the fourth zone. The number of Negroes and their relative numbers had also more than doubled in the outer-

[69] See E. Franklin Frazier, "Negro Harlem: An Ecological Study," *American Journal of Sociology*, XLIII (1937), pp. 72-88.

[70] See Clyde V. Kiser, *Sea Island to City* (New York, 1932), pp. 19-20.

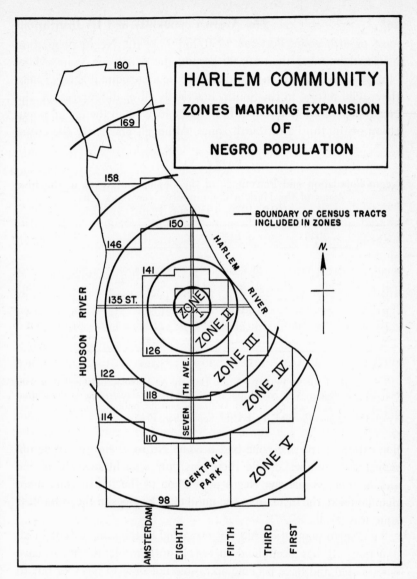

MAP XXI

Harlem Community: Zones Marking Expansion
of Negro Population.

Reproduced with permission from *The Negro Family in the United States* by
E. Franklin Frazier. Copyright 1939 by the University of Chicago Press.

most or fifth zone. Between 1930 and 1940 the Negro population increased by more than 80,000 despite the depression years. Many Negroes came to Harlem in order to secure more equitable relief than they could receive in the South. Practically all of the increase in the Negro population is accounted for by the increase in the Negro population of the third and fourth zones. Although practically the entire

TABLE XVI

Negro Population and Percentage of the Population Negro in the Five Zones of the Harlem Community, New York City, 1910, 1920, 1930 and 1940 *

	1940		1930		1920		1910	
ZONE	NUMBER	PER CENT	NUMBER	PER CENT	NUMBER	PER CENT	NUMBER	PER CENT
I	11,818	99.7	12,585	99.0	9,053	77.2	1,856	18.3
II	74,824	88.8	72,214	87.8	43,734	52.1	13,172	18.9
III	93,732	56.7	64,368	41.4	21,661	13.1	6,145	4.4
IV	89,278	48.5	40,312	22.7	2,058	1.0	1,879	1.0
V	16,550	7.1	14,415	6.2	6,742	2.5	5,775	2.3
Total	286,202	42.3	203,894	30.9	83,248	11.4	27,827	6.7

* Source: E. Franklin Frazier, "Negro Harlem: An Ecological Study," *American Journal of Sociology*, Vol. XLIII, pp. 72-88, and *Census Tract Data on Population and Housing, New York City: 1940.* Welfare Council Committee on 1940 Census Tract Tabulations for New York City. September, 1942.

population of the first zone had become Negro, there was an actual decrease in numbers, while there was only a slight increase in the second zone. While the Negro population of the fourth zone more than doubled, the increase in the number of Negroes in the outermost zone was small.

The Negro population has not expanded to the same extent in all directions. It has been held in check until residential areas have deteriorated and have become accessible not only to Negroes but to Italians and Puerto Ricans as well. In other instances, white residential areas have put up a stubborn resistance even when surrounded by Negroes. Sometimes the location of light industry has doomed an area as a residential area and Negroes following some immigrant groups have entered the area. The extent to which the Negro popula-

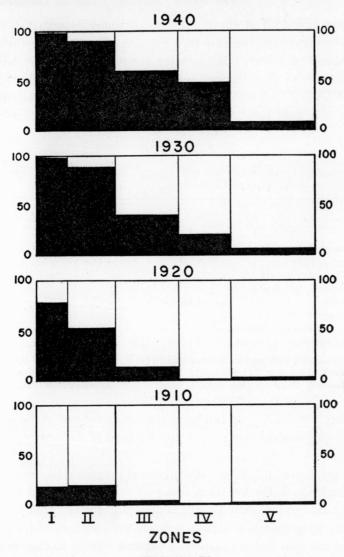

DIAGRAM IV

Percentage of the Population Negro in Each of the Five Zones of
Expansion of the Harlem Negro Community, 1940, 1930, 1920
and 1910.*

* Based on Table XVI.

tion has expanded in the five zones has coincided with the predominant type of structures in these five zones. The Negro population had almost completely taken over the first two zones in 1930, when the majority of the structures were nonresidential in character (See Table XVII). Nine-tenths of the residential structures in these two zones were built before 1900.[71] But what was more significant was

TABLE XVII

Percentage of Population Negro and Types of Structures in Five Zones of the Harlem Community, New York City *

	Zone				
	I	II	III	IV	V
Percentage of population Negro in 1930	99.0	87.8	41.4	22.7	6.2
Percentage of structures that were nonresidential in 1934	83.8	78.2	59.8	42.5	28.0
Percentage of nonresidential structures that were rooming- and lodging-houses in 1934 †	34.2	32.0	31.5	23.0	18.5

* Reproduced with permission from *The Negro Family in the United States* by E. Franklin Frazier, p. 313. Copyright 1939 by The University of Chicago Press.
† Rooming- and lodging-houses are classified as nonresidential structures.

the fact that the Negroes had become a substantial part of the population only in those zones where about a third of the nonresidential structures were rooming- and lodging-houses. The relation between the expansion of the Negro population and the physical condition of the buildings in the five zones is not so obvious because of the rehabilitation of the nonresidential structures in the first zone.[72]

The expansion of the Negro population was associated with a process of selection and segregation of elements similar to that in the larger urban community. There has been a tendency for older persons and unmarried persons to be concentrated in the center of Harlem while married couples with children are found in the outer zones.

[71] See Frazier, *The Negro Family in the United States*, Table 50, p. 638.
[72] *Ibid.*, p. 314.

OCCUPATIONAL STATUS AND INCOME OF NEGROES
IN NORTHERN CITIES

In northern cities the occupational differentiation of Negro communities has advanced beyond that in either southern or border cities. This is especially true in the case of New York City and Chicago (See Table XVIII). In both of these cities, one out of every 30 employed Negro men is in professional or semiprofessional occupations as over against one in every 45 in southern cities. The contrast be-

TABLE XVIII

Percentage of Employed Negro Males in Each Employment Status in
Four Northern Cities with a Total Negro Population
of 100,000 or More: 1940 *

EMPLOYMENT STATUS	NEW YORK	CHICAGO	PHILADELPHIA	DETROIT
Professional and Semi-professional	3.5	3.3	2.8	2.2
Proprietors, Managers	5.0	2.7	2.8	2.4
Clerical	10.5	10.1	6.6	5.2
Craftsmen	8.0	9.2	8.6	13.5
Operatives	19.7	20.1	20.4	28.9
Domestic Service	2.7	1.4	3.2	1.0
Service Workers	35.5	31.4	23.4	20.0
Laborers	13.2	20.1	30.0	25.2

* *Sixteenth Census of the United States: 1940. Population.* Vol. III. "The Labor Force."

tween northern and southern cities is even more important than the figures indicate because a large proportion of the Negroes in professional occupations in southern cities are ministers, whereas in northern cities only a small proportion are ministers and Negroes are found in practically all professional occupations. Then the proprietors and managers of business in northern cities constitute a larger proportion of employed Negro men. The proportion of employed Negro men in clerical occupations in New York City and Chicago is even higher than in the District of Columbia where large numbers are employed in the federal government. The proportion of employed Negro men in skilled occupations is almost the same in New York, Chicago, and Philadelphia as in southern cities, while the proportion is much higher in Detroit. The proportion of semiskilled operatives is about the same in northern cities as in southern cities. On the other hand, there is a much larger proportion of service workers in the northern cities, and a smaller proportion in common labor than in southern cities.

The income of Negro families in the northern cities is higher than in southern cities. Nevertheless, the income of Negro families is far below that of white families. In 1935-36, the median income of native-born nonrelief Negro families was $1,350 as compared with $2,110 for white families of the same status.[73] The median income for Negro wage earners was $1,270 as compared with $1,980 for Negro clerical workers, whose median income was only $200 less than that for white clerical workers. When relief and nonrelief families are considered together, half of the Negro families in New York City had an income of less than $980. The income of Negro families in Chicago was even less than that in New York City. About two-thirds of the Negro families in Chicago had incomes less than $1,000.[74] The low income of Negroes in northern cities is due partly to the job "ceiling" which restricts them to the lowest paid and least desirable occupations.[75] Negro women comprise 50 per cent or more of the domestic servants in the larger cities of the north while Negro men monopolize such jobs as porters and are found in larger numbers as waiters. In industry Negro men are found largely in the unskilled occupations requiring strength.

The "job ceiling" in northern cities is a manifestation of prejudice, based upon color or racial descent, in a modern urban industrial community where the secular process of competition normally determines one's employment status.[76] In the northern city there is a color

---

[73] United States Department of Labor, *Family Income and Expenditure in New York City, 1935-36*, Vol. 1, "Family Income" (Washington, 1941), p. 19.

[74] United States Department of Labor. Bureau of Labor Statistics, *Family Income and Expenditure in Chicago, 1935-36*, Vol. I, "Family Income" Bulletin 642 (Washington, 1938), p. 8.

[75] See Drake and Cayton, *op. cit.*, Chapter 9, for a thorough analysis of the job "ceiling" in Chicago.

[76] The conflict between the principle of competition and the principle of caste in determining the pattern of race relations in the northern city will be considered in detail in Chapter XXVIII.

line, so to speak, but the color line is not fixed because it is not supported by deeply rooted traditions and sentiments. Among the heterogeneous populations of the large cities, there is lacking the traditional background of attitudes concerning the status of the Negro. The profit motive and competition are constantly nullifying the effects of tradition and prejudice. Moreover, the Negro possesses political power which can be utilized to prevent the crystallization of fixed patterns of discrimination, especially, in time of crisis and during the shifts in power.

URBAN NEGRO COMMUNITIES IN THE WEST

Up to 1940 scarcely more than one per cent of the Negroes in the United States were found in the West. About five-sixths of the Negroes in the West were in cities, the largest urban Negro community being in Los Angeles where about a third of all the Negroes in the West were resident. In San Francisco, Seattle, and Portland, there were much smaller communities with from 2,000 to 5,000 Negroes. This situation was changed when an estimated 250,000 Negroes were drawn to these cities in response to the demand for war workers.[77]

The small Negro community in Seattle increased 300 per cent over the number in 1940 as the result of the influx of Negroes during the War emergency.[78] This has affected the spatial distribution of Negroes as well as the character of the Negro community. While Negroes had been widely dispersed, there were four areas of concentration. One of these areas, the center of the cultural life of the Negro community, was inhabited by the conservative home-owning families. In another area close to Japanese residents and near the center of the city there were two Negro hotels and a small but more heterogeneous group of Negroes. The third area of Negro concentration, which was an "overflow" area from the second area, was an area of much social disorganization. The fourth area was an intermediate community between the first and second areas. The influx of Negroes caused some

---

[77] Cf. Henry S. Shryock, Jr. and Hope Tisdale Eldridge, "Internal Migration in Peace and War," *American Sociological Review*, Vol. 12, p. 32.

[78] Robert W. O'Brien, "Seattle" in "Race Relations on the Pacific Coast," *The Journal of Educational Sociology* (November, 1945), pp. 146-57.

dispersion of the Negro population but on the whole it resulted in overcrowding in the area evacuated by the Japanese and in areas already occupied by Negroes. At the same time, the Seattle Housing Authority has pursued a policy of integrating Negroes in some of its projects and in setting up segregated projects. In the matter of employment, Negro workers had to face at first the exclusionist policy of unions. But after a time they were able to break down barriers not only in war industries but in other fields of employment. Because of the conflicting social forces in Seattle, the pattern of race relations has not become crystallized though the Negro made some progress toward integration during the war years.

The increase in the size of the Negro community in Portland, Oregon, was even greater than in Seattle.[79] From less than 2,000, the Negro population increased to 22,000 during the War emergency. The sudden influx of Negroes from all parts of the country with the exception of New England and the state of Delaware was generally resented by the small group of law-abiding and self-sustaining Negroes who had become accommodated to their place in Portland. The vast majority of Negroes were in unskilled and service occupations. As the result of the influx of Negro war workers, a large Negro ghetto was created and discriminations in regard to civil rights were instituted. Ninety-six per cent of the Negro war workers were employed in shipbuilding. Since shipbuilding was a war-born industry, the cessation of hostilities resulted in the unemployment of Negro workers. The Negroes are not disposed, however, to return to the South, whence most of them came. The problem of integrating the Negroes into the community is complicated by the fact that they are from rural backgrounds and have little education and no familiarity with modern farm machinery.

Until the War emergency the less than 5,000 Negroes in San Francisco were lost among the more than 600,000 inhabitants.[80] There was hardly a Negro district since in even the area of greatest Negro

[79] Edwin C. Berry, "Portland" in "Race Relations on the Pacific Coast," *loc. cit.*, pp. 158-65.

[80] Joseph James, "San Francisco," in "Race Relations on the Pacific Coast," *loc. cit.*, pp. 167-78.

concentration there were many whites and Japanese, and a small number of Chinese and Filipinos. The vast majority of Negroes were employed in service occupations. Many Negroes, especially the few professionals, had more white than Negro friends. With the influx of Negroes from the South, the Negro population increased fivefold. When San Francisco became conscious of the Negro minority, the racial pattern which had become established in regard to the Oriental was applied to the Negro. When Negroes began pouring into the city they were crowded into the area evacuated by the Japanese. Employers attempted to restrict Negroes to unskilled and service occupations.[81] Moreover, the Negro worker was excluded from the boilermakers' union and the machinists' union. But as the result of the Fair Employment Practices Committee and the manpower shortage management was forced to change its attitude and the unions issued work permits. The majority of Negroes were employed in shipbuilding and in longshore work. But later Negroes were not only up-graded in industry but they were employed on the trolleys and buses. The greatest difficulty facing the Negro has been the problem of housing. Restrictive covenants and the opposition of real estate dealers to public housing have been responsible for this situation. There is no fixed policy as yet in the treatment of Negroes in restaurants and other places of public service and recreation. The sudden growth of the Negro community has made it self-conscious and has caused it to associate its fight for equality and integration with other minority groups.

The largest Negro community in the West has long been in Los Angeles. It had grown from 15,579 in 1920 to 38,894 in 1930 and by 1940 there were 63,774 Negroes in the city. Then the War emergency brought about 75,000 to the city. This influx caused the Negro community to become one of the largest in the country. The area formerly occupied by the Japanese became overcrowded with Negroes and there was much doubling-up in the Negro area. There was opposition at first to the employment of Negroes in defense work and later when Negroes were employed, they were restricted to the lowest paid unskilled jobs.[82] The problem of Negro labor in Los Angeles was brought

[81] See *The Negro War Worker in San Francisco*. A Project Administered by the Y.M.C.A., May, 1944, pp. 61ff.   [82] Weaver, *op. cit.*, p. 23.

out in the efforts to up-grade Negroes in transportation. After much evasion on the part of management and labor, both were willing to accept the directives from the F.E.P.C. when the government showed in a wildcat strike in Philadelphia that it was determined to carry out a policy of nondiscrimination.[83] The problems of the Negro in Los Angeles are similar to those of the large number of Mexicans. There is first the problem of providing jobs according to individual competence and secondly the problem of providing decent housing facilities.

Our analysis of the character of Negro communities in the towns and cities of the United States has been concerned mainly with their physical base and the economic status of the residents. Since about 50 per cent of the Negro population is urbanized, our analysis has included the physical setting of a half of the Negroes in the country in relation to the white population, the manner in which they make a living, and how their earnings compare with those of their white neighbors. In a general way we have sketched the pattern of race relations in the cities of the different regions. The analysis of urban Negro communities here together with the analysis of rural communities in the foregoing chapter provide a knowledge of the physical and economic setting in which various institutions and other types of associations have developed in the past and function at present. However, before studying these institutions and other forms of associated life, we shall study the emergence and the present character of social stratification in these communities.

[83] *Ibid.*, pp. 171ff.

CHAPTER XII

Social and Economic Stratification

THE roots of the social and economic stratification of the Negro population go back to the period of slavery. Under the influence of slavery as a social institution, significant social distinctions appeared among the slaves. These social distinctions were related to the rôle of the slaves in the social and economic organization of the plantation. There was the distinction, first, between those who served in the house and those who labored in the fields. Very often those who served in the house bore even in their physical features the mark of the master race. Then, there was a division of labor on the plantation which provided an outlet for individual talent and skill. The skill of the artisan was not only recognized by his owner but it gave him a superior status among his fellow bondsmen. Following the Civil War and Emancipation, these social distinctions continued to play a rôle among the freedmen. Those who, through association with the white race in the master's house had acquired the elements of white culture tended to set themselves apart. The superior position of this group was often associated with a lighter skin complexion. Likewise, the skilled artisan, conscious of his superiority, tended to disassociate himself from the masses of unlettered and uncouth former field hands.

Other distinctions came into existence. The ambitious and the thrifty who acquired land set themselves apart from the less efficient and the lazy and the impoverished. Those who had been free before Emancipation looked down upon all of those who had become free as the result of the fortunes of war. These various types of social distinctions created a class structure in the Negro community that existed until the mass migrations during and following World War I. Then as the result of urbanization, which accelerated the occupational differ-

273

entiation of the Negro population, the class structure of the Negro community became more complex and some of the older social distinctions lost their significance.

SOCIAL DISTINCTIONS AMONG THE SLAVES

"We were not of a common lot," wrote an ex-slave with pride in his autobiography, and then explained that slaves recognized a social distinction between house slaves or personal servants and field slaves.[1] In Chapter III, we saw how the house slaves and personal servants in the cast off clothes of their masters appeared at the social functions on the plantation as a "privileged class" and enjoyed great prestige among the slaves who were "excluded from the dwelling of their owners."[2] Among the house slaves and personal servants themselves, there were distinctions in rank. Those who had a responsible position in the household and enjoyed the confidence of the masters stood highest in the slave hierarchy. Sometimes the child of a favorite servant was given the privilege of developing some skill or of following his inclination in regard to a vocation. This often meant that he was apprenticed to a skilled artisan and became in turn a skilled artisan. Although the skilled artisans did not enjoy the social status accorded the more responsible house servants, they had a social rank above that of the field hands. These skilled artisans, who had achieved their position because of their superior intelligence, developed a pride in their workmanship and in their important rôle in the division of labor on the plantation.[3]

Where race mixture occurred, the mulatto was conscious of his relationship to the master race and generally felt himself superior to the unmixed Negroes.[4] The lighter skin color generally involved certain advantages that confirmed this feeling of superiority. Often those of mixed ancestry were taken into the house as house servants, where they enjoyed superior cultural contacts or they might be given special privileges because of their relation to the master. Thus they came to identify themselves with their masters and held themselves apart from the other slaves.

[1] Robert Anderson, *From Slavery to Affluence* (Nebraska, 1927), pp. 29-30.
[2] See pp. 55-56 above. [3] See p. 57 above. [4] See p. 54 above.

In fact, there was a general tendency on the part of the slaves to identify themselves with their masters. This identification carried with it certain social distinctions for among the slaves those who were owned by wealthy and aristocratic masters were likely to have a higher status than those who were the slaves of the poorer and less distinguished whites.

SOCIAL STRATIFICATION AMONG THE FREE NEGROES

Since the class of free Negroes that grew up during slavery continued to be recruited from the ex-slaves, it was natural that the social distinctions recognized among the slaves were carried over into freedom. We have already noted that mulattoes and mixed-bloods were a conspicuous element among the Negroes who were free before the Civil War.[5] The fact of white ancestry did not in itself confer upon one a higher social status among the free Negroes. Generally, white ancestry was associated with certain economic and social advantages which the blacks as a group did not possess. It was often associated with greater literacy or a fair education or considerable mechanical skill. In some sections many of the mulattoes had managed to become land-owners or even the owners of slaves.

Within these free Negro communities there were social distinctions that, though they might have their roots in slavery, had a functional relation to these communities. In northern cities there had always been a small group of free Negroes, generally of mixed ancestry, who had held themselves aloof from the majority of Negroes from the South.[6] This group usually consisted of artisans, tradesmen, and the higher type of personal and domestic servants, who maintained a decent standard of living and became homeowners.[7] This group constituted a sort of upper class which was increased from time to time by

[5] See pp. 67-68 above.

[6] See E. Franklin Frazier, *The Negro Family in Chicago* (Chicago, 1932), pp. 231-38.

[7] See *A Statistical Inquiry Into the Condition of the People of Colour of the City of Philadelphia* (Philadelphia, 1849). In the survey of 4,262 heads of families, there were 315 owners of real estate, valued at $194,318, consisting "of 41 mechanics, 78 labourers, 49 tradesmen, 35 coachmen and hackmen, 28 waiters, 20 hair-dressers, and 11 professional men—preachers, physicians, etc., and 53 females, 46 of whom were widows," (p. 14).

the migration of fairly well-off free mulattoes from the South. It was, however, in the large free communities in the South that the class structure achieved its greatest development. It was in these communities that gradations in economic status and conventional family life established on a traditional basis provided a solid basis for social stratification.

In the free Negro communities in Charleston, S. C., and New Orleans, the class structure reached its highest development.[8] In both cities, the majority of the free Negroes were of mixed ancestry. Many of these free Negroes of mixed ancestry were skilled artisans and had a secure position in the economic organization of these cities. There were, however, differences in social status among the free Negroes which were based upon family background and economic status. At the bottom were the free Negroes with little skill and small incomes. There was also a large class of substantial artisans with stable family life and moderate incomes who formed a middle class. At the top of the social pyramid were the families that possessed considerable property including slaves and could boast of aristocratic white ancestry or the absence of a tradition of slavery.[9] Moreover, in both cities but more especially in New Orleans, many of the upper-class mulattoes were descendants of the wealthy planters who had fled from San Domingo during the revolution in 1790.[10] In New Orleans many of the upper-class families among the free Negroes were descendants of the soldiers who had fought under Jackson in the War of 1812.

SOCIAL STRATIFICATION FOLLOWING EMANCIPATION

The class structure which evolved after Emancipation was based partly upon the social distinctions that had developed among the slaves and partly upon the class distinctions that existed among the

[8] There was a similar development in Washington, D. C. and Baltimore and on a smaller scale in Richmond, Va., Louisville, Ky., and other southern cities.

[9] In Charleston, the absence of a tradition of slavery among two free black families made them eligible for membership in the church attended by the free mulattoes. They were not acceptable in marriage nor were they expected to attend the more intimate social functions to which they were invited.

[10] Grace King, *New Orleans: The Place and the People* (New York, 1928), p. 342. In fact, under the French rule some of these upper-class mulatto families became assimilated into the French upper class.

Negroes who were free before the Civil War. But at the outset, Negroes of free ancestry held themselves aloof from the former slaves and tended to form an upper class in the Negro communities. For example, in North Carolina, there was cleavage between the free "ishy" (issue), the term applied to those who had been free before the Civil War, and the new "ishy," the term applied to those who had been freed as the result of Emancipation.[11] In Kansas, according to the testimony of an ex-slave, the feeling was so bitter, "that those who became free by the war were called in derision by the freeborn, 'contraband.' "[12] As the freedmen acquired land and education, the distinctions between these two groups faded, though in some isolated rural communities of the South this distinction persisted until the present century.[13]

In Charleston, South Carolina, and New Orleans, the class distinctions which had developed before the Civil War were too deeply rooted to be swept away by the changes resulting from Emancipation. The Civil War meant the disintegration of the mulatto group that had occupied an intermediate status between the whites and the Negro slaves. But these mulatto aristocrats who had wealth and education continued to have a strong feeling of superiority toward the emancipated blacks and sometimes resisted as fiercely as the whites their enjoyment of political rights. Some of the descendants of the free mulattoes were elected to office under the Reconstruction governments and developed a certain community of interest with the emancipated blacks. But in their marriages and other intimate associations they held themselves aloof from the emancipated blacks. When white domination was re-established, the color line was drawn so as to include the descendants of the former free people of color and the former slaves in the same category, and both were subjected to the same restrictions. This brought about some solidarity

[11] David Dodge, "The Free Negroes of North Carolina," *Atlantic Monthly*, LVII, 20-30.

[12] Henry Bruce, *The New Man. Twenty-nine Years a Slave. Twenty-nine Years a Free Man* (York, Pa., 1895) p. 79.

[13] For example, in a rural community in North Carolina in the 1930's, a landowner objected to his daughter's marriage to the son of another landowner because the latter's ancestors had been slaves.

of interest and sympathy between the groups, but on the whole they withdrew within the narrow circle of their relatives and friends, refusing even to send their children to the schools provided for Negroes. Some families migrated to other sections of the country where they became a part of small groups of upper class mulattoes or they became lost in the white race. The less affluent skilled artisans likewise formed their own "creole" community from which the emancipated blacks and their descendants were excluded.

SOCIAL STRATIFICATION IN RURAL COMMUNITIES

In the social stratification of the rural Negro communities in the South, both social and economic factors have played a rôle since Emancipation. Following the Civil War, the Negro landowners who had been free before the Civil War constituted an upper class. In some places those of mulatto origin had their own churches and schools and did not associate freely with the blacks. But, as a rule, in the rural South, as the freedmen acquired land and maintained a conventional family life, the distinctions based upon free ancestry and color have become less important. Landownership, stability of family life, and education have increasingly become the bases of upper-class status. It should be pointed out, however, that in rural areas where social relations tend to be informal, social status and social distinctions are less marked, except in such matters as marriage, than in urban areas.[14] Consequently, such factors as landownership

---

[14] In Charles S. Johnson, *Growing Up in the Black Belt* (Washington, D. C., 1941), pp. 73-75, Johnson has provided a highly generalized and formal set of criteria for the division of the rural Negro population into three classes. On the basis of estimates, the rural Negro population is distributed as follows: Upper class, 6 per cent; middle class, 12 per cent; and lower class, 82 per cent. According to Johnson the "folk Negro" is a part of the lower class, but should be differentiated from the rest of this class. Concerning this differentiation, it should be pointed out that it is difficult to understand why the author assigns the "folk Negro" to a lower class status in the rural Negro communities. The "folk Negro" represents a culture group or a society characterized by a high degree of solidarity and certain traditional ways of acting and thinking. Among the "folk Negro" social distinctions are recognized, though there are no developed class strata. When the Negro folk society is broken up through its incorporation into a larger social unit characterized by "civilized" or urban ways of living or through the migration of the Negro folk to cities, the "folk Negro" acquires a class status in the larger social unit or in the city to which he migrates.

and education are not as significant as stable family relations and other aspects of behavior which affect the integrity of communal relationships. Moreover, there are wide variations in respect to social stratification between the rural areas in different states and even within the same state. In the plantation areas of the South, social stratification depends less upon landownership and education than in North Carolina and Virginia where the rural Negro population is more differentiated both economically and socially. As a rule, in the plantation areas where the majority of the Negro farmers are tenants, the more prosperous farmers who maintain stable family life and support the churches and lodges have a higher social status than the poorer sharecroppers with unstable and uncertain family relations. On the other hand, in Virginia and North Carolina there is a greater tendency for three classes to become differentiated in the Negro population. The well-to-do landowners with family traditions constitute an upper class and are differentiated from small-holders and tenants with stable family life. The latter, who form a middle class, are differentiated from the unstable farm laborers and loggers and laborers in turpentine mills at the bottom of the social pyramid.

EMERGENCE OF SOCIAL CLASSES

In cities, where there has been a greater occupational differentiation of the Negro population, a more complex class system has been developing over the years. But at first, there was little relation between occupation and social status. For example, in Athens, Georgia, at the beginning of the present century, the upper class in the Negro community included five teachers, two physicians, three in the United States mail service, three barbers, two tailors, one bookkeeper, two carpenters, two shoemakers, two waiters, one editor, one real estate agent, two ministers, three blacksmiths, one cook, one restaurant keeper, one farmer, and one plumber.[15] The small upper class in the smaller urban communities was often differentiated from the great mass of Negroes who formed a lower class. There was always a tend-

[15] W. E. B. DuBois, *The Negro in the Black Belt: Some Social Sketches.* Bulletin of the Department of Labor, No. 22 (Washington, 1902).

ency toward some differentiation among the lower class on the basis of stable family life and conventional standards of sex behavior.

In recent years a study was made of social classes as opposed to economic classes among Negroes in a small city in a rural "Black Belt" county in Mississippi.[16] In their study of social classes based upon empirical data, the authors point out the relatively slight differentiation of Negro classes. The social differentiation which the authors found in this small community were undergoing changes because of the increasing mobility of the Negro population and the change in the evaluation of white ancestry. Indicative of these changes are the questions asked about "a person who is 'pushing' into the upper class":

(1) What has been his education? (2) Has he professional or semi-professional status? (3) Are his language, manners, and dress "polished"? (4) Is he black? (5) In the case of women, have they had sexual relations with white men? The approved answer to these last two question must be negative.[17]

At the beginning of the century, even in the larger urban communities, occupation was of little importance in determining social status. For example, in Philadelphia at the opening of the century, DuBois was able to identify four classes in the Negro population:

Grade 1. Families of undoubted respectability earning sufficient income to live well; not engaged in menial service of any kind; the wife engaged in no occupation save that of house-wife, except in a few cases where she had special employment at home. The children not compelled to be breadwinners, but found in school; the family living in a well-kept home.

Grade 2. The respectable working-class; in comfortable circumstances, with a good home, and having steady remunerative work. The younger children in school.

---

[16] In defining a social class, the authors write: "In the sense in which a social class is conceived, therefore, its membership can be identified empirically upon the basis of either of two types of information: (1) by records of *common participation of individuals in noneconomic groups*, such as in churches, associations, and clubs and at large dances, teas, picnics, weddings and funerals; and (2) by the verbal expression by individuals of their *willingness* to associate with other persons in these social relationships." *Deep South* by Allison Davis, Burleigh B. Gardner and Mary R. Gardner, p. 238. Copyright 1941 by The University of Chicago Press.   [17] *Ibid.*, p. 246.

Grade 3. The poor; persons not earning enough to keep them at all times above want; honest, although not always energetic or thrifty, and with no touch of gross immorality or crime. Including the very poor, and the poor.

Grade 4. The lowest class of criminals, prostitutes and loafers; the "submerged tenth." [18]

DuBois points out that his scheme of social stratification is based on "moral considerations" rather than income.[19] The fact that he uses "moral considerations" rather than occupation and income does not mean that he has used subjective evaluations. They were the criteria which were generally accepted as the basis of social status among Negroes. In fact, the first stage in the evolution of social stratification was characterized by a class structure in which social distinctions rather than occupation and income played a decisive rôle in social status.[20] In this first stage in the development of social stratification, white ancestry and family descent were important factors in de-

[18] *The Philadelphia Negro* by W. E. B. DuBois, pp. 310-11. Publications of the University of Pennsylvania Series in Economy and Public Law No. 14. Published for the University, Philadelphia, 1899.

[19] *Ibid.*, footnote, p. 311.

[20] In 1877, a colored citizen of Washington wrote a satire on "Washington's Colored Society" in which he described the three classes as follows: "The first class consisted as it does now of Negroes, who were slaves in the District of Columbia befo' de wah and who obtained their liberty by paying the *master* class more than they were really worth. The second or middle class consisted as it does now to a large extent of Negroes, who took advantage of the emancipation proclamation of a gentleman named Abraham Lincoln, sometime President of the United States. The third or poor class consisted of all Negroes as it does now, who never had any master but who were only nominally free at best, and were in an immeasurably worse condition than either of the former when they were in bondage. . . . The upper class, (i.e.) all Negroes who bought their freedom or were set free before the war of rebellion, undertook at an early day in the history of the Negroes of the District of Columbia to mark out the boundary and the habitation not only of the 'Free niggers' but also of those who but for the kindness of Mr. Lincoln might possibly have been groveling in darkness and superstition to a greater extent than they are today. The objection raised against this last named class seemed to have arisen from the fact that the prolific and inventive genius of the immortal Ben Butler had transformed them into 'Contraband of war' a technicality—which shows not only wisdom and humanity but marvellous sagacity and hind sight." Quoted from manuscript document in *The Negro Family in the United States* by E. Franklin Frazier, pp. 397-98n. Copyright 1939 by The University of Chicago Press.

termining upper-class social status.[21] But since white ancestry and family membership conferred upper-class status only when they were associated with social factors, the upper class like the middle and lower class was essentially a social class.

THE DEVELOPMENT OF SOCIOECONOMIC CLASSES

A new stage in the evolution of the class structure in Negro communities had already appeared in Boston at the outbreak of World War I. In a study published in 1914, Daniels described four main classes based upon "clearly defined economic-social distinctions" which determined "rank and place in the total scheme of the Negro community." [22] At the bottom of the social pyramid was the shiftless and vicious element, which formed about 10 per cent of the Negro population. Next came the "rank and file, the common people," comprising 70 per cent of the entire Negro population, who derived a living from domestic and personal service and common labor. This class had incomes ranging from less than a minimum necessary for bare existence to an amount sufficient to "provide common comforts and pleasures." The middle class, which formed approximately 18 per cent of the Negro population, included waiters, Pullman porters, janitors and artisans as well as some professional people and proprietors of small business. The members of this class were generally thrifty and owned homes in the better Negro neighborhoods. At the

21 The author of the satire on "Washington's Colored Society" writes derisively of those who boast of white ancestry: '"There is another element in this strange heterogeneous conglomeration, which for want of a better name has been styled society and it is the species of African humanity which is forever and ever informing the uninitiated what a narrow escape they had from being born white. They have small hands, aristocratic insteps 'and wear blue veins, they have auburn hair and finely chiselled features. They are uneducated as a rule (i.e.) the largest number of them, though it would hardly be discovered unless they opened their *mouths* in the presence of their superiors in intellect, which they were very careful not to do. In personal appearance, they fill the bill precisely so far as *importance* and pomposity goes—but no farther. They are opposed to manual labor, their physical organization couldn't stand it, they prefer light work such as 'shuffling cards or dice' or 'removing the spirits of Frumenta from the gaze of rude men' if somebody else becomes responsible for the damage. Around the festive board, they are unequalled for their verbosity and especially for their aptness in tracing their ancestry." Quoted in *The Negro Family in the United States* by E. Franklin Frazier, p. 399n. Copyright 1939 by The University of Chicago Press.

22 John Daniels, *In Freedom's Birthplace* (Boston, 1914), pp. 174-83.

top of the social pyramid was the small upper class—2 per cent of the Negro population—the majority of whom were of light complexion and lived in superior residential districts and among white neighbors.[23] The upper class was comprised of outstanding professional and literary people who were of northern birth or of long northern residence.

In Boston the emergence of economic-social classes among Negroes had been a slow evolution over a period of three centuries. A similarly slow evolution was occurring in cities in other parts of the country. But this process was greatly accelerated by the sudden urbanization of the Negro population during and following World War I.

IMPACT OF NEW CLASS DISTINCTIONS UPON OLDER CLASSES

When the new class distinctions based upon occupation and income first appeared among urban Negroes during World War I, the older upper class families became alarmed. The reaction of a member of an upper class family in a city in Georgia is typical:

There was a time when A. could boast of many aristocratic and cultured families. Men who have made places for themselves in the world have come from these old families. X. and Y. are representative

[23] The author distinguishes the upper class "from a sort of 'smart set,' which may be described as an excrescence growing out of the several classes which have been noted. There are a host of Negroes who labor to create an impression of superiority by dressing far beyond their means and by attempting to assume the ways of culture. The members of this race—so far as they have opportunity—naturally seek to attain polished manners. Such aspirations are entirely in their favor so long as they are kept within appropriate limits. It is when they are perverted that they become objectionable. Many a Negro, who sports a silk hat and stick on Sunday, 'totes' quarters of beef in the market on Monday. Time was when one was amazed at seeing on the street so many Negroes who had all the earmarks of the idle rich. But ere long one discovered that most of these persons were Pullman porters and hotel waiters. . . . They devote most of their time and money to aping the ways of white 'society.' They have many clubs with fancy and foreign names, and give *bals masques*, *tableaux vivants*, and tournaments at bridge. Their daughters 'study' music, art, or dramatics just long enough to make a show of being 'accomplished.' Their sons endeavor to look and act like college students or men-about-town. Lightness of complexion is almost indispensable to a place in this set, whose members taboo the word 'Negro,' always refer to themselves as 'colored' 'ladies' and 'gentlemen,' and talk much of the slights to which they are subjected." Daniels, *op. cit.*, pp. 179-81.

of the kind of character that A. of a generation ago afforded. That day has passed into oblivion; and the select people who remain are those of that generation. When my mother married, she sent out five hundred invitations in the city. I doubt that I could send fifty to such intimate friends as those to whom my mother's were sent. There just simply isn't any "society" in A.

The large group that stands in the front rank of A.'s society is composed of the "rat" type. "And how did the 'rats' push to the front ranks?" you ask. Social standards began to drop about twenty-seven years ago when several professional men—a doctor and a lawyer, in particular, who now live in Chicago—in the interest of their professions, opened their homes to the entertainment of persons regardless of their social standing. Several years ago, a bootlegger and speakeasy proprietor brought his wife to the city. She was very pretty, except for the dark and sunken rings about her eyes from dissipation. In six months' time, she led A.'s "exclusive social set." And sad to say, there were some young people who if they had stayed together could have made up a small élite social group. But being afraid that they would not enjoy all the real social life, they "let down the bars," became intimate with the bootlegger's wife and visited her home. I live at home through my vacation without contacts, for the best is too bad.[24]

Similar complaints were expressed by members of the old upper-class families in the metropolitan communities of the North. For example, one evening as the Old Settlers Club met in a house on South Parkway in Chicago, their meeting was disturbed by the laughter and gaiety of Negroes entering a theater and ballroom across the street. One member remarked to the group: "Listen to that barbarism. The riffraff that has come to Chicago is destroying all that we have built up."

When these old families saw their ascendancy in the Negro communities menaced, their protests against the degradation of morals and manners was not entirely unjustified. There was often cause for genuine contempt for the crudeness and exhibitionism of those who

[24] Quoted from manuscript document in *The Negro Family in the United States* by E. Franklin Frazier, p. 413. Copyright 1939 by The University of Chicago Press. In *Deep South*, the authors state that members of the upper class complained: "Things had gone from bad to worse. . . . At present upper class standards were so 'low' that 'the best families are associating with bellhops and taxi-drivers.'" *Deep South* by Allison Davis, Burleigh B. Gardner and Mary R. Gardner, p. 240. Copyright 1941 by The University of Chicago Press.

had acquired prominence because of education and a relatively good income. They appreciated the difference between a man or woman without real culture and family traditions who had acquired a formal college education—and that often in an inferior Negro college—and a man or woman with a background of several generations of stable family life and conventional conduct. In the North these old families had had several generations of more or less close contacts with the whites, not only as servants but in schools and other institutions. In the South these old families had ceased to have close contacts with the aristocratic whites. But the heritage of conventional behavior which they had acquired had become a part of their family traditions. Moreover, they had sent their children to the colleges and academies established by northern white missionaries after the Civil War, where the students had received more than a formal education. They lived in close personal contacts with the white New England teachers who molded their characters and made possible their cultural identity with whites. The culture of these old families was not, therefore, a hollow pretense or a caricature of white civilization.[25]

In some instances these old families sought a refuge within the narrow circle of families with a similar background or in the memories of a world that had vanished. But being unable to resist the march of events, they gradually intermarried or merged with those elements who, through the occupational differentiation of Negro population, reached the top of the new class structure.

OCCUPATIONAL DIFFERENTIATION AND SOCIAL CLASSES IN SOUTHERN AND BORDER CITIES

Even in the largest Negro communities in the South, the occupational differentiation of the Negro population has not progressed far. In Atlanta, Birmingham, Memphis, and New Orleans, where there are Negro communities of 100,000 or more, only 6 to 9 per cent of the men are in professional, business, and white-collar occupations. Another 10 per cent of the employed men have achieved the status of

[25] Because of the isolation of these old families, their culture often became ingrown and highly formalized. See Frazier, *The Negro Family in the United States*, pp. 409-12.

skilled workers. As the result of the slow occupational differentiation of the Negro population, socioeconomic classes have been slow in emerging. Many of the social as opposed to occupational and economic bases of social stratification have continued. Yet the small upper class is composed largely of the more successful businessmen and those in the professions. Because of family background and certain personal qualities, including a light complexion, some persons in clerical occupations have upper-class status. The middle class is not as closely correlated with occupational status as the upper class. It is composed of skilled and semiskilled workers, the higher type of domestic servants, and the more responsible service workers, including waiters, janitors, beauticians, and practical nurses. The middle class is differentiated from the lower class, chiefly by its more stable family life and its integration into the institutional life of the Negro community. The lower class, which comprises about two-thirds of the Negro population in these cities, includes semiskilled workers, domestic servants, service workers, and laborers.

In the large Negro communities of the border cities, the occupational differentiation of the Negro population has not progressed as far as in the northern cities. But, as we have seen, in the District of Columbia and St. Louis, the professional and clerical groups are much larger than in southern cities. This has created a larger upper-class group based upon occupation and income.

In Baltimore, Washington, and St. Louis, post office employees, old family retainers, and domestic servants in the wealthier families have ceased to have upper-class status. In Washington, D. C., because of employment provided by the federal government, there is a relatively large professional class and a clerical group of the same relative size as that in Chicago and New York. Consequently, those of upper-class status include almost entirely people of professional status, businessmen, and those in clerical occupations. On the whole, the social stratification of the Washington Negro community, which is typical of the border cities, may be described as follows:

1. *Lower Class.*
The lower class has a larger proportion of dark or black Negroes than the middle or upper class. Many of them are recent migrants

from the rural South. Among this class there is considerable family disorganization. The lower class includes laborers, many service workers (barbers, charwomen, porters, janitors, etc.), many domestic workers, and semi-skilled workers. The group is characterized by a high rate of illiteracy, low incomes and poverty. The social life of the more stable elements revolves about the Church and the lodge. The less stable elements account for the high degree of criminality in the Negro community.

2. *Middle Class.*

The middle class includes a larger proportion of Negroes of lighter complexion who have had a longer residence in the city. Unlike the lower class, with whom they are anxious not to be identified, the middle class exhibits considerable "race pride" and strives to be respectable. Members of this class maintain a stable family life and place considerable value upon conventional sex behavior. For a livelihood middle class families depend upon wage earners in skilled and semi-skilled occupations, domestic service and the service occupations. The more ambitious of the middle-class families in the Negro community seek through education, the professions, or business to make themselves eligible for upper class status. They may even disown their families if identification with them would prove a handicap because of their occupation, color, or morals. And since the upper class is often of fair complexion, the associates whom they seek in friendship and in marriage will most likely be of fair complexion. In such selections, they are not simply seeking to identify themselves with a group because of its light skin complexion but mainly because they wish to improve their status.

3. *The Upper Class.*

The upper class in the Negro community has long had a reputation for snobbishness toward dark or pure-blooded Negroes. To a stranger in the Negro community it might appear that a fair complexion alone determined admission to this class. But, in fact, such factors as family and general culture, occupation and income, and personal achievement and morals help to determine membership in this class. The majority of those of fair complexion will possess a good family background, will be of professional and business standing, and enjoy good incomes as well as a reputation for respectability. Among the women of fair complexion there will be a few of middle or even lower-class origin, who because of education or personal qualities have married men who could give them upper class status. Among the men there will be a larger proportion of men of brown or dark complexion. Many of these men represent elements in the middle class who moved up in social status. At the present time, a growing race consciousness and the rise of members of the darker middle and lower classes have tended to neutralize the snobbishness of the light upper class. If light-skinned Negroes feel an antipathy toward the darker members of the community, they usually conceal it and only confess it among intimates.

Among the upper class there is still much talk about "culture," but it generally turns out that "culture" is restricted to the social amenities, since it is difficult to find among this group many who read good books or have a genuine appreciation of literature or art or music. Rather it is in the matter of conspicuous consumption that the upper class expresses most explicitly its position and role in the social stratification of the Negro community. A teacher or physician is not simply a professional worker, but generally regards himself as a member of an aristocracy which requires certain standards of consumption. High standards of consumption are often made possible by the fact that upper-class married women in the border cities, unlike those in the South, engage in professional and clerical occupations. Thus fine homes, expensive clothes, and automobiles give an appearance of wealth which is one of the chief values of this class. In order to maintain these standards some families live beyond their means, or, as one investigator found some years ago, the head of the family engages in so-called "sundown" occupations.[26] But it also happens that the wife with a secure and fairly large income from teaching is the main support of the family, while her husband, doctor or businessman with low income, presents a "social front" for the family. Though the upper class is relatively small in numbers, it is important in the Negro com-

[26] "Many homes were found in which the head of the family worked regularly at two jobs. This is especially true of those heads of homes that have governmental positions. The early closing hours enable the employee to engage in another occupation during the evening. Several government clerks were found practicing law, selling real estate, printing, waiting on table, or working at gasoline filling stations after the closing hours of the department in which they were employed. The 'sundown occupations' greatly enhance the economic status of the family. The average salary of Negro male government employees ranges from $125 to $150 per month, which is by no means adequate to maintain the standard of living which is characteristic of the average government clerk. Those who desire the comforts of a well-appointed home, the luxuries of an automobile, frequent entertainments, and membership in a number of social clubs are forced to supplement their salaries received from the government by additional money secured from spare-time jobs. It is often the case, therefore, that, instead of the income of the head of the home being merely $150 a month, it approximates $250 or $300 a month." William H. Jones, *The Housing of Negroes* (Washington, D. C., 1929), p. 117.

munity because it provides the standards and values, and symbolizes the aspirations of the Negro community.[27]

DEVELOPMENT OF SOCIOECONOMIC CLASSES IN NORTHERN CITIES

When one turns to the North, one finds that the emergence of social classes based upon occupation and income has been retarded in the smaller Negro communities. For example, in New Haven, where Negroes "have little professional and less business and clerical opportunity," the "able youth are drawn elsewhere by the attraction of greater economic or professional opportunity." [28] The old families were undermined because they lacked an economic base. At the present time there is only a partial differentiation of a cultured upper class which includes "doctors, lawyers, dentists, social workers, teachers, and the ministers of the large, long established churches." [29] But because of limited occupational opportunities, men in personal and domestic service and menial occupations with a college education move in upper-class circles, though they are usually rated as middle class. Through its clubs and other associations and contacts outside of New Haven, the top layer struggles desperately to maintain its exclusiveness within this small Negro community.

It is in the large Negro communities in northern cities that a complex class structure based upon occupation and income as well as social distinctions is emerging. In these communities, as we have seen, the occupational differentiation of the Negro population has progressed more than in southern or border cities (See Tables XIII and XIV). This has resulted in new types of social distinctions, based to some extent upon education but more especially upon income or the ability to maintain certain standards of living. At the same time the social distinctions which determined status in the Negro communities have lost their force.

Even in the large Negro communities in northern cities, a light complexion continues to have value in the selection of friends and

[27] Cf. *Negro Youth at the Crossways* by E. Franklin Frazier, pp. 24-28. Copyright 1940 by American Council on Education.
[28] Robert A. Warner, *New Haven Negroes. A Social History* (New Haven, 1940), p. 184.   [29] *Ibid.,* p. 189.

mates in marriage.[30] Moreover, a light complexion is often associated
with upper-class status.[31] But what is important is the fact that a
light complexion no longer determines social status nor has the support of a mulatto upper class in the Negro community. In the large
urban communities of the North, the Negro, like other people, wins
a place not because of family but through competition. A brown-
skinned young man from Charleston, S. C., where color-caste had
placed insuperable barriers between his family and his mulatto neighbors, tells how these barriers broke down in New York City. He writes:

There were three Negro families in our block and immediate vicin-
ity, the R.'s, S.'s, and our family. The rest of the people of the community were Irish-Catholics with the exception of the L.'s and M.'s,
wealthy Jews. To these whites we were considered thrifty, intelligent,
progressive Negroes, but under their breath, "niggers." But to the R.'s,
a very fair, "blue-blood" Charleston, family we were inferior and far
below them in social status. Although more members of my family
had been to high school and college, and our home was more preten-
tious than theirs, they were obsessed with the idea of being our superiors. They were of an old free, mulatto Charleston family, who had
been there for years and years, while we were upstarts in Charleston,
who had lived there for just about twenty years or so. We were members of the Methodist church; whereas the R.'s were members of the
high tone St. Marks Episcopal Church, where for many years nothing
darker than an octoroon attended.

. . . . .

The R. children never walked on our side of the street, that is, in
front of our door. When they wanted to go to Mrs. S.'s little shanty,
they would walk on their side and cross in the middle of the block to
reach her home. Not even has death been able to bring about the
slightest communication between the families. When Jimmy died at
the age of 17, we sent no condolences. Although when I finished high
school, Mr. R. spoke to me for the first time, the separation still goes
on. We live on one side of the street, and they live on the other. An
insurmountable barrier separates us—social caste. But, interestingly,
the children of the two families have met in other cities; for example,
in New York. There the barriers were broken down and my brother

[30] See St. Clair Drake and Horace R. Cayton, *Black Metropolis* (New York,
1945), pp. 496-506.
[31] See W. Lloyd Warner, Buford H. Junker, Walter A. Adams, *Color and Human Nature* (Washington, D. C., 1941), *passim*.

took one of the R. girls to many dances. In Charleston that could never have happened.[32]

In a city like Charleston, South Carolina, a light complexion is a more important factor in determining social status than in Washington, D. C., and a light complexion in Washington is more important than in Chicago or New York City. A person of light complexion with money to spend in New York or Chicago may not want to be embarrassed in the larger community because of a dark-skinned acquaintance. But within the Negro community the dark-skinned acquaintance may, because of education and income, be a social equal. In the large urban communities in the North, it is one's occupation, education, and income or standard of living rather than family and color that determine status. Then, too, in the large city, one's social status is not determined so much by one's morals as by one's public behavior. In the northern city, as color and family descent decline in importance as the basis of upper-class status, the character of the class structure of the Negro community approximates that of the Western world generally, where social status is correlated with occupational status, income, and education.

In the large Negro communities in the north, three fairly well-defined classes—upper, middle and lower—have come into existence. Although Negroes in the northern city do not suffer the same restrictions as Negroes in the South, the character of the class structure of the Negro community in the northern city has been determined largely by the fact of its segregation in American life.[33] The Negro upper class has its present status, primarily, because of its position in a segregated social world. If members of the Negro upper class were integrated into American society, their occupations and incomes would place them in the middle class.[34] But, as Myrdal has pointed out, partly because of "petty monopolies" created by the attempt to

[32] Quoted in *The Negro Family in the United States* by E. Franklin Frazier, pp. 406-08. Copyright 1939 by The University of Chicago Press. In *Deep South*, the authors note that, "One need no longer be olive, yellow, or white, however, or even brown with 'good' hair, to be a member of the upper class." *Deep South* by Allison Davis, Burleigh B. Gardner and Mary R. Gardner, p. 247. Copyright 1941 by The University of Chicago Press.

[33] Cf. Gunnar Myrdal, *An American Dilemma* (New York, 1944), p. 693.

[34] This has been recognized by Robert A. Warner, *op. cit.*, p. 189.

maintain a "color or racial caste system," Negroes with superior education and in certain occupational and income groups have achieved an upper-class status within the segregated Negro world. With these basic facts in mind, let us see what kind of people are found at the top of the social pyramid, how their behavior is distinguished from that of those beneath them, and what values are implicit or revealed in their style of living.[35]

THE UPPER CLASS

In the northern cities, the Negro professional man, especially the doctor or dentist, figures prominently in the upper class. Members of these two professional groups find in the large Negro community in the North a rich source of income as well as a relatively free environment.[36] Likewise, the Negro lawyer, the more successful at least, will be found in the upper class. It is in the border and especially the northern cities that the Negro lawyer will find the most fertile field for the practice of his profession. Moreover, the position of the Negro lawyer in the northern city is supported by the political power of the Negro, whereas in the South his practice is restricted because of the traditional status of the Negro. Public school teachers are likewise found in the upper class. Where the Negro public school teachers are not numerous, they gain a certain prestige by the uniqueness of their position. But as their numbers have increased, their class position has been determined by a complex of factors involving family, color, income, personal factors, and style of living. The same is true of the growing number of social workers. Negro public administrators who have recently made their appearance in the northern cities derive their social prestige partly from their occupations and partly from economic and social distinctions.

As we have seen in the previous chapter, men engaged in business

[35] The best, and one might say only, documented descriptive analysis of the class structure of the Negro community in the northern city today is to be found in Drake and Cayton's *Black Metropolis*, Chapters 19-22. In the analysis here, the writer has depended partly upon the materials presented in these chapters and partly upon the materials which he collected during a survey of the Harlem community in New York City.

[36] In Chicago, Detroit, New York, and Philadelphia there were 648 Negro physicians or 19 per cent of all the Negro physicians in the United States in 1940.

and in clerical occupations comprise a much larger proportion of employed males in northern cities than in southern cities. In New York City, where the largest proportion of employed Negro men are found to be proprietors and managers, one out of every 20 is in business. The Negro businessman in the northern city has appeared in response to the varied needs of these large Negro

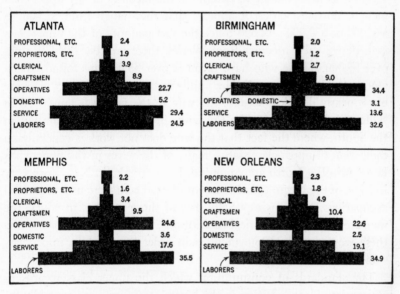

DIAGRAMS V, VI, VII, VIII

Percentage of Employed Negro Males in Each Employment Status in Four Southern Cities: 1940.*

* Based on Table XII.

communities in the North. In both Chicago and New York City, slightly more than one out of every ten employed Negro men are in clerical occupations. The relatively large clerical group has grown up partly because of the growth of Negro business but more especially because of the political power of Negroes which has made employment in the municipal government possible. Both of these groups have tended to increase the size of the upper class in the North. Although the more successful businessmen are at the top of the upper class, many of those in clerical occupations have gained admission to the upper class because their occupational status involves high educational qualifications and they are able to maintain certain standards of living. As among whites, in order to gain access to the upper class in northern cities, a Negro must have an income which will enable him to maintain a certain standard or style of living.

As far as it is possible to determine the incomes of the upper-class men in northern cities, it appears that they range from $3,000 to $40,000 or $50,000 a year.[37] Since the vast majority of the upper-class men derive their incomes from salaries, there are few with incomes over $5,000. Those who have incomes over $5,000 are found chiefly among the businessmen.[38] The family incomes of the upper class are often nearly doubled because the wife in the family is employed in professional services. Unlike the wives in the upper-class families in the South, where the fact that the wife does not work is generally an indication of upper-class status, many of the wives in the upper-class families in the North are employed. For example, in New York City in 1940, of the Negro women employed 4 per cent were in professional occupations.[39] This is especially true of those families in which the men are employed in clerical occupations. Very often the reasons why these women seek employment is in order to maintain upper-class standards of consumption.

The standards of consumption which the upper class regards as appropriate for its position in the Negro community are generally set by the wealthiest members of the upper class. They include the type of home which one should occupy or own and manner in which it should be furnished. In the southern and border cities homeowner-

[37] Cf. Drake and Cayton, *op. cit.*, p. 529. In his study of Negro college graduates, Charles S. Johnson, *The Negro College Graduate* (Chapel Hill, N. C., 1938), p. 155, found that 172 out of 3,120 men reporting had incomes of $5,000 or more.

[38] During the Depression years some Negro doctors were on relief. But during World War II, Negro doctors were prosperous, on the whole, some having incomes amounting to $25,000 or $30,000 a year. Many Negro professional men supplement their incomes from their professions with profits from business. Carter G. Woodson, *The Negro Professional Man and the Community* (Washington, D. C., 1934), pp. 104-05, found that 40 per cent of the Negro doctors were engaged in business operations.

[39] *Sixteenth Census of the United States: 1940 Population*, Vol. III, Part 4 (Washington, D. C., 1943), p. 40.

ship is high among the upper class. Ownership of homes in the northern city is determined, of course, to some extent by the general character of the city. But in recent years, even in New York City, the more prosperous among the upper class have bought homes outside the city. The furnishings of the upper-class homes generally reflect the desire for comfort and luxury, while taste in the selection of furnishings

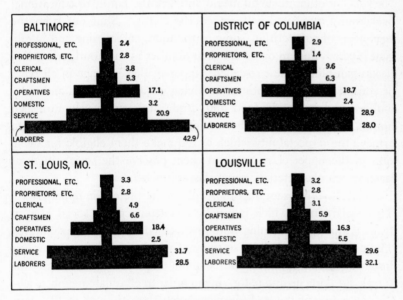

DIAGRAMS IX, X, XI, XII

Percentage of Employed Negro Males in Each Employment Status in Four Border Cities: 1940.*

* Based on Table XIV.

varies according to the general culture of the family. Likewise, in the matter of clothes, the cost of one's clothes and the amount of clothes which one possesses are regarded as an indication of upper-class status. Sometimes whites who work or associate in other ways with Negroes in professional and clerical occupations are at a loss to understand why their colored fellow workers dress better than they themselves. The same tendencies are apparent in the make of an automobile which a member of the upper class buys.

Since income and pecuniary valuations are beginning to play such an important rôle in upper-class status, there has naturally arisen a conflict between economic and social distinctions, as a basis of upper-class status. In Negro communities especially in the North, there has appeared a class of Negroes who are eligible for upper-class status from the standpoint of income but who have gained their wealth through "rackets" or other unlawful means and lack the family or educational background associated with upper-class status.[40] Shut out from the legal areas of competition, some of the more enterprising and intelligent Negroes find an outlet for their abilities in such outlawed activities as gambling. These so-called "upper shadies" engage in all types of conspicuous consumptions, involving expensive clothes and automobiles and luxury in food and drink, and expensively furnished homes. At the same time they are often conscious of their failure to achieve the respectability which would make them eligible for inclusion in the upper class. Some of them observe the social ritual, at least, which characterizes upper-class-status behavior.

Social ritual plays an important rôle in the life of the upper class.[41] This social ritual, which is usually characterized as "social life," is focused upon entertaining and involves considerable expenditures. The numerous social clubs, in some of which there is much duplication of membership, are organized about cliques. These clubs are constantly breaking up and re-forming in order to eliminate members who do not represent the exclusiveness which they attempt to maintain. But most of these clubs are similar in that they undertake to provide lavish entertainment in expensively equipped homes. At one time bridge played by men and women in separate clubs or in mixed groups was the chief form of entertainment. But bridge has been replaced by poker in recent years and high stakes are becoming associated with higher social status, especially among the smart set. Social dancing as a form of entertainment is no longer indulged in by the older members of the upper class; though it continues to be the chief form of

---

[40] See Drake and Cayton, *op. cit.*, pp. 546-50, on the "upper shadies."

[41] In the free mulatto castes in the South during slavery and in the upper class in Negro communities until the urbanization of the Negro the social ritual became highly formalized and almost assumed the character of a religious rite. See Frazier *The Negro Family in the United States*, pp. 409-12.

entertainment among the younger set. The younger members of the upper class not only form social cliques, but they are dominant figures in the Greek letter fraternities and sororities. In recent years these organizations have widely publicized their civic interests, though as a matter of fact they are primarily the center of "social" activities.

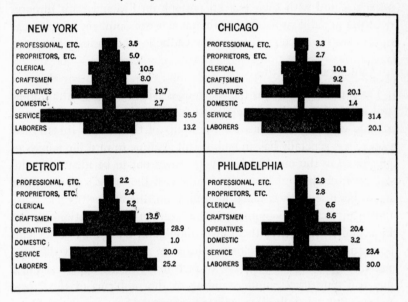

DIAGRAMS XIII, XIV, XV, XVI

Percentage of Employed Negro Males in Each Employment
Status in Four Northern Cities: 1940.*

* Based on Table XVIII.

The social position of the upper class in the Negro community is indicated by its institutional affiliations. Its members are generally affiliated with the Episcopal, Presbyterian, or Congregational church.[42] As among whites, the church affiliation of the upper class is due partly to the traditional association of their families with these churches, and partly to the tendency of Negroes of middle- or lower-class status to

[42] In Washington, an upper class group of light complexion split off from a long established Baptist Church and set up their own organization because they wanted to avoid association with middle and lower class people whom the pastor sought to please by an emotional type of service.

become affiliated with these churches when they achieve a higher status. Sometimes professional and businessmen maintain their membership in the Baptist and Methodist churches for economic reasons. Usually, the upper class prefers membership in the Congregational, Episcopal, or Presbyterian church because the sermons and mode of service accord with their general outlook on life and their ideas of decorum in public worship. For the same reason some members of the upper class have been turning to the Catholic Church in recent years.

UPPER-CLASS VALUES

Despite the attitude of the upper-class Negroes toward the middle and lower classes, they generally profess considerable race pride and affiliate with organizations for the uplift of the "race." In fact, the upper class generally has an ambivalent attitude toward the masses of Negroes. On the one hand, they are eager not to be identified with the poor, crude, and ignorant members of the "race"; on the other hand, because of their racial identification, they are extremely sensitive to any derogatory opinions of the Negro or discriminations against him. Quite often, they themselves indulge in derogatory statements concerning the Negro's color and behavior and even justify discriminations against the lower class. In fact, many of the upper class lack any real sympathetic understanding of the problems of the Negro masses. But generally, they will join efforts to fight for the rights of the Negro and take pride in serving in organizations for the improvement of the Negro. Therefore, they help to support such organizations as the National Association for the Advancement of Colored People and the National Urban League. At the same time these organizations provide clerical and professional employment for the increasing numbers of educated Negroes.

Because of their privileged position behind the walls of segregation, members of the upper class generally do not contemplate without misgivings the complete integration of the Negro into American life. The Negro business and professional men who enjoy monopolies in the Negro community do not want to meet the competition of men and institutions in the larger community. To illustrate the manner in which the interests of this class determine its attitudes toward race relations, one might cite the case of the Negro public schoolteacher. In the border cities and in segregated systems in the North, the Negro schoolteachers justify, by various rationalizations, the existence of separate schools. But in New York City, where Negro teachers receive appointments according to merit, they stand for the complete integration of Negroes. Likewise, the general opposition of the Negro upper class to intermarriage stems from the fear that it will lose its unique social status. Those upper-class Negroes who have a genuine feeling of "race pride" feel that intermarriage would destroy the possibility of perpetuating their family lines through marriage with Negro families of similar social status. But more generally, intermarriage is regarded as a menace by the upper-class Negro woman because it threatens the security of her privileged position. Consequently, the white woman from a respectable middle-class family is designated a "poor white" woman.

The isolation of upper-class Negroes from the white world is responsible for the values which determine their style of life. The general economic and political conservatism of the upper class stems from its position in the Negro community rather than from its economic position in American life. The great time and effort expended upon "social life" are results of the limited opportunities for participation in the larger community. This isolation is likewise responsible for its conspicuous consumption in order to maintain the outward appearance of an upper class.[43] The great concern of the upper class with respectability has arisen from its great desire not to be identified with the masses of Negroes and partly from the manner in which it wants to appear before the white world. Since it is not a completely isolated social world, the Negro community represents in some aspects a pathological phenomenon which is reflected in the personalities of the members of the upper class.

The struggle to play an upper-class rôle in the isolated Negro com-

[43] DuBois writes: "A white Philadelphian with $1,500 a year can call himself poor and live simply. A Negro with $1,500 a year ranks with the richest of his race and must usually spend more in proportion than his white neighbor in rent, dress and entertainment." *The Philadelphia Negro* by W. E. B. DuBois. Publications of the University of Pennsylvania Series in Economy and Public Law No. 14. Published for the University of Pennsylvania, 1899.

munity, while one's income, education, and family background fit one for a middle-class status in the larger community is probably responsible for the so-called instability of many upper-class Negroes.[44] The conflict in rôles increases in the North where the Negro is being integrated into the larger community. The Negro professional man or clerical worker often feels under great compulsion to keep up the requirements of upper-class behavior in the Negro group and at the same time act in the rôle of a middle-class professional or white collar worker in the community at large. As the Negro becomes increasingly integrated into the larger community, the professional man or woman or clerical worker is escaping from the obligations of the upper-class rôle in the Negro community and can orient his behavior with reference to his middle-class status. This seems to be happening in the larger cities of the North.

THE MIDDLE CLASS

The emergence of a clearly defined middle class of any size and significance in the Negro community has coincided with the growing occupational differentiation of the population. Consequently, it is in the large urban communities of the North that a fairly large, well-defined middle class has appeared.[45] In the northern city there is a large group of clerical workers, skilled industrial workers, responsible

[44] Professor Warner, in "American Caste and Class," states that, "It seems possible that the instability of many of the individuals of the upper class (as compared, let us say, with the Negroes of the lower positions) may be due to the instability and skewness of the social situation in which they live. They are always 'off balance' and are constantly attempting to achieve an equilibrium which their society, except under extraordinary circumstances, does not provide for them." "American Caste and Class" by W. Lloyd Warner. *American Journal of Sociology*, Volume XLII, 237. Reprinted by permission of *American Journal of Sociology*. It seems that this observation would apply to the North rather than to the South. In the South the upper-class Negro has achieved, on the whole, "an equilibrium" within his own society and heretofore, at least, only a relatively few intellectuals are in conflict with "caste" restrictions. In the North, on the other hand, where the Negro community is not as isolated, conflicts in status and patterns of behavior arise.

[45] According to Drake and Cayton, *op. cit.*, pp. 522-24, about 30 per cent of the Negroes in Chicago have middle-class status. This is slightly higher than the percentage obtained for Washington, D. C., in 1930, by a more formal division of the population in which skilled and semiskilled workers representing 26.4 per cent of the population were treated as middle class. See Frazier, *Negro Youth at the Crossways*, pp. 21-23.

persons in the service occupations, and firemen, policemen, and other types of workers in protective service. There has thus come into existence a relatively large group of workers with a background of stable family life, a good elementary or high school education, and an income adequate to support a respectable way of living. Since the class structure in the Negro community is fluid, the upper layers of the middle class merge with the upper class, while the lower layers are hardly distinguishable from the lower class.[46]

Because of their fairly secure and adequate incomes, Negroes of middle-class status are able to maintain what they regard as a desirable mode of life. This desirable mode of living includes, first, certain standards of home and family life. In the larger cities the middle class constantly struggles to escape from those neighborhoods inhabited by the lower class. This is often difficult because of rents and the restrictions upon the mobility of the Negro population. Nevertheless, the middle class endeavors to isolate itself from the environment of the lower class by moving into apartments occupied by people with similar standards. Since in middle-class families there is often a tradition of homeownership, which may have its roots in the South, Negroes of middle-class status endeavor to buy homes out of their savings. This ambition is generally thwarted because of the multiple dwellings in the large cities.

Even when Negroes of middle-class status cannot escape from an undesirable physical environment, they endeavor to maintain a stable and conventional family life. In the middle-class family, the husband and father assume responsibility for the support of the family. He often takes pride in the fact that his wife does not have to aid in the support of the family. Both parents are usually interested in the welfare and future of their children. They are not simply interested in the physical welfare of their children but they want their children to conform to conventional moral standards. They want their children to

[46] The term "middle class" as used here refers to the class having an intermediate status between the upper and lower classes in the Negro community. Only a relatively small upper layer of this class is "middle class" in the general American meaning of the term. Moreover, "middle class" as used here is essentially a social class though occupation and income play some part in determining its place in the class structure of the Negro community.

avoid the behavior associated with lower-class status. Moreover, they want their children to take advantage of the educational opportunities which they themselves did not enjoy.

The stability of the middle-class family is often tied up with its affiliations with the institutions in the Negro community. The vast majority of Negroes of middle-class status are affiliated with the church. Although some of the more emancipated upper layers of the middle class may scoff at religion, they usually come from families which were closely identified with the church. But the religion of the middle class is different from that of the lower class. The middle class takes its religion seriously and believes that religion and morality are inseparable. At the same time Negroes of middle-class status believe that religious services should be decorous and that people should avoid the more extravagant forms of religious ecstasy. For the middle class the lodge also is an important form of associated activity. In the large cities the more secular Elks lodge becomes more attractive than the more sacred types of fraternal organizations. Likewise, for many of the middle-class families in the larger cities, affiliation with various social clubs where card playing and dancing are the chief forms of recreation represents a new outlook on life. But the middle class will seldom go in for "society," which is the prerogative of the upper class.

Just as the middle class looks down upon the ways of the lower class, it attempts to discover flaws in the behavior of the upper class. The flaws which it attempts to discover in the upper class are moral lapses. Perhaps the chief value of the middle class is respectability; and respectability in not only correct public behavior but moral conduct. The moral conduct and respectability of the middle class is bound up to some extent with its race consciousness. For the middle class is extremely race conscious. Failure to maintain respectability and moral conduct is a reflection upon the "race," i.e., the Negro. The race consciousness of the middle class is also tied up with the desire to rise in the world. Middle-class Negroes are ambitious for their children to get an education and rise in the Negro world. At the same time they are ambitious to prove the ability of Negroes to rise in the white man's estimation if not in the white man's world.

THE LOWER CLASS

At the bottom of the class structure in the Negro community in the northern city is the lower class, which comprises about two-thirds of the Negro population.[47] In the lower class are found the great body of unskilled workers who earn a precarious living and those who subsist on irregular employment and relief. In this class are many of the most recent migrants from the South, especially those who have little education or are illiterate. However, this class is set off from the middle class not merely because of occupation and low income or even illiteracy. The lower class is distinguished from the middle class because of certain forms of behavior which are associated with lower-class status.[48]

The shiftlessness and irresponsibility of lower-class Negroes are due partly to their lack of education and partly to the lack of economic opportunity for the great masses of Negro men.[49] Since emancipation the masses of Negro men have constantly been drawn from the southern plantations into a fluctuating labor market. Because of the uncertainty and seasonal nature of work in lumber and turpentine camps, many of them have become footloose wanderers. In the towns and smaller cities of the South, they have provided the cheap and casual labor which was needed. Their position in northern cities has scarcely been better except where there has been a demand for large numbers of unskilled workers. But usually the lower-class husband and father must share the economic burden with his wife, who often finds more secure employment in domestic service.

In the northern city the lower class tends to be concentrated in those areas where the Negro first gains a foothold in the city. In these areas the lower-class Negroes are crowded into tenements and dilapidated houses which are held for speculative purposes. In these deteriorated slum areas are found second-hand clothing stores, taverns, cheap movies, and the lighter industries. Moreover, these areas are characterized by the absence of what constitutes a real neighborhood.

---

[47] That two-thirds of the Negro population has lower-class status is indicated in a number of studies. See Daniels, *op. cit.*, p. 177; Frazier, *Negro Youth at the Crossways*, pp. 22-25; Drake and Cayton, *op. cit.*, p. 523.

[48] See Drake and Cayton, *op. cit.*, Chapters 20 and 21.   [49] *Ibid.*, pp. 582ff.

The public schools located in these areas not only reflect in their physical appearance the general deterioration but have scarcely any relation to the life of the residents. Even the church which plays such an important rôle in the life of the middle class is absent or is represented by the numerous "store front" churches. Consequently, the behavior of the lower class is free from the control of neighborhood influences and the control of other institutions.

The absence of neighborhood controls is associated with a general lack of participation in the institutions of the community. Various studies have shown that Negroes of lower-class status are not affiliated with many forms of organized activities. Even in their religious affiliations they tend to become associated with the "store front" churches and churches outside the regular denominations. In those churches they find escape from their poverty and frustrations in a highly emotionalized type of religious service. But such church affiliations have little influence on their morals and manners. The shiftlessness and lack of ambition which characterize lower-class behavior are generally associated with a lack of race pride. For the lower-class Negro, as opposed to the middle class, tends to accept the estimation which whites place upon the Negro's ability and racial characteristics.

There is an element among the lower class that is quiet and exhibits good manners in public. There are lower-class families that struggle to maintain stable and conventional family life. They may humbly accept the fact that they are poor in worldly goods as a part of God's plan but they believe that even the poor may live righteously. Or they may believe that by living honestly and justly and rearing their children properly, their children because of education will rise to a higher status.

IMPORTANCE OF SOCIAL STRATIFICATION

It has been necessary to present this extended analysis of the evolution of social stratification or socioeconomic classes in Negro communities for two reasons. First, since the development of socioeconomic classes has been associated with the amalgamation of the races and the increasing occupational differentiation of the Negro population, it provides a measure of the process of acculturation and integration of the Negro into the American community. Secondly, the institutions and other forms of associated life and various phases of culture in the Negro community can be understood only when studied in relation to its class structure. Therefore, this chapter and the two preceding chapters on the analysis of the physical, economic, and social organization of both rural and urban communities provide the background for the remaining chapters in this section on the institutional structure of the Negro community.

CHAPTER XIII

The Negro Family

IN THE last three chapters, we analyzed the basic economic organization and sketched in general outline the social structure of Negro communities. In this chapter and those that follow, we shall study in more detail the important institutions and associations which comprise these communities. We shall consider first the family which, resting largely upon a habitual and sentimental rather than an institutional basis among the majority of Negroes, is the basic and most important social group. Throughout its development, the Negro family has been influenced in its internal social and psychological organization as well as in its formal structure by the economic and social forces which have determined the character of Negro communities.

THE NEGRO FAMILY DURING SLAVERY

In a previous chapter we have seen how difficult it is to establish upon a factual basis any connection between the development of the Negro family in the United States and the African family system.[1] The attempts to explain the sex behavior and familial life of American Negroes by reference to African culture traits rest upon speculation and specious analogies. Among some isolated groups of Negroes in the New World, as for example in Haiti and Jamaica, it appears that elements of African culture have been retained in the Negro family.[2] But even in Brazil, where conditions were more favorable for the survival of the African family system, one can scarcely find traces of the

[1] See Chapter I, pp. 10-14.
[2] See Melville J. Herskovits, *Life in a Haitian Valley* (New York, 1937), pp. 81-121; and Martha W. Beckwith, *Black Roadways: A Study of Jamaican Folk Life* (Chapel Hill, 1929), p. 54.

African family system today.[3] Therefore, in tracing the development of the Negro family we shall simply analyze the known economic and social factors in the American environment which offer a sufficient explanation of the past development and present character of the Negro family.[4]

During the early development of the plantation system the excess of males in the Negro population resulted in casual associations for satisfaction of sexual hunger.[5] But soon there was no lack of women and mating ranged from purely physical contacts, sometimes enforced by the masters, to permanent associations in which deep sentiment between spouses and parental affection toward children created a stable family group. At the same time the character of the sexual contacts and family life of the slaves was determined to some extent by the master's attitudes toward his slaves. Some masters with no regard for the preference of their slaves mated them as they did their stock. There were instances where Negro males were used as stallions.[6] In a world where patriarchal traditions were firmly established, even less consideration was shown for the wishes of the female slaves. But this was not the whole story, for the majority of masters either through necessity or because of their humanity showed some regard for the wishes of the slaves in their mating.

Since African mores and traditions ceased to control the sexual impulses and determine the forms of mating, their behavior in this regard was subject to individual impulse and sexual attraction. It appears that from the beginning spontaneous attraction played an important

[3] E. Franklin Frazier, "The Negro Family in Bahia, Brazil," *The American Sociological Review*, Vol. VII, pp. 465-78.

[4] The discussion which follows is based almost entirely upon E. Franklin Frazier, *The Negro Family in the United States* (Chicago, 1939), which contains a detailed analysis, supported by documents and statistics, of the points presented in this chapter.

[5] A visitor to America made the following observations: "Those [slaves] who cannot obtain women (for there is a great disproportion between the number of the two sexes) traverse the woods in search of adventures, and often encounter those of an unpleasant nature. They often meet a patrol of whites, who tie them up and flog them, and then send them home." Berguin Duvallon, "Travels in Louisiana and the Floridas, in the Year 1802," pp. 79-94, in *Journal of Negro History*, II, 172.

[6] See, for example, Edward Kimber, *Itinerant Observations in America*. Reprinted from the *London Magazine*, 1745-46 (Savannah, Ga., 1878), pp. 37-38.

part in mating. Moreover, there was rivalry among the males for the sexual favors of the females. This rivalry was kept under control by the master in the interest of order on the plantation. But rivalry did not manifest itself solely in the display of brute force. There came into existence a form of courtship in which tender feelings and attention to the wishes of the woman played an important part in winning her favors. In addition to these psychological factors there were social forces within the plantation organization that tended to humanize the sexual impulses of the slaves and place moral restraints upon their mating. The plantation, as we have seen, was a social as well as an industrial institution in which there was a division of labor and an opportunity for the expression of the individual talents.[7] Within the social world of the plantation, there were social distinctions, involving obligations and expectations in regard to behavior. Consequently the sexual conduct and mating of the slaves were not without moral restraints.

Where slavery became a settled way of life and the plantation organization acquired a patriarchal character, the slave family achieved some degree of permanence. The master's concern for the moral welfare of the slaves included a close supervision of their sex behavior and marital relations. On some plantations there were slave families including three generations that had "married" according to slave customs under the close supervision of their mistresses. Such family groups generally included the father and husband as well as the mother and her children. This was especially true where the father was, for example, a skilled mechanic and had acquired a responsible position in the plantation organization.[8] The solidarity and permanence of such families were due to a number of factors. Habitual association in the same household played some part. But, in addition, genuine affection often developed between the spouses and between the parents and children. Where the family was permitted privacy and permitted to cultivate its own gardens and engage in other common activities, family unity was given substantial basis in common

[7] See Chapter III above.
[8] See for example J. W. C. Pennington, *The Fugitive Blacksmith: or Events in the History of J. W. C. Pennington* (London, 1850).

interests. Thus under the most favorable conditions of slavery the Negro family did among certain elements of the slave population acquire considerable stability. But very often the exigencies of the slave system, such as the settlement of an estate, might destroy the toughest bonds of conjugal affection and parental love.

Because of the conditions imposed by the slave system, the mother was the most dependable and the most important member of the Negro family. The idealized picture of the Negro mother during slavery has represented her as a devoted nurse of the master's children.[9] But there is also plenty of evidence of the devotion of the slave mother to her own offspring. Despite the hardships and suffering which pregnancy and childbirth often involved, the slave mother often exhibited a fierce devotion to her children. In the case of young children, masters were compelled in their own interest to recognize the biological dependence of the child upon the mother. But, in addition, they were forced to recognize the affectional and sentimental ties between the Negro mother and her offspring. A Negro father might be sold and separated from his family, but when the Negro mother was sold the master was forced to take into account her relation to her children. The bonds of affection between mother and offspring were generally developed in the slave cabin where the Negro mother nurtured her brood and was mistress. Even if she were separated from her children she often visited them at night to care for them and find affection and solace from her cares. On the other hand, the father was often a visitor to the cabin two or three times a week, while his interest in his children might only be adventitious. He was compelled not only to recognize the mother's more fundamental interest in the children but her authority in the household. Thus there developed among the slaves a type of family that was held together principally by the bonds of blood and feeling existing between the mother and

[9] Writers on Negro slavery, especially apologists for the system, have represented the Negro mother or "Mammy" as a devoted nurse of the children of the master and as indifferent to her own children. The attitude of the Negro woman toward the children of the master was conditioned by her association with the white children and the rewards which her rôle as substitute mother brought her. Likewise, her attitude toward her own children was determined by what pregnancy and childbearing meant to her. See Frazier, *The Negro Family in the United States*, pp. 42-57, for a full discussion of this point.

her offspring and the sentimental ties that often developed between the children in the same household.

Although it is difficult to estimate the extent to which members of the slaveholding class had sexual relations with the slaves, there is sufficient evidence of widespread concubinage and even polygyny on the part of the white masters. The maternal family organization, i.e., the family in which the mother was the head and main source of support, was fostered partly by the sexual association between the males of the white race and the slave women on the plantation. In the cities where the slaves were released from the plantation discipline and there were free Negroes, the associations between white men and Negro and mulatto women were generally casual.[10] Mulatto children resulting from these relationships were often neglected and became public charges. The sexual relations between the white men and colored women, slave and free, were undoubtedly due at times to physical compulsion on the part of white men. Moreover, mutual attraction also played some part in securing the compliance of the colored woman. But, it appears from available evidence, that the prestige of the white race and the advantages resulting from these associations were generally sufficient to secure the acquiescence of the colored woman. The character of the family groups resulting from the association of the men of the master race and the women of the subordinate race varied considerably.

At the bottom of the scale was the Negro woman who was raped and became separated from her mulatto child without any violence to her maternal feelings; or the slave woman who submitted dumbly or out of animal feeling to sexual relations that spawned a nameless and unloved half-white breed over the South. . . . Sexual attraction gave birth at times to genuine affection; and prolonged association created between white master and colored mistress enduring sentiment. There were instances where white fathers sold their mulatto children; but more often they became ensnared by their affection for their colored offspring.[11]

[10] In Charleston and more especially in New Orleans associations between white men and mulatto women often developed into stable alliances.

[11] *The Negro Family in the United States* by E. Franklin Frazier, p. 85. Copyright 1939 by The University of Chicago Press.

There were white men who acknowledged their offspring and gave them an education and a start in the world. There were white slave-holders who neglected their wives and gave their affection and their worldly goods to their colored mistress and their mulatto offspring.[12] In some cases the white masters even separated themselves from white society and lived entirely with their colored mistresses and mulatto offspring. But since such unions were rare and without the legal and moral support of the communities, the black or mulatto woman was generally the head of the household.

FAMILY LIFE AMONG THE FREE NEGROES

The family life of many of the Negroes who were free before the Civil War was less stable than that of the better situated slaves. This was especially true of the impoverished Negroes who crowded the slums of the cities of the North as well as the South. Among these elements in the free Negro population there was much sexual prom-iscuity and family relationships were loose and uncertain. Though there was less moral degradation in the rural areas, nevertheless, the family life of the free Negroes in the poorer regions of the South rested upon a precarious basis. On the other hand, there was emerg-ing among the free Negro workers a class of skilled artisans whose family life conformed to the family pattern of the white laboring class. In some cases the tradition of stable family life had been built up during several generations of freedom and economic security. Or the tradition of stable family life might even have its roots in slavery. Very often the male head of the family had bought his freedom and that of his wife and some of his children. This class continued to in-crease in areas where slavery was becoming less profitable up to the Civil War.

However, it was chiefly in Charleston, South Carolina, New Or-leans, and a few other areas that the free Negro families acquired to

---

12 Although many white women in the South, accepting masculine prerogatives in a patriarchal system, resigned themselves to the situation, others gave vent to their jealousy and displeasure by acts of cruelty to the slave women and their mulatto offspring. The same reaction on the part of white women occurred in Brazil. See Gilberto Freyre, *Casa Grande & Senzala* (Rio de Janeiro, 1943), Vol. 2, pp. 539-40.

a marked degree an institutional character. Marriage as a legal relationship became a part of the mores of this group as they took over the familial behavior of the whites and the stability and continuity of their family life became rooted in property as well as traditions. Moreover, members of these families were accorded a superior social status by the community. In Charleston as well as in New Orleans a number of the free colored families were descended from the mulatto refugees who fled from San Domingo during the revolution in the latter part of the eighteenth century. The community of free mulattoes in New Orleans was much larger and had a longer history than the free colored people of Charleston. When thousands of well-to-do and cultured mulatto refugees from Haiti poured into New Orleans in the latter part of the eighteenth century the government found it necessary to relax the laws restricting the freedom of this class in regard to dress or to move about at will. At the time of the Louisiana Purchase this class had become an important element in the population and formed an intermediate social stratum between the whites and the slaves. Since these families were of mulatto origin they had taken over the culture of the whites. Moreover, their white forebears had frequently given them educational advantages as well as property. The imprint of this cultural heritage was apparent in the personalities of the members of these free families. They were dignified and undertook to support a literary and artistic culture. They took pride in their white ancestry, which included many whites of distinction. They were intensely conscious of their superior status in a society where Negro blood was the badge of slavery. In New Orleans the traditions of a large number of the free mulatto families went back to the rôle of the mulattoes in the defense of the city against the British in 1814. Many of them sent their children to France to be educated, thus preserving a mode of life that was similar to that of their French neighbors but alien to their Anglo-Saxon neighbors as well as the mass of black slaves.

The patterns of family life developed in this group were as different from that of the great mass of the Negro population as the type of family life which developed among those isolated communities of Negro, Indian, and white descent scattered in various parts of the country.[13] In some cases these communities originated in the eighteenth century.[14] In such communities patriarchal family traditions were firmly established during the pioneer days. These families generally cherished their white and Indian ancestry. But sometimes the Indian character of these communities has been completely effaced and they are classified as Negro communities.[15] Therefore, in tracing the roots of the Negro family in the United States it is necessary to take account of the rôle of these families in the development of the Negro family life.

DISORGANIZATION AND REORGANIZATION OF NEGRO FAMILY LIFE AFTER EMANCIPATION

The immediate effect of the Civil War and Emancipation upon the family life of the slaves was to disrupt the customary relationships and destroy whatever control the master exercised over the sex and family life of the slaves. When the invading armies disrupted the plantation organization, thousands of Negroes were set adrift and began to wander footloose about the country. Not only were the sentimental and habitual ties between spouses severed but even Negro women often abandoned their children. Among the demoralized elements in the newly emancipated Negroes promiscuous sexual relationships and frequent changing of spouses became the rule. The northern missionaries who came South during and following the Civil War were often perplexed by the confusion in marital relations. On the other hand, the disorders arising from the Civil War and Emancipation often provided a proof of the strength of marital and family ties that had developed during slavery. Many mothers kept their children with them and cared for them at a tremendous sacrifice. Describing the fleeing refugees, Higginson wrote, "Women brought children on their shoul-

[13] See Frazier, *The Negro Family in the United States*, Chapter XI, "Racial Islands."

[14] See, for example, William and Theophilus G. Steward, *Gouldtown: A Very Remarkable Settlement of Ancient Date* (Philadelphia, 1913).

[15] For the origin of some of these communities we have historical evidence; but for others one must depend upon the traditions which have been preserved concerning the pioneers. See *Legislative Petitions, Archives of Virginia, King William County, 1843*. Quoted in J. H. Johnston, "Documentary Evidence of the Relations of Negroes and Indians," *Journal of Negro History*, XIV, pp. 29-30.

ders; small black boys carried on their backs little brothers equally inky, and gravely depositing them, shook hands." [16] Moreover, it was noted by the missionaries and others who were in a position to observe the newly emancipated blacks that there was a general disposition on the part of the Negroes to search for their kinfolk.

The development of the Negro family following the confusion which ensued as the result of Emancipation was influenced by a number of social and economic factors. The heroic efforts of the northern missionaries, who attempted to place marriage on a legal and institutional basis, bore fruits wherever they labored. They were supported in their efforts by the Negro church organizations with intelligent ministers and a core of stable families. Moreover, the schools in which the missionaries labored became centers in which sexual mores were taught and enforced and institutionalized family relations were cultivated. Despite the important contributions which the missionaries made to stabilizing family relations, the operation of more fundamental social and economic forces in the life of the Negro were to determine the character of his family life.

The family life of the emancipated Negro was influenced to a large extent by his social development under slavery. Even during slavery some of the freedmen had engaged in semi-free economic activities in order to support their families. Among the better situated slaves, the family had acquired considerable stability and the transition to freedom did not result in disorganization. The father had developed a deep and permanent attachment to his wife and an interest in his children. As a freedman he remained on the plantation as a tenant and assumed responsibility for his family.[17] The more ambitious freedmen were not willing to continue as tenants but began to acquire land.

In acquiring land the Negro husband and father laid the foundation for patriarchal authority in the family. His interest in his wife and children no longer rested upon a purely sentimental or habitual

[16] Thomas Wentworth Higginson, *Army Life in a Black Regiment* (New York, 1900), p. 235.

[17] As a rule the freedmen were unwilling to continue to work in gangs as during slavery; but insisted upon having the land divided so that each family could work as an independent unit.

basis but on an economic tie. In some cases the interest of the father in his wife and children began when he bought them from their owners before Emancipation. But it was only after the Emancipation when the former slave established himself as a freedman that this phase of the development of masculine authority in family relations became important. Even among the freedmen who were tenants, it was customary for the father and husband to make contracts with the landowners and assume responsibility for their families.

. This development of the family was associated with the development of other phases of the institutional life of the Negroes. The churches were under the control of men and the control which it exercised tended to confirm the man's interest and authority in the family. Moreover, in the Bible, which for the freedmen was the highest authority in such matters, they found a sanction for masculine authority. The families that had been free before the Civil War played an important rôle in consolidating masculine authority in the Negro family. Although in some localities the prejudice of this group toward the newly emancipated blacks prevented intermarriage at first, gradually the more successful freedmen married into the families that had been free before Emancipation.

During the latter part of the nineteenth century and the first decade of the present century, two general tendencies were apparent in the development of the Negro family. First, there was an ever increasing number of stable families with a pattern of family organization similar to the American pattern. These families, which were to be found in both rural and urban communities throughout the country, were sharply differentiated from the Negro masses. The emergence of this group of stable families is roughly indicated in the growth of home-ownership up to 1910. By 1910 a fourth of the Negroes in rural areas and 22 per cent of the Negroes in cities were homeowners.[18] A part of the homeowning families formed an upper class in Negro communities, while the remaining homeowning families represented the slow emergence of a middle class. The second general tendency is represented in the development of family life on a habitual and sentimen-

[18] See Frazier, *The Negro Family in the United States*, pp. 246-47.

tal basis among the Negro masses in the rural South. The migration of Negroes to cities, especially the mass migrations to northern cities during and following World War I, has affected both of these developments. In the discussion which follows, we shall consider the changes which have occurred between the two World Wars and the present status of the Negro family.

HIGH PROPORTION OF FAMILIES WITH FEMALE HEADS

As we have seen there has been an excess of females in the Negro population since 1840.[19] However, the excess of females has been characteristic of the cities rather than the rural areas. In fact, the excess of males in the rural-farm Negro population has been increasing during the past two decades.[20] At the same time, there has been a decrease in the ratio of males to females in the rural-nonfarm Negro population to the point that there was a slight excess of females in 1940. It is not possible to determine the effect of these changes in the sex ratio on the marital status of the rural Negro population over the past fifty years. As has been shown in a number of studies, there is considerable uncertainty concerning the real marital status of the Negroes in the rural South.[21]

In Table XIX, we have the proportion of nonwhite (Negro) families in the rural and farm areas of the South with female heads and the marital status of the female heads of families.[21a] Women are heads of more than a fifth of the Negro families in the South. In the rural-nonfarm areas the proportion of Negro families with female heads is about the same as that for the South as a whole. But in the rural-farm areas the proportion of families with female heads is only one-half as great as that for the entire region, and one-third as great as the proportion in urban areas. The larger proportion of families with

[19] See pp. 180-81.

[20] See *Sixteenth Census of the United States, 1940. Population* "Characteristics of the Population," 2, Part I, pp. 19-20.

[21] See Frazier, *The Negro Family in the United States*, pp. 108 ff; Hortense Powdermaker, *After Freedom* (New York, 1939), pp. 152 ff; Charles S. Johnson, *Shadow of the Plantation* (Chicago, 1934), pp. 40-44.

[21a] A female head of a family is a woman—single, widowed, divorced, or if married her husband is not living with the family—who is regarded as head of the family.

female heads among owners than among tenants in rural areas is most likely due to the fact that landlords prefer to have tenant families with male heads or in the absence of legal marriage, families with a male who plays the rôle of husband. In view of the uncertainty concerning the real marital status of Negroes in rural regions, several facts should be noted in regard to the marital status of female heads of families. First, the husband is absent in a fifth of the families of tenants as compared with a tenth of the families of owners. Secondly, a

TABLE XIX

Percentage of Nonwhite Families With Female Heads and Marital Status of Female Heads of Families by Tenure for Urban and Rural South: 1940 *

TENURE	PERCENTAGE OF FAMILIES WITH FEMALE HEADS	*Families With Female Heads*				
		TOTAL	HUSBAND ABSENT	WIDOWED	DIVORCED	SINGLE
Total	21.7	100.0	21.6	62.2	4.9	11.3
Owner	24.5	100.0	11.5	77.4	3.4	7.7
Tenant	20.9	100.0	25.4	56.5	5.4	12.7
Urban	31.0	100.0	24.6	57.9	5.1	12.4
Owner	29.5	100.0	12.4	76.0	3.2	8.4
Tenant	31.5	100.0	27.9	53.0	5.6	13.5
Rural-Nonfarm	22.7	100.0	18.2	65.6	5.1	11.1
Owner	27.5	100.0	11.7	76.7	3.7	7.9
Tenant	20.1	100.0	22.8	57.6	6.1	13.5
Rural-Farm	11.6	100.0	16.7	70.9	3.9	8.5
Owner	16.4	100.0	9.6	81.1	3.2	6.1
Tenant	10.3	100.0	19.7	66.5	4.2	9.6

* Based upon *Sixteenth Census of the United States: 1940. Population and Housing Families.* "General Characteristics," p. 31.

much larger percentage of the female heads of owner families than of tenant families are described as widowed. Widowhood is the real marital status of a larger proportion of owners than of tenant women who are returned in the federal census as widows. Then, the greater proportion of divorced women among the tenant families with female heads is indicative of the greater instability of the tenants. Finally, the larger proportion of single women who are head of tenant families undoubtedly reflects the large amount of illegitimacy in these rural communities.

THE NEGRO FAMILY ON THE PLANTATION

Among a large proportion of the Negroes in the plantation South, courtship begins at an early age through mutual attraction and often involves sexual relations. Where sex relations result in pregnancy, the young people may or may not marry.[22] The birth of a child imposes certain obligations upon the mother because the mores of the Negro community make the relation between mother and child the most sacred of human relations. In fact, a certain distinction attaches to being fruitful or the fulfillment of one's function as a woman. On the other hand, marriage has not become a part of the mores. The father of the child may suggest "marriage" because he wants a woman to provide a home for him and he in turn is willing to provide subsistence for his family. The woman's response to his offer of "marriage" depends upon the attitude of her parents or her desire to start a new family. In the isolated rural communities where this type of so-called "sexual freedom" is permitted there are, nevertheless, certain restraints placed upon sex relations. During a period of courtship a girl is supposed to have one man only. Since in becoming pregnant she imposes economic burdens upon her family, she is obligated out of consideration for her parents to keep this in mind. The father of her child is likewise under obligation to help take care of the child. But in such communities the moral restraints of the larger community are absent. The women generally do not have a sense of guilt in regard to having children outside of marriage. When the couple decide upon marriage, which is generally of the common-law type, they enter into a cooperative relationship. The permanence of the "marriage" depends not only upon affection and sentiment but often upon the extent to which they can "work together" on the farm. Moreover, even after the men and women have entered "marriage," they may not have a sense of guilt when they have outside affairs. They seem to have fulfilled their

[22] Early sex relations account for the high birth rates among young Negro families. For the age group, 10 to 14, the birth rate for Negro women is 3.1 as compared with 0.2 for white women; and for the age group, 15 to 19, 102.7 for Negro women as compared with 42.1 for white women. Bureau of the Census. *Vital Statistics of the United States: 1940.* Part I, p. 9.

obligation to their mates by giving him or her preference in their affections.

In the isolated rural communities, especially among the lower classes, these courtships and forms of marriage do not result in personality conflicts or in social disorganization. In the less isolated communities there are personality conflicts because of the influence of the dominant mores and the control exercised by those conventional family groups that attempt to enforce American family mores. Moreover, outside of the plantation region where there are communities of rural Negroes who have assimilated American standards of family behavior and there are schools and other agencies of communication, the family behavior described is confined largely to the lower classes. In the upper-class families there is supervision of the behavior of young people and legal marriage is a prerequisite to the founding of a family. Throughout the rural South these upper-class families place great value upon morality in sex and family relations and the father is recognized as the head.[23]

As the result of the sex and marital practices which we have described, the Negro family in the rural areas assumes certain peculiar forms of organization. It is not possible to secure a measure of the extent of the various forms in the Negro rural population. However, for the South as a whole, we have statistics on the distribution of the population in private households with relation to the head of the household (See Table XX). Since there is a much higher percentage of families with female heads among nonwhites (Negroes) than among whites, a smaller proportion of Negro women than of white women is in the relationship of wife to the head of the family. There are, however, other differences which reflect divergences in family organization and practices, such as the larger proportion of "grandchildren," "other relatives," and "lodgers" in Negro families. The larger proportion of "servants or hired hands" is also indicative of certain features of the Negro family rather than of the greater employment of servants in the household. The significance of these statistical differences will become clear as we study the organization of the Negro family.

[23] See Frazier, *The Negro Family in the United States*, Chapter XII, "The Black Puritans."

The maternal Negro family, or the family in which the mother is the head, functions in its most primitive form as a natural organization in the rural areas of the South.[24] Historically, it had its origin as we have seen during the slavery period when the mother was the most dependable element in the family. Since Emancipation the maternal family has been supported by the folkways and mores of the rural communities. The matricentric family grows into a type of matriarchate in which the grandmother is the dominant figure. The mother acquires the status of a grandmother when her daughters become mothers and bring their children into the household.[25] Because of her age and experience the grandmother exercises authority over the members of the family and assumes responsibility for their welfare. The grandmother is a repository of folk wisdom and is called upon during the major crises of life. She attends the sick and the dead; but her superior wisdom and authority are recognized chiefly in matters concerning childbirth. She is often the "granny" or midwife who supplies young mothers with knowledge concerning babies and attends them during the crisis of childbirth. In 1940 four-fifths of the live births of Negroes in Mississippi and South Carolina were attended by midwives as compared with a fourteenth of white live births in these states.[26] In Virginia and Tennessee the percentage of live births of Negroes attended by midwives was 58.6 and 26.1 respectively.

The "matriarchal" type of family among rural Negroes in the South is an extended family in that it includes several generations and nephews and nieces and adopted children. This is indicated to some extent by the statistics in Table XX in the larger percentage of grandchildren and "other" relatives in Negro private households than in white households. There is not, however, a larger percentage of "parents" in Negro private households because the persons who would normally be in the relationship of "parent" to the head of the household are themselves the grandparents, who are often the heads of the household.

[24] Ernest W. Burgess and Harvey J. Locke, *The Family. From Institution to Companionship* (New York, 1945), p. 161, use the term "matricentric" to designate the type of family organization described here.

[25] See Frazier, *op. cit.*, Chapter VIII.   [26] Burgess and Locke, *op. cit.*, p. 165.

The extended Negro families are not all matriarchal in organization. Among the upper-class families in the rural South there are semi-patriarchal families of the extended type. The development of the semipatriarchal type of family has been related to the acquisition of land. Moreover, the extent of homeownership in the rural-farm area of the South is related to the socioeconomic status of the inhabitants of the rural area. More than a fifth (Table XXI) of the farm families, including farmowners and renters owned their homes, while among the farm laborers only one family in twenty was a homeowner. Land-owners and homeowners often exercise authority over their married sons as well as their unmarried daughters. But generally their sons are "emancipated" upon reaching maturity and establish their own families on an independent basis.

TABLE XX

Percentage Distribution of Population in Private Households by Heads and Relation to Head and by Color and Sex for the South: 1940 *

	Nonwhite		White	
	MALE	FEMALE	MALE	FEMALE
HEAD	39.5	10.3	44.4	6.5
RELATIONSHIP TO HEAD				
Wife	——	31.9	——	40.9
Child	41.5	38.2	45.2	40.8
Grandchild	5.4	4.8	2.1	1.9
Parent	0.6	2.4	0.9	2.5
Other Relative	6.3	6.7	4.1	4.3
Lodger	6.2	4.8	3.1	2.3
Servant or Hired Hand	0.5	0.9	0.2	0.5

* *Sixteenth Census of the United States: 1940. Population.* Vol. IV. "Characteristics by Age." Part I, p. 114.

THE NEGRO FAMILY IN SOUTHERN TOWNS AND CITIES

In the towns and smaller cities of the South, these various forms of family organization tend to persist with certain modifications. The maternal family plays a larger rôle because of the opportunities for the employment of women in domestic service and the grandmother continues to be the head of a large proportion of Negro families. On the other hand, the extended family tends to disintegrate and the growth of the semipatriarchal type of family is encouraged as the chance for homeownership is increased. It is, however, in the larger cities of the South that the effects of urbanization and the occupational differentiation of the Negro population are manifested in the organization of family life. There is, first, a decline in the size of the family or the number of children to women of childbearing age. For example, the number of children under five years of age to 1,000 Negro women 15 to 49 years of age in Atlanta, Birmingham, and Memphis was 170, 177, and 163 respectively as compared with 472 for Negro women in the rural-farm South.[27] In the cities of the South a much larger proportion—nearly a third as compared with a tenth for rural areas—of

TABLE XXI

Percentage of Nonwhite Families With Employed Head That Were Homeowners in Each Occupation Group in the South: 1940 *

OCCUPATION	TOTAL	URBAN	RURAL-NONFARM	RURAL-FARM
Professional and Semiprofessional	49.3	49.6	45.1	56.7
Farmers and Farm Managers	23.1	54.7	45.9	22.4
Proprietors, Managers, etc.	48.0	42.5	62.2	75.0
Clerical, Sales, etc.	41.4	37.3	62.4	68.8
Craftsmen, Foremen, etc.	34.7	29.7	46.2	41.5
Operatives	21.6	20.7	21.9	29.6
Domestic Service	17.3	13.9	28.5	15.6
Service Workers	27.9	25.0	43.6	37.9
Farm Laborers	10.2	20.0	25.6	5.0
Laborers	20.5	16.1	25.8	29.1
TOTAL	21.9	21.3	29.6	19.3

* Based upon *Sixteenth Census of the United States: 1940. Population and Housing Families.* "General Characteristics," p. 43.

Negro families have female heads. As one may observe in Table XIX the proportion of families with female heads is slightly higher among tenants in urban areas than among owners. There are even more striking differences between female heads of families who are owners and tenants in regard to marital status. In the tenant families with female heads over a fourth of the husbands are absent as compared with an

[27] *Sixteenth Census of the United States: 1940. Population* "Differential Fertility 1940 and 1910," pp. 78, 231, 233.

eighth of the owner families; and three-fourths of the owners are widowed as compared with a little more than half of the renter families.

There is a tendency for the upper- and middle-class families to become segregated into the better areas of the Negro community. These families are distinguished from the lower-class families in regard to the extent of homeownership. In Table XXII, we have the amount of homeownership among the different occupational groups

TABLE XXII

Percentage of Nonwhite Families With Employed Head, That Were Homeowners in Each Occupation Group in Four Southern Cities: 1940 *

OCCUPATION GROUP	ATLANTA	BIRMINGHAM	MEMPHIS	NEW ORLEANS
Professional and Semi-professional	46.4	35.7	53.3	32.3
Proprietors, Managers, etc.	29.0	36.4	33.3	36.4
Clerical, Sales, etc.	33.3	19.0	50.0	23.9
Craftsmen, Foremen, etc.	10.1	17.9	30.2	17.8
Operatives	9.6	20.1	19.1	7.1
Domestic Service	8.0	8.5	14.9	3.2
Service Workers	14.5	7.9	22.0	8.4
Laborers	9.1	10.5	16.9	7.7
TOTAL	12.7	14.0	21.1	9.4

* Based upon *Sixteenth Census of the United States: 1940. Population and Housing Families*, p. 290.

in four southern cities with Negro communities numbering over 100,000. In New Orleans where homeownership is comparatively low, the difference in pattern of homeownership among the various occupational classes is most pronounced. Homeownership is lowest for the domestic workers with low incomes and considerable family disorganization. It is higher for laborers and unskilled workers in industry and even higher for service workers among whom there are many stable and ambitious families. Among the skilled workers or craftsmen, homeownership is twice as high as among the service workers. It is among the white-collar workers—professional and clerical workers and proprietors—that homeownership assumes considerable importance and that the most stable families with a semipatriarchal organization are found.

THE NEGRO FAMILY IN BORDER CITIES

In the border cities, as in the cities of the South, the various types of family organization described above tend to persist. There has been, however, in the border cities a comparatively large group of stable families with a semipatriarchal organization over a long period. Many of these families have their roots among the Negroes who were free in these cities before the Civil War. Moreover, the constant migration

TABLE XXIII

Percentage of Nonwhite Families With Employed Head, That Were Homeowners in Each Occupational Group in Three Border Cities: 1940 *

OCCUPATIONAL GROUP	BALTIMORE	WASHINGTON, D. C.	ST. LOUIS, MO.
Professional and Semi-professional	53.1	59.6	35.1
Proprietors, Managers, etc.	18.2	23.1	9.3
Clerical, Sales, etc.	30.0	37.0	19.4
Craftsmen, Foremen	9.0	19.5	10.4
Operatives	12.2	20.6	4.2
Domestic Service	8.0	7.4	6.5
Service Workers	11.9	18.5	8.1
Laborers	5.3	14.6	7.1
TOTAL	11.1	20.4	8.8

* Based upon *Sixteenth Census of the United States: 1940. Population and Housing,* "General Characteristics," pp. 290-91.

of Negroes from the South has brought to the border cities many stable families. There is a tendency for the various patterns of family life to correspond to the class structure of the Negro communities in border cities.[28] Although among the lower class there is considerable family disorganization and many families have only a mother or grandmother as head, there is a core of stable families even in this class. It is, however, among the middle class, embracing about a fourth of the Negro community, that one finds the largest group of stable families of a semipatriarchal type. In border cities as in southern cities the extent of homeownership in the various occupational groups provides a rough indication of family stability in the different classes (See Table XXIII). In the District of Columbia, where Negro women

[28] See pp. 285-89 above.

of this class have an opportunity for desirable employment, some of these families tend to become equalitarian in their organization, that is, the husband and wife have equal status in the family.

However, it is among the upper-class families that the equalitarian type of family is most pronounced. Unlike the wives in upper-class Negro families in the South, many of the wives in the upper-class families in the border cities are employed in professional and clerical occupations. This not only gives the wives a certain degree of independence but enables the family to maintain certain standards of consumption. Because of their standards of consumption and their values upper-class families have few children and there are many childless couples. A study in 1937 of 114 colored faculty members of Howard University revealed that those who had been married ten years or more had an average of 1.1 children per family. Of the entire group studied, 60 per cent indicated that they had voluntarily restricted their families.[29] Likewise, in a study of 65 families among the Washington colored elite it was found that 36 of the 65 families had no children and that in the remaining 29 families there were only 43 children or an average of less than 0.7 of a child per family for the entire group.

THE NEGRO FAMILY IN NORTHERN CITIES

The effects of urban living upon the character and organization of Negro family life are most pronounced in the large cities of the North.[30] The mass migration of Negroes to the cities of the North resulted in considerable family disorganization. In a later chapter this phase of Negro family life will be considered among the problems of the adjustment of the Negro to American civilization. Here we are concerned primarily with the forms of family organization which have evolved in the urban areas of the North. In the Negro community in the northern city, as we have seen, there is a selection and segregation

[29] See Frazier, *The Negro Family in the United States*, p. 442.

[30] It appears, however, that increases in the sex ratio among Negroes in southern cities has a greater influence on marriage rates than in northern cities. See Oliver C. Cox, "Sex Ratio and Marital Status Among Negroes," *American Sociological Review*, Vol. 5, p. 942.

of various elements in the Negro population.[31] There is a selection and segregation on the basis of age and sex, a process which is related to the marital and family status of the population. The proportion of females and children in the population increases in the successive zones of the cities as one moves from the center outward, marking the expansion of the Negro community.[32] There is a selection and segregation of the population on the basis of marital status. This can be seen in the case of the Harlem Negro community in New York City (See Table XXIV). The decrease in the percentage of men and women single from the first to the fifth zone is associated with a progressive increase in the proportion of men and women married. The

TABLE XXIV

Percentage of Negro Males and Females Fifteen Years of Age and Over, Single, Married, Widowed, and Divorced, in the Five Zones of the Harlem Negro Community, New York City, 1930 *

MARITAL STATUS	SEX	ZONE I	ZONE II	ZONE III	ZONE IV	ZONE V
Single	M	42.6	38.5	35.3	34.0	31.1
	F	30.9	27.6	26.3	25.6	23.5
Married	M	49.8	56.0	60.3	62.3	64.2
	F	50.5	54.8	57.6	59.8	60.1
Widowed	M	7.3	4.7	3.6	2.9	3.8
	F	17.6	16.4	15.0	13.0	14.4
Divorced	M	0.2	0.5	0.4	0.6	0.5
	F	0.6	0.8	0.7	1.1	1.6

* Reproduced with the permission of The University of Chicago Press, from *The Negro Family in the United States*, p. 318.

progressive increase in the proportion married is correlated with a decrease in the proportion widowed. This reflects not so much a difference in the death rates of men and women as a difference in the institutional character of the family. Because of the increasing importance of legal marriage, there are proportionately fewer deserted women and unmarried mothers who call themselves widows and there is an increase in the percentage of women divorced. The small percentage of divorced persons in the zones in and near the center of the

[31] See pp. 257 ff. above.
[32] See E. Franklin Frazier, *The Negro Family in Chicago* (Chicago, 1932), pp. 117-18; and Frazier, *The Negro Family in the United States*, pp. 315-16.

community does not mean greater stability of family life in these areas but rather that separations are irregular and without legal sanctions as probably were also the unions in the first place.

The differences in marital status in the successive zones of expansion of the Negro community are indicative of the selective effects of urban life on the Negro family. In Zone I, which is the business and recreational center of the Negro community, family life tends to disappear as in the center of American cities.[33] Although the concentric zones marking the expansion of the Negro population are not homogeneous in culture, they nevertheless reflect the growing influence of family life in the successive zones. Not only is this indicated in the increase in the proportion married but in the birth rates and in the number of children (See Table XXV). In the first zone only 66 children were born in 1930 to each 1,000 Negro women of childbearing age and there were only 115 children under five to each 1,000 women 20 to 44 years of age. The birth rates and the ratio of children to women of childbearing age increase regularly in the successive zones. In the fifth zone on the periphery of the Harlem community the ratio of children to women of childbearing age is almost equal to the ratio in the rural-farm South.

The progressive stabilization of family life in the zones marking the expansion of the Negro is indicated in some cities by the regular increase of the rate of homeownership in the successive zones. In the District of Columbia the rates of homeownership among Negroes for the five zones in 1940 were: 2.5, 9.3, 17.3, 27.9, and 51.2.[34] The same phenomenon was observable in Chicago in 1930, where the rates for the seven zones were: 0.0, 1.2, 6.2, 7.2, 8.3, 11.4, and 29.8.[35] These increases in the rate of homeownership are related to the tendency for the higher occupational classes to become concentrated in the areas on the periphery of the Negro community. This is seen in Table XXVI, where the percentage of homeownership for the different occu-

[33] See Burgess and Locke, *op. cit.*, pp. 118-19.

[34] An interesting aspect of this process is that the rates for white homeownership closely paralleled the rates for Negroes. They were for the five zones; 2.2, 9.7, 20.7, 31.9, and 53.9.

[35] Frazier, *The Negro Family in Chicago*, p. 127.

pational classes is given. Higher rates of homeownership for the higher occupational groups are most marked in Chicago, Detroit, and Philadelphia. Although it is not so pronounced in New York City with its numerous apartment houses, homeownership there too is higher among the higher occupational classes.

TABLE XXV

Number of Children Under Five to 1,000 Negro Women, 20 to 44 Years of Age and Number of Children Born to 1,000 Negro Married Women, 15 to 44 Years of Age, in the Negro Harlem Community, New York City: 1930 *

ZONE	WOMEN 20-44	CHILDREN UNDER 5	RATIO OF CHILDREN TO WOMEN	MARRIED WOMEN, 15-44 (ESTIMATED)	NUMBER OF BIRTHS	BIRTHS PER 1,000 MARRIED WOMEN 15-44
I	4,141	476	115	2,495	165	66.1
II	23,612	4,160	176	15,087	1,230	81.5
III	21,107	4,749	225	13,883	1,276	91.9
IV	12,498	3,940	315	8,552	1,211	141.6
V	3,872	1,790	462	2,833	477	168.4

* Reproduced with permission from *The Negro Family in the United States* by E. Franklin Frazier, pp. 321 and 322. Copyright 1939 by The University of Chicago Press.

FAMILY LIFE AMONG THE VARIOUS CLASSES

Because of the extent to which class differentiation has evolved in the large northern cities, the organization of Negro family life must be studied in relation to the class structure in these communities. It may be well to begin at the bottom of the class structure, since as one considers the higher levels the effects of urban living from the standpoint of reorganization of the family in the urban environment become more pronounced. The lower-class families are physically segregated to a large extent in the deteriorated areas where Negroes first secure a foothold in the community. It is among this class that one finds the large proportion of families with female heads. This is the result of the economic insecurity of the men and illegitimacy. Because of the precarious hold which women of this class have on men, their attitudes alternate between one of subordination to secure affection and one of domination because of their greater economic security than their spouses.[36] But there is in the lower class a "church centered" core of families that endeavor to maintain stable family relations despite their economic insecurity and other exigencies which make family life unstable. Even during periods of comparative prosperity the employment of women may prove a disintegrating factor since these families lack a deeply rooted tradition.

TABLE XXVI

Percentage of Nonwhite Families With Employed Head That Were Homeowners in Each Occupation Group in Four Northern Cities: 1940 *

OCCUPATION GROUP	NEW YORK	CHICAGO	PHILADELPHIA	DETROIT
Professional and Semi-professional	6.5	20.6	32.4	30.8
Proprietors, Managers, etc.	7.1	22.9	10.3	26.7
Clerical, Sales, etc.	8.6	18.1	33.3	50.0
Craftsmen, Foremen	9.6	6.8	6.8	21.1
Operatives	3.3	3.7	10.2	17.9
Domestic Service	2.6	4.0	14.3	5.6
Service Workers	4.1	7.1	12.9	19.1
Laborers	5.0	5.5	5.9	11.1
TOTAL	4.9	7.9	20.4	19.2

* Based upon the *Sixteenth Census of the United States: 1940. Population and Housing,* "General Characteristics," pp. 290-91.

The occupational differentiation of the Negro population in the northern city, as we have seen, has made possible the emergence of a substantial middle class.[37] The middle class is comprised largely of clerical workers and persons in the service occupations, though there are professional workers and some business persons in this class.[38] But, perhaps, the most important accession to the middle class in the northern cities has been the families of industrial workers, especially the skilled workers. It is among this occupational class that the male head of the family has sufficient economic security to play the con-

[36] St. Clair Drake and Horace R. Cayton, *Black Metropolis, A Study of Negro Life in a Northern City* (New York, 1945), pp. 583-84.

[37] See pp. 300-02 above.

[38] Cf. Drake and Cayton, *op. cit.,* p. 661. See also pp. 300-01 above.

ventional rôle of provider for his family without the aid of the wife. This was indicated in a study of the industrial employment of Negro men and the employment of Negro married women in 75 northern and southern cities with a total population of 100,000 or more in 1930. It was found that the proportion of married women employed declined as the proportion of employed Negro males in industry increased.[39]

Although the husband or father in the middle-class Negro family is generally recognized as the head of the family, the wife or mother is not completely subordinated. There is often a division of labor in the management of the household and a spirit of democracy in the family. The dignified and respected position of the wife and mother is due partly to the tradition of independence among Negro women. The spirit of democracy often springs from the fact that there is considerable cooperation in order that the family may purchase a home or that the children may obtain an education. The education of children means that the family is "getting up" in the world. To be respectable and to "get up" in the world are two of the main ambitions of middle-class families. Therefore, it is not unusual that parents in middle-class families make tremendous sacrifices to enable their children to get a college education.[40] At the same time the children of the middle class are not as a rule spoiled as are often the children in the upper class. They are generally subjected to strict discipline but they are not treated with the harshness which is often found in the case of children in lower-class families. The boys who begin at any early age to earn money in such jobs as running errands and selling newspapers generally develop a sense of responsibility and habits of industry. Consequently, the ambitious and thrifty middle-class families are the mainstay of the Baptist and Methodist churches and other institutions in the Negro community.

We come finally to the upper-class families in the large cities of the North. The upper-class Negro families do not derive their support from invested wealth but rather from professional and other kinds of services. Yet because of their class position, their outlook is often that of a wealthy leisure class. Many heads of upper-class families can tell

[39] The coefficient of correlation was —0.67. See Frazier *The Negro Family in the United States,* pp. 461 and 616-18.   [40] *Ibid.,* pp. 473-74.

success stories of their rise in the world, but these stories are very seldom concerned with becoming heads of business enterprises. As a rule the stories tell of their struggle to achieve a professional education. Moreover, the wives of these upper-class men like upper-class wives in the border cities are sometimes employed in professional occupations.

Where the wife is employed the upper-class family is generally equalitarian in its organization. But even where the wife is not employed, the wife in the upper-class family enjoys considerable equality in the family and freedom in her activities and contacts in the community. In some upper-class families, where the wife is economically dependent, she nevertheless determines to a large extent the manner in which the family income is spent. She herself may be the object of much conspicuous consumption since she becomes the symbol of her husband's economic position. Whether engaging in "social life" or aiding in "civic" activities, she behaves according to the expectations of her class position. Since respectability is taken for granted in this class, the unconventional behavior of husband or wife is not allowed to become a matter of public knowledge. When unconventional behavior of husband or wife becomes public, it generally means the divorce court. An important feature of the expectations of her class is that while respectability is taken for granted, the wife is supposed to appear as "refined" and "cultured." [41]

Among the upper class in the northern city there are many childless couples and relatively few children in families with children. Men and women who have struggled to achieve a high position in the Negro community are not inclined to have the standards which they attempt to maintain lowered by the burden of children. Moreover, since these men have often experienced many privations to achieve an education, they want to spare their children similar hardships. As a consequence the children of the upper class are often spoiled. The parents attempt to satisfy their children's wishes and try often to maintain them in the manner of the children of the rich. Upper-class parents in border and southern cities often send their children to the colleges in the North that represent, in their opinion at least, a certain

[41] Cf. Drake and Cayton, *op. cit.*, p. 531.

exclusiveness. There is some evidence to support the rumors which have often circulated in Negro communities that mulatto women sometimes have refused to have children by their black husbands. A sampling of Negro families in three southern cities, secured from the unpublished data of the 1910 federal census, revealed that couples in which the husband was black and the wife was a mulatto had fewer children on the average than either the couples in which both husband and wife were black or both husband and wife were mulatto.[42] In contemplating marriage, upper-class Negroes in the North as well as in the South take into consideration the color of their prospective mates, especially its effect upon the color of their children.

Among upper-class families there is much individualism. Husbands, wives, and children insist as a rule upon the right to follow their own interests. This individualism becomes very conspicuous among the so-called "emancipated" and "sophisticated" elements in the upper class. Many of these "families" are really childless couples. Their outlook on life is not only individualistic but secular. They represent a new type of intelligentsia in the Negro group. They are acquainted with the latest and best literature; they are concerned with movements within and without the Negro group. They associate freely with white middle-class intellectuals. Among this group may be found many of the "interracial" couples, since the intelligentsia does not exhibit the same hostility to intermarriage as the more conservative and isolated elements in the upper class. Thus they provide a bridge for the complete integration of the Negro in the northern city.

In this chapter we have traced the development of the Negro family and its organization in relation to the emerging class structure of rural and urban communities. It was shown how the family acquired a stable character during slavery as the result of the social and economic organization of the plantation. Then, it was shown how the family first became established on an institutional basis among the Negroes that were free before the Civil War. The analysis revealed the disorganizing effects of the Civil War and Emancipation and the

[42] The samples were taken from Birmingham, Alabama, Charleston, South Carolina, and Nashville, Tennessee. See Frazier, *The Negro Family in the United States*, Appendix B, Table 26, p. 603.

subsequent reorganization in the rural South. Then we saw how the migrations to cities, especially the mass migrations to northern cities, produced a new crisis in the family life of the Negro. The experience with city life, it was seen, has not resulted simply in the disorganization of the family, held together chiefly by habit and sentiment, but in the reorganization according to middle-class patterns, thus reflecting the new class structure in urban communities. The family has been, thus, not only the most important form of organized social life among Negroes, but it has been the means by which the new forms of adjustment have been mediated to succeeding generations.

From the study of the family we shall turn to a study of the Negro church, which next to the family represents the Negro's most important organized social adjustment to American life.

CHAPTER XIV

The Negro Church

THE Negro Church," according to DuBois, "is the only social institution of the Negroes which started in the African forest and survived slavery," [1] and this fact, he stated later, accounts for its extraordinary growth and vitality.[2] In support of this claim, he states that the transplanted African priest "early became an important figure on the plantation and found his function as the interpreter of the supernatural, the comforter of the sorrowing, and as the one who expressed, rudely, but picturesquely, the longing and disappointment and resentment of the stolen people." [3]

But from the scanty and fragmentary reports on the religious behavior of the imported Negro slaves, it would be difficult to establish any connection between African priests and the preachers on the plantations. It would be even more difficult to establish any relation between African religious practices and the Negro church which developed on American soil.[4] It appears from the historical evidence that the religion of the American Negro and his church organization grew out of his experiences on American soil. While it was probably true that at first the Established Church succeeded only in giving "a veneer of Christianity," it was also true that the Negro found in the evangelical faiths—Baptist and Methodist—a set of practices and be-

---

[1] *Some Efforts of American Negroes for Their Own Betterment* edited by W. E. B. DuBois, p. 4. Published 1898 by Atlanta University Press.

[2] *The Negro Church* edited by W. E. B. DuBois, p. 5. Published 1898 by Atlanta University Press.   [3] *Ibid.*

[4] In the latter part of the sentence quoted at the beginning, DuBois states that "under the leadership of the priest and medicine man, afterward of the Christian pastor, the church preserved remnants of African tribal life and became after emancipation the centre of Negro social life." *Some Efforts of American Negroes for Their Own Betterment*, p. 4.

liefs and an opportunity for emotional expression that were related
to his everyday experiences in the new environment. Thus the religious behavior of the Negro and the character of his church organizations have been shaped throughout their development by white
patterns as well as the social and cultural forces within the more or
less isolated social world of the Negro.

THE SOCIETY FOR THE PROPAGATION OF THE GOSPEL IN FOREIGN PARTS

From the beginning of the importation of slaves into what is now
the United States, Negroes received Christian baptism. The initial
opposition to the Christianizing of the Negro tended to disappear
when laws made it clear that slaves did not become free through the
acceptance of the Christian faith and baptism.[5] Although slaves were
regularly baptized and taken into the Anglican Church during the
seventeenth century, it was not until the opening of the eighteenth
century that a systematic attempt was made on the part of the established Church of England to Christianize the Negroes in America.
This missionary effort was carried out by the *Society for the Propagation of the Gospel in Foreign Parts,* which was chartered in England
in 1701.[6] Within a year a missionary was sent out by the *Society* to
the Yammonsee Indians of South Carolina. But when these savage
Indians proved themselves to be hostile to missionary efforts, the representative of the *Society* turned his attention to the more receptive
Negro and Indian slaves.[7] In spite of the opposition of many planters,

[5] See pp. 24-27 above.
[6] C. F. Pascoe, *Two Hundred Years of the S. P. G.: An Historical Account of
the Society for the Propagation of the Gospel in Foreign Parts* (London, 1901),
Vol. I, pp. 1-7. Interest in the conversion of the Negroes was stimulated by three
addresses by Bishop Gibson of London in 1727. (1) "An Address to Serious
Christians among ourselves, to Assist the Society for Propagating the Gospel, in
carrying on the Work of Instructing the Negroes in our Plantations abroad."
(2) "Letter to the Masters and Mistresses of Families in the English Plantations
abroad; Exhorting them to encourage and promote the Instruction of their Negroes in the Christian Faith." (3) "Letter to the Missionaries in the English
Plantations; exhorting them to give their Assistance towards the Instruction of the
Negroes of their Several Parishes, in the Christian Faith." *Ibid.,* p. 8.
[7] *Ibid.,* pp. 12-13. The missionary had to direct his attention also to the white
colonists whom he found "in such a wilderness and so destitute of spiritual
guides and all the means of grace" that they approached the "heathenism" of the
Negroes and Indians. *Ibid.,* p. 13.

the Negroes responded eagerly to the missionary efforts, providing in some congregations a half of the communicants. In 1743 two Negroes were purchased and trained as teachers in a school operated by the *Society* in Charleston, South Carolina. By this time the *Society* had established missions in all the colonies along the Atlantic seaboard. In the North as well as in the South, Negroes were taught in the mission schools and brought into the Established Church.

During this same period the Negro slaves came under the influence of the Moravians, the Presbyterians, the Quakers, and the Catholics. As early as 1738 the Moravians established missions exclusively for Negroes.[8] The Quakers, who began their missionary efforts among Negroes toward the close of the seventeenth century, were generally opposed by the slaveholders because they favored the manumission of the slaves.[9] In 1747 the Presbyterians began their missionary efforts among Negroes in Virginia where according to reports they met with an eager response on the part of the blacks.[10] The efforts of the Catholic missionaries were centered largely in Maryland and Louisiana. Because of their position in the former colony, which was once under Catholic control, the Catholic priests who worked among Negroes generally aroused suspicion.[11] In Louisiana the Catholics were more successful because of the French and the presence of refugees from the former French colony of Haiti.[12]

Unfortunately, the missionaries who worked among the Negroes in the eighteenth century have not left us records of the religious behavior of their converts. Concerning the success which he had had with Negroes who had been instructed in Christian principles by two white women, the Reverend Taylor wrote in 1713:

Upon these gentlewomen's desiring me to come and examine these negroes . . . I went and among other things I asked them, Who Christ was. They readily answered, He is the Son of God, and Saviour of the World, and told me that they embraced Him with all their hearts as such, and I desired them to rehearse the Apostles' Creed and

---

[8] See Charles C. Jones, *The Religious Instruction of the Negroes in the United States* (Savannah, 1842), pp. 30-34.

[9] DuBois, *The Negro Church*, p. 21.   [10] Jones, *op. cit.*, pp. 35-37.

[11] John T. Gillard, *The Catholic Church and the Negro* (Baltimore, 1929), p. 14.   [12] *Ibid.*, pp. 16-19.

the 10 Commandments, and the Lord's Prayer, which they did very distinctly and perfectly. 14 of them gave me so great satisfaction, and were so very desirous to be baptized, that I thought it my duty to baptize them and therefore baptized these 14 last Lord's Day. And I doubt not but these gentlewomen will prepare the rest of them for Baptisme in a little time.[13]

We do not know to what extent the converted blacks resumed their old "heathen" ways or combined the new religious beliefs and practices with the old. The leaders of the *Society for the Propagation of the Gospel in Foreign Parts* were aware of the difficulties in converting adult Africans.[14] Therefore they directed their attention primarily to the Negro children who had not acquired to any appreciable extent the African practices. Moreover, the missionaries of the *Society* required the prospective members of the church to undergo a period of instruction before being baptized and admitted to communion. Under such circumstances a relatively small and selected group of Negroes, probably those closely associated with the whites, were Christianized. In addition, the opposition of the planters and the small number of missionaries tended to restrict the number of black converts. Rev. Clement Hall, a missionary in North Carolina, reported in 1752 that in seven or eight years he had been able to travel 14,000 miles, "Preach about 675 sermons, Baptize 5,783 White children, 243 Black children, 57 White adults, and 112 Black adults." [15] The influence of the Moravians, Presbyterians, Quakers, and Catholics was apparently as restricted as that of the Anglican Church. It is estimated that there were 3,000 Negroes among the 15,800 Catholics in Maryland in 1785.[16] Despite the reported success in the conversion of Negroes, a survey of the situation indicates that only a small proportion of the slaves in the colonies were included among even the nominal Christians.[17]

[13] Quoted in *Classified Digest of the Records of the Society for the Propagation of the Gospel in Foreign Parts* (London, 1893), p. 16.

[14] See "The Bishop of London's Letter to the Masters and Mistresses in the English Plantations" quoted in Jones, *op. cit.*, p. 16.

[15] *Digest of the Records of the S. P. G.*, p. 24.

[16] Gillard, *op. cit.*, pp. 14-15.

[17] Marcus W. Jernegan, "Slavery and Conversion in the American Colonies," *The American Historical Review*, Vol. XXI (April, 1916), pp. 504-27.

THE PROSELYTING EFFORTS OF THE METHODISTS
AND BAPTISTS

What Woodson has aptly called "The Dawn of the New Day" in the religious development of the Negro occurred when the Methodists and Baptists began proselyting the blacks.[18] The proselyting efforts of the Methodists and Baptists, as well as the more restricted missionary work of the Presbyterians, were a phase of the Great Awakening which began in New England and spread to the West and South.[19] From its inception in New England, the Great Awakening was characterized by its appeal to the masses who fainted, and became convulsed during the revival meetings.[20] When the Methodists and Baptists began their revivals in the South, large numbers of Negroes, being attracted by this form of religious behavior, were taken into the churches of these two sects. However, it was not until after the Revolutionary War that the large masses of the Negro population, in the North as well as in the South, became converts and joined the Baptist and Methodist churches. During the closing years of the eighteenth century the revivals in Tennessee and Kentucky tended to re-enforce the mode of conversion characteristic of the Methodist revivals and were utilized in some places by the Baptists and Presbyterians.[21]

As we have noted in a previous chapter, the appeal of the Baptists and Methodists to the Negro has been ascribed recently by some scholars to the Negro's African background.[22] It has even been asserted that the emotionalism of the revivals and camp meetings was due to the participation of Negroes.[23] It is unnecessary, however,

[18] Carter G. Woodson, *The History of the Negro Church*, 2nd ed. (Washington, D. C., 1921), Chapter II.

[19] Joseph Tracy, *A History of the Great Awakening* (Boston, 1892), 81-82.

[20] *Ibid.*, pp. 216-30.

[21] See Catherine C. Cleveland, *The Great Revival in the West, 1797-1805* (Chicago, 1916) and Elizabeth K. Nottingham, *Methodism and the Frontier* (New York, 1941).　　[22] See pp. 15-16 above.

[23] This is the opinion of Professor Herskovits referred to on p. 16 above. In Nottingham, *op. cit.*, p. 204, one finds the following statement: "The bodily contortions which constitute the holy dance (of the Methodists) bear the stamp of Negro influence." As Professor Faris has pointed out in "The Mental Capacity of Preliterates" in *The Nature of Human Nature* "The social situation in which the American Negro found himself has, in all probability, furnished the pattern

to indulge in such speculation in accounting for the response of the Negro to the proselyting of the Baptists and Methodists. The Baptist and Methodist preachers, who lacked the education of the ministers of the Established Church, appealed to the poor and ignorant and the outcast. In the crowds that attended the revivals and camp meetings there were numbers of Negroes who found in the fiery message of salvation a hope and an escape from their earthly woes. Moreover, the emphasis which the preachers placed upon feeling as a sign of conversion found a ready response in the black slaves who were repressed in so many ways. But there were even more fundamental psychological factors in human nature which offer an explanation of the response of the slaves to the religion of the Methodists and Baptists. The slaves, who had been torn from their homeland, from family and friends, and whose cultural heritage had disintegrated or had lost its meaning in the new environment, were broken men. The bonds of a common tradition, of religious beliefs and practices, had been broken and the Negroes had become "atomized" in the American environment. Here was an appeal, emotional and simple, that provided a new way of life and drew them into a union with their fellow men. It drew them into a common union at first with whites, but later formed a stronger common bond with members of their own race.

PARTICIPATION OF SLAVES IN THE RELIGIOUS LIFE
OF THEIR MASTERS

During the period of slavery, the Negroes in the South participated in the religious life of their masters. This was especially true where the plantations acquired the character of a social as well as an industrial institution. Moreover, the house servants often attended the family prayers. In a report to a meeting on the religious instruction of Negroes in South Carolina, one master reported:

---

by means of which he was guided in his religious life." Reprinted by permission from *The Nature of Human Nature* by Ellsworth Faris, p. 274. Copyrighted, 1937, by the McGraw-Hill Book Company, Inc. This opinion is based upon Professor Faris' observations of Congo Negroes who have been subjected to different religious faiths. In each of the three churches which he observed, the religious behavior of the Negroes conformed to the pattern which they had been taught and in none of them was there emotional excitement. *Ibid.*, pp. 275-76.

The number of people on my place is 116, of which number 13 are communicants of the Episcopal Church with one or two exceptions. There are 13 baptized infants and one candidate for adult baptism. Rev. J. S. Hanckel is the only minister, and my wife and myself the only teachers employed among the people. I read the service and teach the catechism to all the people, every Sabbath afternoon. After family prayers on Wednesday night, I teach those who come voluntarily to be instructed. The children are taught constantly during the week by Mrs. M. and our sons, and know the catechism and several hymns. The children learn more readily than the adults: but many of the latter are very consistent and worthy professors.[24]

In the following report from another section of South Carolina, a minister gives information on the distribution of the Negroes among the different denominations and the practice of reserving the galleries for Negroes:

I think there is quite as large a portion of the negroes in the churches generally, as the whites, particularly of the Baptist and Methodist denominations—not so many in the Presbyterian. About one-fourth of the members in the churches are negroes. In the years 1832, '3 and '4 great numbers of negroes joined the churches during a period of revival. Many, I am sorry to say, have since been excommunicated. As the general zeal in religion declined, they backslid. 2. Our churches are furnished with galleries, or portions are set apart for the accommodation of the negroes. They pay good attention, and preserve order. There are a few licensed preachers among them of the Baptist and Methodist order. It has been thought they do some good. They hold meetings only by permission, and not frequently. 3. Our ministers often address the negroes in their discourses. There are some mistresses who instruct their servants at home, and, to their credit be it said, that they pay more attention to the instruction of the negroes than masters; and to their efforts we are indebted for so many well-ordered negroes.[25]

The following longer report from Georgia provides detailed information on the distribution of the Negroes according to denominations, the relations of whites and Negroes in the churches, and the duties of the Negro ministers:

[24] *Proceedings of the Meeting in Charleston, South Carolina, May 13-15, 1845 on the Religious Instruction of the Negroes* (Charleston, South Carolina, 1845), p. 42.   [25] *Ibid.*, pp. 20-21.

There are 4,212 negroes in the District of the county in which I reside and labour. Upon a rough estimate 1,000 of them are members of the different churches: say 350 to the congregational church: 550 to the Baptist—and 100 to the Presbyterian and Methodist. 2. There is one Presbyterian minister who devotes the whole of his time—and one Baptist minister who devotes the half of his time to the religious instruction of these people. There is one coloured minister connected with and under the supervision and control of the Congregational Church, who preaches to the coloured congregation of that church between morning and afternoon services in the white Church, when the white missionary is not present: he performs marriages—attends funerals, &c., but administers no ordinances, this is always done by our white ministers. He also visits as he is able, and receives permission, the different plantations, and holds prayer-meetings with the people and attends to their spiritual affairs. There are coloured watchmen, regularly appointed in both the congregational and Baptist churches. Their duties are expressed by their name. They conduct plantation prayers in the evening where they reside, in connection with prominent members of the Church, of their own colour, and on other plantations when invited and permitted. They exhort the people: give instruction to inquirers—assist members in their Christian walk—warn and reprove, and report cases of delinquency. They are appointed by and are amenable to the white churches. We have no coloured churches independent of the whites. Such organizations we do not deem expedient.[26]

A visitor to the South, who thought that Negroes were "easily excited, and upon no subject so much so, perhaps, as religion" reported as follows on their behavior during church services:

Many of them are truly pious, but the religion of most of them is made up of shouting, which is an incontrovertible argument or proof, with them, of conversion. This shouting is not produced generally by the sermon, for few are able to understand a very plain discourse, of which every sentence will contain words wholly incomprehensible to them. But they always listen with great attention, and so they would do were the sermon delivered in any tongue. A few of the more intelligent and pious Negroes, who can understand most of the sermon, perhaps become affected, and unable, like their better disciplined masters, to control their feelings, give vent to them in groans and shouts. Those about them catch the infection, and spread it, till

[26] *Ibid.*, p. 59.

the whole Negro portion of the audience in the gallery, becomes affected ostensibly by religious feeling, but really by a kind of animal magnetism, inexplicable and uncontrollable.[27]

This same observer attended a beautiful chapel in Tennessee, costing $3,000, which had been erected in the slave quarters or as he said, "in an African village on the plantation." The minister in this church was white and the daughter of the master played the organ.

Upon entering it, I found the body of the floor occupied by black men and women of the plantation, seated in chairs with the utmost decency and quiet, and all neatly and cleanly attired. We took our seats in the gallery, while Isabel placed herself at the organ to play a voluntary. Until the old gentleman who officiated entered, I had time to look at the interior of this bijou of a church. . . . The singing was very remarkable. The African women all sing well, having naturally soft voices; with the organ, and a full fifty fine voices swelling in harmony with it the effect was fine. . . . The responses were all full and timely; for the slaves soon learn words by ear; and many of them go through the whole service, save the psalter, without a mistake. The sermon which was printed, was read well by the elderly layman; it was simple, suitable, and practical. After service, the gray-headed old slaves stood respectfully without the door, and, with uncovered heads, bowed to the colonel and ladies, the latter of whom stopped to speak to some of them, and to make kind inquiries of the old "aunties," as all female slaves are affectionately termed, as the term "uncle" is applied to old men.[28]

Similar reports were made on other parts of the South. However, as one minister pointed out, the relations between whites and Negroes were closer in the up-country of South Carolina, where there were relatively few Negroes than in the low-country where they were more

[27] (J. H. Ingraham) By a Yankee, *The Southwest* (New York, 1835), Vol. II, pp. 263-64. The author adds the comment: "The majority of the religious slaves are of the Methodist denomination, some of which sect may be found on every plantation in the country, but few of them are practical Christians. They are apt to consider the name as the thing. But I have met with individual exceptions, which reflect honour upon their race, and which I now recall with real pleasure one of the most touching and eloquent prayers I have ever heard, I recently listened to from the lips of an old Negro (who sometimes preached to his fellow slaves), as he kneeled by the pallet of a dying African, and commended in an appeal,— which for beautiful simplicity and pathos, is seldom equalled—his departing spirit to God." *Ibid.*, p. 264.

[28] J. H. Ingraham, *The Sunny South* (Philadelphia, 1860), pp. 67-68.

numerous.[29] Similarly, in Mississippi where there were large plantations, which tended to be industrial in character, Negroes received
little religious instruction and had less opportunity for association
with whites in their religious services. A minister reporting from Mississippi wrote concerning the slaves: "There are in this valley multi-
tudes who have no body to look after their souls. The harvest is great,
but the laborers are few." [30]

RELIGIOUS SELF-EXPRESSION AMONG THE SLAVES

Not all of the religious life of the enslaved Negroes was shared
with their masters. In many places Negro preachers were allowed to
conduct services among the slaves. Thus there grew up what has
been aptly called "the invisible institution" of the Negro church.[31]
The growth of the "invisible institution" was encouraged where the
Negroes were isolated most from the whites. This was the case on the
larger plantations and in a state like Mississippi where, as was noted
above, the religious education of the slaves was neglected and there
were few white ministers who gave their time to Negroes. Even in
those areas where the various denominations admitted Negroes into
the churches, the practice of licensing Negro ministers tended to
encourage the growth of the "invisible institution," since the white
ministers were never as close to Negroes as the Negro preachers who
sprang up among them. An ex-slave, writing concerning the life on
the plantation, made the following significant statement concerning
the religious life of the slaves.

We people on the plantation had our church services the same as the
white folks. We did not always have a church to hold our services in,
but we usually had a preacher, and sometimes white preachers would
hold services for us, to which special services all the colored folks
were invited. Our preachers were usually plantation folks just like
the rest of us. Some man who had a little education and had been
taught something about the Bible, would be our preacher. The colored folks had their own code of religion, not nearly so complicated
as the white man's religion, but more closely observed. . . . When

[29] *Proceedings, op. cit.,* p. 24.   [30] *Ibid.,* p. 66.
[31] George F. Bragg, *History of the Afro-American Group of the Episcopal
Church* (Baltimore, 1922), p. 39.

we had meetings of this kind, we held them in our own way and were not interfered with by the white folks.[32]

Where the Negroes were permitted to conduct their services in their "own way" there was more freedom for expression and their church services were characterized by "shouting" and other ecstatic forms of religious behavior. Moreover, there was an opportunity for preachers to arise among them who expressed the slave's feelings and attitudes. In the cities of the South the "invisible institution" was able to grow even more than in the rural areas. A white minister in Columbia, South Carolina gave the following report in 1845:

In the Baptist church in Columbia, of which I am pastor, there are 372 coloured communicants. I am assisted in my ministerial labours among them by two licensed coloured preachers in the town, and four others at various plantations. These preachers hold meetings with the people at least two evenings each week. We have also three watchmen in the town, and one on each plantation. I personally visit the coloured members at the plantations once in three months, with the consent of the owners, and occupy, at present, three preaching stations on some week-day night for the purpose.[33]

The most distinguished preacher to arise among the slaves on the southern plantations was John Jasper. He is described as "an aristocrat," whose mode of dress, manner of walking, and lofty dignity gave evidence of his "aristocratic education." [34] Jasper was sold several times and learned to work in a tobacco factory in Richmond. "At first," according to his biographer, "his tempestuous, ungrammatical eloquence was restricted to Richmond, and there it was hedged in with many humbling humiliations. But gradually the news concerning this fiery and thrilling orator sifted itself into the country, and many invitations came for him to officiate at country funerals." [35]

[32] Robert Anderson, *From Slavery to Affluence: Memoirs of Robert Anderson, Ex-Slave* (Hemingford, Neb., 1927), pp. 22-23.

[33] *Proceedings of the Meeting in Charleston, South Carolina, May 13-15, 1845 on the Religious Instruction of the Negroes* (Charleston, South Carolina, 1845), p. 31.

[34] William E. Hatcher, *John Jasper, the Unmatched Negro Philosopher and Preacher* (New York, 1908), pp. 30-35.

[35] *Ibid.*, p. 38.

THE FOUNDING OF INDEPENDENT NEGRO
CHURCH ORGANIZATIONS

Some of the "humbling humiliations" by which John Jasper was "hedged in" were doubtless due to the presence of the better educated preachers among the free Negroes. For it was among the free Negroes that the Negro church as an institution had its birth. The movement began among the free Negroes in the North that had been emancipated during the period of the American Revolution.[36] The "self-assertion" on the part of Negroes "culminated in the protest of Richard Allen, the founder of the African Methodist Episcopal Church." [37] Allen, who was born a slave in Philadelphia and sold into Delaware, early came under the influence of Methodist preachers and was converted in 1777. In the same year, he and his brother were permitted to purchase their freedom from a kind master for $2,000 in depreciated Continental currency.[38]

After becoming free, Allen followed odd jobs but remained intensely religious and became a preacher in 1780. Because of his talents as a preacher he was allowed to travel with white ministers and even given assignments by Bishop Asbury. When he went to Philadelphia in 1786, he was invited to preach in the St. George Methodist Church. Allen wanted to establish a separate church for Negroes but was opposed by white and Negro members. But when the number of Negro members increased in the St. George Methodist Church, Negroes were removed from the seats around the wall to the gallery. Mistaking the part of the gallery which they were to occupy, Allen, Absalom Jones and another Negro member were almost dragged from their knees as they prayed.[39] They left the church and together with other Negro members founded the Free African Society.

Because of differences in the Free African Society, Jones and Allen developed different plans in regard to the organization of separate Negro churches. Jones became the founder of the St. Thomas African

[36] Woodson, *op. cit.*, pp. 72-73.   [37] *Ibid.*, p. 73.
[38] Richard Allen, *The Life, Experience and Gospel Labors of Rt. Rev. Richard Allen* (Philadelphia, n.d.), p. 12. See also Charles H. Wesley, *Richard Allen Apostle of Freedom* (Washington, D. C., 1935), pp. 15-17.
[39] See Wesley, *op. cit.*, pp. 52-53.

Protestant Episcopal Church and Allen the founder of the African Methodist Episcopal Church. Allen believed that the Methodist rather than the Episcopal Church was suited to the religious behavior and outlook of the masses of Negroes. The movement for an independent church organization spread to Negro Methodist churches in Baltimore and other cities in the South. As a result, Negro leaders of Methodist churches, with the exception of those in the South, met in Philadelphia in 1816 and established the African Methodist Episcopal Church with Richard Allen as its first bishop. The movement spread to New York City and the cities in the South. The African Methodists were suspended in Charleston following the attempted uprising led by Denmark Vesey in 1822.

Toward the close of the eighteenth century there was a secession of Negro Methodists from the white churches which resulted in the organization of the African Methodist Episcopal Zion Church. In 1796 a group of Negroes, most of whom were members of the John Street Methodist Church in New York City expressed the desire "for the privilege of holding meetings of their own, where they might have an opportunity to exercise their spiritual gifts among themselves, and thereby be more useful to one another." [40] In 1799, when their members had increased in the white church, they were permitted to have a building of their own. Later they requested the right to have a Negro minister. Then they decided to withdraw from the white organization and set up their own organization separate from the African Methodist Episcopal Church. Through the work of missionaries, their influence spread to other cities and the African Methodist Zion Church was established in 1821 with James Varick, one of the leaders, as the first bishop in 1822.

During the last quarter of the eighteenth century the Negro Baptists began to establish independent churches in various parts of the country. The first of these churches were established in Southern cities. In 1776 the Harrison Street Baptist Church was organized in Petersburg, Virginia; in 1785 the First African Baptist Church in Savannah; and in 1790 the African Baptist Church of Lexington, Kentucky. Early in the nineteenth century independent Negro Bap-

[40] Quoted in Woodson, *op. cit.*, p. 78.

tist churches were organized in Boston, Philadelphia, and New York City. As we have seen, Absalom Jones had established a separate Episcopal Church for Negroes in Philadelphia. Another Episcopal Church for Negroes, St. James, was organized in New York City in 1818 and later another in Baltimore. Although the Presbyterians were more receptive to the Negroes than the Episcopalians, they did not succeed any more than the latter in attracting the Negroes. Prior to the Civil War there were scarcely 20,000 Negroes in the Presbyterian Church.[41] Likewise, the Congregationalists who aided the fugitive slaves and assisted the Negro in many other ways were not able to compete with the appeal of the Methodist and Baptist churches.

As the result of the Civil War still another Negro Methodist Church came into existence. When the split occurred in the Methodist Church in 1844 over the question of slavery, there were Negro churches connected with the Methodist Episcopal Church in the North. The Methodist Episcopal Church South continued its work with the Negro. But after the Civil War, the small Negro membership which remained in the Methodist Episcopal Church South was permitted to organize a separate body. Thus there came into existence the Colored Methodist Episcopal Church in 1870, in Jackson, Tennessee.

THE GROWTH OF NEGRO DENOMINATIONS
AFTER THE CIVIL WAR

Because of the social disorganization following the Civil War and Emancipation, the religious education and church life of the Negro were disrupted. It was under such conditions that the "invisible institution" of the Negro church which had taken root among the Negroes, especially on the plantations, became visible and merged with the independent Baptist and Methodist Negro organizations. From the Civil War to World War I, the different Negro church organizations continued to expand. The rapid growth of Negro church organizations during this period was a phase of the emancipation of the Negro from white guidance.[42] However, when "white supremacy"

[41] *Ibid.*, p. 97.
[42] Cf. Gunnar Myrdal, *An American Dilemma* (Harper, 1944), pp. 860-61.

was restored, the Negro church became an effective agency in accommodating the Negro to his subordinate position in southern society. By far the largest number of Negroes were attracted to the Baptist churches. In 1916 there were about 3,000,000 Negroes in the nearly 22,000 Baptist churches in the country.[43] Next came the African Methodist Episcopal Church with 548,355 members in 6,633 churches.[44] The African Methodist Episcopal Zion Church and the Colored Methodist Episcopal Church had each about a quarter of a million members in 2,716 and 2,621 churches, respectively. There were over 300,000 members in Negro churches affiliated with the Methodist Episcopal Church (North). There were only 23,329 Negro members in 265 Congregational and Christian churches, and about the same number of Negroes in the Protestant Episcopal Church. There were also more than 50,000 Catholics and about the same number of Presbyterians and Negro Baptists affiliated with the Northern Baptist Convention. Practically all of the Negro members in these churches were organized in separate institutions. The remainder of the 4,602,805 Negro church members were scattered in small numbers in various churches.

In 1936 there were 38,303 Negro churches of all types in the United States, about two-thirds of which were in rural areas. The Negro churches had a total membership of 5,660,618, with less than half of the membership in rural areas.[45] The average number of members per church was twice as great in urban areas—219 compared with 109—as in rural areas. From the standpoint of sex distribution, there were 60.5 males per 100 females in the membership of Negro churches. The value of the edifices of the 34,200 churches reporting was $164,531,531 with a debt of about 20 million dollars. The average value of rural edifices was about $2,000 or one-fifth the average value of the urban churches. Expenditures for the 37,308 churches reporting amounted to almost 18 million dollars or an average of $1,353 for urban churches and $413 for rural churches. There were enrolled in the Sunday Schools of the 35,021 churches reporting about two

[43] Bureau of the Census, *Religious Bodies: 1936 Vol. I. Summary and Detailed Tables* (Washington, 1941), pp. 900-01.
[44] *Ibid.*, pp. 902-03.   [45] *Ibid.*, pp. 850-63.

and a half million scholars, about evenly divided between the urban and rural churches.

NEGRO CHURCHES IN THE SOUTH

In 1936 the majority of the Negro churches—23,744 or 62 per cent—were located in the rural South, while 25 per cent—9,486—of the Negro churches were in the urban areas of the South.[46] Thus about seven-eighths of the Negro churches in the country are in the South. More than two-thirds of the Negro churches in the rural South are of the Baptist denomination and most of the remaining churches are Methodist (See Table XXVII).[47] In the rural South, as Johnson has pointed out,

TABLE XXVII

Number of Negro Churches and Membership According to Denomination in the Urban and Rural South: 1936 *

DENOMINATION	Churches			Membership		
	TOTAL	URBAN	RURAL	TOTAL	URBAN	RURAL
Negro Baptists	20,577	5,590	14,987	3,109,381	1,247,648	1,861,733
Colored Primitive Baptists	942	293	649	41,918	16,569	25,349
Lutherans: Negro Mission	66	26	40	6,553	3,366	3,187
African Methodist Episcopal	3,622	920	2,702	343,983	150,672	193,311
African Methodist Episcopal Zion	1,927	536	1,391	325,111	129,538	195,573
Colored Methodist Episcopal	1,927	521	1,406	249,316	95,313	154,003
Colored Cumberland Presbyterian	132	38	94	10,162	3,249	6,913
TOTAL	29,193	7,924	21,269	4,086,424	1,646,355	2,440,069

* Based upon Bureau of the Census, *Religious Bodies: 1936. Vol. II, Parts 1 and 2, Denominations, Statistics, History, Doctrine, Organization, and Work* (Washington, 1941).

The church is the one outstanding institution of the community over which the Negroes themselves exercise control, and because it stands so alone in administering to their own conception of their needs, its

[46] See Benjamin E. Mays and Joseph W. Nicholson, *The Negro's Church* (New York, 1933), Chapter XVI, concerning "Overchurching in Rural Areas."

[47] Table XXVII does not include figures for the Methodist Episcopal Church and other smaller denominations. In all the states with the exception of Delaware, Montana, and Washington, where the African Methodist Episcopal Church was the leading denomination and Maryland where the Methodist Episcopal Church (North) was the leading denomination, the Baptist was the leading denomination in respect to number of churches and membership. *Religious Bodies: 1936.* Vol. I, p. 83.

function is varied. The religious emotions of the people demand some channel of formal expression, and find it in the church. But more than this, the church is the most important center for face-to-face relations. It is in a very real sense a social institution. It provides a large measure of the recreation and relaxation from the physical stress of life. It is the agency looked to for aid when misfortune overtakes a person. It offers the medium for community feeling, singing together, eating together, praying together, and indulging in the formal expression of fellowship. Above this it holds out a world of escape from the hard experiences of life common to all. It is the agency which holds together the subcommunities and families physically scattered over a wide area. It exercises some influence over social relations, setting up certain regulations for behavior, passing judgements which represent community opinion, censuring and penalizing improper conduct by expulsion.[48]

The majority of the Negro churches in the South are small, unpretentious wooden structures. The following description of the Damascus Baptist Church in Macon County, Alabama, is typical of the rural churches in the plantation South:

The church is a small, painfully conventional boxlike structure with gabled roof and a small bell tower over the entrance. It has once or twice been whitewashed but it is now gray under the long assault of time and the elements. Two giant oaks at the rear, dripping with a Spanish trailing moss, give shelter for the horses and mules of the communicants. Back of the schoolhouse with its broken windows and sagging shutters is a small cemetery with boards and short tombstones jutting up at odd angles to mark the mounds of departed members . . . Inside the church there are three rows of plain wooden benches. The walls of the interior are of white, painted, horizontal boards, and the ceiling, as far up as could be reached, is painted a vivid green. At the end of the room is a very cluttered rostrum. The inclined pedestal has the center; the pastor's seat is directly behind. Then there are three small benches for the choir, two hat racks, and an old clock which is out of order. On the wall back of the rostrum is a large calendar with a picture of Lincoln, an even larger placard announcing a "drive" for $225,000 on behalf of Selma University in 1927, a framed crayon portrait of a former pastor, a placard warning

[48] *Shadow of the Plantation* by Charles S. Johnson, p. 150. Copyright 1934 by The University of Chicago Press.

in red letters of the danger of malaria, and two framed certificates. Beside the rostrum is a coal stove.[49]

The services in the rural churches are characterized by general participation on the part of the congregation.[50] After the congregation has assembled, someone—usually a deacon or prominent member—"raises a hymn," that is, begins singing. The noise dies down and as the singer's voice grows in volume, the congregation joins in the singing. The singing is followed by a prayer by a deacon, which is approved by "Amens" on the part of the congregation. Then follows more spontaneous singing and a prayer. After this comes the sermon, which is characterized by much dramatization on the part of the minister. Members in the audience express their approval by "Amens," groans and such expressions as "Preach it," and "Yes, Lord." As the minister reaches the climax, "shouting" or a form of ecstatic dancing begins. The contagion often spreads until most of the congregation is "shouting." As the "shouting" dies down, someone—very likely the minister, who has not lost control of the services—"raises a hymn." Afterward the minister turns to such practical matters as the collection and announcements concerning future services.

The ministers in these rural churches are older men with a meager education. Scarcely more than two-fifths of them have more than a grammar school education.[51] Moreover, there is much turnover among the rural ministers, especially among the Baptists, where their tenure depends upon their personal inclinations and the extent to which they satisfy the demands of their congregations. The ministers are generally men who have been "called" to preach and therefore they tend to emphasize the mystical aspects of religion and their sermons are otherworldly. Since they themselves "got religion," they place great emphasis upon "getting religion" as prerequisite to church membership.[52] Consequently, the revival continues to play an important

[49] *Shadow of the Plantation* by Charles S. Johnson, pp. 153-54. Copyright 1934 by The University of Chicago Press.

[50] See *ibid.*, pp. 154-62 for a description of a service.

[51] Mays and Nicholson, *op. cit.*, pp. 238-41. See W. A. Daniel, *The Education of Negro Ministers* (New York, 1925) concerning schools for the education of Negro ministers.

[52] See Hortense Powdermaker, *After Freedom* (New York, 1939), pp. 253-73 on "Getting Religion."

rôle in the church services, though there are indications that the revival is not as important as formerly.

The pattern of religious services in the towns and smaller cities of the South is similar to that in the rural communities.[53] In southern cities as in the rural areas, the Negro population is "overchurched." A study in 1933 of Negro churches in seven southern cities revealed that there were 1,075 churches with a combined adult membership of 263,122 or 245 per church.[54] In this study it was pointed out that, "If the white people of Atlanta had proportionately as many churches as the Negroes have, white Atlanta would have 386 churches rather than 136. If the Negroes of Atlanta had proportionately as few churches as the whites, they would have 68 instead of 184." [55] However, in Atlanta and other larger cities of the South, there are differences in the character of the religious services in the Baptist and Methodist churches corresponding to the class differences in the Negro population. In the smaller churches of these denominations and those in which the lower classes are concentrated, the services are similar to those in the rural areas. On the other hand, the solid members of the middle class and a small number of upper-class Negroes are found chiefly in the churches with a more dignified form of religious service. Moreover, in the larger cities of the South, Congregational, Episcopal, and Presbyterian churches become more important in the religious life of the Negro. The relatively small congregations affiliated with these denominations are comprised largely of upper-class Negroes.

THE IMPACT OF THE NORTH ON THE RELIGION OF NEGRO MIGRANTS

The migrations of Negroes to northern cities affected the character of their churches as well as other phases of their life. The number of Negro churches continued to increase until 1926 but the census for 1936 showed a decline of 10.1 per cent. Nevertheless, the number as well as the membership of Negro Baptist churches continued to increase up to 1936. The decrease in the number of churches and in

[53] See *ibid.*, pp. 232-52.　　　[54] Mays and Nicholson, *op. cit.*, p. 204.
[55] *Ibid.*, p. 210.

Negro membership occurred in the various independent Methodist churches and in the Methodist churches connected with the white Methodist Church. There was also a decrease in the number of Episcopal and Presbyterian churches and in the membership in these denominations. But there were significant increases in the number of churches and in the membership of the Roman Catholic Church and in the number and membership of various sectarian churches. In order to understand the significance of these changes in the religious life of the Negro and in the character of his church organizations, it will be necessary to study the situation in a number of northern cities.

TABLE XXVIII

Number of Negro Churches and Membership According to Denomination in the Urban and Rural North: 1936 *

DENOMINATION	Churches			Membership		
	TOTAL	URBAN	RURAL	TOTAL	URBAN	RURAL
Negro Baptists	2,357	1,822	535	648,684	602,339	46,345
Colored Primitive Baptists	67	60	7	1,979	1,845	134
Lutherans: Negro Mission	14	12	2	2,260	2,224	36
African Methodist Episcopal	868	638	230	163,265	122,769	13,496
African Methodist Episcopal Zion	288	240	48	86,350	81,775	4,575
Colored Methodist Episcopal	108	87	21	17,832	16,962	870
Colored Cumberland Presbyterian	13	7	6	506	318	188
TOTAL	3,715	2,866	849	920,676	828,232	65,644

* Based upon Bureau of the Census, *Religious Bodies: 1936. Vol. II, Parts 1 and 2, Denominations, Statistics, History, Doctrine, Organization, and Work* (Washington, 1941).

In 1936 less than a tenth of the Negro churches were in the North and more than three-fourths of the Negro churches in the North were in cities.[56] The majority of the Negro churches were, as in the South, of the Baptist denomination while most of the remainder were Methodist (See Table XXVIII). But in the large cities of the North there are many small churches—"storefront" churches and various sectarian churches.

In northern cities, as in the South, most upper-class persons form

[56] In the West there were only 401 Negro churches with a total membership of 50,000. All except 52 of the churches, with a total membership of only 2,185, were located in urban areas.

the majority of the comparatively small congregations of the Episcopal, Presbyterian, and Congregational churches. The ministers in these churches are educated men and their sermons are generally of a scholarly character. Usually there are a few large Baptist and Methodist churches in which the more solid members of the middle class are concentrated. But in the numerous smaller Baptist and Methodist churches the church-centered elements of the lower class are concentrated. According to Drake and Cayton,

It has been estimated that of the approximately 30,000 lower-class persons who were actually affiliated with churches, about a sixth belonged to three very large lower-class churches (each having more than 1,500 members); another sixth were distributed among a score of medium-sized lower-class churches (each with 200 to 500 members); about one-third of the total group were worshiping in remodeled stores, garages, theaters, houses, and halls; and another third were members of churches in which higher-status members predominated. Lower-class neighborhoods were plentifully supplied with small Baptist and Holiness churches.[57]

The lower-class people carry over into the northern city their traditional attitudes in regard to religion. There is great emphasis upon "Sin" and the "Devil." The chief sin against which the preachers constantly carry on warfare is loose sex behavior. The emphasis upon sex is, of course, a reflection of the sex pattern among the lower class. Since the lower-class churches are attended largely by women, many of whom are deserted or have other irregular marital relations, the church helps to accommodate the women of this class to their fate. The sermons in the lower-class churches reflect the Negro's naïve conception of the strange world about him. The complex and puzzling world of the city is usually pictured as a "wicked world," which will be destroyed by God. Therefore, the faithful should keep themselves uncontaminated by the wickedness of the world. The wickedness of the world consists largely of dancing, card playing, and drinking. The first step toward salvation involves conversion. The conversion experiences are losing much of their dramatic qualities in the city,

[57] *Black Metropolis* by St. Clair Drake and Horace R. Cayton, pp. 612-13. Copyright 1945 by Harcourt, Brace and Company, Inc.

though the services in these churches are characterized by much of the same emotionalisms found in the small rural churches of the South.

The emergence of the "storefront" church in the urban environment is of peculiar interest because it represents, on the whole, the adaptation of the small rural church to city life. Consequently, it is not surprising that the "storefront" church is more characteristic of the northern than of the southern city. In Chicago 75 per cent of the nearly 500 churches in the Negro community were "storefront" churches. Moreover, the location of these churches in relation to the spatial pattern of the Negro community indicates their relation to the economic and cultural organization of the community. The "storefront" churches are clustered in the poorer areas of the Negro community in which the newcomers from the South are concentrated.[58] The existence of these churches is due partly to the poverty of their members and the fact that the members may participate more freely —in praying as well as "shouting"—in the services. There is, however, a more important reason why "storefront" churches flourish in the northern city. In the large churches the Negro from the South, being lost in the mass of members, has no status and longs for the warmth and sympathetic relationship which is provided in the face-to-face association in the small church. Some of the ministers are, of course, charlatans, who take advantage of the ignorance and simple faith of their followers.[59] Then there are the so-called "jack-leg" preachers— untrained and seeking an escape from manual labor—who find in the "storefront" church a chance for employment or a chance to supplement their regular income. The regularly established churches have failed to provide the type of church or the trained ministry required by recently urbanized Negroes. But, on the whole, the "storefront" church owes its existence to the fact that it provides an opportunity for self-expression and social contacts.

[58] Mays and Nicholson, *op. cit.*, p. 219. See also Drake and Cayton, *op. cit.*, pp. 632-36; E. Franklin Frazier, *The Negro Family in Chicago* (Chicago, 1939), p. 276.

[59] In Chicago over 700 preachers were competing for 500 churches. Many of these preachers were "jack-leg" preachers or men without any formal training who had received the "call" to preach. Drake and Cayton, *op. cit.*, pp. 629-30.

THE INCREASE IN NEGRO SECTS AND CULTS
IN NORTHERN CITIES

The most radical transformation in the religious life of the folk Negro is revealed in the various sectarian churches which have sprung up in the northern city. In Chicago over a fifth of the Negro churches are affiliated with various "holiness" denominations and another tenth with "spiritualist" churches. There are in addition to the various "holiness" and "spiritualist" churches other cults or sects which are nationalistic in their orientation. In his study of these cults in the northern cities, Fauset gives four compulsions, "the supernatural being, the personality of the leader, relief from physical and mental illness, and race consciousness," which appear to be responsible for the attraction of Negroes to the cults. In the case of the first compulsion, which is characteristic of all the cults, there is the desire to get closer to "some supernatural power, be it God, the Holy Spirit, or Allah." [60] The influence of the personality of the leader is likewise a common characteristic of the cults. The other two compulsions—physical and mental illness and race consciousness—are of greater importance because they have a peculiar relation to the Negro's adjustment to the northern environment.

The migration of the folk Negro to the northern metropolis often produces a severe crisis in his life. It often results in the disruption of family relations which provided emotional as well as a certain degree of economic security in the South. Generally it means the loss of friends and neighbors who gave the Negro the sense of "belonging" to a social group. Moreover, in the large city church, as we have pointed out, the folk Negro does not enjoy the face-to-face contacts and the status which the church in the South afforded. The folk knowledge and folk practices which provided a guide to life in the South lose their meaning especially in time of crises involving sick-

[60] Arthur H. Fauset, *Black Gods of the Metropolis* (Philadelphia, 1944), p. 76. Raymond J. Jones, *A Comparative Study of Cult Behavior among Negroes with Special Reference to Emotional Group Conditioning Factors* (Washington, 1939), classifies the various cults in five types: Faith Healing, Holiness, Islamic, Pentecostal, and Spiritualist. Fauset, *op. cit.*, has shown that in the various cults there is much overlapping of the types presented in Jones' study.

ness and death. Consequently, the folk Negro seeks new ways to meet these crises and attempts to find a new meaning for his existence in the world of the city. In the cults in which "faith healing" plays an important rôle he finds a "cure" for both physical and mental ills. "Faith healing" appeals to him because it combines elements, similar to the folk beliefs of the southern Negro with an "intellectual" element acquired through the reflection which is forced upon the Negro in the city. In the cults in which "holiness" or sanctification is important, he is able to resolve the moral conflicts created by the conflict between the simple mores of the South and free and easy ways of the city.

The most important cult to appear among Negroes in the northern city has been the Father Divine Peace Mission movement. This movement, which involves "faith healing" and "holiness" or sanctification, began in an obscure town on Long Island. It attracted Negroes from Harlem who disturbed the peace with their noisy religious behavior and thereby caused its leader, Father Divine, to run afoul of the law. As the result of the prosecution of Father Divine and the death of the judge who tried him, which his followers regarded as an act of divine displeasure, he became a Messiah. When he entered the impoverished Harlem community during the depth of the Depression in 1932, the Negroes were in a state of hopelessness.[61] Father Divine thus became the embodiment of a deliverer who had appeared to heal the physically and mentally sick and feed the hungry. Physical ailments were redefined as the result of straying from the "faith" in Father Divine and death became a weakness which the faithful had to overcome. Mental illness or doubt and conflicts were to be resolved simply by thinking of Father Divine and saying "Thank you, Father." [62] At the same time, "one must refrain from stealing, refusing to pay just debts, indulging in liquor in any form, smoking, obscene language, gambling, playing numbers, racial prejudice or hate of any kind, greed, bigotry, selfishness, and lusting after the opposite sex." [63]

[61] See Robert A. Parker, *The Incredible Messiah* (Boston, 1937) for a thorough study of the development of the movement in relation to the psychological, social, and economic backgrounds of Negroes in Harlem.
[62] Fauset, *op. cit.*, p. 63. [63] *Ibid.*, p. 64.

One may discover in this cult a number of elements which reveal a new orientation of the Negro to life in the city. There is a sacred text, so to speak, which reflects the growing literacy of the Negro in the city. This sacred text is the *New Day*, a weekly newspaper which contains the advertisements of nationally known firms as well as local stores. The absence of the Bible is indicative of a certain sophistication or emancipation from traditional modes of thought and behavior. The *New Day* deals with the current issues of the day as interpreted by Father Divine to his followers. There are fourteen planks in the "Righteous Government" platform which serves as a guide to the faithful in their daily contacts. At the same time, the faithful are given an opportunity to indulge in ecstatic forms of religious behavior. These sporadic expressions of religious behavior are a part of living "evangelically," which involves communion with Father Divine. In their day to day existence, the faithful are encouraged to engage in business enterprises which have been, on the whole, successful.

In the Father Divine Peace movement, there are also whites among the faithful and any form of racial prejudice is strictly forbidden. By teaching amity in race relations this movement represents one form of adjustment of the Negro to whites in the urban environment of the North. Thus it stands in marked contrast to those cults which have fostered racial chauvinism and racial exclusiveness. The latter type of adjustment to race relations in the northern city has achieved its most extreme expression in the Moorish Science Temple of America. This cult was founded in 1913 by a twenty-seven-year-old Negro with little formal education, who was born in North Carolina.[64] After becoming acquainted with some phases of oriental philosophy, "he became obsessed with the idea that the salvation for the Negro people lay in the discovery by them of their national origin, i.e., they must know whence they came, and refuse longer to be called Negroes, black folk, colored people, or Ethiopians. They must henceforth call themselves Asiatics, to use the generic term, or, more specifically, Moors or Moorish Americans." [65] The reflections of the leader of this cult

[64] See Fauset, *op. cit.*, pp. 41-51.   [65] *Ibid.*, p. 41.

have been set down in a secret text, Holy Koran, which is not, of course, the Mohammedan Koran.

This movement with its "temples" spread from Newark to Chicago where hundreds of Negroes flocked to the new teacher. Those who became full members of the cult were changed from Negroes to Asiatics. One of the important beliefs inculcated by the leader was that "a star within a crescent moon had been seen in the heavens" and that this sign was a portent of the coming dominance of the Asiatics and the destruction of the whites. The members wore fezzes and publicly exhibited their contempt toward the whites. Because of the increasing conflicts with whites, including the police, it was necessary for the prophet, Noble Drew Ali, to warn his followers to restrain themselves. As the movement grew, conflicts within the organization resulted in the murder of one of the leaders. The prophet was arrested for the murder but was never brought to trial because he died while free on bond. Despite the death of the leader, the movement continued to grow for awhile and spread to other metropolitan areas. Although the movement is still in existence, it has ceased to attract large numbers of Negroes.

This movement, like the Divine movement, combined certain elements in the history of the Negro with new definitions of the Negro's experiences in the city. Although the members of the cult were taught that Christianity is the white man's religion and that Islam was the religion of Asiatics (Negroes are regarded as Asiatics), in their service Christian hymns were set to words which embodied Moslem instruction. A striking feature of the religious services was that the emotionalism characteristic of Negro churches was lacking. In fact, there was little singing except in the form of chants. Members of the cult were required to pray three times a day turning their faces to the East, and to observe dietary restrictions and keep the body clean. The most important feature of the cult was that while it forbade "radicalism" and enjoined loyalty to the country, it offered a transformation of the Negro's personality which enabled him to adjust to the racial discriminations in the northern city.

CHANGES IN THE ORTHODOX DENOMINATIONS

In the northern city the orthodox Baptist and Methodist churches have undergone changes which, though less dramatic, have been important in the adjustment of the Negro church to the urban environment. These changes have been brought about by changes in the mental outlook of the Negro in the city. Because of the greater literacy and experience of the northern Negro it has been necessary for their ministers to have more education.[66] Then, too, the sophisticated Negro in the northern city has a more secular attitude toward the problems which he faces. Consequently, the ministers in the orthodox Baptist and Methodist churches have been forced to direct their sermons to mundane affairs as well as otherworldly matters. The urbanized Negro has increasingly sought in the church an answer to the problems of making a living and a guide for the exercise of his newly acquired political rights. In some of the orthodox churches, the ministers have attempted to continue to stress the supernatural aspects of religion and have taken a conservative attitude toward unions and the political affiliations of the Negro. This attitude has not been always unrelated to the fact that they have received contributions from wealthy white industrialists. But the pressing economic needs of Negroes, especially during the Depression, and their growing knowledge of the relation of economics and politics, have forced the majority of Negro ministers to relate their churches more or less to the social and economic problems of the Negro.[67]

The changes in the character of Negro Baptist and Methodist churches have been most striking in those churches under the dynamic leadership of outstanding ministers. The development of the Abyssinian Baptist Church in Harlem provides an example of the extent to which the orthodox Negro church in the northern city may become secularized in its outlook and in its function.[68] This church began as an orthodox Baptist Church in which many "respectable" Negroes

[66] Cf. Mays and Nicholson, *op. cit.*, pp. 47-48.

[67] See *Whither The Negro Church?* Seminar held at Yale Divinity School, New Haven, Conn. April 13-15, 1931. See also Drake and Cayton, *op. cit.*, pp. 424-29.

[68] See Adam Clayton Powell, Jr., *Marching Blacks* (New York, 1945), pp. 93ff.

of the day worshiped. After the church moved to Harlem, it began to cater to the needs of the thousands of Negroes who migrated from the South during and following World War I. A large structure costing nearly $400,000 was erected with three auditoriums and a community house. The father of the present minister, Adam Clayton Powell, Jr., had to fight the more conservatively religious elements in the church but by the time the membership had reached 11,000 the conservatives had been submerged. This new "social gospel institution," as the young minister who succeeded his father calls it, was equipped to serve the recreational and other needs of young and old. Moreover, the church has been the meeting place for organizations fighting to break down prejudice and secure employment for Negroes in the stores of Harlem. Because of his leadership in the secular interests of the people of Harlem, the minister of this church was the first Negro from Harlem to be elected to the Congress of the United States.

The changes in the character of the orthodox Baptist and Methodist churches in the northern cities are due principally to changes in the religious outlook of the middle class in the Negro community. There have also been changes in the character of the churches attended largely by upper-class Negroes which are indicative of the adjustment which these churches are making to the urban environment of the North. In Harlem, the Negro Presbyterian Church, probably the largest of this denomination in the country, under the leadership of a prominent minister, William Lloyd Imes, carried on a fight for the economic, political, and civil rights of Negroes. Its church activities have included many social features which were designed to help the Negro in his adjustment to urban life. Likewise, the Negro Protestant Episcopal Church, one of the oldest in the country, has maintained a community house and provided social services for the Negroes of Harlem.

There have been other changes in the religious affiliation of Negroes in the northern city which have been the result of more radical changes in the religious outlook of Negroes. There have appeared in northern cities a few institutional churches which attract Negro churchgoers with a broad humanistic as opposed to a strictly religious outlook on life. There is an increasing number of ministers with university education who are concerned with economic and social problems. The churches are the meeting place for clubs with various interests and Sunday forums for the discussion of social and economic problems. For some Negroes who have become emancipated from the orthodox Negro churches, the institutional churches are too secular in their outlook. Consequently, these people are likely to become affiliated with Christian Science churches and the Bahaist movement. While affiliation with these churches offers the means of resolving mental and moral conflicts, it is also related to the status of the Negro. In joining these churches, some Negroes have sought a church which does not practice segregation and in which they might feel at home. Then, too, Negroes and whites who have intermarried have often sought a congenial group in the Bahaist Church. These same motivations have often prompted Negroes to join the Catholic Church.

In its relations with the Negro the Catholic Church has faced a number of obstacles, both outside and within the Negro group.[69] One of the "external" obstacles has been the fact that the masses of Negroes have been concentrated in the South, where there has been much prejudice against the Catholic Church. Then, too, the Church has been forced to set up separate churches, for which there were no trained priests. Even more important than these "external" obstacles have been those "internal" obstacles or conditions existing within the Negro group. The most important of the "internal" obstacles has been the existence of Baptist and Methodist Negro church organizations, which remain one of the chief organized expressions of the race consciousness of the Negro masses. Moreover, the Negro has become accustomed to a type of church service which is opposed to the restraint characteristic of the worship in the Catholic churches. Despite these "external" and "internal" obstacles, and until recent years the belief of Catholics concerning the emotional nature of the Negro and his lack of moral restraint, the Catholic Church has given

[69] See Gillard, *The Catholic Church and the Negro*, pp. 212-57. This book contains a history of the relation of the Negro to the Catholic Church up to 1929.

more attention to the evangelization of Negroes since their migrations to cities.

It appears that the immediate effect of the migration of Negroes to cities was a decline in the number of Negro members of the Catholic Church.[70] This resulted from the disruption of missions in the South and the border states and the general disorganization of the Negro population as the result of the migrations. Around 1930, the Catholic Church began to give serious attention to the migrants. In some cities the Church directed its attention to the economic needs of the Negroes during the depression years. In fact, it seems that many urban Negroes were attracted to the Catholic Church during this period of economic stress. But the efforts of the Church have not been confined to giving aid to Negroes. It has undertaken to provide recreational and educational facilities for Negro youth in cities. For example, in Chicago the Catholic Church has opened parochial schools which provide a full-time program while many of the public schools in Negro neighborhoods are run on double shifts.[71] Only recently the Church has provided a first-class high school in Montgomery, Alabama, for Negroes. The archbishop of St. Louis has instructed the parochial schools to admit Negroes and has at the same time censured the whites who opposed the ruling.

From all indications the efforts of the Catholic Church to attract Negroes are proving successful. This success has been the result primarily of its attention to the problems of Negro youth in cities. The disruption of the Negro folk culture together with family disorganization has tended to alienate Negro youth from their traditional religious heritage. The Catholic Church through its systematic approach to the educational and recreational problems of Negro youth, a program involving the personal relations of the priest to these activities, has created a new religious orientation of the Negro in the city. Moreover, the Catholic Church has come out in recent years in the defense of the Negro's right to full participation in American culture. The general position of the Church has been set forth in recommendations developed in a four-day Seminar on Negro Problems,

[70] See *ibid.*, pp. 263-64.
[71] See Drake and Cayton, *op. cit.*, footnote, pp. 412, 415.

called by the National Catholic Welfare Conference in July 1946.[72] The recommendations included an endorsement of a permanent federal Fair Employment Practices Committee, a condemnation of unions excluding Negroes and of segregation in housing, and a strong defense of the civil rights of the Negro.

The new interest of the Catholic Church in the Negro during the past two decades has been paralleled by a new attitude on the part of white Protestantism toward the Negro. This new attitude has been manifested in the pronouncements of national organizations rather than in changes in the policies of local churches in regard to admitting Negroes to membership. When the three branches of the Methodist Church were united in 1939, the plan for the incorporation of the Negro members of the *Methodist Episcopal Church* represented a concession to the *Methodist Episcopal Church, South*, which had split from the parent body in 1844 over the question of slavery. A central jurisdiction was set up which included Negro churches and over which Negro bishops elected by the Negro constituency presided.[73] The Negro membership is opposed, it appears, to this form of segregation but, according to one of their bishops, will accept the un-Christian arrangement "on account of the Christian childness of some American Methodists who need a little coddling until they can grow into full manhood and womanhood in Jesus Christ." [74] The need for "coddling," it was pointed out, existed among the local Methodist churches in the North as well as in the South.

On the other hand, the Federal Council of Churches in Christ took an unusual step at its meeting in Columbus, Ohio, in 1946 when it pledged to end racial discrimination and urged member churches to work toward the goal of racially mixed churches.[75] The General Assembly of the Presbyterian Church (Northern) has come out against racial segregation as un-Christian. The General Council of Congre-

[72] See *Seminar on Negro Problems in the Field of Social Action*, National Catholic Welfare Conference, November, 1946, Washington 5, D. C.

[73] See *Doctrines and Discipline of The Methodist Church* (New York and Cincinnati, 1912).

[74] See article by Joshua C. Williams, "Shall We Continue the Control Jurisdiction?" *The Central Christian Advocate*, November 13, 1947.

[75] See "The New Social Rôle of American Churches," *A Monthly Summary of Events and Trends in Race Relations*, December, 1946.

gational Christian Churches accepted a report condemning racial discrimination within the churches. Despite these pronouncements by national church organizations, Negroes have not been integrated to any significant extent into the white churches. The present situation in regard to the Congregational Christian churches was brought out in a recent survey. In 1944 about 5 per cent of the Congregational churches were "special" Negro churches.[76] Responses to inquiries sent to 3,800 ministers of Congregational Christian churches revealed that 388 churches had both white and nonwhite members. In 123 of the 388 churches there were white and Negro members in the same church; and in 75 churches there were Negroes and other nonwhite peoples and whites. The Negro membership of these churches consisted in most cases of one to four persons. Among the Congregational churches in New England there is a general disposition to set up separate churches for Negroes or to admit one or two in exceptional cases. There is less resistance to the participation of Negroes in such activities as Sunday School and Vacation Bible School than to full adult membership in the churches.

In considering the relationship of the Negro to white churches, it should be pointed out that in recent years small interracial churches have sprung up over the country. As a rule these churches have two pastors, one Negro and the other white, with the membership including nonwhite members other than Negroes.

The development of the religious life of the Negro and his church organizations in the United States has paralleled other phases of his adjustment to American life and his gradual integration into American society. Whatever remained of his African religious heritage was rapidly lost and the Negro assimilated the forms of religious life found in the American environment. The process of assimilation was determined by the extent to which the Negro was integrated into the religious life of his masters. In the South, the Baptist and Methodist churches because of their appeal and their type of services enabled Negroes under favorable conditions to share largely in the religious

[76] See L. Maynard Catchings, "The Participation of Racial and Nationality Minority Peoples in Congregational-Christian Churches," *The Journal of Negro Education*, Vol. XV, pp. 681-89.

life of the masters. However, the Negro church as an institution had its birth among the free Negroes in the North who seceded from white Methodist churches. The growth of the Negro Methodist Church as an independent organization was restricted in the South, though independent Methodist and Baptist churches sprang up among the free Negroes. After Emancipation the independent Negro church organizations, the Baptist churches and the various Methodist denominations, experienced a rapid growth since the thousands of Negroes who were only nominal Christians became affiliated with these churches. The rapid growth of Negro church organizations was a part of their emancipation from white dominance, though the Negro church became one of the most effective agencies in accommodating the Negro to his subordinate status in the South.

With the migration of Negroes to northern cities, the Negro church has lost much of its former influence. At the same time the Negro church has undergone certain transformations in adapting itself to the urban environment. The "storefront" church, in which the simple folk from the South find a congenial form of worship, has made its appearance in the northern city. Various cults and sects have sprung up in answer to the mental and moral conflicts of the frustrated and disillusioned migrants. The orthodox churches have added secular interests in order to hold the urbanized Negro who has acquired a new attitude toward his problems. During the crisis produced by World War II both Protestant and Catholic churches recognized the segregated Negro church as a violation of the spirit of Christianity but practically no progress has been made in admitting Negroes to membership in local white churches. Yet, it is probable that as the result of rivalry between the Protestant and Catholic churches, the Negro will be increasingly admitted to membership in local churches.

CHAPTER XV

Mutual Aid and Fraternal Organizations

AMONG Negroes, as among other peoples in various parts of the world, organization for mutual aid in times of stress constituted the earliest form of social cooperation. Under the slave system cooperation for mutual aid could not exist because any form of independent collective action on the part of the slaves constituted a threat to the institution of slavery. Among the free Negroes both in the North and in the South, in contrast, mutual aid, very often in connection with their religious organizations, was the occasion for their earliest attempts at social cooperation. After Emancipation cooperation for mutual aid in times of crises—sickness and death—became a part of the rural folkways. During the same period more formal types of mutual aid societies such as fraternal organizations began to flourish. These organizations had their most rapid growth when the Negro was concentrated in rural areas. But as the Negro became urbanized, these more or less sacred types of brotherhoods became less important. At the same time, both the rural mutual aid societies and the fraternal organizations had to compete with the growing influence of the more rational forms of organizations—the insurance companies. In the urban environment, a fraternal organization like the Elks, which is more suited to the temper of the Negro in the secular environment, has come to play a more important rôle.

PATERNALISM AND INDIVIDUAL EXPRESSION OF
CHARITY UNDER THE SLAVE REGIME

"The plantation," writes Phillips, "was of course a factory, in which robust laborers were essential to profits." [1] But he goes on to point out

[1] Ulrich B. Phillips, *Life and Labor in the Old South* (Boston, 1929), p. 197.

that many of the larger plantations had infirmaries and physicians on contract for regular visits, day nurseries, and made provisions for the aged and infirm. The home of a well-to-do slaveholder, he said, was likely to be a "magnificent negro boarding house," which provided food for slaves and their dependents and friends.[2] Under the most favorable conditions of slavery, provisions were doubtless made for the Negroes during illness and when they were no longer able to work. Moreover, the death of a faithful slave not only was an occasion for sorrow but his burial was attended with ceremony and a tombstone might commemorate his devotion to his master's family. But such attention to the physical and spiritual needs of the slaves was a part of a patriarchal system and affected a favored minority of the slaves. The compassion which the slave felt for his fellow bondsmen in time of illness and death and his solicitation for the needs of the aged and infirm was an individual matter. An old "granny" would attend a mother during the crisis of childbearing; an old slave might attend the sick; a slave preacher might offer comfort to the dying.[3] But collective action on the part of the slaves was prohibited because masters feared that any concerted action among the slaves could lead to revolt. Consequently, the earliest forms of social cooperation among Negroes appeared among the free Negroes.

DEVELOPMENT OF MUTUAL AID AMONG FREE NEGROES

The earliest of the societies organized among the free Negroes for mutual aid was The Free African Society, founded in Philadelphia in 1787.[4] This organization, as we have seen, was formed following the secession of the Negro leaders, Jones and Allen, from the St. George's Church.[5] At the time, however, Negroes were migrating to Philadelphia in large numbers and the need of cooperation for mutual aid was becoming urgent. This "curious sort of ethical and beneficial brotherhood" was under the direction of Jones and Allen who exercised a "parental discipline" over its members. The avowed purpose of this

---

[2] *Ibid.*, p. 205.   [3] See p. 342n. above.
[4] W. E. B. DuBois, *The Philadelphia Negro* (Philadelphia, 1889), pp. 19-20.
[5] See pp. 345-46 above.

organization was to "support one another in sickness, and for the benefit of their widows and fatherless children." Three years later, in Charleston, South Carolina, the Brown Fellowship Society was organized among the free people of mixed-racial ancestry. The Preamble of the Rules and Regulations of the Society begins as follows:

Whereas we, free brown men, natives of the city of Charleston, in the State of South Carolina, having taken into consideration, the unhappy situation of our fellow creatures, and the distresses of our widows and orphans, for the want of a Fund to relieve them in the hour of their distresses, sickness and death. . . .[6]

The membership of the Society was restricted to 50 persons, who each paid an admission fee of fifty dollars.[7] In addition to giving assistance to widows and orphans and maintaining burial grounds for its dead, the Society provided for the education of the children of its members. This organization, it should be pointed out, was composed of free colored persons who were fairly well-off economically and constituted a sort of intermediate caste in a society based upon slavery. They accepted the dominant values in southern society and were not disposed to challenge the slave system.

The widespread development of organizations for mutual aid among the free Negroes was the result of their economic insecurity in the cities. This was especially true of northern cities where, as we have seen in Chapter IV, the Negro led a precarious existence because of his inability to compete with European immigrants. For example, in Philadelphia in 1813 there were 11 benevolent societies.[8] By 1838 the number of such societies, mostly small groups, had increased to 100, with 7,448 members.[9] The members of these societies paid in $18,851, received $14,172 in benefits, and the societies had $10,023 on hand. In 1848, there were 8,000 members in 106 societies. Seventy-six of these societies had 5,087 members, whose contributions of 25 cents to 37½ cents a month totaled $16,814.23. The 681 families

---

[6] *Rules and Regulations of the Brown Fellowship Society, Established at Charleston, South Carolina, 1st November, 1790* (Charleston, 1844).

[7] E. Horace Fitchett, "The Traditions of the Free Negroes in Charleston, South Carolina," *Journal of Negro History*, Vol. 25, p. 144.

[8] Abram L. Harris, *The Negro as Capitalist* (Philadelphia, 1936), p. 20.

[9] DuBois, *op. cit.*, p. 222.

that were assisted by these 76 societies received $1.50 to $3.00 a week as sick benefits and $10 to $20 as death benefits. In Baltimore there was a benevolent society of colored men as early as 1821 and by 1835 there were 30 such societies with memberships from 35 to 150.[10] In Richmond and Petersburg, Virginia, burial societies were organized in 1815.[11] These mutual aid organizations represented the beginning of the insurance companies among Negroes. The development of Negro insurance companies will be considered in the chapter on "Business Institutions." Here we are concerned with the growth of fraternal organizations among Negroes as a form of social cooperation for mutual aid.

THE ORGANIZATION OF SECRET SOCIETIES

Contrary to the assumption that secret societies among Negroes represent a continuation of African traditions,[12] the development of these societies occurred among Negroes who were farthest removed culturally from their African background. They developed among the free Negroes in the North who had taken over the culture of the whites and participated to some extent in the white man's world. The oldest of these societies was the Masonic Order, which was organized in Boston in 1775.[13] Prince Hall, a Negro of West Indian origin, and fourteen other Negroes were initiated into an army lodge connected with a regiment of British soldiers. It was not until twelve years later that the Negro Masons were granted a warrant by the Grand Lodge of England under the name of the "African Lodge, No. 459." Prince Hall became the first Grand Master of the first Grand Lodge of Negro Masons. He issued licenses to Negroes who had become Masons in England to form a lodge in Philadelphia and later issued a license to a group of Negroes in Providence, Rhode Island.[14]

[10] James M. Wright, *The Free Negro in Maryland, 1634-1860* (New York, 1921), p. 250.
[11] Luther P. Jackson, "The Early Strivings of the Negro in Virginia," *Journal of Negro History*, Vol. 25, p. 33.
[12] See Herskovits, *The Myth of the Negro Past*, pp. 161ff.
[13] See Harold Van Buren Voorhis, P. M., *Negro Masonry in the United States* (New York, 1940), pp. 3-22.
[14] Booker T. Washington, *The Story of the Negro* (New York, 1909), Vol. II, pp. 149-51.

Out of these local lodges grew a National Grand Lodge. Despite the opposition of whites, a Masonic lodge comprised of Negroes was organized in Louisville, Kentucky, in 1850.

The next oldest secret fraternal order to be established among Negroes was the Odd Fellows. This organization grew out of the Philomathean Institute in New York City and the Philadelphia Company and Debating Society, whose members "saw the need of societies for mutual aid and protection in case of sickness and distress." [15] When they applied in 1842 for admission to the "Friendly Society" of Odd Fellows, their application was refused. Through Peter Ogden, a Negro who had been initiated into a lodge in Liverpool, they then applied directly to the English lodge. Their application was accepted and permission was granted to establish the Philomathean Lodge in New York City in 1843. Later Negro lodges of the Odd Fellows were set up in Pennsylvania and Connecticut.

Before the Civil War two other national secret organizations—the Galilean Fishermen and the Nazarites—were set up among the free Negroes. Both of these secret orders were organized in Baltimore, the home of two other secret societies, the Samaritans and the Seven Wise Men.[16] In Baltimore and Philadelphia numerous other secret societies were organized before the Civil War but these societies never became national organizations.

DEVELOPMENT OF SECRET SOCIETIES AFTER EMANCIPATION

Following the Civil War several other national secret societies were organized. The Galilean Fishermen, which was organized in Baltimore in 1856, became incorporated in 1869. The International Order of Twelve of the Knights and Daughters of Tabor was organized in 1871, though it had its beginning before the Civil War. From the available sources, it appears that the founder of this society was Reverend Moses Dickson, who was born in Cincinnati, Ohio, in

---

[15] Charles H. Brooks, *A History and Manual of the Grand United Order of Odd Fellows in America* (Philadelphia, 1893), pp. 19-20.
[16] Washington, *op. cit.*, pp. 153-55.

1824.[17] In his youth he learned the barber's trade and traveled on the boats that plied up and down the Ohio and Mississippi River. As the result of what he saw of slavery he resolved to do something to free the slaves. Dickson together with eleven other Negro men decided in 1844 to study the situation and meet in St. Louis in 1846. According to the plan the twelve men met in 1846 and formed a secret organization known as the Knights of Liberty. It was agreed that the members should disperse and spend ten years organizing local secret societies which would bring about the emancipation of the Negro. Although it is claimed that by 1856 there were 47,240 Knights of Liberty, the plan for freeing the slaves was abandoned and nothing further is known of the plans. It is known, however, that the Knights of Liberty became actively connected with the Underground Railroad. The leader, Dickson, enlisted in the Union army and after the Civil War disbanded the Knights of Liberty. In 1871 he organized the first Temple and Tabernacle of the Knights and Daughters of Tabor in Independence, Missouri. The object of this secret order was "to help to spread the Christian religion and education" and the members were advised to "acquire real estate, avoid intemperance, and cultivate true manhood." It was claimed that around the end of the last century the order had nearly 200,000 Sir Knights and Daughters in the eighteen Grand Jurisdictions from Maine to California and from the Great Lakes to the Gulf of Mexico.

The organization and development of the Grand United Order of True Reformers occupies an important place in the development of secret societies among Negroes because it became one of the most important financial institutions among Negroes following the Civil War. The founder of the organization was a Reverend Washington Browne who was born a slave in Georgia in 1849.[18] During the Civil War he ran away from a new master and made his way to the North, where he received a meager education. After Emancipation he returned to Alabama, where he joined a movement of the Good Templars

[17] *Why You Should Become a Knight and Daughter of Tabor*, p. 13, Pamphlet in The Moorland Foundation, Howard University, Washington, D. C. See also Washington, *op. cit.*, pp. 158-60.

[18] W. P. Burrell and D. E. Johnson, *Twenty-five Years History of the Grand Fountain of the United Order of True Reformers* (Richmond, Va., 1909), p. 12.

against the whiskey ring. After observing the various benevolent and burial societies among Negroes, he decided that Negroes should have a separate organization adapted to their needs. In 1876 he succeeded in bringing together in a single organization, the Grand Fountain of True Reformers, twenty-seven Fountains with 2,000 members. However, Browne made little progress in creating a mutual benefit organization. On the other hand, the promulgation of his ideas in a newspaper known as *The Reformer* brought him into contact with the Organization of True Reformers in Virginia. He was invited to Richmond, where he was made Grand Worthy Master of the Virginia organization.

The True Reformers first created a real estate department to meet its needs for office buildings. In 1889 a bank was established to serve as a depository for the order. The order began publication in 1892 of *The Reformer*, which had a weekly circulation of 8,000 in 1900. The order then ventured in the field of charity, organizing an Old Folks Home in 1898. This institution was located on land outside Richmond, which was laid out in town lots and sold to Negroes. Other business ventures of the order included a grocery and general merchandise store, a hotel, and a building and loan association. Since the story of the business undertakings forms an important chapter in the development of Negro business, it will be considered in a later chapter.

The Independent Order of Good Samaritans and Daughters of Samaria has a unique position in the development of secret societies among Negroes. The purpose of this lodge was "to carry forward the work of temperance reform," "to secure sympathy and relief for the unfortunate and distressed families of those who pledge themselves to abstain from intoxicating drinks," and "to elevate the living, to comfort the widowed and fatherless in the hour of their affliction." [19] Soon after its establishment in 1847, Negroes were admitted to the order and organized into separate District Grand Lodges.[20] The participation of the Negroes was limited in a number of ways. They

---

[19] Howard H. Turner, *Turner's History of the Independent Order of Good Samaritans and Daughters of Samaria* (Washington, 1881), pp. 25-26.
[20] *Ibid.*, pp. 18-19.

were permitted to take part in the general conventions, but their representation was limited and they could vote only on matters concerning themselves.[21] As the Negro membership increased, the whites began to drop out, with the result that the Negroes gained controlling power in the order.[22] The year 1877, when a Negro was elected Grand Sire, marked a turning point in the order. From then on the order became a Negro organization and increased in influence among Negroes.

The beginning of the Colored Knights of Pythias is of special interest because Negroes were able to become initiated and learn the rituals by passing for white.[23] According to the official account, the petition of a group of colored men was denied at the Supreme Lodge meeting in New York in 1870. In order to circumvent this action a number of colored men who could pass for white applied for membership and were initiated into the order. These men proceeded to set up a Supreme Council of the order and organized a lodge in Vicksburg, Mississippi, in 1880. This action was justified on the grounds that since the exclusion of colored men violated the purpose of the order, which was to extend friendship, charity, and benevolence among men, Divine Providence had made it possible for Negroes to acquire the ritual. The order of the colored Pythians grew rapidly and by 1905 there were 1,628 lodges with 70,000 members in 26 states and territories.

During the period following the Civil War and the first decade of the present century the Negro secret societies had their greatest growth.[24] This was because of the fact that following Emancipation the Negro was thrown upon his own resources and social cooperation for mutual aid in the time of crisis became a necessity. The pattern of the secret fraternal organization had already become established among the free Negroes. To the emancipated Negroes, the secret

[21] Edward N. Palmer, "Negro Secret Societies," *Social Forces,* Vol. 23, p. 209.
[22] Turner, *op. cit.,* p. 39.
[23] E. A. Williams, *History and Manual of the Colored Knights of Pythias* (Nashville, Tennessee, 1917), pp. 13-15.
[24] It was during this same period that there was a phenomenal growth of fraternal organizations throughout the United States. See Frank H. Hankins, "Fraternal Orders," *Encyclopaedia of the Social Sciences,* Vol. 6, p. 423.

fraternal order had a special attraction. There was, of course, the attraction of uniforms and the pageantry of the lodges. But there was a more fundamental attraction. The secret society welded the Negroes together in a sacred brotherhood for mutual aid and common loyalty in a hostile white world. In fact, it was charged by the whites that the lodge meetings were "often plotting places where groups of Negroes devise plans and encourage thoughts against the white man." [25] Although the Negro enjoyed a freedom of expression in the lodge that he did not have outside, there is no evidence that the lodge was a place where plots were formed against the whites.

Another charge brought against the secret fraternities by the whites was that they encouraged the Negro to waste time and money.[26] It was even said that the opportunity to handle money encouraged dishonesty and graft among Negroes. It was true, of course, that Negroes gave much time to their lodges, which afforded the chief form of social participation outside the church. Moreover, it is probably true, as one writer has pointed out, that the Negro "lodges are an effort not so much to escape life as to embellish it." [27] There was probably the normal amount of graft and dishonesty which are found in all such human associations. But these organizations have had a positive value in that they enforced "upon the masses of the people habits of saving and of system which they would not otherwise have been able or disposed to learn." [28]

MUTUAL AID SOCIETIES AND FRATERNAL
ORGANIZATIONS AMONG RURAL NEGROES

Following Emancipation, when the landless Negroes were thrown upon their own resources, mutual aid societies began to flourish in the rural communities. In many cases the various benevolent societies that had existed among the free Negroes in the cities began to recruit members from among the rural folk. But, at the same time there sprang up benevolent societies that were indigenous to the rural communities. These societies were organized to meet the crisis of illness

25 Howard W. Odum, *Social and Mental Traits of the Negro* (New York, 1910), pp. 140-41.   26 *Ibid.*, p. 142.
27 Charles W. Ferguson, *Fifty Million Brothers* (New York, 1937), p. 200.
28 Washington, *op. cit.*, p. 170.

or death. Consequently, they have generally been known as "sickness and burial" societies. From the beginning, the burial societies have been more popular than the societies providing "sickness benefits." However destitute of worldly goods the rural Negro has been, he has often borne his lot patiently as long as he was consoled by the prospect that he would be "put away right," i.e., given a decent burial. Even the poorest member of the community would scrape together a few pennies each month in order to pay his dues in the "burial 'sociation" or the " 'nevolent." The lament of an old woman in Alabama, "If I die today or tomorrow I ain't got a penny to bury me," voiced the despair of one who had lost the last consolation that life had to offer.

The majority of these benevolent societies have been associated with the churches in the rural areas. The names of these societies reveal the influence of the Bible as well as the simple religious conceptions of the Negro folk. They bear such names as "Love and Charity," "Builders of the Walls of Jerusalem," "Sons and Daughters of Esther," "Brothers and Sisters of Charity," and "Brothers and Sisters of Love." [29] The local "sickness and burial" societies should be distinguished from the Negro lodges of fraternal organizations, which are state and national in scope. Although they have been influenced by the state and national organizations, they represented originally the spontaneous efforts of the rural Negro folk to meet the major crises of life through social cooperation. At the present time these simple mutual aid societies have taken on some of the characteristics of the lodges and fraternal organizations. In two rural counties in Georgia, Raper made a study of 87 Negro lodges and societies.[30] Among the 87 lodges and societies, there were 13 Knights of Pythias, 9 Masons, one Odd Fellows, 12 Courts of Colanthe, 8 United Gospel Aids, and one or more of the various local, state, and national lodges and beneficial societies. The majority of the nationally affiliated organizations owned their lodge halls while the majority of the local societies met in churches or in halls belonging to other organizations. The local societies were found to be unstable. They were

---

[29] See Arthur F. Raper, *Preface to Peasantry* (Chapel Hill, 1936), p. 374.
[30] *Ibid.*, pp. 373-81.

constantly dissolving and reforming and often failed to meet their obligations to their members. In the local organizations, which tend to be essentially mutual aid societies, widows and children were given aid by the lodge or individual members and sick members were given ten cents weekly or a pound of sugar, molasses, flour, meat, or potatoes.

The existence of the lodges and mutual aid societies is constantly affected by the impact of outside economic and social forces upon these rural communities. The failure of banks in the "Black Belt" has often caused thousands of these local organizations to disband or to fail to meet their obligations. Then as the insurance companies have extended the field of their operations into the rural communities, the less secure lodges have had to compete with the insurance company, a more rational and secular form of business organization. The lodge has enjoyed a certain advantage because it offered a personal touch in case of illness and provided pageantry in time of death, which the insurance company did not provide. Nevertheless, since the insurance company offers greater security, it has continued to make inroads into the field of mutual aid provided by the lodge and the benevolent society. Finally, the migration of Negroes from rural areas in recent decades has tended more than any other factor to disrupt these traditional organizations.

The national Negro fraternal organizations as well as the rural mutual aid societies have been affected by the fact that the insurance companies have become increasingly more secure and are supported by the urbanized Negro population. The Negro fraternal orders suffered from the same weaknesses as the white orders in regard to their insurance features. Negro orders had the system of assessments in the case of death or even less sound policies of payments. In the eighties of the past century the white fraternal orders realized that their salvation lay in the adoption of sound actuarial methods.[31] But only a few Negro organizations undertook to reform their unsound insurance system and these reforms did not go beyond the adoption of the "step rate" or the attempt to relate assessments to age by increasing the premium with the increase in age.[32] As a result the Negro organiza-

[31] Hankins, *loc. cit.*, p. 427.   [32] Palmer, *loc. cit.*, p. 211.

tions were often forced to default in their obligations or abandon their insurance features.

EFFECT OF URBANIZATION ON FRATERNAL ORGANIZATIONS

The mutual aid societies and fraternal organizations first arose in the cities, where the free Negroes faced the hazards of securing a livelihood in a highly competitive environment. Moreover, they had to face the insecurity of city living without the support of families and neighbors which they had in the rural environment. The fraternal organizations offered economic relief in times of sickness and provided a decent burial. But these organizations attracted the Negroes for other equally important reasons. They offered the moral support that had once been provided by the family in that they formed a type of sacred brotherhood. In their credo and rituals they emphasized love and charity as mutual obligations between men. These organizations appealed to Negroes especially because they gave men who had been set adrift in the city a status in the new environment. Members of these societies not only acquired status within the lodges but through the insignia and especially the military uniforms they were lifted above the anonymous masses.

The fraternal organizations continue to attract the less sophisticated urban Negroes. But, on the whole, the urban environment has caused the older fraternal organizations to lose much of their appeal. The city is providing an increasing number of opportunities for social participation and has opened up many new forms of recreations. Moreover, as the Negro acquires an education and a more secular outlook, these societies with their religious outlook have become less congenial. Then, too, as the result of education and a more secular attitude toward life, Negroes are seeking security in the insurance company.[33] The only national secret society which has increased its membership since the mass migrations to cities has been one which was more con-

[33] In the towns of the South, Negroes are urged to support the fraternal organizations with their insurance features and business enterprises on the grounds of "race pride." See Hortense Powdermaker, *After Freedom* (New York, 1939), pp. 122-25.

genial to the changed outlook and interests of the urbanized Negro.[34] This organization is the Improved Benevolent and Protective Order of the Elks of the World.

The colored Order of Elks was founded by a Pullman porter who claimed to have "come in contact with enough workings" of the order to organize a lodge in Cincinnati in 1898.[35] The white Elks were unable to suppress the colored Elks because the latter had the ritual copyrighted, a formality which the former had neglected. In 1906 there was an attempt on the part of the New York legislature to suppress the colored Elks. In their eighth annual report the colored Elks made the following statement:

Like all other secret and benevolent organizations that have been organized, the white order of Elks will not permit colored persons to become members. But there are colored Elks now. How and where they got their secret work is known to many white Elks of this country. Some may try to deprecate the colored Elks, but we have the same ritual that the white Elks have. Our membership has grown to over 5,000. The letter 'I' stands for 'Improved.' The difference between white and colored Elks is this: The white order is known as the Benevolent Protective Order of Elks. Ours is known as the Improved Benevolent Protective Order of Elks of the World.[36]

At that time the order reported 80 lodges with 61 remitting taxes to the Grand Lodge. The growth of the order was slow until the 1920's when J. Finley Wilson, the dynamic leader, became the Grand Exalted Ruler. When he was elected in 1922, there were 32,000 members of the order. By the next year the membership had increased to 107,000. The order has continued to grow until in 1946 it could boast of 1,000 lodges and 500,000 members. Included in this membership are Junior Elks and Daughter Elks. During the period of its growth the colored Elks have accumulated much wealth in government bonds and real estate. According to the report for 1946, the various lodges of the

[34] This statement is based upon reports of persons connected with the various organizations since there are no available statistics on the present membership of Negro secret fraternal societies. One estimate gives the membership as 2,500,000 with property owned valued at $20,000,000. Ferguson, *op. cit.*, p. 184.

[35] Ferguson, *op. cit.*, pp. 192-93.

[36] Quoted in *Economic Cooperation Among Colored Americans* edited by W. E. B. DuBois, p. 126. Published 1907 by Atlanta University Press.

order own $30,000,000 in United States War Bonds and $25,000,000 in Elks' Homes and other property.

That the phenomenal growth of the colored Elks has been the result of its appeal to the awakened interests of the urbanized Negroes becomes apparent when one studies its program. One cannot deny that there has been an appeal in its colorful parades with their crack drill teams and military uniforms.[37] But there has been a more fundamental appeal in the program. The order has a Grand Commissioner of Education whose Department boasts of having given $500,000 in college scholarships to Negro youths. Although competition for these scholarships often takes the form of oratorical contests, many scholarships have been awarded with less ostentation. There is a Civil Liberties Department which aims to protect the civil rights of Negroes. This Department has engaged in law suits to secure the civil rights of Negroes. Other activities include a health program and a program to reduce juvenile delinquency. The order has made gifts of iron lungs to the hospitals connected with the two Negro medical schools. Thus in various ways the colored Elks have not only dramatized the new aspirations of the urbanized Negro masses but they have lent their aid in the achievement of these aspirations.

Although the Elks represent the aspirations and new outlook of the urbanized Negro masses, the structure of the organization bears the impress of the class stratification of the Negro community. The membership of the organization is composed mostly of the middle class in the Negro community with a large contingent from the lower class. This middle class in the Negro community has been increasing in size and importance during the past two decades. Members of this class who are not eligible for membership in the college fraternities or exclusive upper-class clubs find in the Elks a form of organized social life which offers them a chance for social participation and some opportunity for recognition. In the smaller cities where the upper class is small or there are not many college graduates, the Elks include upper-class Negroes as well as those of middle-class status. On the other hand, the more stable elements of the lower class, especially

[37] Cf. Ferguson, *op. cit.*, pp. 193-94.

those striving to achieve middle-class status, also tend to affiliate with the Elks.

The national leader of the Elks, unlike the more sedate leaders of the older fraternal organizations, has had a wide and colorful career and possesses a dramatic personality that appeals to the urban masses. However, he has gathered about him educated and professional Negroes who hold the strategic offices in the organization. The organization thus gains a certain prestige in the community while receiving its support chiefly from the masses. Under different circumstances, upper-class Negroes, especially intellectuals (some are still so inclined), would view the organization with amusement if not disgust. As it is, the educated and professional leaders can justify their membership in the organization on the grounds that its aims are socially useful. At the same time, through membership in the organization, the educated and professional leaders establish contacts which are necessary and profitable in their professional relations with the masses. The professional men who hold offices in the Elks not only gain prestige among the masses but also secure comfortable incomes in some instances. The vast body of members of the Elks organization enjoy the distinction gained from wearing the insignia and uniforms, participation in the parades, association with outstanding members of the community in recreational clubs, and the support which they give to the advancement of the Negro. Moreover, in those sections of the country where Negroes are denied the right to participate in the political life of the community, other fraternal organizations as well as the Elks provide a substitute field for political activities.

EMERGENCE OF GREEK LETTER SOCIETIES AMONG "THE TALENTED TENTH"

Around the opening of the present century, the number of college graduates and professional men among Negroes was extremely small. At the same time this group, which DuBois designated "The Talented Tenth," [38] was increasing in numbers and becoming more conscious of its common interests. Because of their relatively small numbers,

---

[38] See W. E. Burghardt DuBois, "The Talented Tenth" in *The Negro Problem* (New York, 1903), p. 75.

Negro college graduates and professional men, especially in the North, were widely scattered and culturally isolated from the masses of Negroes. In order to bring together these men with a similar background and outlook in life, there was organized in Philadelphia in 1904 the Sigma Pi Phi Fraternity, which has come to be known simply as the Boulé (Greek word for council).[39] This organization has included in its membership some of the most distinguished Negroes in the United States. While this fraternity has slowly spread to other sections of the country, generally the border cities, it has remained, on the whole, aloof from the affairs of the Negro population. The general aim and outlook of the organization appears to be governed still by that of the isolated "aristocracy of talent" which comprised its membership 40 or more years ago. This seems to arise from the fact that the organization represented a certain social exclusiveness as well as an "aristocracy of talent." The spirit of social exclusiveness with some exceptions has persisted while the emphasis on intellectual and professional attainment has disappeared. The annual meetings of the Boulé are widely publicized in the Negro press as a phase of the activities of the older members of the social elite in the Negro community. The rapidly increasing Negro college and professional graduates are being absorbed in Negro college fraternities.

The first Greek letter fraternity to be organized among Negro college students was the Alpha Phi Alpha Fraternity. This fraternity grew out of an organization of Negro students at Cornell University during 1905-06.[40] Because of race prejudice these students were not eligible for membership in the white fraternities and were excluded from general participation in the social activities of the University. Consequently, a common interest developed among them and they organized a social and literary group which became a Greek letter fraternity in 1906. The following year a chapter of the fraternity was set up at Howard University and later other chapters were set up at Negro and white colleges. By 1935 there were 59 undergraduate college chapters

[39] See *The Boulé Journal*, Vol. 13 (April, 1946), a history of the society and a roster of its present members.
[40] Charles H. Wesley, *The History of the Alpha Phi Alpha* (Washington, D. C., 1935), pp. 21-22.

and 47 graduate chapters in the various cities of the North and South. Since 1914 the fraternity has published a journal known as the *Sphinx*. As the result of a demand on the part of the more thoughtful members that the fraternity develop a program that would be beneficial to Negroes generally, the fraternity inaugurated a "Go-to-High School-Go-to-College Week" in 1920. Since then the fraternity has increasingly associated itself with movements for the welfare of the Negro.

The second Greek letter society to be organized among Negro students was the Omega Psi Phi Fraternity. This society, the first fraternity to be established in a Negro college, was started at Howard University in 1911. The organization of this society was stimulated partly by the presence of a chapter of Alpha Phi Alpha Fraternity, which had acquired a dominant position in the student body. There were also other factors that were responsible for the organization of a second fraternity. The Alpha Phi Alpha became an exclusive social set that was accused of snobbishness toward the darker students and those not from prominent families. Chapters of the Omega Psi Phi Fraternity were set up first in other Negro colleges and later in white colleges. Then graduate chapters were set up in various cities of the country. By 1945 there were 133 undergraduate and graduate chapters in the nine districts into which the country is divided. A part of the program of the Omega Psi Phi Fraternity has been to maintain close contacts between undergraduate and graduate chapters. In recent years the fraternity has undertaken a "program of action." The purpose of this program has been to stimulate the members of the local chapters to participate in activities directed to the welfare of Negroes. A recent effort in this direction has been the interest of the fraternity in the housing of Negroes.

A third Greek letter college fraternity, the Phi Beta Sigma Fraternity, was organized at Howard University in 1914. Immediately thereafter chapters of this fraternity were set up in other colleges—mostly Negro. By 1929 there were 28 undergraduate and 27 graduate chapters in the various cities of the country. Like the other Greek letter societies, this fraternity has initiated a number of prominent Negroes into its graduate chapters. The fraternity publishes a magazine, *The*

Crescent, and during the spring of each year the fraternity conducts a "Bigger and Better Negro Business Week."

The organization of the Kappa Alpha Psi Fraternity, the fourth college fraternity, in 1911 by the Negro students at the University of Indiana was due to the growing race consciousness among the increasing number of Negro students in the colleges of the midwest. At the present time there are 60 undergraduate chapters of this fraternity in both white and Negro colleges and 50 graduate chapters in the various cities of the country.

There have been two Greek letter sororities that have achieved national importance among Negro college women. The first of these was the Alpha Kappa Alpha Sorority which was organized at Howard University in 1908. The young women who started this society got the idea from talks with one of the white teachers at Howard. From the first chapter the society has spread into white as well as Negro colleges. In 1946 there were 72 undergraduate chapters and 94 graduate chapters with a total membership of 6,000. The sorority has sponsored two projects which have significance for the Negro masses. One of these projects—The Health Project—has attracted nationwide attention.[41] This project has carried medical care in the form of dental care, treatment for syphilis, diphtheria, and smallpox to Negroes in several rural counties in Mississippi. The second project is the Nonpartisan Council which has maintained a lobby in the nation's capital. The Nonpartisan Council has closely scrutinized all legislation affecting the Negro and has mobilized Negro opinion and organizations to bring pressure upon congressmen and federal officials. The influence of this society has been broader than any other Greek letter society.

The second sorority, Delta Sigma Theta, which also was organized at Howard University, was established in 1913. In this organization, as in the other Greek letter societies, the members were drawn together in order to enjoy a common social life. But like the other sorority it has become the focus of the activities of Negro college women who are interested in the social problems of the Negro. The

[41] "Cotton Field Volunteer Clinic," *Survey Graphic,* September, 1940. See also under the same title, *Reader's Digest,* September, 1940.

sorority has a five-point program which includes the promotion of education; the support of a permanent Fair Employment Practices Committee; support of local child welfare programs; aid to unmarried mothers and delinquent girls; and financial and other support of programs of intercultural relations.

These various Greek letter societies have acquired a far greater importance in the Negro community than similar organizations in the white community. Although they began as social clubs with some interest in scholarship among undergraduates, they soon became the focus of the organized activities of the professional and intellectual leaders among Negroes. Consequently, the center of power and influence of the Greek letter societies has shifted from the young undergraduates to the men and women in the graduate chapters.

Moreover, these societies very often evoke the deepest loyalties and warmest devotion of their adult members. This is vividly indicated in the remark of a college professor who once exclaimed that there was three things that he loved: his God, his wife, and his fraternity. As the number of college graduates has increased, these fraternities have lost much of their exclusiveness in respect to color and the status of one's family. Membership in a Greek letter society gives one a certain status in the community but it is no longer an indication of upper-class status. It represents rather a striving for status and the achievement of some recognition on the part of middle-class and even some lower-class Negroes who gain at least the symbols of an improved status. Yet as a rule upper-class Negroes continue to control the Greek letter societies. Although these societies continue to place considerable emphasis upon "social" activities, they have influenced increasingly the opinions and attitudes of Negroes generally in regard to their problems. This development has been accelerated as the Negro population has become urbanized and the Negro has become more conscious of the relation of his problems to the larger world.

The organization and growth of mutual aid associations and secret fraternal societies among Negroes have been in response to social and economic forces within Negro life as well as the result of the relations of the races. The mutual aid societies and the secret fraternal organizations first appeared among the free Negroes. Both types of organizations grew up in response to the needs of the Negro and reflected the influence of white patterns. The emancipation of the Negro caused the older fraternal organizations to increase rapidly and brought into existence new fraternal organizations to serve the needs of the emancipated blacks. These organizations introduced discipline among Negroes, encouraged social cooperation, and inculcated habits of savings. Among the emancipated Negroes in the rural areas there sprang up mutual aid societies that provided for such crises of life as sickness and death. Both the secret fraternal organizations and the rural mutual aid societies have felt the impact of urbanization and the growing influence of the more rational form of business organization—the insurance companies. Some of these insurance companies are owned and operated by Negro business and professional men and women, many of whom are college graduates. The Negro college graduate has created his own secret fraternal organizations—the Greek letter fraternities.

CHAPTER XVI

Business Enterprise

T HE first ventures in business enterprise by the Negroes in the United States were made by those who were free before the Civil War. During this period the money which the mutual aid associations, discussed in the preceding chapter, were able to accumulate was used to some extent in small business undertakings. Following the Civil War, the Freedmen's Saving and Trust Company, which was established to instill habits of thrift among the freedmen, tended to cultivate the spirit of business enterprise and to give the freedmen experience in business. Despite the failure of this undertaking, it succeeded in creating a nucleus of Negro businessmen who became leaders in the organization of fraternal insurance societies and banks. The spirit of business enterprise, which was encouraged by Negro leaders, culminated in the organization of the National Negro Business League in 1900. The expression of the spirit of business enterprise among Negroes has been manifested mainly in the establishment of numerous banks, which have had a high rate of failures. However, from the standpoint of successful operation, Negro insurance companies represent the Negro's major achievements in the field of business. The vast majority of Negro business enterprises have continued to be small establishments catering to the wants of a segregated world not served by the business enterprises of the larger white community.

NEGRO BUSINESS VENTURES BEFORE THE CIVIL WAR

Before the Civil War, the free Negroes in both southern and northern cities engaged in small business ventures, most of which were based upon the skills which the Negro had acquired in personal services.[1] For example, the leading barber in Natchez, Mississippi, was a Negro. A free Negro barber in Richmond, Virginia, who employed a free mulatto and two slave assistants, earned considerable money from his shop on Main Street. The livery stable business was another field in which the free Negro ventured. In Washington, D. C., and Richmond and Petersburg, Virginia, and other cities, free Negroes owned and operated livery stables which were patronized by wealthy whites. Many free Negroes who had acquired skill in tailoring set themselves up in the tailoring and clothing business. In New Orleans and Charleston free Negroes were especially successful as tailors and counted among their clients many of the wealthiest white families. It was perhaps in cooking and the preparation of foods that the free Negroes secured the widest reputation for competence. In Charleston, South Carolina, a free Negro owned and operated one of the best taverns in the South.

In northern cities the free Negroes who operated taverns and restaurants enjoyed a wider reputation for their success in this field. In New York City they operated eating houses that numbered among their clientele members of the leading families. Free Negroes in Philadelphia were especially successful as caterers. Although free Negroes in the North were not as important in the skilled occupations as in the South, they engaged in a larger variety of small businesses. In Chicago, Cincinnati, and Detroit they were successful as tailors. In Cincinnati a few free Negroes operated successful businesses in the field of merchandising and pickling and preserving. There were successful Negro contractors in Cincinnati and other cities in Ohio. One of the largest industrial undertakings of the free Negroes was centered in Philadelphia, where James Forten operated one of the largest sail-making plants. Forten's achievement in Philadelphia was rivaled by that of three mulattoes in Charleston, South Carolina, where two operated one of the finest factories for the manufacture of agricultural machinery and one, Anthony Weston, was for three decades famous as a millwright.

[1] Abram Harris, *The Negro as Capitalist* (Philadelphia, 1936), pp. 10ff.

THE FREEDMEN'S BANK AND NEGRO BUSINESS

Following Emancipation the growth of business enterprise among the freedmen was based partly upon the achievements of the Negroes who had been free and partly upon the experiences of the emancipated Negroes during slavery. DuBois undertook to show how the evolution of the Negro businessman after Emancipation grew out of the experiences of Negroes under slavery.[2] "It is easy to see," he wrote, "how the Barber, the Caterer and the Restaurant keeper were the direct progeny of the House-servant, just as the Market-gardener, the Sawmill Proprietor, and the Florist were descended from the Field-hand." This evolution is confirmed only in part in the development of Negro businesses. The barber, the caterer, and the restaurant keeper often used the experience which they had acquired during slavery as a basis for their business undertakings after Emancipation. There is also evidence that some of the slave mechanics became businessmen following their emancipation. On the other hand, there is no evidence that the Negro florist is descended from the field hand or that the Negro grocery and general merchandise store is a form of the "store house" from which "rations" were distributed on the plantation.

One is on surer ground when one relates the development of the spirit of business enterprise to the Freedmen's Bank.[3] The Freedmen's Bank grew out of the necessity to safeguard the unclaimed savings of Negro soldiers and laborers and the desire to serve the financial interests of the emancipated Negroes.[4] At first, a plan had been worked out for the Negro soldiers to make allotments to relatives and to deposit their pay with the government instead of squandering it. Then military and free labor banks were established, the first of these being organized in New Orleans in 1866. In the same year similar banks were set up in Norfolk, Virginia, and in Beaufort, South Carolina. At the close of the Civil War, the deposits in the Beaufort bank, the only bank for

[2] *The Negro in Business* edited by W. E. B. DuBois, pp. 8-13. Published by Atlanta University Press.

[3] See Walter L. Fleming, *The Freedmen's Savings Bank* (Chapel Hill, 1927) for the history of the bank.   [4] Harris, *op. cit.*, Chapter 2.

which information is available, amounted to $200,000. In order to protect the unclaimed deposits and the wage and bounty payments due Negro soldiers, Congress was induced to incorporate the Freedmen's Saving and Trust Company. At the end of the first year, there were 14 branch banks, and by 1871 a total of 34 banks had been established. In 1871 the total deposits amounted to nearly 20 million dollars and the total drafts about 17.5 million dollars, thus leaving 2.5 million dollars due depositors.

Since the federal government had incorporated the Freedmen's Bank and it was controlled by white friends of the Negro, Negro depositors assumed that their savings were protected by the government. Therefore, they rushed to place their small savings in the bank. In 1872 there were at least 70,000 depositors in the banks scattered over the country. Although few Negroes were employed in the bank at first, the employment of Negroes as clerks gave the Negro hope in the field of business enterprise. Unfortunately, through mismanagement, owing partly to pious but incompetent missionaries and partly to irresponsible plunderers who were typical of financial speculators following the Civil War, the bank became shaky in 1873. In order to restore the confidence of Negroes in the bank, Frederick Douglass was elected president in 1874. In spite of the efforts of Douglass, who lent the bank $10,000 out of his personal funds, the bank was forced to close its doors in 1874. When the Freedmen's Bank closed, it owed its 61,131 depositors nearly $3,000,000, 62 per cent of which was paid in dividends between 1875 and 1883.

There has been a tendency for some Negro leaders to regard the failure of the Freedmen's Bank as a major catastrophe in the economic development of the Negro. According to DuBois,

Not even ten additional years of slavery could have done so much to throttle the thrift of the Freedmen as the mismanagement and bankruptcy of the series of savings banks chartered by the nation for their special aid.[5]

Undoubtedly, the failure of the Freedmen's Bank caused hardship for thousands of impoverished Negroes who had only recently been

[5] *The Souls of Black Folk* by W. E. B. DuBois. Copyright 1903 by W. E. B. DuBois, p. 36. Reprinted by permission of A. C. McClurg & Co.

released from slavery. Moreover, the failure of the bank tended to discourage to some extent the habits of thrift which it had fostered. But as Harris has stated:

it seems to us that the effect of the failure of the bank was not as psychologically disastrous as it was pictured by [Negro leaders]. If the setback to the Negro's economic progress had been as profound as described by these leaders, it is hardly likely that the Negro would have been found organizing banks of his own in less than fifteen years after the failure of the Freedmen's Bank.[6]

Despite its failure, the Freedmen's Bank apparently succeeded in instilling into many Negroes the ideal of business enterprise. The Bank gave training to Negroes as clerks and bookkeepers and Negro businessmen and property holders were associated with the branches of the Bank in Washington, D. C., Norfolk and Richmond, Virginia. It was such men who formed the nucleus of the businessmen who became the leaders in Negro banks and fraternal insurance societies.

NEGRO LEADERS BECOME ADVOCATES OF
"NEGRO BUSINESS"

From the 1880's on, as Professor Harris has pointed out,

the Negro masses, urged by their leaders, were led to place increasing faith in business and property as a means of escaping poverty and achieving economic independence. Although ostensibly sponsored as the means of self-help or racial cooperation, as it was sometimes called, through which the masses were to be economically emancipated, Negro business enterprise was motivated primarily by the desire for private profit and looked toward the establishment of a Negro capitalist employer class. One of the clearest expressions of the growing tendency to look upon the development of Negro capitalists and business enterprise as the basis of racial economic advancement is to be found in the proceedings of the Fourth Atlanta University Conference (1898) on "The Negro in Business." [7]

The best expression of this point of view was stated in 1898 by the late John Hope, who later in becoming president of the Atlanta University system, hoped to train the future leaders of Negro business

[6] Harris, *op. cit.*, p. 45.   [7] *Ibid.*, pp. 49-50.

enterprises. In Hope's 1898 address appear the following statements concerning the rôle of business enterprise in the Negro's economic development.

Industrial education and labor unions for Negroes will not change this condition. They may modify it, but the condition will not be very materially changed. The white man will meet the Negro on the same ground and work for the same wages. That much we may as well take for granted, calculate the consequences of, and strive by every means to overcome this falling off in our old-time advantages. . . . We must take in some, if not all, of the wages, turn it into capital, hold it, increase it. This must be done as a means of employment for the thousands who cannot get work from old sources. Employment must be had, and this employment will have to come to Negroes from Negro sources. This phase of the Negro's condition is so easily seen that it needs no further consideration. Negro capital will have to give an opportunity to Negro workmen who will be crowded out by white competition; and when I say Negro workmen I would include both sexes. . . . Employment for colored men and women, colored boys and girls must be supplied by colored people. . . .

We are living among the so-called Anglo-Saxons and dealing with them. They are a conquering people who turn their conquests into their pockets. . . . Business seems to be not simply the raw material of Anglo-Saxon civilization—and by business I mean those efforts directly or indirectly concerned with a purposive tendency to material development and progress, with the point in view of the effort bringing material profit or advantage to the one making the effort; and I would include all such efforts whether made in peace or war. I was saying, business seems to be not only simply the raw material of Anglo-Saxon civilization, but almost the civilization itself. It is at least its mainspring to action. Living among such a people is it not obvious that we cannot escape its most powerful motive and survive? To the finite vision, to say the least, the policy of avoiding entrance in the world's business would be suicide to the Negro. Yet as a matter of great account, we ought to note that as good a showing as we have made, that showing is but as pebbles on the shore of business enterprise. . . .[8]

Among the resolutions adopted at this conference were the following:

[8] *The Negro in Business* edited by W. E. B. DuBois, pp. 56-59. Published by Atlanta University Press.

1. Negroes ought to enter into business life in increasing numbers. The present disproportion in the distribution of Negroes in the various occupations is unfortunate. It gives the race a one-sided development, unnecessarily increases competition in certain lines of industry, and puts the mass of the Negro people out of sympathy and touch with the industrial and mercantile spirit of the age. Moreover the growth of a class of merchants among us would be a farsighted measure of self-defense, and would make for wealth and mutual cooperation.

2. We need as merchants the best trained young men we can find. A college training ought to be one of the best preparations for a broad business life; and thorough English and high school training is indispensable.

3. Negroes going into business should remember that their customers demand courtesy, honesty, and careful methods, and they should not expect patronage when their manner of conducting business does not justify it.

4. The mass of the Negroes must learn to patronize business enterprises conducted by their own race, even at some slight disadvantage. We must cooperate or we are lost. Ten million people who join in intelligent self-help can never be long ignored or mistreated.[9]

At this conference, which was devoted to Negro business, DuBois reported that there were 1,906 Negro businessmen.[10] Nearly half of these businessmen were located in six southern States—Georgia, Texas, Alabama, Tennessee, South Carolina, and Virginia. Over a fifth of the Negro businessmen had grocery stores, while general merchandise dealers and barbers with $500 or more invested accounted for a sixth of the total. Next in order of importance from the standpoint of number came publishers and printers, and undertakers, who have remained until the present some of the most important businessmen in the Negro community.

THE NATIONAL NEGRO BUSINESS LEAGUE

Two years after the Atlanta Conference on the Negro in business, Booker T. Washington took the initiative in founding the National Negro Business League.[11] The general purpose in forming the League,

[9] *The Negro in Business* edited by W. E. B. DuBois, p. 50. Published by Atlanta University Press.   [10] *Ibid.*, pp. 7-8.
[11] Booker T. Washington, *The Negro in Business* (Chicago, 1907), pp. 268-75.

according to Washington, was to extend its influence to "the remotest corners of the land through the organization of local leagues of businessmen and women, and thus encourage, more and more of our people to enter business." At the end of five years there were 320 local leagues and in 1915 it was reported that there were 600 local leagues which had received their inspiration from the annual national meetings.[12] The inspiration which the representatives of the local leagues received at national meetings came through hearing the success stories of Negro businessmen. In fact, after the founding of the League, stories concerning the successful business undertakings of Negroes were constantly played up in Negro publications.[13] When the National Negro Business League celebrated its Silver Jubilee in Chicago in 1924, it was reported that Negroes operated 65,000 businesses and had accumulated wealth amounting to $1,700,000,000.[14] This figure included the ownership of homes, farms, and churches for which the League could hardly take credit.[15] However, the main purpose of these meetings was to inspire Negroes to enter business and to create the faith that their economic salvation was to be found in this field.

In the realm of more concrete aims, the organization by the National Negro Business League in 1930 of a National Negro Housewives League might be cited. This organization was concerned with the problems of the Negro as a consumer.[16] Through the organization of Negro women the League was able to be of service to Negroes during the wartime shortages and to secure representation on OPA price panels. At one time the membership in the Business League included a subscription to the *Service Magazine* but recently the Business League has established *The Journal of Negro Business*. In connection with the League mention should be made of the fact that Negro businessmen have organized 21 Negro Chambers of Com-

[12] William A. Aery, "Business Makes Men, Especially if the Men Are Negroes," *Survey*, Vol. 34 (1915), p. 550.

[13] See, for example, Clement Richardson, "The Man Who Turned Gravel to Dollars," *The Southern Workman*, Vol. 43 (1914), pp. 211-15.

[14] "Growth of Negro Business," *Literary Digest*, Vol. 81 (1924), p. 62.

[15] Even the figure 65,000 businesses is questionable in the light of recent surveys of Negro business enterprises.

[16] Joseph A. Pierce, *Negro Business and Business Education* (New York, 1947), pp. 207-09.

merce. These organizations have announced a wide diversity of objectives, but they have lacked vitality and have often been short-lived.

THE NEGRO IN THE FIELD OF BANKING

When the actual achievements of Negroes in the field of business are studied this faith is found to be based upon meager accomplishments that affect only slightly the economic status of the Negro in American life. The field in which the Negro made his major business ventures was in banking. "The rapid organization of independent Negro banking," writes Harris, "followed in the wake of the expansion of fraternal insurance and burial societies that took place in the first twenty years of the post-Civil War period." [17] The first banks organized and owned by Negroes were the Savings Bank of the Grand Fountain United Order of True Reformers in Richmond, Virginia, and the Capital Savings in Washington, D. C., in 1888. The bank of the True Reformers was authorized to serve as a depository for the Order and to engage in general banking. In 1889 the Mutual Trust Company was established in Chattanooga, Tennessee, and in 1890 the Alabama Penny Savings and Loan Company was organized in Birmingham, Alabama. The latter bank was organized by a preacher, as well as the Nickel Savings Bank which was started in Richmond, Virginia, in 1896. In 1903 the St. Luke's Savings Bank was organized in Richmond to serve as the depository of the Independent Order of St. Luke.

The growth in the number of Negro banks was rapid. Between 1899 and 1905 at least 28 Negro banks were organized and for the period 1888 to 1934 Negroes established at least 134 banks. The majority of these banks had been organized in 14 southern states and the District of Columbia. Twenty-five had been organized in Virginia, 14 in Georgia, 12 in Mississippi, and 11 in North Carolina. Of the 15 Negro banks established in three northern states, eight had been started in Pennsylvania, six in Illinois, and one in Detroit, Michigan. At the time of Harris' study in 1936, there were only 12 of the 134 banks still

[17] Harris, *op. cit.*, p. 46. The discussion here is based upon Harris' work, which is a definitive study of Negro banking through the fourth decade of the twentieth century.

in existence. During the early twenties there were more than 30 banks, but from 1928 to 1931 Negro banks suffered the greatest number of failures. During the thirty-year period, 1899-1929, the resources of Negro banks had grown, reaching a peak of nearly 13 million dollars in 1926. The decline in resources which began in 1927 was accelerated after 1929. It is estimated that the total resources of Negro banks was about $7,000,000 in 1931.

The high rate of failures of Negro banks is related to the character of Negro business enterprises. There are no important commercial and industrial enterprises in Negro communities; and if Negro banks and insurance companies are not included, Negro businesses are comprised in four classes. There are, first, the recreational and amusement establishments; second, real estate; third, retail trade; and fourth, and by far the largest class, personal service.

In thus limiting the scope and the liquidity of the Negro bank's investments and loans, the character of Negro business becomes the fundamental factor in its instability and economic weaknesses. While a few of the Negro banks studied would not have failed had they been conducted by judicious and experienced officers, most of them would have failed even if they had had expert management. Lack of experience and technical bank training, dishonesty, fraud, and speculation, are all too prevalent among Negro banks in relation to their size and the amount of business done by them, but they are not primary causes of their failure and weakness. Given sound and honest management, the Negro bank would still face one fundamental and perhaps insuperable obstacle to successful operation, namely, the inherent characteristics of Negro business enterprise.[18]

The increased activities of Negro banks during the early part of World War II brought their resources up to the 1931 estimate. According to the report of the United States Department of Commerce the increased activity has been due "to sound business acumen and favorable economic conditions, stimulated by the war economy." [19] The aggregate deposits of the 11 reporting banks for 1941 amounted to $7,509,405, or an increase of over 20 per cent over the previous year. More significant, however, was the fact that United States govern-

[18] *Ibid.*, pp. 172-73.

[19] United States Department of Commerce, "Second Annual Report of Banking Institutions Owned and Operated by Negroes," Release, April, 1942, p. 1.

ment obligations absorbed a large share of the increase in the bank resources. For the year 1941 the total of such holdings amounted to $1,406,124, or an increase of $490,168 over the previous year. The total business loans were $3,375,530, or an increase of about 33 per cent, while the total resources of the 11 banks rose to $8,636,453, which represented an increase of about 16 per cent over the previous year.[20]

The first Negro building, loan, and savings association was organized in Portsmouth, Virginia, in 1883.[21] In 1929 there were over 80 such associations but by 1938 the number had declined to 48. The failure of at least 50 associations has been the result of lack of experience, inefficiency, depreciation of property values, and failure to gain stockholders. In 1945 there were only 24 associations in existence, 13 of these being in the North. The assets of these 24 associations ranged from $8,185 to $506,981, with approximately one-half of the associations having assets under $50,000. The two associations with assets over half a million dollars were in Norfolk, Virginia, and Durham, North Carolina.

NEGRO INSURANCE COMPANIES

Although the ventures of Negroes in the field of life insurance have been marked by many failures, it is in this field that they have achieved their most outstanding success in business. The roots of life insurance among Negroes are to be found among numerous ventures dating from the eighteenth century.[22] Throughout the pre-Civil War period numerous beneficial and mutual aid societies among the free Negroes attempted to provide a type of insurance for their members. After Emancipation the fraternal orders entered the field of insurance.[23] The Grand United Order of True Reformers took the lead

[20] In 1945 the most recently organized of these 11 banks had been in existence 12 years and the oldest 42 years. Pierce, *op. cit.*, p. 153. See this work for an analysis of the condition of these banks in 1945. The facts for 1945 reveal essentially the same conditions as those presented for 1941.

[21] Pierce, *op. cit.*, pp. 158-60. See also *ibid.*, Table 58, p. 327.

[22] James B. Browning, "The Beginnings of Insurance Enterprise Among Negroes," *Journal of Negro History*, Vol. XXII, pp. 417-32.

[23] Carter G. Woodson, "Insurance Business Among Negroes," *Journal of Negro History*, Vol. 14, pp. 209-11.

by incorporating an insurance feature in their organization. Other fraternal organizations, including the Masons, Odd Fellows, and Knights of Pythias, followed the example of the True Reformers. The fraternal orders ran into difficulties with their insurance ventures mainly because they did not operate on a sound actuarial basis. There was also much mismanagement since these organizations were not under the supervision of any governmental authority.[24]

In the wake of the success of the True Reformers, there sprang up all over the South small mutual aid beneficial associations.[25] Most of these passed out of existence but they contributed to the growth of insurance among Negroes. These beneficial associations not only provided training and experience for Negroes but some of them developed into substantial industrial insurance companies. These insurance companies grew up partly as a reaction against the discrimination on the part of white companies. Those that have survived have either changed their policy of mutual assesssment or become legal reserve companies.

The emergence of legal reserve insurance among Negroes was related to the experience of Negroes with the fraternal organizations. The first legal reserve company was started by a young Negro physician in Mississippi, Dr. W. A. Attaway, who foresaw and predicted the failure of the insurance ventures of the fraternal organizations.[26] With the aid of a white banker and capitalist, he organized an insurance company with $50,000 capital in 1909, which with a capital of $100,000 in 1910 became a legal reserve company. During the next twelve years the company extended its operations into Arkansas, Tennessee, and Texas. In 1922 the Mississippi Life Insurance Company, as it was named, had a premium income of $881,668 and outstanding insurance amounting to about 15 million dollars. After 1933, the fate of this company became tied up with the Standard Life Insurance Company of Atlanta, Georgia.

Only three months before the Standard Life Insurance Company was organized as a legal reserve company in 1913, the North Carolina

---

[24] W. J. Trent, Jr., *Development of Negro Life Insurance Enterprises*, Master's Thesis. University of Pennsylvania, 1932, p. 22.
[25] *Ibid.*, p. 33ff.   [26] *Ibid.*, pp. 39ff.

Mutual Insurance Company, formerly the North Carolina Mutual and Provident Association, became the second legal reserve Negro insurance company. The North Carolina Mutual represented the transformation of the fraternal insurance society into a business organization.[27] One of the leaders in the organization, John Merrick, operated a barber shop, which brought him into contact with white businessmen. He interested a Negro physician, A. M. Moore, and other Negroes who had acquired the spirit of business enterprise in the insurance scheme. The business aspect of the enterprise was emphasized from the beginning. These same men organized a bank in 1908 and in 1920 the Durham group of Negro businessmen, which included C. C. Spaulding, launched the Bankers Fire Insurance Company. Within twelve years after the insurance enterprise became a legal reserve company in 1913, it had $42,000,000 of insurance in force and assets amounting to $2,000,000.

The organization of the Standard Life Insurance Company was due chiefly to the efforts of a Negro, Herman Perry, who had been an agent for several white insurance companies. He began in 1908 to raise the $100,000 required for a legal reserve insurance company. It was not until five years later that he secured the required capital and launched the Standard Life Insurance Company of Atlanta. He went into the field and within a short time wrote $250,000 insurance without commission. He surrounded himself with the best trained and influential Negroes as directors, officers, and employees. Within a short time it became the largest and most influential legal reserve company owned by Negroes. In 1922, the Standard had nearly 23 million dollars of life insurance in force, an annual premium income of about $1,200,000 and assets of $2,000,000. As the result of the success of this venture, Perry, the founder and president of the Standard, organized a number of subsidiaries including real estate companies, two banks, a printing company, and a pharmacy. When the Standard became pressed for money during its various financial operations, in order to increase its income it took over the Mississippi Life Insurance Company, which was later sold to a white company.

<hr/>

[27] See E. Franklin Frazier, "Durham: Capital of the Black Middle Class," in Alain Locke (Ed.), *The New Negro* (New York, 1925), pp. 33-40.

Despite this questionable maneuver the subsidiaries of the Standard were taken over by whites who held mortgages on the subsidiaries.

The National Benefit Life Insurance Company, which began in Washington, D. C. as an assessment association in 1898, reinsured the policyholders of the Standard in 1925 in order to save the greatest monument to Negro business enterprise.[28] At the time the National Benefit took over the Standard Life, it had over 40 million dollars of insurance in force. During the following year the National Benefit wrote 30 million dollars more but the company had entered upon an inflationary policy, which is revealed when one studies its capital and surplus. Moreover, the company began to change its policy from investment in bonds to investment in real estate and money was shifted to policy loans and "other assets." As a result, the National Benefit collapsed and the collapse was followed by numerous litigations. According to Mitchell, the factors involved in the collapse were unwise expansion, excessive operating costs, reinsuring of the Standard Life, manipulation of capital stock, lack of sound investments, and lack of prudent management.[29]

Following the mass migrations of Negroes to northern cities, three Negro insurance companies were established in the North. In 1929, the Liberty Life Insurance Company was established in Chicago and the Supreme Life and Casualty Company in Columbus, Ohio, and four years later the Northeastern Life Insurance Company in Newark, New Jersey. When these companies began to get into difficulties they were consolidated in the Supreme Liberty Life Insurance Company in 1939. These three companies had a combined capital of $400,000, insurance in force amounting to 25 million dollars and 1,090 employees. During the decade 1920 to 1930 two other insurance companies were organized in Chicago, one in Los Angeles and 11 in southern cities. In 1939 the 26 companies reporting had insurance in force amounting to over 200 million dollars and assets for 27 companies totaling almost $15,000,000. According to the report of the National Negro Insurance Association, which was established in

[28] See James B. Mitchell, *The Collapse of the National Benefit Life Insurance*, The Howard University Studies in the Social Sciences, Washington, D. C., 1939.
[29] *Ibid.*, p. 123.

1921, for the year 1939 the 28 companies reporting had nearly two million policyholders, contributing annual premiums amounting to over 14 million dollars.[30] To the beneficiaries of industrial policyholders these companies paid $1,809,396 and nearly two million dollars for the relief of the physically disabled. The policyholders' reserves of these 28 companies amounted to nearly $18,000,000, and the 8,508 employees of all classes received nearly 6 million dollars, while the stockholders received $80,000 in cash and $275,000 in stock dividends.

For the year 1945, the 44 member companies of the National Negro Insurance Association reported nearly 4,000,000 policies in force, of which 3,860,890 were health and accident and nearly 80,000 unspecified.[31] The total amount of insurance issued by 41 reporting member companies amounted to $723,225,311, of which ordinary policies accounted for $157,435,734. For 39 reporting member companies over a million policies representing over 180 million dollars were lapsed during 1945 because the insured stopped making payments. The premium income of 44 member companies amounted to 38 million dollars or nine-tenths of their income in 1945, while the total disbursements of these companies reached more than 30 million dollars. The employees of these companies received nearly $14,500,000 in salaries. However, despite this impressive showing it is estimated that one large white insurance company has insurance in force on Negro lives amounting to more than twice the insurance in force in all the Negro insurance companies.[32]

RETAIL STORES CONDUCTED BY NEGROES

Except for a few relatively spectacular developments, Negro business has consisted mainly of small retail stores. In 1939 there were nearly 30,000 Negro owned retail stores in the United States. From 1929 to 1939 the increase in the number of Negro owned retail stores was about the same as the increase for white owned retail stores (19.5 per cent and 19.9 per cent respectively).[33] The sales in Negro stores

[30] M. S. Stuart, "Insurance a Natural," *The Crisis*, Negro Business Anniversary Number. April, 1941, pp. 110-41.

[31] See Pierce, *op. cit.*, pp. 110ff.   [32] *Ibid.*, p. 117.

[33] U. S. Department of Commerce, "Retail Negro Proprietorships—The United States—1939." August 29, 1941, p. 3.

in the latter year were only 72.5 per cent of the former year as compared with 87 per cent for white owned stores. Then, too, whereas the number of full-time employees in white owned stores was the same in 1939 as in 1929, the number of full-time employees in Negro

TABLE XXIX

Number of Negro Owned Retail Stores According to Major Business Groups, 1929, 1935 and 1939 *

MAJOR BUSINESS GROUPS	1939	1935	1929
Food Group	11,038	9,008	10,755
General stores (with food)	149	321	761
General Merchandise group	83	68	128
Apparel group	333	232	477
Furniture—household—radio group	65	74	149
Automotive group	46	45	148
Filling stations	1,268	783	799
Lumber—building—hardware group	41	44	147
Eating and drinking places	12,610	8,568	7,918
Drug stores	548	608	712
Other stores	6,646	3,005	2,975
TOTAL	29,827	22,756	24,969

* United States Department of Commerce. Bureau of the Census, 1941, p. 4.

owned stores had decreased 15.1 per cent. The amount of the payrolls of Negro owned stores had decreased even more in comparison with white owned stores. In 1939 the payrolls of white owned stores were about 90 per cent of the amount for 1929 while the payrolls of Negro owned stores in 1939 were only two-thirds of the amount for 1929.

The majority—70 per cent—of these stores were located in the southern States. The largest number of unincorporated retail establishments owned by Negroes was in Texas, where there was also the largest number of employees of Negro owned stores. On the other hand, although only 27 per cent of the stores were in the North, their sales amounted to nearly 40 per cent of the total sales of the retail stores and the payrolls of stores in the North accounted for 50 per cent of the total. Moreover, nearly 40 per cent of the employees were in stores in the North. Three northern States—New York, Illinois, and Ohio—accounted in the order named for 8.9, 8.4, and 7.7 per cent or taken together 25 per cent of the total payrolls of Negro stores in the entire country.

The present character of Negro business in cities has been depicted in recent surveys. One of these was concerned with Negro business in

TABLE XXX

Number of Negro Owned Retail Stores, Sales, Personnel, Payroll and Stocks According to Geographic Divisions in 1939 *

GEOGRAPHIC DIVISION	NUMBER OF STORES	SALES (000)	Employees		PAYROLL	STOCKS ON HAND END OF YEAR, AT COST
			FULL TIME	PART TIME		
North	8,272	$29,028	4,106	1,319	$2,727,000	$1,326,000
South	20,825	39,364	5,756	2,014	2,344,000	1,543,000
West	730	3,074	358	225	305,000	173,000
TOTAL	29,827	71,466	10,220	3,558	5,386,000	3,042,000

* U. S. Department of Commerce. Bureau of the Census, August 29, 1941, p. 10.

Louisville, Kentucky.[34] In Louisville as in other cities the first business ventures among Negroes developed out of the experiences of the Negroes who were free before the Civil War. During the ante-bellum period, it appears that Negroes had a monopoly of the drayage and hauling business. Following the Civil War Negroes continued to carry on this business, and engaged as well in businesses based upon their experiences as domestic and personal servants. When the study of Louisville was made in 1942, there were still 30 drayage and hauling businesses operated by Negroes despite the growing competition. A little more than 40 per cent of the Negro businesses were small retail stores, almost a half of which were ice-coal-wood dealers. These ice-coal-wood dealers had an average investment of $200 while their average monthly sales amounted to $165 and less than $150 in monthly net profits. The service-amusement group of businesses were comprised chiefly of barber and beauty shops and four poolrooms. Among the investment and occupation group were three shoemakers,

[34] A *Study of Business and Employment Among Negroes in Louisville*. By Associates of Louisville Municipal College, University of Louisville, Louisville Urban League, Central High School (Louisville, Ky., May 1, 1944).

four taxicab companies, 30 hauling-drayage businesses and numerous junk peddlers. Four insurance companies and 14 funeral directors made up most of the investment-managerial group. The 354 Negro businesses which were studied employed a total of 752 employees, one-fourth of whom were employed in the four insurance companies. The wages of the employees ranged from free meals to $25 to $30 a week while the average monthly net profit of 348 establishments was less than $150.

NEGRO BUSINESSES IN NORTHERN CITIES

The study of Negro business in Chicago by Drake and Cayton provides a broad and realistic account of the status of Negro business in the large cities of the North.[35] The authors devote two chapters to Negro business, one of which deals with legitimate business enterprises. However, the very title of this chapter indicates the unrealistic belief which Negroes have concerning the extent and significance of Negro enterprises as sources of employment.[36] Among Negroes in Chicago, as in other cities, there is the belief in the "Double-Duty Dollar" or the belief that by patronizing Negro businesses the dollar which the Negro worker earns provides a living for the worker and at the same time creates jobs for other Negroes as well as a wealthy class among Negroes. This myth, which has almost acquired the character of a sacred dogma, is preached from the pulpits of the largest Negro churches as well as in the smallest "storefront" churches. This faith, as the authors point out, results from the Negro's participation in "two social worlds—the larger community of the city, state, and nation and the smaller, socially isolated, and spatially separated Negro world."

As participants in the general American culture, they are exposed to a system that places a high premium upon business success and white-collar occupations. Financial power and economic control bring those political and social rewards which have traditionally been supposed to serve as incentives to thrift, enterprise, and hard work. Negroes,

---

[35] St. Clair Drake and Horace R. Cayton, *Black Metropolis* (New York, 1945), Chapters 16 and 17.

[36] See *ibid.*, Chapter 16, "Negro Business: Myth and Fact."

using the same school textbooks as whites, reading the same papers, attending the same movies, and in constant contact with the white world, tend to incorporate the general ideals of American life. Inevitably, they measure progress since slavery partly in terms of the positions of power and prestige which Negroes attain in the business world.[37]

The objective reality of the rôle of Negro business in the economy of the city of Chicago or any other city for that matter differs from the myth and faith of Negroes in Negro business enterprises. There are no Negroes on the board of directors in La Salle Street; no Negro dealers have a seat on the Stock Exchange or deal in the grain pit. Negroes do not own skyscrapers and there are scarcely any Negro buyers, traveling salesmen, or jobbers.

In the early days of Negro business in Chicago, Negro enterprises were not operated for an exclusively Negro clientele.[38] Following the Civil War, Negroes operated such businesses as barber shops and livery stables and served as draymen. There was an especially successful tailor and a number of wigmakers, masseurs, and caterers. By 1885 there were 200 enterprises in 27 different fields. Even as late as 1900, the Negro market was relatively unimportant so far as Negro businesses were concerned. During the fifteen years prior to the mass migrations from the South, the number of Negro businesses reached 500. The majority of these enterprises were in the service field, with barber shops and moving and storage establishments forming the majority of the enterprises.

It was the mass migrations from the South during and following World War I that created the Negro market in Chicago. Negro businesses sprang up to serve the more than two hundred thousand Negroes. Conspicuous among the Negro businesses were the two banks and four insurance companies. During the depression the two Negro banks failed and many of the larger business establishments were wiped out. At the same time the smaller businesses increased in number because unemployed Negroes with small savings opened small stores as a means of securing a living. Another result of the de-

[37] *Black Metropolis* by St. Clair Drake and Horace R. Cayton, p. 433. Copyright 1945 by Harcourt, Brace and Company, Inc.   [38] *Ibid.*, pp. 433ff.

pression was that Negroes undertook to organize their purchasing power in order to create jobs for Negroes and to urge Negroes to patronize Negro owned enterprises. These aims were to be accomplished through the boycott of white businesses in Negro neighborhoods that refused to employ Negroes. Negroes succeeded in breaking the color-line in some white stores.[39] But, on the whole, this movement did not affect greatly either the extent of Negro employment or the character of Negro business enterprises.

In 1938 there were about 2,600 Negro businesses in Chicago.[40] Of the ten most numerous establishments there were 287 beauty parlors, 257 groceries, 207 barber shops, 163 tailors, cleaners, and pressers, and 145 restaurants. The remaining five most numerous types of businesses—coal and wood dealers, taverns, undertakers, shoe repairing, and dressmakers—were represented by less than 100 establishments. In Negro neighborhoods there were 2,800 white business establishments. However, as the authors of *Black Metropolis* point out, "*While Negro enterprises constituted almost half of all businesses in Negro neighborhoods, they received less than a tenth of all money spent by Negroes within these areas.*" [41] (Italics in the original.)

The situation of Negro business enterprises in the Harlem Negro community in New York City was similar to that in Chicago:

A survey of 52 of the 78 census tracts in the Harlem area or those in which one per cent or more of the total population was Negro showed that Negroes conduct 1928 or 18.6 per cent of the 10,319 businesses. The main type of businesses conducted by Negroes differ considerably from the chief businesses in which whites are engaged. More than a third—36.5 per cent—of the Negro businesses provide personal services such as barber shops, beauty parlors and cleaning and pressing shops where little capital is needed. On the other hand, the same percentage—36.3—of the businesses conducted by whites provide for the

[39] In New York City as well as in Chicago these tactics helped to stimulate anti-semitism among Negroes. Moreover, in Harlem in New York City, the mass pressure for the employment of Negroes worked a hardship on the owners of stores which depended upon the family for labor. See Harris, *op. cit.*, p. 183.

[40] *Black Metropolis* by St. Clair Drake and Horace R. Cayton, p. 438. Copyright 1945 by Harcourt, Brace and Company, Inc.

[41] *Ibid.*, p. 438. "A business census of 1935 revealed that only 5 per cent of the $11,000,000 which [Negroes] spent on groceries was spent with Negroes." *Ibid.*, p. 438.

basic needs of the community. These businesses include grocery stores, meat markets, bakeries, coal and ice companies, restaurants, clothing, department and furniture stores. Only 18.4 per cent of the Negro businesses in the community provide for such basic needs. Moreover, a closer inspection of the types of businesses in this general class shows that the majority of Negro businesses are restaurants.[42]

The findings of the most recent survey of Negro business indicates that there has been little change in its general character during the past 50 years.[43] As stated in a preliminary announcement of the conclusions: "The 10 most frequent businesses operating in the South today are restaurants, barbershops, grocery stores, cleaning and pressing establishments, shoe repair shops, undertakers, confectionary stores, taverns and filling stations." The prominence of undertaking establishments among Negro business enterprises points to an important feature of Negro businesses; namely, the monopoly enjoyed by some Negro businesses. The 3,000 Negro undertakers, who constitute about a tenth of the undertakers in the United States, cater to a need of Negroes which whites refuse to serve. Consequently, Negro undertakers enjoy a monopoly in this field, though among Negro undertakers themselves the competition is keen.[44] It was revealed in the study that 48 per cent of all Negro businesses were service establishments and that 81 per cent of all Negro businesses were in Negro neighborhoods and 18 per cent in mixed neighborhoods. The vast majority—85 per cent—of Negro businesses were one-man establishments; while of the remainder 9 per cent were partnerships, 3 per cent corporations, and 1 per cent cooperatives. Only slightly more than 15 per cent of the operators of Negro businesses kept records; and in the case of those with records 60 per cent of them were kept by the proprietors. The median annual volume of income varied with the amount and character of formal business education which the proprietors had received. The median annual income for operators with no formal business education was about $3,000; for those who took business courses in high school, $4,800; for those with training in

---

[42] The Mayor's Commission on Conditions in Harlem, *The Negro in Harlem* (New York, 1936), pp. 23-24. Unpublished report.
[43] Pierce, *op. cit.*   [44] Pierce, *op. cit.*, pp. 193-94.

private business schools, $4,600; and those with business education in college about $8,700.

Of the 12 cities covered by the survey, Atlanta had the largest number (845) of Negro businesses.[45] Washington stood second with 696 businesses including one bank and the home office of a life insurance company. The facts brought out concerning Negro business in Washington present a picture of Negro business under very favorable circumstances.[46] There were 58 types of business enterprises, two-thirds of which were beauty shops, barbershops, restaurants, grocery stores, and undertakers. Eating places, stores of the food group, and drugstores accounted for 60 per cent of the retail stores. Beauty shops, barbershops, cleaning and pressing establishments, and undertakers comprised 85 per cent of the service businesses. Nearly nine-tenths of the Negro businesses in Washington were single proprietorships; slightly more than 7 per cent partnerships and less than 3 per cent corporations. The median volume of business for all types of enterprises was about $4,500 in 1943. The average number of persons employed in the business establishments was 3.8 and their average weekly salary amounted to 31 dollars.

In the 12 cities covered by the survey there were no wholesale businesses and only 19 manufacturing businesses. Five of the manufacturing businesses were engaged in making caskets and eight in manufacturing cosmetics. In fact, it was in the manufacture of cosmetics that Negroes—women—first achieved a spectacular success.[47] In New York City the late Madame C. J. Walker, who popularized the straightening of hair, is reported to have accumulated over a million dollars from the manufacture of hair and skin preparations.[48] A Mrs. A. E. Malone, in St. Louis and later in Chicago, acquired a large for-

[45] The twelve cities included Atlanta, Washington, D. C., Memphis, New Orleans, St. Louis, Houston, Richmond, Savannah, Cincinnati, Durham, N. C., Nashville, and Baltimore.

[46] *Business Enterprise Owned and Operated by Negroes in Washington, D. C.,* 1944, A Special Report of the Project to Study Business and Business Education Among Negroes. Atlanta University, Atlanta, Ga. This report was a completed mimeographed section of the larger study.

[47] A little more than a third of Negro businesses are conducted by women.

[48] See Carter G. Woodson, *The Negro in Our History* (Washington, D. C., 1928), p. 461.

tune through the manufacture of the Poro hair and skin products. The numerous beauty shops, which constitute a large proportion of Negro business undertakings, have provided outlets for these products.

This study included a survey of cooperatives among Negroes. Information was secured on 11 cooperatives located in seven states and seven cooperatives in the District of Columbia.[49] All of the cooperatives in the District of Columbia were organized in recent years and were in the planning stage or just beginning to operate. The only outstanding cooperative, which has been operating five years, had a capital of $9,000 and sales amounting to $4,000 a week. The 11 cooperatives outside the District of Columbia were organized within the last decade. The annual volume of business of most of the cooperatives was less than $10,000. One outstanding exception was the Georgia State College Cooperative Association (Savannah), which conducts a bookstore and a cafeteria, and sells clothing, confectionery, and groceries with an annual volume of $25,000. The most important cooperatives were in Hampton and Richmond, Virginia. In the former city there was a cooperative meat and grocery store which did an annual business amounting to $34,000 and a similar store was in Richmond with an annual volume of business amounting to $100,000.

WHY HAS NEGRO BUSINESS REMAINED
INSIGNIFICANT?

The facts brought out in the latest survey of Negro business only tend to emphasize the generally recognized fact that Negroes have failed to develop business enterprises commensurate with their achievements in other phases of American civilization. A number of explanations have been offered to account for this failure. These explanations include both economic and social factors. Among the economic factors there is first the competitive disadvantage which the Negro suffers because of the small size of the average Negro business.[50] The Negro businessman also experiences greater difficulties in securing credit because of the marginal position of Negro enterprises. Thus the Negro

[49] Unpublished report by H. Naylor Fitzhugh on "Negroes in Consumer Cooperatives."
[50] Gunnar Myrdal, *An American Dilemma* (New York, 1914), pp. 307ff.

businessman must depend upon an immediate cash turnover and cannot extend credit to his Negro customers who must make their purchases on credit. Moreover, since Negro businesses must depend upon customers in Negro neighborhoods, these neighborhoods which are generally poor cannot support prosperous Negro enterprises. Finally, Negro businessmen cannot get good locations because white real estate owners prefer white businessmen. The explanations in terms of social factors include first the failure of Negroes to be "loyal" to Negro business enterprises. In the recent survey of Negro business, 46 per cent of the Negro consumers stated that operators of Negro business were slow; 44 per cent that they were careless; 29 per cent that Negro business was inefficient; and 23 per cent that it was discourteous.[51]

As Myrdal points out, these various explanations appear inadequate when one compares the Negro's poor achievements in business with the more successful achievements of other alien groups. He points out first that stores and restaurants operated by Orientals gave employment to an average of four persons per store (proprietors and employees) as compared with 1.6 for Negro establishments and that Oriental operated stores had net sales of $89,000,000 as compared with $101,000,000 for Negro owned stores though the Negro population was 50 times as great as the Oriental population. Moreover, he points out that the failure of the Negro caterer, barber, and skilled mechanic as entrepreneurs is attributable partly to inefficiency as well as racial discrimination and political pressures.

All of these factors, social as well as economic, have contributed to the failure of the Negro to develop businesses on a large scale. In considering the various economic factors it is customary to include such factors as desirable sites and the availability of capital. But when one considers such a factor as efficiency, one is dealing with a social as well as an economic factor. Efficiency in business involves judgment and foresight in the matter of risks and habituation to the tasks involved in business. Most often the Negro leader or educator has conceived such matters in terms of formal education and has asserted that the Negro can overcome his inefficiency through formal education given in

[51] *Atlanta University Bulletin, 1947.*

business courses. For two generations the Negro leaders, from Booker T. Washington to the most obscure Negro preacher, have implied that the Negro could be interested in business by preaching to him the value and necessity of engaging in business enterprise. As we have seen, neither of these techniques has increased in any appreciable degree the success of the Negro businessman or the significance of Negro business in the economy of either the Negro community or the larger community. Therefore, it is necessary to search further for the cause of the failure of the Negro businessman even in the field of retail business.

Although no systematic study has been undertaken of the social causes of the failure of the Negro to achieve success as a business man, it appears from what we know of the social and cultural history of the Negro that it is the result largely of the lack of traditions in the field of business enterprise. This absence of traditions in the field of business enterprise becomes apparent when one examines the present character and social origins of all classes in the Negro community. It is obvious that the slaves had no traditions or experience that would enable them to engage in business operations. Among the free Negroes there were those who had maintained taverns and had been skilled artisans. Neither of these occupations provided much experience in business enterprise. When Emancipation came to the great mass of the Negro population, the ventures in business enterprise were undertakings in activities that were foreign to their training and cultural heritage. In brief, from Emancipation to the present time business enterprise has been something alien to the cultural heritage of the Negro.

The Negro peasant in the South has no experience in buying and selling, which are at the heart of the spirit of business. The attempts of the schools to teach business have only revealed the failure of formal education to inculcate habits and values that were alien to the traditional culture of a group.[52] The exhortation and preaching of

[52] It might be noted in this connection (see Pierce, *op. cit.*, p. 37), that 65.2 per cent of Negro business operators entered business for economic reasons and 10.1 per cent because of "family connections and influence," whereas 21.4 per cent of 56 Negroes who had achieved outstanding success in business entered this field because of "family connections and influence" and only 35.7 per cent because of economic reasons.

Negro leaders have failed because they are essentially a magical technique applied to the social process.

The manpower shortage created by World War II opened up employment for Negroes in white business establishments. This experience will provide Negroes with greater and more important education in business than all the business courses in Negro schools provide at present. If this experience is utilized for building up their own small businesses it will lay a broader foundation for a tradition in business enterprise. The graduates of business courses in Negro colleges will continue as in the past to seek employment in the larger Negro enterprises such as banks, insurance companies, and newspapers.

Even if a large section of the Negro population acquired efficiency and traditions of business enterprise, these achievements cannot become the basis of a segregated economy. As Myrdal has pointed out, there is no future for a segregated financial system which at best is only a poor substitute for what the Negro needs: the integration of Negroes into white dominated economic institutions or those of the general community.[53] There are indications that Negroes with business education and training are beginning to be employed in white business institutions. This trend is especially marked in New York City partly as the result of the operation of the Ives-Quinn Law forbidding discrimination in employment.

The development of business enterprise among Negroes has had a long history, dating from the eighteenth century. However, despite its long history, business enterprise among Negroes has played an insignificant rôle in the economy of the nation. Although the business enterprises developed by Negroes since Emancipation have been larger and more diversified than those developed by the Negroes who were free before the Civil War, they have not been of greater importance in the national economy. The failure of the Negroes to develop larger and more important business undertakings is explained in part by such economic factors as their general poverty and the inaccessibility of credit. But there have also been social and cultural factors that help to explain this phenomenon. Important among these are exclusion from employment in white business establishments in which

[53] Myrdal, *op. cit.*, p. 318.

Negroes could learn business methods and the general absence of a tradition of buying and selling. In a few business undertakings such as insurance companies and newspapers, a business tradition is being built up in the families that own some of these enterprises. Although newspapers represent some of the largest business enterprises among Negroes, a discussion of them has been placed in a later chapter because of their rôle in the development of public opinion among Negroes and their general social significance irrespective of their rôle as business enterprises.

PART 4

Intellectual Life and Leadership

FROM an analysis of the character of the Negro community and its institutions we turn to a consideration of its intellectual life and leadership. In the first two chapters, the development and present status of educational institutions, on the elementary, secondary, and higher levels, are presented in relation to public support and private philanthropy. Next, the Negro newspaper is studied not only as a business institution but as an expression of the aspirations of the Negro and in relation to formation of public opinion. Then Negro literature is analyzed not so much from the standpoint of literary values as from the standpoint of the Negro's conception of himself and his outlook on American life. Social movements and the development of race consciousness are analyzed in relation to the changing status of the Negro in American society. In a final chapter the rôle of Negro leaders and the intelligentsia in their relations to institutions and various aspects of community life is traced.

Intellectual Life and Leadership

CHAPTER XVII

Elementary and Secondary Schools

THE development of schools among the Negroes in the United States represents largely the influence of social forces outside the Negro community. Unlike the development of the family and mutual aid associations, the emergence of the earliest schools among Negroes was the direct result of the philanthropic efforts of whites.[1] The earliest schools among Negroes developed in the North where free Negroes were permitted to share in the culture of the white community. On the other hand, in the South the development of the schools among the free Negroes was largely the result of self-effort. Since the formal education of the slaves was forbidden, whatever education they received was because of the exigencies of slavery or the caprice of individual slaveholders.

After Emancipation the development of education was the result partly of the efforts of missionaries from the North and partly of the efforts of the freedmen who, armed with political power, regarded education as a means to equality with the whites. After the overthrow of the Reconstruction governments the Negroes received on the whole about the same meager public education as the "poor whites." But with the "rise of the poor whites," the Negroes lost the equality that they had enjoyed. After the Negroes lost political power they received only a small share of public funds for education. While there has been an increase in recent decades in the public funds allotted to the edu-

[1] In Brazil where Negroes were able to re-establish some phases of their African cultural heritage, the Mahamodan Negroes conducted schools in which the Koran was taught. See Niña Rodrigues, *Os Africanos no Brasil* (São Paulo, 1935), pp. 89-90.

cation of Negroes, the provisions for the public education of Negroes is inferior to that for whites in the South. On the other hand, the mass migrations of Negroes to northern cities has enabled a larger proportion of Negro children to receive a standard American education than at any time in the history of the Negro.

EDUCATION OF THE NEGRO BEFORE THE CIVIL WAR

"The first real educators to take up the work of enlightening American Negroes," writes Woodson, "were clergymen interested in the propagation of the gospel among the heathen of the new world." [2] Educational work carried on by the German Protestants from Salzburg, who were opposed to slavery, helped to reconcile them to slavery as a means of inducting the heathen into the Christian faith. Spanish and French explorers and settlers were committed to a policy of educating the black slaves as a part of indoctrinating them with Christianity. The English were slower to follow a similar policy until the provincial statutes and the declarations of the Bishop of London established the principle that conversion did not lead to manumission.[3] The efforts of the English to educate the Negro slaves were carried out by *The Society for the Propagation of the Gospel in Foreign Parts.* In 1705 the Reverend Samuel Thomas of Goose Creek Parish in South Carolina began his educational work. Nine years later the *Society* opened a school in New York City where there were 200 Negro pupils in 1708. Despite opposition, the *Society* carried on the education of the Negro and the Indian in Virginia, Maryland, and North Carolina. The *Society* met less opposition in Pennsylvania, New Jersey, and other northern States while in New England the education of the Negro was regarded as an obligation of the master toward his servants. The most liberal and influential religious group interested in the education of the Negro was the Quakers. In the South the work of the Quakers was checked while in the North they exerted a strong influence far beyond their own circle.

[2] *The Education of the Negro Prior to 1861* by Carter G. Woodson, p. 18. Copyright 1915 by G. P. Putnam's Sons. This book, which is a definitive study of the education of the Negro prior to the Civil War, contains a wealth of information that can be referred to only briefly in this chapter.

[3] See pp. 335-36 above.

The education of the Negro was influenced by the philosophy of the American Revolution. In the attack upon slavery as a violation of the "natural rights" of man, the opponents of slavery espoused the right of the Negro to be educated for citizenship. Some of the conservative leaders of the Revolution thought of education as a part of a gradual process of emancipation. But men like Benjamin Franklin favored and encouraged the full education of the Negro. Although Thomas Jefferson did not believe in the intellectual equality of Negroes and whites and did not envision the incorporation of Negroes into the white community, he thought that they should be given an industrial and agricultural education. The philosophy of the "natural rights" of man was not able, however, to overcome the opposition of the planters in the South to the education of the Negro. Following the Revolution abolitionists and the more liberal sects, the Quakers, Baptists, Methodists, and Presbyterians continued playing an important rôle in the education of the Negro. Outstanding leaders among the abolitionists were Anthony Benezet and Thaddeus Kosciusko, the Polish general. Benezet and Kosciusko left considerable wealth for the education of the Negro.

The educational work of the Baptist and Methodist churches was a part of their training of a Negro ministry and Negroes in the "Sabbath-schools." The work of the churches was limited in the South when the slaveholders passed stringent laws against the instruction of the slaves and placed limitations upon the education of the free Negroes. There was much clandestine education of slaves, especially in southern cities, while the education of free Negroes was often carried on in defiance of the law or at least with the connivance of the law enforcement agencies.[4]

Negroes enjoyed the best educational opportunities in the cities of the North. As early as 1798, a separate school for colored children was opened in Boston by a white man. It was not until 1820, however, that the city of Boston opened its first primary school for colored children. During the last quarter of the eighteenth century abolitionists opened a school for Negroes in New York City. Some indication of the extent of school attendance is provided in the statistics for

[4] Woodson, *op. cit.*, pp. 205ff.

Philadelphia, where in 1859 there were 1,031 pupils in public schools; 748 in charity schools, 211 in benevolent schools; and 331 in private schools.[5] These statistics show that the education of the Negro before the Civil War was largely the work of philanthropic whites and voluntary organizations among the free Negroes. In Table V, we have seen the extent of literacy and school attendance among free Negroes in 16 cities in 1850.[6]

DEVELOPMENT OF NEGRO SCHOOLS AFTER EMANCIPATION

The first day school for Negroes to be established in the South as the result of the Civil War was opened in 1861. This school, opened less than six months after the beginning of the Civil War, was the work of the American Missionary Association. It was opened to take care of the refugees from the neighboring plantations whom General Butler had designated "contraband of war." The first teacher of this school was a young "free woman of colour" from the North who had been educated in England. During the following year, other schools were established by the Association and other missionary agencies in Portsmouth, Norfolk, Newport News, Virginia; at Newburn and Roanoke Island, North Carolina; and at Port Royal, South Carolina. Thus began the invasion of the South by the much maligned New England "school marms" whose passion for humanity and high ideals had caused them to devote their lives to the regeneration of the emancipated blacks.

As the Union Armies penetrated farther into the South, the representatives of missionary societies and churches sent funds and teachers to aid in the problems of adjusting the Negro to new conditions of freedom. The men and women who went to the South were not adventurers and grafters, as the apologists for slavery have represented them. The majority of these men were inspired by a high idealism and faith in human freedom and equality. Many of them sacrificed wealth and comfort and condemned themselves to a life of hardship and self-denial in their efforts to educate the freedmen. Nor was their desire to provide for the health and education of the

[5] *Ibid.*, p. 147.   [6] See pp. 72-74 above.

freedmen misled and impractical idealism. The necessity of the education of the freedmen was recognized by General Banks in Louisiana, who was the first to make a systematic effort "to establish a regular system of free public schools for Negro children." [7] This effort grew out of a communication from President Lincoln to Banks in which he had stated that "some provision should be made for the education of the young blacks." [8]

The attitude of the South toward the education of the freedmen was determined not only by the traditional attitudes toward the status of the Negro but also by the outlook and interests of the various groups that emerged as the result of the collapse of the traditional class structure which gave rise to three elements in southern society. There were the conservatives, who attempted through the "Black Codes" to reinstate as far as possible the servile status of the Negro. This class was opposed to any form of education of the Negro. There were the moderates, who realized that slavery was dead and that the new status of the Negro should be recognized in creating a new society in the South. In this moderate group were many large plantation owners who were willing to provide some education for the Negro in order to secure a stable and reliable labor supply. The third group was comprised of the unpropertied whites and small farmers, who had no real interest in the slave system. Because of cooperation of this group with Negroes during the early years of Reconstruction, they have been called renegades and "scalawags." [9] This group cooperated with Negroes in establishing public schools during the early years of Reconstruction though later they became aligned against the Negro's struggle for education and citizenship.

The creation of the "Bureau for Freedmen, Refugees and Abandoned Lands" by an act of Congress in 1865 represented an attempt on the part of the government to systematize and assume responsibility for adjusting the freedman to his new status. One of the major functions of the Bureau was the education of the freedmen. The gen-

[7] *The Education of the Negro in the American Social Order* by Horace M. Bond, p. 26. Copyright 1934 by Prentice-Hall, Inc.

[8] Quoted in *ibid.*, p. 26.

[9] In a novel, *Freedom Road*, Howard Fast has presented the cooperation of these whites and the black freedmen during the beginning of Reconstruction.

eral policy of the Bureau was to erect school houses and provide the various missionary societies with funds for the salaries of teachers.[10] There was much opposition on the part of the conservative southern whites to the educational efforts of the Bureau. School houses were burned and both white and Negro teachers were beaten and expelled from the communities in which they worked. As the landless and poor white farmers were won to the cause of "white supremacy," they too joined the opposition to Negro education. It is interesting to note, however, that the *Montgomery Advertiser* stated in an editorial in 1867 that the education of Negroes should provide employment for the widows of Confederate veterans or ex-soldiers of the Confederacy rather than northerners.[11] Bond has made the following objective statement of the contribution of the Freedmen's Bureau to the education of the Negro.

Whatever its faults, the Freedmen's Bureau may justly be credited with the establishment of a widespread and fairly well organized system of free schools for Negroes in the South. In the five years of its operation, it was instrumental in the initiation of 4,239 separate schools. The extent of its work can further be gauged by the fact that it employed 9,307 teachers and instructed 247,333 pupils. The total expenditures for the schools operated under the protection of the Bureau amounted to more than three and one-half million dollars. To this sum the benevolent societies added more than a million and a half, and a conservative estimate of the contribution of Negroes in tuition fees and gifts to these schools is not less than a million dollars.[12]

ATTITUDE OF THE SOUTH TOWARD STATE SUPPORTED SCHOOLS FOR NEGROES

When one turns to the question of public, tax-supported schools for Negroes in the South, one finds opposition on the part of all the

[10] See Bureau of Education, *Negro Education*. Bulletin, 1916, No. 38 (Washington, 1917), Vol. I, pp. 268-95, for an account of the work of the Freedmen's Aid Societies. During the period 1862-74 the receipts of these societies amounted to $4,000,000 including a million dollars from foreign sources. The contributions of Negroes to the Freedmen's Aid for the years, 1862-70, amounted to nearly half a million dollars. *Ibid.*, pp. 296-97.   [11] Bond, *op. cit.*, p. 33.

[12] *The Education of the Negro in the American Social Order* by Horace M. Bond, p. 29. Copyright 1934 by Prentice-Hall, Inc.

state legislatures. This opposition was due partly to the aristocratic tradition in the South that had always been opposed to the education of children at public expense. During the years prior to the Civil War the poor white classes had become more articulate and insistent in their demands for public support of education. Some success had been achieved by the poor whites in the Piedmont regions of Tennessee, Virginia, and North Carolina where Negro slavery was being undermined by soil exhaustion and the decline of the plantation system. But, on the whole, the aristocratic slaveholding class had succeeded in nullifying the attempts of the poor whites to gain more than statutory provisions for a very limited support of public education.

Opposition to public schools for Negroes was the result of other reasons than the traditional attitude toward tax-supported schools for the masses. It was the result largely of the fact that education symbolized and tended to give the Negro a status inconsistent with what was regarded as the Negro's proper place in the social order. The argument, advanced after the Civil War, that education was needed to produce an enlightened electorate applied to the poor whites but not to the Negro.

West Virginia, which became a separate political unit in 1863, was the first southern state to make provisions in its constitutions for the "equal though separate" education of the Negro. In those sections of Florida and Louisiana that were under the jurisdiction of the Union military forces and in the border states, there were efforts to set up public school systems for Negroes. In the border states support for the Negro public schools was from the taxes paid by Negroes. This was true even in the District of Columbia, where in 1862 Congress passed a bill setting aside 10 per cent of the taxes paid by Negroes for the support of Negro schools.[13] The question of the public support of Negro education was tied up with the status of the Negro in the nation. The legal status of the Negro in the nation was finally decided by the Fourteenth and Fifteenth Amendments, which established the citizenship rights of the Negro.[14] The passage of these

[13] *Ibid.*, p. 44.
[14] W. E. B. DuBois, *The Negro Common School* (Atlanta, Ga., 1901), p. 38.

amendments to the Constitution was made possible by "congressional Reconstruction" of the southern states.

In the border states, which were not under the military control of the Union Armies, the legislatures gradually made provisions for the public education of Negroes out of public funds after the separation of schools on the basis of taxes paid by the two races was declared unconstitutional. On the other hand, the governments set up under the military authorities in the South made constitutional provisions and enacted laws for the equal education of Negroes and whites. In five States—Arkansas, Florida, Louisiana, Mississippi, and South Carolina—Negroes were elected superintendents of education. Three of these men were graduates of northern colleges. Although two of the five superintendents were charged with corruption, the other three were acknowledged by southern whites to be honest and efficient.

The chief consequence of the Reconstruction governments upon education in the South was that public, tax-supported education for the masses was established as a democratic right. However, the education of whites and Negroes in the same schools was not attempted on a large scale. In Louisiana and South Carolina where attempts were made to educate the children and youths of two races in the same schools, there was some violence or the whites gradually boycotted the schools. The Negro leaders accepted, on the whole, the separate schools as an inevitable consequence of the traditional attitudes of whites toward the association of the races. But they lost a strategic position when they were assured by philanthropic whites that if they surrendered the right to mixed schools they would receive their share of public funds.[15]

In fact, for some years following the overthrow of the Reconstruction governments, the Negro schools were maintained on an equal basis with the whites. This was the result of a number of factors. There was first the continued voting power of Negroes who supported candidates who promised educational privileges. There was also the tacit promise of the South to the North that in depriving the Negro of political rights, the Negro would still enjoy educational rights

[15] See Bond, *op. cit.*, pp. 53-56.

which would prepare him for citizenship. The situation has been well stated by Bond:

If the South pleaded that Negroes were unfit for citizenship, if Henry Grady, as its representative, asked for tolerance on the part of the North for its treatment of Negroes, the North was willing to acquiesce if assured that conditions would not be allowed totally to revert to antebellum strictures upon the mobility or education of the Negro. If the Negro was not yet ready for citizenship, it was implied that the South should prepare him for his gradual assumption of the role. If the Southern States, immediately upon the end of Reconstruction, had deprived the Negro not only of citizenship rights but also of educational privileges, it is doubtful whether the North would have shown the same complaisance which it did exhibit. In the same way, then, that Southern candidates advised their supporters to avoid riots, brawls, and other disturbances which might give some Northern Republican a chance to "wave the bloody shirt," the leaders of the conservative regime pledged themselves and their parties to a continued participation of the Negro in educational privileges, while they quietly but firmly stripped him of his political power.[16]

In fulfilling their tacit promise to the North, the southern conservatives who came to power in 1876 were interested at the same time in keeping down taxes. As a consequence, they restricted the educational expenditures for both races. In some states, there was a decline in the school enrollment. In this connection it is worthy of note that the salaries of white and Negro teachers remained the same even in Mississippi for a decade after 1876.[17] The domination of the conservatives was of short duration for the poor whites were clamoring for an improvement in their status and education was regarded as the chief means to this end.

THE "RISE OF THE POOR WHITES" AND INEQUALITIES IN EDUCATION FOR THE NEGRO

The growing demand of the poor whites for educational facilities is reflected in the statistics on school enrollment for the two races between 1880 and 1895. In the southern states as a whole, the enroll-

[16] *The Education of the Negro in the American Social Order* by Horace M. Bond, pp. 82-83. Copyright 1934 by Prentice-Hall, Inc.
[17] *Ibid.*, pp. 96-97.

ment of whites increased 106 per cent during this period as compared with 59 per cent for Negroes. To meet the demands of whites for education, a formula was worked out in Mississippi which became a pattern for the South. This formula consisted of the diversion of state funds, based upon per capita appropriation for children of school age, from Negro to white schools.

The first step in carrying out the formula was the inauguration of a system of uniform examination for teachers. The salary range for the different grades of certificate made it possible to pay a first-grade Negro teacher $25 per month and a first-grade white teacher $55. In the diversion of the per capita state appropriation from Negro to white children, the white children in "black" counties or those with a predominantly Negro population fared better than the white children in "white" counties.

The development of inequalities in the education of whites and Negroes was a phase of the so-called "rise of the poor whites" in the 1890's. It was during this period, as we have seen, that the Negro was disfranchised by constitutional provisions and his subordinate status was given a legal basis in the South.[18] The demagogic leaders of the poor whites attributed their inadequate schools to the fact that money had been wasted in the education of the Negro. This was the beginning of a campaign against the education of the Negro. The Negro was described as an inferior being incapable of taking advantage of the education that was provided for him. In Alabama Booker T. Washington used his influence to defeat the bill before the legislature which was designed to limit the appropriations for Negro schools. But in 1890 the influence of Washington, who was beginning his campaign to make the education of the Negro acceptable to the South, was insufficient to overcome the class interests involved in the bill.[19] As a result of the policy of restricting the public support for Negro education, during the first decade of the present century the education of the Negro had improved very slightly since 1875.

[18] See p. 155ff. above.

[19] Bond, *op. cit.*, p. 107. See also the same author's *Negro Education in Alabama: A Study in Cotton and Steel* (Washington, D.C., 1939) for the most penetrating study to date of the influence of economic and social factors, including class and race, in the education of the Negro.

In 1912 the fifteen southern States and the District of Columbia spent $36,649,827 in teachers' salaries on the education of 3,552,431 white children and $5,860,876 in teachers' salaries for the education of 1,852,181 Negro children 6 to 14 years of age.[20] Thus there was spent $10.32 for each white child and $2.89 for each Negro child. The disparity between the per capita spent for Negro and white children increased with the increase in the percentage of Negroes in the population of the counties of the South. For example, in those counties where Negroes constituted less than 10 per cent of the population, the per capita for Negroes was $7.23 as compared with $7.96 for whites, whereas in the "Black Belt" counties, where Negroes constituted 75 per cent and over of the population, the per capita for Negro children was $1.78 as compared with $22.22 for white children. In addition to appropriation for the common or elementary schools, the southern states appropriated $6,429,991 for secondary or higher schools for whites and only $355,720 for Negro agricultural and mechanical schools. In the entire South there were only 64 public high schools for Negroes, 45 having four-year courses and 18 three-year courses.[21] The majority of the public high schools were located in the border states of the South. There were less than 25,000 Negro children enrolled in secondary schools and about a half of these pupils were enrolled in privately supported schools.

RÔLE OF PHILANTHROPY IN NEGRO EDUCATION

Within a few years after Emancipation, a number of philanthropic foundations began to aid Negro education in the South. The Peabody Fund, which was established in 1867 through a gift of $1,000,000 by George Peabody, aided in establishing common schools for Negroes. The trustees of the Fund had certain notions concerning race relations since the fund made the provisions in 1871, when white and colored teachers were receiving the same pay, that Negro schools should receive two-thirds of the allotment made to white schools. The trustees opposed the Civil Rights Bill pending in Congress in 1873 and gave $800 to Fisk University in 1869 in preference to

[20] Bureau of Education, *Negro Education*, Vol. 2, pp. 9-11.
[21] *Ibid.*, pp. 15-16.

Berea College, where Negroes and whites were educated together. In 1880, the Peabody Fund established the Peabody Normal College in Nashville for the training of white teachers and began making contributions to Negro and white normal schools. The Peabody Fund was dissolved in 1914 and $350,000 was turned over to the John Slater Fund.[22]

The John F. Slater Fund, which was established through a gift of $1,000,000 by John F. Slater of Norwich, Connecticut in 1882, was devoted at first to private schools offering higher education and to vocational work in public schools. But because of the influence of Booker T. Washington, the Fund changed its emphasis to industrial education. Another change in the character of the educational work supported by the Fund occurred in 1910 when Dr. James H. Dillard became the general agent. Under his direction the Fund began to support a program of teacher-training for the graduates of the poor rural Negro elementary schools, who generally became the teachers in these schools. By such a program the quality of education was improved without arousing opposition to a program of high school education for Negroes. However, the result of this program was that a program of secondary education for Negroes was gradually incorporated into the public system of education. By 1929 there were 368 county training schools for Negroes receiving $135,866 from the Slater Fund aided by the General Education Board. The important fact, however, is that nearly two million dollars of public tax funds were also spent on these schools.[23]

Dr. Dillard was also responsible for increasing the effectiveness of another philanthropic fund interested in the education of the Negro in the South. The Jeanes Fund was created through a gift of $200,000 in 1905 by Miss Anna T. Jeanes, a Quaker woman of Philadelphia, who wanted to aid the "little county schools." At first the plan was to employ a "Jeanes" teacher who would be stationed in a demonstration center in the county. Under a new plan, accepted by Dr. Dillard, the "Jeanes" teacher became a supervisor of the Negro schools in the county. In 1929 there were 313 Jeanes supervisors in 311 coun-

[22] Bond, *op. cit.*, pp. 131-33.   [23] *Ibid.*, pp. 133-35.

ties, receiving $104,095 from the Jeanes Fund and nearly $200,000 from public funds.[24]

The most important contribution of northern philanthropy to the elementary education of the Negro in the rural South has come from the Julius Rosenwald Fund. The interest of the Fund in the education of the Negro in the rural South was due to a visit of Julius Rosenwald to Tuskegee Institute in 1911.[25] Although Rosenwald had pledged $25,000 to Tuskegee Institute, he was anxious to relieve the conditions in the rural communities. He agreed to help Booker T. Washington build schools in the rural South by supplementing the contributions of the counties and individuals in the communities. The administration of the program was placed first under the direction of a member of Tuskegee Institute staff but was later placed under the direction of an office set up in Nashville to administer the fund. The first six rural schools built in Alabama were built at a cost of $5,354.14, to which Rosenwald contributed $1,976.76 and Negroes, local white residents, and the state of Alabama the remainder. At the time of Washington's death in 1915, 80 rural schools had been built in Alabama, Georgia, and Tennessee. When Rosenwald died in 1932, 5,357 school buildings had been erected with a pupil capacity of 663,615, which meant that between 25 and 40 per cent of all Negro children were in Rosenwald schools. These schools had cost $28,408,520, to which the Fund had contributed 15 per cent, the Negroes 17 per cent, local white friends 4 per cent, and public tax funds 64 per cent. Thus the Fund had stimulated the public authorities as well as the Negro to make substantial contributions to the elementary education of the rural Negro.

INEQUALITIES IN EDUCATIONAL PROVISIONS FOR NEGROES

Despite the stimulation and the substantial financial assistance provided by philanthropic funds for the education of the Negro in the South, the educational facilities for Negro children have remained

[24] *Ibid.*, pp. 135-37.
[25] *Ibid.*, pp. 140-43. See also M. R. Werner, *Julius Rosenwald* (New York, 1939), pp. 128-35.

much inferior to those provided for white children. This has been shown by Bond in the study of the development of Negro education in Alabama and North Carolina and the City of Nashville, Tennessee.[26] During the year 1907-1908 the ratio of per capita expenditure for white children to that for Negro children in terms of teachers' salaries was $5.67 to $1.00. The ratio was not substantially reduced until after 1920. By 1929-1930 the ratio had been reduced from a peak of $6.46 to $1.00 in 1919 to $4.15 to $1.00. Although North Carolina had enjoyed the reputation of being the fairest southern State in expenditures for Negro education, the same pattern was observable. In North Carolina around the opening of the century, as in Alabama when Negroes had political power, the expenditures for Negro and white children were nearly equal. By the year 1907-1908, the ratio of per capita expenditure for white children to per capita expenditure for Negro children was $2.10 to $1.00. A quarter of a century later, 1932-1933, the ratio of per capita expenditure for white children to that for colored children was $2.09 to $1.00.

In four selected counties of Alabama, arranged according to the proportion of Negroes in their population, it was found that the ratio of per capita expenditure for white children to that for Negro children increased with the proportion of Negroes in the population. For example, in Walker County, where Negroes constituted 13 per cent of the population in 1910 and 9.7 per cent in 1930, the ratio of per capita expenditure for white children to that for Negro children was $1.37 to $1.00 in 1929-1930. On the other hand, in Lowndes County in the "Black Belt," where Negroes constituted 90 per cent of the population in 1910 and 91.2 per cent in 1930, $25.26 was spent on each white child as compared with $1.00 spent on each Negro child. There had been very little change since 1910. The same tendency for the ratio of per capita expenditure for the children of the two races to vary according to the proportion of Negroes in the population was found in the counties of North Carolina. In the case of Nashville, Tennessee, it was found that during the 62-year period from 1870 to 1932, there had been very little change in the ratio of per capita expenditure for the two races. In 1870-1871, the ratio of per capita

[26] Bond, *op. cit.*, pp. 152-67.

expenditure for white children to that for Negro children was $1.56 to $1.00, while in 1931-1933 the ratio was $1.59 to $1.00.

The continued disparity between expenditures for white and Negro children is not completely revealed in terms of expenditures for teachers' salaries. In spite of the tendency in some parts of the South for the disparity to be reduced in regard to teachers' salaries, considerable discrimination against Negroes continues in regard to expenditures for buildings, equipment, and such new services as transportation. The situation in North Carolina, which represents the best situation in the South, has been described as follows:

In 1924-1925, for example, $6,667,797 was spent on new buildings and sites for rural North Carolina white children, compared to $444,285 for the same purpose for rural Negro children. Per capita expenditures for teachers' salaries were proportionately three and one-quarter times as large for white children as for Negro children, but building expenditures were almost seven times as large for whites as for Negroes. In servicing a debt incurred largely through building schoolhouses for white children, rural North Carolina spent in 1924-1925, $6,875,870, a sum more than four times as large as the expenditures in the same year for teachers' salaries for the thirty per cent of the school population which was made up of Negroes.

Another item for expenditure, increasingly large in the last few years, is that of transportation. In 1929-1930, rural North Carolina spent $2,181,130 in transporting 172,286 white children to school, but almost two hundred thousand dollars less for the salaries of teachers for 190,817 Negro children enrolled in North Carolina rural schools in this year. Indeed, in 1929-1930, North Carolina spent more money for school trucks for white—$325,290—than it did for new schools for Negro children—$209,911. On repairs to furniture, apparatus, equipment, heating, lighting, and plumbing, the white rural schools of North Carolina spent in 1929-1930 several thousand more dollars than was spent for all new buildings and sites for Negro children.[27]

STATUS OF NEGRO EDUCATION DURING THE
PERIOD OF THE NEW DEAL

During the depression years Negro schools suffered curtailment in regard to both the length of the school term and teachers' salaries.

[27] *The Education of the Negro in the American Social Order* by Horace M. Bond, pp. 164-65. Copyright 1934 by Prentice-Hall, Inc.

Even where there was a policy of making the same proportion of curtailment of support for the schools of the two races, the Negroes suffered more than whites. Reduction of expenditures for Negro schools cut into the heart of the inferior teaching programs provided them, whereas curtailment of expenditures for white schools often only eliminated extracurricular activities. During the period of recovery initiated by the New Deal, a study of the "Special Problems of Negro Education" was undertaken by an Advisory Committee on Education appointed by the President of the United States in 1936.[28] The facts presented in this study indicate the situation of Negro schools in the middle of the third decade of the present century.[29]

In 1933-1934 there were in the 18 southern and border states which require the separation of the races in schools, slightly more than 10,000,000 children 5 to 17 years of age enrolled in schools, 24 per cent of whom were Negro children.[30] However, in regard to school attendance there were significant differences between the children of the two races. In regard to children within the compulsory school-age, 7 to 15 years, 84 per cent of the colored children as compared with 91 per cent of the white children were in schools. The difference in percentage of the children of the two races attending schools varied for different states. For example, in Alabama 79 per cent of the Negroes of school-age as compared with 92 per cent of the white children were in schools. Almost the same difference between the attendance of the children of the two races existed in Georgia and South Carolina. On the other hand, in West Virginia and Kentucky almost the same percentage of Negro children as white children were attending schools. The difference in the percentage of white and Negro children attending schools was more marked in the rural areas than in the cities of these states.[31] This was due to the fact that a

[28] Doxey A. Wilkerson, *Special Problems of Negro Education* (Washington, 1939).
[29] The discussion which follows is based principally upon the facts revealed in this study.
[30] These 18 states were: Alabama, Arkansas, Delaware, District of Columbia, Florida, Georgia, Kentucky, Louisiana, Maryland, Mississippi, Missouri, North Carolina, Oklahoma, South Carolina, Tennessee, Texas, Virginia, West Virginia.
[31] In the District of Columbia, which is completely urbanized and under the federal government, 98 per cent of the white children as compared with 96 per cent of the Negro children were enrolled in schools.

higher percentage of Negro children attend school in the urban areas than in the rural areas. For example, in the rural areas of Alabama 62 per cent of the Negro children, 5 to 17 years, were attending school as compared with 72 per cent of the Negro children in urban areas. In Florida the difference was most marked, where 60 per cent of the rural Negro children as compared with 77 per cent of the urban Negro children were in schools. The regularity of attendance of enrolled Negro children was slightly less (78 out of 100 enrolled Negro children as compared with 81 out of 100 enrolled white children) than that of white children.

Not only was a larger number of Negro children than white children out of school, but the school term for Negro children was shorter than that for white children in the South. In the eighteen states with separate school systems the average length of the school term for whites was 167 days as compared with 146 days for colored children. The difference in length of school term was greatest in Louisiana, where the term for white children was 175 days as compared with 128 days for colored children. While in most of the states the Negro children would require one extra year to complete the eight years of schooling given white children, in Mississippi, Louisiana, and South Carolina, they would require from two and a half to four and a half extra years to receive the eight years of elementary education given white children.

The majority of the Negro children attending school were concentrated in the first four grades of the elementary school. Over 70 per cent of the Negro children as compared with 50 per cent of the white children were below the fifth grade. Even more striking was the fact that nearly 47 per cent of the Negro children as compared with 28 per cent of the white children were in the first and second grades. These differences were due to the inadequate school facilities for Negroes and the greater tendency of Negro children to drop out of school. Out of every 100 Negro children who entered the first grade only 14 reached the first year of high school while 49 out of every 100 white children who entered the first grade reached that level. The irregular attendance of Negro children and the tendency on their part to drop out of school were related to the lack of transportation facili-

ties. In ten of the southern states more than twelve million dollars
was spent on the transportation of school children; yet Negro children
who constituted 34 per cent of the school population received less
than 3 per cent of this fund. In Mississippi no money was spent on
the transportation of Negro children and in Georgia and South Carolina less than half of one per cent was spent on Negro children.

The inferior type of education which was provided for the Negro
child was due partly to the fact that Negro teachers were required to
teach more children than white teachers. For the eighteen states there
was an average of 34 pupils per white teacher and 43 pupils per Negro
teacher. In Alabama, Georgia, Louisiana, Mississippi, and South Carolina the difference was even greater, ranging from 10 in Mississippi
to 19 in South Carolina.[32] It was estimated that nearly 16,000 additional Negro teachers would have to be added in order to equalize the
number of pupils per teacher for the two races.

This extra teaching burden was placed upon Negro teachers who,
especially on the elementary level, had had less training than white
teachers. According to the National Survey of the Education of Teachers in 1930-1931, it was found that 23 per cent of the Negro teachers in
elementary schools as compared with 6 per cent of the white teachers
in 17 southern states had not received any formal education beyond
high school. In the rural areas the difference in educational status was
even greater, the proportion of Negro teachers with training beyond
high school being 5 per cent as compared with 36 per cent for white
teachers. On the secondary level, the difference in the educational
status of the teachers of the two races was less marked. Twenty-eight
per cent of the Negro teachers and 21 per cent of the white teachers
had not received four years of college work, while 11 per cent of
Negro teachers as compared with 25 per cent of white teachers had
done graduate work.

The inferior educational status of Negro teachers was related to the
low salaries paid Negro teachers. The average annual salaries paid
Negro teachers in 17 states in 1935-1936 ranged from $282 in Georgia

[32] In West Virginia the situation of Negro teachers was better than that of
white teachers since there were 22 pupils per Negro teacher and 33 pupils per
white teacher.

to $2,376 in the District of Columbia.[33] There were variations in the differences in the salaries of white and colored teachers in the southern states. In Mississippi Negro teachers received on the average only 32 per cent and in Georgia and South Carolina 37 per cent as much as white teachers. In Alabama, Georgia, and Louisiana, the average salaries of Negro teachers was only slightly higher in relation to the salaries of white teachers than in Mississippi and Georgia and South Carolina. Even in North Carolina, Negro teachers received only two-thirds as much as white teachers. The disparity between the salaries of white and Negro teachers has been justified on the grounds that the standard of living of Negroes in the South is lower than that of whites. But this, as Myrdal has pointed out, is an example of the popular rationalizations which are used to justify economic discrimination.[34]

Inequalities in the educational provisions for white and Negro children were greatest in respect to school plant and equipment. In the 18 states with separate schools there were 24,405 public elementary and 2,305 public high schools for Negroes in 1935-1936. Over a half— 55 per cent—of the elementary schools were 1-room schools and another 19 per cent were 2-room schools. A large proportion of the Negro schools were housed in churches, lodge halls, old stores, and tenant houses.[35] In the 10 southern states for which data were available the value of school property used for school purposes for whites amounted to $836,301,648 as compared with $68,914,048 for Negro children.[36] Thus while the enrollment of Negro children constituted 30 per cent of

[33] Statistics for West Virginia where salaries for 1931-1932 were almost the same were not included. In the District of Columbia salaries of white and colored teachers are the same.

[34] "The rationalizations amount to this: since Negroes are poor and always have been poor, they are inferior and should be kept inferior. Then they are no trouble but rather a convenience. It is seldom expressed so bluntly. Expressions like 'standard of living' and 'cost of living' are employed because they have a flavor of scientific objectivity. They avoid hard thinking. They enable one to stand for the *status quo* in economic discrimination without flagrantly exposing oneself even to oneself." *An American Dilemma* by Gunnar Myrdal, vol. I, p. 218. Copyright 1934 by Harper & Brothers.

[35] In Mississippi nearly two-fifths of the Negro schools were housed in these nonpublic buildings.

[36] The ten southern states were: Alabama, Arkansas, Florida, Georgia, Maryland, Mississippi, North Carolina, South Carolina, Texas, and Virginia.

the total enrollment, the value of the property used for Negro schools constituted only 8 per cent of the total. The differential for certain states was, of course, greater than that for the combined 10 states. For example, in Mississippi, where Negro children constituted 49 per cent of the total enrollment, the value of Negro school property was only 7 per cent of the total; and in South Carolina, where Negro children constituted 46 per cent of the total enrollment, the value of Negro school property was only 12 per cent of the total. When the value of school property was estimated in terms of per white and per Negro pupil, for every dollar represented in school property for each white child only 19 cents was invested in school property for each Negro child. Moreover, it should be pointed out that 32 per cent of the Negro school property was in Rosenwald schools.[37]

In the field of secondary education, the provisions for Negro children were much inferior to those on the elementary level. By the mid-thirties the enrollment of white children in public high schools in the South was almost the same—55 per cent—as compared with 60 per cent for the nation as a whole. But for the year 1933-1934 only 19 per cent of the Negro children of high school age were in high schools. In the 18 states with separate schools 1,077 Negro high schools reported a total enrollment of 163,331 pupils. Although slightly more than two-thirds of the Negro children of high school age were in rural areas, less than a half of the high schools were in rural areas whereas the majority of the white high schools were in rural areas. From the standpoint of enrollment, only 21 per cent of the Negro children of high school age were in rural high schools. There were 230 counties in the South where Negroes constituted 12.5 per cent or more of the total population, that had no high school facilities for Negroes and 195 other counties with a similar proportion of Negroes with no four-year high schools for Negroes. Private secondary schools provided education for 4 per cent of the Negro children enrolled in secondary schools, while the junior college movement had hardly secured a foothold in Negro education.

During the latter half of the decade, 1930 to 1940, there were some

[37] In 12 States, Louisiana and Tennessee being added to the ten given above.

improvements to be noted in the educational provisions for the Negro in the South.[38] Despite the fact that there was a decrease in the number of Negro children 5 to 17 years of age between 1930 and 1940, the percentage of the Negro school population in this age group enrolled in the 18 states with separate schools increased from 82.8 to 85.9. What is even more significant is that while Negro children enrolled in the elementary schools scarcely changed, the increase in the number enrolled in the high schools amounted to 35 per cent. The greater regularity of attendance of the Negro pupils was indicated by the fact that the percentage of enrolled pupils in daily attendance increased 3.1. The average number of days attended by each Negro pupil in elementary and secondary schools combined increased from 113 in 1935-1936 to 126 in 1939-1940. Nearly a quarter of the Negro pupils in the South were enrolled in high schools and for the year 1939-1940 there were 30,009 Negro high school graduates.

In spite of these gains in the education of the Negro in the southern states, important inequalities continued to exist. The proportion of 1- and 2-teacher schools for Negro children had not declined.[39] Although the teaching load of Negro teachers had declined, Negro teachers still had on the average 7.5 more pupils than white teachers. More striking still were the inequalities in salaries paid Negro and white teachers despite comparable training and experience. In Alabama, Georgia, Louisiana, Mississippi, and South Carolina, the average salaries of Negro teachers were less than half the average salaries of white teachers. In terms of current expense per pupil in average daily attendance during the year 1939-1940, the southern states spent $58.69 on each white child as compared with $18.82 on each Negro child. The greatest disparity was in Mississippi where $52.01 was spent on each white child and $7.36 on each Negro child.

[38] See Federal Security Agency, U. S. Office of Education, *Statistics of the Education of Negroes.* Circular No. 215 (June, 1943). By David T. Blose and Ambrose Caliver.

[39] As we have noted 74 per cent of the schools in 18 states in 1934-1935 were 1- and 2-room schools. According to *Statistics of the Education of Negroes,* p. 7, 82 per cent of the Negro elementary schools in Alabama, Arkansas, Delaware, Louisiana, Maryland, Mississippi, South Carolina, and Virginia are still 1- and 2-teacher schools.

DISCRIMINATION IN APPORTIONMENT OF
FEDERAL FUNDS

So far we have considered inequalities in the education of the Negro where only the appropriation of state funds was involved. But there has been discrimination also in the distribution of federal funds. The largest and most important educational program subsidized by the federal government involves vocational education. It was initiated in 1917 with the passage of the Smith-Hughes Act. The appropriations provided by this act and the scope of its program have been supplemented and enlarged by three subsequent acts.[40] The funds provided by these acts are apportioned among the states on the basis of their rural population for vocational agriculture and on the basis of their urban population for home economics and trade and industries. During the year 1934-1935, there were 260,826 pupils enrolled in federally aided vocational courses in the 18 states with separate school systems.[41] Although Negroes constituted 21 per cent of the population of these 18 states, there were only 73,428 Negro pupils or 16 per cent of the total and these pupils were beneficiaries of only 10 per cent of the expenditures.

The inequalities in the apportionment of federal funds become more apparent when they are considered from the standpoint of the three types of vocational education programs. The white pupils were almost evenly divided among the three types of program, 36 per cent being in agriculture, 34 in home economics, and 30 per cent in trade and industries. On the other hand, 55 per cent of the Negro pupils were enrolled in vocational agriculture, 29 per cent in home economics, and only 16 per cent in trade and industries. The unequal expenditures for whites and Negroes varied for the different types of vocational education. Negroes received 12 per cent of the federal funds for vocational agriculture though they constituted 24 per cent of the rural population; 9 per cent of the expenditures for home economics though they constituted 21 per cent of the total population;

[40] The George-Reed Act in 1929; the George-Ellzey Act in 1934; and the George-Deen Act in 1936.
[41] Wilkerson, *op. cit.*, pp. 92ff.

and only 5 per cent of the expenditures for trade and industries though they constituted 17 per cent of the urban population.[42] Instead of receiving $777,735, which was their share of federal funds, Negro pupils received only $354,934 or stated otherwise, $422,801 was diverted from Negroes to whites for vocational education. Although data are not available, there is good reason to assume that Negroes did not receive as great a proportion of state and local appropriations for vocational education as of federal funds.[43]

The main result of the discrimination against Negro pupils in regard to vocational education has been that Negro pupils have not received the industrial education provided white pupils. The small share of federal funds which have been allotted to Negroes has been devoted mainly to vocational agriculture and home economics (farming and domestic service in the popular sense), occupations which are regarded as proper for the Negro. The United States Office of Education has been responsible for permitting the opposition of southern whites to technical training for Negroes to determine the distribution of federal funds for the vocational education of Negroes. As a consequence, when the United States entered World War II, Negroes lacked training in industrial skills which an equitable distribution of federal funds for vocational education in trade and industries would have provided. The results of the failure to provide the proper vocational education for Negroes have been well summed up by Weaver:

At that time [in 1936], less than 2 per cent of the male Negro skilled mechanics in the nation had depended entirely upon formal trade school education as a means of preparation for skilled work; only 2.3 per cent had depended upon vocational education and apprenticeship, 7.0 per cent had been trained by a combination of vocational education and experience and 5 per cent had depended upon a combination of vocational education, apprenticeship and experience. In the Middle Atlantic states, 3.6 per cent of the skilled male Negroes

[42] Negro schools received only 11 per cent of the expenditures for teacher training in Land Grant colleges.

[43] Charles H. Thompson, "The Federal Program of Vocational Education in Negro Schools of Less than College Grade," *Journal of Negro Education*, Vol. 7, p. 317. This article provides a thorough analysis of the discrimination in the apportionment of federal funds for vocational education in the southern states.

listed trade schooling as their principal method of preparation. In the South Atlantic states, where vocational education for Negroes has been emphasized (in words), only 1.5 per cent of the skilled Negro men reported vocational education as the means of preparation for their occupation. As a matter of fact, over 91 per cent of the Negro male skilled workers in the South had not received any vocational training, a higher proportion than that for the nation as a whole, where 83.6 per cent had had no such training. In those regions where vocational education had been most helpful in preparing Negro men for skilled work, it was centered in unsegregated school systems (in the North).[44]

EDUCATIONAL PROBLEMS OF NEGROES IN THE NORTH

During and following World War I, hundreds of thousands of Negroes crowded into the Negro areas of northern cities. The main institution of the larger community with which the tens of thousands of Negro families had contact was the public school. In fact, some of the migrants had left the South in order that their children might have an opportunity for education. In the northern city the Negro child not only was required to attend school but he enjoyed more nearly equal education with white children. As a consequence of the mass migrations to northern cities a larger proportion of Negro children had access to the standard American education than at any time in the history of the Negro.

The mass migrations of Negroes from the rural South naturally created educational as well as social problems. There was the problem of acquainting the Negro children with the physical school plants in the northern city. Then there was the problem of inducting them into the routine which has become a part of the organization and functioning of urban schools. However, the most important problem was that of adjusting the Negro children to the curriculum of the school in the northern city.[45] First, there was much retardation. The Negro

[44] See *Negro Labor, A National Problem* by Robert C. Weaver, pp. 43-44. Copyright 1946 by Robert C. Weaver. Reprinted by permission of Harcourt, Brace and Company, Inc.

[45] E. George Payne, "Negroes in the Public Elementary Schools of the North," *The Annals*, Vol. 140, The American Academy of Political and Social Science, 1928, pp. 224-33.

child who had been in a third or fifth grade in the South was not prepared for the same grade in the North. In the South the Negro child had attended school only from three to six or seven months during the year. Moreover, the quality of education as well as the quantity of education which he had received was far inferior to that provided in the North. In the North Negro children had to become accustomed to attending school with white children and to having white teachers. The white teachers themselves were not prepared to deal with the problems which the influx of Negroes from the South, especially the rural South, presented. In fact, the problems presented by the Negro often aroused latent attitudes and confirmed stereotyped beliefs concerning Negroes.

The immediate reaction of the white community to the problems created by the presence of large numbers of Negroes from the South was that Negroes should be restricted to segregated schools. In some cities of the North, especially those near the border states, a system of segregation came into existence despite the legal right of Negroes to attend all public schools. Because of the problems facing Negro children in northern cities many articles were written to prove the advantages of segregated schools for Negroes in the northern cities.[46] It was argued that segregated schools offered the most realistic manner in which to deal with the Negro migrants from the South, that Negro students are inspired to achieve when they have Negro teachers, that there are more graduates from segregated high schools than from mixed high schools. Negro children were supposed to enjoy all these advantages in segregated schools while receiving the same education as white children. On the opposite side appeared articles that showed that segregated schools were always inferior, that separate schools were created by selfish race-leaders, and that they caused greater misunderstanding between the races and encouraged separation in other relations of the races.

As a matter of fact, the arguments in favor of separate schools for Negroes were often based upon certain implicit assumptions concern-

---

[46] See articles presented in *The Journal of Negro Education*, Vol. IV (July, 1935). See also L. A. Pechstein, "The Problem of Negro Education in Northern and Border Cities," *The Elementary School Journal*, Vol. 30, No. 3.

ing Negroes. Generally they implied that the Negro was not a fit associate of white children or that they were inferior.[47] Moreover, there is much hypocrisy on the part of whites who argue that separate schools should be established for the benefit of Negroes. Usually Negroes who argue for separate schools "are either citizens with sons and daughters to employ, or politicians looking for extra opportunities for petty graft and patronage."[48] Of course, sometimes race-conscious Negroes favor segregated schools as a defensive measure. In the case of both white and Negro proponents of separate schools, there is evidence of a lack of understanding of the larger cultural problems of Negroes in the urban environment.

Before considering these problems, it is necessary to know what is the actual situation of the Negro as regards public education in northern cities.[49] First, it should be noted that 12 northern (including western) states forbid segregation; two states, Wyoming and Indiana, have permissive legislation for separate schools; and 14 states are silent on the question of segregation.[50] Nevertheless, there are segregated schools in the North and whether there is segregation or not is not determined by the existence of the laws forbidding segregation, the absence of such laws, or permissive legislation. Although it has not been determined statistically how many schools are segregated, one estimate gives one-fourth of the schools as segregated, one-half as being mixed schools and one-fourth as being schools in which Negroes

[47] See Bond, *op. cit.*, pp. 384ff. for critical examination of arguments on both sides of the question.

[48] *The Education of the Negro in the American Social Order* by Horace M. Bond, p. 385. Copyright 1934 by Prentice-Hall, Inc.

[49] See L. D. Reddick, "The Education of Negroes in States Where Separate Schools Are Not Legal," *The Journal of Negro Education*, Vol. XVI (1947), pp. 290-300, and in the same issue, pp. 301-10, Reid E. Jackson, "The Development and Character of Permissive and Partly Segregated Schools." This special issue of *The Journal of Negro Education*, which is devoted to "The Availability of Education in the Negro Separate School," contains the status of educational facilities for Negroes in each of the states with separate school systems.

[50] States forbidding segregation in education: Colorado, Connecticut, Idaho, Illinois, Massachusetts, Michigan, Minnesota, New Jersey, New York, Pennsylvania, Rhode Island, and Washington. States with permissive legislation for separate schools: Wyoming and Indiana. States silent on the question of segregation: California, Iowa, Maine, Montana, Nebraska, Nevada, New Hampshire, North Dakota, Ohio, Oregon, South Dakota, Utah, Vermont, and Wisconsin. Jackson, *op. cit.*, p. 301.

are thoroughly integrated.[51] A tabulation of 35 cities in 16 northern and western states indicated that there were definitely no Negro teachers in the schools of 13 cities and that there were Negro teachers in the same buildings as white teachers in 16 cities.[52] In at least six cities Negro teachers did not teach white children; but in all of the 35 cities white teachers taught Negro children. In six of the cities Negroes were principals of Negro schools, while only in New York City and Chicago were there Negro principals of schools with white students.

The problems of the Negro in the public schools in the northern city are very similar to those of immigrant children. In the northern city, as we have seen, Negroes are generally crowded into slum areas. This is owing primarily to their poverty though their cultural background is a factor not to be overlooked. The school buildings in the areas of Negro settlement are old and overcrowded.[53] But as in the immigrant community, there are areas in the Negro community which are differentiated on the basis of occupation, income, education, and general culture. The character of the schools in these areas reflects these differences. The Negro suffers, however, certain social handicaps which are not as great in the case of the immigrant. There is an attempt to restrict the Negro to the least desirable and lowest paid jobs. The normal expansion of the Negro population is restricted because the Negro is identified by his color. These barriers to the integration of the Negro into the urban community not only restrict his gradual integration into the school system but affect the incentives and the interest of Negro school children.

There are important factors in the cultural background of the Negro that have an unfavorable influence on the relation of the Negro children to the public school in the northern city. There is a large amount of family disorganization among Negroes in northern cities which results from the impact of city life upon the simple family

---

[51] See Reddick, *op. cit.*   [52] *Ibid.*, p. 299.

[53] In Chicago there is much overcrowding in the schools located in Negro communities. For example, in 1938 in Chicago 13 of the 15 schools running on "shifts" were in Negro neighborhoods. Even as late as 1944 the claim of the school board that this system had been abolished was disputed by Negro leaders. As a result Negro children spent half of the day in school and the other half of the day on the streets. Drake and Cayton, *op. cit.*, p. 202n.

organization which developed in the South. This affects not only the school attendance of Negro children and their behavior in school but it affects their learning and their interest in school.[54] The influence of the cultural background is intensified where the Negro child is segregated and does not expect the reward of an improved economic status when he has completed his education. The situation is aggravated by the tendency on the part of vocational guidance teachers to discourage Negro students from preparing themselves for jobs other than those traditionally held by Negroes.

EDUCATIONAL ADVANTAGES ENJOYED BY NEGRO CHILDREN IN THE NORTH

Despite the problems and disadvantages which Negro children face in northern cities, they have been able to acquire more education than Negro children in southern cities. This is revealed when one compares the education of Negroes 25 years old and over in the four northern cities with Negro populations of over 100,000 with Negroes of the same age group in similar cities in the South. (See Tables XXXI and XXXII.) Nearly twice the percentage of adult Negroes in southern cities as in northern cities have received no schooling.[55] About the

TABLE XXXI

Negro and Total Population 25 Years Old and Over, by Years of School Completed, for Four Southern Cities: 1940 *

YEARS OF SCHOOL COMPLETED	Atlanta		Birmingham		Memphis		New Orleans	
	NEGRO	TOTAL	NEGRO	TOTAL	NEGRO	TOTAL	NEGRO	TOTAL
No School Years Completed	6.4	3.0	8.5	4.1	6.3	3.2	8.2	4.0
Grade School: 1 to 4 years	30.8	14.1	29.9	14.2	28.2	13.9	32.0	16.2
5 to 6 years	26.2	15.6	23.9	13.8	24.8	14.4	25.0	18.4
7 to 8 years	18.2	20.7	20.7	23.8	24.3	24.2	22.1	28.3
High School: 1 to 3 years	8.2	15.5	8.5	15.2	9.0	16.2	6.7	10.5
4 years	4.4	17.2	4.7	16.4	4.0	16.5	3.3	13.0

* *Sixteenth U. S. Census: 1940, Population*, Vol. II, Pts. 1, 2 and 3, Table 39; and Pt. 6, Tables B-39 and C-39.

[54] Truancy was prevalent among girls in both high schools in the Negro community in Chicago. Drake and Cayton, *op. cit.*, p. 656.

[55] Some of the Negroes 25 years old and over in the northern cities were, of course, born in the South. If Negroes born in the North could be separated from those born in the South the differences between the cities of the two sections would be even greater than the tables indicate.

same relation is found in respect to Negro adults who have completed only four years of elementary education. For example, in Chicago 15 per cent of the adult Negroes have had only four years of elementary education as compared with 30 per cent for Birmingham, Alabama. Whereas the percentages for the four southern cities vary only slightly, there is considerable variation for the northern cities. In New York City about one-eighth of the adult Negroes have completed one to four years of school whereas in Philadelphia a fifth are in this class. Moreover, the proportion of Negro adults who have had only 5 or 6 years of education in Philadelphia is close to that of southern cities. But when one considers the group with seventh or eighth grade education the difference between southern and northern cities is marked. Roughly about a third of the adult Negroes in northern cities as compared with less than a fifth in Atlanta to about a fourth in Memphis have had a seventh or eighth grade education. The same outstanding differences are found in regard to secondary education. About twice the proportion of adult Negroes in the northern cities as in the southern cities have completed one to three years or four years of high school education.

TABLE XXXII

Negro and Total Population 25 Years Old and Over, by Years of School Completed, for Four Northern Cities: 1940 *

YEARS OF SCHOOL COMPLETED	*Chicago*		*Detroit*		*New York*		*Philadelphia*	
	NEGRO	TOTAL	NEGRO	TOTAL	NEGRO	TOTAL	NEGRO	TOTAL
No School Years Completed	3.4	4.1	3.7	3.1	3.4	7.6	5.0	5.1
Grade School: 1 to 4 years	14.7	7.5	17.2	8.9	12.8	7.2	19.6	8.1
5 to 6 years	17.5	8.6	20.0	10.6	17.0	7.8	23.3	12.2
7 to 8 years	33.3	39.7	29.1	32.5	35.6	40.9	30.1	39.9
High School: 1 to 3 years	15.1	15.2	16.5	18.8	14.7	12.7	11.9	14.3
4 years	9.4	14.7	8.4	16.6	9.6	12.4	5.0	12.1

* *Sixteenth U. S. Census: 1940, Population*, Vol. II, Pts. 2 and 3, Table A-39; Pt. 5, Table C-39; Pt. 6; Table B-39.

The above tables also enable us to compare the education of Negroes with that of the total population of these eight cities. In the four southern cities the proportion of Negroes without schooling is twice that of the population as a whole.[56] The proportion of Negroes without schooling in the northern cities is about the same as that of the entire population with the exception of New York City, which has a large proportion of foreign-born whites who have had no schooling. Both northern and southern cities show about the same disparity between the proportion of Negroes and the total population who have received only one to four years of education. On the other hand, the disparity between the education of Negroes and the entire population in southern cities is most striking in respect to those who have attended high school. In southern cities the proportion of Negroes with one to three years of high school education is about three-fifths the proportion for the population as a whole, while in northern cities the proportion for Negroes approximates that of the population as a whole. Even more striking is the fact that the proportion of Negroes with four years of high school education in southern cities is only one-fourth that for the total population. The proportion of Negroes with four years of high school education in northern cities ranges from one-half to three-fourths of that for the entire population.

EDUCATION OF NEGROES DURING WORLD WAR II

World War II focused the attention of the nation on the educational deficiencies of the Negro. A four months' study during the summer and early fall of 1941 revealed that five times as many Negro as white registrants for Selective Service were rejected.[57] This was the result largely of the illiteracy of the Negro registrants since more than a third of the Negro rejections were owing to educational deficiency. About eleven times as many Negro registrants (12.3 per cent as compared with 1.1 per cent) as white registrants were rejected because they were unable "to read and write the English language as well as a student who has completed four years in an American grammar

---

[56] The disparity between the schooling of Negroes and whites in southern cities as compared with northern cities is even greater than is indicated by these figures since Negroes constitute a larger proportion of the population of the southern cities than of northern cities and thereby lower to a greater extent the school attainments of the population as a whole of southern cities.

[57] *Selective Service in Wartime.* Second Report of the Director of Selective Service, 1941-42 (Washington, 1943), p. 289.

school." [58] The high rejection rate for Negro registrants was related to the inadequate educational provisions of the southern states for Negroes.[59] The rejection rate among Negro registrants was lower in 26 states than in 10 southern states. This situation caused the nation to become more conscious of the necessity to educate the Negro if he were to assume his responsibilities at least in modern warfare. At least one southern newspaper did not fail to point to the fact that white boys were being killed while Negro boys were being rejected for military service because of their lack of education.

During World War II, it appears that the gains in educational opportunities which the Negro made during the decade, 1930 to 1940, were consolidated but there is little indication of significant improvements since the war. In the 17 southern states where separate school systems are maintained the average length of the school term for Negroes had increased from 156 days in 1939-1940 to 164 days in 1943-1944 as compared with 173.5 days for white pupils.[60] The average daily attendance of Negro pupils in 1943-1944 was 81.4 per cent as compared with 83.6 per cent for white pupils. The salaries of Negro teachers had increased approximately 50 per cent between 1939-1940 and 1943-1944. In North Carolina and Tennessee, Negro and white teachers with the same training were receiving equal or approximately the same salaries. Despite these improvements, 60 per cent of the Negro pupils were enrolled in classes below the fifth grade. High school facilities for Negro pupils would have to be increased threefold in order to accommodate the same proportion of Negro pupils as white pupils in high schools. The wide difference in the expenditure per white and per Negro pupil has shown little change despite the increase in the expenditures per Negro child. The great disparity between the equipment provided the white pupils and expenditures for their transportation and similar provisions for Negro pupils continues

[58] See American Teachers Association Studies, *The Black and White of Rejections for Military Service* (Montgomery, Ala., August, 1944), p. 2. This study presents a thorough statistical analysis of the relation of white and Negro rejections to the educational provisions of the different states for the two races.

[59] See *ibid., passim.*

[60] See *The Journal of Negro Education*, Vol. XVI, pp. 439 ff. and United States Office of Education, *Biennial Survey of Education in the United States. Statistics of State School Systems, 1943-44*, Chapter II (Washington, 1946), p. 12.

to exist. There is no evidence that separate educational facilities will ever provide equal educational advantages.

EDUCATION OF NEGROES AS A NATIONAL PROBLEM

The inequalities in the education of Negro and white children in the South are the result partly of the inability of the South to support separate school systems for the two races that would measure up to national norms.[61] Consequently, there has been agitation for federal support for education which would enable those sections of the country with low per capita wealth to bring their school systems up to national norms. However, there is no evidence that federal aid to education under state and local control would insure equal educational facilities for Negro children in the South.[62] We have seen how the southern states have constantly diverted federal funds to the education of white children.[63] As a result there has been much agitation on the part of Negroes that proposed federal programs for aid to education contain specific stipulations for their share in federal funds on the basis of their numbers in states with separate school systems. A number of bills for federal aid to education which were introduced into the Congress in 1947 contained provisions for the "just and equitable" distribution of funds for a minority race in states with separate school systems.[64]

Since the inferior educational facilities provided for Negro children are an inevitable consequence of separate schools, there is a growing opinion among Negroes that court action should be taken to abolish separate schools.[65] Already through the National Association for the

[61] See Bond, *op cit.*, Chapter XII, "Financing Separate Systems," for a thorough analysis of the situation in the South.

[62] *Ibid.*, pp. 437ff. See also Howard H. Long, "Federal-Aid-to-Education Legislation." Current Trends, *The Journal of Negro Education*, Vol. XIII (1944), pp. 252-54.   [63] See pp. 438-40 above.

[64] In Senate Bill 472, a just and equitable apportionment for minority races is defined as "not less than the proportion that such minority race in such State bears to the total population of that State."

[65] See articles in *The Journal of Negro Education*, Vol. IV on legal status of separate schools and court action as a remedy. Concerning the present situation, see George M. Johnson and Jane Marshall Lucas, "The Present Legal Status of the Negro Separate School," *The Journal of Negro Education*, Vol. XVI, pp. 280-89.

Advancement of Colored People, Negroes have won cases in the Supreme Court respecting discrimination in the salaries of Negro teachers.[66] The attack on the segregated public school system has received encouragement from court decisions concerning separate schools for Mexicans and children of Latin origin in Orange County, California. In 1946 the District Court handed down an injunction' restraining the school authorities from setting up segregated schools for Mexican children.[67] This order was confirmed by the United States Circuit Court in 1947.[68] The Negro's attack upon the segregated school as being a denial of democracy has been strengthened by the report of the President's Committee on Civil Rights.[69] One of the specific recommendations of the Report was the prohibition of segregation in the public school system of the District of Columbia through congressional legislation.

The increasing extent to which public schools have become available for Negro children has been an index of their increasing participation in American culture. Where segregated school systems have existed, Negro children have been limited to that extent in their participation in American culture. The segregated school has always provided inferior educational facilities and has been the means of maintaining the social subordination of the Negro. In the unsegregated schools of the North the Negro child has come close to obtaining a standard American education and has to that extent participated in the general American culture. In recent years, especially as the result of the world crisis resulting from World War II, there is a growing recognition of the fact that the segregated school is a violation of the American democratic creed.

[66] See Leon A. Ransom, "Education and the Law," Current Trends, *The Journal of Negro Education*, Vol. XI, pp. 224-28; pp. 568-70; and Vol. XIII. pp. 128-30. See also The National Association for the Advancement of Colored People, *Teachers' Salaries in Black and White*. Pamphlet Reprinted February, 1942.

[67] See *Federal Supplement*, Vol. 64, pp. 544-51.

[68] See *Federal Reporter. Second Series*. Vol. 161, F2d., pp. 774-85.

[69] *To Secure These Rights*. The Report of the President's Committee on Civil Rights (Washington, 1947).

CHAPTER XVIII

Institutions of Higher Education

THE evolution of Negro institutions of higher education moved parallel to the development of elementary and secondary schools in the South. The Freedmen's Bureau and the various Freedmen's Aid Societies not only established common schools for Negroes following the Civil War but organized secondary schools and colleges for the training of teachers and the education of leaders. During this same period the different Negro denominational churches began to establish colleges. Later, the land-grant colleges for Negroes, made possible by the second Morrill Act, were organized in each of the southern states. These so-called Negro colleges and universities in the South were engaged principally in secondary education. Increasingly the Negro colleges devoted themselves to work on the college level as public support of secondary education for Negroes developed in the South. The number of Negroes attending northern schools has increased tremendously and Negroes are beginning to demand admission to the state-supported universities of the border and southern cities.

COLLEGES FOR NEGROES FOUNDED BEFORE THE CIVIL WAR

A number of schools for the higher education of Negroes were projected before the Civil War.[1] In Pittsburgh Avery College was operated from 1852 until after the Civil War. Ashmun Institute, which was renamed Lincoln University in 1866, was established by

---

[1] Horace M. Bond, *Education of the Negro in the American Social Order* (New York, 1934), p. 37.

the Presbyterians in Chester County, Pennsylvania, in 1854, though it did not open until 1857. Wilberforce University was established at Tawawa Springs, near Zenia, Ohio, by the Methodist Episcopal Church in 1856. This school was located in an area where southern planters had settled their mulatto offspring and other manumitted slaves on farms. In 1862 the African Methodist Episcopal Church bought the property. Despite these sporadic pre-Civil War attempts to create institutions of higher education for Negroes, the development of Negro institutions of higher education was mainly the result of the work of the Freedmen's Bureau and missionary societies following the Civil War.

DEVELOPMENT OF NEGRO COLLEGES FOLLOWING THE CIVIL WAR

In his 1866 report on his observations during a tour of inspection in 1865, the Bureau's general superintendent of education, J. W. Alvord, noted the eagerness on the part of the emancipated Negroes throughout the South to secure an education.[2] In a number of the cities of the South there was a much higher percentage of the Negro than white children attending schools. He noted that one school in New Orleans with 300 pupils and taught by "cultured colored men" could be favorably compared with an ordinary school in the North. But the number of "cultured colored men" was small and consequently there was a need for institutions in which teachers of the emancipated Negroes could be trained. The need was especially urgent because Negroes indicated a preference for Negro teachers. According to the calculations of the superintendent, 20,000 teachers were needed immediately for the more than a million Negro children who were eager for an education. A year later the superintendent reported that there were 581 Negro students enrolled in the 11 "high or normal" schools, among the 1,208 schools with 77,998 pupils.[3] In the same report the superintendent urged the improvement of the normal schools and suggested that higher institutions of education should be endowed and scholarships provided for students.

[2] Dwight O. W. Holmes, *The Evolution of the Negro College* (New York, 1934), pp. 45-46.   [3] Holmes, *op. cit.*, p. 46.

The report of the general superintendent of education on July 1, 1867 indicated that a number of institutions of higher education had been set up. His report six months later contained the following statement concerning these institutions:

Higher schools, and those for the preparation of teachers, have been aided in equal distribution through the several states. The principal of these, as assisted by the bureau, all of them made permanent institutions by charter of the respective states where they are located, are as follows: National Theological Institute, Washington, D. C.; Howard University, Washington, D. C.; Saint Martin's School, Washington, D. C.; Normal School, Richmond, Va.; Berea College, Berea, Ky.; St. Augustine's Normal School, Raleigh, N. C.; Wesleyan College, East Tennessee; Fisk University, Nashville, Tenn.; Storer College, Harpers Ferry, W. Va.; Atlanta University, Atlanta, Ga.; Robert College, Lookout Mountain, Tenn.; Marysville College, Tenn.; Alabama High and Normal Schools; St. Bridgit's Parochial Schools, Pittsburgh, Pa.; South Carolina High and Normal Schools. The total amount granted to these institutions is $168,000.[4]

By 1870 the rôle of the Bureau in establishing institutions of higher education was completed and the various denominational churches took over the task.

The Baptists instituted Shaw University at Raleigh in 1865, Roger Williams at Nashville and Morehouse at Atlanta in 1867, Leland at New Orleans in 1869, and Benedict at Columbia in 1871; and the Free Baptists established Storer at Harpers Ferry in 1867. The Methodist Episcopal Church instituted Walden at Nashville in 1865, Rust at Holly Springs in 1866, Morgan at Baltimore in 1867, Haven Academy at Waynesboro in 1868, Claflin at Orangeburg in 1869, and Clark at Atlanta in 1870. The Presbyterians already had their important school in Pennsylvania, called Ashmun Institute, now Lincoln University, founded in 1854; to which was added Biddle University in 1867. The Episcopal Church instituted St. Augustine's at Raleigh in 1867.[5]

At first, much of the work of the various denominations was carried on through the American Missionary Association. But gradually the

4 *The Evolution of the Negro College* by Dwight O. W. Holmes, p. 47. Copyright 1934 by Dwight Oliver Wendell Holmes. Reprinted by permission of the Bureau of Publications, Teachers College, Columbia University.

5 United States Bureau of Education, *Negro Education*, Bulletin 38 (Washington, 1917), Vol. I, pp. 252-53.

different denominations undertook the advanced education of the Negro as independent agencies. Consequently, the support of the work of the American Missionary Association was left to the Congregational churches and the Association concentrated its efforts on the education of teachers. The following schools were founded by the American Missionary Association:

In 1865 it had Avery Institute at Charleston, Ballard Normal at Macon, and Washburn at Beaufort, N. C.; in 1866 Trinity at Athens, Ala., Gregory at Wilmington, N. C., and Fisk University at Nashville; in 1867, Talladega College in Alabama, Emerson at Mobile, Storrs at Atlanta, and Beach at Savannah; in 1868, Hampton Institute in Virginia, Knox at Athens, Ga., Burwell at Selma, Ala., since removed to Florence, and Ely Normal, now a public school in Louisville; in 1869, Straight University at New Orleans, Tougaloo in Mississippi, LeMoyne at Memphis, and Lincoln at Marion, Ala.; in 1870, Dorchester Academy at McIntosh, and the Albany Normal in Georgia.[6]

There were other institutions established by various denominational churches. The Society of Friends established schools in Arkansas and South Carolina. The Presbyterians established several schools, the most outstanding of which was Knoxville College in Knoxville, Tennessee, established by the United Presbyterians in 1875. The Southern Methodist Episcopal Church founded Paine College at Augusta, Georgia, in 1884. The most important institution for the higher education of Negroes set up at this time was Howard University, chartered in 1867 by the federal government. Although the primary purpose in establishing it was to provide for the higher education of Negroes, the charter provided "for the education of youth in the liberal arts and sciences" with the provision that there should be no discrimination as to race.

During this period Negro church boards began to establish institutions for the higher education of Negroes. As we have seen the African Negro Methodist Episcopal Church acquired Wilberforce University before the Civil War. Following the Civil War this church organization established Western University in Kansas in 1864; Allen Uni-

[6] *Ibid.*, Vol. I, p. 253.

versity in Columbia, South Carolina, in 1881; Morris Brown University in Atlanta in 1885; and schools in other cities in the South. The African Methodist Episcopal Zion Church incorporated Livingstone College in 1879 and the institution began work on its present location in Salisbury, North Carolina, in 1882. The Colored Methodist Church opened Lane College in Jackson, Tennessee, in the same year and established schools in Birmingham, Alabama; Holy Springs, Mississippi; and Tyler, Texas. The colored Baptists carried on their educational work in connection with the Home Mission Society of the Northern Baptists.

THE ESTABLISHMENT OF HAMPTON INSTITUTE
AND TUSKEGEE INSTITUTE

The establishment of Hampton Institute and Tuskegee Institute at a later time forms a part of the history of the development of institutions of higher education of Negroes. Hampton Institute was located in the area where the first missionary efforts in the education of the freedmen were undertaken. The school was founded as a part of the plan of the American Missionary Association to establish a normal school for the training of Negro teachers for the schools in the area.[7] General Samuel Chapman Armstrong, who had served in the Civil War, is regarded as the founder of Hampton because the American Missionary Association entrusted him with the task of opening and heading the school in 1868. Moreover, Armstrong was largely responsible for shaping the educational policy of the institution. Armstrong's ideas concerning the education of the freedmen had undoubtedly been influenced by his own observation of the Manual Labor School at Hilo, Hawaii, where he was born and spent his early years. His educational policy regarding the freedmen is summed up in the following:

the past of our colored population has been such that an institution devoted especially to them must provide a training more than usually comprehensive, must include both sexes and a variety of occupation, must produce moral as well as mental strength, and while making its

7 L. P. Jackson, "The Origin of Hampton Institute," *The Journal of Negro History,* Vol. 10, pp. 131-49.

students first-rate mechanical laborers must also make them first-rate men and women.[8]

The development of Tuskegee Institute by Booker T. Washington, the most distinguished graduate of Hampton Institute, was the result of the influence of the latter institution. When the Negroes of Tuskegee, Alabama, were given an appropriation of $2,000 for a normal school in return for their political support of a member of the Alabama legislature, they sent to Hampton Institute for someone to head the school. Armstrong recommended for the position Washington, who was teaching in West Virginia. The history of the development of Tuskegee Institute from its humble beginnings to one of the largest endowed and most influential Negro institutions in the United States is an oft-repeated and familiar story.[9] In the more dramatic accounts of the growth of Tuskegee, Washington is pictured leading his pupils in hewing down trees and clearing the way for a great institution. He is pictured as a teacher who changed the aspirations of illiterate Negroes for classical culture to a determination to cultivate the soil efficiently and acquire land. In a more objective appraisal of the work of Washington, the director of the Bureau of Education's survey of Negro education in 1916 makes the following statement:

He was wise enough to keep in close communication with Hampton and its management, to look for encouragement to the generous supporters of that institution, and to draw revenues from the same sources of maintenance; he was also able enough to handle the enterprise, to conquer opposition, and overcome obstacles that would have disheartened an ordinary man; and he had so happy a gift of conciliation as to win the friendship and admiration of the southern white people whenever the opportunity could be found, and to gain from them a moral support that was worth more than money to his work. Thus, in the course of time, Booker T. Washington's school became as famous as Hampton, acquired a property of about the same value, and became the recipient of an equal revenue. A score of other industrial schools have been successful, acquiring a good deal of property and

8 Quoted in *ibid.*, p. 148.
9 Booker T. Washington, *Up From Slavery* (New York, 1910).

gaining revenues for maintenance so ample as to indicate a partiality of donors in the North for schools of this order.[10]

The significance of the wording in the last sentence should not be overlooked. The "partiality of donors in the North for schools" of the "order" of Hampton and Tuskegee had tremendous significance, as we shall see, for the development of Negro institutions of higher education.

LAND-GRANT COLLEGES FOR NEGROES

The development of land-grant colleges for Negroes was related to the growth of schools for industrial education and the development of institutions of higher education. The Morrill fund, which was established by an act of Congress in 1862, was designed to maintain an agricultural and mechanical college in each state. The institutions which were established in the South as the result of this act were all for white youth. In three states, however, a substantial part of the Morrill fund was made available to Negro institutions. In Virginia Hampton Institute received a third of the grant, while Claflin College in South Carolina was given a part of the grant received by the state. In Mississippi, three-fifths of the Morrill fund was assigned to Alcorn University, but when this was found to be too much for its needs, the appropriation was given to another Negro school. In 1878 the funds were restored to Alcorn and the name of the school was changed to Alcorn Agricultural and Mechanical College.[11] During the following year Kentucky granted one-twelfth of its income from the Morrill fund to a Negro school. When the Morrill Act was amended in 1890, it was specified that Negroes in each state should receive an equitable share of the increase in funds provided by the revised Act. Consequently, within a few years land-grant colleges for Negroes were organized in 17 of the southern states.

HIGHER EDUCATION OF THE NEGRO AND HIS
STATUS IN THE SOUTH

The organization of the Negro land-grant colleges occurred at the time when the inferior status of the Negro in the South was being fixed

[10] United States Bureau of Education, *Negro Education*, p. 258.
[11] Holmes, *op. cit.*, pp. 150-51.

in law as well as custom.[12] The establishment of institutions of higher education by the various missionary societies in the North and the Freedmen's Bureau had been based upon certain assumptions concerning the status of the Negro in American life. Holmes has summarized these assumptions as follows:

First, the Negro having been rescued from the hell of slavery and two and a half centuries of unrequited toil, was worthy of everything the nation could bestow upon him by way of recompense, including citizenship and all the necessary means to meet its requirements. Second, it was plain duty of a Christian nation to discharge this obligation to the freedmen promptly by providing them with the same means of mental and moral development that has proved effectual in the advance of white people. Third, the Negro possessed the same mental capacity as the white man, his apparent mental inferiority being due to the debasing effect of slavery. Fourth, without education the freedmen would rapidly degenerate and become a national menace not only to the South but to the entire nation. Fifth, the South had neither the means nor the inclination to offer to the Negro the educational opportunities that he needed and deserved to fit him for citizenship. Sixth, on the above assumptions, the people in the North must of necessity undertake to promote the education of the Negro in the South.[13]

Although the attitudes of southern whites toward the higher education of the Negro varied, they were opposed completely to those held by northern missionaries and philanthropists. The views of southern whites were:

First, the ignorant whites opposed any kind of education for the Negro because they themselves were ignorant and unschooled and could not bear the idea of the Negro receiving education which had been, up to that time, the prerogative of the upper class. Second, the better class of whites in the South realized that some kind of education should be given to the Negro, but believed that the nature of this education should be determined by the South and that the teaching should be done at first by Southern white people and later by the Negroes themselves. Third, there was a strong feeling in the minds of the Southerners that the Northern teachers in the missionary schools

[12] See Chapter VIII.
[13] *The Evolution of the Negro College* by Dwight O. W. Holmes, pp. 68-69. Copyright 1934 by Dwight Oliver Wendell Holmes. Reprinted by permission of the Bureau of Publications, Teachers College, Columbia University.

were teaching the Negroes not only to aspire to social equality but
to distrust and hate the white people of the South among whom they
would have to live.[14]

As a result of the clash in these two viewpoints, the early missionaries
among the freedmen were ostracized at first because they were regarded as a menace to social order. As suspicion subsided, they were
ridiculed for their faith in the intellectual potentialities of the Negro.
Then as the enthusiasm of the North cooled and its idealism faded,
the support of the Negro colleges declined. Thus the ground was laid
for the great controversy over the relative merits of industrial as opposed to higher education of the Negro.

INDUSTRIAL EDUCATION VS. LIBERAL EDUCATION

The main burden of the attack upon higher education was that
it was impractical and did not prepare the Negro for the world in
which he lived. The position of those opposed to higher education was
well expressed in the following words of Booker T. Washington:

For nearly twenty years after the war, except in a few instances, the
value of the industrial training given by the plantations was overlooked. Negro men and women were educated in literature, in mathematics and in the sciences, with little thought of what had been taking
place during the preceding two hundred and fifty years, except, perhaps, as something to be escaped, to be got as far away from as
possible. As a generation began to pass, those who had been trained
as mechanics in slavery began to disappear by death, and gradually it
began to be realized that there were few to take their places. There
were young men educated in foreign tongues, but few in carpentry
or in mechanical or architectural drawing. Many were trained in Latin,
but few as engineers and blacksmiths. Too many were taken from the
farm and educated, but educated in everything but farming. For this
reason they had no interest in farming and did not return to it. And
yet eighty-five per cent of the Negro population of the Southern states
lives and for a considerable time will continue to live in the country
districts.[15]

[14] *Ibid.*, pp. 69-70.
[15] *The Negro Problem* by Booker T. Washington and W. E. B. DuBois, pp.
12-13. Copyright 1903 by James Pott & Company.

The case for higher education was stated by W. E. B. DuBois, a graduate of Fisk University, who received his doctorate from Harvard University in 1895:

The Negro race, like all races, is going to be saved by its exceptional men. The problem of education, then, among Negroes must first of all deal with the Talented Tenth; it is the problem of developing the Best of this race that they may guide the Mass away from the contamination and death of the Worst, in their own and other races. Now the training of men is a difficult and intricate task. Its technique is a matter for educational experts, but its object is the vision of seers. If we make money the object of man-training, we shall develop money-makers but not necessarily men; if we make technical skill the object of education, we may possess artisans but not, in nature, men. Men we shall have only as we make manhood the object of the work of the schools—intelligence, broad sympathy, knowledge of the world that was and is, and of the relation of men to it—this is the curriculum of that Higher Education which must underlie true life.[16]

The statements of these leading proponents of industrial and higher education for Negroes indicate on the surface that each proponent excluded the type of education advocated by the other. But as a matter of fact Washington stated that he "would not confine the race to industrial life, not even agriculture," although he believed that the majority of Negroes were better off in the rural districts. He believed that industrial education would inculcate habits of thrift, a love of work, and encourage homeownership and that industrial education would provide a secure foundation for professional education and public positions of responsibility. DuBois on his part readily admitted that "all men cannot go to college but" he maintained, "some men must." Moreover, he would not deny "the paramount necessity for teaching the Negro to work, and to work steadily and skillfully." Nor would he "seem to depreciate in the slightest degree the important part industrial schools must play in the accomplishment of these ends." But DuBois insisted that industrialism was "drunk with its own vision of success, to imagine that its own work can be accomplished without providing for the training of broadly cultured men and women to teach its own teachers, and to teach the teachers

16 *Ibid.*, pp. 33-34.

of the public schools." [17] Finally, as DuBois pointed out in 1903 Washington through his energy and enthusiasm changed the program of industrial education "from a by-path into a veritable Way of Life." [18]

This final criticism of DuBois went to the heart of the issue, which was really concerned with the status of the Negro in American life. This was recognized by Gunnar Myrdal, in the most recent study of the Negro problem in the United States, where he points out that "the political caste problem" rather than "pedagogical advantages" was "always and necessarily" involved in the advocacy by the white South of industrial education for Negroes. [19] The problem of "industrial versus higher education" was not really concerned with pedagogical values or the extent to which one or the other type of education would prepare the Negro to participate more efficiently in American life. For the majority of southern whites industrial education meant training for domestic service and unskilled labor occupations which were regarded as appropriate to the status of the Negro in the South. To the more sophisticated southern whites, industrial education meant that the Negro would not receive the broad culture of the upper class. Although many northern white supporters of industrial education for Negroes gave a vague sentimental support to industrial education, some of them believed that they were helping the Negro to become an efficient industrial worker. The attitude of Negroes toward industrial education depended upon a number of factors. On the whole, the Negro in the North and upper-class Negroes in the South were opposed to industrial education. On the other hand, the great masses of ambitious Negroes with a plantation background were glad of the opportunity to get any type of education.

A CRITICAL EVALUATION OF INDUSTRIAL
EDUCATION FOR NEGROES

When industrial education is examined from the viewpoint of the values imputed to it by its supporters, it is seen that it failed to accom-

[17] *The Negro Problem* by Booker T. Washington and W. E. B. DuBois, p. 61. Copyright 1903 by James Pott & Company.

[18] W. E. B. DuBois, *The Souls of Black Folk* (Chicago, 1926), p. 42.

[19] Gunnar Myrdal, *An American Dilemma* (New York, 1944), Vol. II, pp. 897-98.

plish the aims of those who favored industrial education. Industrial education did not train Negroes to become domestic servants and laborers. In the industrial schools Negro students acquired literacy and access to a larger world of ideas than was realized by the average southern white who supported this type of education. To this extent the Negro was made dissatisfied with his status in the southern community. Although the Negro student did not receive the broad culture which the more sophisticated whites opposed, many Negro students got a vision of a larger world that caused them to seek a higher education. Moreover, what was more important from the standpoint of both southern and northern whites, who honestly believed that industrial education prepared Negroes to become efficient industrial workers, industrial education did *not* prepare Negroes for industrial occupations.

First, it should be pointed out that some of the proponents of industrial education for the Negro were unconscious of the technological changes which had occurred in American industry. Although technological developments in the South had not kept pace with those in the North, it seems that even Washington was not conscious of the changes in the South. Industrial education provided by the Negro schools was concerned with handicrafts which were rapidly being supplemented or displaced by machine production. Training in handicrafts had an educational value but it did not prepare Negroes to become industrial workers. It is quite possible that northern industrialists who supported industrial education for the Negro were unaware of this fact. Nevertheless, even if the proponents of industrial education and their supporters had been aware of this fact, they were not prepared to face the costs involved in providing the machinery necessary to train the Negro in the skills required in modern industry.

There was also the factor of the white industrial worker in southern industry. Although the average southern white was favorable to "industrial education" for Negroes, he was not willing to encourage the competition of Negro industrial workers. The impact of the industrial revolution upon the South manifested itself in the textile mills from which Negro workers were excluded. Consequently, the southern white worker was opposed to training the Negro in industrial skills which would make him able to compete with white workers.[20] It is understandable why in recent years Latin was retained in southern Negro high schools while technical courses were substituted for the classical tongue in the white high schools.[21] All this emphasizes the fact that industrial education was involved in the question of the status of the Negro and had, on the whole, only a symbolic value in the education of the Negro. Moreover, industrial education had only a sentimental value for those northern industrialists who supported industrial education for the Negro while they refused to employ the graduates of the industrial schools in their plants in the North. The graduates of Tuskegee Institute and other industrial schools became teachers and leaders in other fields requiring an academic education.[22]

CHARACTER OF NEGRO INSTITUTIONS OF HIGHER
EDUCATION UP TO THE FIRST WORLD WAR

When one turns to the so-called institutions of higher education for Negroes what does one find to be the character of education which they provided for Negroes? Conceived in its broadest terms, the aim of the institutions for the higher education of Negroes was to make men of chattels. As Bond has said:

Boys and girls came from the environment of slavery and were transported to a place where the students of Mark Hopkins, Theodore Wōolseley, Charles Finney, and Henry Fairchild sought to do with Negro students what these men had done with them. They succeeded in an uncommon way. If the colleges took students from "life," it was from a life in which there was no idealism and very little intelli-

[20] In view of these facts, the following reasons given for the failure of the graduates of industrial schools to enter industrial occupations appear ridiculous. In Weatherford, *Negro Life in the South* (New York, 1910) it is stated that "the graduates of Tuskegee, true to the Negro nature when left to choose and follow his own career, by a great majority follow other than industrial pursuits when they are graduated." *Negro Life in the South* by W. D. Weatherford, pp. 49-50. Copyright 1910 by Association Press. This Negro nature "is his natural disinclination to do manual work, and his inordinate desire to 'shine' in society." *Ibid.*, p. 52.

[21] Bond, *op. cit.*, p. 362. The fact should not be overlooked, as Bond has pointed out, that the teaching of Latin is less expensive.

[22] Charles S. Johnson, *The Negro College Graduate* (Chapel Hill, 1938), pp. 92-94.

gence. The teachers insisted that the institutions they managed should have both.[23]

But, in fact, the Negro students who were drawn into these institutions were not only the raw field Negroes. There was a process of selection involving general intelligence and literacy, general culture, and economic status. When these institutions of higher education were organized much of the education was on a secondary level and there were classes for pupils on the elementary level. The missionary teachers from the North, true to their democratic ideals, often placed their own children in the classes with Negro children. At Howard University, the first students to enroll in the colleges were five white students, the children of the professors.[24] But it should not be forgotten that many of the children who enrolled in these institutions were the children of the Negroes who had been free before the Civil War. The children of the free Negro were generally prepared to begin a secondary education. The secondary education offered by these institutions was the same as that given in the best academies in the North.

The education in these schools was in the classical tradition. This was not strange when one considers the educational tradition of the secondary schools and colleges of the period. Although there were courses in Latin and Greek and mathematics, there were also courses in English literature and political economy. The sneer that Negro graduates of these institutions "with their little Latin and less Greek" were not prepared for the practical necessities of life betrays not only prejudice in regard to the intellectual capacities of Negroes but ignorance of the development of education in the United States.[25]

[23] *The Education of the Negro in the American Social Order* by Horace M. Bond, pp. 361-62. Copyright 1934 by Prentice-Hall, Inc.

[24] Holmes, *op. cit.*, p. 51.

[25] John C. Calhoun once stated that "if a Negro could be found who could parse Greek or explain Euclid, I should be constrained to think that he had human possibilities." *The Education of the Negro in the American Social Order* by Horace M. Bond, p. 146. Copyright 1934 by Prentice-Hall, Inc. It is not improbable that in choosing a classical education some Negro students wished to meet this challenge. Once Negro college graduates boasted that the Negro president of one Negro University (Wilberforce) had not only parsed Greek but had written a Greek grammar.

Moreover, it was natural that the men and women educated in the best schools in New England should have set up the same ideals in the colleges which they established for Negroes.[26] The process of establishing these institutions was slow and on a sound basis. When in the beginning there were not enough students for the college program, they were encouraged to go to a northern college. Then, too, the whites who built these schools generally educated their own children along with the Negro students.[27]

The institutions of higher education established by the Negro church organizations did not maintain the standards of those set up by the white missionaries from the North. The teachers and trustees in charge of these schools did not possess the education or background of traditions which the white teachers from New England brought to their task. The Negro colleges in the South that have acquired distinction have been those which were built upon the traditions of the New England colleges. The colleges which grew out of the efforts of the Negro church organizations have reflected throughout their history the ill effects of the intellectual isolation of Negro church organizations.

There is one fact that cannot be gainsaid concerning the rôle of institutions of higher education in the development of the Negro: They produced the first generation of educated Negroes following the Civil War. It was in these schools that the teachers were prepared to teach in the public schools for Negroes. It was in these schools that Negroes received their preparation for medicine, dentistry, and law. As DuBois pointed out in 1903:

Out of the colleges of the North came, after the blood of war, Ware, Cravath, Chase, Andrews, Bumstead and Spence to build the foundations of knowledge and civilization in the black South. Where ought they to have begun to build? At the bottom, of course, quibbles the

26 See Myron W. Adams, A *History of Atlanta University* (Atlanta, 1930), pp. 16-17.

27 When a legislative committee of Georgia became conscious of this in 1887, the state withdrew its annual grant of $8,000, passed legislation providing a fine and imprisonment for the trustees and white teachers at Atlanta University. Atlanta University maintained its position and a later bill condemning the University was passed and state support withdrawn. *Ibid.*, pp. 24-29.

mole with his eyes on the earth. Aye! truly at the bottom, at the very bottom; at the bottom of knowledge, down in the very depths of knowledge there where the roots of justice strike into the lowest soil of Truth. And so they did begin; they founded colleges, and up from the colleges shot normal schools, and out from the normal schools went teachers, and around the normal teachers clustered other teachers to teach the public schools; the college trained in Greek and Latin and mathematics, 2,000 men; and these men trained full 50,000 others in morals and manners, and they in turn taught thrift and the alphabet to nine millions of men, who to-day hold $300,000,000 of property. It was a miracle—the most wonderful peace-battle of the 19th century, and yet to-day men smile at it, and in fine superiority tell us that it was all a strange mistake; [28]

By 1909, 3,000 college graduates had completed their work in 32 institutions.[29] Only eight of these institutions at the time had 100 or more graduates. In 1909 there were 15 schools with 20 or more students enrolled in college courses. The schools with the largest enrollment of college students were Howard University, Lincoln University in Pennsylvania, and Fisk University. On the basis of the standards set up by the Carnegie Foundation for the Advancement of Teaching, there were 11 first-grade colleges and 3 second-grade colleges. The remaining 18 of the 32 Negro colleges approximated in varying degrees the work of the second-grade colleges.

The situation of institutions of higher education for Negroes at the time of World War I was given in a report sponsored jointly by the United States Bureau of Education and the Phelps-Stokes Fund. According to that report, "Under a liberal interpretation of college work, only 33 of the 653 private and State schools for colored people are teaching any subjects of college grade." [30] Only three of the 33 schools teaching subjects of college grade—Howard University, Fisk University, and Meharry Medical College—according to the report, had

[28] *The Negro Problem* by Booker T. Washington and W. E. B. DuBois, pp. 46-47. Copyright 1903 by James Pott & Company.

[29] W. E. B. DuBois and A. G. Dill (Eds.), *The College-Bred Negro American* (Atlanta, 1910), *passim*. See also E. Horace Fitchett, "The Role of Claflin College in Negro Life," *The Journal of Negro Education*, Vol. XII (1943), pp. 42-68; and by the same author, "The Influence of Claflin College on Negro Family Life," *The Journal of Negro History*, Vol. XXIX (1944), pp. 429-60.

[30] United States Bureau of Education, *Negro Education*, Vol. II, p. 16.

"student body, teaching force, equipment, and income sufficient to warrant the characterization of 'college.' " [31] As one may see in Table XXXIII, nearly half of the college students and practically all of the professional students were enrolled in these three colleges. Out of a total of 12,726 students enrolled in these 33 institutions, nearly 10,000

TABLE XXXIII

Characterization of 33 Schools Teaching Subjects of College Grade and Classification of Their Students *

CHARACTERIZATION	NUMBER OF SCHOOLS	NUMBER OF STUDENTS	STUDENTS IN COLLEGE SUBJECTS	IN PROFES- SIONAL SUBJECTS	ALL OTHER STUDENTS
College	3 †	2,411	722	972	717
Secondary and College	15	5,486	675	22	4,789
Schools Offering College Subjects	15	4,829	246	0	4,583
TOTAL	33	12,726	1,643	994	10,089

* United States Bureau of Education, *Negro Education* (Washington, 1917), Vol. II, p. 16.

† Howard University, Fisk University, and Meharry Medical College.

were in elementary and secondary grades of the 30 schools and did not measure up to college grade.[32] The 15 institutions characterized as "secondary and college" were limited in their teaching force and equipment, though a few required thoroughness in the work provided for the relatively few college students. On the other hand, the 15 institutions offering college subjects had neither the equipment nor the teachers to maintain college classes.[33] Even two of the three institutions of college grade—Howard University and Fisk University—had

[31] *Ibid.*, p. 16.

[32] This report showed that at the same time there were about 500 Negro students in Northern colleges and professional schools.

[33] The section of the report on Negro colleges contained the following criticisms: (1) There were too many institutions attempting to maintain so-called college departments. (2) The duplication of college work in many cities was due not only to the personal ambition of college presidents but to the desire of the various denominations to have pupils of the church attend their own schools. (3) The colleges have been handicapped by the tenacity with which they keep to the classical tradition. This tendency was due partly to the early traditions and partly to the fact that the limited income of these schools prevented the introduction of modern subjects.

students below the college level. Howard University had 373 students in its academy or secondary department and Fisk University 112 students in elementary grades and 169 students in its secondary school. Within a few years both of these institutions abolished their secondary departments.

Howard University and Meharry College provided complete courses in medicine, dentistry, and pharmacy, while Shaw University offered a two-year course in these fields. Howard University also offered a full law course and maintained a school of religion. In fact, there were 14 institutions that had special equipment and teachers for training ministers. It was found that few of the students in the courses in religion offered by any of the schools had completed even a high school education, while the number of college graduates was negligible.

DEVELOPMENT OF HIGHER EDUCATION FOR
NEGROES AFTER WORLD WAR I

During the decade following World War I there was a definite change in the attitude of the South and the foundations toward the higher education of the Negro. The controversy over the relative merits of industrial and higher education gradually lost its significance. It was increasingly recognized that the Negro required educated leaders in the professions as well as training in industrial skills. Moreover, there was a growing recognition that, as DuBois had phrased it a quarter of century previously, Negro education should provide for the talented members of the race. The migration of hundreds of thousands of Negroes to the urban areas of the North, where they had access to the same education as whites, tended to emphasize the necessity to provide for the higher education of the Negro in the South.

However, it was the Negro colleges themselves that took the lead in bringing their work up to standard.[34] Since the Negro colleges in the South were not recognized by the Southern Association of Colleges, the American Medical Association rated Negro colleges on the basis of the 1917 Survey of Negro education. Because of dissatisfaction with this rating, the Association of Negro Colleges took steps in 1925

[34] Holmes, *op. cit.*, pp. 181ff.

to have another survey of Negro colleges. The survey, which covered 79 institutions, including Howard University in the District of Columbia and Wilberforce University in Ohio, showed that considerable progress had been made since 1916. There were four general types of control of these 79 colleges:

Twenty-two publicly supported institutions under State ownership and control, including land-grant colleges, normal and teacher-training colleges.

Nine universities and colleges owned, governed, and controlled by independent boards of trustees and privately supported.

Thirty-one universities and colleges under ownership and control of northern white denominational church boards and privately supported.

Seventeen privately supported colleges owned and governed by negro denominational church organizations or conferences.[35]

There were 13,860 students enrolled in these schools in 1926-1927. They had a total of 418,695 volumes in their libraries or an average of 5,200 to each college. The average annual expenditures for their libraries for the years 1922-1927 amounted to $107,410. While these 79 schools had a total endowment of $20,713,796, more than two-thirds of this amount represented the combined endowment of Hampton Institute and Tuskegee Institute. This left an average endowment for the remaining 76 schools of about $86,000. Seventy-eight schools had a combined annual income of $8,560,551 or an average of $109,752 per school. It is obvious from these figures that despite the progress noted in the report, Negro colleges functioned under serious handicaps. They lacked adequate financial support, a condition which was reflected in lack of scientific equipment and library facilities. Moreover, there was a deficiency in the preparation of the teachers in these colleges.

One of the results of the survey was the acceptance on the part of the Southern Association of Colleges and Secondary Schools of the responsibility for rating Negro colleges in the South. According to the rating of the association in 1932, there were six "A" class and 22

[35] See U. S. Bureau of Education, *Survey of Negro Colleges and Universities.* Bulletin 1928, No. 7 (Washington, 1929), p. 5.

"B" class four-year colleges; and four junior colleges, only one of which was accorded an "A" rating.[36] The six four-year "A" colleges included Talledega College in Alabama; Atlanta University, Morehouse College, and Spelman College in Atlanta; Fisk University in Nashville; and Hampton Institute in Virginia. All of these schools, with the exception of Hampton, it will be noted, were founded by the white missionaries from the North who established schools for the higher education of the Negro. Eleven of the 22 four-year colleges with a "B" rating were likewise colleges which had been founded by northern church boards. Among the remaining 11 colleges with "B" rating there were nine state schools, one Catholic school, and Tuskegee Institute. There were only 1,849 students enrolled in the class "A" colleges and 6,164 in the class "B" colleges, while the junior colleges had 552 students.

During the 1920's the resources of Negro colleges were devoted increasingly to work on the college level. Moreover, there was a movement toward the consolidation of Negro colleges. There were 12 cities in the South where there were two to five Negro colleges.[37] In New Orleans there were three colleges: Straight University under the American Missionary Association, founded in 1869; New Orleans University under the Methodist Episcopal Church, founded in 1873; and Xavier College, established by the Roman Catholic Church in 1915. Representatives of church boards supporting Straight University and New Orleans University came together with representatives of the Julius Rosenwald Fund and the General Education Board and projected Dillard University. By the arrangement, the two church boards contributed $1,000,000, the two foundations $750,000, and the citizens of New Orleans with the cooperation of the Chamber of Commerce $250,000 for the site of the new university. The first unit of the University to be built was the Flint-Goodridge Hospital. The

[36] Fred McCuiston, *Higher Education of Negroes* (A Summary), (Nashville, Tenn., 1933), p. 26. Colleges receiving the "A" rating met the same standards as white colleges. Colleges receiving a "B" rating did not meet in full one or more of the standards but the general quality of their work was such as to warrant the admission of the graduates to institutions requiring a bachelor's degree for entrance.

[37] Holmes, *op. cit.*, p. 197.

new university is now located on a large campus, where a college program is provided for its students.

In Atlanta there were five Negro colleges: Atlanta University, Clark University, Morehouse College, Spelman College, and Morris Brown University. None of the so-called universities were real universities. Atlanta, Morehouse, and Spelman were, as we have seen, among the class "A" colleges. Clark University was a class "B" college and Morris Brown University, under the African Methodist Episcopal Church, was not considered in the rating by the Southern Association of Colleges. In 1929 an agreement was reached by Atlanta, Morehouse, and Spelman by which the three schools became affiliated in an organization known as the Atlanta University system. Atlanta, according to the arrangement, was to carry on professional and graduate work while Spelman and Morehouse were to take care of the college work. The General Education Board gave $1,500,000 toward the $3,000,000 required for new buildings and to capitalize the annual gifts and pledged up to $1,700,000 toward the $3,400,000 endowment fund for expansion. In addition the Board gave $75,000 annually for current expenses and $450,000 for a library for the university system.

During the period of these developments, public support for the higher education of Negroes in the South was slowly increasing. By 1931 the average income of 32 public colleges was $142,060 as compared with an average of $68,080 for 60 private colleges. However, only one of the public colleges—Virginia State College—received "A" rating by the Southern Association of Colleges. During the year 1937-1938, three-fourths of all the Negro college students enrolled in public institutions were in land-grant colleges.[38] Yet despite the increasing burden of Negro land-grant colleges, these institutions have continued to receive only a small proportion of funds spent on land-grant colleges in the South.

During 1935-36, the 34 white and Negro land-grant colleges in the 17 Southern States received, from all sources, about $55,000,000. Of this amount, about $4,400,000 (8 per cent) went to the 17 Negro institutions. Whereas the average white college received nearly

[38] Doxey A. Wilkerson, *Special Problems of Negro Education* (Washington, 1939), p. 72.

$3,000,000 the average Negro college received slightly more than $260,000.[39]

When one considers the amount of money which the Negro institutions received from the more than a dozen permanent and emergency federal funds, the discrimination against the Negro schools is found to be even greater.[40] Of a total of $17,755,638 which the white and Negro land-grant colleges in the South received in 1935-1936, the Negro schools received only $928,971, or 5.2 per cent. Only in the case of the funds provided by the Morrill-Nelson and Bankhead Jones Acts, which provided that colored schools should receive an equitable share, did Negro schools receive a sum commensurate with the proportion of Negroes in the population. But Negro schools received no share of the federal funds for agricultural research, forestry extension, agricultural and home economics extension, and military training.

MEAGER PUBLIC SUPPORT OF THE HIGHER
EDUCATION OF NEGROES IN THE SOUTH

The extent to which Negroes in the South must depend upon private philanthropy and the meager share of federal grants to land-grant colleges for higher education becomes apparent when one considers the state appropriations to Negro institutions. All of the southern states maintain universities and teachers colleges from which Negroes

[39] *Ibid.*, p. 76.
[40] In what is obviously an apology for the failure of the southern states to give Negroes an equitable share of the land-grant college funds appears the following statement (United States Bureau of Education, *Negro Education*, pp. 259-60), "The total income of these grants in that year [1893] was $128,349, to which were added the State appropriations and gifts from other sources till the entire expenditures amounted to $349,580. This was for 14 schools." "The generosity of these provisions," it is added, "may be better understood by a comparison with the cost of maintaining other schools for colored people." Then it is pointed out that the American Missionary Association spent $175,607 on its Negro schools and that the Presbyterians, Methodists, and Baptists spent a sum that did not exceed this amount. It is obviously misleading to compare the meager share which Negro land-grant schools received from federal and state funds with what church boards in the North spent upon Negro schools. Unless one accepts the implicit assumption that Negroes do not have the same legal rights as whites, it seems strange to designate as "generosity" the fact that the southern states have given Negro students a fraction of their rightful share of both federal and state funds.

are excluded. Each state makes a small appropriation to one or more institutions for Negroes. In Table XXXIV one can see to what extent these Negro institutions share in state funds in six states which are representative of the South.[41] In Alabama where Negroes comprised about 35 per cent of the population, $1,905,713 was appropriated to several institutions for whites while the Negro institution in Montgomery received only $76,616.[42] In Florida the Negroes re-

TABLE XXXIV

State Appropriations to Institutions of Higher Education for Whites and Negroes in Six Selected Southern States: 1937–38 *

STATE	WHITE INSTITUTIONS	NEGRO INSTITUTIONS
Alabama	$1,905,713	$ 76,616
Florida	1,945,290	164,840
Georgia	1,303,516	89,596
Mississippi	589,128	55,233
North Carolina	1,997,477	199,999
South Carolina	1,445,863	82,500

* U. S. Office of Education. *Statistics of Higher Education 1937–38* (Washington, 1941), Table 20, pp. 194 ff.

ceived a larger share of the funds for higher education. On the other hand, in Georgia Negroes who constituted about 35 per cent of the population received about 7 per cent of the appropriation for higher education. In Georgia additional small appropriations were made to two junior colleges for Negroes but this was offset by much larger appropriations for a number of junior colleges for whites. The situation in Mississippi was about the same as that in Georgia except that the general expenditures for higher education in Mississippi are low, while in South Carolina Negroes received even a smaller share of state appropriations for higher education.[43] Although Negroes constituted

[41] These figures do not include appropriations to junior colleges, very few of which are provided for Negroes in the South.

[42] Tuskegee Institute received about $27,000 to carry on the work which the state failed to provide for Negroes and a Negro junior college received $20,000. This was offset to some extent by the appropriation of about $9,000 to a white junior college.

[43] See E. Horace Fitchett, "The Relation of Income to Adequate Educational Opportunities," *The Journal of Negro Education*, Vol. XI, pp. 44 ff.

about 43 per cent of the population of South Carolina, the only Negro institution to get any share of the state appropriation received less than 6 per cent of the total appropriations for higher education. Even in the comparatively liberal state of North Carolina, where Negroes constitute about 28 per cent of the total population, only a tenth of the appropriation for higher education was given to Negro schools. In 1943-1944, Negro institutions in 17 southern states and the District of Columbia received only 5.8 per cent of the funds appropriated for public institutions of higher education. This was the same proportion as in 1929-1930.[44]

Despite the inadequate provisions for the higher education of Negroes in the South, some progress has been made in the work of publicly supported institutions. When the Southern Association of Colleges and Secondary Schools accepted the responsibility for rating Negro schools in 1930, no publicly supported four-year Negro college was given a class "A" rating. By 1939 there were seven Negro colleges supported by the states which were given this rating.[45] During the year 1937-1938, about two-thirds of the graduates of the 98 Negro colleges finished the colleges with class "A" rating.[46]

GRADUATE EDUCATION IN NEGRO INSTITUTIONS

From time to time over a period of thirty or forty years attempts were made at Howard University and Fisk University to provide graduate study. In fact the Master of Arts degree was granted occasionally by both institutions. But recognized graduate study in Negro colleges began at Howard University in 1921.[47] In 1927 graduate study was established at Fisk University and Hampton Institute; and in 1929 at Atlanta University. Xavier University, a Catholic school in New Orleans, established graduate study in 1933; Virginia State College in 1937; and Prairie View State College in 1938. Thus by 1938 there were three publicly controlled and three privately controlled institutions and one church school offering graduate instruc-

[44] Martin D. Jenkins, "The Availability of Higher Education for Negroes in the Southern States," *The Journal of Negro Education*, Vol. XVI, pp. 468-69.

[45] Fred McCuiston, *Graduate Instruction for Negroes in the United States* (Nashville, Tenn., 1939), pp. 29-30.

[46] *Ibid.*, p. 19. [47] *Ibid.*, pp. 38ff.

tion. There was a total of 448 regular students enrolled in six of these institutions.[48] Howard had 259 students, Fisk 79 students, and Atlanta 73 students. During the year 1938-1939, 106 Master's degrees were awarded by five of these schools.[49] During this period about 40 per cent of the students were enrolled in education; 20 per cent in English; and slightly less than 20 per cent in history. From 1919 to 1938, six of these institutions (Prairie View excluded) awarded 686 Master's degrees, half of which were awarded by Howard University.

When these schools began graduate study, they labored under many handicaps.[50] With their limited resources, they were engaged in the task of building up standard colleges. Then there was the problem of providing the personnel to give courses on a graduate level. Even Howard University, which had the largest qualified faculty, was faced with this problem. The teachers in Negro colleges were already over-burdened with teaching responsibilities. The addition of graduate work meant that both undergraduate and graduate instruction would suffer. Moreover, as we have seen, these colleges lacked library facilities and laboratory equipment for their undergraduate instruction. Under such circumstances the introduction of graduate education meant as a rule that the Negro student would receive a second or third-rate graduate education just as he had received an inferior college education.

These considerations have not prevented the increase in the number of Negro colleges with graduate study. In 1938, the Supreme Court ruled in the case of Gaines vs. the University of Missouri that the University should admit Gaines as a student to its law school. This decision established the legal right of Negroes to enjoy the educational privileges provided by the states for whites. Even before this decision a few of the southern states paid a part of the expenses incurred by Negroes who went outside the state to secure education not offered in Negro institutions. Since 1938 five southern states have made ap-

[48] There were only summer students in graduate courses at Hampton Institute. There were 528 summer students enrolled in six institutions (Xavier had no summer students).

[49] Prairie View and Xavier did not award degrees.

[50] See E. Franklin Frazier, "Graduate Education in Negro Colleges and Universities," *The Journal of Negro Education*, Vol. II, pp. 329-41.

propriations for graduate study in the Negro institutions supported by the state. By the fall of 1945 there were 14 Negro colleges and universities that were providing graduate study.[51] There were 576 students enrolled in graduate study in twelve of these schools.[52] For the school year 1944-1945 through the summer of 1945, the 14 schools conferred 248 Master's degrees. Although nearly 40 per cent of the graduate students were enrolled at Howard University, nearly a half of the Master's degrees were awarded by Atlanta University.

The development of professional education has been much slower in the Negro colleges. As we have seen, Howard University began with a full university program including professional courses. The Atlanta School of Social Work was incorporated into the Atlanta University system, which also included a Library Science department with an enrollment of 25 students in 1945.[53] Lincoln University in Missouri had added a law school to satisfy the Gaines decision. The North Carolina College for Negroes had 10 students in law and five in library science in the fall of 1945. Xavier University had 54 students in pharmacy during the year 1945-1946. Lincoln University in Pennsylvania and Virginia Union University had students in theology. The Meharry Medical College, which recently became a class "A" medical college, had 235 students in medicine and 106 in dentistry in 1945-1946. Howard University is still the only Negro institution which merits the title of "university" in the sense that it includes all the professional schools. In the fall of 1945, there were 262 students in medicine, 136 in dentistry, 89 in pharmacy, 87 in law, 80 in social work, and 36 in theology.

UNIQUE POSITION OF HOWARD UNIVERSITY
IN HIGHER EDUCATION OF NEGROES

The development of Howard University, the only institution of higher education supported by the federal government, is in a certain sense a historical accident. As we have seen, Howard University was one of the schools which received support from the Freedmen's Bu-

[51] Martin D. Jenkins, "Enrollment in Institutions of Higher Education for Negroes, 1945-1946," *The Journal of Negro Education*, Vol. XV, p. 237.
[52] Graduate courses were offered in the summer sessions only at Alabama Teachers College and Hampton Institute.   [53] Jenkins, *loc. cit.*, pp. 236ff.

reau. In fact, the school was named after General O. O. Howard, who as commissioner of the Freedmen's Bureau had taken the initiative in acquiring a site for the new university as well as securing support for it.[54] General Howard also served from 1868 to 1873 as the president of the University. In 1879 Congress began to make appropriations to Howard University, which amounted to $215,900 during the next ten years. When Reverend Wilbur P. Thirkield became president in 1906 he sought larger appropriations from Congress. During the next six years the annual federal contribution increased from less than $50,000 to nearly $100,000 in 1912. In 1910 Congress appropriated $174,800, including $80,000 for a science building. The federal appropriations continued to increase until they amounted to $591,000 in 1925-1926. The General Education Board also made a generous contribution of $130,000 toward the equipment of the medical building. During this period the subcollegiate department was abolished and the enrollment of college students increased from 1,080 in 1917-1918 to 3,123 in 1925-1926.

In 1926 the Board of Trustees of Howard University elected the first Negro president, Reverend Mordecai W. Johnson. One of the first achievements of the new president was to secure the legalization of the federal appropriations to Howard University since there had been no legislation authorizing such grants. From time to time southern congressmen had challenged the legality of such grants which, in their opinion, were affording an education for Negroes beyond their mental capacity and above their station in American life. Such objections were generally opposed by the argument that the southern states failed to provide for the higher education of Negroes. In 1928 Congress enacted a law authorizing the appropriations to Howard University with the proviso that no part of the appropriations should be used for religious instruction. Following the enactment of this law, a conference was called in 1929 to consider the future development of the University. The members attending this conference included representatives of both houses of Congress, representatives from the U. S. Bureau of Education, the Bureau of the Budget, the Julius Rosenwald Fund, and Howard University. The plan presented by

[54] Holmes, *op cit.*, pp. 50ff.

the Bureau of Education and tentatively accepted by the members of the conferences was as follows: Congress was to contribute a sum equal to two-thirds of the budget or an annual average sum of $1,100,000 during a period of 10 years while the physical plant was being completed. The trustees were to raise an endowment within at least 15 years so that at the end of the 10-year period the federal government could reduce its contribution to one-half of the annual budget. The execution of the plan was affected by the depression, which resulted in a decline in the student enrollment. Nevertheless, the federal appropriations for salaries, general expenses, and buildings continued to increase during the depression period. For the year 1944-1945 the federal appropriation amounted to $912,002.74 for salaries and expenses and $172,469.18 for war training. During the year 1944-1945 the University had a total income of $1,995,732, and the total assets of the University as of June 30, 1945 amounted to $10,453,570.44, including $6,342,877.86 for grounds and buildings. The student enrollment began to increase during the period of economic recovery and mounted during the war period. For the year 1945-1946 there were nearly 5,000 students enrolled in all divisions of the University.

NEGRO INSTITUTIONS OF HIGHER EDUCATION
AND RACE RELATIONS

It has been apparent in the discussion so far that the development of institutions of higher education for Negroes has been related to broad social and economic forces in American life and to the changing character of race relations. Of special interest is the organization and general character of these institutions both in relation to the Negro community and in relation to the white community. The first factor that deserves attention concerns the question of the administration of these schools. The schools that were set up by the Freedmen's Bureau and missionary societies in the North had white presidents and in the beginning all of the teaching personnel was white. Qualified Negroes were gradually added to the faculties of these institutions and much more slowly Negroes have been elected to the presidencies of these schools. These changes in Negro institutions have been the result of a number of factors. First, there are no longer white men and women of the caliber of the older northern missionaries who want to go South. But there are even more important factors. As Negroes themselves became prepared to assume the direction of these institutions, they have felt that they had a prior right over the claims of even the best prepared and most sincere northern whites who might be interested. This is related in turn to a growing race consciousness on the part of Negroes. From the beginning the state institutions for Negroes and the institutions founded by the Negro church organizations had Negro administrative and teaching personnel. In fact, some of the Negroes who had been prominent in politics became the heads of Negro schools when Negroes were excluded from politics in the South.

Under the white administrators there was a more or less mild type of paternalism. This paternalism was related to the religious zeal and idealism of those who were engaged in a great task of human uplift. As the younger generations of Negro students have entered these schools, there has been some protest against the paternalistic character of the administration. But, on the whole, the protest has not been against the older missionaries who have gradually died off or retired. It has usually been directed against the whites who have succeeded them. When Negro administrators succeeded the white heads, they carried on the tradition of paternalism. In the state schools and those conducted by the Negro church organizations, this paternalism has often assumed the character of an autocracy. As a consequence, the administration of nearly all Negro institutions of higher education is not only autocratic but the administration has become the most important element in the organization of these schools. The autocratic power wielded by the president is generally derived from the fact that the president is appointed by whites or represents the choice of the white community.[55] The wishes of the faculty in even purely educational matters are generally subject to the arbitrary rule of the presi-

[55] In one state institution the president paid his teachers with a personal check, altered at will their monthly salaries, which were based upon verbal agreements, and would discharge them in the middle of the month if he became dissatisfied with them.

dent. The subordinate administrative personnel are appointed to carry out the will of the president. It has been difficult for Negro college teachers to escape from such a situation because they could not find employment in white schools. Thus the Negro institution of higher education has tended to become a feudal type of organization. In the institutions controlled by Negro church organizations the feudal character of the school organization has been more pronounced since the school administration is a part of the church organization in which the church officials exercise autocratic power.

In view of the character of the organization of Negro institutions of higher education, it is not strange that a struggle for status involving power has been more important than efforts to achieve educational values and build up scholarship. In the schools founded by the New England missionaries a traditional classical education took root. But as these schools and others have expanded and assumed the character of universities, no tradition of scholarship and learning developed. Individual scholars in a few of the larger schools have begun to carry on research and make contributions to learning. But as a rule they must do this in an atmosphere where emphasis is placed on other values.[56] The emphasis upon other than educational values has been aptly called "detours in the education of the Negro." One of these "detours" is the notion that Negroes need a particular kind of "moral" education.[57] Negro college heads even more than white college heads place the development of "moral" character above intellectual development and efficiency. Without giving any thought to the mechanism by which any college can develop moral character, whites approve this emphasis in Negro schools because it fits into their prejudices. It has

[56] In commenting on the death of Dr. E. E. Just, the noted Negro biologist, *Science* stated: "Just's scientific career was a constant struggle for opportunity for research, the breath of his life. He was condemned by race to remain attached to a Negro institution unfitted by means and tradition to give full opportunity to ambitions such as his." Vol. 95 (Jan. 2, 1942), p. 11. A Negro scholar, Lewis K. McMillan, in an article, "The American Negro in Higher Education," *The Crisis*, August, 1947, has made a caustic criticism of Negro institutions of higher education. A. A. Medved, a member of the Board of Education of the Northern Baptist Convention, replied to McMillan in an article, "Look at the Record." *The Crisis*, November, 1947.

[57] See Buell G. Gallagher, *American Caste and the Negro College* (New York, 1938), pp. 179-87.

the approval of the segregated Negro community which is more concerned with the symbols of status than with real scholarship and learning. A real scholar is still an oddity in the segregated Negro community since his behavior is at variance with the style of living of the upper class with which he is generally identified.

The character of the Negro institutions of higher education has been determined, of course, to a large extent by the type of students which they attract. The colleges suffer the initial handicap of having to draw the majority of their students from inferior high schools. Northern students who attend Fisk University and Howard University are better prepared than those from southern schools.[58] Although many students come from the professional and business class, the majority come from the lower economic classes, in which the parents have little education.[59] The average Negro who enters the Negro college has had little contact with books and has not developed reading habits. Moreover, when he enters college he does not find an atmosphere where educational values and scholarship are highly respected. The intellectual discipline is often lax, partly because concessions must be made to the inadequate preparation of the students. Since education provides the chief means for social mobility in the Negro group, the mass of the student body is generally dominated by non-educational values cultivated by the children of the business and professional classes. As the great masses of the Negro population with essentially a plantation background are drawn into the colleges the difficulties of maintaining college standards are increased. Since Negro institutions which are undertaking graduate study draw their students principally from Negro colleges, they are faced with the same difficulties as the Negro colleges.

PRESENT STATUS OF NEGRO INSTITUTIONS
OF HIGHER EDUCATION

In 1939, at the request of the Association of Colleges and Secondary Schools for Negroes, Congress charged the United States Office of

[58] Cf. Ambrose Caliver, *A Personnel Study of Negro College Students* (New York, 1931), pp. 118-19.

[59] *Ibid.*, pp. 18 ff. See also Ambrose Caliver, *A Background Study of Negro College Students* (Washington, 1933).

Education with the responsibility of making a study of the higher education of Negroes.[60] In 1940 there were 118 institutions for Negroes which offered one or more years of college work.[61] Among these schools there were 33 publicly controlled and 52 privately controlled four-year colleges and three publicly controlled and 30 privately controlled schools which offered less than a four-year college course. In 114 of these institutions there were 44,000 resident undergraduate students. Of 102 institutions for which information was available, there were 33 colleges with 19,920 students enrolled rated "A" by the regional associations. These colleges had 50 per cent of the total enrollment in Negro colleges. There were 20 institutions with a "B" rating with 8,133 students, while the remaining 49 nonaccredited colleges had 11,740 students. Information on 20 public and 16 private colleges showed that, between 1930 and 1938, students' fees in public institutions had increased 96 per cent and in private institutions 17 per cent.[62] The value of the property holdings of public institutions had increased 40 per cent while that of private institutions had increased 41 per cent. The value of the equipment in public institutions had increased 25 per cent as compared with 55 per cent for private institutions.

On the other hand, there had been a decrease of 2 per cent in the endowment of private institutions and a decrease of 53 per cent in the amount of gifts to these institutions. In order to meet the loss of revenue from gifts, a number of the private Negro colleges (32 in 1948) organized with the support of outstanding white and Negro leaders

[60] U. S. Office of Education. *National Survey of the Higher Education of Negroes* (Washington, 1942), 4 vols. The first volume "deals with socio-economic factors, as a background for understanding the educational problems involved." This volume, which is basic to the entire study, was written by Ina Corinne Brown. "The second and third volumes deal mostly with the data gleaned from the Negro colleges and universities themselves, including statistics, historical and current, on students, staff, income and expenditures, and curricula maintained, the results of tests of freshmen and seniors, economic and other factors in the status of Negro high-school seniors, student health, college libraries, and a comprehensive qualitative evaluation of the total program of a representative group of Negro colleges." The second and third volumes were prepared by a number of specialists, including Miss Brown, in different fields. The fourth volume presents a summary of the principal findings. It was prepared by Ambrose Caliver, Senior Specialist in the Education of the Negro in the United States Office of Education. (Vol. 1, p. vii.)   [61] *Ibid.*, Vol. IV, p. 17.   [62] *Ibid.*, Vol. II, pp. 5-6.

the *United Negro College Fund* in 1944. The Fund appeals annually for financial support to the country as a whole rather than to the small group of philanthropists who formerly supported these private institutions. In view of the small amount of money, about $1,300,000, which is raised annually by the 32 colleges, contributions to the *Fund* are chiefly symbolic of the new attitude of the public toward the higher education of Negroes.

During recent years the enrollment of the 20 public and 16 private colleges has been 57 per cent male and 43 per cent female while the graduates were 60 per cent female and 40 per cent male. The typical freshman in the Negro college was described by the *National Survey* as follows:

The typical freshman in institutions of higher education for Negroes is 19 years of age. He attended Southern urban public elementary and secondary schools, which were, of course, attended altogether by Negro children and staffed, in the main, by Negro teachers. His father is in an occupation of low socio-economic level and his mother is a housewife. The annual income of the parents is reported to be $852. The cultural level of his home background, therefore, is probably not high and the financial status of his parents is such as to make the support of a college student burdensome. In spite of this fact he does not expect to meet some of his expenses by part-time work and he does not anticipate receiving scholarship aid from the college.

The performance of the typical freshman on psychological and achievement examinations is not of a high order.[63] . . . On a non-standardized test of knowledge about the Negro his score of 37 reveals an essential lack of knowledge about the history, literature, and social problems of his racial group.

The typical freshman plans to major in one of the academic fields and to enter teaching as his life's work.[64]

[63] For example, on the Test of Reading Comprehension the typical Negro freshman earned a raw score of 42.5 which stands at the 4th percentile. The percentile position of a given score in a distribution of scores indicates the percentage of scores falling below and above a given score. Therefore, the above score means that the typical Negro freshman has less reading comprehension than 96 per cent of the freshmen in the country whose reading comprehension is considered as normal for students of that grade.

[64] Office of Education, *National Survey of Higher Education of Negroes*, Vol. II, pp. 42-43.

After four years of college life the typical senior in a Negro college is 22 years, 6 months of age.

The elementary and secondary schools he attended were public schools located in a Southern city; he has, consequently, from the elementary school through the college never had any contact with white persons either as classmates or as teachers. His father ranks slightly higher in the scale of occupations than does the father of the typical freshman but still is in an occupation of low socio-economic level. His mother is a housewife. The annual income of the parents is reported to be $1,048. The cultural level of his home background, therefore, is probably not high and the financial status of his parents is such as to make the support of a college student burdensome. This fact is reflected in his statement that the predominant factor in his choice of a college was "financial," and that he contributed greatly to his own self-support during his college years.

His achievement on objective tests of subject-matter achievement is low. The raw scores (and the corresponding percentile ranks in terms of the test norms for end-of-year sophomores) which he earned on the several tests administered are as follows:

	Raw score	*Percentile rank*
General culture (total) . . .	93	10
Social studies	28	11
Literature	16	20
Fine arts	12	18
Science	25	25
Mathematics	9	16
Reading comprehension . . .	50	12
General knowledge of the Negro	52	. .

These relatively low scores reflect the cumulative result of sub-average educational facilities from the elementary school through the college. On a non-standardized test of knowledge about the Negro, this typical Negro college senior reveals an essential lack of knowledge about the history, literature, and social problems of his racial group.

The typical senior has majored in one of the academic subjects, is prepared to enter the occupation of secondary school teaching and expects to continue in this occupation as his life's work, in accordance with his aim when he entered college. He is planning to enter a northern graduate school within the next three years to work toward an advanced degree.[65]

[65] *Ibid.*, Vol. II, p. 43.

Striking individual differences were found among both college freshmen and college seniors. Male students, as a whole, were found superior to female students on almost all the tests that were given. One
of the most important differences was that between students from
northern and southern schools. The superiority of freshmen from
northern schools over those from southern schools was found to persist throughout the colleges.

A study of the faculties of 24 of the institutions revealed that these
institutions compared favorably with the institutions in the North
Central Association in the percentage of the staff holding the Master's
degree. But the Negro institutions were found to be deficient in the
number of staff members holding the doctorate and a large proportion
of those with the doctorate were in one institution.[66] This study also
confirmed what was stated above that the atmosphere of most of the
institutions was not conducive to scholarly activity and that the faculty morale was low. Low morale in the faculties was attributed to
low salaries, uncertain tenure, and the autocratic and paternalistic
administrations which characterize these institutions.

The facts revealed concerning Negro institutions of higher education in the *National Survey* and in our analysis of other sources of
information are the result primarily of the social and mental isolation
of the Negro community and its institutions. The segregation of the
Negro has meant inferior elementary and high schools. It has meant
that Negro colleges, being excluded from the benefit of public funds,
have had to depend upon philanthropy. The cumulative effects of an
inferior elementary and high school education have been reflected in
the type of student who enters the Negro college and the type of student who graduates from the Negro college. The setting up of graduate work in the Negro colleges has only aggravated the bad effects
of segregation. This is evidently recognized in one recommendation
of the *National Survey* where it is stated:

That, in order to develop qualified leaders to attack the difficult problems of the southern region, the institutions of higher learning for
white persons (a) work out ways and means of making their facilities
available to Negro scholars and graduate students; and (b) assist in

66 This institution was obviously Howard University.

providing opportunities, facilities, and leadership for the development of research among Negroes, particularly on problems peculiar to the South.[67]

At the present time there are only three Negro colleges, Fisk University, Howard University, and North Carolina College for Negroes that are recognized by the American Association of Universities and Colleges. Since the college departments of Fisk and Howard have provided the highest quality of college education for Negroes for over 75 years they undoubtedly deserve this recognition. But it is very questionable whether North Carolina College for Negroes should have been given a rating that only provides the basis for the legal fiction that the state provides the same type of higher education for Negroes as it offers whites.

RECENT ATTACKS ON SEGREGATION IN HIGHER EDUCATION

As the conviction has grown among Negroes that a segregated system of education means an inferior type of education, they have begun to attack the principle of segregation itself. The change in attitude toward segregated institutions of higher education and the provisions which some southern states have made for the education of Negroes outside of the states is indicated in a number of legal cases.[68] In the first case the Supreme Court of the state of Oklahoma handed down a decision in 1947 affirming the decision of a trial court that a young Negro woman, Ada Sipuel Fisher, who had applied for admission to the Law School of the University of Oklahoma, should not be admitted to the State University because it was a crime in Oklahoma for a Negro to attend a white school. When this case was carried to the Supreme Court of the United States, the court ruled that Negroes were entitled to receive in state institutions equal education of any type that white persons can obtain in such schools and that Negroes are entitled to receive such education as quickly as other persons. On

[67] Office of Education, *National Survey of Higher Education of Negroes,* Vol. IV, p. 49.

[68] George M. Johnson and Jane Marshall Lucas, "The Present Legal Status of the Negro Separate School," *The Journal of Negro Education,* Vol. XVI, pp. 285-89.

the basis of this decision District Judge Justin Hinshaw ruled that Mrs. Fisher must either be admitted to the Law School at the University of Oklahoma, until a separate law school for Negroes could be established or the University would have to close its law school to new students. Instead of admitting Mrs. Fisher, the University set up a law school for Negroes in committee rooms in the State Senate Building, gave them access to the State Law Library, and employed three faculty members including the dean of the Negro law school.

In April, 1947, a trial court in Louisiana dismissed the mandamus petitions of two Negro students to compel the State Medical and Law Schools to admit them on the grounds that they had not made the proper demand on the state Negro school which has neither a medical nor law school. In the third case, a Negro student appealed to the court to compel his admission to the Law School of the University of South Carolina. When an appeal was taken to the United States Supreme Court by the State of South Carolina, the Supreme Court sustained the ruling of the District Federal Court to the effect that the state must provide law education for Negroes or admit them to the State University. The fourth case is of particular significance because the appellate court of Texas sent the case back to the trial court for "further proceedings." These "further proceedings" included the testimony of several experts from Negro and white universities showing that it was not possible for Negroes to secure in a segregated school a legal education equal to that available to whites in the state university. Nevertheless, in May 1947 the trial court dismissed for a second time the petition of the Negro student. Although the state of Texas has gone ahead in building up a separate Negro university it is likely that the question whether Negro students are receiving education equal to that provided for white students will be carried to the United States Supreme Court.

It has become clear that only "a policy of non-segregation in higher education would satisfy the letter and the spirit of the decisions of the Supreme Court." [69] As the result of the decisions of the Supreme

[69] See American Council on Race Relations, "Memorandum on Racial Segregation in Higher Education." Mimeographed release.

Court Maryland and West Virginia and more recently Delaware have begun to integrate Negroes into the state graduate and professional schools. Even in Oklahoma, despite the opposition of some of the press to the Supreme Court decisions and the present failure of the liberal forces to give effective support to the Supreme Court rulings, the white students themselves have expressed their disapproval of the continued exclusion of Negro students. There are many other indications that the white students of the South are inclined to accept Negro students in graduate and professional schools and that the possibility of integrating Negro students is greater than the most vocal elements in the South are ready to admit.

The futility of the attempts to provide "separate but equal" graduate and professional education for Negroes in the South has been fully demonstrated in Arkansas, Missouri, and Oklahoma. In Arkansas a plan has been set up to accept Negro students but to teach them in separate classes. The expensiveness of such a plan, which may involve the setting up of a separate class for one student, not to mention its absurdity, will bring about its termination. The state of Missouri built a new building for a School of Journalism on the Lincoln University campus for Negroes at a cost of $65,000 in 1941, and a faculty costing $13,000 annually was employed. During the three years, 1941 to 1943, the student body increased from two to 14 and then declined. In order to maintain a separate college at Lincoln University the state spends $697 per capita for 1,228 Negro students and $229 per capita for 17,010 white students at the University of Missouri. In the state of Oklahoma, where $15,500 was spent for the salaries of the dean and two professors in the Law School established for Negroes, the young woman for whom the school was set up refused to attend.

Recently there has been a proposal to set up regional graduate and professional schools for Negroes. As a first step in this direction, a number of governors in southern states have become interested in making Meharry Medical School, which was in financial straits, a regional school for the training of Negro doctors. A bill was submitted to the Congress of the United States to authorize the establishment of Meharry as a regional college in order to comply with the decisions of the Supreme Court respecting equal educational facilities for Negroes. This bill, which was defeated, was opposed by the National Association for the Advancement of Colored People and other Negro and white groups. The opposition to the regional plan was based upon the fact that it was not only an evasion of the Supreme Court decisions that the states provide equal education within their borders but it would perpetuate the segregation pattern and would not insure equal education for Negroes.

The basic issue of segregation in the education of Negroes was well stated in the report of the President's Committee on Civil Rights:

Segregation has become the cornerstone of the elaborate structure of discrimination against some American citizens. Theoretically this system simply duplicates educational, recreational and other public services, according facilities to the two races which are "separate but equal." In the Committee's opinion this is one of the outstanding myths of American history for it is almost always true that while indeed separate, these facilities are far from equal. . . .

. . . we believe not even the most mathematically precise equality of segregated institutions can properly be considered equality under the law. No argument or rationalization can alter this basic fact; a law which forbids a group of American citizens to associate with other citizens in the ordinary course of daily living creates inequality by imposing a caste status on the minority group.[70]

The President's Commission on Higher Education pointed out the undesirable effects of segregation upon the education of whites as well as Negroes:

Although segregation may not legally mean discrimination as to quality of the facilities it does so in fact. . . . Segregation lessens the quality of education for the whites as well. To maintain two school systems side by side—duplicating even inadequately the buildings and teaching personnel—means that neither can be of the quality that would be possible if all the available resources were devoted to one system, especially not when the States least able financially to support

[70] *To Secure These Rights*. The Report of the President's Committee on Civil Rights (New York, 1947), pp. 81-82.

an adequate educational program for their youth are the very ones that are trying to carry a double load.[71]

The majority of the Commission agreed that

If education is to make the attainment of a more perfect democracy one of its major goals, it is imperative that it extend its benefits to all on equal terms. It must renounce the practices of discrimination and segregation in educational institutions as contrary to the spirit of democracy. Educational leaders and institutions should take positive steps to overcome the conditions which at present obstruct free and equal access to educational opportunities. Educational programs everywhere should be aimed at undermining and eventually eliminating the attitudes that are responsible for discrimination and segregation—at creating attitudes that will make education freely available to all.[72]

At the same time that legal attacks are being made on segregated institutions of higher education for Negroes in the South, changes are occurring in the practices of northern institutions in respect to the Negro. First, there has been a growing tendency to omit racial identification from application blanks and registration cards in northern universities. Then there has been the report of the Temporary Commission on the Need for a State University in the State of New York, which recommended to the governor that public funds, either state or local, should be made available to educational institutions only upon the condition that such institutions admit students on the basis of individual merit without regard to race, color, creed, or national origins and that scholarships and fellowships provided by the state or local governments be awarded on the same basis.[73] Following the submission of these recommendations the New York State Legislature enacted a law forbidding racial and religious discrimination in the admission of students to private colleges, universities and professional schools.[74]

The most important change in the policies of northern colleges and

---

[71] *Higher Education for Democracy.* A Report of the President's Commission on Higher Education (Washington, December 1947), p. 34.

[72] *Ibid.,* p. 34.

[73] U. S. Office of Education, *Higher Education* (April 1, 1948), p. 174.

[74] *New York Times*, March 14, 1948, p. 57.

universities in regard to Negroes has been the appointment of Negroes to their teaching staffs. Probably the first Negro to teach in a "white" university was Richard T. Greener, the first Negro graduate of Harvard University, who was a professor of Latin and Greek at the University of South Carolina during the Reconstruction period.[75] Since then only one or two Negroes have been appointed to the teaching staffs of white colleges until recent years. During World War II northern colleges began to appoint Negroes for summer school terms or as special lecturers. Sometimes these appointments were encouraged and supported by the Julius Rosenwald Fund, the General Education Board, and the American Friends Service Committee.[76] A study of appointments of Negroes to northern institutions for the years 1945-1946 and 1946-1947 showed that 45 Negroes had been appointed to the faculties of northern institutions.[77] Twenty-three of the 45 Negro teachers were on regular appointments. From the summer of 1945 to the summer of 1947 a total of 52 Negroes had been appointed to the faculties of northern universities; 26 of these Negroes had continuing assignments.[78]

The development of Negro institutions of higher education was a natural outgrowth of a segregated system of education. They emerged just after the basic tenets of American culture respecting human equality had been tested in a Civil War. Those who had sincerely held these beliefs built educational institutions that would provide an opportunity for the black freedmen to find the fullest expression for their intellectual capacities. At first these institutions were dependent upon private philanthropy and only gradually did they secure even a minimum of financial support from public funds. Consequently, these institutions have suffered from inadequate financial support, poorly trained teachers, and the absence of a tradition of scholarship and learning. Moreover, they have helped to perpetuate the mental isolation of the Negro. Since they have been controlled

[75] Ivan E. Taylor, "Negro Teachers in White Colleges," *School and Society*, Vol. 65, p. 370.   [76] See *ibid.*, pp. 370ff.

[77] William C. Haygood, "Negro Teachers in White Institutions," *The Phi Delta Kappan*, Vol. 28, pp. 74-75.

[78] Communication from *The American Council on Race Relations*. Chicago, Illinois.

largely by the dominant white group, they have been an agency in maintaining the subordination of the Negro. As the Negro has gained a broader outlook through education and the mobility resulting from the migrations to cities and two world wars, he is beginning to revolt against this violation of the democratic creed upon which the nation is based.

CHAPTER XIX

Negro Press and Literature

THE earliest literary efforts of American Negroes were poetic in form and not only showed the influence of the contemporary literary culture of the whites but contained reflections on the Negro's condition in the new environment. For a half century, from 1790 to 1840, the literature of the Negro emanated from the church organizations set up by free Negroes and gave evidence of the growing race consciousness of this group in the North. During this period a Negro college graduate established the first Negro newspaper.

From 1840 to the end of the Civil War, the writings of the Negro were directed chiefly against slavery. These writings generally appeared in the form of biographies and autobiographies of ex-slaves or in a number of newspapers that sprang up at this time. After Emancipation the literary efforts of the Negro found expression in biography, history, theology and oratory, and even sociological works. It was during this period that the various religious and fraternal organs began to appear in large numbers.

During the last decade of the nineteenth century the Negro newspaper, both as a medium of communication and as a business venture, was beginning to acquire some significance. These developments continued into the twentieth century with the appearance of a few Negro writers with a more sophisticated literary interest in the Negro's past. In the wake of the mass migrations to northern cities came a literary renaissance in which Negro writers undertook a re-evaluation of the Negro's past history in America. During this same period the Negro newspaper developed in response to the increased literacy and sophistication of the urbanized masses. Negro newspapers have continued to become more important as business organizations and as molders of public opinion as well as reflectors of the outlook of the Negro. The increasing literary contributions of the Negro, which are gaining ever wider acceptance, have revealed not only greater technical competence in expressing his frustrations but have shown the growing sophistication of the Negro in the modern world.

EARLY LITERARY EFFORTS OF THE NEGRO

The earliest literary efforts of the Negro in the American environment are to be found in the poetic creations of Jupiter Hammon, a slave belonging to a family on Long Island. Hammon, about whose life little is known, was born about 1720 and lived until after the United States was established as a nation.[1] It appears that Hammon received no formal instruction beyond elementary training in reading and writing. He was allowed time to engage in preaching and it is likely that in addition to reading the Bible and hymn books he was acquainted with English religious poems. The few ventures of Hammon in prose did not have any literary value. His poetry, however, reveals the influence of his religious environment and the New Testament. Although it was artless and crude on the whole, it reveals a keen sense of sound and a sincerity of feeling that make it a unique contribution to American poetry in the eighteenth century. One of his best poems, addressed to Phillis Wheatley, embodied the theme that through divine providence she was brought from heathen Africa in order that she might acquire the true religion and teach it to others.[2]

Phillis Wheatley was between seven and eight years of age when she was brought from Africa to America in 1761. She was bought by a wealthy Boston tailor and merchant to serve as a maid for his wife.[3] With only the education provided by her master's family, Phillis Wheatley gained considerable mastery of the English language within less than two years. Her poetry, unlike that of Hammon with its touch of originality, is distinguished chiefly as an achievement in imitation. Her work was "sophisticated rather than primitive, artificial

[1] Vernon Loggins, *The Negro Author* (New York, 1931), pp. 9-16.
[2] *Ibid.*, p. 14.   [3] *Ibid.*, pp. 17-29.

rather than spontaneous, polished rather than crude." [4] An interesting feature about her poetry was that with the exception of a few specific references there was nothing in it to identify it as the work of a Negro. In fact, her poetry was typical of the sentimental poetry which was being turned out by the versifiers in America and England during the eighteenth century. Her precocity was revealed by the fact that as a mere child she was able to imitate the idiom of Alexander Pope. Phillis Wheatley's works revealed a deep religious feeling and reflected her Puritan training. At the same time they contained a musical quality which indicated that in another environment, she might have been an ornament in American literature.

NEGRO LITERARY EXPRESSION FROM 1790 TO 1840

During the latter half of the eighteenth century a few prose writers appeared among Negroes. Outstanding among the prose works produced by Negroes were a thoughtful protest against slavery, Benjamin Banneker's *Almanac,* and the *Life of Olaudah Equino or Gustavus Vassa.* It was not, however, until the last decade of the eighteenth century that there began to appear the prose expression of Negro leaders which ushered in a new period in the literary efforts of the Negro in American life. During the last decade of the eighteenth century separate Negro church organizations, as we have seen, were established by the free Negroes in the North.[5] The leaders in these organizations were men who had been born slaves but had secured their freedom. They supplemented the little formal education which they had been able to secure by self-education. Their revolt against the subordinate position of the Negro in the white church was indicative of the growing race consciousness among this class in the North. In a pamphlet published in 1794 Richard Allen and Absalom Jones answered the attack that had been made upon the conduct of Negroes during the yellow-fever epidemic in Philadelphia in 1792 and 1793. Although the writing was crude it was courageous and honest. Later Allen wrote his autobiography, a book on the doctrine and discipline of the African Methodist Episcopal Church of which he was the

---

[4] *The Negro Author* by Vernon Loggins, p. 16. Copyright 1931 by Columbia University.   [5] See Chapter XIV above.

founder, and a forceful argument against the colonization of the free Negro. Jones' independent literary production was confined to a Thanksgiving sermon, which showed signs of assistance from others. Two publications by Daniel Coker, one of the leaders in the establishment of the African Methodist Episcopal Church, gave indications of a superior educational background. One publication was a well written antislavery tract and the other an account of a voyage to Africa.

Outstanding among the free Negroes of the North who used the pen in defense of the rights of the free Negro was Robert Purvis, who was born in Charleston, South Carolina. He was sent by his wealthy white father to Philadelphia to receive a sound private education. His father willed him a relatively large fortune which enabled him to live as a man of leisure. His work, *Appeal of Forty Thousand Citizens Threatened with Disfranchisement to the People of Pennsylvania,* was written to voice the sentiments of a convention of colored people. The Appeal, which contained information on the progress of the free colored people, was based on the principle of no taxation without representation.

David Ruggles stands out as the most radical and most fearless of the free Negroes in New York who defended the rights of free Negroes. Ruggles attracted attention as the secretary of the Committee of Vigilance, an organization which undertook the protection of free Negroes especially when they were arrested under the pretext of being fugitive slaves. His literary works, which were chiefly controversial, were distinguished by their sharpness in tone and biting sarcasm. For example, in one of the pamphlets, which he wrote in a reply to an attack on the American Anti-Slavery League in which the author charged that the abolitionists approved intermarriage, he retorted: "What of it? It is not repugnant to nature." [6] Ruggles has the distinction of having published the first Negro magazine, *Mirror of Liberty,* though the magazine was short-lived.[7]

There were Negro leaders who wrote in a more conciliatory vein

[6] Loggins, *op. cit.,* p. 80.
[7] Charles S. Johnson, "The Rise of the Negro Magazine," *Journal of Negro History,* Vol. XIII, pp. 7-21.

than did Ruggles. One such leader, Prince Hall, the founder of Negro masonry, had admonished Negroes to "kiss the rod and be still, and see the works of God." [8] But it appears that this type of conciliatory sentiment was drowned by the more radical expressions of Negro leaders.

The most violent antithesis to the conciliatory attitude was to be found in the famous *Appeal* of David Walker. As we have seen, at one time the state of Georgia offered $10,000 for Walker if taken alive because of the *Appeal*.[9] Walker, a free Negro, left North Carolina because in his words, "If I remain in this bloody land, I will not live long." [10] It seems that Walker learned to read and write in Boston, where he became a successful clothing merchant. Although the *Appeal*, published in 1829, caused even some of the most radical abolitionists to oppose Walker, it went through three editions. In the "Preamble" of the *Appeal* Walker states his conviction that as the result of his observations during travels, Negroes are the most "degraded, wretched, and abject set of beings that ever lived since the world began." In Article I he gives a description of the sufferings of Negroes and expresses his contempt of Negroes who marry whites. In Article II he describes the ignorance of Negroes and advises them to change their status by the acquisition of education. The first section of the book is a satire on American Christianity with an exhortation that the slaves rise up against their masters. Although other Negroes wrote in a similar tone, their work did not gain the attention of Walker's *Appeal*.

The prose writings of the Negro during the period 1790 to 1840 are not only a measure of the extent to which he had acquired literacy and thereby broken down his mental isolation but they also contain the reflections of the Negro upon his anomalous position in American life. The reflections of the Negro upon his position were expressed in agitation and some of this agitation found expression in the earliest Negro newspaper. Samuel Cornish, a Presbyterian Minister, and John B. Russworm, a graduate of Bowdoin and the first Negro college

[8] See Loggins, *op. cit.*, p. 85.   [9] See p. 97 above.
[10] Quoted in *The Negro Author* by Victor Loggins, p. 85. Copyright 1934 by Columbia University Press.

graduate in the United States, established the first Negro newspaper in the United States in 1827.[11] Cornish resigned after the first issue and Russworm conducted the paper until 1829, when he resigned to go to Liberia. Cornish resumed the editorship of the paper, the name being changed to *Rights For All*. A second Negro newspaper, which scarcely survived two issues, was published in 1831. Then a third Negro newspaper, the *Colored American*, which was established in 1837 and continued for four years, was also edited by Cornish.

During the first four decades of the nineteenth century, some ex-slave biographies began to appear. But there were important literary expressions of the Negro's attitude toward his status in American life. The works of two Negro writers merit mention. One was a minister of the Congregational church in Connecticut and Vermont and the other a slave in North Carolina. The work of Lemuel Haynes, the Congregational minister, is of interest because he was the offspring of a white mother and an African father and married a white woman and became integrated in the New England community. After being abandoned by his white mother, he became a bonded servant of her employer. His term of indenture expired in 1774 and he joined the "Patriot Army" in 1776 after two years of service as a "minute man." He supplemented the meager education which he had received as a bonded servant in the home of a pastor, where he had learned Greek and Latin. He was ordained as a minister in 1785 and after serving as a pastor in Connecticut accepted a call in Vermont. He enjoyed the friendship of the presidents of Amherst College and Yale University. Haynes' literary works consisted of sermons, the most famous being "Universal Salvation" and letters containing moral anecdotes and remarks on the Scriptures. His works reflected the mysticism of his Puritan environment.

A more interesting figure during this period was George Moses Horton, who was a slave in North Carolina and remained in slavery until Emancipation. Horton brought out his first book of poems, *The Hope of Liberty*, in 1829. The book was reprinted in Philadelphia in

[11] See I. Garland Penn, *The Afro-American Press, and Its Editors* (Springfield, Mass., 1891), pp. 26ff; Frederick G. Detweiler, *The Negro Press in the United States* (Chicago, 1922); and Loggins, *op. cit.*, pp. 78-79.

1837. As a poet Horton has been placed among the "psychological *genre* so well illustrated by the singing, life-drunk and wine-drunk François Villon and Robert Burns." [12] The poems in *The Hope of Liberty* deal with love, death, religion, and nature. These same subjects were treated in a later book of poems, *Naked Genius*. However, the latter book does not contain the crudities of the first book and there is a spirit of merriment toward himself as well as life in general. Horton's poems did not possess the naturalness of Hammon's poetry nor did they exhibit the sophisticated imitation of Phillis Wheatley. He had undoubtedly read Pope, Milton, and other English poets, but what was inspired by reading these authors was essentially his own creations.

NEGRO LITERARY EFFORTS DIRECTED AGAINST SLAVERY

From 1840 until the close of the Civil War, the Negro author expressed himself in most of the fields of literature. By 1840 the agitation over slavery had become nationwide. In the North the free Negroes were subject to even more discriminations than formerly. However, the Negro was gaining white friends who were defending his rights. Although some Negroes were able to get a higher or professional education under extreme difficulties, few of the outstanding leaders were college-trained men. The outstanding leaders among Negroes were men who were educated by the antislavery agitation. It was in the field of controversial writing on slavery that the Negro had his best opportunity for self-expression.

There were three Negro writers during this period who made outstanding contributions to the literary efforts of the Negro. There was Alexander Crummell, never a slave, who was born in New York City in 1819. After receiving some education in the United States and being ordained an Episcopal minister, he went to England, where he received the degree of Bachelor of Arts from the University of Cambridge in 1853. After receiving the degree from Cambridge he went to Africa where he remained 20 years. However, just before his departure

[12] *The Negro Author* by Vernon Loggins p. 107. Copyright 1931 by Columbia University Press.

for England he delivered a eulogy on the life of Thomas Clarkson, which became an important part of the growing literary expressions of Negroes. The major portion of the literary work of Crummell belongs to the period between the Civil War and the last decade of the nineteenth century.

Unlike Crummell, who was a pure Negro and free, William Wells Brown, whose mulatto mother according to rumor was a daughter of Daniel Boone, was the son of a white man and was born a slave in Kentucky. After escaping from slavery and working as a free Negro in Cleveland and Buffalo, Brown was legally emancipated in 1854. He was a self-educated man and became a devoted follower of Garrison, the abolitionist. In addition to his many contributions to the abolitionist press, he wrote a narrative of the rise and fall of Toussaint L'Ouverture and an autobiography, which was published by the Massachusetts Anti-Slavery Society in 1847. The story of his life is one of the most readable of the slave autobiographies and despite its sensationalism, the simplicity of the account marks it as a genuine creation of the author. Later Brown wrote songs, probably with the cooperation of others, for abolition meetings. He wrote a book on his travels in Europe and a novel, *Clotel, or the President's Daughter,* the heroine of which was supposed to be the colored daughter of Thomas Jefferson. In 1863 Brown brought out a history of the Negro containing a discussion of Egypt and Ethiopia and biographies of Negroes.

Frederick Douglass, who was born a slave in Maryland in 1817, was the most outstanding contributor to the literary efforts of Negroes during this period. Douglass ran away from slavery and started his career as a speaker by relating his experiences as a slave at an abolitionist meeting. Soon it became apparent that Douglass was an ideal orator for the abolitionist cause. This was due not so much to the fact that he could give a realistic account of his life as a slave as to his intellectual power and logic in his indictment of slavery. From 1841 to 1845, Douglass traveled as an antislavery agent under Garrison's direction. Then he went to England to lecture for two years. The experience in England helped to mature Douglass in his outlook. After he returned to the United States in 1847, he began his career as an independent journalist. In 1860 Douglass returned to England because he was accused of complicity in John Brown's raid at Harpers Ferry.

Douglass' contributions to Negro literature during this period fall under three heads: oratory, autobiography, and journalism. Before he began writing anything for publication, he had established himself as an orator. Even by 1843 he was included with such distinguished orators as Phillips and Garrison for lectures in Boston. His power as an orator was recognized by the opponents as well as the advocates of abolition. When he returned from England in 1847 his supremacy as an abolitionist orator was undisputed. His speeches from then until the end of the Civil War form a body of passionate though logical oratory unsurpassed by the work of his contemporaries. Although Douglass' first autobiographical work, *Narrative of the Life of Frederick Douglass*, published in 1845, conformed to the pattern of the conventional slave autobiography, it was superior to any autobiography that had been published by a Negro. Because of its simplicity, the work conveyed the deep feeling of the author and the dramatic incidents were fused with the logical argument. A decade later, Douglass published his second autobiography, *My Bondage and My Freedom*. The second work was distinguished by greater accuracy and a broader and deeper appreciation of human nature. Three years before Douglass published his first autobiography, he had begun to write letters to the *Liberator* and the *National Anti-Slavery Standard*. When he returned to the United States in 1847, he decided to use the $2,000 contributed by abolitionists in England in an independent journalistic enterprise. His first paper, the *North Star*, the name being symbolic of the slave's guide to freedom, was modeled after the abolitionist papers of the day. In 1850 the name of the paper was changed to *Frederick Douglass' Paper*. The purpose of the paper was to attack slavery in all of its forms and to advocate universal emancipation. Douglass' paper gradually lost its distinctively Negro character and became a political organ, devoting more space very often to Presidential messages and reports of speeches of congressmen than to matters pertaining directly to the Negro.

The period 1840 to 1865, when Negro writers were especially prolific in their literary efforts, is characterized by a wide variety of literary undertakings. William C. Nell made a serious attempt to write an extensive history of the Negro in the United States; James McCune Smith undertook to show what the Negro might accomplish in western civilization; and a Negro physician, Martin R. Delany, undertook sociological studies of the Negro in the United States as well as the study of Negroes in Africa. Moreover, Negroes began to write histories of the Negro church. Numerous autobiographies of Negroes appeared, one of the outstanding of which was *The Fugitive Blacksmith* by James W. C. Pennington, who had received the degree of Doctor of Divinity from the University of Heidelberg. There was much poetry published by Negroes during this period, the best known poet being a free Negro woman, Frances E. W. Harper, who was born in Baltimore in 1825.

THE "LITERATURE" OF THE SLAVES

So far we have considered the literary efforts of the Negroes who were free before the Civil War. These literary efforts were the expressions of individuals and did not embody the aspirations and outlook on life of the mass of the Negro population. In the technical meaning of the word there was no literature expressing the hopes and aspirations of the great body of Negroes who were slaves. But in the sociological meaning of the term, the folk songs of the Negro represented the literature of slavery.[13] The Negro folk songs, as Park shows, were a poetic expression of the inner life of the Negro slaves. The secular folk songs, which embodied the reflections of the slaves on the incidents of their daily life, did not long outlive the occasions that called them forth. On the other hand, the religious folk songs or the spirituals have continued their hold and influence. The spirituals arose out of communal excitement and expressed the deep unconscious wishes of the slaves. They contained the slaves' ecstatic visions of another world which provided a compensation for the present world of woes and unfulfilled wishes. These rude hymns of the slaves, like litera-

[13] See Robert E. Park, "Negro Consciousness as Reflected in Race Literature," *American Review*, Vol. I, pp. 509-17, for a summary of the evolution of Negro literature, especially poetry, from the standpoint of its sociological implications.

ture in general, embodied their hopes and fears and were handed down orally from one generation to another.

BARREN YEARS OF NEGRO LITERARY EXPRESSION

From the close of the Civil War until the last decade of the nineteenth century, the literary efforts of the Negro lacked the inspiration of the previous twenty-five years. It was a period when the Negro was forced to deal with the realities of his new status rather than the visions of a new world of freedom. Negroes continued to publish autobiographies. Douglass brought out his *Life and Times of Frederick Douglass* in 1883; Elizabeth Keckley, the ostensible author of *Behind the Scenes*, published an account of her life in the Lincoln household; and John M. Langston in his *From the Virginia Plantation to the National Capital* told the story of his remarkable career. In 1883 George Washington Williams published his *History of the Negro Race in America*, a dignified work, which was reviewed favorably by serious magazines. Five years later he brought out his *The Negro in the American Rebellion*, which because of the facts presented was regarded as a fairly respectable history. It was in the writings of Negro church leaders, however, that one finds the most characteristic literary expressions of this period. In the eighties appeared such histories of the Negro church as Reverend A. Wayman's *My Recollections of African M. E. Ministers* and Bishop Tanner's *An Outline of Our History and Our Government* and Reverend E. K. Love's *History of the First African Baptist Church*. During this same decade there were published many addresses and sermons of Negro preachers. The finest achievements of Negro pulpit oratory were to be found in Crummell's *The Greatness of Christ*. In the nineties a flood of histories of Negro churches and sermons continued to flow from the press. However, in a book like Bishop H. M. Turner's *The Black Man's Doom* condemning the Supreme Court's decision declaring the Civil Rights Act unconstitutional, one can see the growing concern of Negro leaders with the status of the Negro during this period.

The literary works of Negroes which are cited above are indicative of the increasing literacy of the Negro after Emancipation. However, when one studies the poetry of the Negro during this period, it is apparent that this growing literacy has caused the Negro's poetic expression to lose its spontaneity and to become pedantic and turgid.[14] For this reason Park has called this period the Dark Ages of Negro poetry. Freedom had brought a change in the Negro ethos and he was trying to prove to himself and to the world that he was a man like other men.

NEGRO LITERARY EXPRESSION DURING THE YEARS OF ACCOMMODATION

The period beginning in the nineties and extending through the first decade of the twentieth century was, as we have seen, a period in which the Negro was forced to accept a status similar to a subordinate caste in the South.[15] It was during this period that the famous controversy between Booker T. Washington and W. E. B. DuBois developed concerning the attitude and strategy of the Negro toward his status in American life. The controversial writings of these two leaders, especially the writings of DuBois, belong in the field of sociological writings. In 1896 DuBois inaugurated the *Atlanta University Studies* of the Negro, which represented the first attempt to study in a scientific spirit the problems of the Negro in American life. DuBois' *The Souls of Black Folk*, published in 1903, contained sociological essays, which commanded attention both because of their penetrating analyses and because of their superb literary quality. The writings of Washington and DuBois will be considered in detail in the following chapter on "Negro Leadership and the Negro Intelligentsia."

During this period beginning in 1890 there was a rapid development in Negro journalism. According to DuBois, there were in 1898 3 magazines, 3 daily papers, 11 school papers, and 136 weekly papers owned by Negroes.[16] The three magazines included two Methodist quarterly reviews. The daily papers were published in Norfolk, Virginia, Washington, D. C., and Kansas City, Kansas. Thirteen of the 70 weekly papers for which information was furnished were published by religious organizations and secret and other societies. Only one of

[14] *Ibid.*, p. 512.   [15] See Chapter VIII above.
[16] W. E. B. DuBois, *The Negro in Business* (Atlanta, 1899), pp. 73-77.

the 66 leading newspapers had been established before the Civil War. In view of the illiteracy of Negroes and their concentration in rural areas, one cannot accept DuBois' statement that nearly all Negro families read Negro newspapers.

The Negro newspapers were springing up in response to the increasing literacy of the Negroes concentrated in cities and presented the opinions of the educated Negroes. In 1901, Monroe Trotter, a graduate of Harvard University, began publishing the *Guardian* in Boston. This paper voiced the opposition of the educated Negro in the North to the conciliatory attitude of Booker T. Washington toward the denial of the citizenship rights of the Negro in the South. On the other hand, the *New York Age* became the defender of Washington's philosophy of racial adjustment in the South. *The Crisis*, the official organ of the National Association for the Advancement of Colored People, began publication in 1910, with W. E. B. DuBois as editor. This magazine represented the new militancy of the educated Negro, especially in the North, aided by liberal whites, toward the growing restrictions upon the citizenship rights of the Negro.

In considering the purely literary contributions of this period, our attention is directed to Booker T. Washington's *Up From Slavery*, originally published serially in the *Outlook*, which appeared at the turn of the century. Although few people, white or colored, realize that it is only one of many autobiographies by Negroes and that it is not the best, it has won a place in American literature similar to Benjamin Franklin's *Autobiography*.[17] It is generally recognized that its pre-eminence among autobiographies by Negroes is not due to superior literary qualities. Its place in American literature is due partly, of course, to the position achieved by its author. But more important than that fact is the sincerity of the book in expressing the personality development of a Negro in the American environment. Washington wrote a number of other books, some with the cooperation of Professor Robert E. Park, but none has achieved a place in American literature. In 1907 Washington published his *Frederick Douglass*, which was a tribute to his distinguished predecessor. This biographical work did not possess the literary merit of *Frederick Douglass* by

[17] Loggins, *op. cit.*, p. 267.

Charles W. Chestnutt or the biographies written by Archibald H. Grimké. Grimké was selected to write *William Lloyd Garrison, the Abolitionist* and *The Life of Charles Sumner, the Scholar in Politics* for the "American Reformers" series. These works, which were worthy contributions to the series, and the work of Chestnutt indicated that Negroes were beginning to take their place in American literature.

The period from 1890 to around 1915 was a period when Negro literary efforts began to show signs of maturing. There were two outstanding figures who represented the tendencies of this period in the development of Negro literature. One was Charles W. Chestnutt, the novelist, and the other Paul Laurence Dunbar, the poet. Chestnutt, who was born in Cleveland in 1858, began teaching, when only 16 years old, in the public schools of the State of North Carolina, from which his parents had migrated to Ohio.[18] After serving two years as principal of the State Normal School in Fayetteville, he engaged in newspaper work in New York City for a short period. He then returned to Cleveland and was admitted to the bar in 1887. In the same year, Chestnutt published a short story, "The Gophered Grapevine," in the *Atlantic Monthly*. This was the beginning of his career as an author of short stories and novels that extended over a period of 20 years. In 1889 appeared his *The Conjure Woman*, a collection of seven short stories, the majority of which had been published in magazines. The short stories in this collection are based upon the folklore of the Negro with which Chestnutt had become acquainted during his residence in the South. This book was not only a sincere work of art but it also exhibited originality and rare skill in its execution. Chestnutt's subsequent volume of short stories and three novels dealing with the color line did not measure up artistically to his achievement in *The Conjure Woman*. Only in "Baxter's Procrustes," a short story in which the Negro does not appear, published in the *Atlantic Monthly* in 1904, did he equal and, in fact, excel his artistic achievement in *The Conjure Woman*. If Chestnutt had written only these two pieces, he would have a distinguished place in the history of the literary development of the Negro.

[18] See Benjamin Brawley, *The Negro Genius* (New York, 1937), pp. 145-51; and Loggins, *op. cit.*, pp. 310-31.

DAWN OF A NEW SPIRIT IN NEGRO LITERATURE

In his *The Souls of Black Folk* DuBois presented a classic picture of the "double consciousness" of the Negro who lived in two social worlds. The "double consciousness" of which DuBois wrote represented the confusion of the Negro ethos in a world where he was free but was not accepted as a full citizen. Paul Laurence Dunbar stands out in the development of Negro literary expression as the first Negro poet who was able to resolve the inner conflict created by this "double consciousness" and view objectively the Negro folk. He made no apology for the Negro folk and without prejudice he represented the Negro truthfully and with sympathy and humor.[19]

Although Dunbar was only in his thirty-fourth year when he died in 1906, he had won a secure place in the history of literary expression among American Negroes. After completing high school in Dayton, Ohio, his birthplace, he was compelled to accept a job as an elevator boy. This did not crush his determination to write poetry, a task to which he had set himself in high school. In 1893 appeared *Oak and Ivy* and in 1895 *Majors and Minors,* two volumes of poetry which were privately printed. The latter work was brought to the attention of William Dean Howells, who wrote a full-page review in *Harper's Weekly* for June 27, 1897. Dunbar was thus able to secure a standard publisher for his third volume, *Lyrics of Lowly Life,* which contained the best poems in his first two volumes and an introduction by Howells. This work established Dunbar in the United States and in England as the first American Negro to give lyric expression to a truly esthetic feeling for Negro life.

Dunbar's literary creations embraced four fields: poems in classic English, dialect poems, short stories, and novels. In his first three novels, dealing with white characters, Dunbar did not distinguish himself as a writer. Even his *The Sport of the Gods,* in which he deals with Negro characters, is a poor specimen of fiction because of its sentimentality and melodrama. Although Dunbar made his most distinctive contribution in his dialect poems, it appears that he wanted to be known as a writer of classic English verse. In a poem of eight

[19] Park, *loc. cit.*

lines, he states that he "sang of life" and his song now and then had a "deeper note" but the world only praised a "jingle in a broken tongue." But the "deeper notes" in his poems in classic English are often sentimental and conventional, though they often express the bitterness and frustration of his brief life. It is possible that Dunbar's attitude toward his dialect poetry reflected the ambivalent attitude of the Negro intelligentsia of his day toward the folk life of the Negro. In his dialect poems he presented in artistic form the rural Negro folk as human beings. His dialect poetry, which still possesses a certain freshness because it was inspired by sincere feeling, will always remain a repository of the colorful and poetic language of the Negro folk.

One of the most important literary contributions at the end of the century, from a sociological standpoint, was the appearance of James Weldon Johnson's "Lift Ev'ry Voice and Sing." Johnson, who was born in Florida in 1871, was graduated from Atlanta University in 1894.[20] While principal of a Negro public school in Jacksonville, Florida, which he succeeded in raising to the status of a high school, he collaborated with his brother, Rosamond, in writing songs. The poem, "Lift Ev'ry Voice and Sing," was written originally for school children who were giving a program to celebrate Lincoln's birthday anniversary. In this poem Johnson endowed the Negro's enslavement and struggle for freedom with a certain nobility. The poem expressed an acceptance of the past and a confidence in the future.[21] Perhaps, it might be said that Johnson's poem tended to cultivate a sense of history among Negroes. At least, this viewpoint is supported by the fact that "Lift Ev'ry Voice and Sing" has become the national hymn for Negroes and is often sung at the opening of their public gatherings.

NEGRO RENAISSANCE FOLLOWING THE MASS MIGRATIONS

Following in the wake of the mass migrations to northern cities during and following World War I, there came what became known as the Negro Renaissance. The "first fruits" of this Negro Renaissance

[20] Benjamin Brawley, *The Negro Genius* (New York, 1937), pp. 206 ff.
[21] Park, *loc. cit.*

appeared in *The New Negro*, edited by Alain Locke, in 1925.[22] One of the contributors to this volume was James Weldon Johnson who wrote on Harlem as the "cultural capital" of the Negro in the United States.[23] The creative work of James Weldon Johnson, whose poem "Lift Ev'ry Voice and Sing" we have discussed, forms a bridge from the period when Negro writers began to write in a sophisticated manner about their past history and the period of the Negro Renaissance. His book, *Fifty Years and Other Poems*, appeared in 1917 when the migration of southern Negroes to northern cities was at its height. In his poem entitled, "O Black and Unknown Bards," he asks:

> How came your lips to touch the sacred fire?
> How, in your darkness, did you come to know
> The power and beauty of the minstrel's lyre?

In this poetic fashion he was really voicing a re-evaluation of the *Spirituals* as a phase of the Negro's past. The dominant spirit of the Negro Renaissance, whether expressed in poetry or the novel, as Park pointed out, was a seeking for a new definition of values.

This new evaluation of the Negro's experience in American life indicated, as Alain Locke stated, that, "The younger generation has achieved an objective attitude toward life." "Race for them," he continues,

is but an idiom of experience, a sort of added enriching adventure and discipline, giving subtler overtones to life, making it more beautiful and interesting, even if more poignantly so. So experienced, it affords a deepening rather than a narrowing of social vision. The artistic problem of the Young Negro has not been so much that of acquiring the outer mastery of form and technique as that of achieving an inner mastery of mood and spirit. That accomplished, there has come the happy realease from self-consciousness, rhetoric, bombast, and the hampering habit of setting artistic values with primary regard for moral effect—all those pathetic over-compensations of a group inferiority complex which our social dilemmas inflicted upon several unhappy generations. Our poets no longer have the hard choice between an over-assertive and an appealing attitude. By the

---

[22] The nucleus of this book was a special issue of the *Survey Graphic* (March, 1925), *Harlem: The Mecca of the New Negro*.
[23] See "Harlem: The Cultural Capital" in *The New Negro*, pp. 301-11.

same effort they have shaken themselves free from the minstrel tradition and the fowling-nets of dialect, and through acquiring ease and simplicity in serious expression, have carried the folk-gift to the altitudes of art. There they seek and find art's intrinsic values and satisfactions—and if America were deaf, they would still sing.[24]

As one studies the poems and pieces of fiction of the authors included in *The New Negro*, the sociological implications of the changed attitude of Negro writers toward the experience of the Negro in American life become apparent. One may take, for example, the two short stories of Rudolph Fisher, "The City of Refuge" and "Vestiges," in which the impact of urban life upon the folk Negro of the South is treated with an understanding and objectivity that is indicative of the new orientation of the Negro toward his experience in American life. Likewise, in Countée Cullen's lyrical poetry, there is no apology for the "brown girl's swagger" and the poet sees the fallen angels in hell smiling when they greet the black girl of "dancing feet." In poetry Langston Hughes could envision the climb of the Negro to civilization associated with the great rivers of the world—the Euphrates, the Nile, and the Mississippi. In America the Negro was the darker brother who ate in the kitchen but tomorrow he would be bidden to "sit at the table when company comes." Many of the writers who were included in *The New Negro* are counted now among the contributors to American literature.

THE EXPANSION OF THE NEGRO PRESS FOLLOWING THE MASS MIGRATIONS

The mass migrations during and after World War I were followed not only by a literary renaissance but by an expansion of the Negro newspaper. Before the development of the Negro communities in northern cities, the relatively few secular Negro newspapers did not have a very large circulation. As T. Thomas Fortune, one of the leading older journalists pointed out, the Negro newspaper had few readers and few advertisers.[25] "It refused to print anything," he adds, "that would damage the good name or morals of the race, and kept all

[24] *The New Negro* edited by Alain Locke, p. 48. Copyright 1925 by Albert & Charles Boni, Inc.   [25] Quoted in Detweiler, *op. cit.*, pp. 60-61.

scandal and personalities, however sensational the news might be, in the background." [26] In fact, one of the reasons that the Negro newspaper did not make a greater appeal to the urban masses was that it "kept all scandal and personalities, however sensational the news, in the background." The masses of Negroes were not interested in the dignified and theoretical discussions of their rights. The first Negro editor and publisher who sensed the demand of the urban Negro for news concerning people, however "scandalous" or "damaging to the race," was Robert S. Abbott. Though Abbott pioneered in this fashion in Negro journalism, it should be noted that he named his paper, *The Defender*, that is the defender of the rights of the Negro. When Abbott started his paper in 1905, it was the size of a handbill. In 1910 *The Defender* began to use headlines, a practice which was ridiculed at first by other Negro newspapers. Although growth in circulation was stimulated by such devices, it was the mass migrations and the issues raised during World War I that were responsible for the phenomenal growth in the circulation of *The Defender*. *The Defender* more than any other Negro newspaper was responsible for stimulating the northward migration of Negroes by picturing the advantages of the North as opposed to southern oppression.[27]

The growing importance of the Negro press was recognized during World War I. In 1918 a group of Negro leaders, including 31 newspaper men, were called together by the War Department and the Committee on Public Information to discuss the relation of the Negro to the War.[28] This group of Negro leaders drew up a "Bill of Particulars" embodying a number of items, among which were a request that the President of the United States denounce mob violence, that the training camps for Negro officers be continued, and that Negroes be granted greater participation in the War effort. As the result of one item in the "Bill of Particulars," a regularly commissioned Negro War correspondent was appointed to report on the western front in France. The new rôle of the Negro newspaper was brought to the attention of the American people in the publication of Kerlin's

26 *Ibid.*, p. 61.
27 See The Chicago Commission on Race Relations, *The Negro in Chicago* (Chicago, 1922), pp. 87-92.   28 Detweiler, *op. cit.*, pp. 68-69.

The Voice of the Negro, 1919.[29] As he stated in his introduction to this book, "The colored people of America are going to their own papers in these days for the news and for their guidance in thinking."[30] The guidance which Negro newspapers were providing was indicated by extracts from 80 selected newspapers on such subjects as Negro leaders, the Negro's reaction to World War I, and the race riots and lynching that followed the War. Although the editor refrained from commenting on the contents, it was obvious from reading them that the Negro newspaper was playing an important rôle in changing the attitude of the Negro toward his status in American life.

In 1922 an analysis was made of the contents of 64 Negro newspapers.[31] Out of a total of 705 news items and 174 editorials, about 21 per cent of the news items and 40 per cent of the editorials were on the subject of racial wrongs or clashes. Nearly 18 per cent of the news items and 7 per cent of the editorials were concerned with race progress and race pride. The welfare efforts, including education, and movements for the solution of the Negro problem accounted for about 22 per cent of the news items and 10 per cent of the editorials. Twelve per cent of the news items and 1 per cent of the editorials were devoted to Negro crime. The remaining 27 per cent of the news items and 40 per cent of editorials were on "all other subjects."

During and following World War I, a number of Negro magazines were established in northern cities.[32] There were two magazines that deserve some attention. In 1917, there appeared *The Messenger*, which was edited by A. Phillip Randolph and Chandler Owen. *The Messenger* was regarded by the editors as a "magazine of scientific radicalism." Their aim was

to appeal to reason, to lift our pens above the cringing demagogy of the times, and above the cheap peanut politics of the old reactionary Negro leaders. . . . Patriotism has no appeal to us; justice has. Party has no weight with us; principle has. Loyalty is meaningless; it depends on what one is loyal to. Prayer is not one of our remedies; it depends on what one is praying for.[33]

[29] See Robert T. Kerlin, *The Voice of the Negro* (New York, 1920).
[30] *The Voice of the Negro* by Robert T. Kerlin, p.ix. Copyright 1920 by E. P. Dutton & Co., Inc.   [31] Detweiler, *op. cit.*, pp. 82 ff.
[32] See Johnson, *loc. cit.*, pp. 16-17.   [33] Quoted in Johnson, *loc. cit.*, p. 17.

Although *The Messenger* advocated socialism and alliance with labor unions, it is doubtful that many Negroes were influenced to join the socialist ranks. It provided rather a mouthpiece for the general dissatisfaction of Negroes. It attacked not only the more conservative Negro leaders but DuBois, the editor of *The Crisis*.[34] As a result of its extremist policy the editors of *The Messenger* were jailed for two and a half days in 1918 and second-class mailing privileges were denied. After the magazine ceased to receive financial support from socialist groups, it lost its radical character and became the organ of the Pullman Porters Union, of which Randolph was the leader.

The second magazine of importance that made its appearance following World War I was *Opportunity*. It began publication in 1923 under the Department of Research and Investigation of the National Urban League. The primary purpose of the magazine was to make available to students, writers, and other interested persons dependable data on the Negro. Under the editorship of Charles S. Johnson the magazine became the medium for cultural expression among Negroes. In the pages of *Opportunity* appeared many of the pieces which formed a part of the Negro Renaissance. *Opportunity*, which has continued publication until the present, has become essentially an organ concerned with the interests of the National Urban League.

THE NEGRO PRESS AND WORLD WAR II

Between World War I and World War II, the circulation of Negro newspapers continued to expand and the influence of the Negro press continued to increase. The expansion in circulation and the growing influence of Negro newspapers were due primarily to the urbanization of Negroes, which resulted in the increasing literacy of the Negro population. In fact, slightly more than two-thirds of the Negro newspapers were established since the end of World War I.[35] Just before World War II, in Chicago, the city in which the Negro press has experienced its greatest development, five weekly papers

[34] See Detweiler, *op. cit.*, pp. 167 ff.

[35] According to the United States Department of Commerce, "Negro Newspapers and Periodicals in the United States; 1943," Negro Statistical Bulletin No. 1 (August, 1944), 67.4 per cent of the 144 Negro newspapers reporting year of establishment were less than 25 years old.

were being published in addition to the Chicago edition of the *Pittsburgh Courier*, which had a circulation of 8,000 or 10,000.[36] The five weekly newspapers were: the *Defender* with an estimated city circulation of 40,000; the *Bee* with 8,000; the *World* with 5,000; the *Metropolitan Post* with 3,000; and the *News-Ledger*, the house organ of a cosmetic company, which distributed about 30,000 free copies.

With the advent of World War II, which stimulated the migration of Negroes to cities and created a new crisis in race relations, the circulation of Negro newspapers increased rapidly and their influence among Negroes gained greater recognition. The Negro newspaper was forced to face the dilemma which the War presented to the Negro. The dilemma which Negro newspapers faced was greater than that of Negro newspapers during World War I because the urbanized Negroes were more sophisticated and more sensitive in regard to their place in American democracy. The Negro press, while protesting its loyalty to the United States, took a determined stand in demanding the complete integration of the Negro into the armed forces and into the industrial organization of American life. It was the *Pittsburgh Courier*, however, which adopted a slogan that resolved the dilemma facing the Negro press. This slogan was "Double V"— victory at home for democracy as well as victory abroad for democracy. The Negro press fought discrimination in the Red Cross and fought senators and congressmen who showed by their utterances concerning Negroes that they were opposed to the major aims for which the War was being waged. It is no exaggeration to say that the Negro press was the major influence in mobilizing Negroes in the struggle for their rights during World War II.

A survey of the Negro press during World War II showed that there were 164 active newspapers in 1943.[37] More than a third—58 out of 164—of the newspapers were published in 20 cities with 50,000 or more Negro inhabitants in 1940. Nearly a third—47—of the Negro newspapers were published in northern states and 10 in the West. Texas led with 12 newspapers and was followed by Pennsylvania with

[36] St. Clair Drake and Horace R. Cayton, *Black Metropolis* (New York, 1945), p. 399.

[37] "Negro Newspapers and Periodicals in the United States: 1943."

11, and Illinois with 9. During the period, July 1, 1942, to June 30, 1943, 144 Negro newspapers, 114 of which were published weekly, had "a combined average net circulation per issue of 1,613,255." The combined average net circulation was greatest in Pennsylvania, Illinois, and New York, in the order named, the total circulation for the three States amounting to almost 600,000. The circulation of Negro newspapers in California, to which Negroes migrated during World War II, almost equaled that of the District of Columbia which was 82,795. It appears that about 60 per cent of the circulation of Negro papers passed beyond state lines. In fact, the so-called "big four" among Negro newspapers—the *Pittsburgh Courier*, the *Chicago Defender*, the (Baltimore) *Afro-American*, and the (Norfolk) *Journal and Guide* have gained their pre-eminence through their circulation outside the states in which they are published. The *Pittsburgh Courier*, with the largest circulation of any Negro newspaper (about 270,812 weekly), has special editions in Chicago, Detroit, Philadelphia, Washington, and several regional and state editions. The *Afro-American*, with a circulation of 229,812, has special city editions in Baltimore (where it appears twice a week), Philadelphia, Washington, D. C., Richmond, Virginia, Newark, New Jersey, and a national edition. The *Defender* (circulation 161,009) has a special national edition, which circulates widely throughout the country. The *Journal and Guide*, with a circulation of 77,462 also has a national edition, which is widely read on the eastern seaboard. As Negro newspapers have grown in circulation, news-gathering agencies have come into existence. The most important news-gathering agency, The Associated Negro Press, was established in 1919.

THE PRESENT RÔLE OF THE NEGRO PRESS

The Negro newspaper suffers from certain limitations which result from its rôle in the Negro community. It came into existence and has continued to grow because the white press has ignored what was considered "news" or of interest in the Negro community. Thus the Negro newspaper is primarily an organ of the "Negro protest." [38] In this respect the Negro newspaper differed from the immigrant press.

[38] Gunnar Myrdal, *An American Dilemma* (Harper, 1944), Vol. 2, pp. 908-12.

Although the latter press is devoted to the interests of immigrant groups, the protest feature is lacking because the various immigrant groups expect to be and are in fact gradually assimilated. The immigrant papers serve the cultural needs of a group speaking a foreign language. Thus the immigrant press is rapidly disappearing, while the Negro press despite the fact that the Negro speaks English is becoming more important. This is because the Negro continues to live in a separate social world and the white press pays little attention to his everyday existence.

The fact that the Negro newspaper is an organ of protest and offers a compensation for the manner in which the Negro is treated in the white press affects the way that news is presented and the content of Negro newspapers. Since Negroes read the white papers, the Negro newspaper is an "additional newspaper." [39] This fact in itself would mean that if the same news were published in the Negro newspaper it would have to be presented with a special slant in order to attract Negro readers. Consequently, general happenings are presented in a manner to be of special interest to Negro readers. But in addition to giving a particular slant to news of general interest, the Negro press must be strongly opinionated in the sense that it must constantly present the protest of the Negro for equal rights. A recent analysis of the front page of 28 leading Negro newspapers showed that two-thirds of the stories dealt with Negro-white relations and only a third with strictly Negro news.[40] Moreover, the Negro newspapers must carry news concerning the people and happenings in the Negro community. Much of the news of happenings in the Negro community is concerned with Negro "society." The compensatory feature of Negro newspapers is especially prominent in the "society" news in that "society" news is an answer to the derogatory attitudes of whites concerning the activities of Negroes. The "society" news also reflects the appeal of the Negro press to the upper and middle classes in the Negro community.

Despite the fact that the Negro newspaper is an organ of protest and reflects the growing race consciousness of the Negro, it contains one feature that tends to contradict these claims. Many of the advertisements in Negro newspapers are concerned with products for

[39] *Ibid.*, p. 915.   [40] *Fortune*, May, 1945, pp. 233-35.

straightening the hair and whitening the skin and love charms and other items to appeal to the credulity of the Negro. A white columnist has often chided the Negro press for carrying such advertisements in view of the professed "race pride" and "race loyalty" of Negro newspapers. The defense offered by Negro newspapers has been weak because they are primarily business undertakings and such advertisements have been a rich source of revenue.

The Negro newspaper has become an agency of social control as public opinion has become important in Negro communities in cities. Negro leaders, especially, are careful about their utterances on race relations and about their activities involving the status of the race because of the watchful scrutiny of the Negro press. Negroes of upper- and middle-class status are sensitive to the publicity that is given unconventional or scandalous behavior by the Negro press. However, the latter type of social control is very similar to gossip in the small town or rural community. When it comes to larger issues, as, for example, the efficiency of a Negro school or a Negro hospital, the Negro press generally fails in its function as an agency of social control. The Negro newspaper as the organ of Negro protest cannot expose the inefficiency or failure of Negro institutions because it would "damage the reputation" of the race or "prove what white people say about Negroes." At the same time the Negro newspaper is an important instrument for attaining political power. It is utilized by white as well as Negro politicians. The Republican and Democratic Parties spend considerable money for advertisements in Negro newspapers and provide emoluments for the publishers and editors in order to secure their support in political campaigns.

LITERARY EXPRESSION SINCE THE NEGRO RENAISSANCE

The development of literary expression among Negroes since the Negro Renaissance in the twenties has brought to fruition the tendencies which were apparent at the time. In commenting on the significance of the Negro Renaissance in 1925, Alain Locke had stated:

The Negro mind reaches out as yet to nothing but American wants, American ideas. But this forced attempt to build his Americana on race values is a unique social experiment, and its ultimate success is impossible except through the fullest sharing of American culture and institutions. There should be no delusion about this.[41]

When Locke reviewed in 1939 the progress of the Negro's literary achievements since the Renaissance in the twenties, he found that the generation of the thirties was "nearer the cultural course" and closer to the social insight which he had predicted in regard to the Negro writer of fiction and poetry.[42] Foremost among the new Negro writers was Richard Wright, who in *Uncle Tom's Children* used the short novel, as Locke points out, "with the sweep and power of epic tragedy." From a sociological standpoint this is not significant so much because of Wright's mastery of the technique of literary expression but rather because it represents a change in the Negro's conception of himself and his rôle in American life. When Wright's *Native Son* appeared, it caused controversy among whites as well as among Negroes. It was argued by some whites and Negroes that a realistic presentation of a Negro boy who was the victim of slum conditions might reenforce certain stereotyped notions concerning Negroes. From a purely literary standpoint, it probably did not measure up to *Uncle Tom's Children*. But what is significant from a sociological standpoint is that it presents the frustrations and tensions of the tragic position of the Negro resulting from social forces in American life. In *Black Boy*, which was also the subject of controversy because some Negro characters were presented as lacking genuine human sympathy, Wright probes more deeply into the personality formation of the Negro from childhood to his entrance upon manhood. While all of this reflects the contemporary realism of American literature, it is indicative of the newer orientation of the Negro toward his life in America.

Some of the most recent literary expressions of American Negroes are contained in an anthology of the writings of the Negro from the eighteenth century until the present.[43] The selections include short

[41] *The New Negro* edited by Alain Locke, pp. 11-12. Copyright 1925 by Albert & Charles Boni, Inc.

[42] Alain Locke, "The Negro: 'New' or 'Newer,'" *Opportunity*, January, 1939.

[43] Sterling A. Brown, Arthur P. Davis, and Ulysses Lee (Eds.), *The Negro Caravan* (New York, 1941).

stories, selections from novels, poetry, folk literature, drama, speeches, biography, and essays, etc. There appears in the comment of the editors a statement, which is significant even if it is not an altogether correct analysis of the literary expression of American Negroes. "In spite of such unifying bonds as a common rejection of the popular stereotypes and a common cause," state the editors,

writings by Negroes do not seem to the editors to fall into a unique cultural pattern. . . . The editors therefore do not believe that the expression "Negro literature" is an accurate one, and in spite of its convenient brevity, they have avoided using it. "Negro literature" has no application if it means structural peculiarity, or a Negro school of writing. The Negro writes in the forms evolved in English and American literature. . . . The editors consider Negro writers to be American writers, and literature by American Negroes to be a segment of American literature. They believe that it would be just as misleading to classify Clifford Odets' plays about Jewish life as "Jewish literature" or James T. Farrell's novels of the Chicago Irish as "Irish literature" or some of William Saroyan's tales as "Armenian literature." . . . The chief cause for objection to the term is that "Negro literature" is too easily placed by certain critics, white and Negro, in an alcove apart. The next step is a double standard of judgment, which is dangerous for the future of Negro writers.[44]

These comments are significant because they emphasize the fact that despite the racial consciousness of the Negro which is found in his literary expression, through participation in American culture and institutions, the Negro's conception of himself is increasingly that of an American. Although the ever-broadening intellectual and social contacts of the Negro may provide the basis of romantic identification with Africa and the darker races and increase the poignancy of his rejection by white Americans, the Negro is, nevertheless, becoming more conscious of his part in the varied culture of America. If the literary expression of the American Negro possesses certain peculiar qualities because of his experiences in American life, this too will become a part of the literary culture of America. This has been

[44] *The Negro Caravan*, edited by Sterling A. Brown, Arthur P. Davis and Ulysses Lee, pp. 6-7. Copyright 1941 by The Dryden Press. See Alain Locke, "Who and What is 'Negro'?" *Opportunity*, February, 1942, for a criticism of this viewpoint. According to Locke, racially and nationally distinctive elements can be completely compatible.

shown in the literary contributions of Negroes during and following World War II.

As an indication of this development, we might take recent novels by four Negro authors. Frank Yerby has written a romantic historical novel, *The Foxes of Harrow*, which became a best-seller. In this novel, which is superior to most novels of this type, Yerby shakes himself "free of the conventional confinement to racial themes." [45] Even where the author deals with race relations, he maintains an honest and truthful balance in this work which is designed chiefly for entertainment. In a second novel of the same character, *The Vixens*, dealing with the Reconstruction period, Yerby has produced a second best-seller. Willard Motley in a first novel, *Knock on Any Door*, which has become a best-seller, has established himself as an important writer. He has avoided the racial theme and chosen an Italian boy for the subject of a novel which is not only an outstanding literary production but a penetrating social document. Although the other two writers, Chester Himes and Ann Petry, deal with race, the manner in which the subject is handled shows none of the conventional treatment of the subject. Chester Himes has written two novels, *If He Hollers Let Him Go* and *Lonely Crusade*, both of which deal with race consciousness. Both novels have their setting on the West Coast and deal with relations between Negro and white workers during World War II. Ann Petry in a first novel, *The Street*, has won recognition as a talented novelist and storyteller. She has chosen Harlem as the setting for her novel dealing with the struggles of a young Negro woman with a son against the disorganization of a slum area. Because of their literary quality and point of view, the works of these four Negro novelists have become a part of the varied literary culture of America rather than a racial literature.

The literary expression of the Negro has been closely tied up, as we have seen, with those social movements which have grown out of the changing relation of the Negro to American life. In the next chapter we shall consider the origin and the nature of social movements among Negroes and their relation to the adjustment and assimilation of the Negro in the American community.

[45] Alain Locke, "Reason and Race," Phylon, Vol. VIII, p. 20.

CHAPTER XX

Social Movements and Race Consciousness

THE Negro's attempt to find a desirable status in American society has been characterized by a number of social movements. These social movements have consisted of deliberately organized efforts to achieve common goals by enlisting the participation and support of the Negro masses. Since any form of concerted action among the slaves was prohibited, social movements among Negroes appeared first among the Negroes who were free in the North before the Civil War.[1] A few attempted insurrections among the slaves exhibited some of the features of incipient social movements and aroused some race consciousness among the blacks. Despite the crisis created by the Civil War and Emancipation, the aspirations and hopes of the freedmen did not crystallize into a social movement. After the overthrow of the Reconstruction governments there was a Negro mass movement, led by "Pap" Singleton, from the lower South to Kansas. The next social movement arose during the first decade of the twentieth century, following the enactment of laws designed to make the Negro a permanent subordinate group in the South. This movement, the Niagara Movement, represented the reaction of the intelligentsia against the compromising leadership of Booker T. Washington. The Niagara Movement merged with the National Association for the Advancement of Colored People, an organization devoted to securing full citizenship rights for the Negro. The Garvey Movement with its nationalistic emphasis, which appeared as the result of World

[1] The various "social movements" included in our discussion range from the more elementary forms of mass movements such as mass migrations to the concerted forms of action on the part of Negro intellectuals.

War I and urbanization, had as we shall see all the essential features of a mass movement. Since the collapse of the Garvey Movement no genuine mass movement appeared among Negroes until A. Phillip Randolph started the March-on-Washington Movement during the crisis created by World War II. Because of its limited aims, this movement soon ceased to inspire Negroes.

SOCIAL MOVEMENTS BEFORE THE CIVIL WAR

The first social movements among Negroes appeared in the movement among the free Negroes in the North for separate church organizations during the last decade of the eighteenth century. This movement arose among the Negroes in the Methodist churches, when their growing numbers had resulted in greater restrictions and segregation. The movement for independent churches revealed that there was developing among the free Negroes a new form of race consciousness involving the question of status and personal dignity. This new race consciousness was not confined to any one community but spread among the Negroes in the cities of the North. During the next thirty or forty years the separate Negro churches became the principal form of associated life for the free Negroes. The churches were more than religious organizations since they were also the centers of social welfare and even economic activities and provided an arena for political contests.

By 1830 the interests and outlook of the free Negroes could no longer be confined to their church organizations. There had been an organized protest against the colonization of free Negroes in Africa as early as 1817 but this had not resulted in a permanent organization. The agitation over slavery was becoming more intense and this agitation was not unrelated to the status of the Negro in the North. The Negro in the North was becoming more conscious of the contradictions between his status and the extension of suffrage and education to the white masses.[2] Moreover, the Negro was becoming more dissatisfied with his precarious economic condition. Out of this growing unrest came the "convention movement" in 1830, in which the leaders

[2] See pp. 79-80 above.

in the Negro churches played the dominant rôle. In the first convention and in the succeeding conventions, the free Negroes made it clear that they considered themselves Americans and condemned the program of the American Colonization Society to colonize free Negroes in Africa. Moreover, at one of the annual conventions, the free Negroes advised Negroes to openly defy the Fugitive Slave law and help their brethren to escape from slavery. The growing race consciousness of the free Negroes in the "convention movement" was thus not directed toward nationalistic or separatist aims but rather toward the achievement of a place in American society.

Among the slaves there was little opportunity for concerted action and consequently there were no social movements except the sporadic attempts at insurrection. In this connection it should be pointed out that Denmark Vesey, the leader of the most important insurrection among the slaves, was a free Negro who had some education and was acquainted with current ideas concerning fredom. Moreover, he knew of the revolution in San Domingo, where the blacks had risen in rebellion against the whites and had succeeded in establishing a Negro republic. In his agitation he always appealed to race pride and endeavored to give the Negro a conception of the place of his race that was opposed to the status that the white man had imposed upon the Negro. He had instructed his lieutenants to recruit urban Negro workers and the "country" Negroes who had few social contacts with whites. The raw "country" Negroes were to be controlled by superstition or the belief that the ways of the Negro were superior to the ways of the white man. Thus he attempted to arouse and intensify race consciousness among the slaves.

After the convention movement subsided in the early fifties, no social movement appeared among Negroes until after the Civil War. The mass migration of Negroes from the lower South to Kansas in 1879, which was described in Chapter VIII, assumed the character of a mass movement.[3] Following a period of unrest growing out of the loss of civil rights and unfavorable economic conditions, "Pap" Singleton, who was known as the "Moses of the Colored Exodus," pro-

---

[3] See pp. 154-55 above.

vided his followers with a vision of a Promised Land in Kansas. The Negro intellectuals who debated the question whether the Negro should leave the South, on the whole, did not participate in this movement.

THE NIAGARA MOVEMENT AND THE NATIONAL ASSOCIATION FOR THE ADVANCEMENT OF COLORED PEOPLE

As we have seen, during the last decade of the nineteenth century and the first decade of the twentieth century, the South succeeded in fixing the lower status of the Negro in law. Booker T. Washington rose to prominence during this period because he represented the acceptance on the part of the Negro of the situation as a *fait accompli*. The Negro intelligentsia in the North challenged Washington's position. In Atlanta J. Max Barber had started a Negro magazine, *The Voice of the Negro*, in protest against the restriction of the citizenship rights of the Negro. But he had been forced to leave the city during the race riot in 1906.[4] In the meantime, W. E. B. DuBois, the acknowledged leader of the Negro intelligentsia, called a meeting of Negro leaders, which met at Niagara Falls in 1905, to organize a movement in defense of the rights of Negroes.[5] Thus the Niagara Movement was launched and the first conference was held at the scene of John Brown's raid, Harpers Ferry, West Virginia, in 1906. The conference resolved:

We shall not be satisfied with less than our full manhood rights. We claim for ourselves every right that belongs to a free-born American, civil and social, and until we get these rights we shall never cease to protest and assail the ears of America with the stories of its shameful deeds toward us. We want our manhood suffrage and we want it now. Second, we want discrimination in public accommodations to cease. Third, we claim the right to associate with such people as wish to associate with us. Fourth, we want the laws enforced against rich as well as poor, against capitalists as well as laborers, against white as well as black. We are not more lawless than the white race; we are

[4] Mary White Ovington, "The National Association for the Advancement of Colored People," *The Journal of Negro History*, Vol. IX, p. 108.
[5] See W. E. B. DuBois, *Dusk of Dawn* (New York, 1940), pp. 87-92.

more often arrested, convicted and mobbed. Fifth, we want our children educated.[6]

Although the Niagara Movement held a number of conferences and conducted a number of cases involving the civil rights of Negroes, it was hampered by the lack of funds. But it happened that liberal whites in the North had become aroused by the growing restrictions upon the rights of the Negro. The insecurity of the Negro was drama-tized in a race riot in Springfield, Illinois, in 1908. This riot provoked a number of articles, the most significant of which was one entitled, "Race War in the North," by William English Walling, which appeared in *The Independent*, September 3, 1908. In this article Walling made the following statement.

Either the spirit of the abolitionists, of Lincoln and Lovejoy, must be revived and we must come to treat the Negro on a plane of absolute political and social equality, or Vardaman and Tillman will soon have transferred the race war to the North.[7]

In response to Walling's appeal, Miss Mary White Ovington began correspondence with him on the subject and this resulted in a meeting with him and Henry Moskowitz in New York City. At this conference it was agreed that a call should be sent out signed by prominent whites and Negroes for a conference on the centennial of the birth of Abraham Lincoln to discuss the status of the Negro in the United States.[8] Oswald Garrison Villard, the grandson of William Lloyd Garrison, who had been called into counsel, wrote the Call. A part of the Call read as follows:

In many states to-day Lincoln would find justice enforced, if at all, by judges elected by one element in a community to pass upon the liberties and lives of another. He would see the black men and women, for whose freedom a hundred thousand of soldiers gave their lives, set apart in trains, in which they pay first-class fares for third-class

---

[6] Quoted in *History of the National Association for the Advancement of Colored People* by Robert L. Jack, p. 2. Copyright 1943 by Edward K. Meador. Reprinted by permission of the Meador Publishing Company.

[7] Quoted in *History of the National Association for the Advancement of Colored People* by Robert L. Jack, p. 4. Copyright 1943 by Edward K. Meador. Reprinted by permission of the Meador Publishing Company.

[8] Ovington, *op. cit.*, pp. 109 ff.

service, and segregated in railway stations and in places of entertainment; he would observe that State after State declines to do its elementary duty in preparing the Negro through education for the best exercise of citizenship. . . . Added to this, the spread of lawless attacks upon the Negro, North, South, and West—even in the Springfield made famous by Lincoln—often accompanied by revolting brutalities, sparing neither sex nor age nor youth, could but shock the author of the sentiment that 'government of the people, by the people, for the people, shall not perish from the earth.' . . . Silence under these conditions means tacit approval. The indifference of the North is already responsible for more than one assault upon democracy, and every such attack reacts as unfavorably upon the whites as upon blacks. Discrimination once permitted cannot be bridled; recent history in the South shows that in forging chains for the Negroes the white voters are forging chains for themselves. 'A house divided against itself cannot stand'; this government cannot exist half-slave and half-free any better to-day than it could in 1861. . . . Hence we call upon all the believers in democracy to join in a national conference for the discussion of present evils, the voicing of protests, and the renewal of the struggle for civil and political liberty.[9]

This conference, which was held in New York City, February 12 and 13, 1909, included W. E. B. DuBois and some of his associates in the *Niagara Movement*. The program adopted by the conference, which led to the formation of the National Association for the Advancement of Colored People in the same year, was as follows:

Abolition of all forced segregation
Equal educational advantages for colored and white
Enfranchisement of the Negro
Enforcement of the Fourteenth and Fifteenth Amendments.

Although the platform, as Miss Ovington points out, does not seem radical today, it "was denounced by nearly every white man who gave to Negro institutions." [10] Even many Negroes thought that the program was too radical and there was pressure from both whites and Negroes to modify it.

But the National Association for the Advancement of Colored People kept to its program and elected W. E. B. DuBois Director of Publicity and Editor of *The Crisis* in 1910. *The Crisis* was a success

[9] Quoted in Ovington, *op. cit.*, pp. 109-10.   [10] Ovington, *op. cit.*, p. 111.

from the beginning. By January 1912, the circulation of *The Crisis* had increased to nearly 16,000 monthly. In 1911, the National Association for the Advancement of Colored People began a vigorous campaign against lynching, despite the difficulty in getting prominent people to speak against lynching. After the first branch was set up in Chicago, branches began to spring up in other cities. By 1916 there were 54 branches, nine locals, and four college chapters with a total membership of 9,500. The mass migrations to northern cities and the issues raised during World War I stimulated the growth of the National Association for the Advancement of Colored People. In 1917, when James Weldon Johnson was appointed national organizer, the membership increased to 11,524 and in 1918 there were 80 branches of the Association. By 1919, the number of branches had increased to 300 and were distributed as follows: there were 122 in the North with 38,420 members; 155 in the South with 42,588 members; and 33 in the West with 7,440 members.[11]

THE NATIONAL URBAN LEAGUE

During the time the National Association for the Advancement of Colored People was becoming the most important organization in the struggle for citizenship rights of the Negro, there came into existence another organization that was primarily concerned with the social welfare of Negroes in cities. As early as 1905 two organizations were formed in New York City: one, the Committee for Improving Industrial Conditions of Negroes in New York, and the other the National League for the Protection of Colored Women.[12] As the result of the studies of George E. Haynes, who was a professor of Sociology at Fisk University, members of both of these committees were brought together into a third committee with broader aims. By 1911 the three committees were fused into an organization under the title of the National League on Urban Conditions Among Negroes, later shortened to National Urban League. The organization soon began to receive financial support from John D. Rockefeller, Jr., Julius Rosenwald, Mrs. William

---

[11] Jack, *op. cit.*, p. 17.
[12] See L. Hollingsworth Wood, "The Urban League Movement," *The Journal of Negro History*, Vol. 9, pp. 117-26.

H. Baldwin, and Alfred T. Stone. From the beginning the Urban League emphasized the interracial character of its program, which was concerned not only with social welfare of Negroes in northern cities but also the training of Negro social workers.

In founding the National Urban League, the leaders had little suspected that within five or six years their organization would become the most important agency in the country in dealing with the mass migration of Negroes to northern cities.[13] From 1912 on Urban Leagues sprang up in the industrial centers of the North to handle the problems of Negro migrants. During World War I they helped to screen the raw recruits to northern industry, assisted them in finding homes, and made available to them the resources of the social service agencies. Moreover, the Urban Leagues served as clearing houses of information on the migrants and became the centers of interracial efforts to assist the migrants in various ways. George E. Haynes, who played an important rôle in the development of the National Urban League, became special assistant to Secretary of Labor Wilson during 1917-1918.

THE MASS MIGRATIONS TO NORTHERN CITIES

The mass migration of Negroes from the South to northern cities was one of the most crucial mass movements in the history of the Negro in the United States. This movement resulted, as we have seen, from changes in southern agriculture as well as the attraction of northern industries, though the latter was the stronger force.[14] But, in addition to these economic forces, there were social forces which played a part in the migration of Negroes to the North. The vision of the North as a Promised Land, which *The Defender* and other Negro newspapers pictured to the southern Negro, offered a solution for the economic problem in the South. The North was not only a place where the Negro would receive higher wages but it was a place where the Negro would be free or where a "man was a man." It offered freedom of movement, chances for employment, the right to vote, and the opportunity for Negro children to get an education. The vision of the North as the Promised Land was communicated to southern Negroes by Negro newspapers. And as the news of the North as a

[13] See statement of George E. Haynes, p. 167 above. [14] See pp. 193-94 above.

Promised Land spread among the southern Negroes, whole communities picked up their meager possessions and joined the hegira to the North. In fact, the leaders in the churches and in the lodges followed the masses instead of leading them to the Promised Land of the North. Even the intellectual leaders of the Negroes were unaware at first of the significance of the flight of the Negro from the feudal South to the freedom of northern cities.

THE GARVEY MOVEMENT

The mass migrations of Negroes to northern cities and the issues of World War I created among Negroes the most important social movement with nationalistic aims that had ever emerged among Negroes. The movement was known as the "Garvey Movement," being named after its leader Marcus Garvey, a West Indian Negro. Garvey, a black Negro, who was born in Jamaica in 1885, had undertaken the organization of a Negro Improvement Association in Jamaica, a scheme which he conceived while visiting England and France.[15] After failing to establish the organization in Jamaica, he came to the United States during World War I. His movement did not make much progress until large numbers of Negroes began to migrate from the West Indies to the United States. With a large nucleus in Harlem the movement under the leadership of Garvey began to make its racial appeal to American Negroes.

The program of the "Garvey Movement" was based upon the thesis that the Negro would never receive justice in a white man's country and that the only solution of the Negro's problem was the establishment of an independent nation.[16] In order to put over his program, Garvey established *The Negro World*, a weekly newspaper. He sought to create a new valuation of everything black or Negro. He organized a uniformed military organization which was to be the vanguard of the African army and he created a corps of "Black Cross Nurses." The first step in establishment of a Negro nation was, according to Garvey,

[15] See W. E. B. DuBois, "Marcus Garvey," *The Crisis*, Vol. 21 (December, 1920 and January, 1921).

[16] See Amy Jaques-Garvey (Ed.), *Philosophy and Opinions of Marcus Garvey* (New York, 1923). See also T. G. Standing, "Nationalism in Negro Leadership," *The American Journal of Sociology*, Vol. XL, pp. 180-92.

the commercial development of Negroes. This was to be achieved by the setting up of grocery stores and restaurants in America and the creation of a fleet of steamships that would bind the Negroes of America to Africa. In selling stock in order to achieve the latter part of his program, Garvey was convicted on the charge of using the mails to defraud and was sent to the federal penitentiary in Atlanta.

As a leader of a mass movement among Negroes, Garvey has had no equal.[17] Although he first attracted mostly West Indian Negroes he quickly succeeded in attracting large numbers of American Negroes. He came to the United States at a time when southern Negroes were migrating to northern cities. The southern migrants were becoming disillusioned about the city as a Promised Land. The migrants found race riots and racial discrimination in the North. This provided proof for Garvey's argument that America was the white man's country. Those that ridiculed this idea were, according to Garvey, "going to find themselves sadly disappointed one of these days, homeless, shelterless, and unprovided for." [18] Hence Garvey offered the disillusioned black masses a new Promised Land, an independent Negro nation in Africa. He invented honors and distinctions and caused the Negro to feel that he was a part of a great cause. Then, too, like all leaders of mass movements, he created victims against whom his followers could direct their hatred. His technique in this respect went amiss sometimes because he tried to set up the distinction between the pure-blooded Negro and those of mixed-racial strains, a distinction with which he was acquainted in the West Indies.

On the whole, Garvey was able to utilize the frustration and disillusionment of the urbanized Negro masses to weld them into a mass movement. He succeeded in attracting large numbers of illiterate and unsophisticated Negroes in the cities, especially northern cities. Although he had his largest following in New York City, the movement attracted large numbers of Negroes in Chicago, Detroit, and Philadelphia. There were also branches of his organization in the larger cities of the South but the Negro in the southern city did not respond in large numbers. In southern cities the Negro masses were largely

[17] See E. Franklin Frazier, "Garvey: A Mass Leader," *The Nation*, Vol. 123 (August 18, 1926), p. 147-48. [18] *The Negro World*, October 18, 1924.

under the control of the church. The appeal of the Garvey Movement was really opposed to the other worldly outlook of the Negro church. However, Garvey was shrewd enough not to challenge Negro ministers, and to utilize the religious heritage of the Negro. When he entered the prison in Atlanta, he sent a message to his followers which revealed the messianic element in the movement.[19] Under the caption, "If I Die in Atlanta," Garvey wrote in *The Negro World*, February 14, 1925, "look for me in the whirlwind or the storm, look for me all around you, for, with God's grace, I shall come and bring with me the countless millions of black slaves who have died in America and the West Indies and the millions in Africa to aid you in the fight for liberty, freedom and life."

The emergence of the Garvey Movement was an extreme expression of race consciousness and nationalistic sentiment which came into prominence during and following World War I. Throughout the history of the Negro in America, the development of race consciousness has been influenced by the varied and changing relations of the Negro to American life. Among the slaves there existed, of course, the consciousness of being different from whites. But where slavery tended to assume the character of a social institution, race consciousness tended to disappear and the slaves tended to identify themselves with the master's family and the slave order. As we have pointed out in regard to Denmark Vesey, race consciousness was deliberately fostered by a free Negro in a conflict situation. But, there was lacking among the slaves common traditions and the moral and psychological conditions to create race consciousness and solidarity, which in turn might generate nationalistic feeling. Following the Civil War the outlook of the rural Negroes in the South was not unlike what it had been under slavery. They tended to accept the valuations of the whites concerning the Negro. Although they were conscious of being black or Negroes, their consciousness of race did not identify them with a historic body of racial tradition. The social consciousness of the rural Negroes tended to identify the Negro with "church communities." Being a Baptist or a Methodist meant more than being

[19] E. Franklin Frazier, "The Garvey Movement," *Opportunity*, Vol. 4 (November, 1926), pp. 346-48.

a Negro. The Methodists and Baptists had a history which determined their outlook on life and directed their destiny.

The impact of urban living upon the Negro changed his outlook on life. Racial conflicts in the North tended not only to intensify the consciousness of being a Negro but it also gave new meaning to being a Negro. Identification with the Negro race meant being a member of a group with a cause if not a history. As in the case of the nationalistic struggles in Europe, the emergence of a racial literature helped in the development of race consciousness.[20] As we have seen, there appeared a Negro Renaissance following World War I. Much of the literature and art of the Negro Renaissance was not only militant but tended to give the Negro a conception of the mission and destiny of the Negro. The Negro newspapers, which began to influence the masses, tended to create a new race consciousness. While the new race consciousness exhibited some of the characteristics of nationalism, it did not involve separation from American life, which was the peculiar aim of the Garvey Movement.

DEVELOPMENTS BETWEEN WORLD WARS

Between the two World Wars, the National Urban League continued to grow. Since the League was concerned with the employment of Negroes in industry, it had to face the problem of the relation of Negro and white workers and the relation of Negro workers to the unions. The problem emerged partly as the result of the policy of exclusion on the part of the unions and the attitude of white workers. In dealing with these problems the League was subjected to much criticism, especially on the part of the younger Negro intellectuals.[21] It was said that because of its dependence upon white philanthropy, the League was evasive in its attitude toward unionism. The critics went even further and charged the League with a policy of expediency and extreme opportunism in regard to the rights of the Negro. In reply to such charges, the League took the position that it was not a Negro mass movement but an interracial undertaking that was

[20] Cf. Robert E. Park, "Negro Race Consciousness as Reflected in Race Literature," *American Review*, Vol. I, pp. 505-17, *passim*.
[21] See Gunnar Myrdal, *An American Dilemma* (New York, 1944), pp. 840-41.

attempting to achieve better economic opportunities for the Negro through conference and discussion rather than mass action.

The League was, of course, correct in its position that it was not a Negro mass movement. In fact, it should be added that the League did not represent the hopes and aspirations of the Negro masses. It was an organization comprised of educated Negroes and philanthropic whites with conservative views concerning Negroes. The League has provided a field of employment for the growing number of educated Negroes who because of racial discrimination would have experienced some difficulty in securing similar employment. Consequently, the Negro leaders in the League have been careful not to antagonize those from whom they secured support in a work which has been beneficial for the masses of Negroes. Although there were some occasions on which it was said that the League had condoned strike-breaking, the official policy of the league had always been opposed to strike-breaking and the officials of the League personally have been in favor of unionism. When one considers the program of the League, which was directed to social welfare as well as the improvement of the working opportunities of the Negro, it appears that the various Urban Leagues maintained a policy in accordance with or slightly in advance of the prevailing public opinion of the communities in which they operated.

During and following World War I, the National Association for the Advancement of Colored People continued its campaign against lynching. Largely because of agitation and publicity on the part of the National Association for the Advancement of Colored People, the Republican Party in the 1920 campaign had urged Congress "to consider the most effective means to end lynching." In 1922 the first antilynching bill was passed in the House but was defeated in the Senate. In 1924, the Republican Party pledged itself to pass antilynching legislation, but its pledge was unfulfilled during the Coolidge and Hoover administrations. Under the Roosevelt administration, two other antilynching bills were introduced into Congress but they were defeated—the first in the House and the second by a filibuster in the Senate. Nevertheless, the publicity given lynching by the National

Association for the Advancement of Colored People was arousing public opinion in the South as well as in the North against this form of lawlessness against the Negro. In addition to the fight against lynching the National Association for the Advancement of Colored People carried on a fight in the courts against residential segregation in cities. The Association won its fight against residential segregation through segregation ordinances in the famous Louisville case in 1917 and successfully defended Dr. Ossian Sweet in the Detroit case in 1925. Dr. Sweet, a Negro physician, moved into a white neighborhood at a time when Negroes were being assaulted for such action. Knowing this, the Sweets carried arms with them when they moved into the house. While the white crowds were surging about their house, the Sweets fired and a white man was killed. Dr. Sweet and his co-defendants were finally exonerated.

The Association carried on a fight in the courts for equal educational opportunities for Negroes, for the right of Negroes to participate in the Democratic primaries in the South, and for the equitable administration of the law. The Association was always on the alert when there was legislation before Congress, such as federal aid to education, to see that the rights of Negroes were protected. In fact, in every field of public and private activity the Association was the organization in the United States that has guarded the rights of the Negro.

The depression that set in in 1929 created considerable unrest among the Negroes in northern cities. Out of this unrest sprang a number of incipient social movements among Negroes. It was during this crisis that there appeared the movement with the slogan, "Don't Buy Where You Can't Work." While this movement was an expression of the growing racial consciousness of the masses, it was also encouraged by local Negro businessmen. On the other hand, the unemployment of large masses of Negroes provided a fertile field for the leaders of radical movements. Negroes began to learn the power of mass action and became acquainted with political ideologies. Many Negroes began to redefine their problems in terms of the class struggle rather than in terms of racial conflict. The Harlem riot of 1935, which began as a race riot, became an assault on property largely because radical whites sided with the Negroes.[22]

During 1935 The National Negro Congress was organized following a conference at Howard University.[23] This conference was held under the joint sponsorship of the Division of Social Sciences at Howard University and the Joint Committee on National Recovery, which was formed during the early days of the New Deal to safeguard the rights of the Negro in the policy making of federal agencies. The idea underlying The National Negro Congress was that there should be a national organization, including all the Negro organizations—religious, fraternal, civic, and trade unions—which would solidify the struggle of the Negroes for equality and enlist the support of the masses. When the first meeting of The National Negro Congress assembled in Chicago in 1936 for a three-day session there were 817 delegates representing 858 organizations located in 29 states and the District of Columbia. A second meeting, attended by 1,149 persons met in 1937, and a third meeting with 900 Negroes and 400 whites met in Washington, D. C. in 1940. The large attendance of whites in 1940 was the result, it was reported, of the influence of the Communist Party. In fact, the third meeting of The National Negro Congress turned out to be the zenith of the Congress. At the third meeting the president, A. Phillip Randolph, who was reported to be affiliated with or sympathetic to the Socialists, charged that the Congress had been captured by the Communists and predicted the doom of any movement directed by whites. After the third meeting, the Congress, partly because of financial difficulties and partly because of the disaffection of Negroes, ceased to attract a large following of Negroes. When one considers the diverse interests that were represented in the organizations officially affiliated with The National Negro Congress, it is obvious that its unity and solidarity rested upon a precarious basis from the beginning.

[22] See Mayor's Commission on Conditions in Harlem, *The Negro in Harlem,* New York, 1936. Unpublished Report.

[23] See Myrdal, *op. cit.,* Vol. 2, pp. 817-19.

SOCIAL MOVEMENTS DURING AND FOLLOWING
WORLD WAR II

The unrest among Negroes which had been created by the depression years was intensified by the crisis in race relations caused by the defense program and World War II.[24] The unrest manifested itself in sporadic local movements with nationalistic aims and more restricted programs for the solution of the Negro problems. Such well-established organizations as the National Urban League and the National Association for the Advancement of Colored People were affected by the unrest of the masses. Although northern industries were not calling, as in World War I, for masses of unskilled laborers, Negroes were moving from the South to the defense areas. During the depression years Negroes had lost some of the gains that they had made in industrial employment, but they did not lose altogether the foothold which they had secured in American industry. They had proved their ability as workers in modern industry when given an opportunity and they were demanding that they be given an opportunity for training for the new demands of the defense industries. Moreover, The Committee for Industrial Organizations had established a new policy in the relation of black and white workers in unionism. The problem which the National Urban League faced in World War I with reference to their wealthy white supporters had been resolved by the course of events in the labor movement. The unions, especially the new industrial unions were absorbing Negro workers, and the Negro workers themselves were demanding entrance to unions since otherwise they would have little chance for employment. Consequently, the National Urban League came out for the unionization of the Negro and his complete integration into American life.

The National Association for the Advancement of Colored People, though a militant organization fighting for the full citizenship rights of the Negro, had to take cognizance of the new upsurge of the Negro masses. One of the weaknesses of the National Association for the

[24] E. Franklin Frazier, "Ethnic and Minority Groups in Wartime, With Special Reference to the Negro," *The American Journal of Sociology*, Vol. XLVIII (November, 1942), pp. 369-77.

Advancement of Colored People had been its lack of the support of the Negro masses though it was fighting for the rights of the Negro masses. At the outbreak of World War II, the Association won the Gaines case before the United States Supreme Court, which upheld the right of Negro students to share all the educational provisions which a state makes for white students.[25] Moreover, the Association intensified its fight for the equalization of the salaries of Negro teachers in the South. Favorable decisions were won in the courts on this issue. During World War II, the Association carried on a fight for the complete integration of the Negroes into the armed forces of the nation. In carrying on this fight and the struggle for equal economic opportunities of the Negro, the Association came into closer touch with the Negro masses.

Therefore, the Association was quick to recognize the significance of the March-on-Washington Movement. While cooperating with this movement, the Association did not attempt to absorb it and kept to its own program. The March-on-Washington Movement was the most spectacular mass movement among Negroes during the War emergency.[26] This movement grew out of the failure to include Negro workers in the defense program. It was organized and directed by A. Phillip Randolph, president of the Brotherhood of Sleeping-Car-Porters. A march on Washington was planned in protest against the exclusion of Negro workers from defense industries. As a result of a conference between the President of the United States and representatives of the March-on-Washington Movement, the President issued on June 25, 1941, Executive Order 8802. The Order reaffirmed the policy of nondiscrimination in government and forbade contractors handling government orders to discriminate against workers "because of race, creed, color, or national origin." [27]

Because of its success in securing a statement on the part of the government against discrimination, the March-on-Washington Movement gained considerable prestige among Negroes. There was an effort to set up local affiliates and create a permanent organization out

---

[25] Jack, *op. cit.*, pp. 13ff.   [26] Myrdal, *op. cit.*, Vol. 2, pp. 851-52.
[27] See President's Committee on Fair Employment Practices, *Minorities in Defense* (Washington, 1941), pp. 15-16.

of the movement. The committee that headed the movement organized support for a permanent Fair Employment Practices Committee and kept up agitation for the civil rights of the Negro. But because of the limited aim of the movement and its technique of bringing pressure through threatening to march on Washington, it was natural that popular support gradually drifted away from the movement.

Although the March-on-Washington Movement gradually ceased to stir Negroes after the Fair Employment Practices Committee was set up, they did not relapse into apathy. The unrest and dissatisfaction of the Negroes became effectively mobilized through the National Association for the Advancement of Colored People. This organization had gradually broadened its appeal to Negroes and lower strata of the Negro population were rallying to its support. The best indication of this fact was the existence in 1946 of 1,200 branches of the Association in 43 states with a total membership of over 520,000. Thus about one out of every 26 Negroes in the United States is a member of the Association today. The widespread influence of the Association is evident in various phases of the struggle of the Negro to achieve equality in American life. Although the Association has remained nonpartisan in respect to politics and has steadfastly refused to influence its members to support any political party, it has exerted considerable influence in arousing Negroes to assert their rights as voters. In addition to urging Negroes to register in the primaries in the South, the Association has provided funds and counsel for court action in order to remove barriers to the Negro's right to franchise. In the South today there are springing up various organizations for the purpose of increasing the participation of the Negro in the political life of that section. Although the Association has no official affiliation with any of these political organizations, it has helped to bring these organizations into existence. Likewise, the Association is constantly enlightening the masses of Negroes concerning the influence of federal legislation in regard to health, hospitals, and education upon their welfare. All of this has some effect upon the political orientation of the Negro, though it is divorced from the structure of political parties. Members of both of the major political parties have increasingly attempted to win the approval of the Association.

Not all of the social unrest among Negroes has been canalized in the expanding local organizations of the National Association for the Advancement of Colored People. Throughout the nation, especially in the cities, numerous organizations are being formed for the democratic rights of Negroes. Some of the organizations are composed solely of Negroes but a far greater number include whites as well as Negroes. One important result of the increasing cooperation of whites and Negroes is that it has neutralized or made impossible such racial or nationalistic movements as the Garvey Movement, following World War I. As the Negro participates in such organizations as the Congress of Industrial Organizations and liberal movements, he tends to lose his racial consciousness and his interests become identified with the aims of these organizations. The identification of his interests and aspirations with these organizations has been made possible because these organizations have supported the Negro in his demands for full citizenship rights.

The Southern Conference for Human Welfare has been one of the most important organizations in which whites and Negroes have cooperated for broad democratic aims. This organization has been concerned with the improvement of the economic, social, political, and educational condition of *all* the people in the South. It made a special appeal to Negroes because of its open attack on the principle of segregation. During 1947, this organization sponsored a number of public meetings in the South where there was no segregation of Negroes and whites. The organization has not enjoyed the munificence of foundations and other organizations which support interracial movements. Although it has sympathetic relations with the labor movement especially the Congress of Industrial Organizations, it has depended upon the voluntary support of liberal groups and individuals. It is because of this fact that it has represented more truly the upsurge of democracy in the South than any other movement. At the same time the influence of the Southern Conference for Human Welfare has been limited because of the charge that it represents a front for Communists. The future of the organization is uncertain since it has been absorbed to some extent into Henry Wallace's third party.

The various social movements which have arisen among Negroes from the eighteenth century until the present have emerged during periods of crises when the relation of the Negro to American society was undergoing changes. The character of these social movements has been determined by the extent to which various strata in the Negro population have been affected by the changing relation of the Negroes to American life. In most of the social movements leaders have appeared who have made articulate the aspirations and hopes of Negroes or the new definitions of their place in American society. In the next chapter, we shall consider the character of various types of Negro leaders and their rôle in the adjustment of the Negro to American society.

CHAPTER XXI

Negro Leaders and the Negro Intelligentsia

THE first important leaders to appear among Negroes were the free Negroes who took the initiative in the establishment of separate church organizations in the North toward the close of the eighteenth century. There was little opportunity for Negroes to rise to positions of leadership among the slaves, since all forms of independent concerted action were suppressed. In some cases runaway slaves and Negroes who were active in the Underground Railroad rose to positions of leadership. After Emancipation leaders appeared in church and fraternal organizations, in education, business, and politics. The most conspicuous leaders among the freedmen were the political leaders who were concerned with the new status of the Negro in American society.

The most outstanding Negro leader during the nineteenth century was Frederick Douglass, who led the demand of Negroes for full equality. The decline in Douglass' leadership coincided with the rise of Booker T. Washington to a position of leadership at a time when the South was reducing the Negro to a subordinate status. The leadership of Washington was in turn challenged by W. E. B. DuBois, the leading representative of the Negro intelligentsia. The mass migration of Negroes to northern cities marked the end of the leadership of Washington and his successors at Tuskegee Institute. One of the results of the mass migrations was the appearance of Marcus Garvey, leader of the most important, though ephemeral, nationalistic movement among Negroes. A more important consequence of the mass migration was the differentiation of economic and cultural interests among Negroes which created a widely differentiated leadership in various areas of life. This new type of functional leadership is becoming a permanent characteristic of Negro leadership as the Negro is increasingly integrated into the American community.

LEADERS OF NEGROES BEFORE THE CIVIL WAR

From the beginning of the introduction of Negroes into the United States, exceptional Negroes appeared in the rôle of leaders. This is shown by the sporadic insurrections during the seventeenth century about which little is known. Likewise during most of the eighteenth century there is evidence that some Negroes acquired the rôle of leaders among their fellow slaves and even among the freedmen.[1] It was not, however, until toward the close of the eighteenth century that leaders of importance appeared among Negroes. These leaders emerged among the free Negroes in the North and they were associated with the movement for separate church organizations. It is important to observe in regard to these leaders that they were men who had acquired the culture of the whites. In no case does it appear that the personality or the outlook of these men was influenced by their African background.

Because of discrimination and segregation, Richard Allen and Absalom Jones and others like them had become intensely race-conscious. But they did not attempt to resurrect on American soil African institutions and practices (about which they knew nothing) but sought to set up independent church organizations which were essentially American institutions. Even those Negroes who had run away from slavery and became leaders were Negroes who had had an opportunity during slavery to acquire some education and skill. The majority of the free Negroes in the North who rose to positions of leadership were completely acculturated. Some of them had enjoyed exceptional educational opportunities as, for example, Robert Purvis, whose activities were discussed in the preceding chapter. The leaders of the "convention movement" which began in 1830 were men who resented the lack of economic opportunities and the existence of civil

[1] See Herbert Aptheker, *American Negro Slave Revolts* (New York, 1943), pp. 162-208.

disabilities because they had taken over so much of American culture. They entered the struggle against slavery because they had become identified through racial discrimination and segregation with the enslaved Negro.

It is likely that some Negro slaves who had only been slightly influenced by American culture attempted to play the rôle of leaders as the result of their African cultural background. But little is known of leadership among the slaves because every form of organized activity was suppressed. The most prominent leaders who were acceptable to the white masters were, of course, the Negro preachers. But even the activities of the Negro preachers were under constant surveillance. The entire slave system was designed to prevent Negroes from achieving prestige among their fellow slaves. The leaders of the insurrections among the slaves were men who managed to circumvent the safeguards instituted to prevent organized activities among slaves under the direction of Negro leadership. Nat Turner was a religious fanatic who succeeded in utilizing the Bible to establish faith in himself on the part of the slaves. Denmark Vesey, a free Negro with unusual intelligence and social understanding, used every means—the Bible, superstition, and appeal to race pride—that could be effective in creating solidarity among the slaves. The failure of Vesey did not result from his lack of insight and understanding but from the failure of his lieutenants to obey his orders. More information is available concerning Negro leaders who assisted in the Underground Railroad Movement because some of them were active in the North. One of the outstanding Negro leaders in the Underground Railroad was Harriet Tubman, who made many trips to the South and led many slaves to freedom.[2]

EMERGENCE OF NEGRO LEADERS AFTER EMANCIPATION

When, following the Civil War, the freedmen were thrown upon their own, Negro leadership began to assume greater importance among them. Some of the most important leaders were the Negroes who had been free before emancipation and had enjoyed educa-

[2] See Earl Conrad, *Harriet Tubman* (Washington, D. C., 1943).

tional and other cultural opportunities. A Negro who had even a meager amount of education was likely to enjoy considerable prestige among the freedmen. As we have observed, the colored teachers of the freedmen were recruited from the Negroes who were free before the Civil War. Then, too, a leadership emerged in response to the organized activities of the freedmen. Since one of the most important organized activities of the freedmen was the church, preachers became the largest and most influential body of leaders among freedmen. Next to the preachers were those who assumed the leadership of the lodges and mutual aid societies which sprang up among the freedmen. The leaders in the fraternal organizations were also, as we have seen, leaders in the earliest business undertakings among the emancipated Negroes.

The most important leaders among Negroes during the Reconstruction Period were the political leaders. The pre-eminence of this class of leadership was not because the simple-minded Negro, as it has often been stated by Negroes as well as whites, sought political office instead of the more important things in life.[3] The political leader among Negroes assumed importance because southern Reconstruction was essentially a revolutionary situation in which power relations and the status of the Negro were undergoing drastic change. It is probable that several hundred Negroes were elected to the legislatures in the southern states and many more were elected to minor local offices.[4] The factors involved in the rise of these men to positions of leadership were the same as those among men the world over. Some had been free before the Civil War and had enjoyed educational opportunities. Others who had been slaves sometimes had

[3] For example, Booker T. Washington stated in his famous Atlanta speech in 1895: "Ignorant and inexperienced, it is not strange that in the first years of our new life we began at the top instead of at the bottom; that a seat in Congress or the State Legislature was more sought than real estate or industrial skill; that the political convention or stump-speaking had more attraction than starting a dairy farm or truck garden." From *Selected Speeches of Booker T. Washington*, edited by E. Davidson Washington, pp. 31-32. Copyright 1932 by Doubleday & Company, Inc.

[4] See Luther P. Jackson, *Negro Office-Holders in Virginia, 1865-1895* (Norfolk, Va., 1945) for the offices which Negroes held and for information on the educational, social, and economic background of the officeholders together with photographs.

been fortunate enough to acquire some education. Even among the
ex-slaves who held office there were many who had managed to acquire some land as well as education. Many of these men possessed
energy, intelligence, and ambition which enabled them to become
leaders. During the period when Negroes enjoyed the franchise 20
went to Congress and two to the United States Senate. On the whole,
the political leaders of the Negro exhibited considerable wisdom
and understanding in a situation where racial feeling and reaction
united to finally destroy democracy in the South.[5]

FROM FREDERICK DOUGLASS TO
BOOKER T. WASHINGTON

The outstanding leader among Negroes during the nineteenth century was, of course, Frederick Douglass.[6] Douglass' life, which extended over a period of 78 years (1817 to 1895), spanned many of
the most important changes in American society as well as the most
important changes in the status of the Negro in the United States.
When he was born, slavery was an established institution in the
South. When he escaped from slavery in 1838, the slavery question
had become the subject of a controversy that threatened the unity of
the nation. As an abolitionist orator, he had become because of his
intellectual powers one of the most prominent figures in the movement. During the Civil War, Douglass led the fight for the right of
the Negro to serve as a soldier and he was among those who urged

5 See Samuel D. Smith, *The Negro in Congress, 1870-1901* (Chapel Hill, 1940),
for the most comprehensive study of the Negroes who were elected to the Congress
of the United States. In regard to these men he reaches the following conclusion:
"From the data and facts examined, it seems clear that the Negroes failed to accomplish much worth while in Congress, during the period under survey. They were all
race-conscious and supersensitive, as was perhaps unavoidable under the circumstances. With some exceptions this resulted in a neglect of their white constituents.
. . . It has been demonstrated in the introductory chapter that the Negroes in
Congress from 1870 to 1901 were rather well equipped by education, previous
political experience, and wealth, and that most of them had considerable white
blood in their veins and were frequently aided by white friends." Reprinted from
The Negro in Congress, 1870-1901, by Samuel Denny Smith, by permission of the
University of North Carolina Press, pp. 143-44. Copyright 1940 by Samuel Denny
Smith.

6 See [Frederick Douglass], *Life and Times of Frederick Douglass* (Chicago,
1882).

Lincoln to issue the Emancipation Proclamation. After Emancipation, Douglass, who was appointed Recorder of Deeds in the District of Columbia and later Minister to Haiti, continued to lead the fight for the equality of the Negro as a citizen in American life. But Douglass lived to see the Negro gradually lose his citizenship rights in the South. It was one of those strange coincidences of history that in the very year in which Douglass died, Booker T. Washington rose to national leadership after his famous Atlanta speech in which he made the statement which was taken to be the basis of future race relations in the South. In that speech he said: "In all things that are purely social we can be as separate as the fingers, yet one as the hand in all things essential to mutual progress."

Kelly Miller, whose position on the Negro problem was intermediate between that of Douglass and Washington, summed up the distinction between the two men as follows:

The radical and conservative tendencies of the Negro race cannot be better described than by comparing, or rather contrasting, the two superlative colored men in whom we find their highest embodiment— Frederick Douglass and Booker Washington, who were both picked out and exploited by white men as the mouthpieces and intermediaries of the black race. The two men are in part products of their times, but are also natural antipodes. Douglass lived in the day of moral giants; Washington lives in the era of merchant princes. The contemporaries of Douglass emphasized the rights of men; those of Washington, his productive capacity. The age of Douglass acknowledged the sanction of the Golden Rule; that of Washington worships the Rule of Gold. The equality of men was constantly dinned into Douglass's ears; Washington hears nothing but the inferiority of the Negro and the dominance of the Saxon. Douglass could hardly receive a hearing today; Washington would have been hooted off the stage a generation ago. Thus all truly useful men must be, in a measure, timeservers; for unless they serve their time, they can scarcely serve at all. But great as was the diversity of formative influences that shaped these two great lives, there is no less opposability in their innate bias of character. Douglass was like a lion, bold and fearless; Washington is lamblike, meek and submissive. Douglass escaped from personal bondage, which his soul abhorred; but for Lincoln's proclamation, Washington would probably have arisen to esteem and favor in the eyes of his master as a good and faithful servant. Douglass insisted

upon rights; Washington insists upon duty. Douglass held up to public scorn the sins of the white man; Washington portrays the faults
of his own race. Douglass spoke what he thought the world should
hear; Washington speaks only what he feels it is disposed to listen to.
Douglass's conduct was actuated by principle; Washington's by pru-
dence. Douglass had no limited, copyrighted programme for his race,
but appealed to the Decalogue, the Golden Rule, the Declaration of
Independence, the Constitution of the United States; Washington,
holding these great principles in the shadowy background, presents
a practical expedient applicable to present needs. Douglass was a
moralist, insisting upon the application of righteousness to public
affairs; Washington is a practical opportunist, accepting the best
terms which he thinks it possible to secure.[7]

In accepting the best terms he thought it was possible to secure,
Washington became not only a conciliator for Negroes but an un-
official political leader in the South. His speeches and public actions
indicated that he accepted the subordinate position of the Negro as
an established fact, based to some extent upon the actual economic
and social position of the Negro. But Washington as the interracial
statesman who enjoyed the confidence of Presidents of the United
States, statesmen, and industrialists, wielded a power in the South
that white politicians recognized. He not only dictated the appointments of Negroes to public office, but white aspirants to appointment
to public offices in the South sought his support.[8] It was possible to
disfranchise the Negro and prevent him from holding public office,
but it was not possible to exclude the influence of the Negro from the
political rivalries of whites. As the dictator of the appointment of
Negroes to public office, Washington was able to control the small
group of the Negro intelligentsia. This control extended into the field
of education where the educated Negro found his chief field of employment. Washington's influence in the appointments of the Republican administration in a region dominated by the Democratic
Party and almost solidified on the subordination of the Negro
was directed toward the alleviation of the lot of the Negro. In

[7] Kelly Miller, *Race Adjustment* (New York, 1910), pp. 19-20.
[8] See E. Franklin Frazier, "The Booker T. Washington Papers," *The Library of
Congress Quarterly Journal of Current Acquisitions*, Vol. 2 (February, 1945), pp.
23-31.

fact, there is good reason to believe that Washington never surrendered in principle the right of the Negro to protest against social discrimination.[9] In his last published article, which appeared in *The New Republic* after his death in 1915, he summarized his objections to segregation. He stated that he regarded segregation as an injustice toward the Negro which not only invited other unjust measures but widened the breach between the two races and that every thoughtful Negro resented the injustice and insincerity involved in segregation.[10]

By the time of World War I the Washington leadership had begun to lose its influence. The successors of Washington at Tuskegee Institute were never able to exercise the influence as leaders which Washington possessed. This was not simply because his successors did not possess his ability or his talent as an interracial statesman. The decline in the influence of the Washington leadership resulted primarily from changes in the objective conditions of the Negro and in his relation to the American community. Even if Washington had lived his influence as a leader would have declined. The most important factor in causing the decline in the influence of the Washington leadership and the failure of his successors at Tuskegee Institute to exercise the same influence as leaders was the migration of Negroes to northern cities.

THE DEVELOPMENT OF A FUNCTIONAL LEADERSHIP

The migration of Negroes to northern cities created large Negro communities in the North and brought about wider occupational differentiation of the Negro population. Out of the diversity of interests which the migrations created among Negroes arose new leaders.[11] Neither Washington nor any other principal at Tuskegee Institute could henceforth have acted as a spokesman for the interests of the various groups in the Negro population. Aside from the fact that the Washington leadership was conciliatory, the essential fact to be noted is that Washington was the spokesman for a mass of

[9] See Gunnar Myrdal, *An American Dilemma* (New York, 1944), Vol. I, pp. 640-41.

[10] "My View of Segregation Laws," *The New Republic*, Dec. 4, 1915, pp. 113-14.

[11] E. Franklin Frazier, "The American Negro's New Leaders," *Current History*, Vol. 28 (April, 1928), pp. 56-59.

inarticulate, illiterate rural folk. As the Negro has acquired education and developed diverse economic and cultural interests, no single person could be their spokesman.[12]

As an example of the manner in which objective conditions have made the Washington type of leadership impossible, one may take the sphere of politics. At one time Washington could dictate the appointment of Negroes to political offices. No principal of Tuskegee Institute could exercise such power at the present time. Negroes have become a part of the political machines in northern cities and political appointments are made in order to insure the political support of Negroes in these cities. In making the political appointments, the President of the United States or the governors of the states consult the political leaders who have influence among Negro voters. Thus as the result of urbanization there has appeared a *functional* leadership among Negroes.

Although the character of Negro leadership has changed, it is still possible to classify Negro leaders in the categories of "accommodation" and "protest" as Myrdal has done; or as "gradualist" and "revolutionary" as Guy Johnson has done. But in view of the changes in the relation of the Negro to the American community, it appears that a more significant classification of leaders would be a functional classification. The position of a Negro leader on the race problem is being determined more by the outlook and ideology of the group which he represents than by the fact that he is radical or conservative. This is, apparently, the reason why Guy Johnson finds there is much confusion as to whether a Negro leader is radical or conservative. Since many Negro leaders believe that the Negro must be integrated

---

[12] Guy Johnson ("Negro Racial Movements and Leadership in the United States," *The American Journal of Sociology*, Vol. XLIII, pp. 68-70) thinks that the "chaotic conditions of Negro thought" and the "conflicting viewpoints" are the result of the transition period in the status of the Negro. He feels that when Negro thought has become integrated, a new leader similar to Booker T. Washington will appear. Our position is that the so-called "chaotic condition of Negro thought" and "conflicting viewpoints" represent the development of diverse interests among Negroes and that as the Negro becomes integrated into American life, these differences in viewpoints will become a permanent feature of Negro life. Consequently, just as among the whites in the United States, no single person can become the symbol or spokesman of the diverse interests of Negroes.

into American society,[13] there is a growing disposition to judge a Negro leader, whether he is an educator, politician, or labor leader, with respect to his stand on the integration of the Negro into particular spheres of American life. In our discussion of the new type of functional leadership five types of leaders will be considered: religious, social welfare, political, labor, and intellectual.

RELIGIOUS LEADERS

We have already analyzed in Chapter XIV the changes which have occurred in the Negro Church as the result of the urbanization of the Negro population during the past twenty-five years. Here we are interested in the new type of religious leadership that has emerged in response to the changes in the religious life of Negroes. The new religious leadership is distinguished broadly by its secular outlook. This secular outlook has been the result partly of broader education and partly of greater sophistication with life. Not only have the educated Negro ministers exhibited a more secular attitude toward life but even many of the semiliterate religious leaders of the smaller churches and various cults show the influence of secularization. The concern of the present-day Negro minister with mundane affairs has been in response to the increasing concern of the Negro masses with problems of employment, housing, and discrimination in the urban environment.[14]

As a consequence of the increasing secularization of outlook, the Negro preacher is concerned with the rights of the Negro. The Negro minister can no longer be interested solely in "getting the Negro in Heaven"; he must be interested in "advancing the Race." [15] Quite

[13] In the preceding chapter we have discussed the Garvey Movement with its separatist and nationalistic aims as a social movement among urban Negroes following World War I. It should be noted here concerning Garvey as a leader that his orientation in regard to the Negro problem was determined partly by the fact that he rose from among the black masses in the West Indies and partly by the contacts provided by European travels. Consequently, his attitude toward the solution of the Negro problem was radically different from American Negro leaders.

[14] Concerning rural Negro ministers, see Harry W. Roberts, "The Rural Negro Minister: His Work and Salary," *Rural Sociology*, Vol. 12, pp. 285-97.

[15] See St. Clair Drake and Horace R. Cayton, *Black Metropolis* (New York, 1945), pp. 424ff. See also A. Clayton Powell, Sr., *Riots and Ruins* (New York, 1945).

often this interest assumes the form of an intense loyalty to various Negro enterprises. Negro ministers advise their members to patronize Negro stores and Negro professional men. They have become especially interested in advising the Negro in the matter of voting. In fact, in a number of instances the Negro minister has merged his religious calling with the secular rôle of political leader. The first Negro congressman from New York City, A. Clayton Powell, Jr., is the pastor of the largest church in Harlem, while Marshall Shepard, the Recorder of Deeds in the District of Columbia, is the pastor of a large Baptist Church in Philadelphia.[16] In Chicago, Archibald Carey, Jr., who is a minister, is also a member of the city council.

The secular outlook of the Negro minister involves an interest in the relations of the Negro to the modern labor movement and social welfare. This has been a gradual development among the ministers as well as the members of their congregations.[17] Slowly the members of the churches have given up their traditional notions of the relations of employers and workers which were supported by their religious ideas. The ministers, on the other hand, were concerned with the material support which they received from the industrialists.[18] But as the Negro industrial worker has become increasingly a part of organized labor, the ministers have been compelled to ally themselves with the interests of the congregations. In the matter of social welfare, the transition from the purely religious outlook has been easier. As we have seen in the chapter on the church, the ministers have instituted programs of social welfare in their churches and conducted forums which were concerned with civic problems.

LEADERS IN SOCIAL WELFARE

Since the mass migrations of Negroes to northern cities, there has emerged a relatively large and influential group of leaders who are primarily concerned with the social welfare of Negroes. In fact, the

16 See A. Clayton Powell, Jr., *Marching Blacks* (New York, 1945).

17 See Brailsford R. Brazeal, *The Brotherhood of Sleeping Car Porters* (New York, 1946), pp. 44ff., concerning the attitude of the ministers and churches toward the organization of the Pullman porters.

18 See, for example, Horace White, "Who Owns the Negro Churches?" *The Christian Century*, February 9, 1938, pp. 176-77.

field of social welfare has provided one of the chief fields of employment for the educated Negro. A large and influential section of the leadership in social welfare is connected with the Urban Leagues in the various cities. The leaders in the Urban Leagues have been identified with the conservative wing of educated Negroes. Their conservative attitude has been a result of the position which they have occupied in the racial pattern in the community. It has been pointed out that they are not leaders of a Negro movement, but leaders in a social welfare program which is supported primarily by the white community. Consequently, the leaders have tended to follow a course that would not alienate their supporters and thereby destroy their program. Although the most publicized phase of their program was to get Negro workers into industry, the local Leagues have performed with greater success the important function of making welfare services available to the Negro. Gradually the leaders have come out for the full cooperation of white and Negro workers and for the integration of the Negro into other phases of the community. An indication of the change in the attitude of some leaders in the Urban League is provided in their action regarding the Taft-Hartley Bill at their meeting on the economic problems of the Negro at Atwater, Massachusetts, in August, 1947. Despite the diplomatic suggestion that a committee be appointed to consider the effects of the Bill on Negroes, the meeting voted a resolution condemning the legislation. However, since the leaders are still bound by their boards and local opinion, especially in the South, they have attempted to secure as much as possible for the Negro within the framework of their organization.

There is an increasing number of Negroes employed in private, but more especially public, social agencies. In northern cities these welfare workers are becoming integrated into the general organization of social welfare. Thus they are becoming less identified as leaders of Negroes. Because of their professional interests, they are drawn into close association with their white fellow-workers. Their complete identification with their white colleagues is limited not only by the attitudes of whites but also by the status and affiliations of the Negro welfare workers within the Negro community. The increasing integration of Negro welfare workers in the general program of social welfare is significant because it is indicative of the manner in which Negroes are becoming assimilated in the urban environment. For example, the public welfare bureau of Cook County, Illinois, is largely staffed by Negroes.

POLITICAL LEADERS

The change in the character of the political leadership of the Negro during the past twenty-five years has been a direct result of the creation of large Negro communities in northern cities. After the Negro was disfranchised in the South, his political leaders became a part of a "rotten borough" system for the distribution of the spoils of victory during the Republican administration.[19] Since the Republican Party in the South played no part in the political issues in the region, the Negro political leaders could only give their support to factions in the Republican Party at its national conventions. The rewards for this support were certain financial considerations in the form of campaign funds and in connection with appointments of whites to offices that Negroes could not fill in the South. There were a few special rewards such as the Office of the Recorder of Deeds in the District of Columbia and the appointment as Minister to Liberia. Such appointments had only a symbolic value for the Negro masses but they were effective in retaining their traditional allegiance to the Republican Party.

In the North a few Negroes had succeeded in being elected to offices including the state legislatures. When the Negroes began to migrate to the northern cities, the white Republican politicians began to capitalize on their traditional allegiance to the Republican Party.[20] At the same time, Negro politicians began to utilize the increasing race consciousness among Negroes to build up political machines. In Chicago, where the Republican mayor, William H. Thompson, became the idol of Negro voters, not only were Negroes elected to office but Negroes were rewarded with jobs. Thus at least for a small section of the Negro population support of the Republican Party rested upon

[19] See Paul Lewinson, *Race, Class and Party* (New York, 1932), pp. 127 to 131, 138ff., concerning the rôle of Negro political leaders after the Negro was disfranchised in the South.
[20] See Harold F. Gosnell, *Negro Politicians* (Chicago, 1935).

more than a sentimental basis. It was, however, the advent of the New Deal that caused the masses of Negroes to become conscious of the relation between politics and economics.[21] The Negro shifted his more or less sentimental support from the Republican Party to the Democratic Party which through the WPA provided him with work and pay.

The political organizations that have grown up in Negro communities in northern cities are part of the political machines in these cities. Out of the political machines has emerged a new type of political leaders. These new leaders are men who have made their way in the rough and tumble of political manipulations. They are generally allied with the graft and rackets that characterize politics in the American city. But they are often men of character who are loyal to the interests of the Negro, though they are often looked down upon by the Negro upper class and the Negro intelligentsia. Nevertheless, being close to the masses and conscious of their aspirations and needs, the best among these political leaders undertake to secure for the masses what is possible in the present organization of society.[22]

LABOR LEADERS

One of the most important indications of the changing relationship of the Negro to American life has been the emergence of the leaders of Negro labor. To be sure, there have always been Negroes who have played an important rôle among Negro workers.[23] But these early leaders of Negro workers were inconspicuous and their work was overshadowed by that of the Negro intelligentsia and Negro politicians. As the result of the urbanization of the Negro population, the entrance of the Negro worker into industry, and changes in American society, there have emerged leaders of Negro labor, whose voices carry more weight than that of the Negro intelligentsia and ofttimes more

[21] See Drake and Cayton, *op. cit.*, pp. 353ff.

[22] Even in the South this change in the political activities of Negroes is observable. Ira Reid pointed out recently in regard to the participation of Negroes in Georgia that the Negro vote "is interested in issues and welfare; its leaders are not to be tempted by the promise of spoils." Ira De A. Reid, "Georgia Negro Vote," *The Nation*, July 6, 1946, p. 14.

[23] See Sterling D. Spero and Abram L. Harris, *The Black Worker* (New York, 1931), pp. 16ff.

than that of Negro political leaders. It was, probably, not a mere accident that one of the most influential labor leaders was one of the editors of *The Messenger*, a magazine which undertook a definition of the Negro problem in economic terms following World War I.

The emergence of A. Phillip Randolph as the first Negro labor leader of national importance occurred at a time when the Negro worker was just securing his foothold in American industry. The Negro Pullman Porter was not a new phenomenon in American industry; he had occupied since the Civil War the traditional position of the Negro, as a servant in the new setting of technological developments in transportation.[24] The Pullman Porter had been affected, however, as Negroes generally had been, by the changes during World War I and had become restive under the paternalistic policy of the Pullman Company. Yet there was a strong anti-union sentiment among the Porters and in the Negro community, based upon traditional notions concerning the friendliness of wealthy whites toward Negroes. When A. Phillip Randolph became interested in the Brotherhood he had to deal with these problems as well as the powerful opposition of the Pullman Company. Through *The Messenger*, which became the voice of the Brotherhood, he carried on an effective educational campaign among the Porters and in the Negro community as well as among whites. Randolph, the son of a Florida minister, who had studied labor economics in two New York colleges, displayed remarkable leadership in winning support from all sides. The success of the Brotherhood in becoming a stable organization and achieving recognition was due largely to his intelligent and wise leadership. As a result of this achievement, he became one of the most influential leaders in the Negro community. His right to this position of leadership was demonstrated when he organized the March-on-Washington Movement, which resulted in President Roosevelt's Executive Order 8802, creating the Fair Employment Practices Committee.

Despite its historic significance, the Negro labor leadership that developed out of the organization of the Pullman Porters was restricted largely to a field in which the Negro worker had a monopoly. The most important factor in the emergence of Negro labor leaders

[24] See Brazeal, *op. cit.*, pp. 1-5.

was the development of industrial unionism in the 1930's. The organizational framework as well as the official policy of the Congress of Industrial Organizations made possible the development of a Negro leadership. An outstanding example of the new labor leader is provided in the career of Willard S. Townsend, a member of the General Executive Board of the CIO. After his college career and a brief period of teaching, he was elected Vice-President of the Chicago local Red Cap union and later President of the International Brotherhood of Red Caps. After the union changed its name to the United Transport Service Employees of America, it transferred its affiliation from the American Federation of Labor to the CIO. Townsend is Secretary of the CIO Committee to Abolish Race Discrimination and serves on the boards of a number of organizations interested in improving race relations. Of this same committee George L-P. Weaver is the director and James C. Carey, chairman. As labor leaders Townsend and Weaver are not only outstanding representatives of Negro labor; they represent the integration of the Negro into the labor movement.[25]

INTELLECTUAL LEADERS

We come finally to the intellectual leaders among the Negroes. We have discussed in preceding chapters the rôle of intellectual leaders or the intelligentsia in the institutional life of the Negro community as well as in social movements. It was from the ranks of Negro intellectuals that DuBois drew his chief support in the Niagara Movement that merged with the National Association for the Advancement of Colored People. Although the Association has gradually won the support of the masses, its direction is in the hands of the Negro intelligentsia and their white friends. At present the Association is able to employ the talents of a large number of Negro intellectuals. Besides Walter White and Roy Wilkins, there is a staff of legal talent which has included Charles H. Houston, Thurgood Marshall, and William Hastie.

At the beginning of the century, DuBois was the chief spokesman

[25] See Willard S. Townsend, "One Problem and a Possible Solution," in Rayford W. Logan, *What the Negro Wants* (Chapel Hill, 1944), pp. 163-92.

of the Negro intelligentsia. "The Talented Tenth of the Negro race," he wrote in 1903, "must be made leaders of the thought and missionaries of culture among their people. No others can do this work and Negro colleges must train men for it. The Negro race, like all other races, is going to be saved by its exceptional men." [26] As a matter of fact, this "aristocracy of talent and character" which was to "raise" the Negro was far removed from the Negro masses in feeling and intellectual outlook. In fact, there were very few who could approach the intellectual stature of DuBois, who had enjoyed the best education that American and European universities could afford. The relatively small number of truly educated Negroes were, like DuBois, isolated and lonely men. They were what sociologists have designated "marginal men." [27] Because of the pattern of race relations in the United States they were condemned to live in two cultural worlds, in neither one of which they felt at home. They were not accepted by the whites while the ignorance, poverty, and primitiveness of the Negro world repelled them. The phenomenon of "marginality" was presented in classic form in the bits of autobiography found in DuBois' writings.[28] The marginal position of DuBois and other Negro intellectuals probably provided a stimulus to an intellectual outlook on life. As the number of educated Negroes has increased, they have become less isolated than DuBois and his early contemporaries were. Nevertheless, the Negro intellectual continues to occupy a marginal position.

In estimating the significance of the achievements of Negro intellectuals, there has been a tendency on the part of friendly whites as well as on the part of Negroes to overestimate their accomplishments.[29] When Negroes have overestimated the achievements of their

[26] Booker T. Washington and W. E. B. DuBois, *The Negro Problem* (New York, 1903), p. 75.

[27] See Everett V. Stonequist, *The Marginal Man* (New York, 1937).

[28] See, for example, W. E. B. DuBois, *The Souls of Black Folk* (Chicago, 1920), pp. 2-3.

[29] Prejudiced and hostile whites have constantly made uncritical comparisons between the intellectual achievements of whites and Negroes. These comparisons have usually involved invidious distinctions which have revealed an ignorance of the influence of culture upon intellectual attainment as well as an ignorance of the cultural history of the western world.

leaders it has been the result of their social and mental isolation or because of compensatory reactions to their inferior status. On the other hand, the overestimation of Negro achievements by whites has been indicative of a feeling of pathos toward Negroes or because they have had, unconsciously perhaps, a double standard in mind. But there have been white scholars who in an objective spirit have rated the achievements of Negro intellectuals as inferior or of little significance. For example, Myrdal states: "Opportunity is a most important prerequisite for achievement; and since the Negro's opportunities have been kept low, his achievements are also small . . . there have been only half a dozen outstanding Negro natural scientists, and perhaps a dozen or so outstanding Negro social scientists." [30] Some competent scholars without racial bias have asserted, however, that the failure of Negro intellectuals to make contributions of a high order cannot be explained on "environmental" grounds or because of the lack of opportunity. For example Hankins, who thinks the backwardness of the Negro cannot be explained by the lack of social opportunity, writes:

But neither condition will account for the full difference between the response of the negro to cultural stimulation and the response of such peoples as the Japanese or the Jews. The contact of the former with western culture has been shorter in time than that of the American negro, but they have not only imitated it in manifold aspects,—they have modified, adapted and improved upon it and made contributions to one of its most difficult activities, scientific research. Moreover, these contributions, notably in the field of medical research and bacteriology, have been of the highest rank. The Jew, in spite of an almost universal anti-Semitism, has made remarkable contributions to every aspect of western culture. It is erroneous to think of the Jews as a race in any strict sense but they may be cited in this connection because they constitute a social group which in many times and places has been more vigorously hated than the negro in many parts of the United States during the last half century. The Jew has not only fought his own battle but he has "come back" with an almost obnoxious persistency and "nerve" after every rebuff. The names of the

[30] *An American Dilemma* by Gunnar Myrdal, Vol. 2, pp. 986-87. Copyright 1944 by Harper & Brothers.

Mendelssohns, the Herschels, the Rothschilds, Heine, Brandeis, Disraeli, among many others, show how diversified the Jewish contribution has been.[31]

In view of such statements, it may be fairly asked why the Negro in the United States has not made intellectual contributions of the first order.

Even as late as 1927, Reuter asserted that, "The total number of really educated Negroes in the country is not sufficient to make a faculty for one first-class college." [32] The relatively few Negroes with graduate education tended to substantiate this statement despite the fact that private philanthropy had spent millions of dollars on the higher education of Negroes and some Negroes had had the benefit of education in northern colleges and universities.

The situation has changed considerably since Reuter wrote in 1927. The change in the intellectual development of the Negro has been most rapid since the urbanization of Negroes following World War I. Prior to World War I only 14 Negroes in the United States had received the degree of doctor of philosophy from recognized American or European universities.[33] The number had increased to 51 by 1929 and during the five-year period from 1930 to 1934, there were 70 Negroes who were awarded doctorates. During the next nine years 247 Negroes were awarded the doctorate. The rapid increase in the number of Negroes who were awarded the doctorate was paralleled by a similarly rapid increase in the number of Negroes attending and being graduated from colleges. Prior to World War I only 4,807 academic degrees—4,171 from Negro schools and 636 from northern schools—had been granted to Negroes.[34] By 1935 the total number had reached over 25,000. For the academic year 1946-1947 there were 68,939 students enrolled in Negro colleges and 2,853 Negro students in northern colleges. The Negro colleges awarded degrees to 5,937

[31] *The Racial Basis of Civilization* by Frank H. Hankins, p. 307. Copyright 1926 by Alfred A. Knopf, Inc.

[32] *The American Race Problem* by E. B. Reuter, p. 289. Copyright 1927 by Thomas Y. Crowell Company.

[33] Harry W. Greene, *Holders of Doctorates Among American Negroes* (Boston, 1946), p. 26.

[34] Charles S. Johnson, *The Negro College Graduate* (Chapel Hill, 1938), p. 8.

graduates in 1947; while northern colleges awarded 115 degrees to Negro graduates in the same year.[35]

BASES OF THE PAUCITY OF FIRST-RATE INTELLECTUAL NEGRO LEADERS

The failure of the Negro to produce outstanding intellectual leaders has usually been attributed to the innate inferior intellectual endowment of the Negro. This explanation seemed plausible when the intelligence tests were first used. The Army tests administered to recruits during World War I indicated that Negroes were inferior in intelligence to whites.[36] However, when the intelligence scores were broken down for regions, it was found that northern Negroes made higher scores than southern Negroes and that Negroes from some northern states made higher scores than southern whites.[37] An attempt was made to explain the higher intelligence scores of northern Negroes by attributing it to selective migration. It was assumed that the intellectually better endowed Negroes had left the South. This hypothesis was shown to be untenable in a study by Otto Klineberg.[38] His study revealed that the intelligence scores of southern Negro children increased with length of residence in the northern city. Moreover, it revealed that Negro children from southern cities started out with higher intelligence scores than those from the rural South but that the latter caught up with the former. Such facts seem to indicate that the low intellectual development of the Negro has been due to his social and mental isolation.

In an article written several decades ago, W. I. Thomas called attention to the effects of social and mental isolation upon the intellectual development of the Negro.[39] He pointed out first how race

[35] *The Crisis*, August, 1947. The Negro graduates of some white colleges were not reported because they did not keep records on the race of students.

[36] R. M. Yerkes, "Psychological Examining in the United States Army," Memoirs National Academy of Sciences (Washington, 1921), Vol. 15.

[37] See Otto Klineberg, *Race Differences* (New York, 1935), pp. 182ff.

[38] See Otto Klineberg, *Negro Intelligence and Selective Migration* (New York, 1935).

[39] W. I. Thomas, "Race Psychology," *American Journal of Sociology*, Vol. XVII (1911-12), pp. 744-47. See in this connection the point made by Buell G. Gallagher, *Color and Conscience* (New York, 1949), pp. 122-27, that Negroes in France, Brazil, and Russia, where they have not suffered discrimination as in the United States, have made first-rate contributions to modern civilization.

prejudice had isolated the Negro from the intellectual currents in American life. In addition, he pointed out how the Jew though isolated in Russia and Rumania was able to rise because of "resources and traditions and techniques of his own." The fact that the Negro has been isolated has often been noted but the lack of "resources and traditions and techniques of his own" has generally been overlooked. In this connection it might be pointed out that graduates of Negro schools who have become intellectual leaders have had supplementary training in northern universities. As we have seen in the chapter on institutions of higher education, these institutions not only lack resources but they have never built up traditions of scholarship and learning. Since the white community has the final authority in appointing heads of Negro institutions, it is doubtful whether it has such matters as learning and scholarship in mind when it selects the heads of Negro institutions. One should also not overlook the generally unfavorable effect of the Negro community upon the intellectual achievements. As was pointed out in Chapter XII, the Negro intellectual or scholar in the Negro world is isolated unless he conforms to the upper-class patterns of behavior, which are opposed to intellectual values.

Negroes who have become the intellectual leaders have broken through the mental isolation of Negro institutions and gained access to a larger intellectual world through attendance at northern institutions. Such men as W. E. B. DuBois and E. E. Just were the products of northern institutions. Unfortunately, those who have managed to escape the mental isolation of the masses have devoted most of their energies to the problems of the Negro. In the past the Negro scholar or intellectual was expected to devote himself to the Negro problem; and, in fact, this was the chief means of finding employment. The pattern of race relations has tended in other ways to distort the real significance of the contributions of Negro scientists and scholars. For example, there is little publicity given to the achievements of Just in the field of biology and Charles H. Turner, an outstanding entomologist,[40] while George W. Carver has been seized upon as a symbol of

---

[40] See Edward Ferguson, Jr., "A Revised List of Papers Published by Charles Henry Turner," *The Journal of Negro Education*, Vol. IX (1940), pp. 657-60.

the intellectual achievements of Negroes. Carver was connected with Tuskegee Institute, which has represented in the public mind the "right" type of education for Negroes. In addition, Carver's physical appearance together with the publicity concerning his great humility made a special appeal to the prejudices of the whites. In fact, any Negro who happens to fit into the white man's conception of the Negro or plays a desirable rôle in "interracial politics" may be built up into an intellectual giant.

Gradually the Negro intellectual is breaking through the racial barriers that have formerly restricted his interests and placed a false valuation upon his achievements. The 1944-1945 edition of *Who's Who in America* listed 91 Negroes, at least 50 of whom had been included because they had achieved distinction in their various fields of interests, rather than because of their official position.[41] Among those listed for distinction in their fields were the singers, Marian Anderson, Roland Hayes and Paul Robeson; the composers, Harry T. Burleigh, R. Nathaniel Dett, William Grant Still, and Clarence Cameron White; the writers, Langston Hughes, Zora Neale Hurston, Richard Wright, and Claude McKay; the editors and publishers, Robert S. Abbott and Carl Murphy; the lawyer, Charles H. Houston. In addition to those listed in *Who's Who* there are many other Negroes who have achieved distinction, measured by universal standards, in medicine, law, and science.[42] First among them should be mentioned Dr. Louis T. Wright, who was elected a fellow in the American College of Surgeons in 1934. He has published many scientific articles in the field of medicine and is recognized as an authority on skull fractures in the field of surgery. Dr. Charles R. Drew distinguished himself during World War II as the director of the blood plasma project for Great Britain. William H. Hastie, a former dean of the Howard University Law School, was appointed federal judge in the Virgin Islands and later the governor of the Islands. Percy L. Julian, who received his doctorate in chemistry at the University of Vienna, and served as a research professor at the DePauw University, has done dis-

---

[41] Jessie P. Guzman (Ed.), *The Negro Year Book. A Review of Events Affecting Negro Life, 1941-1946* (Tuskegee Institute, 1947), pp. 15-16.
[42] See *ibid.*, pp. 25-26.

tinguished work as a research chemist in industry. There are several young Negro mathematicians who have already gained some recognition. David H. Blackwell, who received his doctorate at the University of Illinois and was a fellow at the Institute for Advanced Study at Princeton, New Jersey, has published original articles and served as a consultant in the Navy Department. J. Ernest Wilkins, with a doctorate from the University of Chicago, has been a fellow at the Institute for Advanced Study and published a number of original studies.

These men are representative of the increasing number of Negro scientists who are distinguishing themselves as scholars and scientists in the universities and in industry.[43] In the northern city, especially, the walls of segregation are being broken down and the social as well as professional contacts of educated Negroes are widened. Consequently, the educated Negro is more likely to have the same interests and patterns of behavior as whites in the same class. He is not restricted to an upper-class rôle as in the more rigidly segregated Negro community in the border or southern city. The recent rapid intellectual advance of the Negro seems to indicate that as his mental and social isolation is broken down his intellectual achievements will gradually measure up to those of other groups.

Our analysis of leadership among Negroes has confirmed Myrdal's general observation that Negro leadership has been related to the pattern of race relations in the United States both with respect to time and place. The earliest group of Negro leaders appeared among the free Negroes in the North when the restrictions and segregation of Negro members of white churches were increasing. The character and influence of Negro leaders throughout the period before Emancipation was determined by the economic position of the Negro and his cultural attainments. Following the Civil War the political leader rose to prominence when the Negro was struggling to secure the status of a citizen. During the period in which the Negro struggled to attain equality Frederick Douglass became the leader of Negroes on the national level. When the Negro was disfranchised and his subordinate status in southern society was embodied in law, Booker T. Washing-

---

[43] See *ibid.*, pp. 44ff., for Negroes in physics and other fields of science.

ton rose to fame as a compromising leader. The mass migrations of Negroes to northern cities changed the character of Negro leadership. With the increasing occupational differentiation of the Negro population, the acquisition of political power, the increasing literacy of Negroes and the resulting differentiation of economic and cultural interests, a functional leadership appeared among Negroes. Since these changes have been associated with the increasing integration of the Negro into American life, the emergence of functional leaders is likely to become a permanent characteristic of Negro leadership as the participation of Negroes in American culture increases.

Problems of Adjustment

PARTS 1 and 2 showed how the Negro community came into existence and acquired its present relation to American life. Part 3 portrayed the character of the Negro community and its institutions and their relation to the American community. Part 4 dealt with the intellectual life and the leadership of the Negro community in relationship to both the Negro world and the larger white world of which it is a part. Part 5 will be devoted to the main problems of adjustment which the Negro has faced. There are first the problems of health and physical survival which are related to the economic and social status of the Negro. Then follows an analysis of the Negro's position in the economic organization and the phenomenon of unemployment and poverty among Negroes. Next comes an analysis of the failure of the Negro's family organization to function in American society. The extent to which Negro adults violate the laws of the community and Negro children become the subject of court action form the subject of a fourth chapter. A fifth chapter contains an analysis of the failure of Negroes to function as responsible members of society because of mental deficiency and mental breakdown. The final chapter in this section is devoted to the nature of race relations and how they have affected the development of the Negro in American society.

CHAPTER XXII

Health and Survival

$\mathbb{A}$ LITTLE more than half a century ago Frederick L. Hoffman, the statistician of the Prudential Life Insurance Company, after a careful analysis of vital statistics on the Negro population, concluded that the increase in constitutional and respiratory diseases among Negroes meant that the gradual extinction of the race was only a question of time.[1] This pessimistic prognosis concerning the survival of the Negro was made at a time when the unfavorable effects of the social disorganization following the Civil War upon the Negro had reached their climax. The consequences of the social disorganization were most marked in cities into which Negroes drifted following Emancipation. During the last decade of the nineteenth century and the first decade of the present century the death rate of Negroes began to decline in urban as well as in rural areas. The mass migrations to northern cities during and following World War I raised once more the question of the ability of the Negro to survive in modern urban civilization. Since the mass migrations to the North the Negro death rate has continued to decline and in spite of a general decline in the birth rate among Negroes, the increase in the Negro population has kept pace with that of the white population.

HEALTH OF THE NEGRO DURING SLAVERY

There are scarcely any reliable data on health and disease among the Negro slaves. There was undoubtedly a high birth rate among the slaves but this was accompanied by a high infant mortality. There

[1] Frederick L. Hoffman, *Race Traits and Race Tendencies of the American Negro* (New York, 1896), p. 329.

are some data on the Negro in Charleston, South Carolina, which indicate that the death rate from tuberculosis was much lower among Negroes than among whites.[2] That this was true of the general Negro population is confirmed by the statistics on the prevalence of tuberculosis among recruits during the Civil War. Of 315,620 white and 25,828 colored recruits examined, those rejected for tuberculosis amounted to 11.4 per 1000 among the whites and 4.2 per 1000 among the Negroes.[3] But it is noteworthy that although the Negro recruits had a smaller rate of tuberculosis than whites when they enlisted, the death rate among Negro soldiers from tuberculosis was over four times as high as among white soldiers. This difference has been interpreted as an indication of the Negro's greater susceptibilty and less resistance to tuberculosis. But as Holmes has pointed out, the tremendous increase in tuberculosis following Emancipation is attributable to the social disorganization, poverty, and ignorance of the freedmen.[4]

INCREASE IN NEGRO MORTALITY
FOLLOWING EMANCIPATION

The death rate in the Negro population unquestionably increased during the 25 or 30 years following the Civil War. Since the only data available for this period are for cities, it is impossible to draw conclusions concerning the rural Negro population. However, it is fairly certain that the effects of social disorganization and poverty upon the freedmen were most severe in the cities. In the registration area, which included only a few northern states, the death rates among Negroes were 32.4 and 30.2 respectively as compared with 20.2 and 17.3 for whites in 1890 and 1900.[5] However, Hoffman reported the same rates for Negroes and whites in his study of 10 cities.[6] The rates were undoubtedly higher since 30 to 40 per cent of Negro deaths in cities were not recorded.[7] Because of the acuteness of the problem, Negro leaders singled out the health problem of the Negro for study. The

---

[2] See *ibid.*, pp. 69-70.
[3] S. J. Holmes, *The Negro's Struggle for Survival* (Berkeley, Calif., 1937), p. 75. This is the most thorough and comprehensive study that has been made of the survival of the Negro in American society. Many of the facts presented in this chapter have been taken from this study.
[4] *Ibid.*, p. 76.   [5] *Ibid.*, p. 40.   [6] *Ibid.*, pp. 38ff.   [7] *Ibid.*, pp. 39-40.

first monograph and part of the second monograph in the Atlanta University Studies of the Negro were devoted to the health of the Negro in cities.[8] DuBois and his collaborators undertook to show the relation of negligence, intemperance, ignorance, and poverty to the high mortality of Negroes.

During the last decade of the nineteenth century and more especially after 1900, there was evidence that the Negro was acquiring greater capacity to survive under the conditions of freedom. In 15 out of 33 northern cities and in 32 out of 34 southern cities the death rate of Negroes declined.[9] During the second decade of the present century the decline in Negro mortality was even more rapid. This was indicated in the life tables for the Negro population in the Original Registration Area. The increase in the span of life for Negroes was due to the decline in infant mortality since the mortality among Negro adults continued to be high and in some cities showed an actual increase. By 1920 the life span of Negroes had increased considerably in the Original Registration Area; but the expectation of life of south ern Negroes who were largely rural was greater than that of northern Negroes who were concentrated in cities.[10]

HEALTH OF WHITES AND NEGROES IN COUNTRY AS A WHOLE

During the present century the expectation of life at birth has gradually increased among Negroes. In 1900 the expectation of life of Negro females was 35 years and that of Negro males 32.5 years, as compared with 51 years and 48 years for white females and males respectively. A Negro female baby born 30 years later could expect to live 49.5 years or two years longer than a Negro male baby. At the same time a white female baby had a life expectancy 13.2 years greater and a white male baby 11.5 greater than Negro babies of the same sex. The difference in the life expectancy of the two races had not changed in regard to females in 1940. As Hauser has shown, "On the basis of death rates for the 3-year period centered in 1940, the aver-

---

[8] See W. E. B. DuBois (Ed.), *Mortality Among Negroes in Cities* (Atlanta, 1896), and *Social and Physical Condition of Negroes in Cities* (Atlanta, 1897).
[9] Holmes, *op. cit.*, p. 42.   [10] *Ibid.*, p. 43.

age future lifetime of white males at 1 year of age was approximately 65 years; in contrast, the average future lifetime of Negro males was 56 years. For females, the figures respectively for white and Negro are 69 years and 58 years." [11]

Hauser's studies in Chicago reveal the wide difference in the mortality of Negroes and whites in a northern city which does not represent an unusual case.

Under 1930 death rates, of an original cohort of 10,000 white males, 7,815 would survive to age 45; but in the Negro population only 5,139 would survive to the same age. That is if 1930 death rates continued, by age 45, 22 per cent of the white males in Chicago would have died; while in contrast, more than twice that proportion, 49 per cent of the Negro males would have died before attaining the same age. Similarly, in accordance with 1930 differential death rates, 18 per cent of the white females as contrasted with 42 per cent of the Negro females would die before reaching age 45.

Within the white and Negro populations, respectively, economic status was an important factor in mortality experience. Among whites, for example, 31 per cent of the males and 24 per cent of the females in the lowest fifth of the population ranked by economic status would die before attaining age 45. In contrast, only 15 per cent of the males and 12 per cent of the females in the highest fifth of the population would die before reaching age 45. Among Negroes, 57 per cent of the males and 51 per cent of the females in the lowest economic class would die before reaching age 45; while this would be true of only 35 per cent of the Negro males and 31 per cent of the females in the highest Negro economic class (the highest Negro economic class is at a lower level than the highest white economic class).

Thus, within the same city, and this is not the unusual case, the chances of survival to age 45 are only half as great for the Negro as for the white population; and only half as great for the lower as for the higher economic groups.

By 1940, as reported in an unpublished study by Evelyn Kitagawa of the University of Chicago, the mortality schedule of the entire population of Chicago had decreased and the differentials, at least by race (data are not available by economic status for 1940), had also appreciably decreased, but a great difference in the mortality experience of the white and Negro races was still evident. If the 1940 death

[11] Philip M. Hauser, "Population Problems in the United States." Unpublished study.

rates persisted, 15 per cent of white males as contrasted with 36 per cent of Negro males would fail to live to age 45; and 11 per cent of white females as contrasted with 29 per cent of Negro females would die before age 45.[12]

Hauser has made a significant contribution to the study of the differentials in the fertility of Negroes and whites by providing "an index of human wastage in population replacement." Assuming that the 1905-1910 birth and death rates had persisted, he shows that according to the Bureau of the Census, 100 women would in their lifetime produce 134 daughters, the figure 134 being known as the net reproduction rate.

To net 134, however, these 100 women in the original cohort would have to produce 179 daughters (the 179 is known as the gross reproduction rate). The difference between these figures, 179 and 134, or 45, represents the number of daughters who would fail to survive through the child bearing period. This number, 45, may be expressed as a percentage of gross reproduction (179 in this case) and may be interpreted, therefore, as the percentage of a cohort of women who would fail to survive through the child bearing ages. The percentage is, in effect, an index of human wastage in population replacement. For the United States as a whole, in 1905-1910, 25 per cent is the index of human wastage in population replacement. (45 divided by 179.)

For the same period, 1905-1910, the net reproduction rate for the white population was 134 and that of the non-white, 133. But the index of human wastage in population replacement for the non-white population was 41, as contrasted with an index of 25 for the white population.

By 1935-1940, the net reproduction rates of both the white and non-white populations had both declined, but the white more rapidly than the non-white. The net reproduction of the white population for this period was 96—4 per cent below replacement level; while that of the non-white population was 114—14 per cent above the replacement level. To achieve this 18 point difference between the white and non-white net reproduction rates, however, required a 35 point difference in gross reproduction rates (141 compared with 106); that is, the non-white index of human wastage in replacement, 19 per cent, was more than twice as high as the white index of human wastage in replacement, nine per cent.[13]

[12] *Ibid.*   [13] *Ibid.*

In Chicago in 1930, Hauser found that the index of human wastage in replacement was more than four times (34 as compared with 8) as high for the lowest economic grouping of Negroes as for the highest economic grouping of the white population. One of the principal causes of the shorter life expectancy of Negroes at birth is their high infant mortality.[14] Although the infant death rate among Negroes has declined over the years, it is still over 60 per cent higher than the infant death rate among whites. While influenza and pneumonia are the chief causes of death of both white and Negro infants, syphilis is of greater importance among Negro infants. In connection with the higher infant death rate among Negroes there should be considered the higher maternal mortality among Negro women. Nearly three times as many Negro women as white women die from conditions associated with pregnancy and childbirth.

After the age of five the rates for the communicable diseases which characterize childhood are about the same for the two races. On the other hand, death rates for tuberculosis, influenza, nephritis, pneumonia, syphilis, homicides, and pellagra are uniformly higher among Negroes than among whites. Tuberculosis, influenza and pneumonia are the main diseases which are responsible for the high death rate among Negroes. These three diseases are responsible for nearly three-fourths of the excess mortality among Negroes under 25 years of age. In fact, about 50 per cent of the excess mortality among Negroes between 10 and 24 years of age is attributable to tuberculosis alone. Although in the older age groups tuberculosis accounts for a smaller proportion of deaths, influenza and pneumonia are important at all ages. For the age group between 45 and 65 years of age nephritis and heart disease are responsible for 40 per cent of the excess mortality. There are geographic differences in the causes of mortality that should be noted. For example, the suicide rate which is generally very low among Negroes is about two and a half times higher in the North than in the South. On the other hand, there are relatively fewer deaths due to homicide and accidents in the North. Likewise,

[14] The discussion which follows is based upon a memorandum on "The Health of the Negro" which was prepared by Harold F. Dorn for Gunnar Myrdal's *An American Dilemma.*

the infant death rate and maternal mortality are lower in the North. But the death rates from tuberculosis and diabetes in the North are almost twice as high as in the South. In the urban South the death rate among Negroes is about 66 per cent higher than in the rural South, while for whites the difference is only 48 per cent. Contrary to the situation among whites, who have an 18 per cent higher death rate in the urban areas than in the rural areas of the North, Negroes have a 6 per cent lower death rate in urban areas than in rural areas. These differences have not yet been explained.

Very little is known concerning the incidence of physical defects and impairments in the general population and practically nothing is known concerning racial differences in this regard. According to the results of a survey of relief families in 79 cities by the Federal Emergency Relief Administration in 1934, there was revealed little difference in the proportion of whites and Negroes reporting serious disability. In regard to dental defects we have more specific information on the children of the two races. A study of 13,000 rural children in Tennessee showed that the average number of defects per child was 4.2 for whites and 2.3 for Negroes. It was also found that 80 per cent of the white and 67.5 per cent of the Negro children were in need of dental care. The results of this study were confirmed by unpublished data from the United States Public Health Service. As measured by an index of dental defects, based upon a computation of decayed, missing, or filled permanent teeth, white boys and girls had indexes of 14.9 and 15.4 and colored boys and girls indexes of 9.3 and 11.9, respectively.

The higher mortality among Negroes than among whites is largely the result of the prevalence of chronic diseases and to a lesser extent the result of other types of illnesses. Information on illness among urban white and Negro families is contained in the National Health Survey conducted by the United States Public Health Service during 1935-1936. Data for four cities—Atlanta, Georgia, Dallas, Texas, Newark, New Jersey, and Cincinnati, Ohio—showed that 5.9 per cent of the colored and 4.5 per cent of the white population were ill on the day visits were made to the families. In regard to these figures it should be pointed out that the colored population included in the survey was of a lower economic status than the white.[15] The larger percentage of Negroes ill at the time of the visits was the result largely of chronic diseases. According to the data secured in the Survey, during 1935 the average Negro living in urban areas was unable to carry on his usual activities for a period of about 11 days because of serious illness. The loss of time because of serious illness was 20 per cent greater for Negroes than for whites.

HEALTH OF NEGROES AND WHITES IN A SOUTHERN STATE

The present situation of the Negro in regard to health in the lower South has been revealed in a study of health and mortality in Louisiana.[16] The data of that study indicate that

the health of Louisiana's colored people, as gauged by mortality rates, is considerably worse than that of her white people. The number of deaths from all causes for this race is about 13.8 per 1000, or one and one-half times as high as that of whites (9.1 per 1000). The whites enjoy this superiority over nonwhites at all ages except 65 years and above; and the differences in favor of the whites persist in all types of residential areas—in rural districts, in small and large cities—a fact which further substantiates their significance.

The most extreme differences between the two races occur with respect to death among infants, indicating that the whites utilize superior skills and resources in caring for and feeding young children. After lethal selection has been operative for some years, the superiority of the whites decreases, and after age 65 the colored people of the State may enjoy a longevity which compares favorably with that of their white fellows. The reported data indicate this to be true in the large cities of the state. In rural areas, however, rates of death for colored and white persons beyond the age of 65 years are very close to each other, and in the small towns and cities (2,500 to 10,000 population) aged as well as younger Negroes are characterized by higher

[15] Forty-two per cent of the colored population was on relief and 88 per cent was either on relief or had annual incomes of less than $1,000, whereas the corresponding percentages for whites were 15 and 34.

[16] Louise Kemp and T. Lynn Smith, *Health and Mortality in Louisiana,* Louisiana Bulletin No. 390 (May, 1945).

rates of mortality than are the whites who live there. But caution should be used in reaching conclusions on this score.[17]

This study revealed that the difference between the mortality of whites and Negroes was most pronounced in the small towns and cities with a population of 2,500 to 10,000. For the state as a whole, pneumonia and influenza killed relatively twice as many Negroes as whites; two and one-half times as many Negroes as whites died from tuberculosis; and syphilis was six and one-half times as deadly to the Negroes as to the whites. The death rate for pellagra, a deficiency disease associated with poverty and poor food habits, was six times as high among Negroes as among whites. Typhoid fever and whooping cough were four times as fatal among Negroes as among whites. Moreover, in the case of the degenerative diseases, the whites had an advantage over Negroes. The death rate from diseases of the heart, which are the primary causes of death for both races, was 20 per cent higher among Negroes than among whites. On the other hand, in the case of cancer, diabetes, appendicitis and congenital malformation the death rates for the two races were about the same and only slightly different in the case of ulcer of the stomach and cirrhosis of the liver. In the cities, diphtheria seemed to be less fatal for Negroes; while in the state as a whole deaths from automobile accidents and suicides were proportionately fewer among Negroes. Thus out of 25 common causes of death, the death rates for 17 diseases were significantly higher for Negroes than for whites.

Despite the poor health showing of the Negroes, they, like the whites, had shown improvement since 1920. The improvements in the health of the Negroes of Louisiana are summarized as follows:

[17] *Ibid.*, p. 19. The authors point out that "It should be remembered that the age data for Negroes are less reliable than those for whites; and that the Social Security Program introduced between 1930 and 1940 may have stimulated some persons to attain age 65 more quickly than normal. At any rate there were reported in Louisiana only 8,999 Negro females aged 55-59 in 1930 in comparison with 10,341 aged 65-69 in 1940. Also the decrease of Negro males in the age group under consideration from 11,099 aged 55-59 in 1930 to 10,417 aged 65-69 in 1940 does not seem sufficiently large. Among white females the corresponding change was from 19,032 in 1930 to 17,108 in 1940, and among white males the decrease was from 19,890 at the beginning of the decade to 15,744 at the close. Thus the apparent slight advantage of the nonwhites aged 65 and over in reality probably is due to the reduction in rate achieved by inflating the population."

In absolute gains in lives saved over the past two decades, Louisiana's colored people seem to have shared to a somewhat greater extent than have her whites, proportionate to their numbers in the population. This is due primarily to the great strides which have been made in controlling certain of the transmissible diseases among Negroes. The most outstanding example of this is in the case of tuberculosis. Colored people were dying in 1920 at the rate of about 234 per 100,000 from tuberculosis while in 1940 the rate had been cut to 95, or by 139 deaths per 100,000 of the population. The whites, for whom the rate was much lower at the beginning of the period, or 80.9, reduced theirs to the rather favorable figure of 38.4, or by 42.5 deaths per 100,000 of the population. Larger absolute reductions were more characteristic of Negro than of white death rates for malarial and typhoid fevers and for diarrhea, with the result that the rates of mortality for all these causes for the two races approximated each other more closely in 1940 than in 1920. In addition, Negroes of the State registered a much larger absolute reduction in deaths from pellagra than did whites, and they seem to have improved their situation a little more with respect to fatal accidents other than those involving motor vehicles. And accidents with motor vehicles which were, in 1940, killing about 20 more whites of each 100,000 than they were in 1920, had increased by only about 15 per 100,000 among colored.

On the other hand, with respect to gains made in the control of other of the causes of death, advances made by whites over the 20-year period were more outstanding than those made by Negroes. The fatality of pneumonia and influenza seems to be yielding somewhat more rapidly among the former, and the measures adopted by whites in curbing deaths from diphtheria and whooping cough are apparently proving a little more effective. Whites have also registered a little success in the control of deaths from syphilis, a cause which seems to have increased in importance in the Negro population. Rather substantial improvement (amounting to a reduction of 12 deaths per 100,000 population) in conditions associated with maternity has been characteristic of both races.

The degenerative diseases as a whole seem to have advanced a little more rapidly in importance as causes of death among colored people. Diseases of the heart are killing about 137 more white persons today out of each 100,000 than they were in 1920; they are responsible for 141 more colored deaths per 100,000 population than they were two decades ago. On an annual basis per 100,000 population, cancer is now killing 37 more whites, and 41 more Negroes, respectively; and deaths from disease of the nervous system, which have increased only by about 8 per 100,000 among whites, have increased by 25 among nonwhites. Deaths from nephritis, which show a slight tendency to decline among whites since 1920, have increased by about 20 per 100,000 among nonwhites. These differences may be accounted for in part by more accurate assignment of deaths by causes at the present time among the state's Negroes, and in part by the fact that as mortality from the transmissible diseases is reduced among them, a larger share of this race lives to reach the advanced ages.[18]

HEALTH AND SURVIVAL OF NEGROES IN CITIES

The rural Negro population in the South, which has accounted for the increase in the number of Negroes, has continued to decline during the past 25 years. Consequently, the health and survival of the Negro has depended increasingly upon his ability to survive in modern urban civilization. A considerable amount of information on this question is provided in the statistics of the Metropolitan Life Insurance Company which had about two million Negro policyholders. The majority of these industrial policyholders are in both southern and northern cities.[19] During the 25-year period, 1911 to 1935, the death rate for white policyholders declined from 1,309.4 to 724.6 while that of colored policyholders declined from 1,854.5 to 1,179.5 per 100,000.[20] The death rate for all forms of tuberculosis declined from 418.3 for colored males to 162.3 and from 398.8 for colored females to 143.1 during the period from 1911 to 1935. On the other hand, during this period the death rate for syphilis increased for colored males from 26.6 to 54.7 and for colored females from 14.9 to 23.6 per 100,000. These figures indicate that the death rate among Negroes in 1935 was about the same as that among whites in 1916 or there was a lag of 20 years.

Chiefly as the result of urbanization there has been a marked decline in the Negro birth rate. The low birth rate among urban Ne-

---

[18] *Ibid.*, pp. 30-31.

[19] See Louis I. Dublin and Alfred J. Lotka, *Twenty-five Years of Health Progress* (New York, 1937), pp. 7-10.

[20] The death rate increased for whites and Negroes during the influenza epidemic in 1917-18.

groes is reflected in the large number of childless Negro couples and the relatively small number of children in Negro families. Kiser's analysis of the National Health Survey data on married women revealed that birth rates among skilled and semiskilled urban Negro workers were considerably lower than those of whites of the same occupational classes and that birth rates among the Negro laboring classes were only slightly higher than those for Negroes in the professional and business classes.[21] The small number of children in urban Negro families was shown in a study of Negro families in Chicago. Miss Graham found in an analysis of every tenth Negro census family that there was an average of only one child per family and that 60 per cent of 2,930 married male heads of families had no dependent children.[22] Thirty per cent of these families had one or two children; 5 per cent three children; and 5 per cent more than three children.

The low fertility of the Negro families is not distributed evenly throughout the Negro population of our cities. There are variations which reflect the influence of economic and social factors in the selection and segregation of various elements of the Negro population with reference to residence. In Chicago, it was found that the area of the lowest fertility was in the "bright light" area where prostitution and other forms of social disorganization were located.[23] Moreover, as in the case of Kiser's findings, the Negro families in the areas of the Black Belt where the migrants settled had about the same number of children to women of childbearing age as the families in areas occupied by the professional and business families. The influence of the selective process with reference to residence on the fertility of the Negro was revealed even more strikingly in the Harlem Negro community.[24] In the center of the Harlem community there were only 66.1 births per 1,000 married women; while in the four other successive zones marking the expansion of the Negro population the birth

[21] Clyde V. Kiser, "Birth Rates and Socioeconomic Attributes in 1935," *Milbank Memorial Fund Quarterly*, Vol. XVII (April, 1939), pp. 139-41.

[22] Irene J. Graham, "Family Support and Dependency Among Chicago Negroes: A Study of Unpublished Census Data," *Social Service Review*, Vol. III, p. 551.

[23] See E. Franklin Frazier, *The Negro Family in Chicago* (Chicago, 1932), pp. 86ff.

[24] E. Franklin Frazier, "Negro Harlem: An Ecological Study," *The American Journal of Sociology*, Vol. XLIII, pp. 72ff.

rate increased regularly to 168.4 per 1,000 married women in the fifth or outermost zone. The ratio of children under five years of age to 1,000 women of childbearing age showed a similar increase for both 1920 and 1930. In the first zone there were 115 children to each 1,000 women of childbearing age and in the fifth zone, 462 in 1930. In the first zone deaths were in excess of births; in the second zone deaths balanced births; while in the third zone there were more than two births to each death.

The selective process which is revealed by the differential birth and survival rates shows the influence of economic status, education, and general culture. The simple peasant folk bring to the city their notions concerning disease and health which form a part of the folk culture in the South. These folk notions and practices form an even greater handicap in the city than in the rural environment.[25] There is much social disorganization and economic insecurity incident to the urbanization of the Negro. This results in the breaking of family ties, the neglect of children, and uncontrolled sex relations. Promiscuous sex relations cause the spread of venereal disease, which brings about much sterility among Negro women. Among the disorganized elements in cities, abortions are resorted to frequently in order to escape the inconvenience of having children. Moreover, the disorganized elements in the Negro community are employed sporadically at low wages as unskilled workers or secure a living in criminal activities. They are generally concentrated in areas where there is much overcrowding and an absence of adequate sanitation.[26] Consequently, it is in the most disorganized areas of Negro communities in cities that one finds the lowest fertility among Negro women.

During the process of selection in the city, those Negroes who because of stable family life, improved economic status and education

25 Even in the rural areas a selective process with reference to survival and economic status is apparent. For example, in a study of three counties located in three different southern states, it was found that the number of Negro children born and living in farm-owner families was larger than that for farm renters and that the number of children born and living in families of farm renters was larger than in families of farm laborers. See E. Franklin Frazier, *The Negro Family in the United States* (Chicago, 1939), pp. 259-60.

26 See U. S. Health Service, *The National Health Survey: 1935-36* (Washington, 1938), p. 10.

are more able to cope with the conditions of urban life tend to become segregated in certain areas. This group includes the more stable workers with some traditions of conventional family life who are ambitious for their children to take advantage of the opportunities offered by the city.[27] Among this group the family is smaller than the rural Negro family but it represents a more rational and intelligent adjustment to life. This more rational and intelligent adjustment to urban living is the result not only of formal education acquired in the schools but also of the educational work of social welfare agencies. Moreover, this group is increasingly taking advantage of the social services, such as prenatal and maternal care, provided by public welfare agencies. Consequently, as this group increases in size among Negroes in cities, Negroes show greater ability to survive in the urban environment.

That the health and survival of the Negro in modern urban civilization is dependent upon improvement in economic status and upon education in regard to health and food habits has been shown in a study of income and food expenditures among tuberculous families in Harlem.[28] In 1940, when 46 per cent of the families surveyed had an average annual income per adult cost unit of less than $300, 66 per cent of them spent less than three dollars per unit per week. In 1943, when 50 per cent of the families had an average income of $500 or more, 66 per cent of the families spent from three dollars to $14.99 per unit cost per week. However, it was shown in another study that the fact that the income in the families had increased considerably and on the average expenditures for food were sufficient for a good diet did not necessarily insure a good diet. Seventy-one per cent of the families

[27] It was revealed in a study of children in black and mulatto families in three southern cities—Birmingham, Alabama, Nashville, Tennessee, and Charleston, South Carolina—that although on the average the same number of children were born in black and mulatto families, from 5 to 7 per cent more children had survived in mulatto than in black families. The higher survival rate in mulatto families was associated with a lower rate of illiteracy and higher socioeconomic status. E. Franklin Frazier, "Children in Black and Mulatto Families," *The American Journal of Sociology*, Vol. XXXIX, pp. 12-29.

[28] Jean Downes, "Recent Changes in Income and Food Expenditures Among Tuberculous Families in Harlem," *The Milbank Memorial Fund Quarterly*, Vol. XXI (April, 1943), pp. 158-63.

had dietary patterns considerably below "the standard pattern believed necessary for the maintenance of good health." [29] After a period of education in food habits under public health supervision, the proportion of families with substandard dietary patterns was reduced to 51 per cent.

HOUSING AND THE HEALTH OF NEGROES

In the chapters on rural and urban Negro communities, there were presented some general facts on the housing of the Negroes. Here we are concerned with the relation of housing of the Negro to his health and survival. According to the 1940 federal census, for the country as a whole 16.3 per cent of the dwelling units occupied by "nonwhites" (though it includes Orientals it is largely descriptive of Negroes) were in need of major repairs.[30] It appears that in respect to housing the Negro was better off in the North than in the South. In the North 28.5 per cent of the dwelling units occupied by nonwhites as compared with 37.9 per cent in the South were in need of major repairs. The difference becomes even more significant when one considers the fact that 18.6 per cent of the dwelling units occupied by nonwhites in the urban South as compared with 4.6 occupied by nonwhites in the urban North had no running water.

One can get a more detailed picture of housing facilities for Negroes from the materials contained in The National Health Survey, 1935-1936, conducted by the United States Public Health Service and other studies.[31] Throughout the rural areas of the South the housing provided Negroes is much inferior to that available to whites. An analysis of unpublished data of the Farm-Housing Survey in 1934 showed that in 11 southern states about a half of the white farm operators as compared with four-fifths of the colored farm operators lived in unpainted frame houses. When the housing of the two races is considered from the standpoint of the foundations upon which the

[29] *Ibid.*, pp. 164-81.

[30] *Sixteenth Census of the United States: 1940. Housing*, Vol. II (Washington, 1943), pp. 18-19.

[31] The data provided in these studies and in unpublished tabulations made for Gunnar Myrdal's *An American Dilemma* (New York, 1944) have been analyzed in Richard Sterner, *The Negro's Share* (New York, 1944), Chapters IX and X.

houses rest, the condition of the floors, the roofs, the exterior and interior walls, and the chimneys, the same inferiority of housing facilities for Negroes is apparent. Nearly a half of the houses occupied by Negroes had foundations and roofs in poor condition as compared with about 30 per cent of the houses occupied by whites. Over a third of the houses occupied by Negroes had floors and exterior walls in poor condition as compared with about a fifth of the houses occupied by whites. Over a half of the houses of Negro farm operators had interior walls and ceilings in poor condition and nearly a third had chimneys in poor condition as compared with a third and about a sixth respectively of the houses of white operators. A larger percentage of the houses of white farm operators than of colored farm operators had piped water and refrigeration. Moreover, in the inferior housing facilities for Negroes there was more overcrowding than among white farm families. Among white owners there was 0.83 person per room; among white tenants and Negro owners, 1.14 and 1.15 persons per room; and among Negro tenants 1.45 persons per room. From the little available evidence it appears that the same disparities in white and Negro housing facilities exist in the villages of the South.

When one turns to the housing of Negroes in the urban areas, one finds that housing available to Negroes is inferior in the case of every phase on which statistics are available.[32] Unpublished tabulations from the Real Property Inventories conducted by the Federal Housing Administration during the years 1936 to 1940 revealed that with the exception of the Woodlawn area in Chicago, Illinois, 25 per cent to 73 per cent of the dwellings occupied by Negroes in 18 cities were in need of major repairs or were unfit for use. In these same cities—7 northern cities and 11 southern cities—the percentage of dwellings in need of major repairs or unfit for use occupied by whites ranged from 2 to 25 per cent. The inferior quality of Negro housing in respect to specific items has been revealed in a Consumer Purchases Study. In four small southern cities—Albany, Georgia, Gastonia, North Carolina, Sumter, South Carolina, and Griffin, Georgia—over 60 per cent of nonrelief normal Negro families had no indoor water supply for the kitchen and more than 75 per cent had none for the bathroom;

[32] Sterner, *op. cit.*, pp. 186ff.

while only 10 per cent of the white families of the same character were without either facility. According to the National Health Survey, in cities of less than 10,000 population, 73 per cent of the white families and only 9 per cent of the Negro families had indoor flush toilets. Even in southern cities of 25,000 to 100,000 population, only 20 per cent of the Negro families as compared with 80 per cent of the white families did not depend upon the communal privy. A larger percentage of Negro families than white families in southern cities depended upon fireplaces for heating. In northern cities the Negro suffers from inadequacies in housing but not to the same extent in regard to toilet and heating facilities because of sanitary and protective measures in the larger cities. Moreover, the available data indicate that there is less overcrowding of Negroes as well as of whites in northern cities than in southern cities.

Although there is much overcrowding in the dilapidated houses occupied by Negroes in the rural areas, especially in the lower South, it does not have the same serious consequences for the health of the Negro as in the cities. Yet as the result of inadequate housing in the rural areas, Negroes are subject to illnesses resulting from exposure. Tuberculosis and influenza are two of the main causes of death among the rural Negroes in the South. It is in the cities, however, that the effects of inadequate housing on the health of Negroes are most marked. For example, Jones found a much higher death rate for respiratory diseases among Negroes living in the alleys of Washington, D. C., than among Negroes living on the streets.[33] In a more systematic study Woofter found a Pearsonian correlation of +.809 between Negro death rates from tuberculosis and congestion in New York City.[34] In the Black Belt of Chicago where Negroes were living 90,000 per square mile as compared with 20,000 whites per square mile in an adjacent area, the Negro death rate for tuberculosis was more than five times the rate for whites in 1940-1941.[35] Although the high tuberculosis rate was caused partly by malnutrition resulting

[33] William H. Jones, *The Housing of Negroes in Washington, D. C.* (Washington, D. C., 1929), pp. 42-43.

[34] T. J. Woofter, *Negro Problems in Cities* (New York, 1928), p. 90.

[35] St. Clair Drake and Horace R. Cayton, *Black Metropolis* (New York, 1945), pp. 203-04.

from poverty and ignorance, it was also the result of overcrowding.

There are indications that the improved housing facilities provided by the public housing programs have been an important factor in the improvement of Negro health in cities. In an attempt to measure the social effects of housing it was found that there was an improvement in the health of Negro families that had been rehoused in public housing projects.[36] Although the rehoused Negroes continued to have a higher mortality from tuberculosis than the whites in the public housing projects, the mortality from tuberculosis among the rehoused Negroes was lower than that of Negroes in the control group. The Negro mortality from tuberculosis in the city of Newark increased during 1942 to 1943 while in the public housing projects the mortality rate from this cause remained less than a half of that for the Negroes in the city. In Newark there was also a reduction in infant mortality, which is responsible for much of the higher mortality among Negroes. The death rate from this cause was less than a third in the two housing projects than in wards outside the projects.[37] In regard to communicable diseases—chicken pox, diphtheria, scarlet fever, et cetera, the improvement in the rates for Negroes was lower in both 1942 and 1943 than for the city as a whole but the improvement over the control group did not appear until 1943. Despite the limitations of this study, it provides a clear indication of the effect of housing upon the health of Negroes.

SOCIAL AND ECONOMIC FACTORS AFFECTING NEGRO HEALTH

Housing is only one of the social and economic factors affecting the health of Negroes. Among the social factors there is first the lower educational status of the Negro population. Because of his illiteracy, the Negro does not have access to scientific knowledge concerning health and disease. Consequently, the great mass of illiterate and semi-literate Negroes acquire their knowledge concerning the nature of

[36] Housing Authority of the City of Newark, *The Social Effects of Housing.* Newark, New Jersey, November, 1944.

[37] In one project the infant mortality rate remained slightly higher than the rate in one of the wards in the control group.

disease and cures for illnesses from folk beliefs and superstitions. This is not only the case with the rural Negro but is characteristic of the recent migrants to urban areas. In the city, especially the northern city, the public school and social agencies are gradually changing the Negro's conception of the nature of disease and attitude toward health. At the same time, however, the large amount of family disorganization among Negroes provides a fertile field for illness and favors the spread of venereal diseases. Many of the stillbirths among Negroes in both rural and urban areas are the result of syphilitic infection. Comparable blood test data for Albermarle County, Virginia, and Chicago, Illinois, showed the average rate of syphilis for Negroes to be seven times that of whites.[38] In a study of the distribution of the general population and the syphilis population by income in Washington, D. C. in 1939, it was found that 77.7 per cent of the Negro population had incomes of less than $1,000 per annum, whereas 86.6 per cent of the Negro syphilis population was in this income class. And while 21.6 per cent of the Negro population was in the income class, $1,000 to $3,000, only 13.0 per cent of the Negro syphilis population was in this income class. Although the influence of the age factor is unknown, it appears that, as in the white group, the incidence of syphilis among Negroes is higher in the low income groups.

The relation of economic factors to the health and survival of the Negro has been revealed more strikingly in other studies. In an unpublished study by Philip M. Hauser, of mortality in Chicago, 1929-1931, it was revealed that there was a definite inverse relationship between the death rate and economic status of both whites and Negroes.[39] The death rate among Negroes living in areas with median monthly rentals of $60 to $74 was two-thirds less than the death rate for Negroes in areas of lowest rentals. The excess of mortality among Negroes compared with whites was 64 per cent in the areas of highest rentals as compared with 82 per cent in the areas of lowest rentals. According to the results of the National Health Survey the members of Negro families on relief had lost four times as much time because of disabling illness as persons in families with an annual income of

[38] Harold F. Dorn, *loc. cit.*   [39] Cited in Dorn, *op. cit.*

$2,000 or more and 2.3 as much time as persons in families with less than $1,000 income. The low income of Negro families influences, as we have seen above, the diet of Negro families. According to a study of the Bureau of Home Economics of the diets of wage earners and clerical workers in 1934-1936, only 11 per cent of the Negro families in the South had diets graded as good and 25 per cent diets graded as fair. The estimated cost of a good diet would have assumed that a Negro family received an annual income of $1,200. But the estimates prepared by the National Resources Committee for 1935-1936 showed that 92 per cent of the Negro families in the South had an income less than $1,250. Despite the limitations of these estimates, the fact seems to be clear that a large proportion of Negroes do not have a diet that is necessary to maintain themselves in physical health.

EFFECT OF RACIAL SEGREGATION
AND DISCRIMINATION

In a discussion of the influence of social and economic factors upon the health of the Negro, special consideration needs to be given to the consequences of racial segregation and discrimination. The effects of racial segregation and discrimination upon health appears first in respect to the opportunities afforded Negroes for hospital care. According to a study in 1938 by the Council on Medical Education and Hospitals of the American Medical Association, the number of beds in general hospitals in Mississippi per 1,000 population was 2.4 for whites and 0.7 for Negroes as compared with 3.3 for the entire country.[40] Although about a half of the population of Mississippi was Negro, only 23 per cent of 72,442 admissions to the 88 general hospitals were Negroes. The Duke Endowment reported in 1938 that in North Carolina and South Carolina 2.1 general hospital beds per 1,000 population were available for white and 1.2 for Negro patients. Thus in the Carolinas as in Mississippi about three times as many whites as Negroes were admitted to hospitals. The limited hospital facilities for Negroes were especially serious in regard to tuberculosis. In 1934 there were in the 13 southern states only 1,666 beds set aside for Negroes whereas during that year 11,385 Negroes died from tuberculosis.

[40] Cited in Dorn, *loc. cit.*

In order to meet the need for hospital facilities, Negroes have established over a hundred hospitals, mainly in the South.[41] Less than a fifth of these hospitals are approved by the American College of Surgeons and only nine are approved by the Council on Medical Education and Hospitals of the American Medical Association for the training of interns.

In the North there is less discrimination against the Negro in respect to the availability of hospital facilities though Negroes are sometimes segregated in separate wards. The discrimination generally is greatest in the case of Negro patients who are able to pay and are not permitted to have private rooms. On the other hand, the vast majority of Negro patients who are unable to pay are increasingly accorded the same facilities as white patients. This is shown in the percentage of white and Negro babies born in hospitals. In the North in 1937 about the same proportion of Negro babies as white babies were born in hospitals; whereas in the southern states, with the exception of Kentucky and Tennessee, a larger percentage of white babies than Negro babies were born in hospitals.[42] According to the National Health Survey, in northern cities nearly the same proportion of Negroes with disabling illnesses as whites in the same condition received hospital care. But in southern cities a smaller proportion of Negroes than whites received hospital care, the difference being greater in the smaller cities. In northern cities Negroes with disabling illnesses were attended by a physician as frequently as whites, but a much larger percentage of Negroes with disabling illnesses than whites received care at public clinics. In southern cities of 100,000 population or over, about the same proportion of Negroes as in northern cities received care at public clinics, but in smaller southern cities a larger proportion of whites than Negroes received such care.

[41] In 1944 there were 124 Negro hospitals in 23 States and the District of Columbia, 12 of which were operated by the federal, state, and municipal governments. See Jessie P. Guzman (Ed.), *Negro Year Book* (1947), pp. 336-38.

[42] The same difference appeared in regard to the percentage of Negro and white births whether attended by a physician or a midwife. In the North 98 to 99 per cent of both Negro and white births were attended by a physician; whereas in the southern states (West Virginia excluded) from 25 to 75 per cent of the Negro births were attended by a midwife and with the exception of Oklahoma (1.9 per cent) 8 to 20 per cent of the white births were attended by midwives.

The inadequate health provisions for Negroes are partly the result of segregation and discrimination in the training of Negro doctors, dentists, and nurses.[43] There are about 4,000 physicians, 1,600 dentists, 9,000 nurses, and 1,400 pharmacists included in the Negro professional personnel in the United States.[44] About 85 per cent of the Negro physicians received their training at the Howard University Medical College in the District of Columbia and Meharry Medical College in Nashville, Tennessee. At the present time about 70 Negro doctors are graduated annually from each of these two Negro schools and about 12 from northern medical schools. The relatively few Negroes graduating from northern medical schools is the result of a general policy of excluding or discouraging the attendance of Negro students. In 1942 there were 3,810 Negro doctors in the United States or a ratio of 1 to 3,379 Negroes; while the ratio for the entire nation was one physician to 750 persons. The ratio of Negro physicians to the Negro population ranged from 1 to 1,002 in Missouri to 1 to 18,527 in Mississippi. Only in St. Louis, Mo. and Washington, D. C. did the ratio of Negro physicians to the Negro population equal the ratio for the total population of the country.

The health of the Negro is inevitably affected adversely by segregation and discrimination in medical care. When the education of Negro personnel is segregated and limited, there is an additional handicap placed upon the Negro's own efforts to maintain a healthy existence. The limitation of the education of Negro doctors to segregated Negro schools has resulted in inferior medical education. The Negro medical schools have been limited both in respect to the caliber of their teaching staff and in respect to their equipment. In the case of one medical school there have been serious limitations upon clinical training in the southern states. The inferior medical education given in the Negro medical schools is reflected in the state board records of

---

[43] Segregation and discrimination in the field of medicine are increasingly attracting the attention of the general public. See for example, Harry F. and Katharine Pringle, "The Color Line in Medicine," *The Saturday Evening Post*, January 24, 1948.

[44] See W. Montague Cobb, *Medical Care and the Plight of the Negro* (New York, 1947), for an excellent analysis of the problem of the medical education of Negroes and the present status of Negro professional personnel. The discussion which follows is based upon this study.

the graduates of these schools. Over a period of 44 years, 1903 to 1946, the graduates of Howard University Medical School and Meharry Medical College have had a record of 16.7 per cent and 28.9 per cent failures respectively as compared with 3.1 per cent failures for the graduates of Harvard University Medical School and Washington University Medical School in St. Louis and 6.2 per cent failures for the graduates of the Emory University's Medical College. The higher percentage of failures at the two Negro medical schools can be attributed partly to the inferior education which Negro students receive in the segregated Negro high schools and colleges in the South and partly to the inevitably inferior standards maintained in segregated professional schools.[45]

Even when the graduates of the Negro medical schools have been inclined to develop their skill, to keep abreast with the latest developments in medicine, and to maintain high standards in the practice of medicine, they have been handicapped by the pattern of segregation and discrimination. Negro graduates of medical schools find it difficult to secure internships except in Negro hospitals. According to Cobb there were only about 158 internships available for Negro doctors in 1947 and 129 of these were available in Negro hospitals. There were only 116 residencies and assistant residencies available for Negro physicians, nearly all of these being in Negro hospitals. The City of Cleveland is an outstanding exception in regard to the admission of Negroes as interns and to residencies. There the integration of the Negro physician has proceeded further than in any other city of the country. In New York City the city-owned Harlem Hospital has had a mixed staff since 1919. Since the so-called "interracial" Sydenham Hospital is in a predominantly Negro area in New York City it is of questionable significance from the standpoint of the integration of Negroes into voluntary hospitals. These hospitals represent exceptions to the general policy of either excluding the Negro physicians from even the hospitals to which they send their patients or the setting up of inferior hospitals for Negroes.

One of the most important barriers to the development of the Negro physician has been the policy of the American Medical Asso-

[45] See Chapter XVII above.

ciation. Negro physicians have been excluded from the Association by the stipulation that membership is contingent upon membership in a physician's local, county, or state association. Consequently, because of the attitude of white physicians in 17 southern states and the District of Columbia, Negro physicians are denied the benefits conferred by membership in the Association. To meet this situation Negro physicians have set up their own organization, the National Medical Association, which publishes its own professional journal. It should be pointed out, however, that during the past year the American College of Surgeons has raised its color bar, which has been in existence since the admission of two distinguished Negro surgeons, one at the time of its organization in 1913 and another in 1934. With the admission of 15 Negro physicians, the total was brought to 17 Negro members, two of whom are graduates of the Howard University Medical School, one a graduate of Meharry Medical College, and the remaining 14 from northern medical colleges. In 1946 the American Nurses Association removed the barrier to Negro membership by providing a direct membership for qualified nurses when they were not accepted in the local societies. Until the color bar in the various phases of medical education and the professional organizations is removed, Negro doctors, dentists, and nurses will continue to be handicapped by inferior training and a lack of opportunity for development.

IS RACE A FACTOR IN THE HEALTH AND SURVIVAL OF NEGROES?

Despite the reduction in mortality among Negroes and the improvements in health as the result of education and improvement in economic status, there is still some question concerning the immunity or susceptibility of the Negro to certain diseases. This is especially true in regard to tuberculosis and syphilis, which show a much higher incidence and mortality among Negroes than among whites. According to the report of the Selective Service: "Venereal diseases remain the most important cause for rejections among Negro registrants. All States having large Negro populations are concerned about this matter." [46] During the period, April 1942 to March 1943, 30.4 per cent of the Negroes were rejected for selective service because of syphilis while during the period April 1943 to December 1943, 11.0 per cent were rejected for this cause.[47] For the period April 1942 to March 1943, 170.8 of each 1,000 Negro registrants were rejected because of syphilis. The rate was over 200 per 1,000 in the District of Columbia, Florida, Indiana, Mississippi, Tennessee, and Texas.[48]

According to Lewis, the Negro has less resistance to the progress of tuberculosis, which, he thinks is due to the absence of a factor that increases resistance or the presence of a factor that decreases resistance.[49] Likewise, in regard to syphilis, he believes that the absence of immunity in the Negro is due to some probable differences in his tissue which makes a difference in the development of the disease.[50] In the absence of comparative studies of Negroes and whites living under comparable economic and social conditions, the statement of Dublin appears to be the only acceptable view concerning this question. He states:

But color, doubtless, does exert more or less influence over the prevalence of, and the death rate from many diseases. Just how much of this influence is due to racial immunity or susceptibility, and how much to racial customs, economic status and environment, is difficult if not impossible to determine. The factor of the "crossing" of the white and Negro bloods beclouds the issue—since the mulatto, the octoroon, et cetera, have both white and Negro blood, although they are classified as "colored." [51]

During the course of his adjustment to American society, the Negro has managed not only to survive but also to increase his numbers. The most rapid increase occurred during the period of slavery when un-

[46] *Selective Service in Wartime.* Second Report of Selective Service, 1941-42 (Washington, 1943), p. 390.
[47] *Physical Examinations of Selective Service Registrants During Wartime* (Washington, D. C., 1944), p. 18. The decrease in percentage of Negroes rejected because of syphilis was due partly to changes in medical standards that permitted registrants with the disease to be inducted.   [48] *Ibid.*, p. 134.
[49] Julian H. Lewis, *The Biology of the Negro* (Chicago, 1942), pp. 151-52.
[50] *Ibid.*, p. 183.
[51] Louis I. Dublin, "The Problem of Negro Health as Revealed by Vital Statistics," *The Journal of Negro Education*, Vol. 6, p. 273.

doubtedly a high death rate was offset by a high birth rate. At the
same time, it appears that residence on the plantation provided certain safeguards against the hazards of such diseases of civilization as
tuberculosis and syphilis. Because of the social disorganization and
competition following Emancipation and the movement to cities, the
Negro increased at a slower rate. Tuberculosis and syphilis made large
inroads among Negroes and there was a marked increase in the death
rate. Around the opening of the century, the decline in the death rate
indicated that the Negro was becoming better adjusted to life as a
freedman. The mass migrations to northern cities created anew the
problem of the survival of the Negro in modern urban civilization.
The continued increase in the Negro population is due to the increase among rural Negroes in the South. According to the calculations of the National Resources Committee, the net fertility (reproduction of females) of the urban Negro population was only .76
as compared with 1.61 for rural Negroes.[52] Those rates were slightly
lower than urban whites and slightly higher than rural whites. The
progress that the Negro has made in surviving in the urban environment has been dependent partly upon increasing knowledge concerning health and the welfare provisions of the northern cities. It
has also been dependent upon the extent to which the Negro has
found economic security and has been able to enjoy the benefits of
civilized living.

As the rate of increase of the Negro population declines, the integration of the Negro into American society will be accelerated. The
mental and social isolation of the Negro will thereby be broken down.
He will gain access to knowledge concerning health and will acquire
the habits of living which are conducive to health. As a result the
differences between the Negroes and whites in regard to the incidence
of diseases and death rates will be minimized.

[52] National Resources Committee, *Problems of a Changing Population* (Washington, D. C., 1938), p. 132.

CHAPTER XXIII

Unemployment and Poverty

UNDER the system of slavery the problem of the employment of Negro labor did not exist except in those areas where the plantation system was being undermined. Even in such areas the Negro slaves who were not needed were sold into the lower South or the slaves might find profitable employment by "hiring their time." Many slaves who hired their time were often able ultimately to buy their freedom. Since the Negroes who were free before the Civil War tended to become concentrated in cities, they faced the problem of finding employment. In southern cities the free Negroes often enjoyed a monopoly in the mechanical trades, whereas in the northern cities where free Negroes had to face the severe competition of immigrant labor, they were an impoverished and submerged group.

Following the Civil War, the entire Negro population was thrown into competition with the whites. On the southern plantation the Negro was able to compete with the landless whites. But in the cities of the South as well as of the North, the Negro was forced to work in domestic service and in the lowest paid unskilled occupations. Consequently, a large proportion of the urban Negro population became dependent or maintained itself on a poverty level. The mass migrations to northern cities during and following World War I gave the Negro worker his first foothold in industry. But the insecurity of his position was revealed during the depression in the thirties when from a half to three-fourths of the Negroes in the cities were dependent upon relief. The defense program and more especially World War II provided the Negro once more with employment. This was achieved partly by action on the part of federal government and partly because of full employment. Since the end of World War II the Negro has held most of his wartime gains. The employment of Negroes on the southern plantations, however, is being threatened by the mechanical cotton picker.

EMPLOYMENT OF NEGROES DURING SLAVERY

To a certain extent the plantation system which evolved in the South represented a racial division of labor.[1] Therefore, the Negro's rôle in the competitive struggle with different white groups was more or less obscured by his fixed status. Even the employment of slave mechanics on the plantations did not arouse opposition among the white mechanics. However, where the economic basis of slavery was being undermined, as in Maryland and Virginia, the profitable utilization of his labor became a problem. Slaveholders in these states found an outlet for their surplus Negroes in the slave markets of the lower South. When diversified farming on a nonplantation basis began to prosper in Virginia after 1830, slave labor became of less importance in the new system of agriculture but there was an increased demand for slave labor in manufacturing and internal improvements.[2] In the cities of Virginia slaves were employed in the tobacco factories and in the production of cotton, iron, and flour.

The utilization of slave labor in manufacture in the South before the Civil War brought to the surface the competition between Negroes and the poor whites. There was agitation against the hiring out of slaves as competitors of white mechanics and artisans. In Georgia the white laboring class succeeded in getting the legislature to pass a law in 1845 prohibiting contracts with slave and free Negro mechanics.[3] On the whole, however, the slaveholders were able to prevent any serious restriction upon the employment of slaves in industrial occupations. It was, therefore, the free Negro mechanics or Negroes who

[1] See Edward B. Reuter, "Competition and the Racial Division of Labor," in Edgar T. Thompson (Ed.), *Race Relations and the Race Problem* (Durham, N. C., 1939), pp. 46-60.

[2] Luther P. Jackson, *Free Negro Labor and Property Holding in Virginia, 1830-1860* (New York, 1942), pp. 48ff.

[3] Sterling D. Spero and Abram L. Harris, *The Black Worker* (New York, 1931), pp. 7-8.

hired their time in cities who felt the brunt of the competition of white labor.

In the cities and towns of the South the free Negro mechanics were able to hold their own. Tobacco manufacture provided the best opportunities for the employment of Negroes in the cities of Virginia. As we have seen, skilled Negro workers enjoyed a monopoly of mechanical trades in Charleston, South Carolina. Likewise in New Orleans, free Negroes were found in large numbers in all of the skilled trades and enjoyed considerable prosperity. Although there were free Negroes in the cities of the South who existed in the midst of poverty and squalor, free Negroes in the South, on the whole, had a much more secure economic position than the free Negroes in northern cities. Among the free Negroes in the North, where the competition of immigrant labor had to be met, there was much pauperism. For example, in Philadelphia in 1837 Negroes formed 14 per cent of the inmates in the county almshouse although they constituted only 7.4 per cent of the population.[4] In fact, the fear of the competition of Negro labor was the basis of opposition to Emancipation among some elements in the white working class in the North.

EMERGENCE OF UNEMPLOYMENT AND POVERTY AMONG NEGROES AFTER EMANCIPATION

After Emancipation, the Negro sharecropper and agricultural laborer as well as the Negro artisan were thrown into open competition with the common white man of the South. But the competition for land never became the cause for serious social conflict.[5] As sharecroppers and tenants, Negroes were restricted in their competitive opportunities and did not become landowners in sufficient numbers to threaten either the white landowners or landless whites. On the other hand, when the Negro mechanic was thrown into competition with the white worker, there was often open social conflict in both the North and the South. Gradually Negro mechanics were supplanted in the South where they had enjoyed a monopoly. According to estimates, at the

[4] W. E. B. DuBois, *The Philadelphia Negro* (Philadelphia, 1899), p. 270.
[5] Rupert B. Vance, "Racial Competition for the Land," in Thompson, *op. cit.*, pp. 102ff.

close of the Civil War, 100,000 of the 120,000 artisans in the South were Negroes.[6] By 1890, the skilled Negro worker had been eliminated as a competitor of the southern whites.

The gradual elimination of the skilled Negro worker was the result of a number of causes. DuBois attributed the plight of the Negro worker in the northern city to the heritage of slavery, the social disorganization following Emancipation, and the racial prejudice against Negroes.[7] It appears that the same causes operated in the South. The gradual elimination of the Negro mechanic in the South was owing partly to inefficiency and personal and social disorganization which prevented skills from being transmitted from one generation to the next. It was with the view to correct this situation that Booker T. Washington inaugurated a system of industrial education for Negroes. But, as we have seen, the system of industrial education established at Tuskegee Institute and other industrial schools was concerned with handicrafts that were becoming outmoded. Moreover, industrial education for the Negro could not meet the competition of white labor. When the Knights of Labor, which was chiefly concerned with the welfare of the masses of workers including Negroes, was superseded by the American Federation of Labor, Negro workers suffered more than unskilled white workers.[8] Since the rising unionism was based upon skills, the masses of white workers as well as the masses of Negro workers were excluded. But, the skilled Negro workers had to meet the organized competition of white workers in the all-white unions.

As a consequence of racial barriers against Negro workers as well as their inefficiency and lack of skill, pauperism and poverty were widespread among Negroes in cities up to World War I. In Philadelphia about 9 per cent of the inmates in the almshouse from 1891 to 1896 were Negroes, although they constituted only 4 per cent of the city's population; and about 9 per cent of Negroes in the main area of Negro concentration were in need of alms. Because of the social disorganization among Negroes and their precarious economic position in northern cities, an issue of *Charities* was devoted to their prob-

---

6 Spero and Harris, *op. cit.*, pp. 159-60.   7 DuBois, *op. cit.*, pp. 282-86.
8 Spero and Harris, *op. cit.*, p. 47.

lems in 1905.[9] In the articles dealing with various aspects of the Negro population in Boston, Chicago, Philadelphia, and Baltimore, there was presented a dark picture of the Negro's plight in modern urban society. Negro workers were confined to the lowest paid forms of unskilled labor and domestic service. Where they had made temporary inroads in the field of industry, it was often as strikebreakers because of the opposition of the all-white unions. The precarious position of the Negro workers in New York City was revealed in a study of their employment published in 1912.[10] There the vast majority of Negro workers were engaged in domestic and personal services at low wages. The precarious position of the Negro worker was attributed to prejudice on the part of both white workers and employers and the inefficiency of Negro workers.

When McCord made his study of dependency among Negroes in 1914, he attributed pauperism among them to the fact that the Negro was a "child race" lacking training and development, whereas whites who became paupers were of "pauper stock." [11] Moreover, he maintained that following Emancipation the Negro had equal if not better economic opportunities than whites because he had the command of the labor situation and did not have to face the competition of labor unions and race prejudice. In addition, he argued, the Negro had political power supported by the United States Army. Despite all this, he concluded, the Negro lost out in competition with whites because of "hereditary racial differences" and as a consequence idle Negroes crowded the streets while agriculture and industry called for skilled and unskilled workers.[12] Within a year or so after these uncritical explanations were advanced concerning the unemployment and poverty of Negroes in cities, Negroes began to migrate to northern cities in response to the demands of northern industry for strong but unskilled workers.

[9] The Charity Organization Society, *The Negro in the Cities of the North* (New York, 1905).

[10] George E. Haynes, *The Negro at Work in New York City* (New York, 1912).

[11] Charles H. McCord, *The American Negro as a Dependent, Defective, and Delinquent* (Nashville, 1914), p. 150.

[12] *Ibid.*, pp. 74ff.

EFFECTS OF MASS MIGRATION TO NORTHERN CITIES
ON EMPLOYMENT OF NEGROES

The migration of Negroes to northern cities during World War I was partly the result of changes in southern agriculture and partly but more especially the result of the attraction of northern industry. The Negroes who eked out a living in southern agriculture and in the cities of the South constituted an industrial labor reserve.[13] Consequently they were drawn into northern industry to fill the vacuum in the labor market when immigrants returned to Europe to bear arms. The great mass of Negro workers from the South entered industry as unskilled workers. In 1910 Negroes constituted 6.4 per cent of the unskilled workers in the steel industry; but by 1920 their percentage had increased to 17. Another example of the new rôle which they began to play in industry is provided in the case of the packing industry in Chicago. In 1910 only 33 of the 4,414 semiskilled workers and 34 of 8,426 laborers in the packing industry were Negroes; while in 1920 there were 1,558 Negroes among the 6,931 semiskilled workers and 1,397 Negroes among the 7,032 laborers.[14]

The migration of Negroes to industrial areas not only enabled Negro men to gain a foothold in industry but it afforded Negro women their first opportunity for industrial employment. Before World War I Negro women had no place in industry except as laborers and semiskilled workers in the tobacco industry.[15] As white women workers moved up the industrial ladder, Negro women began to take their places in the jobs traditionally held by white women such as textiles, clothing, food, tobacco, and head- and footwear. From 1910 to 1920, the number of Negro women in manufacturing and mechanical industries increased from 67,937 to 104,983.[16]

The entrance of Negroes into modern industry during World War I reduced unemployment among them and increased their earning capacity. In the South where there was industrial expansion during

[13] See Spero and Harris, *op. cit.*, pp. 144ff. and Wesley, *Negro Labor in the United States*, pp. 282ff.   [14] Spero and Harris, *op. cit.*, p. 153.

[15] United States Department of Labor, *Women's Bureau Bulletin*, No. 20, (Washington, 1922), pp. 5-6.   [16] Spero and Harris, *op. cit.*, p. 152.

the postwar period Negroes found employment as unskilled workers in turpentine, iron, and steel, and the fertilizer industry. At the same time Negroes found increasing opportunities for employment in domestic service and in such service occupations as janitors, porters, etc. But the Negro had to face in the North as well as in the South racial barriers to his employment in industry.[17] During the depression in 1921, Negro workers were laid off in larger numbers proportionately than white workers. For example, in Detroit where Negro males comprised 5 per cent of the male workers, they represented 16 per cent among the 20,000 unemployed.[18] But on the whole, during the prosperous years of the 1920's Negro workers did not suffer much from unemployment though they were concentrated in domestic service and unskilled occupations.

EFFECTS OF THE DEPRESSION ON EMPLOYMENT OF NEGROES

The depression that began in 1929 revealed the insecurity of the Negro's position in industry. The Unemployment Census of January 1931 revealed that unemployment among Negro workers in the cities was in some instances twice as high as among white workers.[19] In Detroit 60 per cent of the Negro workers as compared with 32 per cent of the white workers were without work. Likewise, in Houston, Texas, 35 per cent of the Negro workers as against 18 per cent of the white workers were unemployed. When the 1937 Unemployment Census was made, Negro men and women in the North were still unemployed to a much larger extent than white workers. In the North the unemployment rates for colored and white workers were 38.9 and 18.1 respectively, while in the South the rates for Negro and white male workers were 18 and 16 per cent. For colored and white women

[17] See Herman Feldman, *Racial Factors in American Industry* (New York, 1931), Chapter II.   [18] *Ibid.*, p. 42.

[19] See Richard Sterner, *The Negro's Share* (New York, 1943), pp. 39-45. See also National Urban League, *Unemployment Status of Negroes*, a compilation of Facts and Figures Respecting Unemployment Among Negroes in 106 Cities (New York, 1931); and National Urban League, *The Forgotten Tenth*, An Analysis of Unemployment Among Negroes in the United States and Its Social Costs; 1932-1933 (New York, 1933).

workers the rates of unemployment were 42.9 and 23.2 respectively in the North and 26.0 and 26.2 respectively in the South. The better showing of the Negro in the South was due, of course, to the fact that the majority of Negro workers were in agricultural occupations. As a result of the depression nearly half of the Negroes in skilled occupations were displaced. In 1940, 17.6 per cent of the colored male workers as compared with 14.2 per cent of the white male workers were unemployed.[20]

The impact of unemployment on the Negro community in northern cities is well illustrated in the statistics for New York City. The number of applicants, nearly all Negroes, at the Harlem office of the State Employment Service increased from 6,609 in 1928 to 28,279 during the year 1930.[21] By September, 1935, there were 24,292 Negro families, exclusive of unattached men and women, on the relief rolls. On the basis of the 1934 census of the New York Housing Authority, these 24,292 Negro families constituted 43.2 per cent of all the Negro families in the Harlem area. But Negro dependency as indicated by these figures was not evenly distributed over the Harlem community. The rate of dependency declined from 709 per 1,000 families in the center of the community, where there was much social disorganization, to 284 per 1,000 families in the outermost zone, occupied by the more stable and economically better off families.[22]

EFFECTS OF NEW DEAL ON ECONOMIC STATUS
OF THE NEGRO

When the program of government financed construction became important in 1932 and 1933, the Negro worker was handicapped because he was trained for small scale construction companies and by the policy of the labor unions.[23] Even when the vast program of public

[20] Robert Weaver, *Negro Labor* (New York, 1946), p. 9.

[21] The Mayor's Commission on Conditions in Harlem, *The Negro in Harlem* (New York, 1936), p. 37. Unpublished Report.

[22] E. Franklin Frazier, "Negro Harlem: An Ecological Study," *loc. cit.*, p. 86. In the Black Belt in Chicago, the number of Negro charity cases declined from eight per 100 residents in the First Zone occupied by the poorer migrants to one per 100 residents in the Seventh Zone where higher economic classes were concentrated. See *The Negro Family in Chicago*, pp. 152ff.   [23] Weaver, *op. cit.*, pp. 38ff.

works was inaugurated under the Public Works Administration, discrimination against the Negro worker was continued. In 1932 the Secretary of the Treasury and in 1933 Secretary Ickes, the Administrator, issued an order to state engineers forbidding discrimination on account of color and religious affiliation. When both orders proved ineffective, it was provided that Negro workers should receive a minimum percentage of the skilled payroll. This quota system proved more effective but did not solve the problem of discrimination on the part of the unions. In fact, the New Deal's policy of protecting the worker's right to organize and the Negro's right to work were often in conflict. Therefore, the Public Works Administration set about securing the cooperation of the unions in issuing work permits to Negroes admitting them to the unions. But the Negro worker still faced the problem of securing training in the new techniques of the building trades.

Despite these initial handicaps in the field of building construction, the New Deal agencies had a profound effect upon the economic status of the Negro.[24] There was first the effect of the relief agencies.[25] In the rural areas of the South the proportion of Negro families receiving relief under the Federal Emergency Relief Administration was not determined solely by need but also by local attitudes and traditions concerning the relation of landlords and tenants. This is shown by the larger proportion of white than Negro families on relief and the variations in the proportion of Negro families receiving relief in the various states and within the same state. In the southern states there were proportionately fewer Negro families than white families on relief in 1935. In these ten states, with the exception of Kentucky, where 10.9 per cent of the Negro families as compared with 17.2 per cent of the white families were on relief, the Negro relief rate was less than 10 per cent. In 21 of 90 counties studied in Georgia, the proportion of Negro families on relief was less than a fourth the proportion of white families receiving relief, whereas in a few counties the Negro relief rate was higher than that for whites. Likewise in Texas, at one

---

[24] *Ibid.*, pp. 14-15.

[25] See Sterner, *op. cit.*, Chapter XII for an analysis of studies of the Negro on relief.

extreme there were three counties where the proportion of Negro families on relief was less than the proportion for white families, while at the other extreme there were 5 counties in which four times proportionately as many Negro families as white families were receiving relief. However, despite the influence of local attitudes and traditions, in Texas 15.1 per cent of the Negro families as compared with 13.0 per cent of the white families were on relief and in Oklahoma 42.5 per cent of the Negro families as compared with 25.2 per cent of the white families received relief.

In the urban areas of the South the Negro families fared better than in the rural areas. From 22 to 46 per cent of the Negro families in the urban areas of 16 southern states and the District of Columbia were on relief as compared with 4 per cent to 18 per cent of the white families. Over a half of the Negro families in border cities and about a third in southern cities were on relief. In some of the border and southern cities the Negro relief rate was from four to seven times the white rate. The differences between the relief rates among Negroes and whites in border and southern cities are clearly revealed when one considers the proportion of Negro families among the total families on relief in certain cities. In the District of Columbia, Norfolk, Virginia, and Charlotte, North Carolina, Negro families comprised from 70 to 80 per cent of the relief families. As a rule Negro families had greater difficulty in securing relief in both rural and urban communities. Moreover, the Negro families received smaller benefits than white families. In 13 southern cities in 1935 Negro general relief grants averaged $24.18 as compared with $29.05 for whites.[26]

The large proportion of Negro families on relief in southern cities revealed the economic insecurity of Negroes in the modern urban economy. This was revealed even more strikingly in the northern cities where 52.2 per cent of all Negro families were dependent upon relief. Although there were instances of discrimination in regard to hiring of personnel, there was no discrimination against Negroes in regard to relief benefits in northern cities.[27] Because of their large

[26] See Sterner, *op. cit.*, p. 236.
[27] See The Mayor's Commission on Conditions in Harlem, *The Negro in Harlem.*

numbers on relief, Negroes gained widespread benefits in regard to maternal and child care and guidance in respect to diets.

After the Federal Emergency Relief Administration was discontinued, employable Negroes were placed on public works projects under the Works Progress Administration, later called the Work Projects Administration. In September 1937, Negro workers constituted 23.3 per cent of the total employed on WPA projects in 11 southern states.[28] During the next four years the proportion of Negro workers among those employed on WPA projects increased to 26.1 per cent in the South and 16 per cent in the country as a whole. In some southern States during this same period the proportion of Negroes on WPA projects declined but in others it increased. The important fact to be noted is that when there was an upswing in employment in 1940, Negro workers continued to depend upon WPA projects. In eight northern states where there were large concentrations of Negroes, the proportion of Negroes among workers on WPA projects was larger, two to four times larger in some cases, than the proportion of Negroes among the unemployed in 1940.

Although Negroes received lower work-relief earnings than whites, in the South, especially in the rural South, their relief-earnings were higher than their earnings in private employment, if the WPA relief was to be maintained on an adequate basis. On the other hand, the Negro unemployed had little opportunity for employment on "Professional and Service Projects." In 1940 there were only 11 Negro supervisors in the 14 southern states as compared with 10,333 white supervisors. Despite the discrimination, "vast numbers of Negroes were enabled to retain work habits and a minimum of health as the result of federal aid." [29]

When the Civilian Conservation Corps was first set up Negro youth had a small share in its program. This was partly owing to the fact that Negro youth was concentrated largely in rural areas. But it was also the result of the policies and practices of the local agencies in the South. For example, in 1939 or six years after the inauguration

[28] See Sterner, *op. cit.*, pp. 239ff., for an analysis of unpublished data on the WPA projects.   [29] Weaver, *op. cit.*, p. 14.

of the CCC program, in the Fourth Corps area comprising eight southern states, Negro CCC enrollees constituted only one-fifth of the total though they comprised one-third of the males 15 to 24 years of age in the area. In other areas Negro enrollees constituted a larger proportion than their relative numbers in the population. Although by 1936 the proportion of Negro enrollees was equal to their relative numbers in the country as a whole, they were not represented to the extent of their needs.

Negro youth shared much more largely in the National Youth Administration program than they did in the CCC program.[30] From the standpoint of their relative numbers in the general population, Negro youth had a higher representation than whites on the out-of-school work program and student works program in 1941. Then, too, Negroes were represented to a greater extent in the administration of the NYA than in that of the CCC. There were 27 states with State Supervisors of Negro affairs and over 500 Negro supervisors of projects. About 300,000 Negro boys and girls had part-time work during the first five years of the operation of the NYA program. Where Negro youth were unable to take advantage of college and graduate student aid, this was the result of the inadequate educational facilities in the South. Moreover, it should be pointed out that though the representation of Negro youth in the NYA equaled or exceeded their relative numbers in the population, because of their poverty they were not cared for in proportion to their needs. At the same time a large number of Negro youth were able to remain in school and to acquire training and work experience because of the NYA program.

Although Negro farmers did not participate to the extent of their needs in the programs of the Farm Security Administration, their economic position was improved by this form of federal assistance. From the standpoint of number of standard loans made to farmers, Negro farmers received loans commensurate with their relative numbers in the population in all the states in the four southern regions with the exception of Tennessee, Georgia, Arkansas, Mississippi, and Oklahoma.[31] But the number of loans was not a true measure of the

[30] See Sterner, *op. cit.*, pp. 261ff.   [31] See *ibid.*, pp. 298ff.

participation of Negro farmers. When the participation of Negro farmers is considered from the standpoint of the number of low income farmers, it is found that whereas 37 per cent of such farmers were Negro, only 23 per cent of the borrowers were Negroes. The importance of the loans is indicated by the fact that the net income of Negro borrowers increased 62 per cent as compared with a 48 per cent increase for white borrowers. Nearly 2,000 Negro farmers also took advantage of the tenant-purchase program which was aimed to enable tenants and sharecroppers to become landowners. Moreover, nearly 1,400 Negro families were settled in 32 homestead projects in 13 southern states in 1940. Negro farmers were aided also by the rental cooperatives which were established in 1939.

During the period of the New Deal the economic status of the Negro was improved in other ways. The policy of the National Recovery Administration in regard to minimum wages tended to weaken the differential based upon race. Even more important was the growth of the industrial unions with their more liberal policy toward Negro workers. The consequences of the new relationship of Negro workers to unionism will be considered in connection with the changes in the economic status of the Negro during and following World War II.

SIGNIFICANCE OF SOCIAL SECURITY

The above facts concerning the low economic status of Negro families tend to emphasize the special significance of the Social Security Act of 1935 for the masses of Negroes. The extent of aid to dependent children provided by the Act may be taken as an indication of the significance of broader social service for Negroes. For 16 states combined in 1942, there were 52 out of every 1,000 Negro children as compared with 25 out of every 1,000 white children receiving aid.[32] The rate of aid to Negro children varied considerably for the different states. In the 10 states with more than 5,000 Negro children in the population, the rate ranged from 14 per 1,000 Negro children in

[32] Federal Security Agency, *Families Receiving Aid to Dependent Children*, Part 1, Race, Size and Composition of Families and Reasons for Dependency. Washington, D. C., 1945.

North Carolina to 173 in Illinois.[33] The rate of aid to Negro children
in six of the states was three to 10 times as high as the rate for white
children. In West Virginia, Louisiana, and Arkansas the rate for
Negro children was only slightly higher than the aid to white children
and in North Carolina less than that to white children. In view of the
low economic status of Negroes and the large amount of family disorganization among them, it is reasonable to assume that relatively
few needy Negro children were given aid. This is supported by the
fact that in these four states a larger portion of Negro children than
white children were not approved for assistance.

ECONOMIC STATUS OF NEGRO JUST PRIOR
TO WORLD WAR II

Despite the beneficial effects of the New Deal upon the economic
status of the Negro, the Negro was a submerged element in the industrial life of the country when America began its defense program.
Between April and October, 1940, the rate of unemployment among
whites declined from 17.7 per cent to 13 per cent, while unemployment
among Negroes remained about 22 per cent.[34] That the barriers to
the employment of Negroes were still intact, is shown by the fact that
in the various areas where there was a man-power shortage thousands of
Negroes were unemployed. Not only were there no facilities for training Negro workers for the war industries but trained Negroes were
not given employment because of race prejudice. The situation in
the South was even worse than in the North.

The low economic position of the Negro just prior to World War
II was indicated by the fact that 48.5 per cent of the Negroes with
incomes from wages or salaries as compared with 16.7 per cent of the
whites having incomes from these sources received less than $500 a
year. (See Table XXXV.) However, there were variations in the incomes of Negroes as in the incomes of whites coinciding with educational attainments. "For example, native white males 25 to 29 years
old who did not finish a single year of school had a median wage or

---

[33] These 10 States include: Illinois, Oklahoma, Kansas, Missouri, Massachusetts,
District of Columbia, West Virginia, Louisiana, Arkansas, and North Carolina.
[34] See Weaver, *op. cit.*, pp. 18-19.

salary income of only $407, those completing college had a median of $1,567. The corresponding medians for Negro males in the same age groups were $316, and $882." Whereas over two-thirds of the Negro males with no education had incomes less than $500, only one-eighth of those with four or more years of college education had such incomes. On the other hand, over a fourth (26.2 per cent) of the Negro males with a college education had incomes of $1,500 and over, while less than 1 per cent of the Negroes with no education had such incomes. Yet only 3.9 per cent of the Negro males with a college education had incomes of $2,500 and over as compared with 34 per

TABLE XXXV

Percent Distribution by Cumulative Income Classes in Selected Education Groups of Native White and Negro Males 25 to 64 Years Old Without Other Income in 1939, for the United States: 1940 *

WAGE OR SALARY INCOME IN 1939	Native White					Negro				
		Years of School Completed					Years of School Completed			
	TOTAL	NONE	GRADE SCHOOL, 7 AND 8 YEARS	HIGH SCHOOL, 4 YEARS	COLLEGE, 4 YEARS OR MORE	TOTAL	NONE	GRADE SCHOOL, 7 AND 8 YEARS	HIGH SCHOOL, 4 YEARS	COLLEGE, 4 YEARS OR MORE
Total	100.0	100.0	100.0	100.0	100.0	100.0	100.0	100.0	100.0	100.0
Less than $500	16.7	52.9	18.6	8.1	3.7	48.5	68.6	36.7	25.4	12.7
Less than $1,000	36.7	79.9	44.8	26.3	12.3	85.2	93.9	79.3	70.1	47.5
Less than $1,500	63.4	91.3	69.8	52.4	27.9	96.6	99.1	95.7	90.4	73.8
$1,500 and over	36.6	8.7	30.2	47.6	72.1	3.4	0.9	4.3	9.6	26.2
$2,000 and over	18.6	3.3	13.3	25.3	51.6	1.1	0.2	1.0	4.5	13.1
$2,500 and over	9.0	1.5	5.4	12.3	34.0	0.2	0.1	0.2	0.6	3.9

* Bureau of the Census, *Population, Special Reports,* Series P-46, No. 5. June 18, 1946. Statistics based on a 5-per cent sample.

cent of the white males of the same educational status. The same disparity appeared on lower educational levels. For example, nearly a half (47.6 per cent) of the white males with a four-year high school education had incomes of $1,500 and over whereas less than a tenth (9.6 per cent) of the Negro males of the same educational level were in this income class.

A more detailed analysis of the incomes of nonfarm Negro families in the South in 1940 has been shown in a recent study.[35] It was found

[35] E. Franklin Frazier and Eleanor H. Bernert, "Children and Income in Negro Families," *Social Forces,* Vol. 25, No. 2 (December, 1946), pp. 178-82.

that in 51 per cent of the Negro families, there were no children and that the median family unit income in these families amounted to $221 per year. As the size of the families increased, the family unit income decreased. In the families with three or more children, in which were found 65 per cent of all Negro children, the family unit income amounted to only $126. The family unit income of different types of families is presented in Table XXXVII. It will be observed that

TABLE XXXVI

Families, Children in Families, and Median Family Unit Income, by Number of Children in Family for the South

(Nonfarm families, 1940, with only wage or salary income in 1939)

		Nonwhite		All Classes * (White and nonwhite)		
NUMBER OF CHILDREN	PERCENT OF FAMILIES	PERCENT OF CHILDREN	MEDIAN FAMILY UNIT INCOME	PERCENT OF FAMILIES	PERCENT OF CHILDREN	MEDIAN FAMILY UNIT INCOME
Total	100	100	184	100	100	330
No child	51	0	221	37	0	435
1 child	19	16	189	26	18	362
2 children	12	19	152	17	24	303
3 or more children (4.252) †	18	65	126	20	58	189

* Thomas J. Woofter, Jr., "Children and Family Income." *Social Security Bulletin* (January, 1945), p. 2.

† 4.322 for male heads of family and 4.076 for female heads—weighted together.

the median income of Negro families was higher where both the husband and wife were present in the family. However, even where both husband and wife were present the family income decreased considerably where there was more than one child in the family. The same was true of the families where there was a male head and some person other than the wife was present.

The facts presented concerning families with only a female head were of considerable importance because in the cities of the South from a fourth to a third of the Negro families are in this category. The median income of these families was extremely low, ranging from $326 to $357 per year and increasing with the number of children in the family. However, the family unit income in these families decreased from $184 where there were no children to $87 in families with three or more children. These figures indicate that from a fourth to a third of the Negro families in the towns and cities of the South were dependent upon the meager earnings of Negro women in domestic service. The situation was not the same in all of the 17 Southern states. In 10 of the states the median income per family unit ranged

TABLE XXXVII

Nonwhite Family Unit Income of Nonfarm Negro Families, by Type of Family, for Southern Region

(Nonfarm families, 1940, with only wage or salary income in 1939)

TYPE OF FAMILY	FAMILY UNITS	MEDIAN INCOME	FAMILY UNIT INCOME
Average family	2.74	$505	$184
Male head with wife:			
No children	2.39	623	261
One child	3.05	629	206
Two children	3.65	612	168
Three or more	4.60	620	135
Male head other:			
No children	1.41	417	295
One child	2.77	590	213
Two children	3.42	605	177
Three children	4.32	592	137
Female head:			
No children	1.77	326	184
One child	2.46	350	142
Two children	3.20	355	111
Three children	4.10	357	87

from $149 in South Carolina to $197 in North Carolina. (See Map XXII.) In Delaware, Virginia, Tennessee, and Kentucky the median income per family unit was between $200 and $249; and in Maryland $293. Negro families were somewhat better off in West Virginia where the median income per family unit amounted to $338; and in the District of Columbia where it was $409.

The extent to which the incomes in Negro families fell below the Bureau of Labor Statistics "cost of maintenance" budget for a four-person manual worker's family has been shown in a study of 14

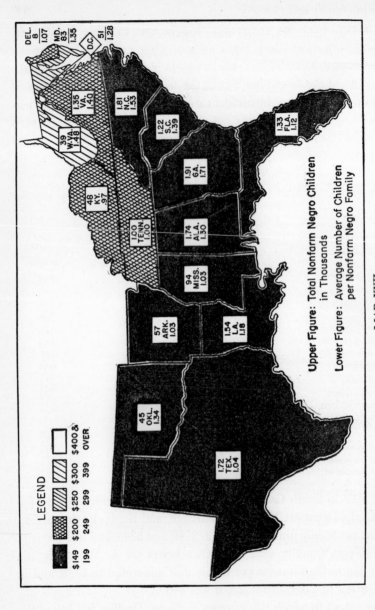

LEGEND

$149	■
199	
$200	(crosshatch)
249	
$250	(diagonal hatch)
299	
$300	(light diagonal hatch)
399	
$400 & OVER	□

DEL.
8
1.07

MD.
83
1.35

51
1.28
D.C.

W.VA.
39
1.48

VA.
1.35
1.40

KY.
48
.97

N.C.
1.81
1.53

TENN.
1.00
1.00

S.C.
1.22
1.39

MISS.
94
1.03

ALA.
1.74
1.30

GA.
1.91
1.71

FLA.
1.33
1.12

ARK.
57
1.03

LA.
1.54
1.18

OKL.
45
1.34

TEX.
1.72
1.04

Upper Figure: Total Nonfarm Negro Children in Thousands

Lower Figure: Average Number of Children per Nonfarm Negro Family

MAP XXII

Nonfarm Negro Children, 1940, and Unit Income of Nonfarm Negro Families, 1939, by State.

cities.[36] (See Table XXXVIII and Diagram XVII.) It was found that the median income per family unit was below the "cost of maintenance" budget in all of the cities with the exception of Los Angeles where Orientals form about a third of the nonwhites. The next fact of significance was that the difference between the median income per

TABLE XXXVIII

Comparison of Median Family Unit Income, 1939, for Nonwhite and All Families and Cost of Maintenance Budget, 1940, in 14 Cities

CITY	Median Family Unit Incomes *		COST OF MAINTENANCE BUDGET	Percentage of Difference Between Maintenance Budget and Family Unit Income	
	NONWHITE FAMILIES	ALL FAMILIES †		NONWHITE FAMILIES	ALL FAMILIES †
North:	Dollars	Dollars	Dollars	Per cent	Per cent
Chicago	377	612	447	—16	+37
Cleveland	334	527	429	—22	+23
Detroit	345	611	442	—22	+38
New York	401	611	467	—14	+31
Philadelphia	381	519	407	— 6	+28
Border:					
Baltimore	324	505	408	—22	+24
St. Louis, Mo.	285	514	426	—33	+21
Washington, D.C.	395	704	461	—14	+53
South:					
Atlanta	239	380	412	—42	— 8
Birmingham	231	349	392	—41	—11
Houston	276	488	401	—31	+22
Memphis	238	309	399	—40	—23
New Orleans	224	355	393	—43	—10
West:					
Los Angeles	412	620	407	+ 1	+52

* The "median family unit income" is the ratio of the median family income to the average number of family units per family in each city.

† Figures from Thomas J. Woofter, Jr., "Children and Family Security" *Social Security Bulletin* (March, 1945), p. 6.

family unit and the "cost of maintenance" budget was less in northern cities than in southern cities. In the northern cities, half of the Negro families have a family unit income from 6 to 22 per cent below the maintenance budget, whereas in southern cities the deficient income for half the Negro families ranged from 31 to 43 per cent. The three border cities occupied an intermediate position in that the deficiency

[36] E. Franklin Frazier and Eleanor H. Bernert, "Adequacy of Income in Negro Families in Selected Cities." Unpublished study.

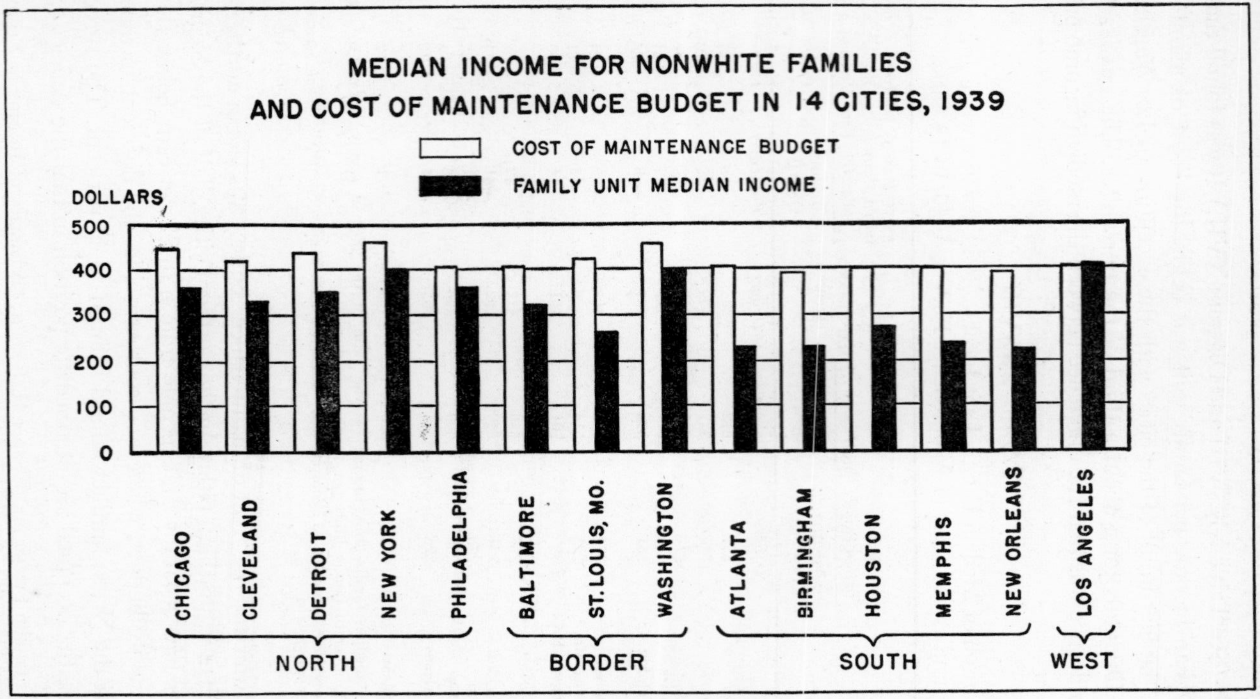
MEDIAN INCOME FOR NONWHITE FAMILIES
AND COST OF MAINTENANCE BUDGET IN 14 CITIES, 1939
COST OF MAINTENANCE BUDGET
FAMILY UNIT MEDIAN INCOME
DOLLARS
500
400
300
200
100
0
CHICAGO
CLEVELAND
DETROIT
NEW YORK
PHILADELPHIA
BALTIMORE
ST. LOUIS, MO.
WASHINGTON
ATLANTA
BIRMINGHAM
HOUSTON
MEMPHIS
NEW ORLEANS
LOS ANGELES
NORTH
BORDER
SOUTH
WEST

DIAGRAM XVII *

* Based on Table XXXVIII.

in the incomes of half the Negro families was the same as in two northern cities and one southern city. From these facts it appears that Negro families were better off economically in northern cities than in southern cities since the median incomes were higher and the extent to which their incomes fell short of "cost of maintenance" budget was less.

CHANGES IN ECONOMIC STATUS OF NEGRO DURING WORLD WAR II

With the inauguration of the defense program in 1940, various government agencies made pronouncements regarding discrimination against Negro workers.[37] For example, the United States Office of Education made a statement to the effect that there should be no discrimination in the expenditure of funds for vocational training. Later the Office of Production Management asked contractors to "examine their employment and training policies" with reference to the utilization of Negro labor. Such pronouncements were the result of the increasing pressure on the part of Negroes and white liberals. Even President Roosevelt added his voice in a memorandum to the OPM, stating that the government could not countenance discrimination against American citizens. These various pronouncements did not increase significantly the employment of Negroes in defense industries. And by 1941 Negroes had become convinced that the government was not translating its announced policy in regard to nondiscrimination into action. Under the leadership of A. Phillip Randolph, president of the Brotherhood of Sleeping Car Porters, a March-on-Washington was organized in order to dramatize the exclusion of Negro workers from war industries. (See Chapter XX.) This resulted in Executive Order 8802 by President Roosevelt on June 25, 1941, reaffirming a policy of nondiscrimination in respect to race, creed, or national origin on war contracts. A Fair Employment Practices Committee was set up to implement the Executive Order.

One of the first evidences of the effect of the Committee was the increase in the employment of Negroes in clerical and professional occupations in the government. In its dealings with the employment

[37] See Weaver, *op. cit.*, pp. 131ff.

of Negroes in private industry, the Committee was successful in some cases but was unable to overcome the combined opposition of management, labor, and local communities in other instances.[38] For example, in 1945 in East Alton, Illinois, where there had been an established rule against the presence of Negro workers, the Committee was unable in the face of the opposition of management, labor, and local leaders, to secure the employment of Negroes in the Western Cartridge Company. On the other hand, the Committee was finally able to secure the acquiescence of the union in regard to the employment of Negroes in the General Cable Company in St. Louis, Missouri. But it required the dramatic appeal of the president of the company, Dwight R. G. Palmer, to secure acquiescence on the part of the white women employees. The Committee succeeded, with the backing of the government, in securing the employment of Negroes as operators on the Philadelphia street cars but failed to achieve a similar victory in the District of Columbia because of its indecision about giving a directive to the Capital Transit Company. The failure of the Committee was due in the final analysis to the fact that southern Democratic leaders were supported by Republicans who were opposed to the agencies created by President Roosevelt.

It was not until 1942 that the color bar against Negro workers began to "bend." [39] Negro employment began to increase in the construction of army cantonments where carpenters were required. This was a field of employment in which Negroes had the requisite skill. Even in this instance pressure on the part of the federal government was necessary to ensure the employment of Negro workers. As the color bar began to bend, it then became apparent that in yielding to southern prejudice, the United States Office of Education through its restricted vocational program for Negro youth in the South had handicapped the Negro worker in his competition with white workers in industry. Even when the Office of Education undertook to train war workers little was done to correct this policy. Only in the North where whites and Negroes were admitted to the same training courses did

---

[38] See Malcolm Ross, *All Manner of Men* (New York, 1948).

[39] See Weaver, *op. cit.*, for comprehensive analysis of the employment of the Negro in war time.

Negroes receive the full benefits of the training. Moreover, the Negro in the North was more favorably situated to take advantage of the war training courses because of the training which he had received through the National Youth Administration.[40]

Some information on the changes in the occupations and incomes of Negro families during the War is provided in a detailed study of the earnings of residents of two Negro housing projects in Atlanta, Georgia.[41] It was found that the average family income of the 1,281 families in the two housing projects increased 65 per cent from 1940 to 1944, despite the fact that there was a decrease of 15 per cent in the average number of income receivers per family. Moreover, in at least 15 per cent of the families studied, there had been a reduction in incomes because of the drafting of male members, generally the chief wage earners, into the armed forces. It was noted that as the income of the principal wage earner increased, there was a tendency for the wives to discontinue work. From 1940 to 1944 the average incomes in one housing project increased from $721 to $1,297 and in the other project from $929 to $1,398. The increases in family incomes were not only due to increases in incomes in the same occupation but also were due to changes to better occupations. In a number of typical cases it was revealed that Negroes whose annual earnings as a janitor had been $360 or as a porter $520 had become machine operators at annual wages of $1,503 or a United States mail clerk at $2,673. A typical case is presented of a maid whose annual earnings had increased from $312 to $2,477 when she became a drill operator. Although this study of Negro residents of a housing project is not typical of the entire Negro labor force, it is indicative of the increased earning power of Negro workers during the War.

The gains which the Negro made in employment during the War were not due simply to the existence of the Federal Fair Employment

[40] See Nettie P. McGill and Ellen N. Matthews, *The Youth of New York City.* New York, 1940. In December, 1939, Negroes comprised 19 per cent of the workers under the NYA. At this time one-half as many Negroes as whites were being transferred from NYA projects to industry.

[41] "Annual Family Earnings and Occupational Earnings of Residents of Two Negro Housing Projects in Atlanta, 1937-44," *Monthly Labor Review,* December, 1945, pp. 1061-73.

Practice Committee. The Committee succeeded in removing the color bar against the upgrading and the introduction of Negro workers into many industries. These two ends were accomplished through the pressure which the Federal Government could exercise and through the provision of training opportunities for Negro workers. In addition, the Committee put pressure upon the United States Employment Service to accept Negro workers for classification and referral as other workers. All of these measures were limited in their effectiveness by local opposition to giving Negro workers equal status with white workers. Especially in the South was the effectiveness of the Committee limited; while in New York State the Committee working through the USES achieved greater success. The effectiveness of the work of the Committee was determined by another factor which influenced the employment gains of the Negro; namely, the existence of full employment. It was in the areas of man power shortage that Negro labor was utilized on a large scale. But even the War emergency was not sufficient to break down the color barriers to the complete integration of the Negro into American industry. In the final report of its work over a period, the Fair Employment Practices Committee made the following statement:

Two fundamentally hopeful facts developed out of the Government's efforts to open wartime opportunities to all workers:

1. Employers and workers abandoned discrimination in most cases where Government intervened.
2. Once the barriers were down, the workers of varying races and religions worked together efficiently and learned to accept each other without rancor.

FEPC during its 5 years satisfactorily settled nearly 5,000 cases by peaceful negotiation, including 40 strikes caused by racial differences. During the last year of the war, FEPC held 15 public hearings and docketed a total of 3,485 cases, settling 1,191 of them. These settlements were not publicized and generally escaped attention. The contrary impression, that FEPC normally met with unyielding opposition, was created by the comparatively few difficult cases which received emphasis through public hearings and public expressions of defiance by some recalcitrant employers and unions.

In fact, the bulk of FEPC's useful work was accomplished by the quiet persuasion of its regional representatives assigned to 15 regional and subregional offices located in major industrial centers.

That is not to say that persuasion alone can end discrimination. The employer's need for war workers, or his patriotism, or dislike of exposure, each in its respective situation was a powerful incentive to stop discrimination. The practice, however, seldom disappeared spontaneously. The intervention of a third party, with authority to act if necessary, was required to start the process in motion.[42]

From the standpoint of the history of Negro workers' relation to American industry, Weaver is justified in his conclusion that during the War the Negro "secured more jobs at better wages and in a more diversified occupational and industrial pattern than ever before." [43]

One of the main factors responsible for the change in the economic status of the Negro during World War II was the new relation of the Negro to the labor unions. The new relation of Negro workers to the unions was inaugurated prior to World War II when the Congress of Industrial Organizations was founded in 1935. According to its constitution, one of the chief aims of the CIO was to ". . . bring about the effective organization of the working men and women of America regardless of race, color, creed, or nationality." [44] Although the CIO and its constituent unions adhered to this stated policy, they had to face traditional prejudices toward the workers and certain traditional attitudes of Negroes toward unionism.[45] Although statistics are not available, it is generally agreed that there was a tremendous increase in unionism among Negroes as the result of the founding of the CIO. It is estimated that there were 210,000 Negro members of the CIO in 1940.[46]

The increase in Negro union membership during World War II was tied up with their integration into industry. Many of the unions

[42] Fair Employment Practice Committee, *Final Report*, June 28, 1946 (Washington, 1947), pp. viii-ix. Negroes filed 80 per cent of the FEPC complaints.

[43] Weaver, *op. cit.*, p. 306.

[44] Herbert R. Northrup, *Organized Labor and the Negro* (New York, 1944), p. 14.

[45] See Horace R. Cayton and George R. Mitchell, *Black Workers and the New Unions* (Chapel Hill, 1939), for a comprehensive study of the integration of Negro workers into the CIO.

[46] See Charles S. Johnson and Davis McEntire, "Minority Labor Groups," in *Yearbook of American Labor* (New York, 1945).

which had closed shop agreements with plants handling government contracts excluded Negro workers. This was especially true of the unions affiliated with the American Federation of Labor. Even where the CIO was disposed to integrate Negro workers, they hesitated because of the fear that in the employee representation elections the AFL would win.[47] At first governmental pressure was ineffective, but gradually in those areas in the North where there was a labor shortage, the war industries began to yield and follow the federal establishments in training Negro machine operators. Then, in the reconverted automobile industry where the CIO unions were in control, Negro workers were upgraded. Gradually, Negro workers were trained and employed in the aircraft industry, which had assumed so much importance during the War. At the beginning of the defense program large numbers of Negro workers, many of whom possessed the requisite skill, remained unemployed in a number of cities while the migration of white workers to these cities was encouraged.[48] That the Negro worker made progress in becoming integrated in American industry during the War is indicated by the increase in the percentage of skilled and semiskilled Negro workers between 1940 and 1944. During this period the percentage of all Negro male workers in skilled indus trial occupations increased from 4.4 to 7.3 and in semiskilled industrial occupations from 12 to 22.4 per cent.[49]

ECONOMIC STATUS OF THE NEGRO
SINCE WORLD WAR II

Upon the conclusion of World War II one of the important problems facing the Negro worker during the reconversion of industry to civilian production was the question of seniority.[50] Since Negro workers were newcomers in many industries and had been recently upgraded, they were more likely to lose their jobs. Then, too, Negroes had made their greatest employment gains in factories which suffered severe cutbacks and war industries that declined after the war. More-

[47] See Weaver, *op. cit.*, pp. 35ff.
[48] United States Congress, *Interstate Migration. Hearings Before the Select Committee to Investigate the Interstate Migration of Destitute Citizens.* First Interim Report (Washington, 1941), pp. 23ff.
[49] *Ibid.*, p. 79.   [50] See Weaver, *op. cit.*, pp. 266ff.

over, Negro workers were concentrated in shipbuilding, aircraft, ammunition, explosives and small industries with little possibility of reconversion. In the latter half of 1945, the reduced employment of Negroes began to reflect all of these factors. "Of the seven war centers studied by FEPC during reconversion, all but Chicago showed a heavier loss of jobs by Negro than by white workers and a necessity on the part of Negro workers to accept the lowest paid jobs. . . . Whereas during the war many Negroes had risen into the skilled, professional, and managerial categories, by 1946 these openings for them had dwindled to a scant few. New York City was an exception." [51]

After the FEPC ceased to function in 1946, the employment of Negroes on equal terms with whites no longer had the support of the federal government. However, four states—New York, New Jersey, Massachusetts, and Connecticut—and four cities—Chicago, Milwaukee, Minneapolis, and Philadelphia—have enacted legislation against discrimination in employment. New York's State Commission Against Discrimination (SCAD) has achieved considerable success in breaking down the barriers to the employment of Negroes.[52] During the period from its inception, July 1, 1945, to July 19, 1947, SCAD received 714 complaints, 18 of which were later withdrawn. Because of lack of jurisdiction, 80 were dismissed and 174 were closed after investigation because of lack of merit. Another 161 were closed after conferences revealed no basis for complaint. Of the remaining 281, 151 were settled by conference and conciliation with members of SCAD and 130 were still pending. It is important to note the absence of any case that was brought before a public hearing or taken to the courts. It appears that employers would rather conform to the law than be charged with discrimination which might result in boycotts, reprisals, or unfavorable publicity. Whereas SCAD has had some influence on the unions which discriminate against Negro workers, it has encountered difficulties, as for example, in the milk delivery trades where the union has offered more opposition than the employers. The success of SCAD has been most conspicuous in placing Negroes in

[51] FEPC, *Final Report*, p. xi.
[52] Herbert R. Northrup, "Proving Ground for Fair Employment," *Commentary*, December, 1947, pp. 552-56.

positions as clerks in stores and other positions from which they were formerly rigidly excluded.

In the South the most important movement toward the integration of Negro workers into industry has been the drive of the CIO which got under way at the beginning of 1946. The CIO has maintained the principle of nonsegregated local unions, though there are some all Negro locals in small mills where the entire working personnel is Negro. This policy has been adopted on the basis of past experience which showed that separate local unions established vested interests among Negro as well as white workers. In connection with the union drive there is an educational campaign designed to reduce racial prejudice and discrimination. The drive of the CIO has been successful, especially in textiles, lumber, and food processing. Negro workers especially have responded wholeheartedly in the union drive. Despite a tendency toward voluntary segregation on the part of whites and Negroes, there is evidence that racial barriers are breaking down. Moreover, there is greater acceptance of the idea of upgrading Negro workers as well as of equal pay. The success of the present drive in the South is due partly to the work of the National Labor Relations Board in establishing the principle of equal pay for Negro workers and the effect of the work of the FEPC during the War.

The importance of the drive to integrate Negro workers into the labor movement in the South is emphasized when one considers their present low economic status especially in the South. In 1946, in the urban and rural-nonfarm areas of the country as a whole, the median income of nonwhite families was $1,834 in comparison with $3,094 for white families.[53] In the north central states and the West, the median incomes of nonwhite families were closer to those of the white families. In the north central states the median incomes of nonwhite and white families were $2,273 and $3,023 respectively and in the West $2,659 and $3,152 respectively. On the other hand in the South, the median incomes of nonwhite families was $1,527 as compared with $2,709 for white families. When one considers the cities only, it is found that 27.9 per cent of the nonwhite families as compared with

[53] Bureau of the Census, *Current Population Reports. Consumer Income.* Series P-60, No. 1, January 28, 1948.

7.7 per cent of the white families in the South have incomes of less than $1,000.

It appears that the Negro worker has not suffered severe unemployment since the close of the War. According to the report of the Census Bureau, during the week of January 4-10, 1948, 5.2 per cent of the male and 3.8 per cent of the female nonwhite labor force as compared with 3.5 per cent of the male and 2.9 per cent of the female white labor force was unemployed.[54] The Bureau of Labor Statistics reported that although the Negro made his greatest wartime gains in factory employment in munition industries (chemical, metals, and rubber), "the proportion of Negroes employed in industrial jobs (craftsmen and operatives) was about the same in 1947 as during the war." [55] However the employment of Negroes as skilled craftsmen and foremen "appears to have declined somewhat since the war's end, in contrast to a significant increase in the proportion of craftsmen and foremen among whites." [56] That the Negro workers have not suffered greater downgrading is the result of the fact that there has been relatively full employment.

SUMMARY

Unemployment and poverty among Negroes have been closely tied up with the demand for their labor in the development of the national economy. At the same time, however, the extent and nature of the employment of Negroes have been conditioned by social attitudes on the part of both white employers and white workers. When white and black workers began to compete on the labor market, Negro tenants and farm laborers were able to hold their own. But in the cities Negro workers were gradually forced out of the skilled trades partly because of the inefficiency of Negro workers but mainly because of the organized opposition of white workers. The demands of northern industry during World War I were able to absorb the surplus Negroes in agriculture and marginal and unemployed Negro workers in cities. When the 1929 depression set in, the insecurity of the Negro's position in

---

[54] Bureau of the Census, *Current Population Reports. Labor Force.* Series P-57, No. 67, February 6, 1948.
[55] *Monthly Labor Review*, December, 1947, p. 664.   [56] *Ibid.*, p. 664.

industry was revealed. Large numbers of Negro workers became the recipients of relief in cities. When the defense program began, the Negro industrial workers were still a submerged group in American industry. Because of government action, the man-power shortage, and the growing importance of the industrial unions with their more liberal policy, Negro workers gained a foothold in American industry. In the future the employment of the Negro and his ability to rise above the impoverished condition of the past will depend upon full employment and his integration into American industry and organized labor as well as the social services provided by the public policies set and supported by the government.

CHAPTER XXIV

Family Disorganization

THE disorganization of family life among Negroes has long attracted the attention of sociologists and other students of the Negro problem.[1] Most of the earlier studies presented a gloomy picture of widespread family disorganization and sexual immorality. For example, a half century ago one investigator concluded that statistics on illegitimacy proved "that neither religion nor education has influenced to an appreciable degree the moral progress of the race." [2] The opinions of a northern-born mulatto, who wrote at the turn of the present century, were not less extreme. He wrote of the "moral putridity" of Negroes and stated that marital immoralities were not "confined to the poor, the ignorant, and the degraded among the freed people, but are equally common among those who presume to be educated and refined." [3] Essentially the same opinion was expressed later by others. Odum, who holds no such opinions today, wrote in 1910 that his observations of the Negro for twenty years led him to the conclusion that the Negro was "as destitute of morals as any of the lower animals." [4] Even as late as 1930, a former chaplain of the Mississippi State Penitentiary concluded in his book on the Negro in the District of Columbia that the high illegitimate birth-rate "is one of the mani-

[1] See E. Franklin Frazier, *The Negro Family in Chicago* (Chicago, 1932), pp. 1-9, for views concerning the demoralization of Negro family life.

[2] Frederick L. Hoffman, *Race Traits and Tendencies of the American Negro* (New York, 1896), p. 236.

[3] William H. Thomas, *The American Negro, What He Was, What He Is, And What He May Become* (New York, 1901), p. 179.

[4] Howard W. Odum, *Social and Mental Traits of the Negro: Research in Conditions of the Negro Race in Northern Towns: A Study in Race Traits, Tendencies and Prospects* (New York, 1910), p. 171.

fest measures of the indifferent success achieved upon the part of the white, during his long contact in mediating the ideals, the morals of Christianity" to Negroes.[5]

EXPLANATIONS ADVANCED TO ACCOUNT FOR FAMILY DISORGANIZATION AMONG NEGROES

Various reasons have been advanced to account for the widespread family disorganization among Negroes.[6] Some of these explanations attributed the widespread family disorganization among Negroes to biological factors. During the first decade of the present century, one student offered the explanation that it was due to "sensual concretism" which distinguishes the Negro from the Caucasian.[7] "In the case of nature's most potent instinct of sex," he went on to explain, "a scarcely appreciable proportion of the race ever makes any effort whatever to keep it within due metes and bounds."[8] According to another writer, the strong sex instinct of the Negro, which cannot be bound by social restraints, only manifests the characteristics of his other animal impulses.[9] In a similar vein wrote McCord, who felt that "a compelling sexual appetite" nullified the desire on the part of the Negro girl to maintain her honor.[10] About the same time an army physician contributed his explanation of loose sex behavior among Negroes. In his opinion, the Negro was "a race without morals" that could only mimic the white race and "many animals below man manifest a far greater amount of real affection in their love-making than do the Negroes."[11] Even as late as the twenties, a writer on social

[5] A. H. Shannon, *The Negro in Washington. A Study in Race Amalgamation* (New York, 1930), p. 111. This is manifestly not only a biased, but also an ignorant book. The author makes the preposterous statement that the high illegitimacy rate among Negroes is due to the fact that they enjoy too much freedom and that, therefore, Negro women desire children by white men.

[6] See Frazier, *op. cit.*, pp. 11-13.

[7] William W. Elwang, *The Negroes of Columbia, Missouri. A Concrete Study of the Race Problem* (Columbia, Mo.), 1904.

[8] *Ibid.*, p. 53.   [9] Odum, *op. cit.*, pp. 259-60.

[10] Charles H. McCord, *The American Negro as a Dependent, Defective and Delinquent* (Nashville, Tennessee, 1914), p. 106.

[11] R. W. Shufeldt, *America's Greatest Problem: The Negro* (Philadelphia, 1915), pp. 46-47. In the same paragraph the author exclaims, "How very, very rare it is that we see two Negroes kiss each other, or exhibit any true sentiment in love-making!"

problems stated that immorality flourished among Negroes "because of their past history in Africa, where the climate tended to the preservation of those with a high birth rate and thus caused the Negro to inherit stronger passions than the white man." [12] Following a similar line of thought, Weatherford wrote in 1924, that such racial traits "built into the race during long centuries" could not "be bred out in a few years or even a few decades." [13]

There were some writers who attributed the disorganization of Negro family life in America not only to racial or biological factors but to the African cultural background. Writing at the beginning of the century, Tillinghast thought that he could trace the weaknesses of the American Negro family to its African roots:

The West African father felt little concern in his children; the mother, while showing impulsive affection for them at times, had no idea whatever of systematically correcting and training them. Thus, at the time the Negroes came to this country there had not been developed in the race strong and enduring parental affections nor more than a very slight sense of responsibility for careful bringing up of children.[14]

Dowd, who held that biological traits were only partly responsible for the loose behavior of Negroes, attempted to show the connection between their sexual incontinence and African cultural traits:

Under the matrilineal family, which has existed from time immemorial in Africa, sexual incontinence is not attended with the evil consequences that necessarily follow from it among the Caucasian races, the traditions of which are those of the patrilineal family. Consequently there have never developed among the Negro races the ideas of chastity which are so consecrated among the Caucasians. The animistic and polytheistic religion of the African Negroes rather promotes sexual incontinence, and exalts it to a virtue, while the religion of the Caucasian regards sexual incontinence as a cardinal sin.[15]

[12] George S. Dow, *Society and Its Problems* (New York, 1922), p. 181.
[13] W. D. Weatherford, *The Negro from Africa to America* (New York, 1924), p. 42.
[14] Joseph A. Tillinghast, *The Negro in Africa and America*, "Publications of the American Economic Association," New York, May, 1902, p. 160.
[15] Jerome Dowd, *The Negro in American Life* (New York, 1926), p. 582.

These attempts, over a period of thirty years, to explain the demoralized sex behavior of American Negroes in terms of hypothetical racial traits were based largely upon certain erroneous conceptions of "primitive" people. This conception, as Faris has shown, fitted into the general hypothetical scheme of human evolution:

The conception of the mind of "primitive man" held by Herbert Spencer had the advantage of aesthetic symmetry and proportion. If animals can be arranged in serried ranks, and if the highest of these is infinitely below the civilized man, there ought surely to be, not only a missing link, but also grades or ranks of men varying in their capacities and possibilities. If this assumption be made, and if the isolated sentences quoted from travelers and residents among savages be duly cited, it is possible to make out a good case, as the classical statement of Spencer shows.[16]

Modern anthropological research has discredited Spencer's conception of the "place" of so-called "primitive" people in the biological evolution of mankind. The behavior of so-called "primitive" people, like the behavior of civilized people, can be explained in terms of their culture. This does not mean, however, that those who have attempted to explain the sex behavior of American Negroes in terms of African culture were on surer ground. Tillinghast's notions of African customs show a lack of any real knowledge of actual conditions, and Dowd reverses the real situation as to the method of reckoning descent in Africa. As a matter of fact, in Africa "the reckoning is so prevailingly patrilineal, that the few cases of matrilineate can scarcely be looked upon as anything but secondary local modifications." [17]

The recent attempts of Herskovits to explain the sex behavior and family life of American Negroes in terms of African culture do not rest upon such generalizations as those of Tillinghast and Dowd about African culture. Professor Herskovits is well grounded in a knowledge of African culture and has a first-hand knowledge of the culture of the area from which Negro slaves came.[18] Yet, as we have seen in

[16] Ellsworth Faris, "The Mental Capacity of Savages," *American Journal of Sociology*, Vol. XXIII, p. 603.

[17] *Anthropology* by A. L. Kroeber, p. 234. Copyright 1923 by Harcourt, Brace and Company, Inc.

[18] See Melville J. Herskovits, *The Myth of the Negro Past* (New York, 1941).

Chapter I, his attempt to relate certain phases of the family life of the American Negro to African culture represents ingenious speculations about superficial similarities between African practices and the behavior of American Negroes.[19] During the past fifteen years, American sociologists have abandoned biological explanations of the sex behavior of Negroes and have rejected the attempt to ascribe such behavior to the influences of African culture.[20] They have analyzed the sex and family behavior in terms of historical and social factors which have molded the Negro family in the American environment.

DISORGANIZATION OF FAMILY LIFE FOLLOWING EMANCIPATION

The Civil War and Emancipation created a crisis in Negro family life.[21] Despite the general insecurity of family ties and the uncertain position of the father and husband during slavery, the Negro family was subject to the discipline of the master. In addition, where conditions were favorable, the Negro family achieved considerable stability because of the character of its internal organization. The Civil War and Emancipation destroyed the discipline and the authority of the masters and uprooted the stable families from their customary mode of living. As a consequence promiscuous sex relations and constant changing of spouses became the rule among the demoralized elements among the free Negroes. There was much confusion concerning marital relationships because of the separation of spouses during slavery. The missionaries who went South to minister to the needs of the freedmen often experienced difficulty in deciding who were the right-

[19] See pp. 12-13 above.
[20] See Edward B. Reuter, *The American Race Problem, A Study of the Negro,* Rev. ed. (New York, 1938), pp. 199ff. It should be pointed out, however, that while in the first edition of this book, published in 1927, Reuter attributed the sex behavior of Negroes partly to social factors in the American environment, he nevertheless included a biological explanation in the statement that "The fact is also often pointed out that the Negroes are by temperamental endowment extrovert and are possessed of strong native sex appetite. These two facts taken together dispose the Negroes to a degree of sex promiscuity not common to other groups." *The American Race Problem* by E. B. Reuter, p. 220. Copyright 1927 by Thomas Y. Crowell Company.
[21] See E. Franklin Frazier, *The Negro Family in the United States* (Chicago, 1939), pp. 89ff.

ful partners in marriages which were to have the sanction, for the first time, of law and religion. Sometimes the missionaries found it necessary to resort to force or the threat of imprisonment in order to get the former slaves to abandon their promiscuous sex relations. But moral instruction and even force were unable to hold in check the widespread family disorganization which ensued when the Negro became a free agent in forming and breaking marital ties.

During the years between Emancipation and the opening of the present century, Negro family life became stabilized to some extent under the modified plantation system. A large proportion of the so-called marriages were, to be sure, "common-law" relationships. But from the standpoint of stability and community recognition, these relationships had the same character as legal marriages. They conformed to customs and mores which had grown up among the rural folk. The mores of these rural communities were little influenced by the laws of white men who regarded with contempt or at least amusement the customs and ways of the segregated Negro communities. Consequently, it was not strange that when whites turned their attention to the customs and practices of the Negro world, they were inclined to regard the large numbers of children born outside legal marriage as an indication of loose sex relations.

One observer of the change in family relations following Emancipation was of the opinion that a quarter of a century after slavery illegitimacy was on the increase.[22] Another student writing during the early years of the present century likewise regarded the absence of legal marriage among 20 of the 40 couples on a plantation in Louisiana as evidence of widespread family disorganization and immorality among rural Negroes.[23] There is no evidence that illegitimacy was on the increase among rural Negroes a quarter of a century after slavery nor that the conditions on the Louisiana plantation were typical of the Negro rural population. It is quite possible that on the industrialized sugar plantations in Louisiana there was much social dis-

[22] Phillip A. Bruce, *The Plantation Negro as a Freeman* (New York, 1889), pp. 19-20.
[23] J. Bradford Laws, *The Negroes of Cinclaire Central Factory and Calumet Plantation, Louisiana* (United States Department of Labor Bulletin 38 [January, 1902]), pp. 102-3.

organization. These observers failed to take into account the folkways and mores that had grown up among the rural Negroes. Among the rural Negroes generally the bearing of children represented the fulfillment of a woman's destiny. The children of an unmarried daughter became a part of her family. Disorganization of Negro family life generally appeared as the result of the impact of outside economic and social forces, as, for example, when the father or husband was drawn into the turpentine or lumber camps or the wife or mother went to town to supplement the family income.

The disorganization of Negro family life has continued on a large scale because of the urbanization of the Negro. But in order to see how urbanization has affected the stability and organization of Negro family life, it is necessary to sketch briefly the major patterns of family life that gradually emerged following Emancipation.[24] There was first the maternal family pattern which was found in its purest and most primitive form in the rural South. This type of family pattern had existed since slavery because the father's function ceased with impregnation or he had no authority in the household. The woman was chiefly responsible for the support of the family and maintained authority over her children and her daughters' children who were often illegitimate. The second type of family grew up among the more stable and ambitious elements in the Negro population. In this conventional pattern of family life the father was the recognized head and assumed responsibility for the support of the family. The third pattern of family life had as its foundation the traditions of stable family life that were built up among the Negroes who were free before the Civil War. The distinguishing feature of these families was that they acquired more than any other large group of Negro families an institutional character. These families were similar to those families which grew up in the isolated communities of Negro-white-Indian families. This fourth pattern of family life was distinguished from the third by a patriarchal authority which rested upon a long history of pioneering and landownership.

[24] See E. Franklin Frazier, "Traditions and Patterns of Negro Family Life in the United States" in Edward B. Reuter (Ed.), *Race and Culture Contacts* (New York, 1934), pp. 191-207 and Chapter XIII above.

FAMILY DISORGANIZATION IN URBAN AREAS

As the rural Negro population was drawn into the towns and cities of the South, family disorganization increased among Negroes. The family system that was adapted to the rural community tended to break up. In the city illegitimate children are not only a serious economic burden but they become an impediment to the disorganized elements who would move about without restraint. At the end of the last century, a little more than a fourth of the Negro births in Baltimore and Mobile were illegitimate.[25] There are no statistics on the extent of illegitimacy before 1900 except in the District of Columbia. In 1878, 9.8 per cent of the Negro births were illegitimate; but during the next year the percentage of illegitimate births rose to 17 per 100 live births. By 1881 a fifth of the Negro births were illegitimate, and the proportion fluctuated between a fifth and a fourth until 1910. The increase in the illegitimacy rate coincided with an unprecedented increase in the Negro population, resulting from an influx of large numbers of southern Negroes.

The disorganization of Negro family life which had become characteristic of the Negro communities in the towns and cities of the South became a serious social problem in northern cities after the mass migrations during and following World War I. Among the million or so migrants there were thousands of men and women who had cut themselves loose from family and friends to seek work and adventure.[26] When many such persons arrived in the northern city, they had already experienced considerable personal disorganization. The simple folk culture of the rural community had been shed or had lost its significance. Their sexual life had become a casual affair in which sympathy and affection played little part. The numbers of these unattached men and women were constantly swollen by the husbands and fathers who had deserted their families when they arrived in northern cities. In fact, family desertion has been one of the chief forms in which family disorganization among urbanized Negroes has manifested itself.

[25] Frazier, *The Negro Family in the United States,* pp. 621 and 623.
[26] *Ibid.,* pp. 272ff.

Although it is difficult to determine to what extent Negro men desert their families, information in a number of studies indicates that they desert families relatively more frequently than men of other racial groups. For example, it was found that during the six years (exclusive of 1914) from 1909 to 1915, Negroes comprised 21.1 per cent of all desertion cases aided by the county agent in Chicago.[27] In New York City where Negro families comprised 5.6 per cent of all families under the care of the Charity Organization Society, they furnished 11.2 per cent of the desertion cases. During the depression year, 1930-1931, the desertion cases among the families receiving assistance from the Society amounted to 14.8 per cent. The proportion of Negro families without male heads is evidently due partly to desertion on the part of the men, since it cannot be accounted for by widowhood, divorce, and legal separation. In 1940, the percentage of Negro families with female heads in cities with a total population of 100,000 or over ranged from 21 to 34.

The majority of the Negro desertion cases handled by social agencies represent recent migrants to the city.[28] It is difficult to determine the real marital status of the couples involved in desertion cases. For example, of 248 major and minor service cases handled by the Central District of the United Charities in Chicago in 1927, the marriage of the couples was verified in only 70 cases. The indefiniteness of the marital status of migrant Negro couples is due partly to the lack of records and indifference on the part of the southern white officials and partly to the fact that marriage has not acquired an institutional character among many migrants from the South.

In view of these facts, family desertion among Negroes involves more than the breaking of marital bonds that have a legal basis. Desertion as a social phenomenon includes those cases of quasi-families in which the "husband" and "wife" have been bound only by the customary practices of the Negro folk. At the same time, it is indicative of the widespread practice characteristic of urban life generally of sexual association on the basis of casual attraction between individuals.

[27] *Ibid.*, pp. 325-26.
[28] See *ibid.*, Chapter XV, and *The Negro Family in Chicago*, Chapter VIII. See also Ruth Reed, *Negro Illegitimacy in New York City*, New York, 1926.

Among the Negro folk the stability of marital relationships is maintained chiefly by the mores and institutions (usually the church) of the rural community and the sympathy and common interests that develop between man and woman. In the rural South a marriage or family supported by these elements may have considerable stability. It represents an adaptation to the economic and social environment and satisfies the wishes of the persons involved. But when this type of married couple or family migrates to the city, it tends to go to pieces. It no longer has the support of the neighbors and institutions of the rural environment and it no longer satisfies the newly awakened interests and wishes of the family members. In the absence of institutional controls and the lack of a family tradition and common interests, the husband or father and sometimes the mother or wife may sever family ties and pursue his or her individual impulses and wishes.

The high rate of illegitimacy among Negroes must likewise be studied in relation to the impact of social and economic forces upon the folk culture. In the Registration Area, the proportion of illegitimate births has increased from 120.1 per 1,000 total births in 1917 to 165.2 per 1,000 in 1943.[29] The statistics for individual cities show wide fluctuations during the present century.[30] But the rate in some cities has remained consistently high. For example, in the District of Columbia, during the year 1940 slightly more than one out of every five Negro births was illegitimate. Little understanding of illegitimacy is provided by attempting to relate the fluctuations to changes in the movement or condition of the Negro population. On the other hand, considerable light is thrown on the problem through analysis of case studies in terms of changes in family structure and the attitudes of unmarried mothers.[31]

In the rural communities of the South, illegitimacy does not appear as a social problem. The child of the unmarried mother generally becomes a part of the more or less amorphous family groups that have grown up in that region. Depending upon the character and status

[29] United States Department of Commerce, Bureau of the Census, *Vital Statistics of the United States* (Washington, 1945), p. 12.

[30] See Frazier, *The Negro Family in the United States*, Tables 33-47, pp. 621-32.

[31] See *ibid.*, Chapter XVI, and Frazier, *The Negro Family in Chicago*, Chapter IX.

of the family and the influence of generally accepted sex norms of the American people, illegitimacy may cause little or no disgrace or sense of guilt. Such free sex practices become a social problem in the urban environment. Illegitimacy occurs among the families that are concentrated in the deteriorated and disorganized areas in which the poorer migrants to the city are concentrated. Illegitimacy among these people does not represent a single type of behavior. There are some unmarried mothers who continue to behave according to the mores of the southern rural community. But in the city children mean increased economic burdens and children born out of wedlock may be the cause of shame and guilt feelings. In the city sex relations and motherhood are thus redefined for the migrants. Sex relations tend to acquire a purely hedonistic character and the burdens of motherhood are something to be avoided. As the women with a rural background achieve some sophistication with city ways, they avoid motherhood by using contraceptives and by resorting to abortions. Whereas in the rural areas they would have rejoiced in giving birth to a child even outside of wedlock, in the city they may attempt to rid themselves of the burden and disgrace by abandoning their child. Since each new wave of migrants brings with them the conceptions of sex and motherhood which they have acquired from the folk culture, illegitimacy continues a major problem in the adjustment to city living.

FAMILY DISORGANIZATION AMONG
"MIDDLE CLASS" NEGROES

Family disorganization among the masses of Negroes with a folk background is manifested in both desertion and illegitimacy. But even those families with a traditional background of stable family life and who constitute a middle class in the Negro community, experience some degree of disorganization in the urban community. The ability of these families to resist the disorganizing effects of urban life are dependent upon a number of factors. Where the family achieves economic security and becomes integrated into the institutions of the community, it is generally able to maintain its stability. In such families, which comprise the most ambitious elements in the Negro community, those who improve their economic and social status in the

city often break away from the old family pattern. Family disorganization among the middle class sometimes results in socially disapproved
behavior; but more often it leads to reorganization of one's personal
and family life on a more intelligent and rational basis to meet the
demands of city life.

Among the middle-class families the breaking of marital ties is a
matter for the divorce court, while the Negro from the isolated areas
of the rural South has only a vague knowledge of the meaning of
divorce.[32] It is part of the middle-class Negro's conformity to moral
codes and maintenance of respectability to have his marital relations
rest upon legality. However, there still survives among this class some
of the traditional opposition to divorce. Although it is difficult to
determine whether Negroes or whites resort to the divorce court more
frequently, it appears that as marriage acquires an institutional character, Negroes are increasingly seeking a legal dissolution of their
marital ties. Divorces with their attendant publicity in the Negro
press provide an index to family disorganization among upper-class
families. The changing character of the Negro community and its
new relation to American life have tended to undermine the values
and such distinctions as color and family descent which gave upper-
class families support and status. In the new world of the modern city,
occupation and income have become more significant than family
identification and Puritanical codes of behavior.

FAMILY DISORGANIZATION AND HOUSING OF NEGROES

It would be erroneous to regard "poor housing," considered as an
isolated factor, as a cause of family disorganization among Negroes.
The type of housing facilities which have been available for Negroes
are related to the economic and social status of the Negro as well as
to such factors as racial segregation and exploitation by white landlords. When the physical character of a dwelling place is considered
in relation to family disorganization, it is necessary to study its effect
upon the relations of the members in the household and upon the
behavior of the individuals in the family. Not only do Negroes live in

[32] See Frazier, *The Negro Family in the United States*, Chapter XVIII.

the least desirable areas and most deteriorated structures but they are crowded into these areas and structures beyond the limits of health, hygiene, safety or decency. In the rural areas, the crowding of parents and children in the same room has certainly had some effect upon the sex knowledge which Negro children acquire at an early age. However, because of the outdoor life of the rural population and the character of their family life, overcrowding does not have the same serious consequences as in the city.

On the other hand, overcrowding and the lack of facilities for normal family living have serious consequences for families in the cities. Because of their poverty it is often necessary for two or even more families to occupy a single house or the same apartment. Thus individual families are denied the privacy which is necessary to family exclusiveness. Even where the family is isolated from other families, very often the Negro family in the city is forced to take in lodgers. In northern cities nearly a third of the Negro families have lodgers, the proportion of families with lodgers being especially high among families with women heads.[33] Often where Negro families occupy a single dwelling unit without lodgers, the space at their disposal provides no privacy for the individual members of the families. Although the lack of privacy for the family and its members has affected the sex and family relations of Negroes, there is really little scientific information on the subject.[34]

The lack of suitable living space and modern housing facilities affects the relations of the members of the family in other ways. Even those Negro families which are disposed to gather for meals are very often denied this opportunity because of the absence of space or facilities. Then there is scarcely any opportunity for recreation or the type of social intercourse which knits the members of a family together. For a large proportion of Negro families in the city, the house

[33] Sterner, *The Negro's Share*, pp. 54-55.

[34] Thomas J. Woofter in *Negro Problems in Cities* (New York, 1928), p. 94, found a Pearsonian correlation of $+.243$ between the density of the Negro population and the rate of illegitimacy. It would be erroneous to conclude from these figures that the mere fact of *physical closeness* of people was a causative factor in illegitimacy since social and cultural factors have been found to be primarily responsible for unconventional sex behavior among Negroes.

is not a home but a place to cook and eat as individuals and sleep at night. When the weather permits it is generally a place from which one escapes. This is true of adults as well as children. This fact probably explains why so many Negroes congregate on the streets of Negro neighborhoods. So far as the children are concerned, the house becomes a veritable prison for them.[35] There is no way of knowing how many of the conflicts in Negro families are set off by the irritations caused by overcrowding people, who come home after a day of frustration and fatigue, to dingy and unhealthy living quarters.

GENERAL EFFECTS OF FAMILY DISORGANIZATION ON NEGRO COMMUNITY

The widespread disorganization of family life among Negroes has affected practically every phase of their community life and adjustments to the larger white world. Because of the absence of stability in family life, there is a lack of traditions. Life among a large portion of the urban Negro population is casual, precarious, and fragmentary.[36] It lacks continuity and its roots do not go deeper than the contingencies of daily living. This affects the socialization of the Negro child. With a fourth to a third of Negro families in cities without a male head, many Negro children suffer the initial handicap of not having the discipline and authority of the father in the home. Negro mothers who have the responsibility for the support of the family are forced to neglect their children who pick up all forms of socially disapproved behavior in the disorganized areas in which these families are concentrated.

Without the direction provided by family traditions and the discipline of parents, large numbers of Negro children grow up without aims and ambitions. The formal instruction provided by the public schools cannot make up for the deficiency in family training. In fact, much of the Negro child's lack of interest in education is attributable to the fact that it is unrelated to the experiences in the family. Moreover, the lack of employment opportunities for Negro youth helps to en-

[35] Juvenile delinquency was reduced among the rehoused families in the projects in Newark, New Jersey. See Chapter XXII above.

[36] See Frazier, *The Negro Family in Chicago*, pp. 223ff.

courage the aimlessness and lack of ambition among Negro youths without a normal family life. Thus family disorganization and social and economic forces in the community unite to create a sense of irresponsibility among Negro youth. Out of such an environment comes the large number of criminals and juvenile delinquents in the cities of the country.

SUMMARY

The widespread disorganization of Negro family life which has existed since Emancipation is the result of the impact of social and economic forces on the simple family organization which evolved in the rural South. After the social upheaval occasioned by the Civil War and Emancipation, the Negro family achieved a fair degree of stability in the rural areas of the South. But constantly the stability of the rural Negro family was undermined by the migration of men and women to the turpentine and lumber camps as well as to the towns and cities. As a result the Negro communities in the towns and cities of the South have long been characterized by widespread family disorganization. The crisis created in Negro life by the mass migrations to northern cities during and following World War I increased the volume of family disorganization. At the same time there has been an increasing stabilization of the Negro family over the years in cities. As the Negro has acquired education and has become integrated into the economic life of our cities, family life has become stabilized among the middle class which has assumed importance in the Negro community. On the other hand, the continued migrations from the rural South to cities, which increased in volume during World War II, has caused family disorganization to remain one of the serious problems of the Negro. Because of its volume, the disorganization of Negro family life has retarded the socialization of the Negro and lowered his economic efficiency. Moreover, it has been partly responsible for criminality and juvenile delinquency which will be considered in the next chapter.

CHAPTER XXV

Crime and Delinquency

ONCE it was the generally accepted opinion that there was no crime among Negroes during slavery. This opinion, as we have seen in Chapter V, has been proved false.[1] Moreover, contrary to certain notions regarding the adjustment of the Negro to a servile status, it appears that most of the crimes during slavery consisted of aggressions or retaliations against whites. When some of the early students of the Negro began the study of crime, they were at great pains to show the high crime rate among free Negroes in the North during slavery.[2] One such writer regarded the high crime rate in the North as well as in the South, during the decades following slavery, as evidence that under the conditions of freedom crime increased among Negroes because their behavior was motivated by passion and license rather than reason.[3]

During the last decade of the nineteenth century and the first decade of the present century there were two notable attempts to assess and interpret the high crime and delinquency rates among Negroes. There was the study of Hoffman, referred to above, in which the author concluded that education had "utterly failed to raise the

[1] See p. 90 above. Typical of the erroneous beliefs concerning crime among Negroes is the statement by Frederick L. Hoffman, *Race Traits and Tendencies of the American Negro* (New York, 1896), p. 217, that "During slavery, the Negro committed fewer crimes than the white man, and only on rare occasions was he guilty of the more atrocious crimes, such as rape and murder of white females, whether from cowardice or respect and devotion to his master, he respected the persons of his master's household, and few indeed are the recorded attempts at insurrection and revolt on the part of the southern slave."

[2] See Charles Otken, *The Ills of the South* (New York, 1894), pp. 227-29.

[3] *Ibid.*, pp. 218ff.

Negro to a higher level of citizenship, the first duty of which is to obey the laws and respect the lives and property of others." [4] In the other study, DuBois analyzed the high criminal rate among Negroes in terms of the social disorganization following Emancipation and the degradation of Negro labor which resulted from an attempt on the part of the South to maintain the Negro in a servile position.[5]

STUDIES OF NEGRO CRIME BEFORE MASS MIGRATIONS TO THE NORTH

In the same year that World War I began, there appeared a study which undertook to analyze and interpret the high rate of criminality among Negroes in the United States.[6] This book was written on the assumption that the Negro was a childlike and primitive race whose "psychical characteristics" tended to ally him with the instinctive and habitual criminal type.[7] However, during the previous year there had appeared a much more thoughtful analysis of Negro criminality in the South.[8] It was shown that the crime rate among Negroes was higher than among whites in both the North and the South though it was lower among Negroes than among some im-, migrant groups. During the four decades following the Civil War, crime had increased in both the North and South, but the crime rate among Negroes in the South had remained about a third as high as in the North. A reasonable explanation of the difference was the fact that the vast majority of the Negroes in the North lived in cities, while the reverse was true in the South and that a far greater number of Negroes in the North than in the South were in the age group in which the incidence of crime is highest. For the years, 1894 to 1905, there was evidence that the incidence of crime among Negroes had decreased slightly or had become stabilized. This was the period in which the incidence of lynchings had reached its peak and had begun to decline. Two other facts of importance concerning Negro

[4] Hoffman, *op. cit.*, p. 228.

[5] W. E. B. DuBois, *Some Notes on Crime* (Atlanta, 1904), pp. 2-9.

[6] Charles H. McCord, *The American Negro as a Dependent, Defective and Delinquent* (Nashville, Tennessee, 1914).   [7] *Ibid.*, pp. 42ff.

[8] Monroe N. Work, "Negro Criminality in the South," in *The Negro's Progress in Fifty Years* (Philadelphia, 1913), pp. 74-80.

crime were brought out by this analysis. The first was that even if all the Negroes who had been lynched on the charge of rape had been included among those legally charged with rape, the criminal rate for this charge, which was lower than for most immigrant groups in the country as a whole, would have been increased less than one-fourth of one per cent. Secondly, it was pointed out that the introduction of the convict lease system in southern prisons, thereby making the convicts a source of income, had caused the southern states to have an interest in increasing the number of convicts, the majority of whom were Negroes.

NEGRO CRIME BETWEEN WORLD WARS

Fifteen years later, a more thoroughgoing analysis of statistics on Negro crime was undertaken by Sellin.[9] It was shown first that both Negro and white investigators had accepted as true a higher criminal rate among Negroes than among whites. This conclusion was based upon statistical data from many sources. For example, in the Superior Courts of North Carolina for the years 1922 to 1925, there were 8.71 indictments per 1,000 Negroes as compared with 4.65 per 1,000 whites. In the Western Penitentiary of Pennsylvania, there were 575 Negroes instead of 42, if the Negro rate had been the same as the rate for whites. The statistical data, it was pointed out, represented *apparent* as opposed to *real* criminality rates and that the ratio between the two was not constant. This fact was especially important in assessing criminality among Negroes because of a number of reasons. There was first the fact of racial discrimination in both the North and the South. In the North the Negro was not only more liable to arrests than whites but in the case of Minneapolis it was found that the police records were altered so that it appeared that many more Negro arrests had occurred than the records showed.[10] Moreover, in northern cities many innocent Negroes have been arrested because the political party in power wanted to refute the charge of the party out of office that Ne-

[9] Thorsten Sellin, "The Negro Criminal" in *The American Negro, The Annals* (Philadelphia, 1928), pp. 52-64.
[10] See Maurine Boie, "An Analysis of Negro Crime Statistics for Minneapolis for 1923, 1924 and 1925," *Opportunity*, Vol. VI, pp. 171-72.

gro criminals were treated with laxity. In the South there has been a long history of the irresponsibility of the police officers towards Negroes. Petty officers of the law had harassed Negro workers and taken their earnings. Because of race prejudice and the social subordination of the Negro, the Negro was more likely to be fined and imprisoned than the white man.

It was further shown by an analysis of statistics that Negroes were convicted more frequently than whites and received longer sentences. For example, in Detroit a much larger percentage of Negroes than whites were convicted for burglary, armed robbery, simple larceny, assault and battery, disturbing the peace, accosting and soliciting, common prostitution, sex crimes, offenses against the state drug and prohibition laws, and embezzling, forgery, and similar crimes. In Detroit during the first six months of 1926, "twice as many Negroes were sentenced to imprisonment as whites for approximately the same kinds of offenses in the aggregate." [11] Moreover, a larger percentage of whites than Negroes were given the alternative of a fine or imprisonment and twice as many whites as Negroes were given suspended sentences or placed on probation. A similar situation was found in Alabama where 48.6 per cent of the Negro defendants were convicted for felonies as compared with 43.8 per cent of the white defendants. Of the whites convicted, 13.5 per cent were given the alternative of a fine or sentence as opposed to only 7.1 per cent of the Negroes convicted; and 30.9 per cent of the Negroes convicted were sentenced while only 15.5 per cent of the whites convicted were sentenced. In the South as a whole there was evidence that Negroes were given longer sentences than white prisoners.

A section of the report of the National Commission on Law Observance and Enforcement was devoted to an analysis of studies of Negro crime and case studies of Negro prisoners in the Sing Sing Prison in New York.[12] The proportion of Negroes in the prison population of Sing Sing was in excess of their relative numbers in the

[11] Sellin, *op. cit.*, p. 63.
[12] See Ira DeA. Reid, "Notes on the Negro's Relation to Work and Law" in National Commission on Law Observance and Enforcement, *Report on the Causes of Crime* (Washington, 1931), Vol. I, Part III, pp. 221-55.

population of New York during the years 1923 to 1927 and the proportion of Negroes in the prison population had increased during this
period. Negro prisoners exceeded their proportion in the prison population for all offenses except forgery. The highest percentages of
offenses for which Negroes had been imprisoned were assault, homicide, and burglary. An analysis of case studies of 80 Negro prisoners
revealed that a number of social and economic factors were associated with Negro crime. In 59 per cent of the cases unemployment
appeared as a factor and in 54 per cent of the cases such social factors as gambling, drinking, criminal associations, appeared as causative
factors in Negro crime.

The information provided in these case studies and data on Negro
crime in other cities pointed to certain conclusions concerning Negro
crime in cities. A large proportion of Negroes in cities consist of migrant males between the ages, 20 to 44, who contribute the largest
proportion of criminals in any racial group. Negro migrants to cities
must find homes in physically deteriorated areas which are also centers of a vicious social environment. In addition, Negro men are constantly faced with unemployment and constantly live on the fringe
of a marginal existence. As a result of these social and economic factors Negro men constitute a disproportionately large part of the criminal element in cities.

In 1940 there appeared a statistical analysis of the rate of Negro
commitments to the Western State Penitentiary of Pennsylvania in
relation to the age and sex distribution of the Negro population in
the 33 counties from which the prisoners came; the degree of industrialization of these counties; and whether the prisoners were native to the
state.[13] During the 30 years, 1906 to 1935, the rate of Negro commitments was, on the basis of the proportion of Negroes in the population,
nearly 10 times as high as the rate for native whites. For the decade
1916 to 1925, when Negroes were migrating to Pennsylvania in large
numbers, the rate of commitments for Negroes was 15 times that for
whites. During the 30-year period the rate of commitments for Negroes for crimes of violence was nearly 30 times as great as that for

[13] Jess Spirer, *Negro Crime, Comparative Psychology Monographs*, Vol. 16,
Number 2 (June, 1940).

whites. The rate for such crimes among Negroes mounted to more than 30 times that of whites during the migration years, 1916 to 1925. Although a larger percentage of white commitments than Negro commitments, 64.1 per cent as compared with 56.1 per cent, were for predatory crimes, the rate for Negroes was nearly nine times that of whites. The rate of Negro commitments for sex crimes was over seven times that of whites for the entire 30 years; but there was a distinct decline during 1916 to 1925.

The comparison between the commitments of out-of-state Negroes and Pennsylvania Negroes revealed that the rate of commitments for the former was 12 times and for the latter five times the rate for whites. In the case of violent crimes, the rate for out-of-state Negroes was nearly five times that of Pennsylvania Negroes. A comparison of the rates of commitments of Negroes from the more industrialized and less industrialized areas did not show any differences. This fact should not be interpreted as indicating that social and cultural factors are not responsible for the high crime rate among Negroes. Within the same community there are vast differences in the economic and social status of the Negro population. In Chicago, for example, the percentage of Negro males in the county jail declined regularly from 9.4 for the First Zone of the Negro community, where the poorer southern migrants settled, to 1.2 in the Seventh Zone, where the higher socioeconomic classes were concentrated.[14] This regular decline in jail commitments coincided with the decrease in the social disorganization of the Negro community.

CRIME IN THE HARLEM COMMUNITY IN NEW YORK CITY

Crimes among Negroes in the northern city may be shown concretely in the case of the Harlem community in New York City.[15] According to the records of the seven police precincts in the Harlem area, during the first six months of 1935, there were 6,540 Negro men and 1,338 Negro women arrested. A little more than 7 per cent of

[14] E. Franklin Frazier, *The Negro Family in Chicago* (Chicago, 1932), pp. 210ff.
[15] Mayor's Commission on Conditions in Harlem, *The Negro in Harlem* (New York, 1936), pp. 97-100. Unpublished manuscript.

the men and about 5 per cent of the women were under 21 years of age. On the other hand, the majority of the men—59.1 per cent—were between 21 and 35 years of age, while over two-thirds—67.3 per cent— of the women were between 21 and 30 years. Among the men, policy or what is known as the "numbers racket" stood first with 2,089, or 31.9 per cent of the total arrests. It is important to note that men arrested on this charge were numerous in all age groups up to 60. The widespread operations of this "racket," which extracts so much money from the community for the benefit of racketeers who have no other interest in Harlem, were due to a large extent to the desperate economic condition of the people who hoped to gain through luck what was denied them through labor. Although policy figured less prominently among the causes for women's arrest, it accounted for 8.6 per cent. The next major cause for arrests among Negro men showed almost the same proportion as policy; this was disorderly conduct, which included 2,023 arrests or 30.9 per cent. Disorderly conduct included many types of misdemeanors, a great many of which were immoral conduct. In fact, most of the 265 arrests of women for disorderly conduct—practically a fifth of the women arrested—were due to immoral conduct. However, the majority of women arrested—801 or 59.9 per cent—were charged with vagrancy, another term often used to designate immoral conduct. Thus it appears that close to 80 per cent of the arrests of Negro women were for immoral sex behavior. In an environment like Harlem, where there was little opportunity for employment for a large number of single women who had broken away from the family, immoral conduct offered a means of livelihood.

Five crimes involving property—burglary, 188 arrests; robbery, 141 arrests; grand larceny, 77 arrests; assault and robbery, 32 arrests; and pickpocketing, 24 arrests—together accounted for 7 per cent of the arrests of men and 3 per cent of the arrests of women. For men the next three crimes of importance were gambling, felonious assaults, and liquor violations. The 421 arrests for gambling constituted 6.4 per cent of the total; while the 334 arrests for violations of the liquor laws amounted to 5.1 per cent. It is especially important to note the figures in regard to crimes against persons since social disorganization in Harlem is conducive to such crimes. Of the 6,540 men arrested, 328 or 5.0 per cent were charged with felonious assault and 35 or five-tenths of one per cent with homicide. Of the 1338 women arrested, 38 or 2.8 per cent were charged with felonious assault and 4 or three-tenths of one per cent with homicide.

Primarily because of their poverty, the people of Harlem can exercise little control over the rôle of the community in the economy of the city. Therefore, Harlem becomes the prey of every influence that is capable of wielding economic power in the community. It has become the location of vice dens and pleasure resorts for whites. White people come to Harlem in order to escape the control of their own communities. In Harlem, they indulge in vicious and antisocial behavior because they are free from the censure of their race and the intimate groups in which their lives are rooted. The Negro, because of his economic condition, is induced to cater to the vicious, immoral, and pleasure-seeking impulses and desires of these whites. Hence, as long as Harlem remains an area in which whites, and Negroes for that matter, can throw off normal social restraints, it will remain a breeding ground for crime and delinquency.

NEGRO CRIME AND THE ADMINISTRATION OF JUSTICE

In an article which appeared in 1941, Guy Johnson presented an analysis of the causes of Negro crime and its relation to the administration of justice.[16] This article was based upon the assumption, "that the fundamental causes of crime in the Negro are the same as in any other group and that the simple fact of race is not sufficient in itself to explain any important group differences in criminal behavior." [17] The significant feature of this article was that it analyzed Negro crime in relation to the lower caste position of the Negro and the influence of caste in the administration of justice. It was pointed out that the lower caste position of the Negro was responsible for the low economic status of the Negro and the concentration of Negroes in

[16] See Guy Johnson, "The Negro and Crime," The Annals, American Academy of Political and Social Science, Vol. 217 (September, 1941), pp. 93-104.
[17] *Ibid.*, p. 93.

ghettos where there is considerable social disorganization. Moreover, it was shown how the lower caste position defined crime on the part of Negroes. As the result of caste, every conflict situation between the races has the possibility of becoming a crime on the part of Negroes. Negroes are suspected or blamed for crimes because they are the victims of frame-ups and are used as scapegoats. The police, who generally use brute force on Negroes, have little respect for the rights of Negroes as citizens or human beings. Even the courts, in their handling of Negro cases, reflect the influence of the lower caste position of the Negro.

From three-fourths to nine-tenths of the victims of murders committed by Negroes in Richmond, Virginia, five counties in North Carolina, and Fulton County, Georgia, were Negroes. The Negro murderers of Negroes were seldom convicted or sentenced to death, while Negroes who killed whites were almost certain to be sentenced to death. The segregation of Negro prisoners and the sentencing of them to the chain-gangs of the South made them the victims of brutality on the part of the white guards who possessed the worst prejudices of the whites. Negroes were not pardoned or paroled as frequently as whites and when they were paroled, it was generally for the purpose of being exploited by whites. Finally, the hypothesis was presented that much intraracial violence among Negroes is due to the frustration and hostilities created by their lower caste position.[18]

MOST RECENT STUDIES OF NEGRO CRIME

The most recent analysis of the extent, nature, and causes of criminality among Negroes has been made by the Swedish social economist, Gunnar Myrdal, in his monumental work on the Negro problem.[19] Basing his statistical analysis upon United States Census data for 1939, he found that 42.4 native whites and 23.6 foreign-born whites per 100,000 population as compared with 134.7 Negroes were received from courts by state and federal prisons.[20] In the southern

[18] For a discussion of the high homicide rate among Negroes, see H. C. Brearley, *Homicide in the United States* (Chapel Hill, 1932), Chapter VI.
[19] Gunnar Myrdal, *An American Dilemma* (New York, 1944), Vol. 2, pp. 966-79.
[20] United States Bureau of the Census, *Prisoners in State and Federal Prisons and Reformatories: 1929* (Washington, 1941).

states, the rate per 100,000 population for Negro felony prisoners received by state and federal prisons from courts was 86.3 as compared with 148.7 for northern and western states. In the South the rate per 100,000 population of prisoners sentenced for felonies was two and a half times that of whites, while in the North the Negro rate was five times that for whites. The percentage of Negroes among those arrested for various offenses and the rate per 100,000 Negro and white population are presented in Table XXXIX.

In analyzing the causes of crime among Negroes, Myrdal showed the influence of the lower caste position of the Negro and the influence of historical factors on the social and economic status of the Negro. He pointed out a factor generally overlooked; namely, how "Caste, especially when it operates to cause legal injustice and insecurity of life and property, prevents the Negro from identifying himself with society and the law." [21]

A disproportionate number of Negro men and women, as measured by their relative numbers in the population, continue to be numbered among the adult offenders in our cities. For example, in 1945 in the District of Columbia, 74.4 per cent of the adult offenders arrested were Negroes, while 25.6 per cent were whites, although Negroes constituted about 33 per cent of the population.[22] More than eight times as many Negroes as whites were arrested for aggravated assault and three times as many Negroes as whites were charged with murder and housebreaking. During the first six months of 1945, Negro women arrested for prostitution and related offenses constituted 62 per cent of all women arrested for these offenses. These figures indicate that the pattern of criminality has changed little over the past half century. There is every reason to believe that as long as the Negro is discriminated against in employment and is forced to live in ghettos where there is considerable social disorganization, criminality among them will continue to be high.

[21] *An American Dilemma* by Gunnar Myrdal, pp. 975-76. Copyright 1944 by Harper and Brothers.
[22] Washington Criminal Justice Association, *Crime in the Nation's Capital* (Washington, D. C., 1946).

TABLE XXXIX

Distribution of Arrests According to Race and Type of Offense (Excluding Those Under Fifteen Years of Age): 1940 *

OFFENSE CHARGED	PER CENT NEGRO OF TOTAL IN EACH	RATE PER 100,000	POPULATION ᵃ
	OFFENSE	NEGRO	WHITE ᶜ
Criminal homicide	40.1	19.8	3.2
Robbery	30.8	31.7	7.6
Assault	44.0	116.4	15.7
Burglary—breaking or entering	24.5	66.3	22.0
Larceny–theft	28.4	138.1	37.4
Auto–theft	14.8	15.4	9.6
Embezzlement and fraud	11.5	17.1	14.2
Stolen property; buying, receiving, etc.	27.3	7.6	2.2
Arson	17.4	1.5	0.8
Forgery and counterfeiting	9.1	5.0	5.4
Rape	22.1	10.4	3.9
Prostitution and commercialized vice	25.4	17.7	5.9
Other sex offenses	14.9	11.1	6.8
Narcotic drug laws	19.3	7.5	2.9
Weapons, carrying, possessing, etc.	45.8	20.3	2.5
Offenses against family and children	15.6	9.7	5.7
Liquor laws	47.2	36.5	4.4
Driving while intoxicated	6.8	15.3	22.4
Road and driving laws	21.6	10.0	3.9
Parking violations	14.3	ᵇ	ᵇ
Other traffic and motor vehicle laws	21.0	15.5	6.2
Disorderly conduct	28.1	64.2	17.6
Drunkenness	12.3	110.3	84.8
Vagrancy	19.5	81.5	36.0
Gambling	41.9	43.2	6.0
Suspicion	27.1	130.6	37.9
Not stated	19.5	6.5	2.9
All other offenses	23.5	69.2	24.1
Total	22.8	1,078.4	391.6

* Reproduced from *An American Dilemma*, by Gunnar Myrdal, Vol. 2, p. 973. Copyright 1944 by Harper and Brothers.

Sources: United States Department of Justice, Federal Bureau of Investigation, *Uniform Crime Reports* (Fourth Quarterly Bulletin, 1940), p. 223; and *Sixteenth Census of the United States: 1940, Population,* Preliminary Release Series P-10, No. 1.

ᵃ Population bases taken as of 1940.

ᵇ Less than one-tenth of one per cent.

ᶜ White includes both foreign-born and native-born, and it includes Mexicans (who are separated in the original statistics).

JUVENILE DELINQUENCY AMONG NEGROES

Criminality, which thrives among Negroes in an environment of poverty and social disorganization, has its roots in juvenile delinquency. For nearly a half century, it appears that Negro boys and girls have constituted a disproportionate number of cases of juvenile delinquency in the cities of the country. For example, in Chicago the percentage of Negro boys among juvenile delinquents increased from 4.7 in 1900 to 21.7 in 1930.[23] The increase was most marked between 1920 and 1925, following the migrations from the South, when the percentage of Negro boys jumped from 9.9 to 17.1. Likewise, in New York City, the proportion of Negro boys and girls among those arraigned in the Children's Court increased from 4.2 per cent in 1919 to 8 per cent in 1925, although the Negro population was only 2.7 per cent of the total in 1920.[24] During this same period the proportion of Negro juvenile delinquents in Indianapolis, Gary and Dayton was three to four times as large as their relative numbers in the population.[25] In three southern cities, Richmond, Memphis, and Charleston, South Carolina, Negro cases were one and a half times as numerous as their relative numbers in the population of these cities.

The situation in the Harlem community in New York City during the five years, 1930 to 1934, was characteristic of the larger cities of the North where there were large Negro communities. During the years from 1919 to 1930, the percentage of Negro children among the children arraigned before the children's court had increased from 4.2 to 11.7.[26] However, from 1930 to 1934, the number of boys and girls arrested for juvenile delinquency had declined. During this five year period 1,503 boys and 183 girls were brought before the court. Among those brought before the court there were 137 boys and girls, the majority under 10 years of age, who were neglected and homeless children. Three of the 1,503 boys arrested were charged with homicide

[23] Frazier, *The Negro Family in Chicago*, pp. 205-06.

[24] Joint Committee on Negro Child Study *A Study of Delinquent and Neglected Children Before the New York City Children's Court in 1925* (New York, 1927), p. 6.

[25] See Thomas J. Woofter, *Negro Problems in Cities* (New York, 1928), p. 227.   [26] The Mayor's Commission, *The Negro in Harlem*, pp. 95-97.

and more than a third of them were arrested for larceny, robbery, stealing, burglary, and unlawful entry. On the other hand, it appears that the delinquency of an equally large number was the result of activities that could be controlled through proper recreational activities. For example, about 20 per cent of the boys were arrested for hitching on trolleys and stealing rides on the subway. Moreover, a relatively large proportion of the arrests were due to such offenses as selling newspapers after seven o'clock and shining shoes. These offenses were certainly related to the general poverty of the community.

Although the juvenile delinquency rate among Negroes has fluctuated over the years, it has remained high. For example, in 1932 Negro delinquents constituted 20 per cent of boys' cases and 24 per cent of the girls' cases handled by 68 courts, not including cases handled by the federal courts.[27] In 1943, Negro and nonwhite children comprised 19 per cent of the juvenile delinquency cases handled by the courts.[28] During World War II there was a general increase in juvenile delinquency cases, the increase being greater for girls than for boys. However, the increase among white girls was greater than among Negro girls.[29] The report on the situation in the District of Columbia is typical of cities with high rates of delinquency.[30] Of the children brought before the juvenile court because of delinquency, 68 per cent were Negro; and of the children brought before the court as "destitute of a suitable home," 31 per cent were Negro. Negro children comprised 77 per cent of the "wards of the Board of Public Welfare who were committed because of delinquency and 52 per cent of those committed because of delinquency or neglect." The report continues:

Case histories in the court and the Child-Welfare Division tell the story for a large number of these children. Mothers who must support the family often go to their places of employment early in the morning

[27] United States Department of Labor, *Juvenile-Court Statistics and Federal Juvenile Offenders: 1932* (Washington, 1935), p. 29.

[28] United States Department of Labor, Children's Bureau, "Social Statistics," Supplement to Vol. 9, No. 12 (June, 1945) of *The Child*.

[29] Elsa Castendyck and Sophia Robison, "Juvenile Delinquency Among Girls," *The Social Service Review*, Vol. XVII (September, 1943), pp. 253-64.

[30] United States Department of Labor, Children's Bureau, *The Public Child-Welfare Program in the District of Columbia* (Washington, 1938).

and return home late at night, leaving the children to shift for themselves. Lack of opportunities for wholesome activities leads the children into forbidden forms of recreation or into lawbreaking—playing ball in alleys, begging, selling without a license, unauthorized use of an automobile which has been left conveniently unlocked, or serious forms of theft or burglary. Nothing, apparently, can be done for the children except to remove them from their homes and place them under the guardianship of the public agency for care in other homes or in institutions. It becomes a never-ending circle of commitments and recommitments.[31]

The situation in the District of Columbia in 1945 was similar to that in 1937. Approximately 73 per cent of the juvenile offenders arrested were Negroes.[32]

NEGRO JUVENILE DELINQUENCY IN RELATION TO
THE ORGANIZATION OF THE URBAN COMMUNITY

Although Negro boys and girls have contributed a disproportionate number of juvenile delinquents, this fact becomes understandable when studied in relation to the economic and social organization of Negro communities in the cities of the country. As the result of his first studies of the relation of juvenile delinquency to community organization, Shaw pointed out that the increase in the number of Negro delinquent cases in Chicago might be the result of the movement of Negroes into deteriorated areas from which white Protestants had moved.[33] In an earlier study in which he calculated rates of delinquency along the main thoroughfares radiating from the Loop, he found that the decline in rates along the radial passing through the area occupied by the Negro population was similar to that along the other radials.[34] When, in a later study, the present writer calculated the rates of Negro juvenile delinquency for the seven zones representing the expansion of the Negro population, it was found that

---

[31] *Ibid.*, p. 9.

[32] Washington Criminal Justice Association, *op. cit.*, 1945, p. 7.

[33] Clifford R. Shaw, *Delinquency Areas* (Chicago, 1929), p. 53.

[34] Clifford R. Shaw, "Correlation of Rate of Juvenile Delinquency with Certain Indices of Community Organization and Disorganization," *Publication of the American Sociological Society*, Vol. XXII (1928), pp. 174-79. Shaw did not separate the Negro from the white cases.

the rates declined from 42.8 per 100 boys, 10 to 17 years, in the First Zone to 1.4 per 100 in the Seventh Zone.[35] That the rate of juvenile delinquency among Negroes as among whites varies in relation to the organization of the community has been confirmed by Shaw and his associates in studies of a number of cities.[36]

The decline in the rate of Negro juvenile delinquency in Chicago coincided with the diminishing social disorganization in the successive zones of expansion. The diminishing social disorganization was indicated by an increase in homeownership, a decrease in the number of adult criminals, and a decrease in family dependency, desertion, and illegitimacy. Associated with the marked decline in juvenile delinquency were a decline in illiteracy and a marked increase in the proportion of Negroes in professional and business occupations. Analysis of case studies of juvenile delinquency revealed its relationship to social disorganization as measured by these various indices. Juvenile delinquency was highest in the areas where the recent migrants to the city were concentrated. In these areas the family failed to function as an agency of social control because of the absence of the father and mothers were forced to assume the support of their families. In these areas there was no true neighborhood life; churches were absent or exercised little social control; and the school had no relation to the life of the people. There were no provisions for recreation and the boys and girls acquired patterns of delinquency from the gangs that were formed spontaneously in the "city wilderness." Juvenile delinquency was thus the product of a complex of economic and social forces characteristic of these areas of social disorganization. It almost disappeared entirely in the areas of the Negro community where the stable families with economic security were concentrated.

Our analysis of crime and juvenile delinquency revealed that a disproportionately large number of Negro adults and children have been brought before the courts since Emancipation. The high crime rates were originally ascribed to some physical or moral deficiency of Negroes. But gradually students have come to study Negro crime in

[35] Frazier, *The Negro Family in Chicago*, pp. 209ff.
[36] See Clifford R. Shaw and Henry D. McKay, *Juvenile Delinquency and Urban Areas* (Chicago, 1942).

relation to such economic and social conditions as poverty, ignorance, and urbanization. In recent years Negro criminality has been studied in relation to the effects of the subordinate status of the Negro. Moreover, sociological studies of the high juvenile delinquency rate among Negroes have revealed that it is not higher than that of whites. when studied in relation to the social disorganization of the areas in which Negroes are concentrated in cities. This new understanding of the nature of Negro crime and juvenile delinquency has helped to redefine these problems. But whether this knowledge will be utilized to reduce Negro crime and juvenile delinquency will depend partly upon the extent to which the Negro is integrated into American life and partly upon the measures which the American community adopts to deal with these problems.

CHAPTER XXVI

Mental Deficiency and Insanity

THERE is a paucity of scientific knowledge concerning the extent of mental deficiency or feeblemindedness in the Negro population. The much more extensive information on the incidence of insanity among Negroes has been the basis of conflicting conclusions. In 1914 a white investigator was of the opinion that millionaires could not "better serve society than to found institutions for the segregation and care of the feebleminded Negro" and that such institutions were more appropriate for the Negro than institutions of higher education.[1] This same investigator thought that the higher death rates of the Negro insane were due to the "unwonted excitements and unwonted strains of self-support" of a complex civilization and that in the attempt of the Negro to adjust to an alien environment "his native primitive preorganization snaps and he is crazy for good and fatally." [2] Although such opinions reflected the current prejudices of whites, they were also indicative of the inferences, based upon certain notions about the relation of race to insanity, of psychiatrists concerning the incidence of insanity among Negroes. Only within recent years have studies appeared which have treated the problem in a more scientific spirit.

FEDERAL CENSUS DATA ON NEGRO FEEBLEMINDED

The United States Census report for 1910 showed that "of the 20,731 persons enumerated in institutions for the feeble-minded on January 1, 280 were Negroes; and of the 3,825 feeble-minded persons

[1] Charles H. McCord, *The American Negro as a Dependent, Defective and Delinquent* (Nashville, 1914), p. 169.
[2] *Ibid.*, p. 168.

admitted to such institutions during the year 85 were Negroes." [3] According to these figures the Negroes in institutions represented a rate of 2.8 per 100,000 population as compared with 25 for whites; while the rate of admissions per 100,000 population was 0.9 for Negroes and 4.6 for whites. As the census points out, these figures are "largely fictitious so far as regards the relative prevalence of feeblemindedness among Negroes and whites." [4] Information contained in later census reports on the prevalence of feeblemindedness among Negroes and whites is likewise inadequate. In 1923, on the basis of the institutionalized feebleminded population the rates per 100,000 were 47.3 for native whites and 9.4 for Negroes.[5] These low rates of feeblemindedness among Negroes are an indication of the lack of institutions for Negroes who are mentally defective. This is borne out by the statistics, which show that in the very states where there are large numbers of Negroes there are few or no provisions for the care of feebleminded Negroes. Moreover, in the South where large numbers of Negroes are in rural areas little effort is made to discover feebleminded Negroes. Even in southern cities feebleminded Negroes are likely to be permitted to wander about until they commit some crime. When they are apprehended there is small probability that they will be treated as feebleminded or admitted to institutions for the mentally defective.

MENTAL DEFICIENCY AMONG NEGRO DRAFTEES

An analysis of 69,394 neuropsychiatric cases excluding rejections identified at recruiting posts and army camps during World War I showed that while 31.5 per cent of all cases were classified as mental defectives, 48.3 per cent of the Negro cases were so classified.[6] The report on physical examinations during World War II contains much information on the rejections of drafted men for educational and

[3] Department of Commerce, Bureau of the Census, *Negro Population: 1790-1915* (Washington, 1918), p. 451.   [4] *Ibid.*

[5] Niles Carpenter, "Feebleminded and Pauper Negroes in Public Institutions," in *The American Negro. The Annals*, Philadelphia, 1928, p. 56.

[6] Pearce Bailey, "Contribution to Mental Pathology of Races in the United States," *Archives of Neurology and Psychiatry*, Vol. 7 (February, 1922), pp. 183-201, summarized in Benjamin Malzberg, "Mental Disease Among American Negroes: A Statistical Analysis," p. 395, in Otto Klineberg (Ed.), *Characteristics of the American Negro* (New York, 1944), pp. 373-99.

mental deficiency by both the draft boards and at the induction stations.[7] It was pointed out in the report that it was never possible to clearly separate registrants found illiterate from those who were mentally deficient.[8] This was especially true after April 1, 1943 when illiteracy *per se* was no longer considered a cause for rejection. During the entire period of the report, April 1942 to December 1943, the rejection rate for illiteracy and mental deficiency was 36.8 per 1,000 white registrants and 128.2 per 1,000 Negro registrants. During this same period, the examination of registrants showed 8.7 per 1,000 Negroes and 5.8 per 1,000 whites to be morons, imbeciles, and idiots. For the first part of this period, April 1942 to March 1943, educational and mental deficiency was the second leading cause for Negro rejections, with syphilis as the first cause. For educational and mental deficiency as a single cause 21.2 per cent of the Negro registrants and 8.1 per cent of the white registrants were rejected. When mental deficiency is considered separately as a cause of rejections, the percentage of Negro rejections for this cause was 3.4 as compared with 2.9 for whites.

In August 1942 and January 1943 the medical standards were modified so that educational deficiency alone was no longer a cause for the rejection of registrants. As a result of the modification of medical standards, educational and mental deficiency became the leading cause for the rejection of Negroes. During the second part of the period, April 1943 to December 1943, 8.5 per cent of the Negroes as compared with 2.8 per cent of the whites were rejected because of mental deficiency.

During the entire period, April 1942 to December 1943, 3.4 per cent of Negro rejections as compared with 2.9 per cent of the white rejections by the local boards and the induction stations were because of mental deficiency. But if one considers the rejections of the local boards and the induction stations separately, it appears that the local boards overlooked mental deficiency in Negroes. For the country as a whole the percentages of rejections of Negroes and whites before

[7] Selective Service System, *Physical Examinations of Selective Service Registrants During Wartime*, Medical Statistics Bulletin No. 3, Washington, D. C., November 1, 1944.   [8] *Ibid.*, p. 38.

local boards because of mental deficiency were 1.4 and 4.5 respectively; but at the induction stations the percentages were 4.8 and 2.4 respectively. Since the examination by the local board physician screened the registrants "in order to eliminate those with manifestly disqualifying defects," the local boards' physicians in the South evidently regarded mentally defective Negroes as "normal" Negroes. This assumption is supported by the fact that in nine states—Alabama, Arkansas, Georgia, Kentucky, Mississippi, North Carolina, Oklahoma, Tennessee, and West Virginia—the percentage of Negroes rejected because of mental deficiency was lower than that of whites both by the local boards and at the induction stations. The statistics for Louisiana deviated greatly not only from those for southern states but for the country as a whole. The percentages of rejections by the local boards because of mental deficiency were for Negroes and whites 1.5 and 4.8 respectively, while at the induction stations the percentages were 18.3 and 5.6 respectively for the two races. Even in New York City it appears that mentally deficient Negroes escaped the attention of local board physicians. The percentages of Negroes and whites rejected by the local boards because of mental deficiency were 1.2 and 2.3 respectively; while at the induction stations 4.5 and 1.1 respectively.

FEDERAL CENSUS DATA ON NEGRO INSANITY

Studies of insanity among Negroes extend over a period of more than 50 years and there are federal census statistics on the Negro insane as far back as 1850. The federal decennial enumerations of the insane for the period, 1850 to 1890, included persons at home as well as in institutions. During the forty-year period, the incidence among whites in the United States increased from 766 in 1850 to 1,977 in 1880 and 1,814 per 1,000,000 in 1890; while the rate for Negroes increased from 175 in 1850 to 912 in 1880 and declined to 886 in 1890.[9] In the North Atlantic Division the rate for both whites and Negroes was higher at each census than in the South. In the North Atlantic

[9] See Benjamin Malzberg, "Mental Disease Among American Negroes: A Statistical Analysis," in Otto Klineberg (Ed.), *Characteristics of the American Negro* (New York, 1944) pp. 373 ff.

Division the rate for whites was 1,009 in 1850, 2,478 in 1880, and 2,384 in 1890; while the rate for Negroes increased from 869 in 1850 to 2,550 in 1890. From these figures it appears that in 1890 there was relatively more insanity among Negroes than among whites in the North.

In fact, the ratio of the insanity rate among whites to the insanity rate among Negroes decreased during the 40 years from 4.4 to 2.0 in the country as a whole; in the North Atlantic Division from 1.2 to 0.9 and in the South Atlantic Division from 5.2 to 2.1. Thus it appears that insanity among Negroes as measured by census figures increased rapidly during the 25 years following the Civil War. It is often assumed that there was little insanity among the slave population and that the increase in insanity among Negroes was due to the removal of the master's protective care. Whether this assumption is true or not, it is true, as we have shown in an earlier chapter, that there was considerable social disorganization and racial conflict during these years and it is quite possible that it resulted in an increase in insanity. Moreover, since the Negro population in the North was concentrated in cities where there was much economic insecurity and social disorganization, it is conceivable that the insanity rate among northern Negroes was higher than among southern Negroes. But the difference indicated by the census statistics may not be a true measure of the difference since the enumeration of the Negro insane depended upon the judgment of the enumerators.

Subsequent federal statistics on insanity have included only the institutional population. According to the federal census of 1904, Negro patients in institutions and Negro admissions amounted to a little more than one-half their relative numbers in the population of the country.[10] Here again one may see how the absence of institutional provisions for Negroes suffering with mental disease causes rates based upon the institutionalized Negro population to be useless. In 1904 the vast majority of the Negro population was concentrated in the South, where there were few provisions for the Negro insane even if their relatives or the public authorities were disposed to commit

[10] *Ibid.*, p. 376.

them to an institution. According to the 1910 federal census the Negro insane in institutions constituted 131.4 per 100,000 population while the rate for whites was 213.2. The admission rates for Negroes and whites were 44.6 and 68.7 per 100,000 respectively. These low rates for Negroes were, as in 1904, due to the fact that Negroes were concentrated in the South. In the North the rates for both the number of Negro patients and the admissions were considerably higher than the rates for whites.[11] The federal census of mental patients in institutions in 1923 used first admissions to determine the incidence of mental disease. According to this census the rate for Negroes was 56.4 per 100,000 population as compared with 69.5 for the white population.[12] A year previous to this census, Laughlin undertook to work out a ratio of insanity among various ethnic and racial elements in the population to the proportion which each element constituted of the total population.[13] He found that the Negro had only 57 per cent of his quota which was much lower than the quotas for native and foreign-born whites and next to the lowest quota which was 42 per cent for the Japanese.

According to the federal census of institutionalized patients in 1933, the incidence of mental disease among Negroes exceeded that of the population of the country as a whole. Moreover, Negroes had a higher rate of first admissions in all except four of the southern states. In view of the absence of adequate institutional care for the Negro insane, the higher rate of first admissions for Negroes is significant. As Negroes have migrated to northern cities, there is greater probability that insane Negroes will be discovered and given institutional care. Moreover, the urbanization of the Negro population has most likely increased the insanity rate among Negroes and these statistics, though inadequate, are a partial index to the effect of urban living upon Negroes.

[11] United States Bureau of the Census, *Negro Population, 1790-1915*, p. 448.
[12] Malzberg, *op. cit.*, pp. 376-77.
[13] H. H. Laughlin, *An Analysis of America's Melting Pot.* Commission on Immigration. November 21, 1922. Quoted in Otto Klineberg, *Race Differences* (New York, 1935), p. 243.

RECENT STUDIES OF NEGRO INSANITY

During the past decade or so a number of significant studies of insanity among Negroes have appeared. One such study undertook to determine the relative incidence of insanity among Negroes as indicated by statistics for state hospitals in Alabama, Georgia, and Illinois and to relate the incidence to socioeconomic factors.[14] According to this study, for the decade, 1923 to 1932, the incidence of the Negro first admissions, per 100,000 population to state hospitals in Georgia and Alabama was only slightly higher than the incidence for whites, while in Illinois the incidence for Negroes was over twice as great as for whites. In Georgia the rate of admissions was higher for the urban than the rural population. Another article appearing about the same time contains an analysis of the incidence of insanity among Negroes in Cincinnati.[15] The admissions to the Cincinnati General Hospital showed a preponderance among Negroes of all types of psychoses except those occurring in later life, such as involutional or arteriosclerotic reactions. Alcoholic psychoses and syphilis of the central nervous system were higher among Negroes than among whites as was the incidence of syphilis with psychoses. There was no evidence, however, that psychoses among Negroes were different from those among whites as regards etiology, diagnosis, psychotic manifestations and treatment. This study confirmed the findings in regard to New York City which will be considered later.

A more recent study is of particular interest because the incidence of insanity among Negroes is contrasted with insanity among whites in relation to the ecological organization of the modern urban community.[16] The area inhabited by Negroes in Chicago, together with hobohemia, rooming house areas, and the areas in which the foreign-born were resident, had the highest rates of schizophrenia. However,

[14] Joseph S. Simeon, *A Comparative Study of the Incidence of Insanity Among Negroes and Whites*, Phelps-Stokes Studies, No. 14, Bulletin of the University of Georgia (Athens, 1938).

[15] Phillip S. Wagner, "A Comparative Study of Negro and White Admissions to the Psychiatric Pavilion of Cincinnati General Hospital," *The American Journal of Psychiatry*, Vol. 95, pp. 167-83.

[16] See Robert E. L. Faris and H. Warren Dunham, *Mental Disorders in Urban Areas* (Chicago, 1939).

schizophrenia rates among Negroes in the city as a whole varied considerably. Like the schizophrenia rates for whites, the rates for Negroes were much higher in rooming house, tenement, and certain types of apartment areas than in areas of single homes. It was further noted but no explanation offered in this study that the catatonic rate for Negroes was high while the paranoid rate was low.

INSANITY AMONG NEGRO DRAFTEES

The most recent statistics on the incidence of insanity among Negroes are to be found in the report on the physical examinations of registrants for selective service.[17] As a result of the examination of registrants, it was found that 50.3 per 1,000 Negroes as compared with 70.6 per 1,000 whites were suffering from mental diseases. The incidence for white registrants was higher for grave mental and personality disorders, major abnormalities of mood, psychoneurotic disorders, chronic inebriety, drug addiction, and mental diseases not classified. Only in the case of psychopathic personality did the rate for Negroes (21.5 as compared with 17.6) exceed that for whites. Likewise, the percentage of Negro rejections for mental disease was lower than the percentage of white rejections for the same cause. For the country as a whole, during the period, April 1942 to March 1943, 5.8 per cent of the Negro rejections and 14.2 of the white rejections were for mental disease. During the period, April 1943 to December 1943, mental disease was responsible for 13.0 per cent of the Negro rejections and 19.2 per cent of the white rejections. In most of the states the percentage of whites rejected because of mental disease was higher than that of Negroes. However, in Massachusetts and the state of New York exclusive of New York City, although the percentage of whites rejected by the local boards was greater than that of Negroes, the percentage of Negroes rejected at the induction stations for mental diseases was greater than that for whites. The same situation was found in New York City where 3.7 per cent of Negroes as compared with 7.2 per cent of the whites were rejected for mental disease by the local boards; while 17.3 per cent of the Negroes as compared with 16.8 per

[17] Selective Service System, *Physical Examinations of Selective Service Registrants During Wartime.*

cent of the whites were rejected at the induction stations because of mental disease. Thus it appears that the more careful examinations by the induction stations revealed mental disease to be as high among Negroes as among whites in the states where the Negro population is concentrated in urban areas.

A CRITICAL ANALYSIS OF INSANITY AMONG NEGROES

The most careful analysis of statistics on the incidence of insanity among Negroes is to be found in the studies of Malzberg.[18] His studies are based on first admissions to all hospitals in the state of New York for the three year period, July 1, 1928 to June 30, 1931. During this period, there were 1,841 Negro first admissions, 95.1 per cent of which were to civil state hospitals, 3.9 per cent to hospitals for the criminal insane, and only one per cent to licensed institutions. A smaller percentage of white admissions were to both the civil state hospitals and the hospitals for the criminal insane; and a larger percentage—4.7— of the whites were admitted to licensed institutions. The average annual rate of admissions per 100,000 population was 150.6 for Negroes and 73.7 for whites.

The distribution of the Negro and white patients with reference to psychoses showed important contrasts. For the Negroes, dementia praecox comprised 29.5 per cent of the admissions; general paresis, 16.6 per cent; manic depressive psychoses, 11.6 per cent; and alcoholic psychoses, 10 per cent. Among the whites general paresis constituted only 9.4 per cent of psychoses and alcoholic psychoses only 5.9 per cent. Whites had a larger percentage of senile psychoses and psychoses with cerebral arteriosclerosis. Since the mean age of Negroes was less than that of whites, it tended to increase the relative frequency of Negroes with dementia praecox and manic depressive psychoses. From these figures, the author concludes, it was clear that mental disease

[18] See Benjamin Malzberg, "Mental Disease Among Negroes in New York State," *Human Biology*, Vol. 7, pp. 471-513; "Migration and Mental Diseases Among Negroes in New York State," *American Journal of Physical Anthropology*, Vol. XXI, pp. 107-13; and "Mental Disease Among American Negroes: A Statistical Analysis," *loc. cit.*, pp. 373ff.

when it occurred among Negroes was much more likely to be general paresis and alcoholic psychoses than among whites.

When Negro and white rates for the various psychoses were determined on the basis of population, the difference between the two races in respect to certain psychoses is greater than that indicated above. The rates of dementia praecox for Negroes and whites are 44.4 and 19.2 per 100,000 population respectively; manic depressive psychoses, 17.4 and 10; general paresis, 25 and 9.4; alcoholic psychoses, 15.1 and 4.3. When the rates of admission were standardized for the age of the Negro and white population the rates of admission for all psychoses were 224.7 for Negroes and 97.4 for whites, the Negro rate thus being 2.3 times that of whites. The standardized rate of first admissions for Negroes in New York City was only slightly (233.3 as compared with 224.7) above that for the state as was also true of the white rate. The standardized rates of first admissions for Negroes in New York City were higher than the Negro rates for the state for general paresis and practically the same for alcoholic psychoses.

An important fact brought out by this study was that Negroes indigenous to the state of New York had a much lower rate of first admissions than Negro migrants. The rate for Negroes born in New York State was 40 per 100,000 as against 186.2 for Negroes born in other states. This difference is of great significance in interpreting the greater incidence of certain psychoses among Negroes as compared with their incidence among whites. Migration results in considerable social disorganization, involving the breaking of family ties and promiscuous sexual relations. The high incidence of paresis, which is the result of syphilitic infection, is doubtless related to social disorganization. Likewise, personal disorganization is often associated with drinking. This probably accounts for the large incidence of alcoholic psychoses among Negroes. Moreover, Negroes are concentrated in domestic service, in which the incidence of mental disease is relatively high for all races.

The facts which have been presented in this chapter concerning mental deficiency and insanity seem to warrant certain conclusions in regard to the Negro's adjustment to American society. First, the available statistics do not provide conclusive evidence that there is more feeblemindedness among Negroes than among whites. It is conceivable, of course, that the slightly higher proportion of Negro selective service registrants rejected because of mental deficiency is indicative of differences in the occurrence of mental deficiency among the two races. The brutalizing effects of slavery and the racial conflicts following Emancipation might have tended to kill off the mentally better endowed Negroes. The isolation of the Negro in rural areas could have provided a favorable environment for the propagation of mentally deficient stocks. Moreover, the ignorance and folk practices of the Negro regarding gestation and the lack of maternal care during pregnancy and childbirth could have produced a disproportional number of "congenital" as opposed to "hereditary" feebleminded Negroes. At any rate the differences between the Negroes and whites are not large enough to be important.

Likewise, in the case of insanity, it does not appear that mental breakdowns have been a conspicuous feature in the adjustment of the Negro to western civilization. In fact, mental disease has not taken as great a toll as have physical diseases such as tuberculosis and syphilis. The latter disease is doubtless responsible for a large percentage of insanity as the Negro becomes urbanized. The increase in mental disease seems to be related to the mobility and the social disorganization incident to urbanization. Therefore, although it is impossible to predict the probable trend of insanity among Negroes, there is the possibility that it may increase as the result of the social disorganization incident to the breaking down of their traditional isolation and during the process of their integration into American society, especially in urban centers.

CHAPTER XXVII

Race Relations

THE development of the Negro community with its separate institutions should be viewed in the light of the changing character of race relations in the United States. This has been revealed throughout our discussion of the character and function of these institutions among Negroes. Because every phase of Negro life in the United States is touched or permeated by the race relations aspect, it appears important to view all of the subjects thus far discussed in the light of the relations between the Negro and white elements, in so far as they are separate segments, of American society. In studying race relations as a social phenomenon, it will be necessary to single out two important features for analysis. These two features are race prejudice and racial discriminations, particularly in their manifestation in public policy.

NATURE OF RACE PREJUDICE

Before analyzing the nature of race prejudice, it is necessary to consider first the nature of prejudice in general. As indicated in the etymology of the word, prejudice is a pre-judgment in the sense that it is a judgment concerning objects and persons not based upon knowledge or experience. The most elemental manifestation of prejudice in this broad meaning of the word is to be found in the personal likes and dislikes and preferences and antipathies which everyone exhibits in regard to food, clothes, and art as well as persons.[1] Although these so-called personal idiosyncrasies, tastes, or prejudices are often deep-seated and appear to be organic reactions, they have been conditioned

[1] See Louis Wirth. "Race and Public Policy," *Scientific Monthly,* Vol. 58, (1944) pp. 302-3.

by the experiences of the individual in his group life. The experiences which are responsible for personal taste and idiosyncrasies are often forgotten. In fact, prejudices may not result from personal experiences with objects or persons. Very often prejudices or dislikes of objects and persons are reactions acquired from other persons or they are attitudes taken over from the culture of the group.

Race prejudice, as Faris has pointed out, is a special form of prejudice directed toward some racial group.[2] Like prejudices and dislikes in general, race prejudice consists of certain preconceived attitudes which are not based upon scientific knowledge or facts concerning a racial group. The very term racial prejudice, it should be noted, suggests an important element in the phenomenon which we are analyzing. Race prejudice is directed not against an individual with certain observable characteristics but against the individual as a member of the category "race." The categoric picture which a prejudiced person carries in his head affects even his perception of an individual identified with a race that is the object of his prejudice. It is probably true that to most white people all Negroes look alike, just as to Negroes who have prejudices against Chinese all Chinese look alike. When a person has prejudice against a racial group, a person identified with the racial group fails to emerge as an individual.[3] With true insight into the nature of prejudice, Sinclair Lewis has the enraged neighbors, who have discovered that Neil Kingsblood has some remote Negro ancestor, declare that they are going to drive out the black, thick-lipped brute.

Since race prejudice is "an attitude with an emotional bias," [4] the reasons which a person offers for his prejudice are "rationalizations" rather than "reasonable grounds" for his attitude. In providing reasons for his attitude he is attempting to make it appear logical or justifiable. For example, whites often justify their prejudice against Negroes

[2] Ellsworth Faris, "The Natural History of Race Prejudice" in his *The Nature of Human Nature* (New York, 1937), p. 354.

[3] This fact has been supported by an experiment in which whites with favorable attitudes toward Negroes were more competent in differentiating new faces among pictures of Negroes from old faces than whites with unfavorable attitudes toward Negroes. See Virginia Seeleman, "The Influence of Attitude Upon the Remembering of Pictorial Material," *Archives of Psychology*, No. 258, September, 1940.   [4] Wirth, *op. cit.*, p. 303.

on the grounds that the latter are lazy, lacking in intelligence, or immoral. When they undertake to justify their prejudice against Japanese, they give other "reasons" since they do not attribute these qualities to Japanese. The relation of rationalizations to race prejudice may be observed in many ways, such as in the changing reasons which have been advanced against the education of the Negro. The first reason advanced for not educating the Negro was that he was not capable of being educated. After numerous Negroes acquired an education, it was argued that education unfitted the Negro for labor and made a criminal of him. The latest rationalization which is heard among some whites is that education makes the Negro unhappy.

The prejudice which one has against a member of a racial group may lead one in a conflict situation to desire to exterminate the object of one's prejudice. But, as in other human relations, a *modus vivendi* is generally established in regard to the racial group which is the object of prejudice. This involves primarily the question of status. During the period of slavery when the inferior status of the Negro was fixed, race prejudice tended to be absent. Whatever racial prejudice was manifested toward the Negro was directed against the free Negro. In a society based upon slavery, there was no place for a free Negro. The reference here to "place" is not to "place" in the spatial sense, but to place in the social sense or *status*.[5] Those who are prejudiced against a racial group are generally eager to keep the members of the racial group in a subordinate social status. This explains why the Negro maid with her cap and apron may enter a hotel from which a Negro college professor or scientist is excluded.

INFLUENCE OF CULTURAL FACTORS ON RACE PREJUDICE

From what has been presented concerning the nature of race prejudice, it is apparent that cultural factors play a rôle in its form and genesis. It is necessary, however, to give special consideration to the cultural factor because of its primary importance in the development

[5] See Robert E. Park, "The Bases of Race Prejudice," *The American Negro. The Annals* (American Academy of Social and Political Science), Vol. 140, pp. 11-20.

of race prejudice. It is generally agreed by scholars and even laymen who have been in a position to observe race relations that race prejudice is not an "instinctive" reaction. Differences in skin color, hair texture, or the contour of one's face do not in themselves arouse race prejudice.[6] Children are, of course, aware of color differences but their attitudes toward a person of a different color are determined by their experiences with a person of a different color. There is no basis for the statement by Duncan that "There is something about the white race that causes the black Negro to be repugnant to it."[7] Because of the emotional dependence of the white child upon her black nurse or mammy in the ante-bellum South, there was no repulsion felt toward the black skin. Nor do white children who play with Negro children feel any repulsion toward their black skins.[8] The Negro child is regarded simply as a human being with the same feelings and emotions as other children. A change in attitude appears as the result of the definitions—gestures, emotional reactions as well as verbal responses—which the child acquires from his parents and white playmates.

As the child grows up his attitude toward Negroes is molded by many cultural factors in his environment. In the South he learns that the Negro is a different kind of a being if, for example, he expresses the desire to have a Negro playmate at his party. In this manner the family may give him at an early age a certain conception of the Negro or what is regarded as the Negro's proper status in relation to whites. When the white child enters school, he learns that Negro children are not eligible to attend the same school because of their color which is defined in terms of race.[9] Likewise, the exclusion of Negroes from

[6] In an early statement on the nature of race prejudice Park wrote that "It is evident that there is in race prejudice, as distinguished from class and caste prejudice, an instinctive factor based on the fear of the unfamiliar and the uncomprehended." See Robert E. Park and Ernest W. Burgess, *Introduction to the Science of Sociology* (Chicago, 1924), p. 578. Later Park based race prejudice on the normal tendency of the mind to react to individuals as members of categories and that these categories involve status. See Robert E. Park, "The Bases of Prejudice," *The American Negro. The Annals*, Vol. 140, pp. 11-20.

[7] Hannibal G. Duncan, *The Changing Race Relationship in the Border and Northern States* (Philadelphia, 1922), p. 17.

[8] One such white child in Atlanta, Ga., thought that the mother of the Negro child had accidentally poured too much iodine on the Negro child.

[9] See Bruno Lasker, *Race Attitudes in Children* (New York, 1929), pp. 115ff., on the effect of institutions on racial prejudices in children.

churches and recreational institutions instill attitudes concerning the place of the Negro in society. In the North, especially in some of the smaller cities where there are few Negroes, the children of the two races may play together and associate in other ways without the children of either race being conscious of racial differences. But usually when the children reach puberty or they begin to have their social affairs in high schools, the white parents and school authorities object to the inclusion of Negroes. In the larger cities of the North with their large Negro communities, Negro and white children grow up largely in different social worlds despite their association in schools.

One might say that the entire culture of the American people has until World War II and the years following stamped the Negro as an inferior human being unfit for assimilation into American life. One might begin with the terms which are used in referring to Negroes. In the South the term "nigger" which expresses contempt has been used generally, while even in the North there have been attempts to rationalize the spelling of the word Negro without a capital "n." Newspapers in the South have generally refused to carry the picture of a Negro unless he has committed a crime. Until recently when the Negro was portrayed in literature he appeared only as a fool or sycophant and in the movies, except where he appears in special pictures, the Negro must appear as a buffoon or a servant. All of these cultural influences tend to instill racial prejudices in the young and confirm the stereotypes of the Negro in the minds of adults.

COMPETITION AND RACE PREJUDICE

To be prejudiced against a racial group involves an unwillingness to compete with members of that group for social position or economic goods. As we have seen, during slavery there was no rivalry between slaveholders and slaves for social position and there was no competition for economic rewards. On the other hand, where the white mechanics were thrown into competition with free Negro mechanics, the former manifested the fiercest kind of race prejudice toward the latter. Following emancipation when the two races often became rivals for offices and social position, race prejudice appeared among the former slaveholding class. Moreover, as both races became involved generally in economic competition, prejudice against the Negro as a race became widespread.

In the history of the labor movement in the North as well as in the South, it is apparent that the exclusion of the Negro worker has been based upon the desire to eliminate him as a competitor. During periods of economic stress, when competition for jobs has been along racial lines, race prejudice has become more acute. The prominence of the economic factor in race prejudice has led some investigators to regard the economic motive as the dominant factor in race prejudice.[10] According to this view, race prejudice exists because something is to be gained and the most important gains are economic. Undoubtedly, economic competition plays an important rôle in race prejudice. However, it should be noted that members of different races may compete without arousing race prejudice. Race prejudice appears only when members of different races who are in competition appear not as individuals but as representatives of races in competition. The desire to eliminate the Negro as a competitor has been rationalized on the grounds of his inefficiency or his inferior mental endowment. Such rationalizations are not confined to those in competition but may be found in theoretical discussions of the relative value of different races.[11]

PERSONAL FACTORS IN RACE PREJUDICE

Although prejudice against another race is determined by the culture of one's group and is accentuated by competition with the race which is the object of prejudice, individual manifestations of racial prejudice are affected by personal factors. The two most important personal factors which appear to be responsible for intense prejudice on the part of individuals are the feeling of insecurity and frustrations. Individuals who are insecure economically or socially and are forced to compete with members of a different race are more likely to exhibit intense race prejudice than those who have a secure social and eco-

[10] See Otto Klineberg, *Social Psychology* (New York, 1940), pp. 391 ff. While recognizing the influence of folkways and customs, Klineberg holds that the economic motive is the dominant motive in race prejudice.

[11] See, for example, Paul Popenoe and Roswell H. Johnson, *Applied Eugenics* (New York, 1933), p. 303.

nomic position.[12] In the South the whites who have enjoyed social and economic security have always manifested less intense prejudice against Negroes than the poor whites. Where individuals have competed with members of a race that is the object of prejudice, they have been disposed to attribute their own failings and shortcomings to the unfair practices or some other derogatory characteristic of the other racial group.

Individual differences in race prejudice are not only characteristic of different social and economic classes. They vary among individuals on the same economic and social level and even among members of the same family. Individuals among the poor whites who achieve social and economic security are less likely to manifest the intense racial prejudice of the less secure and less successful members of their class or their own family. However, those individuals who have not completely escaped from the insecure social and economic position of the poor whites are likely to have intense prejudices. It is often among the small businessmen whose economic and social position is insecure that the most intense prejudice is shown toward the Negro, especially those Negroes who are acquiring education and economic security. In a region like the South, where large numbers of whites are economically and socially insecure and are often frustrated in their attempts to escape from their insecurity, the intense race prejudice becomes almost a collective neurosis. A crime committed by a Negro may become the occasion for attacking innocent Negroes. The Negro becomes the scapegoat for their failures and frustrations. In fact, over many years the Negro has been the scapegoat in the South for the ignorance and poverty of the region.

DISCRIMINATIONS ARISING FROM RACE PREJUDICE

In the discussion so far, race prejudices might appear to be a matter of private concern, but as Wirth has pointed out, prejudices "are by no means purely private, either in origin or in their consequences." [13] As a private matter race prejudice may lead one to refuse to have a member of a different race as a dinner guest or as a partner in mar-

[12] Wirth, *op. cit.*, p. 304. See also Hortense Powdermaker, *Probing Our Prejudices* (New York, 1944), pp. 30-33.   [13] See Wirth, *op. cit.*, p. 306.

riage. Because of racial prejudice, one may not sit next to a member of a different race in a railway coach or on a streetcar. These manifestations of race prejudice are of private concern. On the other hand, where such prejudices become the basis of laws against intermarriage and segregation in transportation, they represent public discrimination and become a matter of public concern.

Both private and public discriminations arising from race prejudice are designed to maintain the Negro in an inferior social status and to prevent Negroes from competing with the whites. In the North the personal manifestations of race prejudice have been more conspicuous in race relations than public discriminations. On the other hand, in the South, race relations have been characterized mainly by public discriminations. In an article which appeared in 1904, Thomas pointed out the difference between the feeling of northern and southern whites toward the Negro:

Of the relation of black to white in this country it is perhaps true that the antipathy of the southerner for the negro is rather caste-feeling than race-prejudice, while the feeling of the northerner is race-prejudice proper. In the North, where there has been no contact with the negro and no activity connections, there is no caste-feeling, but there exists a sort of *skin*-prejudice—a horror of the external aspect of the negro—and many northerners report that they have a feeling against eating from a dish handled by a negro. The association of master and slave in the South was, however, close, even if not intimate, and much of the feeling of physical repulsion for a black skin disappeared.[14]

The difference between the feeling of northern and southern whites toward the Negro, which Thomas has indicated, is important in the consideration of discriminations against the Negro. In the North much of the discrimination against the Negro has been arbitrary because it reflects individual prejudices, involving in some cases physical repulsion, against the Negro. The whites in the South have been concerned with keeping the Negro in an inferior social position and preventing him from competing with whites. One might say that until a decade or so ago, in the minds of northern whites there was no *place*

[14] William I. Thomas, "The Psychology of Race-Prejudice," *The American Journal of Sociology*, Vol. IX, pp. 609-10.

for the Negro in the social structure, whereas in the South the Negro had a *place* but it was an inferior *place* or inferior social status in the social structure. The public discriminations which are supported by law as well as custom in the South have led some investigators to regard race relations in the South as a caste system.[15]

The pattern of race relations in the South has some of the features of a caste system. There is the legal prohibition against intermarriage and there are strong taboos against sexual contacts between Negro men and white women which have a quasi-religious sanction. Negroes are restricted to menial occupations and in the relations of the races the superior position of whites and inferior position of the Negroes must be recognized. There are symbols and an etiquette in race relations which support the taboos and the relative social positions of the two races. All of this represents or has represented a certain "ortho-

[15] According to Warner, the social organization of the South involves two kinds of stratification; a caste system and a class structure in each caste. W. Lloyd Warner, "American Caste and Class," *The American Journal of Sociology*, Vol. XLII, pp. 234-37. In his Introduction to *Deep South*, Warner elaborated his theory of caste and undertook to show why the term was a truer description of the character of "race relations" than race prejudice. Allison Davis, Burleigh B. Gardner and Mary R. Gardner, *Deep South* (Chicago, 1941), pp. 7-8. In the latest statement of his position in "A Methodological Note" at the end of St. Clair Drake and Horace R. Cayton, *Black Metropolis* (New York, 1945), pp. 769-82, Warner undertakes to show that while there is a "noticeable difference" between race relations in the deep South and in Chicago, the same type of status relationship exists between the races. Hence, he claims that the term "caste" describes the character of race relations in Chicago as well as in the deep South. Anyone acquainted with race relations in this country knows that there is a fundamental difference between the status of Negroes in Mississippi and in Chicago. The "caste" hypothesis of race relations has not remained unchallenged. See Oliver C. Cox, "The Modern School of Race Relations," *Social Forces*, Vol. 21, pp. 218-30. See also Oliver C. Cox, *Caste, Class and Race; A Study in Social Dynamics*. Garden City, New York, 1948. We shall only point out some of the most important criticisms of this supposedly new conceptual approach to race relations in the United States. The approach is designated as "supposedly new" because numerous writers had previously used the term "caste" to describe race relations. But they have used the term in a less formal fashion, possibly because they recognized that many phases of race relations lacked the character of a caste system. The term caste is an essentially static concept, while race relations involve group conflicts and attitudes which are constantly changing. Moreover, the studies which were supposedly guided by the "caste" hypothesis have on the whole been a documentation of the concept. They have failed to deal with the dynamic aspects of race relations and show under what conditions the patterns of race relations have changed and how attitudes of whites and Negroes have changed.

doxy" in race relations.[16] Although in some rural and semirural areas of the South, race relations have conformed closely to this orthodoxy, there have always been certain features in race relations which are not congruent with and are opposed to a caste system.

First, it might be pointed out that there is no consistent pattern of race relations in the South. One of the important phases in race relations in the South involves the segregation of the races. The variations and contradictions in the patterns of segregation are so great as to preclude the logic underlying a caste system.[17] The taboos and restrictions placed upon the relations of the races and etiquette observed vary not only according to areas and classes but according to the education and economic power of Negroes. Moreover, the so-called caste restrictions are more effective in the rural areas and small towns than in the cities where there is greater enlightenment and more mobility. Finally, and this is of crucial importance, Negroes who comprise the so-called lower caste do not accept the discriminations, and expect some day to see them abolished. The discriminations against the Negro are opposed to the political and religious ideals which are accepted by both whites and Negroes. Race relations in the South represent an accommodation or external adjustment which always involves a latent conflict. The conflict is increasingly becoming overt in the legal battles of the Negro for political and economic equality and the abolition of segregation.

EFFECTS OF DISCRIMINATION ON THE NEGRO

We have already seen the effects of racial discrimination on the health and survival of Negroes and on their employment and ability to enter into economic competition with whites. Here we are concerned with the effect of discriminations on the aspirations and achievements of the Negro and on his general outlook on life.

The theory of separate but equal educational and other facilities has never worked out in practice. Separate education for Negroes has always meant inferior schools and inferior teaching personnel for Negro children. Inferior schools have caused a high rate of illiteracy

16 See Thomas P. Bailey, *Race Orthodoxy in the South* (New York, 1908).
17 See Charles S. Johnson, *Patterns of Negro Segregation* (New York, 1943).

to continue among Negroes since Emancipation. The resulting mental isolation of Negroes which continued a half century was only partially broken down by the mass migrations of Negroes to northern cities during and following World War I. Because of the discriminations in regard to employment the Negro has been kept in the lowest paid and unskilled occupations, and thus there has been no premium placed upon exceptional skill and talent among Negroes. If Joe Louis and Roland Hayes had remained in the South they would probably never have developed the desire to excel in their respective fields. Even if they had developed the desire to achieve skill and excellence in their respective fields, they could never under the system of racial discrimination in the South have acquired the necessary training and education.

Some persons have advanced the opinion that the oppression of the Negro in the United States has spurred the Negroes to achieve what they would not have otherwise accomplished. For example, in comparing the racial situation in Brazil with that in the United States, Pierson makes the following statement:

It is possible that the Brazilian blacks and mixed-bloods, lacking as they do in most cases the sense of inferiority long characteristic of the Negro in the United States, particularly of the mixed-blood, have been less activated by personal ambition. Feeling themselves less under the necessity of demonstrating to a hostile white world their individual talents and abilities, they have not had the same incentive for social advancement and, consequently, have not, perhaps, as a group, risen in class as rapidly as has the Negro in the United States.[18]

In regard to this statement it should be noted first that Pierson has introduced some confusion about what he means by a Negro. In the United States, blacks and mixed-bloods, including those without any sign of Negro ancestry, are classified as Negroes. On the other hand, when one refers to Negroes in Brazil, one means black people. As is well known, more than 50 per cent of the Brazilian population is comprised of mixed-bloods. These mixed-bloods have played a conspicu-

[18] *Negroes in Brazil* by Donald Pierson. Copyright 1942 by The University of Chicago Press, p. 349.

ous rôle in Brazilian life for a hundred years.[19] Since there is no way of distinguishing Indian and Negro ancestry among mixed-bloods, Indian ancestry is often played up. It is obvious, then, that Pierson does not mean to say that blacks and mixed-bloods in the United States have achieved more than the majority of the Brazilian population. The fact is that Brazil provides the instance in which the absence of race prejudice or caste based upon racial descent has enabled blacks and mixed-bloods to rise to distinction, measured by universal standards, in most fields of human achievements.[20] On the other hand, in the United States racial discrimination and color-caste have restricted even the mixed-bloods, who enjoyed some initial cultural and economic advantages over the blacks. Only when the Negro in the United States has been able to escape from the more oppressive forms of discrimination has he made noteworthy achievements. Since the mass migrations from the South, beginning with World War I, the Negro has made more gains in civilization than during his entire previous history in the United States.

While, on the one hand, white Americans have denied the Negro the right to compete with whites, on the other hand they have given millions of dollars in philanthropy to aid him in overcoming the effects of discrimination. In a sense the Negro has always been the ward of the nation, so to speak, or the ward of some philanthropic interests. Consequently, the Negro has never been permitted to achieve the full stature of a man through competition with whites. Many of his leaders have owed their pre-eminence to the fact that they have played the rôle of mediators in a pattern of race relations based upon the economic dependence and social subordination of the Negro. The dominant white interests have singled out mediocre Negroes for the rôle of "great Negroes," while Negroes of superior mental endowment and courage have been crushed as irresponsible radicals.

[19] E. Franklin Frazier, "A Comparison of Negro-White Relations in Brazil and in the United States," *Transactions of the New York Academy of Sciences*, Series II, Vol. 6 (May, 1944), pp. 251-69.

[20] Gallagher has called attention to the fact that "other nations which do not discriminate against the Negro have been enriched by minority contributions in such proportions as to dwarf into insignificance the achievements of the Negro in the United States." Buell G. Gallagher, *Color and Conscience: The Irrepressible Conflict* (New York, 1946, p. 123).

Thus a factual and objective basis for the charge that the Negro is a "child" race has been provided in the whole system of racial discrimination. It is no wonder that since the Negro has been treated and regarded as a "child" race, whites have not taken him seriously. In fact, as the result of the system of discrimination, the Negro has not been permitted to play a serious rôle in the economic and social life of the nation. However, as the Negro population has become urbanized and the Negro worker has become integrated into the labor movement, the Negro is ceasing to be the ward of philanthropy. Moreover, as the result of the Negro's increasing political power, he is beginning to occupy strategic positions in American life. For example, the appointment of a Negro as the governor of a territorial dependency was symbolic, at least, of the adult status which the Negro is acquiring in American life.

One of the truly remarkable phases of race relations in the United States is the fact that whites and Negroes do not know each other as human beings. Most of the sentimental talk of southern whites to the effect that they know Negroes simply reveals the barriers which have been erected between the races since Emancipation. Southern whites know the stereotype of the Negro which provides a certain moral justification for the white's behavior and attitudes toward Negroes.[21] Nor has the northern white known the Negro since he has only reacted to a different stereotype.[22] White Americans do not know Negroes for the simple reason that race prejudice and discrimination have prevented normal human intercourse between the two races. The so-called liberal white man or "friend" of the Negro generally views the Negro with a feeling of pathos or a patronizing attitude. For example, the emotional gifts of the Negro have been exalted while his intellectual inferiority has been accepted as true.[23] Often in appraising the intellectual and artistic achievements of Negroes, there is a tendency to appraise them according to standards inferior to the generally

[21] See John Dollard, *Caste and Class in a Southern Town* (New Haven, 1927), Chapter XVI.

[22] See Daniel Katz and Kenneth W. Braly, "Racial Stereotypes of One Hundred College Students," *The Journal of Abnormal and Social Psychology*, Vol. 28, pp. 280-90, and by the same authors, "Racial Prejudice and Racial Stereotypes," *ibid.*, Vol. 30, pp. 175-93.   [23] Faris, *op. cit.*, p. 365.

accepted standards. The unexpressed pathos seems to be: it is good for the poor Negro.

As the result of racial barriers, the attitude of pathos on the part of whites is matched by a tendency toward idealization of whites on the part of Negroes. For example, in a study of racial stereotypes of 100 students in a Negro college in Virginia of whom 80 were from the South, over 50 listed the traits, "musical," "superstitious," and "very religious," as characteristic of the Negro, while 63 regarded "intelligent," 37 "industrious," and 36 "scientifically minded" as characteristic of white Americans.[24] In fact, the Negro knows white people only through stereotypes, except where for his own protection he must adjust his behavior to real white people. As a result of being forced to adjust his behavior to the demands of whites, the Negro has developed certain personality traits. The form which this adjustment takes from childhood on depends upon what section of the country he lives in and upon his class position in the Negro world.[25] Because of their economic security, upper-class children are shielded from the cruder expressions of race prejudice, while the lower-class children are exposed to the most brutal manifestations of racial antagonisms. The children in each class are taught to acquire certain attitudes and techniques in dealing with whites. No matter what technique is used, it involves a certain amount of deception and there is much suppressed antagonism because of daily frustrations.

EMERGENCE OF THE NEGRO AS A MINORITY

As the result of the various forms of racial discrimination which have created barriers to mutual understanding and appreciation between whites and Negroes, the Negro has emerged as a minority in

[24] James A. Bayton, "The Racial Stereotypes of Negro College Students," *The Journal of Abnormal and Social Psychology*, Vol. 36 (1941), pp. 97-102.

[25] The following studies projected and financed by the American Youth Commission of the American Council on Education contain a wealth of information on how race prejudice or the "minority" status of the Negro affects the development of the personality of Negro youth. Allison Davis and John Dollard, *Children of Bondage* (Washington, D. C., 1940), E. Franklin Frazier, *Negro Youth at the Crossways* (Washington, D. C., 1940), Charles S. Johnson, *Growing up in the Black Belt* (Washington, D. C., 1941), and W. Lloyd Warner, Buford H. Junker, and Walter A. Adams, *Color and Human Nature* (Washington, D. C., 1941).

American life.[26] Although he has always been excluded from participation in American life, his status has not always been exactly that of a racial or cultural minority. While under the system of slavery the Negro had a place in the social organization; he was not a true racial or cultural minority. Following the Civil War, especially during the Reconstruction Period, an attempt was made to completely integrate the Negro into the life of the South. The resulting racial conflict and the so-called restoration of "white supremacy" tended to exclude the Negro from participation in the life of the South. During this period the North repudiated its idealism in regard to the Negro and the country became intensely conscious of its "Negro problem." However, the Negro was not regarded as simply a group with a different racial and cultural background as, for example, the Italians or Poles. He was regarded as an inferior human being and his poverty, ignorance, and social disorganization as well as his folk culture were considered an inevitable consequence of his inferiority.

During the period of rigorous exclusion from American life, the Negro worker lost his former position as an important element among skilled workers in the South. This gave birth to the belief among Negro leaders that the masses of Negroes could only find economic salvation in the creation of a separate Negro economy. It was during this same period that the Negro church organizations experienced their greatest growth. These church organizations embodied to a greater extent than any other institutions the cultural traditions of the Negro. There were, however, other institutions such as schools and fraternal organizations which were becoming the repositories of the collective achievements, the aspirations and traditions of the Negro group. In these developments there was being laid the basis for the emergence of the Negro as a racial or cultural minority. The vast majority of Negroes, however, were still rural folk without any real consciousness of group identification based upon a common history or a common culture.

The emergence of the Negro as a true racial or cultural minority was not achieved until after World War I. The Negro worker be-

[26] Louis Wirth, "The Problem of Minority Groups," in Ralph Linton (Ed.), *The Science of Man in the World Crisis* (New York, 1945), pp. 347-72.

came an important element in American industry for the first time. The social and mental isolation of the black masses was destroyed through the movement of over a million Negroes to cities. The masses of Negroes became race-conscious in the sense that they became identified with a group with a history and a destiny. There was a new orientation and a new valuation of the Negro's experience in America. This was brought about by the appearance of a group of Negro writers and artists who ushered in a Negro renaissance. Not only was the Negro affected by these developments; the Negro became redefined in the minds of white America. Although the Negro continued to be excluded from full participation in American life, gradually a new conception of the Negro as a cultural minority was created. By the time the United States entered World War II, the Negro had emerged as a racial or cultural minority among the ethnic minorities in American life.

As a racial or cultural minority the Negro occupies a unique position. He has been in the United States longer than any other racial or cultural minority with the exception, of course, of the American Indian. Although the Negro is distinguished from other minorities by his physical characteristics, unlike other racial or cultural minorities the Negro is not distinguished by culture from the dominant group.[27] Having completely lost his ancestral culture, he speaks the same language, practices the same religion, and accepts the same values and political ideals as the dominant group. Consequently, when one speaks of Negro culture in the United States, one can only refer to the folk culture of the rural Southern Negro or the traditional forms of behavior and values which have grown out of the Negro's social and mental isolation. Moreover, many of the elements of Negro culture which have grown out of his peculiar experience in America, such as music, have become a part of the general American culture.

Since the institutions, the social stratification, and the culture of the Negro minority are essentially the same as those of the larger community, it is not strange that the Negro minority belongs among the assimilationist rather than the pluralistic, secessionist or militant minorities.[28] It is seldom that one finds Negroes who think of them-

[27] *Ibid.*   [28] *Ibid.*, pp. 354 ff.

selves as possessing a different culture from whites and that their peculiar culture should be preserved. Perhaps, only in the case of the Negro church where there are vested interests supported by certain cultural traditions, can one find any desire to maintain a separate culture. The only movement involving a secession from America has been the Garvey Movement. But as we have seen this movement appealed to a relatively small number of disillusioned Negroes who had recently migrated to the city. The movement collapsed when the leader was imprisoned and deported upon release from prison. The Negro minority is striving for assimilation into American life. The Negro has striven as far as possible to efface or tone down the physical differences between himself and the white majority. He does not take seriously the notion of a separate Negro economy. In his individual behavior as well as in his organized forms of social life he attempts to approximate as closely as possible the dominant American pattern. Whenever an opportunity for participation in American culture is afforded he readily seizes it; that is, so far as his past experiences and preparation permit him to take advantage of such opportunities.

DEALING WITH RACE PREJUDICE AND PUBLIC DISCRIMINATIONS

As a racial or cultural minority seeking assimilation into American life, the Negro faces both private prejudices and discriminations based upon public policy. As Wirth has pointed out, these are two different problems and require different types of remedies.[29] Personal prejudices involving certain stereotypes and emotional biases concerning Negroes may be modified by education, propaganda, and broader social experience. The increasing mobility of the American population has done much to modify the naïve prejudices of whites against Negroes. Moreover, increased opportunities for whites and Negroes to associate in common activities have modified these personal prejudices. The work of the interracial committees established in the South following World War I was based upon the sound assumption that association in activities of common interest would modify if not efface racial prejudices. Although the relations between Negroes and whites

[29] See Wirth, "Race and Public Policy," pp. 306 ff.

in these early adventures in interracial cooperation were characterized by a certain social distance and tabooed subjects, racial stereotypes were undermined and emotional biases were broken up. Even more effective in destroying individual prejudices have been the literature and art which have enabled white people to enter sympathetically into the lives of Negroes.

The problem of dealing with public discriminations based upon law and custom involves changes in the structure of our society, especially in the South. Usually changes in the social structure are brought about during periods of crisis. The crisis in race relations created by World War II has had implications for changes in the social structure. In various parts of the country, rural as well as urban, racial tensions appeared.[30] The Negro was no longer willing to accept discrimination in employment and in housing without protest. Moreover, the treatment of Negro soldiers, especially by southern whites who resented a Negro in uniform, tended more than any other factor to stir up resentment among Negroes against their traditional status in American life. The Negro's demand for a new status in American life was summed up in a volume, *What the Negro Wants*,[31] containing statements by 14 Negro leaders representing conservative and radical opinions on race relations and equally as diverse economic and political philosophies.

In the South liberals joined with Negro leaders in setting forth principles which they thought should guide the changes in the relations of the races.[32] The declaration of principles was based upon a statement by southern Negro leaders in Durham, a later statement by a group of southern white leaders in Atlanta, and a statement by a collaboration committee composed of representatives of both groups. The Negro leaders came out for political and civil rights and while expressing themselves as "fundamentally opposed to the principle and practice of compulsory segregation" of races, classes or creeds they thought it was "sensible" to deal with "discrimination and neglect." The conference of white leaders emphasized the legal rights of the

[30] See Charles S. Johnson and Associates, *To Stem This Tide* (Boston, 1943).
[31] Rayford W. Logan (Ed.), *What The Negro Wants* (Chapel Hill, 1944).
[32] *The Southern Regional Council, Its Origin and Purpose*, Atlanta, Ga.

Negroes and their right to education and employment. The final statement, which was vaguer and dealt with generalities concerning democracy, left the question of segregation untouched. On the other hand, the Negro was warned that insistence upon complete equality in the South would result in a racial war in which the Negro was bound to be the loser.[33] This counsel of wisdom or veiled threat did not deter the Negro press in the northern and border states in their demand for full equality. The demand of Negro leaders for equality during the War was, in fact, a strategic move during a crisis situation. Even the northern leaders in demanding equality and that segregation be abolished did not believe that it could be achieved immediately. The southern Negro leaders were attempting in a more conciliatory manner to gain as much as possible during a period of change.

In spite of the great opposition to changes in public policies regarding discrimination, there are evidences that the "rising tide of democratic sentiment and enlightenment" is having its influence upon public policies. The Supreme Court has handed down decisions to the effect that Negroes as interstate passengers are entitled to the same accommodations as whites; that the Negro has a right to participation in the primaries in the South; and that he has a right to the same educational advantages as whites. The most important attack on public policies supporting racial discrimination has been the President's program of Civil Rights legislation before the Congress of the United States. This legislative program grew in part out of the Report by the President's Committee on Civil Rights and the Report of the President's Commission on Higher Education. The proposed program of Civil Rights for Negroes, involving antilynching legislation, a permanent Fair Employment Practices Committee, and legislation against segregation in transportation has aroused southern politicians.

Despite the opposition of southern politicians to federal legislation guaranteeing the civil rights of Negroes, there are many indications that there is a rapidly growing public opinion in favor of the civil rights of the Negro. This is indicated by the state and city Fair Employment Practices laws; the State Committee Against Discrimina-

[33] Virginius Dabney, "Nearer and Nearer the Precipice," *Atlantic Monthly* (January, 1944), pp. 94-100.

tion and laws against discrimination in education in New York; the numerous Mayors and Governors Commissions on Race Relations; and the resolutions and programs of the various church organizations supporting the civil rights of Negroes. The fact that the platforms of both the Democratic Party and the Republican Party contained planks that indicated in general support of the Negro's civil rights indicates that the state of public opinion in the country is such as to make possible fundamental changes in public policies which support racial discrimination.

CONCLUSION

CHAPTER XXVIII

Prospects For Integration of the Negro Into American Society

THIS study has been concerned primarily with the development of the Negro community and its institutions or the emergence of the Negro as a racial minority. As a racial minority, the Negro has been excluded from the "melting pot" philosophy which included the various ethnic groups in the country.[1] This fact was vividly expressed by Charles Francis Adams in a speech in Richmond, Virginia, in 1908, in which he stated:

The American system, as we know, was founded on the assumed basis of a common humanity, that is, absence of absolutely fundamental racial characteristics was accepted as an established truth. Those of all races were welcomed to our shores. They came, aliens; they and their descendants would become citizens first, natives afterward. It was a process first of assimilation and then of absorption. On this all depended. There could be no permanent divisional lines. That theory is now plainly broken down. We are confronted by the obvious fact, as undeniable as it is hard, that the African will only partially assimilate and that he cannot be absorbed. He remains an alien element in the body politic. A foreign substance, he can neither be assimilated nor thrown out.[2]

At the time when this statement was made, there was deep concern as to the future of the Negro in American society. Emancipation had destroyed the accommodation which had existed between whites and

---

[1] Louis Wirth, "Problem of Minority Groups," in Ralph Linton (Ed.), *The Science of Man in the World Crisis* (New York, 1945), p. 358.
[2] Quoted in Robert E. Park and Ernest W. Burgess, *Introduction to the Science of Sociology* (Chicago, 1924), p. 760.

blacks during slavery. The last threads of sentiment between the two races were dissolving as the Negroes moved into the cities. The attempt to reduce the Negro to a subordinate caste in the South had not solved the problem, while in the North wherever Negroes were found in large numbers, they remained outside the industrial organization and were regarded as an unassimilable element.

During the four decades which have elapsed since the speech of Adams, many important changes have occurred in the Negro, in the relation of the Negro community to American life, and in the relation of the American nation to a changing world. In view of these changes, what are the prospects for the integration of the Negro into American life?

CHANGES IN THE NEGRO

Let us begin by considering the changes which have occurred in the Negro. Up to the first decade of the present century the vast majority of the Negroes were peasant folk dwelling on the plantations of the South. A third of the southern Negroes were illiterate while less than a half of the Negro children of school age were attending school. The lack of educational facilities together with the barriers that Emancipation and Reconstruction had erected between the races had tended to arrest the acculturation of the Negro.[3] This was all changed as the result of World War I which drew nearly a million Negroes out of the social and mental isolation of the world of the Negro folk. As Negroes have continued to be drawn into cities, especially northern cities, the tempo and the character of their acculturation have changed. The tempo was quickened because they were brought into contact with many phases of American culture with which they had no contact in the rural isolation. Suddenly exposed to a multiplicity of patterns of behavior and new modes of thought, the Negro has often adopted bizarre forms of behavior in order to secure

[3] See Melville J. Herskovits, *Acculturation, A Study of Culture Contact* (New York, 1938), pp. 2-32, for a critical analysis of the processes involved in acculturation. See also Bronislaw Malinowski, *The Dynamics of Culture Change*, edited by Phyllis M. Kaberry, (New Haven, 1945), pp. vii ff., where the author emphasizes the fact that when two races with different cultures come into contact each takes over some elements of the culture of the other.

recognition. Moreover, many of the newly acquired patterns of behavior and ways of thinking have not affected the deeper layers of his personality which were molded by the family and the folk culture. But on the whole the urbanized Negro has sought to conform to the new environment. Thus, slowly the Negro, like the European immigrant, has acquired the manners and customs of America and as these new ways have become a part of his family heritage he has been transformed into a new person. The extent to which this transformation has occurred has been in proportion to his schooling and his participation in other phases of American culture.

Although the folk Negro has become transformed through education and wider participation in American life, the fact of his color has continued to retard the degree of his integration into American life. Despite the policy which defines as a Negro any person with Negro ancestry, the mixed-blood in the United States as elsewhere has enjoyed many advantages. Moreover, the mixed-blood has served as a channel by which the culture of the whites has been communicated to the Negro group.[4] Under the conditions of city living, the mobility of the Negroes of mixed ancestry has been increased. Because of the anonymity of the city they have been able to "pass" for white or for southern Europeans and South Americans.[5] There have been a number of estimates of the number of Negroes who have passed into the white race; but it is impossible to know definitely the number who change their race.[6] It is well known that many Negroes "pass" for white in order to secure employment in occupations which are closed to Negroes. Some Negroes experience considerable inner conflict in "passing" for white, while others feel completely at home in the white

[4] See Louis Wirth and Herbert Goldhamer, "The Hybrid and the Problem of Miscegenation," in Otto Klineberg (Ed.), *Characteristics of the American Negro* (New York, 1944), pp. 249-369, for the most comprehensive and critical analysis of available information on Negro-white mixtures in the United States. See also Edward B. Reuter, *The Mulatto in the United States* (Boston, 1918) and by the same author, *Race Mixture* (New York, 1931).

[5] See Wirth and Goldhamer, *op. cit.*, pp. 312 ff.

[6] See John H. Burma, "The Measurement of Negro 'Passing,'" *The American Journal of Sociology*, Vol. 52 (July, 1946), pp. 18-22; and E. W. Eckard, "How Many Negroes 'Pass,'" *The American Journal of Sociology*, Vol. 52 (May, 1947), pp. 498-500, for the most reliable estimates on the number of Negroes who "pass" for white each year.

world. Those who feel an inner conflict despite their physical and cultural identification with whites remain as unassimilated as the dark Negroes. On the other hand, there are mixed-bloods who have identified themselves inwardly with whites and have become assimilated in the white race. The children of such people have no history or memories to connect them with Negroes.

Because of his high visibility, the Negro of dark complexion and pronounced negroid features experiences a different problem of integration. However, one should not overlook the fact that how the Negro appears is determined to a large extent by the manner in which the Negro is defined by our culture. As we have seen in the last chapter the categoric picture of the Negro as given in our culture has changed. The Negro who is presented, for example, in the advertisement of a popular brand of whiskey today is a kindly, dignified human being, entirely different from the grotesque apelike caricature of a human being that was used thirty or forty years ago to advertise shoe polish. Moreover, it should be noted that as Negroes dress as other Americans and acquire their manners and ways in their public conduct, their visibility tends to decrease. Finally, as Negroes are found increasingly in occupations and in rôles which they did not formerly occupy, the association of a dark complexion and negroid features with an inferior social status tends to disappear.

CHANGES IN THE NEGRO COMMUNITY

There have been important changes in the character of the Negro community and its relation to the white community which are facilitating the integration of the Negro into American life. First, it should be noted that a smaller proportion of the Negro population is concentrated in the South and the Negro population has become more evenly distributed in that region. Moreover, as we have shown during the course of this study, the Negro has become more integrated into the economic life of the nation. Forty years ago the Negro had lost his important position as a skilled worker in the South and he had no place in northern industry. As the result of World War I the Negro gained a foothold in industry and as the result of the development of the industrial unions and World War II, he has become an important element among the industrial workers of the country. Moreover, as the result of his political power in the northern states and Fair Employment Practices legislation the barriers to the employment of Negroes are being removed. Thus the economic basis for a separate communal life which was provided to some extent by the concentration of Negroes in agriculture has been destroyed.

The increasing occupational differentiation of the Negro population is affecting the structure of the Negro community. Forty years ago the Negroes were concentrated in agriculture and domestic service. In the cities there had appeared, often in the neighborhood of the Negro colleges, a small upper class comprised of a few professional men and the more stable and respectable elements of various occupational statuses. As the result of the mass migrations to northern cities, the occupational differentiation of the Negro population was accelerated. The process has continued until at present in the North Negroes are found in most of the occupations. Even in the South where the process has been much slower because of the lack of political power and employment opportunities, education has provided the Negro with the knowledge and skills to serve the Negro communities. As the result of these changes, in the North the various classes in the Negro communities are developing common interests with members of the same classes in the white community. For example, Negro industrial workers are being integrated into the unions and Negro and white social workers and teachers are being drawn together outside their professional interests. The employment of Negro teachers in northern universities has been especially significant for the changing status of the Negro. Although racial barriers have prevented similar developments in the South there is a growing recognition of the individual Negro's occupational and professional status which is providing a basis of common interests between the races. Despite these changes, Negro life continues to flow within the separate institutions of the more or less segregated Negro community. In the South the separate public schools and recreational facilities erect barriers between children who might otherwise forget racial differences. There are also the separate churches, theaters, and even separate businesses which serve the wants of the Negro. Even in the North where the public educational and recreational facilities favor the integration of the Negro into the American community, the separate churches and social clubs and other associations embodying the cultural interests of the community maintain the separation of the races. While these separate institutions have played an important rôle in the acculturation of the Negro since they have provided the channels through which the Negro has taken over American patterns, they are nevertheless barriers to the integration of the Negro into American life. The persistence of segregation in the case of certain types of institutions while other types of institutions absorb the Negro seems to be related to certain fundamental facts of human relationships.

INTEGRATION: FROM SECONDARY TO PRIMARY GROUP CONTACTS

An attempt has been made to define the typical stages in the developing relationships of immigrants or minority groups and the dominant white group in the United States. Bogardus has developed the theory of a "race-relation cycle" based upon the recurrent behavior on the part of native white Americans toward the Oriental and the Mexican.[7] In the first phase there was an attitude of curiosity toward the stranger; and in the second stage, the stranger was welcomed because of the demand for his labor. In the third stage, however, the immigrant became the object of industrial and social antagonism because he was a competitor and sought improvement in his status. There followed a fourth phase when through legislation the immigrant was excluded or restricted in his enjoyment of economic, political, and social rights. In the fifth phase, there appeared "fair-play" movements which helped immigrants to retain confidence in American ideals and helped Americans to maintain their reputation before the world. Then followed a phase of acquiescence in which antagonism died down, and a final phase in which the children of immigrants had to face the problem of assimilation.

[7] Emory S. Bogardus, "A Race-Relations Cycle," *The American Journal of Sociology*, Vol. XXXV, pp. 612-17.

It is possible to relate the development of Negro-white relations to the stages described in the "race-relations cycle." For example, many features of present Negro-white relations indicate that they have entered the fifth, sixth and final stages depending upon the section of the country. However, instead of attempting to fit Negro-white relations in the various parts of the country into this scheme, we shall undertake to discover in what areas of human relations integration is progressing most rapidly and in what areas there is greater resistance to integration. This procedure appears to be more profitable since it involves at the same time the rôle of the institutions in the Negro community in the process of integration.

The process of integrating the Negro into American life may be represented by a gradient as indicated in the title of this section. The Negro is being integrated first into those areas of American life involving secondary contacts as opposed to primary contacts,[8] or secular as opposed to sacred relations. Yet the fact of status is involved in the relations of the races. It appears that as a rule status is more important where contacts are primary or tend to be intimate than where contacts are impersonal. The Negro was first integrated into the economic organization when he performed a specialized form of labor as a slave. Antagonism developed toward him as a competitor and this antagonism has continued on a wide scale until the last decade or so. But gradually the Negro worker is being integrated into industry. In fact, it is in the economic relations of American life that the Negro is gaining his greatest acceptance today. In the South where the CIO is carrying on an educational campaign against discrimination in connection with its union drive and has an established policy of nonsegregated unions, there is a growing acceptance of the Negro's right to work according to his skill and on the basis of equal pay. There is still a barrier to the employment of Negroes in "white collar" occupations along with whites because of the status involved in such occupations. On the other hand, in the North the Negro is

[8] See Charles H. Cooley, *Social Organization* (New York, 1909), Chapter III, on the nature of primary group relations, and Ellsworth Faris, "The Primary Group: Essence and Accident," *American Journal of Sociology*, Vol. 38 (July, 1932), pp. 41-50, for a critique of the concept of primary groups.

gradually winning the right to work in "white collar" occupations. Increasingly, the public is becoming accustomed to being served by Negro clerks and white workers are exhibiting less opposition to Negro workers in such occupations.

However, in the South the barriers to the admission of Negroes to theaters and other public recreational institutions show few signs of weakening. Even in the District of Columbia, Negroes are excluded from theaters and movie houses despite nationwide protest. The fight against the segregated public schools in the capital of the world's greatest democracy is only beginning to enlist the support of national leaders. There is no likelihood that the separate public schools in the South will be abolished soon, though there is a growing opinion among white students in the state institutions of some southern states that Negro students should be admitted. In the North where there has been no legal segregation in the matter of public education, there have been segregated schools and the employment of Negro teachers has been restricted or Negro teachers have been placed in Negro areas. Throughout the North opposition to this type of segregation and discrimination has been growing in recent years. Indicative of the changes which are occurring is the recent action of the states of New Jersey and New York in abolishing all forms of segregation in public education. Moreover, in the North the exclusion of Negroes from public places of amusement and recreation is not as great today as formerly.

While these changes are taking place in regard to public institutions where contacts are secondary or more or less impersonal and secular, there is little evidence that even in the North the Negro is gaining acceptance in those institutions and associations where contacts are more intimate and personal. For example, it appears that Negroes will be "integrated" into theaters and public places of recreation and amusement in northern cities sooner than in the churches. During the past decade or so Negro actors have increasingly been integrated on the American stage while the traditional opposition to Negroes in the audience has been diminishing.[9] Despite the professions of the

[9] See Edith J. R. Isaacs, *The Negro in the American Theatre* (New York, 1947).

Christian churches concerning brotherhood and even their inter-racial programs, churches consist largely of family groups and embody the cultural traditions of certain classes. The same might be said concerning the Negro church organizations which derive their support from family groups and embody the cultural traditions of the Negro minority. Moreover, the Negro churches like other separate institutions in the Negro world represent certain vested interests which Negroes particularly functionaries of these institutions are unwilling to surrender.[10]

When one considers the various associations in which human relations are free and informal and more especially the most intimate of social groupings, the family, where human relations tend to be sacred, one can get a measure of the moral isolation of the Negro in American life. Probably, the Negro has felt more keenly his moral isolation in the midst of American life than the various forms of oppression and discrimination because these are only a reflection of his moral isolation. To be counted in or to belong, as Sterling Brown has pointed out, is what the Negro wants in America at the present time.[11] Of course, other racial and ethnic minorities experience to some degree the same moral isolation. But other racial minorities such as the Chinese and Indians are not numerous and have an ancestral cultural heritage and the ethnic minorities are all defined as white and are being assimilated. The Negro is a large racial minority without an ancestral cultural heritage to fall back on. While he is essentially an American, he is still regarded as an alien without even the romantic sentiment with which the Chinese or Indian is invested. The more the Negro escapes from the world of the folk and conforms to the dominant American patterns of behavior and thought, the more keenly he feels his moral isolation. The more he participates in American life, the more he feels that certain areas of intimate association with whites are closed to him.

Yet there are signs that among certain groups, especially in the

[10] E. Franklin Frazier, "Human, All Too Human. The Negro's Vested Interest in Segregation," *Survey Graphic*, January, 1947.

[11] See Sterling A. Brown, "Count Us In" in Rayford W. Logan (Ed.), *What the Negro Wants* (Chapel Hill, 1944), pp. 308-44.

larger cosmopolitan communities, the barriers to intimate association are being broken down. For example, among the more liberal and radical labor groups, Negroes participate freely in their social activities and are at home within their family circle. Then, too, among certain intellectual and artistic groups, the participation of Negroes on a basis of complete intimacy and acceptance has increasingly become a commonplace occurrence. As the Negro achieves competence in the various professional fields, there is a growing disposition to accept him as a social equal, generally within a restricted circle, since prejudices against such contacts are strong among the more conventional members of the professional groups. The final and strongest barrier to complete acceptance is, of course, the disapproval of intermarriage. There is little reliable information on this phase of race relations.[12] Probably not more than three per cent of Negro marriages in the large northern cities are across race lines. The vast majority of whites and Negroes who intermarry are found in semiskilled and unskilled occupations. More Negro men than Negro women marry across race lines; and about a third of the white bridegrooms are foreign born. The members of the professional classes of both races who intermarry are generally the more sophisticated and emancipated members of the middle class. There is as much opposition among the conventional members of the Negro upper and middle classes to intermarriage as among the same elements in the white group. Despite these barriers to intermarriage it should be noted that intermarriage is not regarded with the same provincial attitude either among whites or among Negroes as in the past.

CHANGES IN THE ORGANIZATION OF AMERICAN LIFE

The changes which we have noted in the Negro and in the Negro community, and in the progress of his integration into American life have been related to the changes in the organization of American life. The America which Charles Francis Adams represented when he

---

12 Louis Wirth and Herbert Goldhamer, "The Hybrid and the Problem of Miscegenation," *loc. cit.*, pp. 249-369, is the latest and most comprehensive source of information on the subject.

spoke 40 years ago is vastly different from the America of today.[13] There have been technological changes which have increased the production of minerals and power and agricultural products. There has been a decline in the rate of population growth and in the volume of immigration, and more important still a new distribution of the population. The most important consequence of the redistribution of population has been the emergence of metropolitan communities. The changes in technology and the development of metropolitan communities have affected the economic organization of American life while the changes in the economic organization have caused wage earners to play a more important rôle in the social organization. At the same time the increasing importance of cities and metropolitan communities in American life has drawn the inhabitants of rural communities out of their isolation. Finally, there has been a growth in governmental functions not only in the field of education, health, recreation and welfare, but in the field of the increasingly complex economic relations which have resulted from technological changes.

These changes in the social organization of American society are having a profound effect upon the status of Negroes. As American society has become more mobile and secular in its outlook, people are no longer bound by sacred traditions and fixed local sentiments. For example, with the appearance of the filling station, there was not the same insistence upon separate toilet facilities as in the case of the railway station. Likewise separation in traveling by air has not been enforced as in the case of railroads. The effect of the increased physical mobility of the population on customary and even legal practices regarding race relations was accentuated during World War II. In the upper tier of the southern states, the constant movement of large numbers of people tended to wipe out segregation on trains. Even under normal circumstances in the larger cities of the South there has been much relaxation of the castelike controls in race relations which have characterized the rural South. In the metropolitan areas of the North, where there is greater anonymity and contacts are more casual

[13] See p. 687 above.

and impersonal, the Negro escapes from most of the caste restrictions of the South. Since Negroes resemble all the races of the earth they tend to lose their identity in the cosmopolitan populations of northern cities. In the process of secularization of human relations the traditional notions of the Negro are dissolved along with taboos and traditional sentiments toward the Negro. The Negro as a racial problem is becoming less important as he becomes a part of the problems arising out of the conflict of economic and class interests in American society.

The changes in the organization of American society have involved developments in communication which in turn have had an influence on attitudes and public opinion regarding the Negro. There has been a wider dissemination of knowledge through the extension of the public school system to the remotest rural areas. The increase in high school and more especially college attendance has brought an increasing number of persons in contact with scientific knowledge concerning races and race relations. Even more important has been the rôle of the radio and the movie in spreading information and in producing greater uniformity of ideas and attitudes. Although the movies have tended to cater to traditional attitudes and prejudices, they have nevertheless increasingly cast the Negro in a rôle different from local and provincial conceptions of him. On the other hand, the radio has increasingly tended to present a new conception of the Negro and his relation to American life. As a consequence of these changes in communication, no section of the country can escape the influence of the public opinion and attitudes which are becoming representative of the country as a whole. For example, the news of the lynching of a Negro in a remote southern rural community is flashed to the whole country and pictures of the scene of the crime are featured in magazines with national circulation. The local community must defend its action or attempt to reconcile it with generally accepted principles of law and justice. Moreover, despite traditional notions concerning states' rights and local autonomy, public opinion is increasingly supporting intervention on the part of the federal government designed to safeguard the Negro's rights.

THE DEMOCRATIC CREED AND CHRISTIAN IDEALS

The extension of the media of communication throughout the nation has resulted in a new interest in the meaning of the democratic creed. Myrdal has called attention to the fact that the American Creed, involving the "ideals of the essential dignity of the individual human being, of the fundamental equality of all men, and of certain inalienable rights to freedom, justice, and a fair opportunity" have become the "highest law of the land." [14] The Creed is accepted by both whites and Negroes. In fact, the Negroes who experience discriminations claim that the Creed is violated but they believe that the nation is ruled by it. Likewise, the whites who violate the Creed experience some sense of guilt and attempt to justify their behavior in terms of the Creed. The appeal of the Negro and his white allies for equality for the Negro gains in persuasive power because it is based upon the American Creed.

World War II and the subsequent crisis have tended to accentuate interest in the meaning of democracy and equality. As soon as the United States declared itself to be the "arsenal of democracy," the question of the right of the Negro to equal treatment under the law and an equal opportunity for employment became a national issue. The federal government was forced to abandon its traditional laissez-faire policy in regard to the rights of the Negro to equal employment opportunities. Moreover, the federal government no longer excused its inactivity in respect to the civil rights of the Negro on the grounds of states' rights but began to prosecute cases of peonage. This did not represent simply arbitrary interference on the part of the federal government since such action was supported by a growing public opinion in the South as well as in the North. After the United States entered the War against Germany, which had based its political creed upon the theory of racial inequality, the section of the American Creed declaring the fundamental equality of all men acquired a new significance. Both public and private agencies set about effacing the traditional notions about the inferiority of the Negro. There was opposition, of course, as in the case of the distribution by the army of

[14] Myrdal, *An American Dilemma*, Vol. I, p. 4.

the pamphlet, *Races of Mankind*, by the two anthropologists, Ruth Benedict and Gene Weltfish. But, on the whole, there was a redefinition of the Negro and the idea of biracialism gave place to the idea of integrating the Negro into American life.[15]

One of the roots of the American Creed, as Myrdal points out, is to be found in Christianity.[16] This was due to the social heritage of America which was colonized by many of the Protestant lower class sects. As we have seen, two of these lower class sects, the Methodists and the Baptists, were originally in favor of the emancipation of the Negro slave. After these churches became established as denominations, they split prior to the Civil War over the question of slavery. However, following the Civil War, there were elements in the southern churches who based their demands for the equitable treatment of the Negro on Christian ideals. Much of the work of the Commission on Interracial Co-operation in the South was based upon an appeal to Christian ideals. The work of the Commission finally bore fruit when the white women of the southern churches condemned lynching as a means of protecting white womanhood.[17] Although this action on the part of the white woman in the churches was partly the result of the growing public opinion against lynching, the influence of emotionalized Christian ideals cannot be denied.

The crisis created by World War II caused both the Protestant and Catholic churches to take a stand on the relation of the Negro to American society. As we have pointed out, the Protestant churches through the Federal Council of Churches in America have taken a stand against segregation and favored the integration of the Negro into American life. Increasingly the Protestant churches have included Negro churches and their ministers in their programs. Like-

[15] For example, it is noteworthy that despite his general condemnation of the demand of Negroes for complete equality, W. T. Couch asks: "Does the white man have no right to attempt to separate cultural from biological integration, and help the Negro to achieve the first and deny him the second?" Reprinted from *What the Negro Wants*, edited by Rayford W. Logan, p. xxii, by permission of the University of North Carolina Press. Copyright 1944 by The University of North Carolina Press. See also New York War Council, Committee on Discrimination in Employment, *How Management Can Integrate Negroes in War Industries*, 1942, prepared by John A. Davis.   [16] Myrdal, *op. cit.*, pp. 9-12.

[17] Commission on Interracial Cooperation, *Southern White Women on Lynching and Mob Violence* (Atlanta, Ga., n.d.).

wise, the Catholic church in the United States has attacked the principle of color caste and opened its seminaries to Negro students. The vindication of the rights of Negroes in terms of Christian ideas has been a part of the struggle of Christianity to survive in the crisis of the modern world. Even before World War II, the Christian churches began to deal with the question of race relations in a number of ecumenical conferences.[18] In a conference in Cleveland in 1945, the Protestant churches of America spoke out boldly against the hypocrisy of dismantling the Japanese Empire while the United States and the European nations continued to maintain their imperial power over the colored peoples of the world. Moreover, the Cleveland Conference took the position that race prejudice was a primary obstacle to world brotherhood.

COLOR AND DEMOCRACY

The struggle of the Negro to achieve equality in American society can no longer be separated from the struggle of colored colonial peoples to attain freedom and independence. It might be pointed out that Negroes because of their increasing education and knowledge of world affairs have identified their struggle for equality with the struggle of the colored colonial races for independence. A mere glance at the Negro newspapers will reveal the extent to which sympathy and understanding between American Negroes and Africans and Asiatics have grown during recent years. Even during World War II there was much sympathy for the Japanese on the part of American Negroes because Japan was a *colored* nation fighting a *white* nation which had drawn a color line even in its armed forces. Such rebellious sentiments might be regarded only as the expression of the resentment of an impotent and repressed minority if the objective conditions in the world today were different. But the struggle of Indonesia and Indo-China for independence are questions of international politics, and the prestige and position of the United States in the arena of international politics are influenced by its treatment of the Negro.

The colored colonial peoples of the world, who have been com-

---

[18] See Buell G. Gallagher, *Color and Conscience: The Irrepressible Conflict* (New York, 1946), pp. 199 ff.

pared to the slum dwellers of our great cities, are demanding the right to enjoy the resources of the lands which they inhabit which involves the right to civilized standards of living.[19] European imperialism which has become identified with the supremacy of the white race has been challenged in Asia and in Africa. Despite the military defeat of Japan, it cannot be denied that white imperialism in Asia has been destroyed. The British Empire has been forced to grant self-government to India; Holland, despite the assistance from the United States, has been forced to meet some of the demands of the Indonesians; while France is unable to re-establish her rule in Indo-China. Even in West Africa the British are faced with the rise of nationalism.[20] As the result of the enlisting of West Africans in the British military forces and their employment as industrial workers, the African Negroes have gained a new conception of themselves as well as of the whites who often worked and fought beside or against them. The shortage of manpower in the colonies was responsible for the employment of Africans in responsible positions in government and in commerce. Consequently, the development of a nationalistic movement in West Africa is not the result of Communistic agitation as the propaganda of newspapers would lead one to believe.

The influence of Russia in the struggle of the colored colonial peoples for freedom and independence is more important than it is represented to be in the propaganda contained in the newspapers of the United States. Russia has provided for the world a solution of the problem of racial and cultural minorities dwelling within a single political community. Despite the criticisms which are brought against the economic and political organization of Russia, even the enemies of Russia are forced to admit that racial prejudice has been minimized and racial discriminations are no longer supported by public policy. The absence of racial prejudice and discrimination in Russia has had a tremendous influence on the American Negro. Moreover, in the arena of international politics, as for example, in the United Nations

[19] W. E. B. DuBois, *Color and Democracy: Colonies and Peace* (New York, 1945).

[20] *Foreign Policy Reports.* "Nationalism in West Africa" by Vernon McKay. Foreign Policy Association, Inc., March 15, 1948.

Organization, Russia has become the champion of the rights of the colored colonial peoples. Even if the United Nations Organization should cease to function, the United States, however powerful militarily, to exercise the moral and political influence which is required for leadership, is faced with the problem of convincing the colored colonial peoples of the world that its espousal of democracy and human equality includes the colored peoples of the world. The most convincing proof of its sincerity in championing democratic rights for all the peoples of the earth would be the granting of equality and democratic rights to its Negro citizens.

A NEW AMERICA IN A NEW WORLD

The integration of the Negro into American society will be determined largely by the reorganization of American life in relation to a new world organization. The so-called "Negro Problem" is no longer a southern problem or even an exclusively domestic problem. Even when the United States was a relatively isolated nation during the Civil War, the question of Negro emancipation played a rôle in its international relations. During World War I when the country was engaged in a struggle "to make the world safe for democracy" the question of the status of the Negro could only be evaded because of the backward condition of the Negro and the existing international situation. But, during the interval between World War I and World War II, the condition of the Negro changed and the international situation which involved the relation of the colored colonial peoples to European imperialism underwent important changes. Japan which was the only colored nation to escape colonial status was able, because of the conflicting imperialistic interests of American and European nations, to become a competing imperialistic power. The crisis provided by World War II provided Japan with what was regarded as an opportunity to extend its imperial power over Asia. Because of the superiority of its industrial and technological resources, the United States was able to defeat Japan. But this defeat did not come until after Japan had destroyed both the prestige and political domination of the white Europeans in the Orient. Then with the setting up of the United Nations Organization, the influence of Russia

with its policy of racial equality and opposition to colonialism provided the colored colonial peoples with a new hope and determination.[21]

The integration of the Negro into American society must be viewed
in relation to the reorganization of American life which has been
necessitated by the new world into which the United States must fit
if it is to survive. We have indicated the changes which have occurred
between two world wars and more especially the changes in race
relations which World War II has brought to a climax. Despite the
present inferior status of the Negro, there have been changes which
represent gains in that the Negro has been regarded increasingly as
other people and has been integrated to some extent into American
life. It is not likely that these gains will be lost. Even if there should
be an economic crisis which generally increases racial antagonism, the
relation of the United States to the rest of the world would prevent a
general reaction against the Negro as a national policy. The American
nation is committed to certain principles, the most important of
which are human freedom and human equality, and in its bid for the
support of the colored majority in the world, the treatment of the
Negro can become its greatest asset.[22]

Hence, the integration of the Negro into American society becomes
from the standpoint of the Americans themselves a question of a
new organization of American life in relation to certain principles and
values which are becoming dominant in the world today. These principles and values were implicit in the American system, from the beginning. There was the assumed basis of a "common humanity" and
the "absence of fundamental racial characteristics." Charles Francis
Adams thought that the theory had broken down because of the

[21] In this connection it should be noted that the new relation of the United
States and the European nations to the colored peoples of the world has changed
the entire character of their missionary work among the peoples of Asia and Africa.
See Kenneth Scott Latourette, "The Present Status of Foreign Missions," *Annals*
(March, 1948), Vol. 256, pp. 63-71.

[22] In concluding his monumental study of the Negro problem in the United
States, Myrdal writes: "America can demonstrate that justice, equality and cooperation are possible between white and colored people. . . . America is free
to choose whether the Negro shall remain her liability or become her opportunity."
An American Dilemma, by Gunnar Myrdal, Vol. II, pp. 1021-22. Copyright 1944
by Harper & Brothers.

presence of the Negro in the United States. He was not aware that many of the "aliens" who, he thought, could be "assimilated" and then "absorbed" did not feel toward the Negro as the old American stock. Nor could he foresee that the provincial America of which he was the spokesman would become the center of a cosmopolitan world. He could not envision the changes which would result from technological developments in transportation and communications. For Adams "democratic institutions" and "freedom" were values which reflected the "genius" or social heritage of a section of European peoples. These values, though undergoing changes in their content to fit changes in the economic and social organization of modern life, have become universal values. They no longer represent the values of any racial group. In America these values are enlisting the support of all racial groups and of all minorities. This does not mean that the struggle for racial equality will not be long and difficult. Even the liberals in the South are still talking about equality for the Negro behind the walls of segregation. But the organized power of white and colored people in the labor movement, in the field of education, and in politics in support of the "assumed basis of a common humanity" is increasing. Thus the extent of the reorganization of American life will depend upon the effectiveness of the alliance or common cause of Negroes and other minorities who share this belief.

I. THE NEGRO UNDER THE SLAVE REGIME

Aimes, H. S., "African Institutions in America." *Journal of American Folklore,* Vol. XVIII, pp. 15–17.

Allen, Rt. Rev. Richard, *The Life Experience and Gospel Labors of Rt. Rev. Richard Allen.* Philadelphia: A.M.E. Book Concern, n.d.

Anderson, Robert, *From Slavery to Affluence: Memoirs of Robert Anderson.* Hemingford, Neb.: The Hemingford Ledger, 1927.

Aptheker, Herbert, "Maroons Within the Present Limits of the United States." *The Journal of Negro History,* Vol. XXIV, pp. 167–184, April, 1939.

——, *Negro Slave Revolts in the United States.* New York: International Publishers, 1939.

——, "The Negro in the Abolitionist Movement." *Science and Society,* Vol. V, pp. 2–23, 1941.

Armstrong, George D., *The Christian Doctrine of Slavery.* New York: C. Scribner, 1857.

Ball, Charles, *Slavery in the United States: A Narrative of the Life and Adventure of Charles Ball, A Black Man.* Lewiston, Pa.: J. W. Shugert, 1836.

Ballagh, James C., *A History of Slavery in Virginia.* Baltimore: The Johns Hopkins Press, 1902.

Bancroft, Frederic, *Slave-Trading in the Old South.* Baltimore: J. H. Furst Co., 1931.

Barnes, Gilbert H., *The Anti-Slavery Impulse: 1830–1844.* New York: D. Appleton-Century Co., Inc. 1933.

Becker, Carl, *The Declaration of Independence.* New York: Alfred A. Knopf, 1942.

Beckwith, Martha W., *Black Roadways: A Study of Jamaican Folk Life.* Chapel Hill: The University of North Carolina Press, 1929.

Birnie, C. W., "The Education of the Negro in Charleston, South Carolina, Before the Civil War." *The Journal of Negro History*, Vol. XII, No. 1, pp. 5–13, January, 1927.

Brackett, Jeffrey R., *The Negro in Maryland*. Baltimore: N. Murray, 1889.

Bradford, Sarah H., *Harriet, The Moses of Her People*. New York: G. R. Lockwood and Son, 1886.

Bruce, Phillip A., *Economic History of Virginia in the Seventeenth Century*. Vol. II. New York: The Macmillan Co., 1907.

Buckmaster, Henrietta, *Let My People Go*. New York: Harper and Bros., 1941.

Cable, George W., "Creole Slave Songs." *Century Magazine*, Vol. XXI, pp. 807–27.

Carneiro, Edison, *Religiões Negras*. Rio de Janeiro: Civilização Brasileira, s.a., 1936.

Catterall, Helen T. (Ed.), *Judicial Cases Concerning American Slavery and the Negro*, 2 Vols. Washington, D. C.: Carnegie Institution of Washington, 1926.

Coffin, Joshua, *An Account of Some of the Principal Slave Insurrections*. New York: The American Anti-Slavery Society, 1860.

Coleman, J. Winston, *Slavery Times in Kentucky*. Chapel Hill: The University of North Carolina Press, 1940.

Coppin, Levi J., *Unwritten History*. Philadelphia: A.M.E. Book Concern, 1919.

Cromwell, John W., *The Early Negro Convention Movement. The American Negro Academy, Occasional Paper No. 9*. Washington, D. C., 1904.

——, "The First Negro Churches in Washington," *The Journal of Negro History*, Vol. VII, No. 1, pp. 64–106, January, 1922.

Dallas, R. C., *The History of the Maroons*, 2 Vols. London: T. N. Longman and O. Rees, 1803.

Daniels, John, *In Freedom's Birthplace*. Boston: South End House Association, 1914.

Davenport, Frederick M., *Primitive Traits in Religious Revivals*. New York: The Macmillan Co., 1917.

Davis, Noah, *The Narrative of the Life of Noah Davis, A Colored Man, Written by Himself at the Age of Fifty-four*. Baltimore: John F. Weishampel, 1859.

Desdunes, R. L., *Nos hommes et notre histoire*. Montreal: Arbour and Dupont, 1911.

Dodd, William E., *Expansion and Conflict*. New York: Houghton Mifflin Co., 1915.

Dodge, David, "The Free Negroes of North Carolina," *Atlantic Monthly*, Vol. LVII, pp. 23–30, January, 1886.

Donnan, Elizabeth, *Documents Illustrative of the History of the Slave Trade to America*, 4 Vols. Washington, D. C.: Carnegie Institution of Washington, 1935.

Douglass, Frederick, *My Bondage and My Freedom*. New York: Miller, Orton and Mulligan, 1855.

Doyle, Bertram W., *The Etiquette of Race Relations in the South*. Chicago: The University of Chicago Press, 1937.

Drewry, W. S., *Slave Insurrections in Virginia, 1830–1865*. Washington, 1900.

DuBois, W. E. B., *John Brown*. Philadelphia: G. W. Jacobs and Co., 1909.

——, *The Negro Family*. Atlanta: Atlanta University Press, 1908.

——, *The Philadelphia Negro*. Philadelphia: The University of Pennsylvania, 1899.

——, *The Suppression of the African Slave-Trade*. New York: Longmans, Green and Co., 1896.

Duncan, H. G. and W. L., "The Development of Sociology in the Old South," *American Journal of Sociology*, Vol. XXXIX, pp. 649–56, March, 1943.

Edwards, Bryan, *The History, Civil and Commercial, of the British Colonies in the West Indies*, 3 Vols. London: G. and W. B. Whitaker, 1801.

Filho, João Dornas, *A Escrãvidão no Brasil*. Rio de Janeiro, 1939.

Fitchett, E. Horace, "The Traditions of the Free Negroes in Charleston, South Carolina," *The Journal of Negro History*, Vol. XXV, No. 2, pp. 139–52, April, 1940.

Fitzhugh, George, *Cannibals All! or Slaves without Masters*. Richmond, Va.: A. Morris, 1857.

——, *Sociology for the South: or the Failure of Free Society*. Richmond: A. Morris, 1854.

Franklin, John Hope, *The Free Negro in North Carolina*. Chapel Hill: The University of North Carolina Press, 1943.

Frazier, E. Franklin, *The Negro Family in the United States*. Chicago: The University of Chicago Press, 1939.

Frederick, Francis, *Autobiography of Rev. Francis Frederick of Virginia*. Baltimore: J. W. Woods, Printer, 1869.

Gaines, Francis P., *The Southern Plantation*. New York: Columbia University Press, 1924.

Gandia, Enrique de, *Francisco de Alfaro y la Condicion Social de los Indios*. Buenos Aires: Librería y editorial "El Ateneo," 1939.

Gray, Lewis C., *History of Agriculture in the Southern United States to 1860*. Vol. I. Washington, D. C.: Carnegie Institution of Washington, 1933.

Greene, Evarts B., *American Population Before the Federal Census of 1790*. New York: Columbia University Press, 1932.

Herrick, Cheesman A., *White Servitude in Pennsylvania*. Philadelphia: J. J. McVey, 1926.

Herskovits, Melville J., "On the Provenience of New World Negroes," *Social Forces*, XII, pp. 252–62, October–May, 1933–34.

——, "Social History of the Negro," in Carl Murchison (Ed.), *A Handbook of Social Psychology*. Worchester, Mass.: Clark University Press, 1935.

——, *The Myth of the Negro Past*. New York: Harper and Bros., 1942.

——, *Life in a Haitian Village*. New York: A. A. Knopf, 1937.

Hesseltine, William B., *A History of the South, 1607–1936*. New York: Prentice-Hall, Inc., 1936.

Higginson, T. W., "Gabriel's Defeat," *Atlantic Monthly*, Vol. X, pp. 337–45, September, 1862.

Hughes, Henry, *Treatise on Sociology, Theoretical and Practical*. Philadelphia: Lippincot, Grambo and Co., 1854.

Jackson, Luther P., "The Early Strivings of the Negro in Virginia," *The Journal of Negro History*, Vol. XXV, No. 1, pp. 25–34, January, 1940.

——, "Religious Development of the Negro in Virginia from 1760 to 1860," *The Journal of Negro History*, Vol. XVI, No. 3, pp. 168–239, July, 1931.

——, "The Virginia Free Negro Farmer and Property Owner," *The Journal of Negro History*, Vol. XXIV, No. 4, pp. 390–439, October, 1939.

Johnson, Guion Griffis, *A Social History of the Sea Islands*. Chapel Hill: The University of North Carolina Press, 1930.

Johnston, Sir Harry H., *A History of the Colonization of Africa by Alien Races*. Cambridge: University Press, 1913.

Johnston, James, "Documentary Evidence of the Relations of Negroes and Indians," *The Journal of Negro History*, Vol. XIV, No. 1, pp. 38–9, January, 1929.

Kemble, Frances A., *Journal of a Residence on a Georgian Plantation in 1838–1839*. New York: Harper and Bros., 1863.

King, Grace, *New Orleans. The Place and the People*. New York: The Macmillan Co., 1928.

List of the Tax Payers of the City of Charleston for 1860.

Lloyd, Arthur Y., *The Slavery Controversy. 1830–1860*. Chapel Hill: The University of North Carolina Press, 1939.

Minutes of the Fifth Annual Convention for the Improvement of the Free People of Colour in the United States, 1835. Philadelphia, 1835.

Narrative of Sojourner Truth. Boston: For the Author, 1875.

Nieboer, H. J., *Slavery as An Industrial Institution*. The Hague: Martinus Nijhoff, 1910.

An Official Report of the Trials of Sundry Negroes Charged with an Attempt to Raise an Insurrection in the State of South Carolina, Prepared and Published at the Request of the Court by Lionel Kennedy and Thomas Parker. Charleston, 1822.

Olmsted, Frederick L., *A Journey in the Back Country*. Vol. I. New York: G. P. Putnam's Sons, 1907.

Olmsted, Frederick L., A *Journey in the Seaboard Slave States*. New York: Dix and Edwards, 1856.

Park, Robert E., "The Conflict and Fusion of Cultures," *Journal of Negro History*, Vol. IV, pp. 111–33, April, 1919.

Parkhurst, Jessie W., "The Role of the Black Mammy in the Plantation Household," *The Journal of Negro History*, Vol. XXIII, pp. 349–69, January, 1938.

Pennington, J. W. C., *The Fugitive Blacksmith: or Events in the History of James W. C. Pennington*. London: C. Gilpin, 1850.

Phillips, Ulrich B., *American Negro Slavery*. New York: D. Appleton and Co., 1936.

—— (Joint editor), *Documentary History of American Industrial Society: Plantation and Frontier Documents: 1649–1863*. Vol. II. Cleveland: The A. H. Clark Co., 1909.

——, *Life and Labor in the Old South*. Boston: Little, Brown, and Co., 1929.

——, "Slave Crime in Virginia," *The American Historical Review*, Vol. XX, pp. 336–40, 1914.

Plummer, Nellie, *Out of the Depths*. Hyattsville, Md., 1927.

Puckett, Newbell N., *Folk Beliefs in the Southern Negro*. Chapel Hill: The University of North Carolina Press, 1926.

Ramos, Arthur, *O Negro Brasileiro*. Rio de Janeiro: Companhia editora nacional, 1940.

——, *The Negro in Brazil*. Translated from the Portuguese by Richard Pattee. Washington, D. C.: The Associated Publishers, Inc., 1939.

Reuter, Edward Byron, *The American Race Problem*. New York: Thomas Y. Crowell Co., 1938.

——, *The Mulatto in the United States*. Boston: R. G. Badger, 1918.

Robertson, James A. (Tr.) *Louisiana Under the Rule of Spain, France, and the United States, 1785–1807*. Cleveland: The Arthur H. Clark Co., 1911.

Robin, C. C., "Voyages . . . de la Louisiane" (Paris, 1807), vol. iii, 169–70, in Ulrich B. Phillips, *Documentary History of American*

Industrial Society: Plantation and Frontier Documents: 1649–1863. Vol. II, p. 31. Cleveland: The A. H. Clark Co., 1909.

Rodrigues, Nina, *Os Africanos no Brasil,* 2a Edição. São Paulo: Companhia editora nacional, 1935.

Ross, Rev. Frederick A., *Slavery Ordained of God.* Philadelphia: J. B. Lippincott, 1857.

Russell, John H., *The Free Negro in Virginia: 1619–1865.* Baltimore: The Johns Hopkins, Press, 1913.

Schoolcraft, H. R., *By a Southern Lady: Letters on the Condition of the African Race in the United States.* Philadelphia: T. K. and P. G. Collins, Printers, 1852.

Sherman, Corinne, "Racial Factors in Desertion," *Family,* Vol. III, p. 224.

Siebert, Wilber H., *The Underground Railroad from Slavery to Freedom.* New York: The Macmillan Co., 1898.

——, "The Underground Railroad in Massachusetts," *Proceedings of the American Antiquarian Society,* Vol. XLV, pp. 25–100, April, 1935.

Smedes, Susan Dabney, *A Southern Planter.* New York: J. Pott and Co., 1894.

Spencer, Herbert, *The Principles of Sociology.* 3 Vols. New York: D. Appleton and Co., 1929.

A Statistical Inquiry into the Condition of the People of Colour of the City and District of Philadelphia. Philadelphia, 1849.

Steward, Austin, *Twenty-two Years a Slave, and Forty Years a Freeman; Embracing a Correspondence of Several Years, While President of Wilberforce Colony, London, Canada West.* Rochester: W. Alling, 1857.

Still, William, *The Underground Railroad.* Philadelphia: Porter and Coates, 1872.

Sumner, William Graham, *Folkways.* Boston: Ginn and Co., 1907.

Sydnor, Charles S., "The Free Negro in Mississippi Before the Civil War," *American Historical Review,* XXXII, p. 772, July, 1927.

Thompson, Edgar T. (Ed.), *Race Relations and the Race Problem.* Durham, N. C.: Duke University Press, 1939.

Thompson, John, *The Life of John Thompson, a Fugitive Slave.* Worcester: J. Thompson, 1856.

Turner, Edward R., *The Negro in Pennsylvania.* Washington, D. C.: The American Historical Association, 1911.

United States Bureau of the Census, *Agriculture in the United States in 1860.* The Eighth Census. Washington, D. C., 1864.

——, *Negro Population in the United States, 1790–1915.* Washington, D. C., 1918.

Villard, Oswald Garrison, *John Brown.* Boston: Houghton Mifflin Co., 1910.

Walker, David, *Walker's Appeal, in four Articles together with a Preamble.* Boston: Published by David Walker, 1856.

Wesley, Charles H., *Negro Labor in the United States, 1850–1925.* New York: Vanguard Press, 1927.

——, *Richard Allen, Apostle of Freedom.* Washington, D. C., The Associated Publishers, Inc., 1935.

Wish, Harvey, *George Fitzhugh, Propagandist of the Old South.* Baton Rouge, La.: Louisiana State University Press, 1943.

Woodson, Carter G., *The African Background Outlined or Handbook for the Study of the Negro.* Washington, D. C.: The Association for the Study of Negro Life and History, Inc., 1936.

——, "The Beginnings of the Miscegenation of Whites and Blacks," *The Journal of Negro History,* Vol. III, No. 4, pp. 335–53, October, 1918.

——, *The Education of the Negro Prior to 1861.* New York: G. P. Putnam's Sons, 1915.

——, *The History of the Negro Church,* 2nd Edition. Washington, D. C.: The Associated Publishers, 1922.

——, *Free Negro Heads of Families in the United States in 1830.* Washington, D. C.: The Association for the Study of Negro Life and History, 1925.

——, "The Negroes of Cincinnati Prior to the Civil War," *The Journal of Negro History,* Vol. I, No. 1, pp. 1–22, January, 1916.

Woodson, Carter G., "The Relations of Negroes and Indians in Massachusetts," *The Journal of Negro History*, Vol. V, No. 1, pp. 45–57, January, 1920.

Wright, James M., *The Free Negro in Maryland, 1634–1860*. New York: Columbia University Press, 1921.

II. RACIAL CONFLICT AND NEW FORMS
OF ACCOMMODATION

Allen, James S., *Reconstruction: The Battle for Democracy*. New York: International Publishers, 1937.

——, "The Struggle for Land During Reconstruction," *Science and Society*, Vol. I, pp. 378–401, Fall–Spring, 1936–37.

Baker, Ray Stannard, *Following the Color Line*. New York: Doubleday, Page and Co., 1908.

Barrow, David C., "A Georgia Plantation," *Scribner's Monthly*, Vol. XXI, p. 836, April, 1881.

Beard, Charles A. and Mary R., *The Rise of American Civilization*. New York: The Macmillan Co., 1927.

Bond, Horace M., *The Education of the Negro in the American Social Order*. New York: Prentice-Hall, Inc., 1934.

Botume, Elizabeth, *First Days Among the Contrabands*. Boston: Lee and Shepard, 1893.

Bruce, Phillip A., *The Plantation Negro as a Freeman*. New York: G. P. Putnam's Sons, 1889.

Buck, Paul H., *The Road to Reunion*. Boston: Little, Brown and Co., 1938.

Clark, John B., *Populism in Alabama*. Auburn, Ala.: Auburn Printing Co., 1927.

Coppin, L. J., *Unwritten History*. Philadelphia: A.M.E. Book Concern, 1920.

Doyle, Bertram, *The Etiquette of Race Relations in the South*. Chicago: The University of Chicago Press, 1937.

DuBois, W. E. B., *Black Reconstruction*. New York: Harcourt, Brace and Co., 1935.

DuBois, W. E. B., *The Negro Landholders of Georgia*, "Bulletin of the Department of Labor," No. 35. Washington, D. C., 1901.

Fish, Carl R., *The Rise of the Common Man*. New York: The Macmillan Co., 1927.

Fisher, Miles Mark, *The Master's Slave—Elijah John Fisher*. Philadelphia: The Judson Press, 1922.

Fleming, Walter L., *The Freedmen's Savings Bank*. Chapel Hill: The University of North Carolina Press, 1927.

——, " 'Pap' Singleton, The Moses of the Colored Exodus," *American Journal of Sociology*, Vol. XV, pp. 61–82.

Hacker, Louis M., *The Triumph of American Capitalism*. New York: Simon and Schuster Publishers, Inc., 1940.

—— and Kendrick, Benjamin B., *The United States Since 1865*. New York: F. S. Crofts & Co., 1937.

Haynes, George E., "Conditions Among Negroes in the Cities," in *The Negro's Progress in Fifty Years*. Philadelphia: The American Academy of Political and Social Science, 1913.

Helper, Hinton R., *Nojoque, A Question for a Continent*. New York: G. W. Castleton and Co., 1867.

Hicks, John D., *The Populist Revolt*. Minneapolis: The University of Minnesota Press, 1931.

Higginson, Thomas W., *Army Life in a Black Regiment*. Boston: Fields, Osgood and Co., 1870.

Kelsey, Carl, "The Evolution of Negro Labor," *Annals of the American Academy of Political and Social Science*, Vol. XXI, pp. 55–76.

Lewinson, Paul, *Race, Class and Party*. New York: Oxford University Press, 1932.

Lewis J. Vance, *Out of the Ditch: A True Story of an Ex-slave*. Houston, Texas, 1910.

Lynch, John R., *The Facts of Reconstruction*. New York: The Neale Publishing Co., 1915.

MacDonald, William (Ed.), *Documentary Source Book of American History, 1606–1898*. New York: The Macmillan Co., 1914.

Marx, Karl and Engels, Frederick, *The Civil War in the United States*. New York: International Publishers, 1937.

Michie, Allan A. and Ryhlick, Frank, *Dixie Demagogues*. New York: The Vanguard Press, 1939.

Miller, Alphonse B., *Thaddeus Stevens*. New York: Harper and Bros., 1939.

The Negro's Progress in Fifty Years. Philadelphia: The American Academy of Political and Social Science, 1913.

Pearson, Elizabeth, *Letters from Port Royal, Written at the Time of the Civil War*. Boston: W. B. Clark Co., 1906.

Pierce, Edward L., "The Contrabands at Fortress Monroe," *Atlantic Monthly*, Vol. VIII, pp. 626–40, November, 1861.

——, "The Freedmen at Port Royal," *Atlantic Monthly*, Vol. XII, p. 296, September, 1863.

——, *The Negroes at Port Royal*. Boston: R. F. Wallcut, 1862.

Randall, J. G., *The Civil War and Reconstruction*. New York: D. C. Heath and Co., 1937.

Roe, Merwin (Ed.), *Speeches and Letters of Abraham Lincoln, 1832–1865*. New York: E. P. Dutton and Co., 1907.

Shugg, Roger W., *Origins of Class Struggle in Louisiana*. Baton Rouge: The Louisiana State University Press, 1929.

Skaggs, William H., *The Southern Oligarchy*. New York: The Devin-Adair Co., 1924.

Simkins, Francis B., *The Tillman Movement in South Carolina*. Durham, North Carolina: Duke University Press, 1926.

—— and Woody, Robert H., *South Carolina During Reconstruction*. Chapel Hill: The University of North Carolina Press, 1932.

Smith, Samuel D., *The Negro in Congress, 1870–1901*. Chapel Hill: The University of North Carolina Press, 1940.

Speech of Hon. Charles Sumner of Massachusetts in the United States Senate, February 6 and 7, 1866. Washington: The Congressional Globe, 1866.

Spero, Sterling D. and Harris, Abram L., *The Black Worker*. New York: Columbia University Press, 1931.

Stephenson, Gilbert T., *Race Distinctions in American Law*. New York: Association Press, 1911.

Steward, T. G., *Fifty Years in the Gospel Ministry*. Philadelphia: A.M.E. Book Concern, 1922.

Stone, Alfred H., *Studies in the American Race Problem*. New York: Doubleday, Page and Co., 1908.

Tebeau, C. W. "Some Aspects of Planter-Freedman Relations, 1865–1880," *The Journal of Negro History*, Vol. XXI, pp. 130–50, April, 1936.

United States Bureau of the Census, *Negro Population, 1790–1915*. Washington, D. C., 1918.

Van Deusen, John G., "The Exodus of 1879," *The Journal of Negro History*, Vol. XXI, pp. 111–29, April, 1936.

Washington, Booker T., *Up from Slavery*. New York: A. L. Burt Co., 1901.

West, Henry L., "The Race War in North Carolina," *The Forum*, Vol. XXVI, pp. 578–91, September, 1898.

Wiley, Bell Irvin, *Southern Negroes, 1861–1865*. New Haven: Yale University Press, 1938.

Woodson, Carter G., *A Century of Negro Migration*. Washington, D. C.: The Associated Publishers, 1918.

Woodward, C. Vann, *Tom Watson, Agrarian Rebel*. New York: The Macmillan Co., 1938.

Work, Monroe N. (Ed.), *The Negro Year Book, 1937–1938*. Tuskegee Institute, Alabama, 1937.

III. THE NEGRO COMMUNITY AND
ITS INSTITUTIONS

Aery, William, "Business Makes Men, Especially if the Men are Negroes," *Survey*, Vol. XXXIV, p. 550, 1915.

Allen, Richard, *The Life, Experience and Gospel Labors of Rt. Rev. Richard Allen*. Philadelphia: A.M.E. Book Concern, n.d.

American Council on Race Relations, *Report*, May, 1948.

Anderson, Robert, *From Slavery to Affluence: Memoirs of Robert Anderson, Ex-Slave*. Hemingford, Nebraska: The Hemingford Ledger, 1927.

Arensberg, Conrad M. and Kimball, Solon T., *Family and Community in Ireland*. Cambridge: Harvard University Press, 1940.

Atlanta University Bulletin, December, 1945. Reprint.

Atwood, J. Howell and Wyatt, Donald W., Davis, Vincent J. and Walker, Ira D., *Thus Be Their Destiny*. Washington, D. C.: American Council on Education, 1941.

Barrow, David C., "A Georgia Plantation," *Scribner's Monthly*, Vol. XXI, pp. 830–36, April, 1881.

Berry, Edwin C., "Portland" in "Race Relations on the Pacific Coast," *The Journal of Educational Sociology*, Vol. XIX, pp. 158–65, November, 1945.

The Boulé Journal, Vol. XIII, April, 1946, A History of the Society and a Roster of its Present Members.

Bragg, George F., *History of the Afro-American Group of the Episcopal Church*. Baltimore: Church Advocate Press, 1922.

Brooks, Charles H., *A History and Manual of the Grand United Order of Odd Fellows in America*. Philadelphia: M.V.P. Chas. H. Brooks, 1893.

Browning, James B., "The Beginnings of Insurance Enterprise Among Negroes," *Journal of Negro History*, Vol. XXII, pp. 417–52, October, 1937.

Bruce, Henry, *The New Man, Twenty-nine Years a Slave, Twenty-nine Years a Free Man*. York, Pa.: P. Anstadt and Sons, 1895.

Burgess, Ernest W., "Determination of Gradients in the Growth of the City," *Publication of the American Sociological Society*, Vol. XXVI, pp. 178–84, 1927.

——, "Residential Segregation in American Cities," *The Annals*, Vol. CXL, p. 110, November, 1928.

—— and Locke, Harvey J., *The Family. From Institution to Companionship*. New York: The American Book Co., 1945.

Business Enterprise Owned and Operated by Negroes in Washington, D. C., 1944. A Special Report of the Project to Study Business and Business Education Among Negroes. Atlanta: Atlanta University.

Catchings, L. Maynard, "The Participation of Racial and Nationality Minority Peoples in Congregational-Christian Churches," *The Journal of Negro Education*, Vol. XV, pp. 681–89.

Classified Digest of the Records of the Society for the Propagation of the Gospel in Foreign Parts. London, 1893.

Cleveland, Catherine C., *The Great Revival in the West, 1797–1805.* Chicago: The University of Chicago Press, 1916.

Committee on Negro Housing, The President's Conference on Home Building and Home Ownership, *Negro Housing.* Prepared by Charles S. Johnson. Washington, D. C.

Corruthers, James D., *In Spite of Handicaps: An Autobiography.* New York: George H. Doran Co., 1916.

"Cotton Field Clinic," *Survey Graphic*, September, 1940. See also under the same title, *Reader's Digest*, September, 1940.

Cox, Oliver C., "Sex Ratio and Marital Status Among Negroes," *American Sociological Review*, Vol. V, p. 942, December, 1940.

Daniel, W. A., *The Education of Negro Ministers.* New York: George H. Doran Co., 1925.

Daniels, John, *In Freedom's Birth-Place.* Boston: Houghton, Mifflin Co., 1914.

Davis, Allison, Gardner, Burleigh B., and Gardner, Mary R., *Deep South: A Social Anthropological Study of Caste and Class.* Chicago: The University of Chicago Press, 1941.

DeCorse, Helen, *Charlottesville—A Study of Negro Life and Personality.* Charlottesville: The University of Virginia, 1933.

Doctrines and Discipline of The Methodist Church. The Methodist Publishing House, Nashville, Tennessee.

Dodge, David, "The Free Negroes of North Carolina," *Atlantic Monthly*, Vol. LVII, pp. 20–30, January, 1886.

Dollard, John, *Caste and Class in a Southern Town.* New Haven: Yale University Press, 1937.

Drake, St. Clair and Cayton, Horace R., *Black Metropolis. A Study of Negro Life in a Northern City.* New York: Harcourt Brace and Co., 1945.

DuBois, W. E. B. (Ed.), *Economic Cooperation Among Colored Americans*. Atlanta, Ga.: Atlanta University Press, 1907.

—— (Ed.), *The Negro Church*. Atlanta University Publications, No. 8. Atlanta, Ga.: Atlanta University Press, 1903.

——, *The Negro in Business*. Atlanta, Ga.: Atlanta University Press, 1899.

——, "The Negro in the Black Belt: Some Social Sketches," *Bulletin of the Department of Labor*, No. 22. May, 1899.

——, *The Philadelphia Negro*. Philadelphia: The University of Pennsylvania Press, 1899.

—— (Ed.), *Some Efforts of American Negroes for their Own Betterment*. Atlanta University Publications, No. 3. Atlanta, Ga.: Atlanta University Press, 1898.

——, *The Souls of Black Folk*. Chicago: McClurg and Co., 1903.

——, *The Negro Problem*. New York: James Pott and Co., 1903.

Faris, Ellsworth, *The Nature of Human Nature*. New York: McGraw-Hill Book Co., Inc., 1937.

Fauset, Arthur H., *Black Gods of the Metropolis*. Philadelphia: The University of Pennsylvania Press, 1944.

Ferguson, Charles W., *Fifty Million Brothers*. New York: Farrar and Rinehart, Inc., 1937.

Fitchett, E. Horace, "The Traditions of the Free Negroes in Charleston, South Carolina," The Journal of Negro History, Vol. XXV, No. 2, pp. 139–52, April, 1940.

Fitzhugh, H. Naylor, "Negroes in Consumer Cooperatives." Unpublished report.

Fleming, Walter L., *The Freedmen's Savings Bank*. Chapel Hill: The University of North Carolina Press, 1927.

Frazier, E. Franklin, "Durham: Capital of the Black Middle Class," in Alain Locke, Editor, *The New Negro*. New York: A. and C. Boni, 1925.

——, "The Negro Family in Bahia, Brazil," *The American Sociological Review*, Vol. VII, No. 4, pp. 465–78, August, 1942.

——, *The Negro Family in Chicago*. Chicago: The University of Chicago Press, 1932.

Frazier, E. Franklin, *The Negro Family in the United States*. Chicago: The University of Chicago Press, 1939.

———, "Negro Harlem: An Ecological Study," *American Journal of Sociology*, Vol. XLIII, No. 1, pp. 72–88, July, 1937.

———, *Negro Youth at the Crossways*. Washington, D. C.: American Council on Education, 1940.

Freyre, Gilberto, *Casa Grande & Senzala*. 2 vols. Rio de Janeiro: Jose Olympia, 1943.

Garnett, William and Ellison, John M., *Negro Life in Rural Virginia: 1856–1934*. Blacksburg, Va.: Virginia Polytechnic Institute, Bulletin No. 295, June, 1934.

Gillard, John T., *The Catholic Church and the Negro*. Baltimore: St. Joseph's Society Press, 1929.

Glazier, Harlan E., *The Color Line in Our Public Schools*. Washington, D. C.: Interracial Committee of the District of Columbia, 1937.

Gray, Lewis C., *History of Agriculture in the Southern United States to 1860*. 2 Vols. Washington, D. C.: Carnegie Institution of Washington, 1933.

Greene, Lorenzo J. and Callis, Myra Colson, *The Employment of Negroes in the District of Columbia*. Washington, D. C.: The Association for the Study of Negro Life and History, 1931.

"Growth of Negro Business," *Literary Digest*, Vol. LXXXI, p. 62, 1924.

Hamilton, C. Horace and Ellison, John M., *The Negro Church in Rural Virginia*. Blacksburg, Va.: Virginia Polytechnic Institute, Bulletin No. 273, June, 1930.

Hankins, Frank H., "Fraternal Orders," *Encyclopedia of the Social Sciences*, Vol. VI, p. 423.

Harris, Abram L., *The Negro as Capitalist*. Philadelphia: The American Academy of Political and Social Sciences, 1936.

Hatcher, William E., *John Jasper, the Unmatched Negro Philosopher and Preacher*. New York: F. H. Revell Co., 1908.

Hagood, Margaret J., *Statistics for Sociologists*. New York: Reynal and Hitchcock, Inc., 1941.

Herskovits, Melville J., *Life in a Haitian Valley*. New York: A. A. Knopf, 1937.

——, *The Myth of the Negro Past*. New York: Harper and Bros., 1941.

Higginson, Thomas Wentworth, *Army Life in a Black Regiment*. New York: Houghton, Mifflin and Co., 1900.

Hoffsommer, Harold, *The Resident Laborer on the Sugar Cane Farm*. Louisiana Bulletin No. 334. Baton Rouge: Louisiana State University, 1941.

——, *The Sugar Cane Farm*. Louisiana Bulletin No. 320. Baton Rouge: Louisiana State University, 1940.

Holley, William C., Winston, Ellen and Woofter, T. J., Jr., *The Plantation South: 1934–1937*. Works Projects Administration. Washington, D. C.: United States Government Printing Office, 1940.

Holmes, S. J., *The Negro's Struggle for Survival*. Berkeley, Calif.: The University of California Press, 1937.

Ingraham, J. H., By a Yankee, *The Southwest*. Vol. II. New York: Harper and Bros., 1835.

——, *The Sunny South*. Philadelphia: G. G. Evans, 1860.

Jackson, Luther P., "The Early Strivings of the Negro in Virginia," *The Journal of Negro History*, Vol. XXV, pp. 25–34, January, 1940.

James, Joseph, "San Francisco," in "Race Relations on the Pacific Coast," *The Journal of Educational Sociology*, Vol. XIX, pp. 167–78, November, 1945.

Jernegan, Marcus W., "Slavery and Conversion in the American Colonies," *The American Historical Review*, Vol. XXI, pp. 504–27, April, 1916.

Johnson, Charles S., *Growing up in the Black Belt*. Washington, D. C.: American Council on Education, 1941.

——, *The Negro College Graduate*. Chapel Hill: The University of North Carolina Press, 1938.

——, *Shadow of the Plantation*. Chicago: The University of Chicago Press, 1934.

——, et al., *Statistical Atlas of Southern Counties*. Chapel Hill: The University of North Carolina Press, 1941.

Johnson, Guion G., A *Social History of the Sea Islands*. Chapel Hill: The University of North Carolina Press, 1930.

Johnson, Guy B., *Folk Culture on St. Helena Island, South Carolina*. Chapel Hill: The University of North Carolina Press, 1930.

Johnston, J. H., "Documentary Evidence of the Relations of Negroes and Indians," *The Journal of Negro History*, Vol. XIV, No. 1, pp. 41–3, January, 1929.

Jones, Charles C., *The Religious Instruction of the Negroes in the United States*. Savannah, Ga.: T. Purse, 1842.

Jones, Raymond J., A *Comparative Study of Cult Behavior Among Negroes with Special Reference to Emotional Group Conditioning Factors*. Washington, D. C.: Published for the Graduate School for the Division of Social Sciences, Howard University, 1939.

Jones, William H., *The Housing of Negroes in Washington, D. C.* Washington, D. C.: The Howard University Press, 1929.

Kennedy, Louise V., *The Negro Peasant Turns Cityward*. New York: Columbia University, 1930.

Kimber, Edward, *Itinerant Observations in America*. Reprinted from the *London Magazine, 1745–46*. Savannah, Ga., 1878.

King, Grace, *New Orleans: The Place and the People*. New York: The Macmillan Co., 1928.

Kiser, Clyde V., *Sea Island to City*. New York: Columbia University Press, 1932.

Laws, J. Bradford, "The Negroes of Cinclaire Central Factory and Calumet Plantation, Louisiana." *Bulletin of the Department of Labor*, No. 38. Washington, 1902.

Leap, William L., *Red Hill—Neighborhood Life and Race Relations in a Rural Section*. Charlottesville, Va.: The Michie Co., 1933.

Lewis, Edward E., *The Mobility of the Negro*. New York: Columbia University Press, 1931.

——, "Recent Farm-Ownership Changes in the Cotton Belt and their Significance for Migration," *Social Forces*, Vol. XIII, pp. 238–44, December, 1934.

Locke, Alain (Ed.), *The New Negro*. New York: A. and C. Boni, 1925.

Long, Herman H. and Johnson, Charles S., *People* vs. *Property*. Nashville, Tenn.: Fisk University Press, 1947.

Long, Howard H., "The Support and Control of Public Education in the District of Columbia," *The Journal of Negro Education*, Vol. VII, pp. 390–99, July 1928.

Lynd, Robert S. and Helen M., *Middletown in Transition*. New York: Harcourt, Brace & Co., 1937.

Mangus, A. R., *Rural Regions in the United States*. Works Projects Administration. Washington, D. C.: United States Government Printing Office, 1940.

The Mayor's Commission on Conditions in Harlem, *The Negro in Harlem*. New York, 1936. Unpublished report.

Mays, Benjamin E. and Nicholson, Joseph W., *The Negro's Church*. New York: Institute of Social and Religious Research, 1933.

Miller, Kelly, "Enumeration Errors in Negro Population," *Scientific Monthly*, Vol. XIV, pp. 167–77, 1922.

Mitchell, James B., *The Collapse of the National Benefit Life Insurance Company*. Washington, D. C.: The Howard University Studies in Social Sciences, 1939.

Myrdal, Gunnar, *An American Dilemma*. New York: Harper and Bros., 1944.

National Housing Agency. Federal Public Housing Authority, *Report S-602*.

——, *Report S-602A*.

National Resources Committee, *Our Cities, Their Role in the National Economy*. Washington, D. C.: United States Government Printing Office, 1937.

The Negro in New Jersey. Report of a Survey by the Interracial Committee of the New Jersey Conference of Social Work in Cooperation with the State Department of Institutions and Agencies. December, 1932.

The Negro War Worker in San Francisco. A Project Administered by the YMCA, May, 1944.

"The New Social Role of American Churches," *A Monthly Summary of Events and Trends in Race Relations*, December, 1946.

Nottingham, Elizabeth K., *Methodism and the Frontier*. New York: Columbia University Press, 1941.

O'Brien, Robert W., "Seattle" in "Race Relations on the Pacific Coast," *The Journal of Educational Sociology*, Vol. XIX, pp. 146–57, November, 1945.

Odum, Howard W., *Social and Mental Traits of the Negro*. New York: Columbia University, 1910.

Palmer, Edward N., "Negro Secret Societies," *Social Forces*, Vol. XXIII, p. 209, October–May, 1944–45.

Park, Robert E., "The Urban Community as a Spatial Pattern and a Moral Order," in *The Urban Community*, edited by Ernest W. Burgess. Chicago: The University of Chicago Press, 1926.

Parker, Robert A., *The Incredible Messiah*. Boston: Little, Brown and Co., 1937.

Pascoe, C. F., *Two Hundred Years of the S.P.G.: An Historical Account of the Society for the Propagation of the Gospel in Foreign Parts*. London, 1901. Vol. I.

Pennington, J. W. C., *The Fugitive Blacksmith: or Events in the History of J. W. C. Pennington*. London: C. Gilpin, 1850.

Phillips, Ulrich B., *Life and Labor in the Old South*. Boston: Little, Brown and Co., 1929.

—— and J. D. Glunt (Eds.), *Florida Plantation Records from the Papers of George Noble Jones*. St. Louis: Mississippi Historical Society, 1927.

Pierce, Joseph A., *Negro Business and Business Education*. New York: Harper and Bros., 1947.

Powdermaker, Hortense, *After Freedom*. New York: The Viking Press, 1939.

Powell, Adam Clayton, Jr., *Marching Blacks*. New York: Dial Press, 1945.

Proceedings of the meeting in Charleston, South Carolina, May 13–15, 1845 on the Religious Instruction of the Negroes. Charleston, South Carolina, 1845.

Raper, Arthur F., *Preface to Peasantry*. Chapel Hill: The University of North Carolina Press, 1936.

Raper, Arthur F., *The Tragedy of Lynching*. Chapel Hill: The University of North Carolina Press, 1933.

Reid, Ira DeA., *The Negro Community in Baltimore. A Social Survey*. The Baltimore Urban League, October 1, 1934.

Rent and Housing Conditions in the District of Columbia. 73rd Congress, 2nd Session, 1934. Senate Document No. 125, Part 2.

Reuter, Edward B., *The Mulatto in the United States*. Boston: Richard G. Badger, 1918.

Richardson, Clement, "The Man Who Turned Gravel to Dollars," *The Southern Workman*, Vol. XLIII, pp. 211–15, April, 1914.

Ross, Frank A., "Urbanization and the Negro," *Publication of the American Sociological Society*, Vol. XXVI, p. 118.

Rules and Regulations of the Brown Fellowship Society, Established at Charleston, South Carolina, 1st November, 1790. Charleston, 1844.

Seminar on Negro Problems in the Field of Social Action. National Catholic Welfare Conference. Washington 5, D. C., 1946.

Shryock, Henry S., Jr., and Eldridge, Hope Tisdale, "Internal Migration in Peace and War," *American Sociological Review*, Vol. XII, p. 32, January, 1948.

Simpson, George E., "Haitian Peasant Economy," *The Journal of Negro History*, Vol. XXV, pp. 498–519, October, 1940.

Smith, T. Lynn, "A Demographic Study of the American Negro," *Social Forces*, Vol. XXIII, p. 384.

A Statistical Inquiry Into the Condition of the People of Colour of the City of Philadelphia. Philadelphia, 1849.

Stepniak, Sergius, *The Russian Peasantry*. London: G. Routledge and Sons, Ltd., 1905.

Sterner, Richard, *The Negro's Share*. New York: Harper and Bros., 1944.

Steward, Theophilus G., *Fifty Years in the Gospel Ministry, From 1864 to 1914*. Philadelphia: A.M.E. Book Concern, n.d.

Steward, William and Theophilus G., *Gouldtown: A Very Remarkable Settlement of Ancient Date*. Philadelphia: J. B. Lippincott Co., 1913.

Stuart, M. S., "Insurance a Natural," *The Crisis*, Negro Business Anniversary Number. Vol. XLVIII, pp. 110–44, April, 1941.

A *Study of Business and Employment Among Negroes in Louisville*. By Associates of Louisville Municipal College, University of Louisville, Louisville Urban League, and Central High School. Louisville, Ky., May 1, 1944.

Supreme Court of the United States. Nos. 72 and 87, 290 and 291.

Thompson, Edgar T. (Ed.), *Race Relations and the Race Problem*. Durham, N. C.: Duke University Press, 1939.

Thompson, Warren S., *Ratio of Children to Women: 1920*. Census Monograph. Washington, D. C., 1931.

—— and Whelpton, P. K., *Population Trends in the United States*. New York: McGraw-Hill Book Co., Inc., 1933.

Tracy, Joseph, A *History of the Great Awakening*. Boston: Tappan and Dennet, 1842.

Trent, W. J., Jr., *Development of Negro Life Insurance Enterprises*. University of Pennsylvania, 1932. Unpublished Master's Thesis.

United States Bureau of the Census, A *Century of Population Growth, From the First Census to the Twelfth, 1790–1900*. Washington, D. C.: United States Government Printing Office, 1909.

——, *Fourteenth Census of the United States*. Vol. II, *Population*.

——, *Fifteenth Census of the United States: 1930*, Vol. III, Part I.

——, *Negroes in the United States*. Washington, D. C.: United States Government Printing Office, 1904.

——, *Negro Population, 1790–1915*. Washington, D. C., 1918.

——, .*Negroes in the United States 1920–1932*. Washington, D. C., 1935.

——, *Plantation Farming in the United States*. Washington, D. C., 1916.

——, *Population Special Reports*, Series P-45, No. 3, March 29, 1945.

——, *Sixteenth Census of the United States: 1940. Population*. Vol. III. "The Labor Force."

United States Bureau of the Census, *Sixteenth Census of the United States. Population.* Washington, D. C., 1941.

——, *Sixteenth Census of the United States: 1940.* Series P-10, No. 1.

——, *Sixteenth Census of the United States. Population,* Vol. III, Part 4, Washington, D. C., 1943.

——, *Sixteenth Census of the United States. Population,* Second Series, Washington, D. C., 1943.

——, *Sixteenth Census of the United States, Population,* Second Series, United States Summary, Washington, D. C., 1943.

——, *Sixteenth Census of the United States,* Vol. II, Part I, 1943.

——, *Sixteenth Census of the United States: 1940. Population.* Vol. IV. "Characteristics by Age." Part I.

——, *Sixteenth Census of the United States: 1940. Population.* "Characteristics of the Population," Vol. II, Part I.

——, *Sixteenth Census of the United States: 1940. Population.* "Differential Fertility 1940 and 1910."

——, *Sixteenth Census of the United States: 1940. Population and Housing, Families.* "General Characteristics."

——, *Religious Bodies: 1936,* Vol. I. *Summary and Detailed Tables.* Washington, D. C., 1941.

——, *Retail Negro Proprietorships—The United States—1937.* August 29, 1941.

——, *Vital Statistics of the United States: 1940.* Part I.

——, *Vital Statistics Special Reports. The Net Reproduction Rate.* May 9, 1941.

——, *Summary of Vital Statistics: United States, 1940.* November 7, 1941.

United States Department of Agriculture. Bureau of Home Economics. *The Farm Housing Survey,* Washington, 1939.

——, Bureau of Home Economics. *Family Income and Expenditures Southeastern Region,* Part I, Family Income, Washington, 1940.

United States Department of Commerce, "Second Annual Report of Banking Institutions Owned and Operated by Negroes," Release, April, 1942.

United States Department of Labor, Bureau of Labor Statistics, *Family Income and Expenditure in Chicago, 1935–36*, Vol. I. "Family Income" Bulletin No. 642, Washington, 1938.

——, *Family Income and Expenditure in New York City, 1935–36*, Vol. I, "Family Income," Washington, 1941.

——, *Family Income and Expenditure in the Southeastern Region, 1935-36*, Vol. I, "Family Income." Washington, 1939.

Valien, Preston, "Southern Negro Internal Migration, 1935–1940." Unpublished paper presented to the Fourth Annual Conference of the Negro Land Grant Colleges Cooperative Social Studies Project. Howard University, Washington, D.C., May 7, 1948.

Vance, Rupert B., *All These People*. Chapel Hill: The University of North Carolina Press, 1945.

——, *Human Factors in Cotton Culture*. Chapel Hill: The University of North Carolina Press, 1929.

——, *Human Geography of the South*. Chapel Hill: The University of North Carolina Press, 1935.

Voorhis, Harold Van Buren, P. M., *Negro Masonry in the United States*. New York: H. Emerson, 1940.

Walker, Harry J., *Changes in Race Accommodation in a Southern Community*. Unpublished Ph.D. Thesis. The University of Chicago, 1945.

Warner, W. Lloyd, "American Caste and Class," *American Journal of Sociology*, Vol. XLII, p. 237.

——, Junker, Buford H. and Adams, Walter A., *Color and Human Nature*. Washington, D. C.: American Council on Education, 1941.

Warner, Robert A., *New Haven Negroes*. New Haven: Yale University Press, 1940.

Washington, Booker T., *The Negro in Business*. Chicago: Hertel, Jenkins and Co., 1907.

——, *The Story of the Negro*. 2 Vols. New York: Doubleday, Page and Co., 1909.

Weatherford, W. D., "Race Segregation in the South," *The Survey*, Vol. XXXIII, pp. 375-77.

Weaver, Robert C., *The Negro Ghetto*. New York: Harcourt, Brace and Co., 1948.

——, *Negro Labor*. New York: Harcourt, Brace and Co., 1946.

Wesley, Charles H., *The History of the Alpha Phi Alpha*. Washington, D. C.: The Foundation Publishers, 1935.

——, *Richard Allen, Apostle of Freedom*. Washington, D. C.: The Associated Publishers, Inc., 1935.

Whither The Negro Church? Services held at Yale Divinity School, New Haven, Conn., April 13–15, 1931.

Why You Should Become a Knight and Daughter of Tabor. Pamphlet in The Moorland Foundation, Howard University, Washington, D. C.

Williams, E. A., *History and Manual of the Colored Knights of Pythias*. Nashville, Tenn.: National Baptist Publishing Board, 1917.

Williams, Joshua C., "Shall·We Continue the Central Jurisdiction"? *The Central Christian Advocate*, November 13, 1947.

Woodson, Carter G., *The History of the Negro Church*. Second Edition. Washington, D. C.: The Associated Publishers, 1921.

——, "Insurance Business Among Negroes," *Journal of Negro History*, Vol. XIV, No. 2, pp. 209-11, April, 1929.

——, *The Negro in Our History*. Washington, D. C.: The Associated Publishers, Inc., 1928.

——, *The Negro Professional Man and the Community*. Washington, D. C.: The Association for the Study of Negro Life and History, Inc., 1934.

——, *The Rural Negro*. Washington, D. C.: The Association for the Study of Negro Life and History, Inc., 1930.

Woofter, T. J., Jr., *Black Yeomanry*. New York: Henry Holt and Co., 1930.

——, *Landlord and Tenant on the Cotton Plantation*. Works Progress Administration. Division of Social Research. Research Monograph V. Washington, 1936.

—— (Ed.), *Negro Problems in Cities*. Garden City, N. Y.: Doubleday, Doran and Co., Inc., 1928.

Woofter, T. J., Jr., "What is the Negro Rate of Increase?" *Journal of the American Statistical Association*, Vol. XXVI, n.s., pp. 461–62, December, 1931.

Work, Monroe N., "Racial Factors and Economic Forces in Land Tenure in the South," *Social Forces*, Vol. XV, pp. 205–15, October–May, 1936–37.

Wright, James M., *The Free Negro in Maryland, 1634–1860*. New York. Longmans, Green and Co., 1921.

IV. INTELLECTUAL LIFE AND LEADERSHIP

Adams, Myron W., *A History of Atlanta University*. Atlanta, Ga.: Atlanta University Press, 1930.

American Council on Race Relations, "Memorandum on Racial Segregation in Higher Education." Mimeographed Release.

American Teachers Association Studies, *The Black and White of Military Service*. Montgomery, Alabama, August, 1944.

Aptheker, Herbert, *American Negro Slave Revolts*. New York: Columbia University Press, 1943.

Bond, Horace M., *The Education of the Negro in the American Social Order*. New York: Prentice-Hall, Inc., 1934.

——, *Negro Education in Alabama. A Study in Cotton and Steel*. Washington, D. C.: The Associated Publishers, Inc., 1939.

Brawley, Benjamin G., *The Negro Genius*. New York: Dodd, Mead and Co., 1937.

Brazeal, Brailsford R., *The Brotherhood of Sleeping Car Porters*. New York: Harper and Bros., 1946.

Brown, Sterling A., Davis, Arthur P. and Lee, Ulysses (Eds.), *The Negro Caravan*. New York: The Dryden Press, 1941.

Caliver, Ambrose, *A Background Study of Negro College Students*. Washington, D. C.: United States Government Printing Office, 1933.

——, *A Personnel Study of Negro College Students*. New York: Teachers College, Columbia University, 1931.

The Chicago Commission on Race Relations, *The Negro in Chicago*. Chicago: The University of Chicago Press, 1922.

Conrad, Earl, *Harriet Tubman.* Washington, D. C.: The Associated Publishers, Inc., 1943.

Detweiler, Frederick G., *The Negro Press in the United States.* Chicago: The University of Chicago Press, 1922.

Douglass, Frederick, *Life and Times of Frederick Douglass.* Chicago: J. S. Goodman and Co., 1882.

Drake, St. Clair and Cayton, Horace R., *Black Metropolis. A Study of Negro Life in a Northern City.* New York: Harcourt, Brace and Co., 1945.

DuBois, W. E. B., *Dusk of Dawn.* New York: Harcourt, Brace and Co., 1940.

——, "Marcus Garvey," *The Crisis,* Vol. XXI, pp. 112–15, December, 1920 and January, 1921.

——, *The Negro Common School.* Atlanta, Ga.: Atlanta University Press, 1901.

——, *The Negro in Business.* Atlanta, Ga.: Atlanta University Press, 1899.

——, "The Talented Tenth" in *The Negro Problem.* New York: James Pott and Co., 1903.

——, *The Souls of Black Folk.* Chicago: A. C. McClurg and Co., 1920.

—— and Dill, A. G. (Eds.), *The College-Bred Negro American.* Atlanta, Ga.: Atlanta University Press, 1910.

Ferguson, Edward, Jr., "A Revised List of Papers Published by Charles Henry Turner." *The Journal of Negro Education,* Vol. IX, pp. 657–60.

Fitchett, E. Horace, "The Influence of Claflin College on Negro Family Life," *The Journal of Negro History,* Vol. XXIX, pp. 43–60, October, 1944.

——, "The Relation of Income to Adequate Educational Opportunities," *The Journal of Negro Education,* Vol. XI, pp. 39–46, January, 1942.

——, "The Role of Claflin College in Negro Life", *The Journal of Negro Education,* Vol. XII, pp. 42–68, Winter, 1943.

Frazier, E. Franklin, "The American Negro's New Leaders," *Current History,* Vol. XXVIII, pp. 56–9, April, 1928.

Frazier, E. Franklin, "The Booker T. Washington Papers," *The Library of Congress Quarterly Journal of Current Acquisitions*, Vol. II, pp. 23–31, February, 1945.

——, "Ethnic and Minority Groups in Wartime, With Special Reference to the Negro," *The American Journal of Sociology*, Vol. XLVIII, pp. 369-77, November, 1942.

——, "Garvey: A Mass Leader," *The Nation*, Vol. CXXIII, pp. 147–48, August 18, 1926.

——, "The Garvey Movement," *Opportunity*, Vol. IV, pp. 346–48, November, 1926.

——, "Graduate Education in Negro Colleges and Universities," *The Journal of Negro Education*, Vol. II, pp. 329–41, October, 1932.

Gallagher, Buell G., *American Caste and the Negro College*. New York: Columbia University Press, 1938.

Gosnell, Harold F., *Negro Politicians*. Chicago: The University of Chicago Press, 1935.

Greene, Harry W., *Holders of Doctorates Among American Negroes*. Boston: Meador Co., 1946.

Guzman, Jessie P. (Ed.), *The Negro Year Book, A Review of Events Affecting Negro Life 1941–1946*. Tuskegee Institute, Alabama: Tuskegee Institute, 1947.

Hankins, Frank H., *The Racial Basis of Civilization*. New York: A. A. Knopf, 1926.

Haygood, William C., "Negro Teachers in White Institutions," *Phi Delta Kappan*, Vol. XXVIII, pp. 74–5.

Higher Education for Democracy. A Report of the President's Commission on Higher Education. Washington, D. C., 1947.

Holmes, Dwight O. W., *The Evolution of the Negro College*. New York: Teachers College, Columbia University, 1934.

Jack, Robert L., *History of the National Association for the Advancement of Colored People*. Boston: Meador Publishing Co., 1943.

Jackson, Luther P., *Negro Office-Holders in Virginia, 1865–1895*. Norfolk, Va.: Guide Quality Press, 1945.

Jackson, Luther P., "The Origin of Hampton Institute," *The Journal of Negro History*, Vol. X, No. 2, pp. 131–50, April, 1925.

Jackson, Reid E., "The Development and Character of Permissive and Partly Segregated Schools," *The Journal of Negro Education*, Vol. XVI, pp. 301–10, July, 1947.

Jaques-Garvey, Amy (Ed.), *Philosophy and Opinions of Marcus Garvey*. New York: Universal Publishing House, 1923.

Jenkins, Martin D., "Enrollment in Institutions of Higher Education for Negroes, 1945–1946." *The Journal of Negro Education*, Vol. XV, p. 237.

——, "The Availability of Higher Education for Negroes in the Southern States," *The Journal of Negro Education*, Vol. XVI, pp. 468–69, July, 1947.

Johnson, Charles S., *The Negro College Graduate*. Chapel Hill: The University of North Carolina Press, 1938.

——, "The Rise of the Negro Magazine," *The Journal of Negro History*, Vol. XIII, No. 1, pp. 7–21, January, 1928.

Johnson, George M. and Lucas, Jane Marshall, "The Present Legal Status of the Negro Separate School," *The Journal of Negro Education*, Vol. XVI, pp. 280–89, July, 1947.

Johnson, Guy B., "Negro Racial Movements and Leadership in the United States," *The American Journal of Sociology*, Vol. XLIII, pp. 57–71.

Kerlin, Robert T., *The Voice of the Negro*. New York: E. P. Dutton and Co., 1920.

Klineberg, Otto, *Negro Intelligence and Selective Migration*. New York: Columbia University Press, 1935.

——, *Race Differences*. New York: Harper and Bros., 1935.

Lewinson, Paul, *Race, Class and Party*. New York: Oxford University Press, 1932.

Locke, Alain, "The Negro: 'New' or 'Newer'," *Opportunity*, Vol. XVII, pp. 4–10, January, 1939.

—— (Ed.), *The New Negro*. New York: A. and C. Boni, 1925.

——, "Reason and Race," *Phylon*, Vol. VIII, pp. 17–27, First Quarter, 1947.

Locke, Alain, "Who and What is 'Negro'?" *Opportunity*, Vol. XX, pp. 36–41, February, 1942.

Loggins, Vernon, *The Negro Author*. New York: Columbia University Press, 1931.

Long, Howard H., "Federal-Aid-to-Education Legislation," Current Trends, *The Journal of Negro Education*, Vol. XIII, pp. 252–54, April, 1944.

McCuiston, Fred, *Graduate Instruction for Negroes in the United States*. Nashville, Tenn.: George Peabody College for Teachers, 1939.

———, *Higher Education of Negroes* (A Summary). Nashville, Tenn.: Committee on Approval of Negro Schools, Southern Association, Colleges and Secondary Schools, 1933.

McMillan, Lewis K., "The American Negro in Higher Education." *The Crisis*, Vol. XLVI–XLVII, August, 1947.

Medved, A. A., "Look at the Record," *The Crisis*, Vol. XLVI–XLVII, November, 1947.

Miller, Kelly, *Race Adjustment*. New York: The Neale Publishing Co., 1910.

Myrdal, Gunnar, *An American Dilemma*, Vol. I. New York: Harper and Bros., 1944.

The National Association for the Advancement of Colored People, *Teachers' Salaries in Black and White*, Pamphlet, Reprinted February, 1942.

Ovington, Mary White, "The National Association for the Advancement of Colored People," *The Journal of Negro History*, Vol. IX, No. 2, pp. 107–116, April, 1924.

Park, Robert E., "Negro Race Consciousness as Reflected in Race Literature," *American Review*, Vol. I, pp. 505–17.

Payne, E. George, "Negroes in the Public Elementary Schools of the North," *The Annals* of the American Academy of Political and Social Science, Vol. CXL, pp. 224–33, 1928.

Pechstein, L. A., "The Problem of Negro Education in Northern and Border Cities," *The Elementary School Journal*, Vol. XXX, No. 3.

Penn, I. Garland, *The Afro-American Press, and Its Editors*. Springfield, Mass.: Willey and Co., 1891.

Powell, A. Clayton, Jr., *Marching Blacks.* New York: Dial Press, 1945.

Powell, A. Clayton, Sr., *Riots and Ruins.* New York: R. R. Smith, 1945.

President's Committee on Fair Employment Practice, *Minorities in Defense.* Washington, D. C., 1941.

Ransom, Leon A., "Education and the Law," Current Trends, *The Journal of Negro Education*, Vol. XI, pp. 224–28, April 1942, and Vol. XIII, pp. 128–30, January, 1944.

Reddick, L. D., "The Education of Negroes in States Where Separate Schools are not Legal," *The Journal of Negro Education*, Vol. XVI, pp. 290–300, July, 1947.

Reid, Ira DeA., "Georgia Negro Vote," *The Nation*, Vol. CLXIII, p. 14, July 6, 1946.

Reuter, Edward B., *The American Race Problem.* New York: Thomas Y. Crowell Co., 1927.

Roberts, Harry W., "The Rural Negro Minister: His Work and Salary," *Rural Sociology*, Vol. XII, pp. 285–97, 1947.

Rodrigues, Nina, *Os Africanos no Brasil*, São Paulo: Companhia editora nacional, 1935.

Science, Vol. XCV, p. 11, January 2, 1942.

Selective Service in Wartime. Second Report of the Director of Selective Service, 1941–42, Washington, D. C., 1943.

Smith, Samuel D., *The Negro in Congress, 1870–1901.* Chapel Hill: The University of North Carolina Press, 1940.

Spero, Sterling D. and Harris, Abram L., *The Black Worker.* New York: Columbia University Press, 1931.

Standing, T. G., "Nationalism in Negro Leadership," *The American Journal of Sociology*, Vol. XL, pp. 180–92.

Stonequist, Everett V., *The Marginal Man.* New York: Chas. Scribner's Sons, 1937.

Survey Graphic. Harlem: The Mecca of the New Negro, March, 1925.

Taylor, Ivan, "Negro Teachers in White Colleges," *School and Society*, Vol. LXV, p. 370.

Thomas W. I., "Race Psychology," *American Journal of Sociology*, Vol. XVII, pp. 744–47, 1911–12.

Thompson, Chas. H., "The Federal Program of Vocational Education in Negro Schools of Less than College Grade," *The Journal of Negro Education*, Vol. VII, pp. 303–18, July, 1938.

To Secure These Rights. The Report of the President's Committee on Civil Rights. New York: Simon and Schuster, 1947.

Townsend, Willard S., "One Problem and a Possible Solution," in Rayford W. Logan (Ed.), *What the Negro Wants*. Chapel Hill: The University of North Carolina Press, 1944.

United States Bureau of Education. *Negro Education*, Bulletin No. 38, 1916, Vol. I, pp. 268–95, Washington, D. C., 1917.

——, *Survey of Negro Colleges and Universities*. Bulletin No. 7, 1928, Washington, D. C., 1929.

United States Department of Commerce, "Negro Newspapers and Periodicals in the United States: 1943," Negro Statistical Bulletin No. 1, August, 1944.

United States Office of Education, *Biennial Survey of Education in the United States. Statistics of State School Systems, 1943–44.* Washington, D. C., 1946.

——, *Higher Education*, April 1, 1948.

——, *National Survey of the Higher Education of Negroes*. 4 Vols. Washington, D. C., 1942.

——, *Statistics of State School Systems of Education*, Vol. II.

——, *Statistics of the Education of Negroes*. Circular No. 215, by David T. Blose and Ambrose Caliver, June, 1943.

Washington, Booker T., "My View of Segregation Laws," *The New Republic*, Vol. V, No. 57, pp. 113–14, December 4, 1915.

—— and DuBois, W. E. B., *The Negro Problem*. New York: James Potts and Company, 1903.

Washington, E. Davidson (Ed.), *Selected Speeches of Booker T. Washington*. Garden City, N. Y.: Doubleday, Doran and Co., Inc., 1932.

Weatherford, W. D., *Negro Life in the South*. New York: Young Men's Christian Press, 1910.

Weaver, Robert C., *Negro Labor, A National Problem.* New York: Harcourt, Brace and Co., 1946.

Werner, M. R., *Julius Rosenwald.* New York: Harper and Bros., 1939.

White, Horace, "Who Owns the Negro Church," *The Christian Century,* February 9, 1938.

Wilkerson, Doxey A., *Special Problems of Negro Education.* Washington, D. C.: United States Government Printing Office, 1939.

Wood, L. Hollingsworth, "The Urban League Movement," *The Journal of Negro History,* Vol. IX, No. 2, pp. 117–26, April, 1924.

Woodson, Carter G., *The Education of the Negro Prior to 1861,* Second Edition, Washington, D. C.: The Association for the Study of Negro Life and History, 1919.

Yerkes, R. M., *Psychological Examining in the United States Army.* Memoirs. National Academy of Sciences, Vol. XV, Washington, D. C., 1921.

V. PROBLEMS OF ADJUSTMENT

"Annual Family Earnings and Occupational Earnings of Residents of Two Negro Housing Projects in Atlanta, 1937–44." *Monthly Labor Review,* pp. 1061–73, December, 1945.

Bailey, Thomas P., *Race Orthodoxy in the South.* New York: Neale Publishing Co., 1908.

Bayton, James A., "The Racial Stereotypes of Negro College Students," *The Journal of Abnormal and Social Psychology,* Vol. XXXVl, pp. 97–102, 1941.

Bernard, L. L., *Instinct. A Study in Social Psychology.* New York: Henry Holt and Co., 1924.

Boie, Maurine, "An Analysis of Negro Crime Statistics for Minneapolis for 1923, 1924 and 1925," *Opportunity,* Vol. VI, pp. 171–72, June, 1928.

Brearley, H. C., *Homicide in the United States.* Chapel Hill: The University of North Carolina Press, 1932.

Bruce, Phillip A., *The Plantation Negro as a Freeman.* New York: G. P. Putnam's Sons, 1889.

Carpenter, Niles, "Feebleminded and Pauper Negroes in Public Institutions," in *The American Negro. The Annals.* Philadelphia, 1928.

Castendyck, Elsa and Robison, Sophia, "Juvenile Delinquency Among Girls," *The Social Service Review*, Vol. XVII, pp. 253-64, September, 1943.

Cayton, Horace R. and Mitchell, George R., *Black Workers and the New Unions.* Chapel Hill: The University of North Carolina Press, 1939.

Cobb, W. Montague, *Medical Care and the Plight of the Negro.* New York: National Association for the Advancement of Colored People, 1947.

Cox, Oliver C., *Caste, Class, and Race; A Study in Social Dynamics.* Garden City, N. Y.: Doubleday and Co., Inc., 1948.

——, "The Modern School of Race Relations," *Social Forces*, Vol. XXI, pp. 218-30, October–May, 1942-43.

Dabney, Virginius, "Nearer and Nearer the Precipice," *Atlantic Monthly*, Vol. CLXXI, pp. 94-100, January, 1943.

Davis, Allison and Dollard, John, *Children of Bondage.* Washington, D. C.: American Council on Education, 1940.

Davis, Allison, Gardner, Burleigh B. and Gardner, Mary R., *Deep South.* Chicago: The University of Chicago Press, 1941.

Dollard, John, *Caste and Class in a Southern Town.* New Haven: Yale University Press, 1937.

Dorn, Harold F., "The Health of the Negro." A Memorandum Prepared for Gunnar Myrdal's *An American Dilemma.*

Dow, Grove Samuel, *Society and Its Problems.* New York: Thomas Y. Crowell Co., 1922.

Dowd, Jerome, *The Negro in American Life.* New York: Century Co., 1926.

Downes, Jean, "Recent Changes in Income and Food Expenditures Among Tuberculous Families in Harlem," *The Milbank Memorial Fund Quarterly*, Vol. XXI, pp. 158-63, April, 1943.

——, "A Study of Food Habits of Tuberculous Families in a Harlem Area of New York City," *The Milbank Memorial Fund Quarterly*, Vol. XXI, pp. 16-18, April, 1943.

Drake, St. Clair and Cayton, Horace R., *Black Metropolis*. New York: Harcourt, Brace and Co., 1945

Dublin, Louis I., "The Problem of Negro Health as Revealed by Vital Statistics," *The Journal of Negro Education*, Vol. VI, pp. 268–75, July, 1937.

—— and Lotka, Alfred J., *Twenty-five Years of Health Progress*. New York: Statistical Bureau, Metropolitan Life Insurance Co., 1937.

DuBois, W. E. B. (Ed.), *Mortality Among Negroes in Cities*. Atlanta, Ga.: Atlanta University Press, 1896.

——, *The Philadelphia Negro*. Philadelphia: The University of Pennsylvania, 1899.

—— (Ed.), *Social and Physical Condition of Negroes in Cities*. Atlanta, Ga.: Atlanta University Press, 1897.

——, *Some Notes on Crime*, Atlanta, Ga.: Atlanta University Press, 1904.

Duncan, Hannibal G., *The Changing Race Relationship in the Border and Northern States*. Philadelphia: The University of Pennsylvania, 1922. Ph.D. Thesis.

Elwang, William W., *The Negroes of Columbia, Missouri. A Concrete Study of the Race Problem*. Columbia, Mo.: Department of Sociology, The University of Missouri, 1904.

Fair Employment Practices Committee, *Final Report, June 28, 1946*. Washington, D. C., 1947.

Families Receiving Aid to Dependent Children, Part 1, Race, Size and Composition of Families and Reasons for Dependency. Washington, D. C.: Federal Security Agency, 1945.

Faris, Ellsworth, "The Mental Capacity of Savages." *American Journal of Sociology*, Vol. XXIII, p. 603.

——, *The Nature of Human Nature*. New York: McGraw-Hill Book Co., Inc., 1937.

Faris, Robert E. L. and Dunham, H. Warren, *Mental Disorders in Urban Areas*. Chicago: The University of Chicago Press, 1939.

Feldman, Herman, *Racial Factors in American Industry*. New York: Harper and Bros., 1931.

Frazier, E. Franklin, "A Comparison of Negro-White Relations in Brazil and the United States," *Transactions of the New York Academy of Sciences,* Series II, Vol. VI, pp. 251–69, May, 1944.

——, "Children in Black and Mulatto Families," *The American Journal of Sociology,* Vol. XXXIX, No. 1, pp. 12–29, July, 1933.

——, *The Negro Family in Chicago.* Chicago: The University of Chicago Press, 1932.

——, *The Negro Family in the United States.* Chicago: The University of Chicago Press, 1939.

——, "Negro Harlem: An Ecological Study," *The American Journal of Sociology,* Vol. XLIII, No. 1, pp. 72–88, July, 1937.

——, *Negro Youth at the Crossways.* Washington, D. C.: American Council on Education, 1940.

——, "Traditions and Patterns of Negro Family Life in the United States," in Edward B. Reuter (Ed.), *Race and Culture Contacts.* New York: McGraw-Hill Book Co., 1934.

—— and Bernert, Eleanor H., "Adequacy of Income in Negro Families in Selected Cities." Unpublished study.

—— and ——, "Children and Income in Negro Families," *Social Forces,* Vol. XXV, No. 2, pp. 178–82, December, 1946.

Gallagher, Buell G., *Color and Conscience: The Irrepressible Conflict.* New York: Harper and Bros., 1946.

Graham, Irene J., "Family Support and Dependency Among Chicago Negroes: A Study of Unpublished Census Data," *Social Service Review,* Vol. III, p. 551.

Hauser, Philip M., "Population Problems in the United States." Unpublished study.

Haynes, George E., *The Negro at Work in New York City.* New York: Columbia University Press, 1912.

Herskovits, Melville J., *The Myth of the Negro Past.* New York: Harper and Bros., 1941.

Hoffman, Frederick L., *Race Traits and Tendencies of the American Negro.* New York: The Macmillan Co., 1896.

Holmes, S. J., *The Negro's Struggle for Survival*. Berkeley, Calif.: The University of California Press, 1937.

Housing Authority of the City of Newark, *The Social Effects of Housing*. Newark, N. J., November, 1944.

Jackson, Luther P., *Free Negro Labor and Property Holding in Virginia, 1830–1860*. New York: D. Appleton-Century Co., Inc., 1942.

Johnson, Charles S., *Growing up in the Black Belt*. Washington, D. C.: American Council on Education, 1941.

——, *Patterns of Negro Segregation*. New York: Harper and Bros., 1943.

—— and Associates, *To Stem This Tide*. Boston: The Pilgrim Press, 1943.

—— and McIntire, Davis, "Minority Labor Groups," in *Yearbook of American Labor*. New York: Philosophical Library, 1945.

Johnson, Guy, "The Negro and Crime," *The Annals of the American Academy of Political and Social Science*, Vol. CCXVII, pp. 93–104. September, 1941.

Jones, William H., *The Housing of Negroes in Washington, D. C.* Washington, D. C.: Howard University Press, 1929.

Katz, Daniel and Braly, Kenneth W., "Racial Prejudice and Racial Stereotypes," *The Journal of Abnormal and Social Psychology*, Vol. XXX, pp. 175–93.

——, "Racial Stereotypes of One Hundred College Students," *The Journal of Abnormal and Social Psychology*, Vol. XXVIII, pp. 280–90.

Kemp, Louise and Smith, T. Lynn, *Health and Mortality in Louisiana*, Louisiana Bulletin No. 390, May, 1945.

Kiser, Clyde V., "Birth Rates and Socio-Economic Attributes in 1935," *Milbank Memorial Fund Quarterly*, Vol. XVII, pp. 139–41, April, 1939.

Klineberg, Otto (Ed.), *Characteristics of the American Negro*. New York: Harper and Bros., 1944.

——, *Social Psychology*. New York: Henry Holt and Co., 1940.

Kroeber, A. L., *Anthropology*. New York: Harcourt, Brace and Co., 1923.

Lasker, Bruno, *Race Attitudes in Children.* New York: Henry Holt and Co., 1929.

Laughlin, H. H., *An Analysis of America's Melting Pot.* Commission on Immigration, November 21, 1922. Quoted in Otto Klineberg, *Race Differences.* New York: Harper and Bros., 1935.

Laws, J. Bradford, *The Negroes of Cinclaire Central Factory and Calumet Plantation, Louisiana.* United States Department of Labor Bulletin No. 38, January, 1902.

Lewis, Julian H., *The Biology of the Negro.* Chicago: The University of Chicago Press, 1942.

Linton, Ralph (Ed.), *The Science of Man in the World Crisis.* New York: Columbia University Press, 1945.

Logan, Rayford W. (Ed.), *What The Negro Wants.* Chapel Hill: The University of North Carolina Press, 1944.

Malzberg, Benjamin, "Mental Disease Among Negroes in New York State," *Human Biology,* Vol. VII, pp. 471–513.

——, "Migration and Mental Disease Among Negroes in New York State," *American Journal of Physical Anthropology,* Vol. XXI, pp. 107–13.

Mayor's Commission on Conditions in Harlem, *The Negro in Harlem.* New York, 1936. Unpublished Report.

McCord, Charles H., *The American Negro as a Dependent, Defective and Delinquent.* Nashville, Tenn.: Benson Printing Co., 1914.

McGill, Nettie P. and Matthews, Ellen N., *The Youth of New York City.* New York: The Macmillan Co., 1940.

Myrdal, Gunnar, *An American Dilemma.* New York: Harper and Bros., 1944.

National Commission on Law Observance and Enforcement, *Report on the Causes of Crime.* Washington, D. C., 1931, Vol. I, Part III, "Notes on the Negro's Relation to Work and Law Observance," by Ira DeA. Reid.

National Resources Committee, *Problems of a Changing Population.* Washington, D. C.: United States Government Printing Office, 1938.

National Urban League, *Unemployment Status of Negroes*, a Compilation of Facts and Figures Respecting Unemployment Among Negroes in 106 Cities. New York, 1931.

——, *The Forgotten Tenth*, An Analysis of Unemployment Among Negroes in the United States and Its Social Costs: 1932–1933. New York, 1933.

The Negro in the Cities of the North, the Charity Organization Society. New York, 1905.

Northrup, Herbert R., *Organized Labor and the Negro*. New York: Harper and Bros., 1944.

——, "Proving Ground for Fair Employment," *Commentary*, Vol. IV, pp. 552–56, December, 1947.

Odum, Howard W., *Social and Mental Traits of the Negro: Research in Conditions of the Negro Race in Southern Towns: A Study in Race Traits, Tendencies and Prospects*. New York: Columbia University Press, 1910.

Otken, Charles, *The Ills of the South*. New York: G. P. Putnam's Sons, 1894.

Park, Robert E., "The Bases of Race Prejudice," *The American Negro, The Annals*, Vol. CXL, pp. 11–20.

—— and Burgess, Ernest W., *Introduction to the Science of Sociology*. Chicago: The University of Chicago Press, 1924.

Physical Examinations of Selective Service Registrants During Wartime, Medical Statistics Bulletin No. 3, Selective Service System. Washington, D. C., November 1, 1944.

Pierson, Donald, *Negroes in Brazil*. Chicago: The University of Chicago Press, 1942.

Popenoe, Paul and Johnson, Roswell H., *Applied Eugenics*. New York: The Macmillan Co., 1933.

Powdermaker, Hortense, *Probing Our Prejudices*. New York: Harper and Bros., 1944.

Pringle, Harry F. and Katherine, "The Color Line in Medicine," *The Saturday Evening Post*, January 24, 1948.

Reed, Ruth, *Negro Illegitimacy in New York City*. New York: Columbia University Press, 1926.

Reuter, Edward B., *The American Race Problem, A Study of the Negro*. New York: Thomas Y. Crowell Publishing Co., 1938.

Ross, Malcolm, *All Manner of Men*. New York: Reynal and Hitchcock, 1948.

Seeleman, Virginia, "The Influence of Attitude Upon the Remembering of Pictorial Material," *Archives of Psychology*, No. 258, September, 1940.

Selective Service in Wartime, Second Report of Selective Service, 1941–42. Washington, D. C., 1943.

Sellin, Thorsten, *The Negro Criminal* in *The American Negro*. *The Annals*, pp. 52–64. Philadelphia, 1928.

Shannon, A. H., *The Negro in Washington, A Study in Race Amalgamation*. New York: Walter Neale, 1930.

Shaw, Clifford R., "Correlation of Rate of Juvenile Delinquency with Certain Indices of Community Organization and Disorganization," *Publications of the American Sociological Society*, Vol. XXII, pp. 174–79, 1928.

——, *Delinquency Areas*. Chicago: The University of Chicago Press, 1929.

—— and McKay, Henry D., *Juvenile Delinquency and Urban Areas*. Chicago: The University of Chicago Press, 1942.

Shufeldt, R. W., *America's Greatest Problem: The Negro*. Philadelphia: F. A. Davis Co., 1915.

Simeon, Joseph S., *A Comparative Study of the Incidence of Insanity Among Negroes and Whites*, Phelps-Stokes Studies, No. 14, Bulletin of the University of Georgia, Athens, 1938.

The Southern Regional Council, Its Origin and Purpose, Atlanta, Ga.

Spero, Sterling D., and Harris, Abram L., *The Black Worker*. New York: Columbia University Press, 1931.

Spirer, Jess, *Negro Crime, Comparative Psychology Monographs*, Vol. XVI, No. 2, June, 1940.

Sterner, Richard, *The Negro's Share*. New York: Harper and Bros., 1943.

A *Study of Delinquent and Neglected Children Before the New York City Children's Court in 1925.* Joint Committee on Negro Child Study. New York, 1927.

Thomas, William H., *The American Negro, What He Was, What He Is, And What He May Become.* New York: The Macmillan Co., 1901.

Thomas, William I., "The Psychology of Race Prejudice," *The American Journal of Sociology,* Vol. IX, pp.593–611.

Thompson, Edgar T. (Ed.), *Race Relations and the Race Problem.* Durham, N. C.: Duke University Press, 1939.

Tillinghast, Joseph A., *The Negro in Africa and America,* "Publications of the American Economic Association." New York: Macmillan Co., May, 1902.

United States Bureau of the Census, *Current Labor Reports. Consumer Income,* Series P–60, No. 1, January 28, 1948.

——, *Current Labor Reports. Labor Force,* Series P–57, No. 167, February 6, 1948.

——, *Negro Population: 1890–1915.* Washington, D. C., 1918.

——, *Population—Special Report,* Series P–46, No. 5, June 18, 1946.

——, *Prisoners in State and Federal Prisons and Reformatories: 1929.* Washington, D. C., 1941.

——, *Sixteenth Census of the United States: 1940. Housing,* Vol. II, Washington, D. C., 1943.

——, *Vital Statistics of the United States.* Washington, D. C., 1945.

United States Department of Labor, Children's Bureau, *The Public Child-Welfare Program in the District of Columbia,* Washington, D. C., 1938.

——, Children's Bureau, "Social Statistics," Supplement to Vol. IX, No. 12, June, 1945, of *The Child.*

——, *Juvenile-Court Statistics and Federal Juvenile Offenders: 1932.* Washington, D. C., 1935.

——, *Women's Bureau Bulletin,* No. 20. Washington, D. C., 1922.

United States Health Service, *The National Health Survey: 1935–1936. Sickness and Medical Care Series. Preliminary Reports.* Washington, D. C., 1938.

Vance, Rupert B., "Racial Competition for the Land", in Edgar T. Thompson (Ed.), *Race Relations and the Race Problem.* Durham, N. C.: Duke University Press, 1939.

Wagner, Phillip S., "A Comparative Study of Negro and White Admissions to the Psychiatric Pavilion of Cincinnati General Hospital," *The American Journal of Psychiatry,* Vol. XCV, pp. 167–83.

Warner, W. Lloyd, "American Caste and Class," *The American Journal of Sociology,* Vol. XLII, pp. 234–37.

——, Junker, Buford H. and Adams, Walter A., *Color and Human Nature.* Washington, D. C.: American Council on Education, 1941.

Washington Criminal Justice Association, *Crime in the Nation's Capital.* Washington, D. C., 1946.

Weatherford, W. D., *The Negro from Africa to America.* New York: George H. Doran Co., 1924.

Weaver, Robert C., *Negro Labor.* New York: Harcourt, Brace and Co., 1946.

Wesley, Charles H., *Negro Labor in the United States.* New York: The Vanguard Press, 1927.

Wirth, Louis, "Race and Public Policy," *Scientific Monthly,* Vol. LVIII, pp. 302–3.

——, "The Unfinished Business of American Democracy," *The Annals,* pp. 1–9, March, 1946.

——, "The Problem of Minority Groups," in *The Science of Man in the World Crisis,* Edited by Ralph Linton. New York: Columbia University Press, 1945.

Woofter, Thomas J., Jr., "Children and Family Income," *Social Security Bulletin,* January, 1945, Washington, D. C.

——, "Children and Family Security," *Social Security Bulletin,* March, 1945, Washington, D. C.

——, *Negro Problems in Cities.* New York: Doubleday, Doran and Co., 1928.

Work, Monroe N., "Negro Criminality in the South," in *The Negro Progress in Fifty Years.* Philadelphia: The American Academy of Political and Social Science, 1913.

CONCLUSION

Bogardus, Emory S., "A Race-Relations Cycle," *The American Journal of Sociology*, Vol. XXXV, pp. 612–17.

Brown, Sterling A., "Count Us In," in *What the Negro Wants*, Edited by Rayford W. Logan. Chapel Hill: The University of North Carolina Press, 1944.

Burma, John H., "The Measurement of Negro 'Passing,'" *The American Journal of Sociology*, Vol. LII, pp. 18–22, July, 1946.

Commission on Interracial Co-operation, *Southern White Women on Lynching and Mob Violence*. Atlanta, Ga., n.d.

Cooley, Charles H., *Social Organization*. New York: Charles Scribner's Sons, 1909.

DuBois, W. E. B., *Color and Democracy: Colonies and Peace*. New York: Harcourt, Brace and Co., 1945.

Eckard, E. W., "How Many Negroes 'Pass,'" *The American Journal of Sociology*, Vol. LII, pp. 498–500, May, 1947.

Faris, Ellsworth, "The Primary Group: Essence and Accident," *The American Journal of Sociology*, Vol. XXXVIII, pp. 41–50, July, 1932.

Foreign Policy Reports, "Nationalism in West Africa," by Vernon McKay. Foreign Policy Association, Inc., March 15, 1948.

Frazier, E. Franklin, "Ethnic and Minority Groups in Wartime with Special Reference to the Negro." *The American Journal of Sociology*, Vol. XLVIII, No. 3, pp. 369–77, November, 1942.

——, "Human, All Too Human. The Negro's Vested Interest in Segregation," *Survey Graphic*, January, 1947.

Gallagher, Buell G., *Color and Conscience: The Irrepressible Conflict*. New York: Harper and Bros., 1946.

Herskovits, Melville J., *Acculturation. A Study of Culture Contact*. New York: J. J. Augustin, 1938.

Isaacs, Edith J. R., *The Negro in the American Theatre*. New York: Theatre Arts, Inc., 1947.

Johnson, Guy B., "Some Factors in the Development of Negro Social Institutions in the United States," *The American Journal of Sociology*, Vol. XL, pp. 329–37.

Logan, Rayford W., *What the Negro Wants*. Chapel Hill: The University of North Carolina Press, 1944.

Malinowski, Bronislaw, *The Dynamics of Culture Change*, Edited by Phyllis Kaberry. New Haven: Yale University Press, 1945.

——, *A Scientific Theory of Culture and Other Essays*. Chapel Hill: The University of North Carolina Press, 1944.

Myrdal, Gunnar, *An American Dilemma*. New York: Harper and Bros., 1944.

New York War Council, Committee on Discrimination in Employment, *How Management Can Integrate Negroes in War Industries*. 1942. Prepared by John A. Davis.

Park, Robert E., "Assimilation," *The Encyclopaedia of the Social Sciences*, Vol. II, pp. 281–83.

Report of the President's Research Committee on Social Trends, *Recent Social Trends in the United States*. New York: McGraw-Hill Book Co., 1933.

Reuter, Edward B., *The Mulatto in the United States*. Boston: Richard G. Badger, 1918.

——, "The Possibility of a Distinctive Culture Contribution from the American Negro," in Kimball Young (Ed.), *Social Attitudes*. New York: Henry Holt and Co., 1931.

——, *Race Mixture*. New York: Whittlesey House, McGraw-Hill Book Co., Inc., 1931.

Wirth, Louis, *Research Memorandum on the Effect of War on American Minorities*. New York: Social Science Research Council, 1942.

—— and Goldhamer, Herbert, "The Hybrid and the Problem of Miscegenation," in Otto Klineberg (Ed.), *Characteristics of the American Negro*. New York: Harper and Bros., 1944.